The USS *Carondelet*

The USS *Carondelet*

A Civil War Ironclad on Western Waters

MYRON J. SMITH, JR.

Foreword by W. DOUGLAS BELL

McFarland & Company, Inc., Publishers
Jefferson, North Carolina, and London

Also by Myron J. Smith, Jr.,
and from McFarland

Tinclads in the Civil War: Union Light-Draught Gunboat Operations on Western Waters, 1862–1865 (2010)

The Timberclads in the Civil War: The Lexington, Conestoga *and* Tyler *on the Western Waters* (2008)

Le Roy Fitch: The Civil War Career of a Union River Gunboat Commander (2007)

Myron J. Smith, Jr., also compiled *The Baseball Bibliography*, 2d ed. (4 volumes, 2006)

Frontispiece: **A drawing of the *Carondelet* by Samuel Ward Stanton, ca. 1968**
(lithograph, after a sketch by L.W. Hastings, USN, published by Middleton, Strobridge & Co., Lithographers, Pike's Opera House, Cincinnati, circa 1864–65. Naval History and Heritage Command, Library of Congress, Currier & Ives).

Library of Congress Cataloguing-in-Publication Data

Smith, Myron J.
The USS *Carondelet* : a Civil War ironclad on western waters / Myron J. Smith, Jr. ; foreword by W. Douglas Bell.
p. cm.
Includes bibliographical references and index.

ISBN 978-0-7864-4524-0
softcover : 50# alkaline paper ∞

1. Carondelet (Gunboat) 2. Mississippi River Valley — History — Civil War, 1861–1865 — Naval operations. 3. United States— History — Civil War, 1861–1865 — Naval operations. I. Title.
E595.C35S52 2010 973.6'245 — dc22 2010006927

British Library cataloguing data are available

On the cover: *The Mississippi in Time of War*, Currier & Ives (Library of Congress)

Manufactured in the United States of America

McFarland & Company, Inc., Publishers
Box 611, Jefferson, North Carolina 28640
www.mcfarlandpub.com

For Fred

Contents

Acknowledgments viii
Foreword by W. Douglas Bell 1
Preface 3

1. Planning the Western Ironclads 5
2. The Building of the *Carondelet* and the City Series Gunboats 20
3. Life Aboard the *Carondelet* 39
4. Fort Henry 50
5. Fort Donelson 70
6. Island No. 10 88
7. Fort Pillow and Memphis 111
8. The *Arkansas* 122
9. Transition, January–March 1863 144
10. Vicksburg 151
11. From Vicksburg to Red River 175
12. Nashville 195
13. War's End 214

Chapter Notes 227
Bibliography 255
Index 273

Acknowledgments

The following persons are gratefully acknowledged for their support, assistance, or encouragement in the preparation of this work in its current and earlier lives. Given that some of those acknowledged are now deceased, titles, where given, reflect those known at the time of the contributor's interaction with the writer.

Mr. Edwin C. Bearss, Office of Archeology and Historical Preservation, U.S. Department of the Interior, National Park Service, Washington, D.C.

Mr. Douglas Bell, Glendale, Arizona.

Mr. William E. Geoghegan, Museum Specialist, Division of Transportation, Smithsonian Institution, Washington, D.C.

Audrey and Howard Wright, Bethesda, Maryland.

Dr. Robert L. Bloom, History Department, Gettysburg College, Gettysburg, Pennsylvania.

Dr. Louis Bouchard, History Department, Shippensburg State College, Shippensburg, Pennsylvania.

Dr. Dean C. Allard, Head, Operational Archives, U.S. Navy Historical Center, Washington, D.C.

Mr. Elmer O. Parker, Assistant Director, National Archives, Washington, D.C.

Dr. Robin Higham, History Department, Kansas State University, Manhattan, Kansas.

Mr. William Tippett, Hernando, Mississippi.

Dr. B.F. Cooling, Industrial College of the Armed Forces, Washington, D.C.

Ms. Teresa Gray, Public Services Archivist, Special Collections and University Archives, Jean and Alexander Heard Library, Vanderbilt University, Nashville, Tennessee.

Personnel at a number of libraries and archives helpfully provided insight and information during the research and writing stages. Among them were the kind folks manning the libraries and special collections/archives of the U.S. Navy Department, Library of Congress, National Archives, University of Tennessee, University of Arkansas, East Tennessee State University, U.S. Army Historical Center, Missouri Historical Society, Tennessee State Library and Archives, St. Louis Public Library, Cincinnati and Hamilton County Public Library, Ohio State University, Nashville Public Library,

As usual, the staff of the Thomas J. Garland Library, Tusculum College, were supportive. Special thanks is extended to Charles Tunstall, reference and interlibrary loan librarian, for his diligent pursuit of titles not in our collection.

I would like to tip my hat to Mr. Douglas Bell, great-great-grandson of Acting Ensign Scott D. Jordan, for his kind foreword. Tennessee state historian Walter T. Durham provided encouragement during several visits to the Garland Library.

Foreword by W. Douglas Bell

The American Civil War was only days old when Federal officials began to plan for the creation and use of warships on the Mississippi River. As the river was then a vital strategic and commercial artery partially blockaded by the Confederacy, the battle for control of the "Father of Waters" would prove to be the major naval campaign of the war, as both sides fought to dominate its navigation.

While the Confederates built up a system of riverbank fortifications backed up by small gunboats, steamboat salvage entrepreneur James B. Eads built seven revolutionary but nearly identical river ironclads near St. Louis. Commissioned in January 1862, these boats spent the remainder of the conflict battling for control of the Mississippi and its tributaries. They led the way in a series of decisive and well remembered engagements from Fort Henry and Fort Donelson through the Battle of Nashville.

Professor Smith's latest book reviews the story of the most famous of these City Series gunboats, the *Carondelet.* In detail, he explains how she was constructed, manned, and fought in more battles than any other U.S. warship prior to World War II. He also looks into the personnel side of the boat's history, through memoirs, diaries, and letters that give a flavor of the daily life aboard. Among those cited are letters from my great-great-grandfather, Acting Ensign Scott Dyer Jordan.

"As I am writing this letter if I raise my eyes from the paper I see roaches in hundreds in any direction which I may look. The table on which I am writing is alive with them. They are continually running over the paper getting in the way of the pen."— so wrote Acting Ensign Jordan to his wife, Judith, in Cape Elizabeth, Maine, from aboard the *Carondelet* in 1863. He goes on in the letter to describe some of their food, "a good bean soup. All hands are very fond of it," and to pass on instruction to the family: "Tell Frank to be a good boy.... Dora must assist you in taking care of Fred and in kissing him for me."

Years later, Scott's great-granddaughter, Floridian Eleanor Jordan West, and her daughter, Maureen, began a "labor of love," tracking down and collecting this letter and more than 100 others from family members. At one point, as they lay in their beds in a motel room in Cape Elizabeth reading the newly collected items, they remarked that they were getting to really know their ancestor. With the letters chronologically assembled, the issue became how to share them with the world.

Over the next several years, Eleanor had the letters transcribed so they were more readable. Attempts to publish them were unsuccessful. Eventually, she enlisted my aid and the transcriptions were scanned, copied and bound into books for the family. In order to expand their distribution, the scanned images were copied to CD-ROM so they could be distributed at no cost to individuals with a love of Civil War history and to libraries and museums with a connection to events mentioned in the letters.

This is the first study to employ the Jordan letters to help paint a detailed and personal picture of the Civil War from the deck of a Union river ironclad. Blended with other sources, citations from this newly compiled repository amplify much of what is known of the famous vessel's service in the period after March 1863. They also throw fresh illumination on those largely unknown moments unrelated in dusty official records or more formal memoirs.

Myron Smith's *Carondelet* provides much insight into the river war and, in the process, well fulfills Eleanor West's dream of sharing Ensign Jordan's personal letters with the world.

W. Douglas Bell is a retired, self-employed computer consultant and a lifelong researcher in family history and genealogy. He has enjoyed using his computer skills to organize and distribute the Civil War letters of his great-great-grandfather, Scott Dyer Jordan.

Preface

The storm broke in April 1861. At 2:30 P.M. on April 13, Maj. Robert Anderson surrendered his beleaguered Fort Sumter, in Charleston Harbor, South Carolina, to the Confederacy. Two days later, U.S. President Abraham Lincoln declared a state of insurrection and called for 75,000 three-month volunteers to quash the revolt. All the years of talk, hope, and work spent in seeking a solution to the economic, political, and social differences that divided the North and the South had ended in failure. The most tragic conflict in American history was "on."

The Mississippi Valley west of the Allegheny Mountains lay partly in the North and partly in the South. When the Southern states enacted ordinances of secession, they claimed as their own that portion of the valley lying within their borders and prepared for its military defense. In the North, planners began to formulate a recovery strategy. One military measure envisioned to support such a plan was the construction of a flotilla of naval vessels for operation on the great inland rivers.

Forty years ago, this writer took an interest in Civil War naval history, but, while in graduate school, found a paucity of readily available published materials. Still, with the support, encouragement, and aid of authorities in the field, an investigation into the creation of the Federal Western gunboat navy was completed, focused on one vessel, the U.S. Steam Gunboat *Carondelet*.[1]

The *Carondelet* was chosen for examination in my original study because, of all the purpose-built river gunboats, she seemed to be the most active and, because she epitomized a revolution in warship construction, quite important. Writing in support of the project, E.J. Pratt, superintendent of the Fort Donelson National Military Park, was emphatic: "the book is needed now."

From Fort Henry through the siege of Vicksburg and from the Red River campaign through the Battle of Nashville, this ship ran up a record for action unsurpassed by any other U.S. Navy warship prior to World War II. She was mentioned frequently in the Civil War literature then available, often because of her most famous exploit, that of running past the batteries at Island No. 10 in April 1862.

While composing his memoirs late in the 1870s, Rear Adm. Henry Walke, last commander of the Mound City Naval Station, paused to consider his first ironclad command, the U.S. Gunboat *Carondelet*. She was "a most successful craft," he proudly recalled. Under the command of half a dozen skippers, the vessel "was in more battles and encounters with the enemy (about 14 or 15 times); and under fire, it is believed, longer and oftener than any other vessel in the Navy." Walke's opinion carried down through the years. In the most popular (and one of the few) histories of the gunboat fleet available in the 1960s, H. Allen Gosnell called *Carondelet* the "most famous of all the river gunboats of the Civil War."

When consulted for their opinions, two famous Civil War historians believed the effort worthy. From his offices at the American Heritage Publishing Company, the late Bruce Catton wrote: "I think a full-dress story of that warship's construction and history is a book that is needed, and I am glad to know that someone has tackled the job — I hope you are able to get the work published." David Donald (who just recently passed away), writing from Johns Hopkins University, was delighted to hear of my "interesting work on the history of the *Carondelet.* That is indeed an exciting subject."[2]

As completed in 1969, my original study centered upon the gunboat's construction and recruiting history. Four major points were covered: (1) the plans for the *Carondelet*'s invention and construction; (2) her actual building and outfitting; (3) the recruitment of her officers and crew; and (4) life aboard. The examination took into account that our subject was one of seven almost-identical boats in the Cairo, or City Series, class of river ironclads. In relaying the foundations of her history, it was necessary to tell and interweave that of her six sisters as well.[3]

In 1982, the 1969 Shippensburg University report was revised in a photocopy publication some have called "privately printed."[4] In addition to drawing upon sources published or uncovered during the intervening dozen years, the new title emended previous errors and omissions. It was simultaneously expanded slightly to include more on the vessel's operational history. A lengthy, updated bibliography was attached, while footnotes were stowed at the end of each chapter.

The book in hand draws on its predecessors and further expands their cursory reviews of the *Carondelet*'s wartime activities. Particular attention is paid not only to the gunboat's encounters with Forts Henry and Donelson, but also to her run by Island No. 10, the Plum Point Bend encounter with the Confederate River Defense Force, her battle with the Confederate armorclad *Arkansas*, adventures in Steele's Bayou and at Grand Gulf, the Red River escape, and her participation in the Nashville campaign. Some time is taken to carefully examine her postwar dismantling and ultimate fate.

Supporting documentation includes the works cited in 1969 and 1982, including some missed which should have been noted. It also comes from a myriad of print titles, book and periodical, not available 40 — or even 12 — years ago. Additionally, we have been fortunate to draw from the letters of officers and crewmen not previously available. Our expanded bibliography demonstrates that no longer is the war on Western waters "the ignored war" Virgil Carrington Jones once called it.[5]

1

Planning the Western Ironclads

The news of Fort Sumter's fall reached a highly excited — and politically divided — public in the city of St. Louis, the largest town in the border state of Missouri, within hours of its occurrence on April 13, 1861. Throughout the state, as in much of the Upper Midwest, sympathies had been divided for months between the Union and what would soon be called the Confederacy. Firebrands and stalwarts supported both with vigor. Many citizens openly worked for secession. Others, however, vowed that Missouri would not join the rebellious South. Among these was the new U.S. attorney general, Edward Bates; postmaster general Montgomery Blair; and the celebrated and ingenious riverman James Buchanan Eads. "Though not large in stature," according to John D. Milligan, the latter "combined vast amounts of confidence and ambition with genuine engineering talents."[1]

When details of the Fort Sumter bombardment and President Lincoln's call-up were received in St. Louis, they were printed in the two local newspapers, the *Daily Missouri Republican* and the *Daily Missouri Democrat*. As accounts appeared, James Eads, like others who relied upon the print press in those days for information, eagerly grasped copies and probably retired with them to his office desk in the Exchange Building on the city's South Main Street, between Market and Walnut streets. There, surrounded by the maps and charts that showed the Middle West and United States, maps that had been his companions since he first entered the salvage business years before, he wrestled with the enormity of events.

Neither a military nor a naval thinker but possessed of detailed regional physical data gained through a lifetime of river work, Eads simultaneously pondered possible Union strategies for the protection and rescue of the Mississippi Valley. The noted salvage expert was convinced by his firsthand knowledge of the geography between Illinois and New Orleans that a defensive posture could not be adopted. Rather, it was his opinion that only aggressive action would defeat the Rebels and save the West. Quickly, he wrote to his friend Bates in Washington and suggested that he had a plan for "vigorous action" that might prove helpful in wresting the Lower Mississippi away from the South.

Bates and postmaster general Blair also believed that the Mississippi should be forcibly reclaimed and that a naval force be created to serve on that stream. The pair had already been in discussions with the chief executive, himself a westerner from Illinois, concerning the movements on the Mississippi River. They knew that "The Father of Waters" was the key to success in the middle of the country — "Hold the stream and you hold all," as Fletcher Pratt put it years later. According to historian Gibson, Bates was "probably the first person to propose to Lincoln" an inland river blockade. Eads' letter gave him with the first actionable plan that he could present to the president and he determined to do so as soon as possible.

Three days after Sumter, Bates advised Eads that the riverman's presence would soon be required in the nation's capital, as "it will be necessary to have the aid of the most thorough knowledge of our Western rivers and the use of steam on them." The attorney general's summons arrived in the Exchange Building on April 24 and caused Eads to immediately entrain for Washington, D.C.

When Eads arrived at the Federal capital several days later, he made his way to the Justice Department, where he and Bates conferred on the engineer's ideas: the Mississippi and its tributaries would be blockaded and then retrieved using, among other resources, a flotilla of gunboats converted from three owned by his Missouri Wrecking Company. Once the Confederacy was divided along the Mississippi and its tributaries, these inland river arteries could be used to crush the divided parts in a large vise-like squeeze.

Bates introduced Eads to navy secretary Gideon Welles and his assistant secretary, Gustavus Vasa Fox. On April 29, the engineer was taken by AG Bates before President Lincoln and the Cabinet to explain his ideas for creating a river navy to aid in a campaign to first blockade and then recover the river valley. Standing before the distinguished assemblage, he offered his recommendations in the rapid, abrupt phraseology that had earned him a reputation as a man with "a hundred horsepower mouth."

The proposed crusade as outlined would be based on an amphibious force operating from the low-lying town of Cairo, Illinois, where the Ohio River flowed into the Mississippi and where those two streams physically separated pro–Union Illinois from the border states of Kentucky and Missouri. Nearly all hearing Eads' words found the concept worthy, save secretary of war Simon Cameron, who thought it ridiculous and impossible to accomplish.[2]

U.S. war secretary Simon Cameron (1799–1889) initially opposed any sort of naval involvement upon the western inland waters, but then changed his mind and demanded exclusive control over construction and deployment of any gunboats. Navy secretary Welles provided his colleague with the expertise of his department, including Cmdr. John Rodgers and Naval Constructor Samuel Pook (Library of Congress, Brady Collection).

James Eads, who also delivered his ideas in writing the same day to an appreciative navy secretary Gideon Welles, also received a positive read on them from Commodore Hiram Paulding, then at the Washington Navy Yard. There was, however, no immediate word from the government on whether or not it would push their implementation, and Eads returned to St. Louis. Other opinions and concepts emerged in the days ahead concerning the future of the Mississippi Valley.[3]

Eads and Bates were not the only ones considering plans to militarily end the Southern insurgency. On April 18, Ohio governor William Dennison and others sought the counsel of Ohio and Mississippi Railroad president George B. McClellan, who was then residing in Cincinnati. McClellan, a well-regarded former U.S. Army engineer captain, was then at the height of his organizational and administrative genius. About the same time, the railroad man, who was seeking a military role for himself in the spreading conflict, sent a report of his own to Dennison on the defense of the Queen City, which he emphasized was "the most important strategical point in the valley of the Ohio." On the strength of this report and recommendations from prominent Buckeyes, Dennison, with Washington's approval, appointed McClellan to head Ohio's militia on April 23.[4] Because the telegraph wires to Washington were down, McClellan sent his report by messenger. As he waited for a response that would take a week to arrive, the new Brig General of Volunteers immediately set to work bringing order out of the chaos that was then rampant in Ohio military circles.

On April 27, "Little Mac," another nickname by which McClellan was known, sent another progress report even though he had yet to receive a reply to his first. A portion of the narrative was a grand strategic recipe "intended to relieve the pressure upon Washington, & tending to bring the war to a speedy close." For starters, key points along the Ohio had to be garrisoned, especially Cairo and Cincinnati. Then victory could be achieved in one of two ways. Send an army through western Virginia and down the Kanawha Valley to Richmond or send a two pronged attack, one pincer via Nashville and the other via South Carolina and Georgia, that would encircle the Rebels. This plan, sent upstairs to the national leadership during the chaotic first weeks of the Rebellion, has been called "the first recorded attempt at an overall strategy for prosecuting the war." It beat Eads' suggestions onto paper by two days and Scott's by a week.[5]

On May 3, Union Army chief Lt. Gen. Winfield Scott replied to McClellan describing his own strategy for crushing the rebellion. The elderly leader, who was largely immobile and was believed out of touch by some, had been a military commander since the War of 1812. He knew war and he knew that any fight with the South would be long and difficult. When President Lincoln called for Union volunteers back in April, Scott warned him that if the South were invaded at any point any time soon, "I will guarantee that at the end of the year you will be further from a settlement than you are now." His unheeded warning would hauntingly return at Bull Run Creek in July. But now it was springtime and Scott had the opportunity to refine and offer his strategic concept in some detail. At the heart of his victory formula lay the idea of strangling the South along the Mississippi and its tributaries, using inland river highways to mount and support amphibious assaults to crush the strong points of the divided parts, eventually reopening the mighty stream to United States commerce.

Scott based his strategy on a powerful U.S. Navy coastal blockade and called for a decisive "movement down the Mississippi to the ocean, with a cordon of posts at proper points ... the object being to clear out and keep open this great line of communication." On the river, such an enterprise would be supported by "from 12 to 27 steam gunboats." He hinted that McClellan would have charge of any enterprise undertaken under the plan as commander of a new military Department of the Ohio that would be announced within days.

This was the famous western river–based "Anaconda Plan." It was often ridiculed, would not be fast or simple to apply, but, in the end was, with modifications, followed as the basis of the Union's war-fighting master strategy. The concept had the advantage of being easy for everyone, from private to president, to understand and get behind. "From this time on," wrote T. Harry Williams, "the occupation of the line of the great river became an integral part of his [Lincoln's] strategic thinking." The Confederacy, for its part, devised no real countermeasures to the Union approach and such preparations as could be made to resist the scheme would, in the end, prove useless.[6]

James B. Eads returned to Washington at the beginning of May, wondering why his proposal, which seemed to have won initial support, was not adopted. After reviewing his ideas with war secretary Simon Cameron, the riverman found the government remained unwilling to commit. The administration was receiving considerable input and "impact statements" from various quarters in the remaining loyal states and required time to absorb varying opinions.

The Cabinet now had access to the plans of Scott, McClellan, and Eads, to say nothing of those from a large number of other Northern celebrities from politicos to newspaper owners. Along the Ohio River, according to historian Ambler, many supported the concept that a fleet of gunboats could not only aid in river defense, but also serve "as an indispensable auxiliary in the aggressive warfare which was to be waged." These folks now looked at the great waterways "in terms of military strategy"—highways over which to move the soldiers who would snuff out the rebellion by carrying the fight south.

A few citizens had concerns that plunging fire from Rebel shore batteries, such as those at Memphis or Vicksburg, could destroy them. The editor of the *Cincinnati Daily Commercial* was not one of these. He insisted in his May 8 issue that protected gunboats could defy shore gunners and could, in any event, be "indispensable as convoys." Additionally, they would give local rivermen choosing to serve aboard a chance to "try their prowess, nothing being too hazardous for them."

Although noncommittal in his immediate response to the Eads presentation, perhaps because he remained unconvinced that such a plan could succeed, secretary of war Cameron was equally convinced that, if there was to be one, an inland river effort was not a marine enterprise. As a result of the positive views of a western riverine offensive now reaching his office, he began to come around to the concept of an amphibious campaign backed up by gunboats. In keeping with long-standing interservice rivalry, however, Cameron resolutely refused to recognize any U.S. Navy jurisdiction over an inland stream. Pointing out that the outfitting of any western river gunboats was army business—sort of "a floating artillery wing," he prepared to change his mind on a western riverine push and to ask Lincoln and his colleagues for support for his turnabout contention.

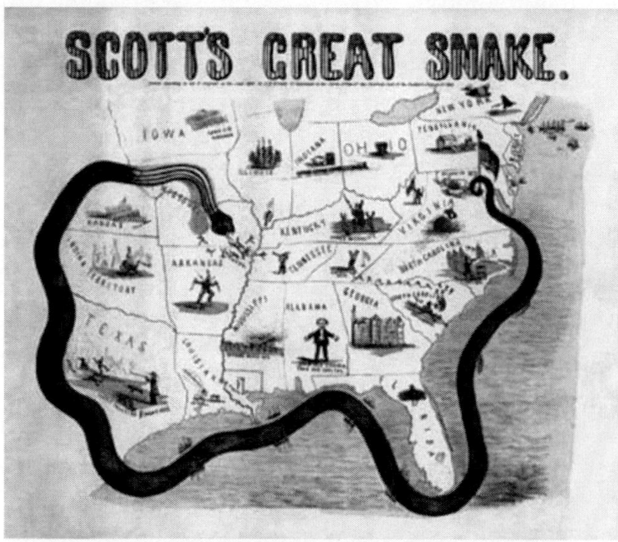

The grand Union strategy devised by Lt. Gen. Scott was called the Anaconda. It included the use of gunboats to support Army amphibious operations on the Western Waters (Library of Congress).

Navy Secretary Welles, meanwhile, was preoccupied with the "immense problems of the Atlantic and Gulf blockade." The great-bearded former Connecticut newspaperman was probably not disappointed when, at the next Cabinet meeting following the Eads presentation, the secretary of war suddenly "claimed jurisdiction over the whole movement." Cameron's powerful associates agreed with his position that any western naval force should really come under the purview of the army. If President Lincoln and the others had required an inland river flotilla plan from Welles, it would have required him to undertake the time-consuming prospect of developing a comprehensive amphibious warfare scheme, as historian Chamberlain put it, "capable alike for assault of fortified positions or to meet attack from such naval combinations as the South might organize."

Hubbub reigned in the capital city and in every department of the Federal government over the next several weeks, while many of the best and brightest military and naval officers quit the Union service to join those of their respective states. The Navy Department had many more pressing concerns than building a few craft out in the middle of the country. So it was that in the confusion, excitement, and interservice rivalries which marked the Federal buildup, the Eads plan was amalgamated into one sponsored, financed, and controlled by the War Department. During these troubled days, apparently, no one remembered to officially notify Capt. Eads concerning the Cabinet's decision on his proposal.

The U.S. War Department officially established the Department of the Ohio on May 10 covering the states of Ohio, Indiana, and Illinois. Maj. Gen. McClellan, at Cincinnati, received command. Efforts at conciliation in the weeks since Fort Sumter were very slow along the Ohio and Mississippi. Fortunately for the North, soldiers were rapidly working on fortifications and artillery positions at Cairo, Illinois. The reporter in town for the *Chicago Daily Tribune* noted on May 19 that batteries had been erected on the Ohio and Mississippi levees for a distance of three miles on each river. Fourteen brass 6-pdrs. and a 12-pdr. howitzer were distributed over the area.[7]

On May 14, the day after the U.S. Army occupied Baltimore, Navy Secretary Welles sent Eads' April 29 proposal over to the War Department where, in light of the recent Cabinet decision, "the subject more properly belongs." He also, and belatedly, wrote the engineer explaining that he had done so. Having undoubtedly already learned the fate of his plan from Bates, or maybe unofficially from Welles himself, Eads prepared for his return to St. Louis.

The first problem facing Secretary Cameron and his generals in implementing the Eads-Scott "Anaconda" strategy was one of materiel. There were no regular Union gunboats on the rivers and western military officers had no idea exactly what was involved with their creation. Turning back to the navy for technical help, Cameron received Welles' promise to speedily make consultants available.

Also on May 14, Cameron wired newly promoted Maj. Gen. McClellan ordering him to confer with Eads and any navy men sent west. The War Department, the secretary noted, now appreciated Eads' ideas, but wanted their man in the field to have an opinion. Once "The Little Napoleon" (yet another McClellan nickname) had heard them out and signed on, he could then place orders for preparation of the boats everyone believed necessary. It likewise appears probable, notes historian Gibson, that, at the time of these interservice interchanges, Lt. Gen. Scott dispatched the army's chief engineer, Brig. Gen. Joseph G. Totten, to the Midwest to review the river transportation infrastructure.

During his days with the railroad, Maj. Gen. McClellan learned something about rivers and steamboats, far less than Eads of course, but probably more than any of the as yet unknown navy people who were coming to help. When the Cincinnatian received the war secretary's directive, sent on the same day as his promotion, the busy Buckeye was completing Ohio's mobilization, turning the mob of men, organizational turmoil, and equipage chaos handed him by Governor Dennison into something approaching an actual army. He was even enjoying himself, announcing to a staff officer that this project was really more fun "than running railroads and adding up columns of dollars and cents."[8]

On May 16, Cmdr. John Rodgers, II, on duty at the USN Hydrographic Office, received anticipated active-service orders. He was probably not consulted prior to their receipt and may have been surprised to learn that he was to report to Maj. Gen. McClellan at Cincinnati "in regard to the expediency of establishing a naval armament on the Mississippi and Ohio Rivers." The new Department of the Ohio commander was to be consulted not only out of courtesy to his command position, but also because, as the chief War Department deputy in the region, he would have charge of building, under authority of the quartermaster general, any waterborne force.

Having accommodated Secretary Cameron, the Navy Department cut orders sending the most knowledgeable available sailor in town out West to serve as nautical advisor to the soldiers. At War Department urging, he would accompany James B. Eads home, stopping at Cincinnati to confer with McClellan and going to Cairo to inspect for possible acquisition one of the largest boats in which the engineer had an interest.

Secretary Welles may have taken the time to brief Rodgers on his mission's restrictions before his departure and emphasized that the assignment came with very limited authority. Although the commander would fall under army orders and funding, he would be allowed to requisition only his own department for sailors and naval ordnance. Conversely, he could make all the recommendations to the War Department that Cameron and his generals would hear. Whatever problems arose under this anomalous permit, Rodgers was expected to work them out with McClellan or local military officers, municipal officials, businessmen, and rivermen. A couple of junior USN officers would be detailed later to help him assist the military, but, in the end, western river gunboats were army business, not that of Welles, and they were not to cost or unduly concern the Navy Department.[9]

The unhappy end of Rogers' Mississippi River saga lay in the future. Now the uncertain prospect of helping to establish a western naval armament demanded his attention. On April 19, he and James B. Eads detrained at Cincinnati, where they were met and escorted to McClellan's headquarters. There the ocean sailor and the considerably younger and much shorter theater commander cautiously began what would become something of an affinity. For his part, the Buckeye general was very happy to have "an officer of Rodgers' standing and ability" assigned to his command. The commander found McClellan agreeable and, in his case at least, not interested in gunboat micromanagement. Quite possibly with Eads present, Rodgers and McClellan discussed what should initially be done on this matter of "interior nonintercourse." It was quickly determined that Rodgers would travel out to Illinois and Missouri with the engineer to learn firsthand what exactly Eads was proposing for the defense of Cairo.

During his journey, the naval commander was to stop not only at the confluence of the Ohio and Mississippi, but at St. Louis and Mound City as well. At those places he was to "obtain all possible information as to the construction of gunboats, floating batteries, etc." McClellan formally directed Rodgers to visit with Eads at St. Louis and to look over the vessels of his Missouri Wrecking Company offered the government in his April communication with Secretary Welles. If they were acceptable and could be converted into warships, "Little Mac" specifically directed Rodgers to "please close the purchase on such terms as you think the interests of the Government require." If Eads' boats wouldn't do, the sailor was to find others that could be turned into gunboats and let the general "know at once the terms on which they can be had."

Although Cmdr. Rodgers had not originally been charged by Secretary Welles with planning anything beyond gunboat ordnance, he was now given to believe by his orders from Maj. Gen. McClellan that he had the authority to act. One historian, Robert C. Suhr, has written that the general, Engineer Eads, and Cmdr. Rodgers "met to discuss the situation on the western rivers." Eads' emphasis on a river blockade, expressed since April, was reviewed. It was after this conference, in which it was decided that "the Union needed three gunboats at Cairo," that "Rodgers took it upon himself to create a flotilla." That he elected not to purchase Eads' boats and turn elsewhere for boats not converted to ironclads would cause him problems. The process of acquiring a trio of boats called "timberclads" is reported in detail elsewhere.

Taking his leave, Rodgers informed his superiors of McClellan's travel orders, though perhaps not his purchasing authority. Next morning, as Rodgers and Eads boarded the Ohio and Mississippi Railroad's direct train for St. Louis, Secretary Welles sent an order to Naval Constructor Samuel M. Pook at the Washington Navy Yard requiring that he head out to Cairo and meet Rodgers. There he would undertake such special duty as the commander might desire based upon the designer's not inconsiderable shipbuilding expertise.[10]

It is perhaps ironic that, in those days of national confusion, Lt. Gen. Scott also attempted to obtain his own picture of Midwest river conditions. At almost the same time that Cmdr. Rodgers was visiting St. Louis, Cairo, and Mound City, Brig. Gen. Totten was travelling up and down the Ohio River putting together a dossier. In the process of visiting with many more people than Rodgers, Totten assembled valuable intelligence for U.S. military leadership. This data had currency not because it was unknown, but because it was written down in a report, with several informational addenda, that brought together insights from many quarters. The same data was communicated, often in little paragraphs, in the river sections of individual local western newspapers, but there was no way to quickly analyze these widely scattered narratives.

Except for local packets, the Mississippi River below Cairo was now closed to commercial navigation for the first time in 60 years. The same suspension also occurred on the Ohio and its tributaries. Though only a few weeks old, the blockade had a devastating impact on river trade as business dried up and insurance companies refused to assume risks. By the end of May both Totten and Rodgers learned, as Eads already knew, that the St. Louis levee, usually bustling and exciting, was quiet. A local reporter told his readers that it was "quiet as a graveyard; steamboatmen feared a total suspension of business; and grass, it was prophesied, would soon be growing on the wharf."

The army engineer, with help from others, not only inventoried available steamboat bottoms, of which there were nearly 400 available for charter or purchase on the Mississippi and Ohio, but also identified the availability of freight and coal barges. Boat-building yards were located at Pittsburgh, Wheeling, Cincinnati, Madison and New Albany, Indiana, and Mound City, with all but the last capable of building engines. Totten understood that his superior, Scott, was interested in having gunboats constructed on the western waters. The 73-year-old had learned that they could be perfectly fitted at any of the five towns mentioned and that, if the government pressed the matter, they could be ready in three months. Knowing nothing personally about gunboat construction or conversion, the veteran did not feel comfortable in completing his memorandum until he returned to Washington because he wanted yet another opinion.

To bolster his report's value, the army's top engineer, while en route back to his headquarters, wrote to the chief of the navy's Bureau of Construction, Equipment and Repair. John Lenthall was a veteran bureaucrat whose knowledge of ship and boat concepts was widely respected. His opinions concerning Totten's findings and requirements would bear weigh. When his colleague's communication came in on June 1, Lenthall went over to his files and brought out a draught for a gunboat upon which he made a few modifications. Himself a blue-water design specialist who "felt slight optimism that armed vessels adequate to fresh-water conditions in the West could be devised," Lenthall, nevertheless, believed that his design might form the basis for a craft "well adapted to operations on the Ohio and Mississippi Rivers." Others interested in such a project could make necessary modifications.

Lenthell's gunboat plans called for a craft 170 feet in length and 28 feet in beam (width), with a depth of hold of 8 feet, 10 inches. When armed (with four 8-inch cannon) and ready, the boat would displace about 435 tons and draw 4 feet, 7 inches of water. Due to the often-shallow river depths and floating debris, the vessel could not have a propeller, but should be a side-wheeler to permit maximum handling. It should be "built in the form of a bateau, the bottom flat and coming up at the ends; thus, all the timbers of the bottom and of the sides would be straight." Three boilers would go into the hold, which would therefore need

Left: **Acting upon a War Department request, the long-time chief of the U.S. Navy's Bureau of Construction and Repair, John Lenthall, offered his ideas for western river gunboats. These were significantly altered by Naval Constructor Samuel M. Pook (Naval History and Heritage Command).** ***Right:*** **A former Connecticut newspaperman and now navy secretary, Gideon Welles (1802–1878) found his department in disarray when the Lincoln administration took office in March 1861. Although grateful for the insights of James B. Eads and willing to send Cmdr. John Rodgers to the inland rivers to assist the War Department, he was not initially interested in establishment of a western naval fleet. Providing initial support in the form of ordnance, naval constructors and expertise, plus a limited number of regular officers, Welles gradually came to see the role of the gunboats in a positive light and supported creation of the Mississippi Squadron (U.S. Army Military History Institute).**

to be deep enough to permit a man to stand up. This bateau arrangement would really be an early "double-ender," a type possessed of a rudder on both bow and stern that could steam either way without "rounding to," the riverman's term for turning around. The type was later employed on eastern rivers such as the James. The diameter of the paddle wheel would be 24 feet and the face of the bucket 7 feet. An 8-foot stoke would be provided by cylinders 18 inches in diameter. It was estimated that the 436-ton vessel described would cost somewhere between $19,000 and $22,000 per copy.

Lenthall sent along his gunboat plans within hours of Totten's return to Washington, complete with written explanations. The designer may also have informed Totten, assuming he had not heard, that Samuel M. Pook, his subordinate and also a top naval constructor, had just gone to Cincinnati and that Cmdr. Rodgers was there to oversee ordnance matters. The army's head engineer, perhaps after consultation with Quartermaster General Meigs, completed his Scott report on June 3. Attaching Lenthall's drawings and explanations, Totten recommended that the Navy authorize an officer of the rank of commander and two lieutenants be sent to the Ohio River with the authority to let gunboat contracts and oversee construction. He further suggested that they have full authority, after consulting with local boat and engine builders as well as Constructor Pook, to make modifications to the Lenthall drawings. The brigadier thought 10 boats could be had for $200,000, but he questioned the idea of advertising for bids for fear that "exposing designs" might be injurious and unnecessary.[11]

A messenger carried the Totten-Lenthall report to Lt. Gen. Scott. Given the press of the aging leader's business, it took most of a week for him to get through it, but he was satisfied with it in the end. On June 10, the document was forwarded to the office of the secretary of war, with a recommendation that 16 of the Lenthall gunboats be contracted—"each with an engine"—and finished in western boatyards by September 20.

Cameron quickly digested Scott's report and, next day, sent Secretary Welles those parts of the document dealing with gunboat construction, requesting that they be executed. He also suggested that some of the main steamboat constructors be consulted so that the government could make use of their experience so far as the practicalities of Lenthall's design were concerned. In addition to Lenthall's findings, Cameron also relayed reports from his Ordnance Department to the effect that the army's rifled 42-pounders, because of their long range, accuracy, "and the moral effect they produced," should form a portion of the armament of each gunboat. He promised to issue orders authorizing that bureau to set aside one or two of the cannon for each boat, along with the necessary ammunition. "The other guns," he added, "it is supposed may be properly supplied by the Navy."[12]

On June 15, Welles replied to Secretary Cameron's message. In view of the demands on the reduced force of his department, the navy boss could not spare any officers to superintend river gunboat construction—indeed, he had none to superintend even the building of oceangoing steamers. Besides, Welles wrote, "it seems to me unnecessary that such superintendents be naval officers." The USN had long since learned that civilians, engineers, and naval constructors—such as Pook—could do the job just as well and thereby free line officers.

Agreeing with Lenthall's observation that the gunboats would prove in many respects different from ocean steamers in their construction, the navy secretary urged his War Department counterpart to consider the idea that it would be well to have them built by "Western men who are educated to the peculiar boat required for navigating rivers." Welles, for his part, would, if Cameron so desired, authorize one of his naval constructors to advise and assist in adapting the vessels to war purposes.

The secretary of war also provided a copy of the Totten-Lenthall report to the industrious quartermaster general, Montgomery C. Meigs. The latter forwarded a copy, via a June 13 covering letter to Maj. Gen. McClellan, to Cmdr. Rodgers. While busily modifying his timberclads, the naval officer was asked, along with the recently arrived Pook, to have as many riverboat construction people as possible look over the Lenthall plans and suggest changes. To add emphasis, Meigs wrote again to McClellan on June 17 saying that it was vital to get up at least two ironclad vessels; as long as they carried cannon (preferably at least three forward), the pair did not "need much speed" and could be "mere scows."

It required the remainder of June for Rodgers and Pook to complete their interviews with builders, captains, and engineers in the Cincinnati area. When they finished, Pook was ready to incorporate all he had learned into extensive modifications of Lenthall's drawings. His boats would be "the first class of vessels designed for war on the rivers."[13] Pook's gunboat specifications called for a shallow, wooden-hulled craft 175 feet overall length, 51.6 feet in beam, and 6 feet deep in the hold. Increasing the beam by 22 feet allowed another five feet in length and offered a superior gun platform able to host greater weight than Lenthall's narrower design. The hold was to be 6 feet from the top of the floor timbers to the top of the gun deck beams, with 7 feet clear height between decks under those beams. In addition to the engines, the hold would also contain a magazine, a shot locker, a shell room, and the coal bunkers.

James Buchanan Eads (1820–1887), a Mississippi River entrepreneur, was among the first to recommend a concrete plan of action to the Federal government for gunboat warfare along the western rivers. His plan, which envisioned the use of armored vessels, was presented to the Navy and War departments and, within a few months, resulted in the receipt of contracts to build seven ironclads designed by Samuel M. Pook. Among them would be the famous *Carondelet* (Library of Congress, Brady Collection).

From his discussions around Cincinnati, Pook learned that the western rivers, unlike the oceans, were almost always smooth. Noting this, he decreased "the ratio of length to breath from Lenthall's 6:1 to 3½:1," thus ensuring "an extremely stable gun platform." The constructor's flat-bottomed gunboat was to have three keels. Pook abandoned Lenthall's "double-ender" concept and the two vulnerable side-wheels in favor of a single center wheel in the after end of the vessel just forward of the stern, "like a ferry-boat." As the noted correspondent Franc B. "Galway" Wilkie later told his readers, this location would cause it "to be as little exposed as possible."

The paddle wheel, 20 feet in diameter, would be accommodated in an opening 18 feet wide running 60 feet forward. The opening was to be "framed with an easy curve from the bottom up to the water line, so as to allow water to pass freely" beneath it. Its presence then could only be detected by the paddle-wheel housing which rose above the after end of the top or, in western parlance, the "hurricane deck." Atop the main deck, Pook drew an oblong casemate, the sides of which rose up 8 feet to a flat hurricane deck; 35 degrees on the sides and 45 degrees forward. The angles, "Galway" noted, would allow the protection to "turn or 'glance off' a missile." This iron-covered casemate, made of oak 8 inches thick on the forward face with 2½ inch oak planking elsewhere, was to enclose the wheel, engines, boilers, and gun deck. It could not, surprisingly, be reached from above save through a side gun port or down the pilothouse companionway to the chart room below.

Within the after section of the casemate, the naval constructor also planned to include a plain large cabin, divided into two staterooms for the captain, two mess rooms, and four two-person staterooms— not much larger than hutches—for the junior officers. Each was to be fitted with berths, a bureau, and a washstand. A table would stand in the captain's main room and in each mess room. On top of the casemate would be a pilothouse (often called a wheelhouse) in which the steering apparatus would be fitted "with wire or chain wheel ropes leading to the upper deck before the smokestacks ... in the most approved plan."[14]

To make his gunboat better able to stand the fire of the huge cannon of that day, Pook called for four athwartship bulkheads below the main deck that divided the hold into 15 watertight compartments. To further guard against shot and shell, he wanted iron plates of sufficient thickness placed in suitable positions around the casemate. This could be done, he believed, with 75 tons of charcoal iron plating (13 inches wide by 7½ to 11 feet long) and rail armor (railroad track iron).[15] The casemate was also to be "pierced" for a sufficient number of gun ports for her own heavy ordnance. Pook recommended the forward end mount three rifled cannon, each broadside with up to seven 68-pounder Columbiads and on the stern three more rifled pieces. This suggestion was similar to the one made by Meigs to McClellan on June 17. In the end, the gun deck was about one foot above water level.[16]

Son of War of 1812 hero Commodore John Rodgers, Cmdr. John Rodgers II (1812–1882) was the architect of the U.S. Army's 1861 Western Flotilla and birth father of the Union's first timberclad gunboats. An intrepid explorer, he was also charged with superintending the initial construction phase of the Pook turtles, while finding time to serve as operational captain of the *Tyler*. Having run afoul of theater commander Maj. Gen. John C. Frémont, Rodgers was succeeded by Flag Officer Andrew Hull Foote in September (Naval History and Heritage Command).

With only a few, but significant, modifications to these plans, this overall revision of the Lenthall design accurately foreshadowed the future appearance of the City Series gunboats.

Indeed, as William E. Geoghegan wrote in 1970, a comparison of the ideas advanced by Lenthall and Pook show very "little similarity" while National Archives historian Elmer O. Parker has recorded that Pook's plans for the seven vessels are each a little different in and of themselves. Historians Fowler and Joiner believed that, in addition to modifying Lenthall's double-ender concept, Pook also crafted his design "more along the recognizable lines of the C.S.S. *Virginia* than of a Union vessel."

While Pook was at his drawing board extensively revising the Lenthall plans he would give to Maj. Gen. McClelland and Cmdr. Rodgers at the start of July, the latter was at work with noted Queen City steamboat engine expert A. Thomas Merritt. The latter agreed to supply a set of plans for the propulsion units required by the naval constructor's design revisions. On July 6, four days after they were passed by McClelland, Rodgers sent QMG Meigs those of Pook's specifications as were completed, promising to send the remainder along as they were completed. The naval constructor actually turned over two sets of plans, one for an elaborate vessel that might cost $214,324 per copy and another, stripped-down version that would come in for about $55,000. Meanwhile, Merritt handed over two sets of plans (one for a paddle wheel design and a second) while another set, for paddle wheels, was acquired from one S.H. Whitmore.[17]

The U.S. Congress, on July 17, appropriated a million dollars to the War Department for "gunboats on the western rivers." Responsibility for their construction fell upon the quartermaster general, who was also to account for all project expenditures. Unhappily, and without his approval, orders were cut for the modification of two additional steamers (one Eads' Submarine No. 7) into ironclads and the building of a fleet of mortar boats.

On Friday, July 19, Meigs dispatched to Secretary Welles the packet of Merritt and Whitmore engine designs received from Rodgers a day or two before. Along with his power plant designs and specifications, both men had enclosed letters of explanation. The logistics general requested that Welles show the three sets of plans to the Navy Department's chief engineer, Benjamin F. Isherwood, and obtain his opinions upon them before the War Department advertised for bids to build the gunboats. Welles referred the power plant drawings to Isherwood, who gave them his immediate attention. After studying them overnight, he reported back to the secretary. In Isherwood's opinion, the regular western paddle wheel engines would be found more reliable and satisfactory than a screw for the same reasons originally given by Lenthall. The usual western river power plant (noncondensing) and high-pressure boilers would be adequate in the muddy and debris-plagued waters.

Isherwood also advised Welles of his agreement with Merritt that the boilers and engines be placed as low as practicable in the holds of the boats "without too much sacrifice of the requirements of mechanical excellence." Indeed, the Cincinnati engineer anticipated that, employing the shortest possible connections, the two engines, placed transversely and side by side, could be fitted into a space of less than 16 feet. A transversely laid auxiliary engine would go 7 feet in front of the other two and the boilers three feet ahead of it. On July 21, Welles returned the engine plans to Meigs, along with a copy of Isherwood's report finished two days earlier. If any further aid or information could be provided, he noted in a cover letter, it would be speedily provided.[18]

While the navy consultants reviewed the Merritt and Whitmore engine plans, QMG Meigs caused preliminary advertisements to be placed in leading western newspapers announcing the acceptance of bids to build the gunboats. The first notice appeared in the *St. Louis Daily Missouri Democrat* on July 29:

Gunboats for the Western Rivers
Quartermaster General's Office
Washington, July 18, 1861

Proposals are invited for Constructing Gunboats Upon the Western Rivers. Specifications will be immediately prepared and may be examined at the Quartermaster's office at Cincinnati, Pittsburgh, and this office. Proposals from boat builders alone will be considered. Plans submitted by builders will be taken into consideration.

M.C. Meigs
QMG U.S.

Once the Pook plans were submitted and approved, the Isherwood report on the gunboat engines was considered, and Merritt's plans adopted, Meigs signed off on the entire project, specification revisions were made available and the *Daily Missouri Democrat,* on August 1, was paid (as were others newspapers) to adjust its advertisement:

Western Gunboats

Proposals for Building Western Gunboats will be received by General Meigs, QM General, Washington City, D.C., until August Fifth when the bids will be opened by him and contracts awarded.

Drawings for inspection and specifications for distribution at the office of The Collector of Customs, St. Louis.

The bids to be endorsed, "Proposals for Western Gunboats."

As the adjusted ads passaged to the western newspapers, three noted residents of St. Louis, including postmaster general Blair's brother, Francis P. Blair, Jr., wrote the quartermaster general that they had learned from a high government source that the War Department was planning to build river gunboats. This eminent lobby reminded Meigs of Missouri's many facilities for steamboat building and suggested that the best locations for gunboat construction were the towns of Cape Girardeau and St. Louis. The latter, besides being a center of machine manufacture, had dry docks and a great number of able workers.

The Missourians' most potent argument was geographical: the gunboats were to be used on the Mississippi and, therefore, they should be built on that stream so that, even when floods came or the river level went down, the ironclads would be available for use. Not so obliquely calling Meigs' attention to his brother-in-law's problems getting the timberclads to Cairo, the correspondents emphasized that constructing the vessels at their location would allow them "to be got out at all seasons of the year, and not high up on the Ohio, where they may [be] tied up and of no use when needed." In a letter written sent along a few days before the bids were due to be inspected, the postmaster general also wrote Meigs to support any claims that might be submitted by St. Louis builders.

In the period since he had first visited Washington, D.C., at the behest of attorney general Bates, James B. Eads did his best to keep in touch with the progress of "his" Mississippi Valley plan; but he received little or no official correspondence on the matter. He read, of course, of Lt. Gen. Scott's "Anaconda," but knew nothing officially about it. Eads was also aware that, in mid–July, the War Department moved to change the army's western commander. The man chosen to succeed McClellan in a new western command was the noted explorer and 1856 Republican presidential candidate, John C. Frémont, "The Pathfinder of the West," as he was nicknamed. The noted explorer also happened to be the son-in-law of the legendary Thomas Hart Benton, mentor of Francis P. Blair, Jr.

It is not known for certain when Frémont first met Capt. Eads, but it is apparent that the engineer and the general had a meeting shortly after the new theater commander came into town and quite possibly as early as July 26. In connection with the mission given BG Asboth,

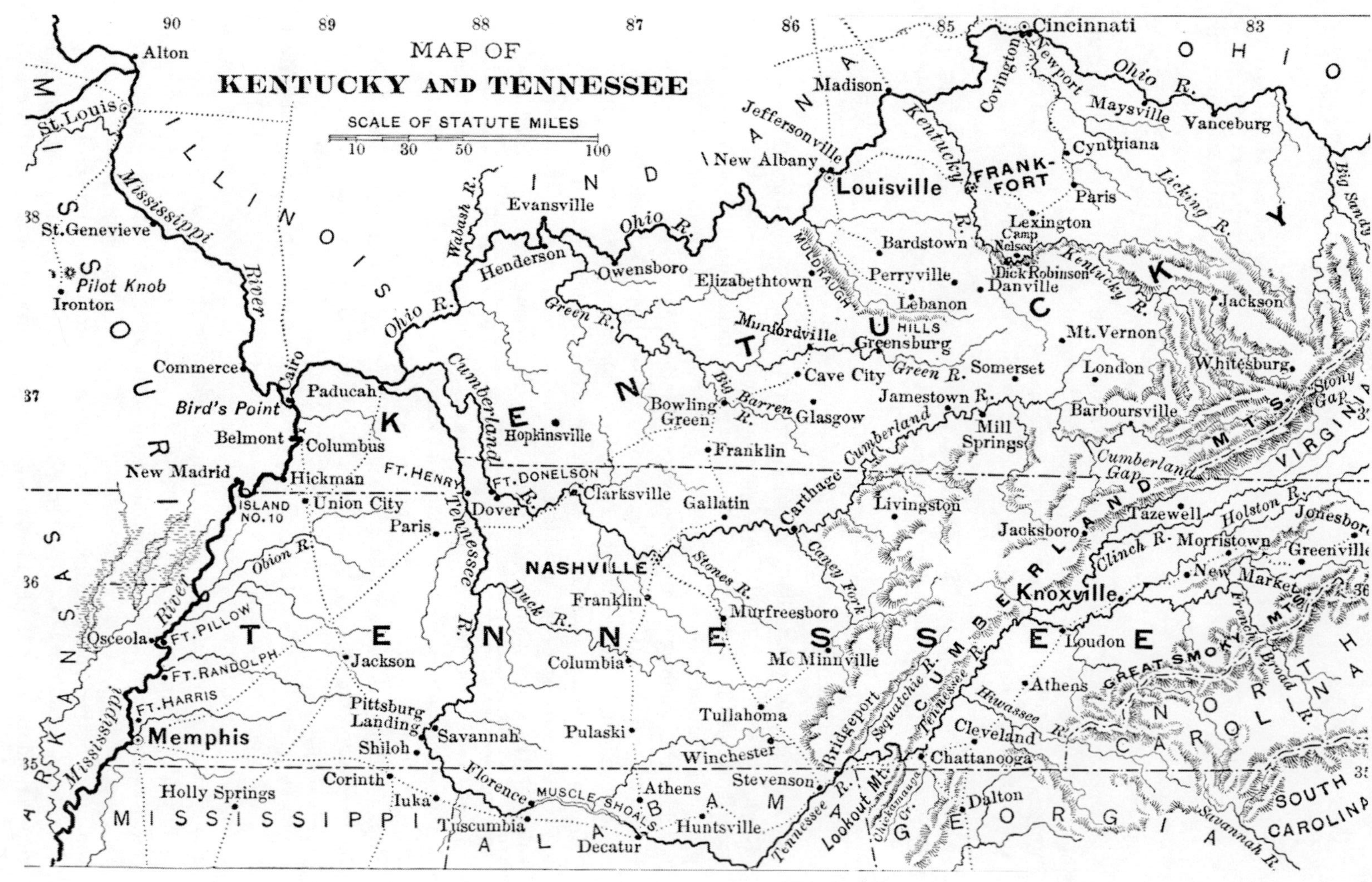
MAP OF
KENTUCKY AND TENNESSEE
SCALE OF STATUTE MILES
10 30 50 100
90
89
88
87
86
85
83
38
37
36
35
MISSOURI
ILLINOIS
INDIANA
OHIO
KENTUCKY
TENNESSEE
VIRGINIA
NORTH CAROLINA
SOUTH CAROLINA
GEORGIA
ALABAMA
MISSISSIPPI
ARKANSAS
Alton
St. Louis
St. Genevieve
Pilot Knob
Ironton
Commerce
Cairo
Bird's Point
Belmont
Columbus
New Madrid
Hickman
ISLAND NO. 10
Union City
Paducah
Evansville
Henderson
Owensboro
Elizabethtown
Madison
Jeffersonville
New Albany
Louisville
FRANK-FORT
Cincinnati
Covington
Newport
Maysville
Vanceburg
Cynthiana
Paris
Lexington
Camp Nelson
Dick Robinson
Danville
Bardstown
Perryville
Lebanon
MULDRAUGH HILLS
Munfordville
Greensburg
Cave City
Bowling Green
Glasgow
Franklin
Hopkinsville
FT. HENRY
FT. DONELSON
Dover
Clarksville
Gallatin
Carthage
Paris
NASHVILLE
Franklin
Murfreesboro
Columbia
McMinnville
Tullahoma
Pulaski
Winchester
Stevenson
Bridgeport
Athens
Huntsville
Decatur
MUSCLE SHOALS
Florence
Tuscumbia
Iuka
Corinth
Holly Springs
Shiloh
Pittsburg Landing
Savannah
Jackson
Memphis
FT. HARRIS
FT. RANDOLPH
FT. PILLOW
Osceola
Mt. Vernon
Somerset
London
Jamestown R.
Mill Springs
Barboursville
Jackson
Whitesburg
Stony Gap
Cumberland Gap
Livingston
Jacksboro
Tazewell
Morristown
Jonesboro
Greenville
New Market
Knoxville
Loudon
Athens
Cleveland
Chattanooga
Dalton
Lookout Mt.
CUMBERLAND MTS.
GREAT SMOKY MTS.
Ohio R.
Licking R.
Big Sandy
Kentucky R.
Green R.
Big Barren R.
Cumberland R.
Wabash R.
Mississippi River
Obion R.
Tennessee R.
Duck R.
Stones R.
Caney Fork
Clinch R.
Holston R.
French Broad R.
Hiwassee R.
Sequatchie R.
Chickamauga Cr.
Savannah R.

Eads undoubtedly made Frémont aware of the availability of Submarine No. 7 and the circumstances under which its earlier conversion had been rejected by the USN western representative. Thereafter, as Nevins reports, "Captain James B. Eads was frequently at headquarters."

On July 27, as the bid notices on gunboats started to appear in the St. Louis and other Ohio River newspapers, Cmdr. Rodgers received a brief telegram at Cincinnati from Secretary Welles: "General Fremont is the successor of General McClellan. Report to him."[19]

Eads had no deeper insight into the Pook or Merritt plans than that discernible from the designs open for examination, but, as one man later put it, he was also not limited by any "moss-grown theories to overcome" relative to gunboat building. With no other enterprise otherwise occupying him, the salvage expert elected to enter the contest and to make an extremely low bid in an effort to win the government contract. Even though he had never seen a real gunboat before (though he may have read of their use in the Crimean War), James Eads was convinced that, because of his knowledge of river steamers, he could build one. After formulating his proposal for what he no doubt considered bargain basement craft, he posted it to Meigs in Washington on August 1. So confident was he of his abilities, Eads even included unique phrasing that would permit the government to penalize him a certain amount of money for every day he was late.

On Tuesday, August 5, eight gunboat bids were opened in the office of the quartermaster general. When all the letter openers were down, it was discovered that Missourian Eads had, indeed, sent in the lowest proposal. Blair's friend stated that he could build from four to sixteen ironclads at $89,000 each and could deliver them to Cairo, Illinois, on or before October 5, 1861. Eads, who had come to the capital city, was notified of his success. With the attorney general at his side, Eads signed a contract in Meigs' office on August 7 to deliver seven gunboats in Cairo "completed and finished" according to Pook's specifications, on or before October 10, 1861. At this time, he was also informed that Cmdr. Rodgers, who had assisted Mr. Pook with the design, would oversee their preparation and appoint a construction superintendent and other subordinates as required.[20] This legal document was very specific regarding payments and penalties.[21]

Seven other Ohio River boatbuilders had also submitted bids, ranging from a high of $110,000 per unit quoted by Madison, Indiana, constructor A.F. Temple down to the $75,000 from New Albany's William Jones. Temple was so upset that he lost the bid that he wrote to his U.S. senator, H.L. Lane, complaining that Eads was not a legitimate builder, but merely a wartime speculator. His appeal fell on deaf ears, largely because none of the other bidders had offered to build so many boats at so low a figure and none volunteered a penalty clause.

Before he could start, Eads was faced with the task of finding four men who would post a bond of $30,000 to insure that he would faithfully perform his part of the contract. With a copy of the agreement in his pocket, the engineer set to work locating his backers and then building seven gunboats from nothing but a rough set of plans in only 64 days. As one student has summed it up: "The program had all the characteristics of a problem contract; subject to political pressures, time constraints, interservice rivalry arising from a Navy design, procured by the Army, and administered by local naval superintendents of shipbuilding, and not least, the difficulties of the new technology of ironclads."[22]

Opposite: **The importance to the North of safeguarding transportation and logistics on the Mississippi and its tributaries and to the South of blockading their use can be easily understood from this map. A map something like this was viewed by leaders in Washington, Richmond, St. Louis, and Nashville as they planned their offenses and defenses. The first six months of the Civil War in the West would be fought by the Western Flotilla in the streams of the territories illustrated (*Battles and Leaders*).**

2

The Building of the Carondelet *and the City Series Gunboats*

It took only a few days for James B. Eads to return to St. Louis following the August 7 contract signing in the Washington, D.C., offices of the U.S. quartermaster general, Montgomery C. Meigs. Riding the rails west, the engineer doubtless considered how he would initiate the gunboat building program.

Before the new ironclad contractor could actually launch his project, four bondsmen had to be contacted. With little talk and much enthusiasm, the quartet (William S. Nelson, Albert Pearce, Oliver B. Filtry, and Barton Bates) each posted $30,000 to guarantee that Eads would faithfully perform his part of the War Department deal. Affidavits were signed by Asa Jones, the collector of the Port of St. Louis, Col. Frank Blair, and Judge Samuel Treat to the effect that the bondsmen each actually had the money they pledged. These papers were all sent to Washington on August 30, 1861.[1]

While the paperwork was completed attesting to his honesty, James Eads started ordering the materials and facilities necessary for the construction of the boats, often tying up the telegraph wires out of St. Louis for hour after frenzied hour. Agents were also dispatched in an effort to secure facilities. In effect, he was becoming a classic prototype of today's program/systems manager.

Next, the constructor went over to Plum Street and purchased a ticket aboard one of the St. Louis & Iron Mountain Railroad trains which made the daily 10 mile trip south to the village of Carondelet, quietly nestled between St. Louis and Jefferson Barracks.[2] Disembarking, he made his way to the facilities of the Carondelet Marine Railway and Drydock Company, sometimes known as Emerson's Ways, located at the bottom of a slope off Marceau Street on the Riviere des Peres, a minor Mississippi River tributary.

Having occasionally employed its services for his own earlier activities, Eads was doubtless familiar with the boatyard that Primus Emerson had established during the 1850s, now the largest in the west and rivaled only by Howard's Madison, Indiana, facility. With Emerson having relocated South, the company was now operated by its president, Roger McAllister, a friend of the salvage expert and the man who had posted the July 6 letter to Meigs expressing an interest in building boats for the Union.

What drew Ead's attention to this particular facility, of course, was the special railway system in its title that Emerson had invented—"the largest and most complete to be found in the West, 'in fact in the United States.'" Coming onto the company grounds, the visitor immediately saw tracks laid out into the river. Over them, a powerful steam engine could haul a steamboat out of the water by car or cradle in about 30 minutes. Out of the stream, it was sent directly into a shiphouse (a very large shed) for repair or, conversely, a new or repaired one could be taken to the water and launched. Laid at right angles to the Riviere des Peres, the six long sheds each held drafting and engineering rooms at their upper ends. By 1861, Emerson's treeless boatyard, in addition to the shiphouses, included a dozen ways, a variety of hoists and cranes, and the marine railway. By now, other boatyards on the Ohio were also modeled after Emerson's concept, but none were as close to St. Louis. So it was that Eads chose to lease this facility for the construction of his gunboats.

Within hours, the energetic Eads was also recruiting workers to perform the actual physical labor on the gunboats. The *St. Louis Daily Missouri Democrat* repeated a belief that 3,000 or 4,000 men would be employed on the project while at least 25,000 people would gain financially from the associated labor connected with the construction of the craft. This associated labor would start just as soon as Eads was able to place orders for lumber and subcontractors set to work on the engines and other parts called for in the Pook specifications. As the correspondent reviewing the launch of the boatbuilding enterprise observed, "The energy displayed by the contractor for building the seven gunboats for the Mississippi River evinces the good judgment exercised by the War Department in confiding this very important business to our fellow citizen, Mr. Jas. B. Eads.... We hazard nothing in saying that the whole fleet will be ready to deal out death and terror to the traitors by the 10th of October next."[3]

Although much of the material was quickly ordered and the Carondelet boatyard was in readiness, a project superintendent to estimate the quality and progress of work was yet to be named. Back on July 22, before the identity of the builder was known, engine designer A. Thomas Merritt applied to Quartermaster General Meigs for the position. After several notes from senators and congressmen were sent supporting the idea, the Ohioan was appointed to the post.

As Naval Constructor Samuel M. Pook had returned east, Cmdr. John Rodgers, by default of his position and western location, was required to take charge, as general superintendent for ironclad construction, and see the project through. A number of issues left unresolved by the designer were handed off to the seaman to resolve, including ordnance, armor, and pilothouses. With the same take-charge approach demonstrated in the acquisition of his timberclads, Rodgers busied himself with the new Eads project. In response to

This largely inaccurate drawing appeared in *Harper's Weekly*, October 5, 1861. The artist may have drawn the illustration of the Eads building project from details provided by others. The representation does, however, provide some idea of the state of construction (notice the boards on the ground), even if not correctly depicting the hull frame appearance.

his brother-in-law's communications, the Maryland-born sailor wrote back from Cincinnati agreeing with the QMG that properly mounted army 42-pdrs. and navy Dahlgrens would be adequate. He recommended that the battery of each boat be slightly smaller than first imagined to avoid trimming by the stern and suggested casemate armor thickness. In addition to Meigs, Rodgers also wrote Bureau of Ordnance chief Capt. Andrew A. Harwood seeking plans for gun carriages and to Eads himself asking that the boats' armor be made from "only the best charcoal iron."

A few days later, Rodgers named John Litherbury to check the building done at Carondelet and ordered him to report to Capt. Eads in Missouri. Litherbury had become familiar with certain gunboat requirements while converting the timberclad *Lexington* at his Cincinnati boatyard.[4]

Cmdr. Rodgers was particularly anxious to secure the armament required by the new gunboats. On August 10, he sent to navy secretary Gideon Welles a requisition for cannon, ordnance equipment, and supplies for the seven gunboats then under construction. Simultaneously, a letter was dispatched to the Navy Bureau of Ordnance and Hydrography telling of the need for 35 rifled 42-pounders and 70 nine-inch Dahlgrens to arm the boats. Capt. Harwood, the Ordnance bureau boss, replied through Welles that these guns were unavailable. In another effort to obtain the needed cannon, Rodgers wrote to QMG Meigs to see if the War Department might provide them. The sailor's brother-in-law recalled the June 11 letter from secretary of war Simon Cameron to Welles in which the former had promised to make available a sufficient number to supply each of the gunboats with not less than two 42-pounders and a supply of ammunition.

While Meigs was digging his copy of Cameron's letter out of his files, Secretary Welles already had the original in hand and was sitting down to write the war secretary to remind him as follows: "Sir: Understanding that the War Office will supply the gunboat flotilla now in process of construction on the Western waters with thirty-five 42-pounder rifled guns, together with projectiles and ammunition, I urgently request ... that the rifled guns be forwarded to St. Louis with the utmost possible expedition." Welles, a one-time Connecticut newspaper editor and astute politician, seldom passed up an opportunity like this one.

The additional great guns requested by Rodgers beyond the 35 would be supplied by the navy from its Buffalo, Erie, and Sacketts Harbor depots. Welles could not supply the gunboats with any small arms due to the pressing needs of seagoing warships employed on the Atlantic and Gulf coasts; but, in his reply to the commander, he promised to make every effort to provide the remainder of the equipment and supplies as required by that officer.[5]

As can be seen in contemporary photographs, construction of the four Carondelet hulls got off to a fine start, with each unit located close to the next with cut timber piled all around. Two were built bow to bow. As more laborers joined the effort, the adjacent town swelled in terms of people and structures. In addition to the various buildings and machinery of the boatyard, new houses were constructed, along with stores, saloons, boardinghouses, restaurants, and even a red light district, turning it into a "muddy, sprawling, roistering little community."

By August 25, most of the structural timbers were in place and observers visiting the Carondelet ways were told that planking would be laid down within a week. Although they had no ribs, the flat-bottomed stern wheelers featured unique frames. Three longitudinal keels, 14 inches wide and 6 inches thick, ran fore and aft while rising as high as the lower port sill; frames for each of the four boats were set on 18-inch centers that measured 4½ inches by 10 inches. The boards covering the bottom were 5 inches thick, while planking over the sides was 4 inches. Planks making up the gun deck were each 10 inches or a shade more on 24-inch centers while 2½ inches of white oak covered ceilings. An early construction alteration made by Eads from the Pook plans concerned the framing. Those employed on the sides of the casemates and bottoms were continued to form sharp knuckles. This added about two feet to the beam of each gunboat.

On August 26, Cmdr. Rodgers wired various river community newspapers that "proposals will be received at Cairo, Ill., 'till August 31, for gun-carriages." The contract was subsequently awarded to the Eagle Iron Works of Cincinnati, where the firm's chief engineer, N.G. Thom, was placed in charge of the work. Along with all the necessary gun implements "such as sponges, ladles, scrapers, and worms," the carriages were to be delivered by October 10, delivery day for Eads' gunboats.[6]

Earlier, on, August 17, James Eads had sent QMG Meigs the first work estimate, a small sum totaling $58,315.40. It was not yet possible, he wrote in the covering letter, to report an estimate on the Mound City project or the 700 tons of iron armor that was being rolled by Gaylord, Son & Company's mills at Newport, Kentucky, and Portsmouth, Ohio. It was also too early to get an estimate on the engines subcontracted to Hartupee and Company of Pittsburgh. The Missourian expressed confidence, however, that he would finish his job by October 10, but he warned the quartermaster chief of the importance of having "money in abundance when work is pushed with extraordinary celerity." He petitioned Meigs to send him quickly "¾ of the value of the enclosed estimate," or $43,736.55. Eads also hoped that Washington would accept the names he had thus far thought up for the boats: *M.C. Meigs, John Rodgers, J.C. Frémont, George B. McClellan, Nathaniel Lyon,* and *N.P. Banks.*

According to Mr. Eads, a previous prediction by the *Daily Missouri Democrat* that 4,000 men would find work on his project was erroneous. In a newspaper interview of August 22, the prime contractor reported that only 200 men were working on the four Carondelet frames. During the next week, however, he planned to add an additional 200

Cairo, at the very tip of Illinois, was a major Federal ground and naval command center from the beginning of the Civil War. Here the new Pook turtles were outfitted once they were sent down from Carondelet or Mound City. In this photo, Cairo is seen from its Ohio Street and Ohio River side, ca. 1864 (Miller's *Photographic History of the Civil War*).

to his gangs. This group, hopefully, would include ship carpenters, who would be paid at the rate of $2 per 10-hour day with $.25 for each hour of overtime. The same day and in the same newspaper, the contractor advertised that "Good Ship Carpenters" could find employment by applying in person at Eads' office in the Exchange Building at St. Louis.

Many of the men hired to build the gunboats were Irish, French, and German and came from yards along the Ohio River, including those at Jeffersonville, New Albany, Louisville, and Cincinnati. Eads also announced that, during the last part of the month, he had decided to build the last three boats at Mound City, Illinois, on the Ohio River just north of Cairo. This move would obviously spread the work around and relieve any cramping of the Carondelet building spaces. As the *Carondelet* was constructed as part of the St. Louis project, the work at Mound City will not be followed here in detail.

Still, the workmen were not happy. During the third full week of August, a number of men and artisans threatened to walk out on strike for higher wages. Pro-Confederacy people in the area openly bragged that they would save the employees the trouble of striking by burning the vessels long before they were finished. To prevent any such event, the local press called for troops to be stationed around the boatyard. On August 28, Cmdr. Rodgers wrote to Maj. Gen. John C. Frémont, the army's newly arrived western replacement for Maj. Gen. George B. McClellan, asking him to assign soldiers to guard the vessels being built at the Marine Ways.[7]

On August 30, Cmdr. Rodgers wrote to Superintendent Litherbury regarding the need for pilothouses. The Cincinnatian was asked to have Eads erect an octagonal, low, wooden "texas," a structure with sloping side, on the hurricane deck atop the casemate of each vessel. It was to be situated forward of the two chimneys. Enemy shot would hopefully bounce off such a pilothouse. While mentioning the hurricane deck, we should note other topside fixtures added now or shortly thereafter. On the length of each side were a line of awning stanchions each 8 feet high, with 10-foot high stanchions down the centerline. Skylights were cut in the deck on each side of the wheelhouse and aft the pilothouse. Two ventilators were set over the fire room and two more abaft the boilers. Four boats were hung from davits just forward of the wheelhouse.

During these hectic summer days, Maj. Gen. Frémont had yet to meet Cmdr. Rodgers. The "Pathfinder of the West" was, however, well acquainted with members of the Blair family and had apparently seen Capt. Eads in St. Louis before the engineer departed Missouri for the ironclad bid opening in Washington. August was only a few days old when postmaster general Montgomery Blair received a letter from the new Department of the West commander. The communication from Frémont asked for new levies, new money, and a new western waters naval commander. The key sentences relative to this account read: "It would serve the public interest if Commander John Rodgers were removed and an officer directed to report to me to have command of the operations on the Mississippi. Show this to President." Two days before Rodgers' call upon Frémont for protection, the Navy Department assigned Capt. Andrew Hull Foote as the commander's replacement. Welles sent a copy of the order to St. Louis, but Rodgers did not receive it because he was with the timberclads at Cairo and it was not forwarded.

Until the day his replacement appeared, Cmdr. Rodgers did not learn from Frémont, the Blairs, Eads, Welles, assistant navy secretary Gustavus Fox, Meigs (who may or may not have known from his brother-in-law Montgomery Blair) or anyone else that his transfer had been requested. Until then, he was allowed to operate his command and provide advice on the construction of the new gunboats completely unaware that his days in the

West were numbered. Lincoln had given Frémont a free hand and, in Rodgers' case, he used it quickly.

A long-time Welles acquaintance, Foote was ordered to Missouri from the New York Navy Yard. In taking charge of naval activities on the Mississippi, the bearded officer was to be particularly careful not to ruffle military feathers or those of prominent businessmen or politicians like Eads or the Blairs. The 56-year-old Foote assumed command of the "naval operations upon the Western rivers, now organizing under the direction of the War Department," on September 6. As a full navy captain, Foote ranked higher than the commander he replaced. Even as a flotilla commander, he was still, however, locally equated with army men wearing colonel's eagles.[8]

In Williamsport, New York, also on September 6, Commander Henry Walke, the Light House Inspector of the Eleventh Lighthouse District and future commander of the *Carondelet*, received orders to report, without a moment's delay, to Capt. Foote in St. Louis. Walke has been pictured as a man "with bushy eyebrows and a broad, humorous mouth, nimble as a fawn." He was tall, thin, and clean-shaven, save for a few chin whiskers, and owned a distinctive receding hairline and an aquiline nose. Always ramrod stiff in appearance, he usually wore a long-skirted naval uniform with gold braid. Among a group of officers marked for removal in the 1850s and then "restored," Walke was court-martialed and reprimanded by the Buchanan administration in January 1861 for his unauthorized landing of supplies at Fort Pickens, Pensacola, a move that probably saved that bastion for the Union but violated his local orders. When Gideon Welles became navy secretary, he was too busy to review the censure and thus Walke found himself stewing in New York.

Flag Officer/Rear Admiral Andrew H. Foote (1806–1863) succeeded Cmdr. John Rodgers in command of the Western Flotilla in September 1861. Foote guided the construction and manning of the Pook turtles and led them during the battles at Fort Henry, Fort Donelson, and Island No. 10 (Library of Congress).

Making his way by train and steamer, Walke soon appeared in Missouri, where his old colleague promptly made him temporary squadron commander of the three timberclads based at Cairo, with the *Tyler* as his personal flagboat. This arrangement with the no-nonsense Walke, which lack of manpower denied Rodgers, gave Foote the opportunity to concentrate his energies almost exclusively upon completion of the gunboats. It also allowed the Pensacola hero, who believed his western posting a demotion, to begin planning his redemption by drive and imagination.[9]

In addition to Walke, other regular naval officers, some of whom would achieve fame and others death, were also transferred to the rivers from areas along the Atlantic coast and the Great Lakes. They would be joined by a large number of "volunteer" naval officers, often captains or mates from the crews of inland steamboats. Many of these men would prove every bit as valuable as any trained at sea before the mast in the mold of Foote or Walke.

As the Navy relocated or recruited the gunboat officers, work continued on the gunboats abuilding in Carondelet and Mound City. In his August 30 letter to QMG Meigs in which he sent his bonds, contractor Eads mentioned that he had some 600 men and 12 sawmills at work on the ironclad enterprise. Again he requested that the percentage of the estimate due him be promptly sent so that he could pay the rapidly growing pile of bills now accumulating on his office desk. Eads knew that the War Department had received, in July, a $1 million appropriation from Congress for gunboat construction, so his disappointment at not receiving a timely disbursement is understandable. He may not have known that some of the funds were being used to pay for the conversion of his own Submarine No. 7 into the giant *Benton* as well as the alteration of the ferry *New Era* into the *Essex* and construction of numerous mortar boats. Two weeks after he was due an initial payment, the engineer posted to Washington the second 20-day estimate. Its cover letter gently reminded the quartermaster general that he had not been paid anything as yet. Although his bills were already over $700,000 (a huge sum in 1861), Eads remained convinced he could meet the October deadline.

The first funds from Washington arrived at the St. Louis office of Capt. George D. Wise, the army assistant quartermaster charged with locally handling and dispersing project funds, during the third week in September. Even after Wise paid Eads, the contractor was in trouble with some of his subcontractors. For example, Hartupee and Company in Pittsburgh had finished the two sets of boilers and engines promised for the project. Unpaid, the firm complained to Washington. With $25,000 involved, Hartupee also wired Eads requesting payment. When the cash did not arrive from St. Louis, Eads did not even acknowledge the complaining telegrams coming in from Pittsburgh. Hartupee's officials then wrote to Meigs concerning Eads' cavalier manner and their lack of payment. What they failed to take into account in the Steel City was the Federal government's failure to pay Eads.

Although contractor Eads had to battle his creditors and subcontractors, he work still continued to move forward. In its September 18 edition, the *Daily Missouri Democrat* painted an interesting picture of the progress being made. According to the pro–Union newspaper, the boats at Carondelet were better than half finished, with the work "done in a model manner, and according to the strictest letter of the contract." With over 800 workers employed, Eads' organizational genius, the writer contended, was "exhibited in [a] noiseless and effective manner." Four barges and a steamboat were reported busy hauling timber from the locations where Eads had mills at work. There were eight mills, the paper noted, located in Kentucky, Ohio, and Illinois, and 13 in St. Louis alone, all cutting the specified white oak into the various sizes of lumber required for the decks and casemates. It was also estimated that before the enterprise was completed it would use 15 million feet of wood and 800 tons of iron plating — in addition to bolts, spikes, nails, engines, and boilers.

The *Daily Missouri Democrat*'s competitor, the *Daily Missouri Republican*— also pro–U.S.— observed, however, that the four boats at Carondelet would probably not be finished until October 15. This more pessimistic report preceded information that Eads had expanded his Carondelet workforce from 484 to 700 during the fourth week of September, the majority being carpenters. As subsequent events would show, the prediction of the *Daily Missouri Republican* was substantially correct. In addition to increasing the number of

Carondelet laborers, Eads now decided to work his construction gangs in different shifts seven days a week and at night. The project's blacksmith, machine, and coppersmith shops, sawmills, foundries, and rolling mills also functioned 24/7 in different shifts.[10]

At Eads' request, a dear friend, the former St. Louis mayor O.D. Filley, stopped in to see QMG Meigs during his late September visit to Washington, D.C. It is unknown what transpired, though a letter from the contractor to the general was turned over. Within a week, Eads had a check for his $43,000. As the month ended, the contractor learned that another disbursement was forthcoming.

The time between the arrival of Capt. Foote and the departure of Cmdr. John Rodgers for the east on October 5 was productively spent. Throwing himself fully into the various tasks assigned by his successor, Rodgers, the one-time explorer, was now, more than ever, involved in the Eads ironclad project.

From August into September, laborers laid out and assembled the bilge (lower hull), projecting it up 45 degrees from the flat bottom to the waterline. An inner skin of 4- and 5-inch planks covered this hull and these were, in turn, reinforced with 2-inch wood. Internal bulkheads were constructed within the bilge hulls. These would not only improve watertight integrity, but provided the spaces for magazines, coal bunkers, shot lockers, and shell rooms. They also provided additional support for the main deck (or gun deck) abuilding above and soon to be planked over. Additionally, below deck, the five 24-foot long boilers were placed into a cradle, the firebox was installed, and the two-cylinder Merritt main and one-cylinder Merritt "doctor" (auxiliary) engines were mounted. At the right moment, the central 20-foot wide paddle wheel would be sited in its protected raceway toward the stern.

Topside, the angled superstructure sloped upwards and inwards to the top of a 12-foot high rectangular wooden casemate. Five-inch planks atop the vertical frames comprised the sides of the casemate, which met the bilge hull at a 4-foot solid waterline timber base known as the "knuckle." Additional protective oak would be applied to the ends of the casemate, 24 inches on the bow and five inches on the stern. When this task was completed and the main and hurricane decks were finished, the entire craft was caulked. Once the armor plate was in hand, it would be riveted into place.

Almost since the project's first day, Gaylord. Son and Company rolled armor protection for the gunboats at its Ohio and Kentucky mills. Specifically, the 700 tons of product was produced in slabs 2½ inches thick, 13 inches wide, and in lengths ranging from 3½ feet to 11 feet. Indeed, the armor plate was rolled under the same sort of forfeiture arrangement that Eads had with the government. Gaylord was liable for a $200 penalty for every day it ran behind schedule. Gaylord's first shipment of armor plate arrived at Carondelet one day ahead of its delivery date. There it would be installed aboard the gunboats. Incidentally, it was Cmdr. Rodgers who earlier came up with the idea of manufacturing the plates with a lip that would permit their easier installation. Now, as his last western service, he decided that the effectiveness of the sheets should be tested.

Together with Superintendent Merritt, Rodgers called upon U.S. Army Lt. Albert Buffington at the St. Louis Arsenal. Would the military man like a bit of sport that would assist the war effort, the sailor inquired. The eager young lieutenant quickly assigned a pair of 10-pounder Parrott rifles and their crews to the duty.

On September 20, Merritt, Rodgers, Buffington, the cannon and their crews, together with a number of iron sheets, were taken by steamboat across the Mississippi to a beach opposite Carondelet on the Illinois shore. There the metal was attached to oak blocks 16 inches thick and set up as targets at a 35 degree angle, the same inclination as the casemate sides of the abuilding ironclads. In the tests which followed, those angles would change. Firing from ranges of 800 yards down to 200, the two Parrotts blasted away, failing to penetrate the armor plate. Satisfied, Rodgers reported to his superiors and to the local newspapermen watching that "the iron resisted beyond all expectations and proved to be of a very superior quality."

Eads sent in his third estimate on October 2. This one covered the $32,000 spent on the Mound City subcontract and the Hartupee and Company engines. Again, Eads pressed Meigs to pay him as soon as possible. Despite the $111,000 disbursement of September 29 (24 days overdue), he remained "cramped and annoyed for money." As of that date, the engineer reported that "all the engines and boilers; all the plate iron for five boats; and nearly all the work on my hulls is completed."

On October 5, as the work on the gunboats went on, the new western naval chief, Capt. Foote, sent another new officer, Cmdr. Roger Perry, to Cairo to take charge of receiving the ordnance and stores for the flotilla. He was to borrow the army wharf boat *Graham* for storing the cannon when they arrived and guard them "as already evil-minded persons have made attempts to render them useless."

As Perry departed, Foote wrote QMG Meigs requesting $130,000 to cover the expenses of the gunboat service. These expenses included wages, advances, and the purchase of clothing, small stores, anchors, chains, hawsers, hammocks, coal, engineers' and carpenters' stores, and "other contingent repairs and supplies." Meigs would also receive a statement from Superintendent Merritt, dated October 6, that Eads had just given him "bills for work

In its issue of February 22, 1862, *Harper's Weekly* includes an illustration of the gun deck of one of the turtles. The picture is quite accurate, "except for a few distortions." Edwin C. Bearss wrote to this author on August 9, 1969. It appears brighter than when its entire length was lit only by kerosene lanterns. There is also insufficient depiction of the chests and side racks for such items as priming wires, fuse wrenches, gunlocks, shot tongs, cups, rammers, sponges, and shell bearers as well as the correct placement of coiled breeching and preventer gear, training tackles, and other hawsers (*Harper's Weekly*, February 22, 1862).

and materials furnished by him for the Gun Boats for the amount of $175,000," including $20,000 worth of armor plating en route from Cincinnati. Although only four days remained under Eads' contract until the boats were to be delivered to Cairo, Merritt pointed out that it would be another week before the first was even launched and a fortnight beyond that before the premier unit could be sent down to the inland naval station.

It would require an additional two days for Merritt to dispatch Eads' estimate to Washington. In the meantime, the superintendent had discovered what he perceived to be a problem concerning the placement of the iron. Although the original specifications demanded 75 tons of protection for each boat, this was not enough to also adequately cover the boilers and engines. Unless those areas were to be left relatively defenseless, another 25 tons of armor was required. Merritt was correct, of course, that the designed protection was not complete, being arranged only about ⅔ of the way back the length of the casemate from the bow. The after third of the casemate, the hurricane deck, boilers, machinery, steam drum, and fantail were not significantly armored, if protected at all, and were vulnerable.

Where it was placed on the vessel sides, the heavy armor provided coverage for a distance 5 feet below the knuckle and 12 feet above. The vertical strakes were nearly 9 feet long and 13 inches wide. Overlapping lips, suggested by Cmdr. Rodgers, each 2 inches wide and a half-inch thick were part of each iron plate and allowed the plates to be held together on the casemates when inch-and-half bolts were pounded through their laps. The deck just forward of the casemate was covered with ¾ inches of iron.

As quartermaster general, Montgomery C. Meigs (1816–1892) worked with navy officers on western waters almost from the first day of the Civil War. It was he who counseled with the Navy Department regarding the design and building of all army gunboats and then arranged the details of the ironclad contracts won by James B. Eads. Meigs' department then dealt with Eads on all matters related to the construction of the *Carondelet* and her sister boats (National Archives).

It was anticipated that the boats would fight bows-on only, Merritt's concern was not universally appreciated. It was, in many quarters, initially believed that 24 inches of oak, the vertically and horizontally placed timbers of which were alternated, and 2½ foot iron slabs on the forward casemate would be sufficient. Even so, lack of plating on the incurving sides of the casemate toward the bow rendered the turtles dangerous even in head-on fighting. Cmdr. Rodgers also determined to provide "2½ inch plating on the outside of the casemate reaching from 2 feet forward of the boiler to abreast of the piston rod guides, making a length of 32 feet." The listed 12-inch side and aft backing was not universally protective.

Plunging shot from above, particularly if it hit a steam drum or boiler, could disable a boat. The *New York Times* would inform its readers on February 8, 1862, that "of course, the boats are not plated on the roof, which consists of 2½ inch plank." It was readily acknowledged that a shot falling through the hurricane deck, even at an acute angle, "would go through, and a heavy shell so entering would blow up the boat." On the other hand, "the chances of this occurring are not as one in a thousand."

The *Mound City* would take a plunging shot into her steam drum in June 1862 and many aboard were scalded to death as she was put out of action. An attack from the rear, such as that made by the *Arkansas* in July 1862 upon the *Carondelet,* could also have terrible results. By the fall of 1862 when she was upgraded following her clash with the Confederate monster, the *Carondelet* had her boilers "perfectly protected with heavy oak casemates, covered with iron."

As summer started to give way to fall, workmen bustled about the hulls, winding their way through huge balks of timber and enormous stacks of lumber, to say nothing of all manner of fittings. Other obstacles included piles of timber ends and carpets of wood chips, plus buckets and boxes crammed with tools, nails, caulk, and other items. Disgusting today but so common a nuisance in those days as to elicit no comment from newsmen was oceans of dung from the horses that hauled heavy loads, especially lumber, from the Iron Mountain Railroad tracks down to the ways. Saws buzzed and hammers banged continuously. A suggestion by navy constructor John Lenthall was also followed. Timber was "used ... directly from the saw," without marking or finishing. The noise became deafening when mauls clanged against rivets so hot they glowed red. The great nails secured the plate armor to the casemate wood, from 26 inches thick on the forward services to 19 inches aft. As a general description, the uninitiated would, in the words of historian Kendall Gott, look upon each craft as "a raft with an iron shed on top."

As the casemates were completed, they were painted black, with the hurricane deck and other exterior decks left with natural wood finishes. The only differentiating color, at least initially, was a distinguishing stack band given each craft. The red stripes of the *Carondelet* appeared a few feet below her chimney tops.

To make certain that the weight of the bow armor plate did not cause the boat to travel low forward and possibly ground or arch up like the spine of a pig and break, the vessels were all equipped with "hog chains." Running fore and aft from four vertical stanchions that were situated just above the fourth gun port, these 2½ inch diameter rods passed through the hurricane and main decks and were anchored at each end of the engine and boilers spaces to the keelsons. These could be adjusted and aided navigation through shallow water.

Within a deep swallowtail inside each casemate, about 28 feet forward of the stern, an 18-foot-wide race was cut to house a single paddle wheel in an iron framework. The 22-foot diameter wheel was given a crank on each side to be operated by pitman rods. The paddle blades, called "buckets," were made of wood and could be readily replaced if damaged. It was hoped that this arrangement would mitigate the obvious hazards of exposed paddle wheel boxes. The relatively small profile of the outside wheelhouse was covered with light armor (critics called it "boiler iron") where it humped above the hurricane deck. Power was, of course, supplied by the below-deck boilers and two-cylinder, inclined, non-condensing, reciprocating Merritt engine. The design and location of the race made it impossible to mount a single rudder—even if it had been sufficient to control steerage. Two rudders—still insufficient to fully control maneuverability in swift water—were mounted on sternposts, one on each side of the race. Wrought iron hinges held the 5-foot high rudders in place.

October 12 was an important milestone in the Eads gunboat enterprise. Two days after the date for delivery specified in the government contract, the first craft, *Carondelet,* was launched to the delight of a large crowd of onlookers. At 4:00 P.M. that Saturday afternoon, the vessel was, according to the reporter from the *St. Louis Daily Missouri Democrat,* "Gradually lowered into the 'father of waters' upon the ways on which it was built, and such was the noiseless, and almost imperceptible manner of the operation, that we found the boat gracefully upon the water and nobody hurt and not even a lady frightened." A rival scribe from the *St. Louis Daily Missouri Republican* was also very enthusiastic. "The launch was conducted in an admirable manner," he testified, "and everything about the Marine Railway worked smoothly."

When launched, the boat was far along in her construction. It would only be a few more days until she was ready for trials. Upon examining the vessel, knowledgeable rivermen proclaimed her building was being "done in a very substantial and smooth manner." Eads was "entitled to great credit for the faithful manner in which he had performed his contract."

A second boat was to be launched on the 15th and the remaining two Carondelet boats by the 17th or 18th. It would only remain "for the 560 workmen" employed to finish fitting them out and this was expected to be completed by November 1.[11] Having been launched just 45 days after Eads signed the contract to build her, the first City Series ironclad would be remembered as the most active. Her name was *Carondelet* and she was the first ironclad gunboat ever launched in the Western Hemisphere.[12]

It would take some time to finish fitting out the new gunboats; indeed, it would take longer than most people expected. As October drew toward a close, Eads urgently informed Capt. Foote that it would be necessary to halt work "on the gunboats for want of funds." The naval officer appealed to QMG Meigs, who found a way to quickly send the $227,750 of Eads' fourth estimate.

Toward the end of the first week in November, Capt. Foote, who would shortly be appointed flag officer, examined the four Carondelet vessels. He was not happy with what he found. In a semiofficial letter to the quartermaster general dated November 7, the bearded seadog commented on what he considered to be a problem of balance. With the armor aboard, Foote complained, the vessels drew 5 feet 10 inches aft, but only 3 feet 11 inches forward, and at anchor, the fantails (that portion of the deck abaft the paddle wheel) was only 13 inches from the water. The naval officer feared that when the two huge rudders and the wheel buckets were installed, they would add to this unhappy ratio in each boat. To solve this problem, Foote recommended that, abaft the wheel, the contractor "cut out the deck and beams covering the clearance, springing a heavy timber arch over the space." Once the arch was finished, the captain suggested that "a light deck" be built upon it.

Contractor Eads also weighed into this dispute, insisting the USN man was wrong. The Missourian believed—correctly as it turned out—that, when fully armed and provisioned, the stern draft would not be increased, but rather equalized as the heavy ordnance, forward of the center of gravity, would lift the stern. After this civilized dispute, Foote developed increasing confidence in Eads. Still, in a private letter to Meigs, the sailor noted that, irrespective of his increasingly high estimate of the contractor's character, he would still bear close watching.

With the coming of winter, it became necessary to transfer the gunboats from Carondelet to Cairo "so that the usual fall of the river as winter sets in will not prove a blockade." The first two gunboats to finish fitting out were the *Pittsburg* and the *St. Louis* and so they were the first dispatched down the difficult 145 mile course, arriving at Cairo on November 28 and 29. Because the craft had not yet shipped their cannon, they were escorted by the timberclad *Lexington.*

On the last day of November, Foote, now a flag officer equal in rank to a brigadier general, notified QMG Meigs that the *Carondelet* and *Louisville* would leave for Cairo shortly. Happily, he also noted success of the engine trials on the two ironclads, which hoisted anchor and, with their escort, departed downriver on December 2. The *Carondelet* and *Louisville* arrived at Cairo on December 5. Meanwhile, Foote, who had taken a train down on December 4, was on hand to greet their arrival. After the boats were tied up, he wired

Above and following page: **Taken at Eads' Carondelet, Missouri, boatyard in the fall of 1861, these two extraordinary photographs depict work on the hulls of the City Series gunboats, one of which may have been the *Carondelet.* In the photograph above, four of the ships are shown under construction in pairs, at two levels on the shore, with casemate side timbers largely installed. Vertical timbers extending above the slanting casemate sides are framing for the ships' paddle-wheel boxes. Note building and flagpole in the right background, the twin rudder posts at the ships' sterns with the paddle raceway between them, and a portion of the copious amount of timber devoted to the project in the foreground. In the opposite page photograph, the main deck on one gunboat is shown, with its boilers in the foreground and casemate timbers at the sides. Another vessel is beyond, with some spar deck beams atop the casemate side timbers and upright framing in place for her wheel box (courtesy National Archives).**

navy secretary Welles of their arrival and pointed out that it would require two weeks for Eads to finish them. The flag officer promised that, while the carpenters worked on, he would have his own men see that the craft were equipped and ready "for service."

Once the welcoming remarks were over and the last "Huzzah" was shouted, the carpenters and mechanics swarmed aboard the two gunboats. The laborers plied their hammers and mauls in endless noise. Visiting the latest arrivals at this new naval station, which would soon become one of the most important in Welles' domain, the editor of the local newspaper was impressed. Back at his desk, he wrote: "We are confident in asserting that the boats built for the service are of such construction and so armed that they can pass any batteries that have been or may possibly be erected at Columbus or any other point on the river."

The work continued apace and the interior arrangements of the boats, like those coming down earlier, soon began to appear very "shipshape." The machinery was adjusted, ammunition taken aboard, and preparations made to receive the cannon. A St. Louis reporter also inspected the work being done at Cairo and commented that "the sound of the hammer and chisel and saw, and the busy notes of industry arising from all marine quarters was especially reassuring."[13]

Even as the workers hammered away, it was not long before new problems turned up. As mentioned earlier, Eads changed some of the Pook drawings to counteract design errors. The major problem encountered this time was with the boilers, which now numbered five instead of the four in the original blueprints. As the *Cairo City Gazette* observed, "The boats are now here and have to undergo some alterations in their machinery, which will give them increased power. This alteration will necessarily delay the expedition down the river for a short time, but it will go soon enough to suit our Southern friends—we mean enemies."

While steaming downriver, engineers in several of the gunboats noticed that their engines had "worked water instead of steam, endangering the engines." To remedy this, it was necessary to enter into new contract arrangements for the relocation of the steam drums "to the top of the boilers." It was also found necessary to armor the octagonal pilothouses.

On December 16, Capt. Foote wired Capt. Wise at Barnum's Hotel, St. Louis, regarding the steam drum problem. Could Wise, the naval officer inquired, after hearing firsthand concerning the difficulty from Superintendent Merritt, make inquires. Had G.B. Allen & Co., Renfrew, Crozier & Co., and Gaty, McCune & Co. really offered the best prices for doing the relocation work? In the end, the necessary modifications, according to the *St. Louis Daily Missouri Democrat*, cost $1,200 per boat.

Off-duty soldiers, of which there were many guarding the tip of Illinois, regularly visited the waterfront to check the boats' progress (security was not as tight then as now, even in wartime). Pointing to their shapes, they often compared the craft to the large mud turtles which inhabited the shores of the Mississippi and Ohio rivers. Eliot Callender, soon to be serving as an ordinary seaman aboard the *Cincinnati*, styled the craft as a product of the "Mud Turtle school of architecture with just a dash of Pollywog treatment by way of relief." Thus the Eads ironclads became know as "Pook Turtles" or just "turtles."

While the reporters, civilians, and off-duty soldiers ambled around the wharf area inspecting and criticizing, the outfitting of the gunboats continued. An even more important inspection of the *Carondelet* and her sisters was that conducted by Superintendent Litherbury on December 21. Once his examination was completed, the Cincinnatian presented his findings to Capt. Foote, who signed off on them and passed them to Eads. In his cover letter, the naval officer, believing matters of funding did not fall under his purview, refused to release the contractor "from any obligation of forfeiture he may be under by terms of his contract" for not completing the boats "within the time specified." He did give Eads a progress summary of expenditures paid ($478,275) since August and the amount ($148,925) still owed. Simultaneously, Foote refused to accept the boats because they were unfinished. Eads had not yet "fully completed them for their armament." The government therefore required him "to do all extra work necessary to this end."

Distressed, Eads informed Foote that he was taking the train to Washington, D.C., in an effort to obtain the unpaid balance of the contract, as well as additional funds ($85,000) incurred for extra work performed by his requirement or that of Cmdr. Rodgers. With business suspended over Christmas, the engineer was unable to visit Meigs before Boxing Day, and to make matters worse, the interview went poorly. The QMG bluntly informed Eads that, regardless of his excuses, the gunboats were not finished and hence the government was due damages.

Unsuccessful in the attempt to get paid, the never-say-die Eads petitioned Meigs again on December 29, the day he took the train back to Missouri. He and his creditors, in a note to the logistics officer, needed to know when they would receive payment "of the accounts left with you."

To hasten this finishing work, Eads, on January 7, 1862, hired and rushed 24 more carpenters and machinists by train from St. Louis to Cairo. The *Carondelet* was commissioned on January 10 and was moved to midstream, where she anchored near the already commissioned *Cincinnati* and *St. Louis.* By January 11, even as machinists continued working on the gunboats' boiler problem, Foote and the laborers managed to get all the cannon aboard and mounted in the dark and hot casemates.[14]

The *Carondelet*'s great guns were her raison d'être. Two of the rifled 7-inch army 42-pounders that war secretary Cameron had ordered sent west and an ancient 8-inch 64-pounder smoothbore were mounted in her bow battery. The stern battery consisted of a pair of old 32-pounder smoothbores, while her broadside was made up of a pair of 42-pounders, a pair of 64-pounders, and four 32-pounders.[15] Various racks and chests near the ordnance contained battleaxes, priming wires, shot tongs, and gun locks. In racks along the inside casemate wall were sponges, cups, and rammers.[16]

In a January 11 report to navy assistant secretary Gustavus V. Fox, Capt. Foote reported that work on all of the City Series gunboats, save the *St. Louis*, was not yet "fully completed, or out of the contractor's hands." The movement of the steam drums to the tops of the boilers onboard the *Carondelet* and her sisters was not finished, though cannon were all or partially mounted.

Topside aboard the craft, the finished pilothouses finally received their protective iron. Armor was affixed to 19-inch thick oak backing on the first three panels and upon timbers 12 inches thick aft. Not known until the *Cairo*'s recovery, the workmen cleverly installed one-half-inch iron flaps over the rectangular ports on each of the eight sides. Each flap had a small circular "peephole" about the size of a silver dollar in its center, and when action pended, the flap could be lowered over the port. Thus "in the hour of battle, the pilot will be peeping out through narrow holes, his hands grasping the [6-foot] wheel and steering the vessel." Inside the pilothouse, as on all river steamers, were cords leading to bells in the engine room for the communication of desired speeds. In addition, the pilothouse contained ready-reference charts, the rough or deck logbook, and such necessary items as speaking trumpets and spyglasses. Access to the chart room and gun deck below was by ladder. Another interesting place aboard the *Carondelet* was her blacksmith shop. It was located about 10 feet abaft the chimneys. All manner of tools were stocked there—vises, hammers, anvils, chisels—for use in repairing iron or metal fixtures and for other assorted tasks.[17]

While the carpenters finished the *Carondelet*'s pilothouse, the great guns were mounted aboard, the matter of the steam drums was resolved, and painters finished applying a coat of black paint to the exterior above the knuckle. Earlier, the interior had been whitewashed and, even before she and her sisters were launched, the hull below the waterline was colored red. All paint was lead-based. Because of their similarities when seen from any distance, each "turtle" was given her own identifying band painted around her chimneys a few feet from the top. The *Carondelet*'s new stack band was red.

Another inspection of the *Carondelet* and her sisters was undertaken on January 15 by several of Capt. Foote's subordinates. Rowed between the vessels, Master Carpenter James R. McGee, together with Cmdrs. Alexander M. Pennock and Roger N. Stembel, thoroughly checked all decks, armament, machinery, and associated spaces and equipment. When the visits were concluded, the team certified that the work was, in fact, "completed according to the terms of the contract with the Government, excepting the time at which they ought to have been finished and delivered at Cairo."

Joseph B. "Mack" McCullagh, the correspondent of the *Cincinnati Daily Gazette,* also had a chance to view the craft during the day and was somewhat less than impressed. Among the first to say in print that the ironclads "present very much the shape of a turtle," the Queen City scribe had his doubts. Although the naval officers supposedly stated publicly that the new vessels were safe, "it does not look so to an outsider," he told his readers in a report sent off that night.

Picking up on the weaknesses noted by Superintendent Merritt (perhaps through an interview with him), Mack revealed in an age of far less media security that "two-thirds of the sides and all the upper deck (or roof) and the stern, including the upper portion of the wheelhouse" were "exposed." Given its central location, the partially iron-covered machinery, he opined, was "better protected than the men, particularly if they should be subjected to a cross-fire." To sum it up, the reporter said he would "dislike exceedingly to be cooped up in one of them under the tremendous fire which they will probably have to encounter at some points on the river."

Meanwhile, the flotilla inspection team filled out a formal certificate, which was presented to Capt. Foote for his signature. The next morning, with Eads and several associates present, Foote signed the form and handed it to the contractor, formally accepting the seven City Series gunboats, now 97 days late. Once that little ceremony was completed, the remaining five gunboats were all placed into commission. One after the other they anchored in midstream among floating ice.

Cmdr. Henry Walke (1808–1896), captain of the timberclad *Tyler*, became the first captain of the *Carondelet* at the close of 1861. The longest serving and best known of the boat's skippers, he would remain aboard for a year. During his tenure, the ironclad fought at Fort Henry, Fort Donelson, Island No. 10 (scene of her greatest success), Fort Pillow/Plum Point Bend, and Memphis before encountering the Rebel ram *Arkansas*. Walke, a noted artist, was tall, taciturn, and not universally beloved, either aboard his boat or throughout the Western Flotilla (Library of Congress).

A few days later, a St. Louis newspaperman was able to inform his readers that the vessels were "fearfully and wonderfully made." Every bit as important, "the gunboats are at last (thank Heaven!) actually done." When about this time the British writer Anthony Trollope saw the turtles "close under the terminus of the railway with their flat, ugly noses against the muddy bank," he believed them quite formidable, "got up" as they were "quite irrespective of expense."

Modestly, Eads, in a letter to the editor of the *St. Louis Daily Missouri Democrat* the following June, took no credit for the design of his turtles. Most of the credit for the gunboats has gone to Pook and Rodgers; however, one scholar has complimented Eads. "Anyone at all familiar with his [Eads']

Along with mortar boats then also under construction, several of the Pook turtles are shown outfitting at the Carondelet riverbank prior to their transfer down the Mississippi to Cairo in December 1861 (*Battles and Leaders*).

quick mind and assertive personality," wrote John D. Milligan in 1984, "would know that the man doubtless contributed ideas to the project as well."[18]

Among the preparatory actions henceforth regularly undertaken by the *Carondelet* and her sisters was coaling. The 140-pounds-per-square-inch Merritt engines, which also ran the steam capstan and pumps, were coal burning. The anthracite fuel was not provided by the ton or hundredweight, as might be expected. Rather, it was loaded through the gun ports into the three bunkers in the hold by the bushel basket or the box. This was not a process that could be accomplished "underway" in the style known by navy men since World War II. The *Carondelet* obtained her fuel from a coal barge lashed alongside. When at an anchorage (permanent or temporary), the craft often moved at a regularly scheduled time to perform this dirty task. While steaming, the gunboat consumed 18 to 20 bushels, or 1,980 pounds, of coal per hour. Range was not as important to the ironclads as fuel availability; hence, coal barges were either kept with the fleet or located at convenient points, such as the mouth of the White River.[19]

Designed for a speed of 9 miles per hour, or approximately 7 nautical knots, the Eads ironclads seldom made this speed due to their weight and the strong river currents. Because the furnaces of the ironclads had no fans and relied upon natural chimney draft to assist the firebox flames, the power output was low. The *Carondelet* was a notoriously slow steamer and she had even worse luck with the current than her sisters. When steaming downriver at reduced speed, her steering ability was almost nil.

Despite these problems, Seaman Callendar fully expected that the ironclad sisters would be able to make up "in style" whatever "they lacked in speed." With her coal, cannon, and stores aboard, the *Carondelet* lay low in the water—much like a swimming turtle. Unhappily, this displacement would mean that she had great difficulty in obtaining extreme elevation with her cannon due to the low gun ports.[20]

Although the government, in the person of Capt. Foote, had accepted the seven Pook turtles, the last chapter in the *Carondelet* construction story—payment—was unfinished because the War Department had yet to cut the final checks. Eads began to worry that he would not be paid for work added beyond that specified in the contract even as his creditors began sending nasty notes or clamoring at his door.

On January 27, Eads informed Meigs that the extra armor work alone resulted in the boats floating 122 tons of iron plating instead of the 75 proposed by naval constructor Samuel Pook. This total was half again what was originally expected and, naturally, caused a cost overrun. During the last week of January, the contractor boarded a train for the Federal City in order to once more see QMG Meigs and restate his case for recompense. Again, the harried quartermaster general appeared out of sorts during his interview with Eads. Meigs was not interested in listening to the Missourian's talk of government-caused delays such as the need for extra armor plating or late receipt of materiel monies due. He was only concerned that the boats were not at Cairo on time. Leaving the army man's office, Eads wired Foote: "I can obtain no assurance of receiving a dollar and must return as I came."

On February 5, Eads again got in touch with Meigs' office. He acknowledged the late completion of the boats, but pointed out that the government had also been late in paying him so that he could proceed. Wrote Eads: "Question, am I liable to forfeiture?" Busy trying to supply the entire Union Army and doubtless tired of the Eads matter which had plagued him for the past six months, Meigs turned the compensation matter over to a member of his staff, O.M. Dorman. The latter studied the engineer's claims that extra work and lack of government payments had held him up, found that Eads position was correct, and returned a report to his chief recommending payment without penalty. QMG Meigs forwarded Eads' claims to the U.S. comptroller, J. Madison Cutts, on February 15. With the papers, he sent along Dorman's study and a note saying that whatever was paid to Eads should come out of December's congressional appropriation for western gunboats.

After himself studying the documents from the three men, Cutts also agreed that Eads was due and issued him $234,781.31 in government bonds— not cash — on February 20 as settlement. After waiting these many months and actually having had what was still his property in action at Forts Henry and Donelson earlier in the month, the patriot was finally able to pay off his creditors.[21]

3

Life Aboard the Carondelet

The *Carondelet* was finished, but she, together with her six sisters, was still unready to play an active role in the developing plans of the Union Army in the west. The reason for this was a lack of enlisted crew. Shipping men for the gunboats was not a simple undertaking, as Cmdr. John Rodgers learned when trying to recruit crews for the timberclads during the summer of 1861. Although it was originally expected that experienced river jacks would quickly enlist, that did not happen. The potential gunboatmen joined the army instead.

Wages aboard the ironclads and other naval craft were low (particularly in comparison to the income of riverboat sailors). A significant cause of poor recruiting was fear of death from scalding should cannonballs impact the ill-protected wheelhouse. Recruitment of Caucasian men to serve aboard the gunboats lagged throughout the war, as Lt. Com. S. Ledyard Phelps told his superior, because it was universally believed "that service on Gunboats will be exceedingly dangerous."

All during the fall and winter of 1861–1862, the flotilla commanders (Rodgers and Flag Officer Andrew Hull Foote) worked diligently to secure crews, pushing their case directly with their superiors at the Navy and War Departments and indirectly through efforts made at recruiting offices (called "rendezvous") in many of the river towns, in addition to those in Cleveland, Cincinnati, Chicago, and Milwaukee. Psychology, bureaucracy , and lack of experience with naval requirements, as well as the needs of the ocean fleet and field armies, conspired against flotilla recruitment.[1]

On January 11, 1862, as the Eads ironclads approached acceptance, Flag Officer Foote reported to Washington that he had only 589 men on hand and, because of continued higher civilian riverboat pay, had been able to attract only about 200 men at the recruiting stations set up along the Ohio River. A thousand were still required.

The *St. Louis Daily Missouri Democrat*, in its January 24 issue, informed the local public of the navy's recruiting problems. The unknown correspondent found it "provoking" that, with the ironclads finally finished, they were not fully manned. Foote had done his best, the paper said, but had received many more promises than sailors. Even Brig. Gen. Ulysses S. Grant, the Cairo district commander, had encouraged ironclad enlistments. Perhaps those of service age did not recognize the benefits of gunboat service: "The pay of the sailor is somewhat more liberal than that of the soldier, and his duties include no long marches or wet encampments. He gets his meals and his grog [under Foote — no way!] with unfailing regularity and has always, besides, a dry bed — luxaries [*sic*] which a soldier can seldom count on." Despite such inducements, no rivermen and few soldiers stepped forward to volunteer.

When he was informed that the ironclads were finished, navy secretary Gideon Welles was also told that, in light of the poor turnout, it would be difficult to make them as efficient as they might be. Foote would send 60 men aboard each boat, leaving 115 enlisted billets per vessel.

Welles interceded on behalf of the gunboat commander once more and, by the end of January, Maj. Gen. Henry Halleck, overall western theater commander, started to allocate some 600 men to the flotilla. Foote also found that he had no choice but to detail most of the crews of some vessels from one to another. For example, the *Carondelet* received most of the bluejackets available to the *Mound City*. By the time of the Fort Henry expedition, all of the billets on the City Series boats *Cairo, Cincinnati,* and *Carondelet,* plus the *Essex,* were filled. Finding sufficient sailors would remain a problem for some time to come.[2]

The City Series ironclads were designed for complements of about 175 men each. This total included 16 or 17 officers, 27 petty officers, 111 seamen, 4 or 5 landsmen, 1 or 2 apprentices, 12 firemen, and 4 coal heavers. The *Carondelet* had openings for 17 officers, but of these, only one, the skipper, would initially be a professional navy man and even that would change as the conflict wore on.

The "mud turtle" Eads ironclads were not only different in appearance from oceangoing sailing ships, but they did not look much like Western steamboats, either. True, they were about the same size as some of the latter, but they were closed up by their casemates and consequently much more uncomfortable. The men who joined the crew of the *Carondelet* would find, upon stepping inside her casemate, that its sloping sides and overhead of just nine feet made the craft somewhat cramped. Even when her gun ports were open, her enclosing armored superstructure made her interior temperature rise on normal days to over 90 degrees and on hot ones to over 100—and that was outside the engine room. Mounted just forward of the wheelhouse, four iron ventilators were not much help. The new boat was noisy, sooty-dirty, and nothing at all like naval vessels on the East Coast or Gulf Coast blockades.

Back on December 23, Flag Officer Foote had received a letter from Cmdr. Henry Walke, still in command of the timberclad task force that made headlines for its service during the November Battle of Belmont. Itching for one of the new boats, Walke applied to transfer himself and his whole crew from the timberclad *Tyler*. The tall ex–Virginian, who called Ohio home, was not alone in seeking to skipper one of the Eads craft. Foote, a one-time messmate of Walke's on the *Natchez*, replied on Christmas Eve that it would be unwise to break up the crews of the timberclads in such a manner. To do so "would be unmilitary and injurious to the flotilla, and unprecedented in the Navy."

Agreeing on January 15, 1862, that the timberclad captain could have one of the ironclads (with a new crew), the flag officer cut orders for Walke to assume command of the *Carondelet.* Shortly after receiving Foote's directive, Walke turned command of the *Tyler* over to Lt. William Gwin and repaired aboard his new boat. Upon his shoulders was now placed the burden of organizing her subordinate officers and crew.[3]

The junior officers aboard the *Carondelet* were "Acting Volunteer" officers, a rank similar to that held by those gallant Royal Navy volunteer officers who manned British escort vessels during World War II. Few if any had received professional naval training prior to making application to join the Western Flotilla. Many were rivermen and former steamboat captains or mates—merchant sailors. None ever became commodores or admirals. The petty officers were normally advanced from the most skilled of the enlisted members of the crew.

The volunteer officers and petty officers worked hard onboard the *Carondelet* and throughout the gunboat squadron, as much was required to whip that new service into shape. Advancement came through demonstration of military courage or excellent seamanship—and a hard driver like Henry Walke would tolerate no less than either. Unlike the situation in the Union army, promotions were not awarded for ability to recruit hands or swing votes. Wrote newsman Albert D. Richardson about the inland navy's nonpolitical officer corps: "They were far freer from envy and jealousy—quiet, unassuming, with no nonsense about them."[4]

The contract pilots aboard the river gunboats have often been singled out for special praise as they were, collectively, perhaps the bravest men aboard. Their position was completely anomalous, being civilians subject to army authority able to legally exercise no authority save that concerning navigation. Despite the fact that Confederate snipers attempted to kill them and thereby disable the boats they were guiding, many came forward for the positions, even knowing the danger.[5]

The officers aboard the *Carondelet* had their quarters in the cabins Samuel Pook had specifically designed into the after section of her casemate. These included four for the junior officers, one each for a dispensary, head, mail room, and wardroom. The two large cabins at the rear of the casemate belonged to Capt. Walke.

Save for the captain, who traditionally dined alone, the boat's officers took their meals in the wardroom, also known as the officers' mess. There were 10 men assigned to the wardroom mess, though none below the rank of ensign. The master's mates, carpenters, and assistant engineers all belonged to steerage. Each officer contributed about $10 per month toward his share of mess provisions beyond government issue. One man was chosen to make all of the purchases, handle the bookkeeping, and maintain mess supplies. By August 1863, the 10 *Carondelet* wardroom officers had acquired for themselves a stock that included a large amount of sugar, 2½ barrels of flour, 50 pounds of cheese, 100 pounds of bacon, one 50-pound box of soda crackers, 6 gallons of honey, and 24 bottles of catsup and Worcestershire sauce.

Aboard the *Carondelet*, as Acting Ensign Scott D. Jordan later wrote home, the men in his mess had their "meals in good shape on a Mahogany table." There they ate from ironstone dishes and used knives, forks, and spoons produced by Rogers and Brothers and the Hartford Manufacturing Company. They were served by four African American waiters (overseen by a white steward), who were allowed to eat at the officers' table once they were finished. The waiters also kept the officers' staterooms in good order, blacked their boots every morning, and washed and mended their clothing and bedding. The African American cooks, on the other hand, "never come to the wardroom under any circumstances."

All of the wardroom officers were smokers or chewed tobacco. They were not as opposed to strong drink as their flag officer and had an excellent liquor locker, "undoubtedly for snake bite." After Memphis was taken in June 1862, there were also soft drinks from such firms as J.H. Kemp of that city.[6]

Whenever they had free time, the ironclad's officers could be seen reading newspapers forwarded from home or elsewhere, enjoying letters or writing them, and even sunbathing. They fished, played cards, and on occasion, took an extra nap in their bunks. A few, like Capt. Walke, an accomplished artist, made sketches of local scenery, other squadron craft, passing civil steamboats, or past battle scenes.[7]

When the *Carondelet* departed for Fort Henry in February 1862, her enlisted crew was quite heterogeneous. It would remain so throughout the war. About all the new tars had in common was that almost none joined the boat with any nautical experience. Aboard the Eads ironclad, as her first commander later remembered, there were more young men than any other vessel in the fleet. The majority of these came from Philadelphia and Boston and were untrained ("without drill"). There were, however, "just enough men-o'-war's men to leaven the lump with naval discipline." The older seamen from the east included Maine lumbermen, New Bedford whalers, New York liners, and Philadelphia "sea lawyers." The foreigners enlisted were mostly Irish, with a few English, Scots, French, Germans, Swedes, Norwegians, and Danes.

African Americans did not initially constitute a significant number of *Carondelet* crewmen; however, in the years ahead, a number shipped aboard, often in times of illness or hot weather or just to fill an increase in empty billets caused by squadron expansion or the end to short-term enlistments. Many of these men were freed or escaped slaves, called "contrabands," and held the lowest ranks and often found themselves at work in the engine room handling coal. The number of African Americans aboard increased after the fall of Vicksburg; for example, on July 15, 1863, eight were enlisted at one time.[8]

Once *Carondelet* seamen came aboard (no matter whether at the beginning of the conflict or later), they were assigned to their duties and stations by the executive officer, initially known as the first master. He also assigned them to a mess, a small unit that, on this particular ironclad, was not unlike that onboard any other Yankee warship regardless of location. Each mess provided dining and social cohesion for from 5 to 10 ratings and each mess had one large wooden "kit" (chest) in which the sailors stored their eating gear — tin cups and plates, spoons, scrub brushes, and an earthen jar of molasses. Every sailor initialed and took care of his own utensils.

In addition to assigning men their duties, messes, and stations, the ship's officers also divided the crew into two 25-man watches, one each port and starboard (left and right). Additionally, each watch also had two quartermasters and a captain of the watch. Acting Ensign Scott D. Jordan in a letter home explained to his wife their further division: "The watches are again divided into 1st and 2nd Starboard and 1st and 2nd Port Watches, making what is called Quarter Watches. So you see you have 1 Quartermaster and 1 captain of the watch always on deck and subject to the Officer of the Deck's orders." Throughout the

Learning to service the *Carondelet*'s cannon was the major drill endured by her seamen. Fighting those pieces was the primary reason they were recruited and to do so efficiently — and without panic in the din of battle — required much practice (National Archives).

Save for the captain, who traditionally dined alone, the boat's officers took their meals in the wardroom, also known as the officers' mess. There were 10 men assigned to the wardroom mess, though none below the rank of ensign. The master's mates, carpenters, and assistant engineers all belonged to steerage (National Archives).

Many men aboard the *Carondelet* engaged in active correspondence with loved ones at home, waiting, as sailors always did, for the next mail steamer. Some bluejackets, however, were sadly without relations but enjoyed sharing the letters or newspapers of their messmates (*Harper's Weekly*, January 28, 1865).

entire day, each watch lasted four hours beginning at 12 midnight and running to the following midnight. So it was, for example, that the *Carondelet*'s gun deck was also divided into three divisions: Bow (First); Broadside (Second); and Stern (Third). Bells run on the half-hour marked the passage of time. At the end of each watch, an entry recording all activities seen or participated in (no matter how trivial) was made in the boat's deck log. To avoid surprise and ensure squadron-wide safety, certain precautions were common to all the boats. Indeed, many were institutionalized when Acting Rear Adm. David Dixon Porter took over the fleet.[9]

Despite the fact that the men were assigned to various duties in separate watches and divisions, many found that, regardless or "urging" from their petty officers, they still did not understand the ways of navy life. One man wrote to his brother:

> If you are ignorant [of your duties], it is nothing more than is the case with everyone, with the exception only of the captain and a few eastern officers.... Indeed, I have been surprised to find so many totally ignorant of their duties and, like myself, have to pick up gradually.... [T]wo thirds of them do not know anymore about their requirements than I do.... [Experience] is not particularly essential [;] all that will be required below the captain can be learned and performed in the course of a few weeks.

Judging from the ironclads' success at Fort Henry less than a month after their commissioning, this young man seems to have been correct in his optimistic conclusion.

The men of the *Carondelet* must have initially presented less than a "smart" appearance to an inspecting officer. While many of the sailors did wear regulation navy uniforms, others were dressed in soldier garb—complete with the insignia of the branch—cavalry, infantry—from which they had volunteered or were drafted. An observer in a letter to kin noted on December 1, 1861 that "As to your uniform, there is none presently required.... It will be necessary to have the navy cap with band and cover; beyond that it will be optional with yourself. If you see fit to get a uniform, one similar to mine ... a sack coat, like the one you wear of blue ... with the pants and vest as the dress uniform, will be what you require. There is no regulation as to overcoats; one can wear what he pleases."

Officers dressed in uniform whenever they were on duty. Despite the fact that awnings were rigged all over the boat during the summer, the need to keep up personal appearances could be extremely uncomfortable. Although coats were required, "we omit wearing our vests when we please so we manage to get along very well," one junior officer recalled in June 1863. A few months later, he also remarked that the workday uniforms were the same as the best uniforms, except manufactured from "a cheaper kind of cloth."

After Acting Rear Adm. Porter took over the squadron in October 1862, he ordered that the crewmen of each boat be examined, morning and evening, to see if they were "comfortably clad, and have their under flannels on." The crew wore government issue shoes with hobnailed soles which were attached to the uppers with wooden pegs. Some of the bluejackets actually wore shoes with horseshoes on the heels. Clothing and small stores were issued to the men once a month under the supervision of one of the boat's officers. They were paid their small wages quarterly.[10]

Crewmen aboard the *Carondelet,* and other vessels of the Union's western navy, had, by modern standards, a poor diet, quite dull. It was not dissimilar from that aboard merchant steamers and, it can be argued, was better than that enjoyed by many big city dwellers. With regard to fresh chow, citizens increasingly encountered by the bluejackets in small river communities were also sometimes better fed—before they were visited by foraging parties from both sides.

The kinds of provisions available to sailors' messes aboard the ironclad can be seen from the manifest of stores taken aboard on one date chosen at random, March 28, 1863:

> 32 barrels of biscuit, 8 barrels of beef, 9 barrels of pork, 9 barrels of flour, 4 barrels of rice, 4½ barrels of dried apples, 4 barrels of sugar, 1⅓ barrels of coffee, 5 barrels of beans, 3 barrels of molasses, 1½ barrels of vinegar, and 2 kegs of pickles.

The beef and pork were salted. Additionally, the galley was stocked with butter, potatoes, and preserved meat. Occasionally, it was possible to get fresh meats ashore for the men, especially beef, or from passing supply steamers, but with the lack of refrigeration, it often spoiled. Fresh-caught fish was enjoyed, as were vegetables, wild fruits and berries, and certain "foraged" goods picked up on boat expeditions. The victuals listed above were, as appropriate, prepared in huge cooper and iron pots on a large cooking range in the galley. This room also had a huge chopping block, complete with a giant two-handed cleaver that the butcher used to chop up the meat before handing it to the various messes. Once the food was prepared, the men ate it sitting on their gun carriages or "sitting cross-legged, like Turks, on the floor [deck]." When battle was imminent, some commanders allowed the men a meal beforehand if there was time, but sometimes it was eaten standing at the guns.[11]

From the time the sailors were awakened and told to "turn to," a typical day in the life of a *Carondelet* sailor was usually fast-moving but occasionally dull. It shared a number of similarities with that of brethren on the ocean blockade, but there were unique opportunities and difficulties on these boats that were never very far away from the land. River jacks did not learn how to furl sails or watch the horizon for ship or storm, but faced the challenges of river navigation and attacks by hidden irregulars, for which they were trained to be attentive and alert. Throughout the remainder of the day, as one reporter put it, the men would "hear the shrill whistle of the boatswain amid hoarse calls of 'All Hands to Quarters,' 'Stand by the Hammocks,' etc." Tardiness in carrying out commands or tasks guaranteed offenders an entry on the Black List, from which unsavory tasks were assigned, such as peeling potatoes. Once the hammocks were stowed and the men had eaten a breakfast of hardtack (hard biscuits) and "colored hot water facetiously called coffee," they were turned to cleaning ship and holystoning the decks. Inspection followed, leading to several hours of big gun drill.

Learning to service the *Carondelet*'s cannon was the major drill endured by her seamen. Fighting those pieces was the primary reason they were recruited, and to do so efficiently — and without panic in the din of battle — required much practice. The 12-member gun crews of the *Carondelet* were divided into three divisions. Given the initial belief that most battles would be fought bows-on, the First Division comprised the two forward-looking 42-pdrs. and an 8-inch Dahlgren. The broadside cannon comprised the Second Division and those in the stern the Third. During their drills, especially those at the guns, sailors stepped "lively," or faced abuse — usually verbal —from the officer in charge or their own mates. Serving a cannon in a slipshod manner could mean death. Safety and speed were essential; uniform (often just bell-bottom trousers and undershirts) and decorum were less important than proficiency. In fact, Flag Officer Foote ordered that all vessels under his command be ready to open fire "within five minutes."

Following an hour off for lunch at noon, the ironclad's crew returned to work, staying engaged in make-work activities or drills, for which each man had a station, until 4:00 P.M. in winter or 5:00 P.M. in summer. The drills, practiced over and over, had become (and would continue to be) the most effective way to turn raw recruits into fighting sailors, readying them to save their lives instantly by obeying commands and executing requirements. Among the drills practiced, usually at different times and sometimes under stopwatch competition, were fire and rescue, man overboard, abandon ship, lowering boats, small arms, and repelling boarders. The men could be sent to battle stations instantly and, when it was a drill, the time required for the crew to drop everything and reach assigned posts was usually set to encourage improvement. Once everyone was assembled, the great guns may or may not have been exercised. All of these oft-repeated tasks welded Capt. Walke's men into a collective unit capable of offering a fight or making a defense.

The *Carondelet*'s sailors usually had no work after supper — with the possible exception of coaling — and were free to "skylark" (amuse themselves) until lights for those not on watch were ordered out at 9:00 P.M. When it was safe or just too hot, the men were often allowed to sleep on deck, though many chose to remain in hammocks slung within the casemate. A correspondent imbedded aboard one of the Eads boats remembered his first night: "By the dim light of the lamp, I could see the great gun within six feet of me, and shining cutlasses and gleaming muskets. Looking out of the ward-room, I could see the men in their hammocks asleep like orioles in their hanging nests. The sentinels paced the deck above and all was silent, but the sound of the great wheel of the steamer turning lazily in the stream, and the gurgling of the water around the bow."

Individual discipline aboard the vessels of the Federal Western Flotilla, and its successor organization, the Mississippi Squadron, was the same as that maintained aboard seagoing men-o'-war. Regular officers (Annapolis graduates) feared career-hampering reprimands from their district or squadron commanders. Volunteer officers were frequently confined to their quarters for rudeness, drunkenness, and other such lapses from the naval code. Two *Carondelet* cases from 1863 illustrate the point; even the best officers could be imprisoned for faulty performance of their duties. In the predawn hours of January 11, as the ironclad was steaming toward Island No. 10, she nearly collided with the light draught ("tinclad") *Brilliant.* As Acting Ensign Oliver Donaldson, promoted from his original post of ship's carpenter, was officer of the deck, he was held responsible for the near disaster and was "put under arrest immediately." Capt. Walke later had him released and restored to duty. On September 17, Acting Master Charles H. Ammerman was confined to his quarters for bad conduct. A month later, he was sent north on the transport *New National* to stand court-martial. He was dismissed from the service on October 9. Until the capture of Vicksburg, Acting Rear Adm. Porter seldom released officers or men from service for any other reason save illness.

Drunkenness and poor conduct were more seriously perceived when it came from the enlisted ranks. Rear Adm. Foote simply could not abide drunken jack-tars and in a general order dated December 17, 1861, threatened to "visit with the utmost rigor ... all who may be guilty of the slightest degree of intoxication." Profanity was strictly forbidden to both officers and men, but could still be heard during heated moments. These and most other serious crimes committed by sailors aboard the *Carondelet* were nearly all punished by the Black List, a period of time confined in irons below deck, demotion or some combination of the three. Dismissals were infrequent and deserters were pursued. The June 1863 fate of the ironclad's Seaman Saul Russel is instructive. On June 10, during the siege of Vicksburg, Seaman Russel was charged with bad conduct. Placed in irons, he was subjected to a court-martial the very next day. Although it got off to a prompt start, the trial lasted off and on until June 18. On that day, the defendant was released from irons and restored to duty, after being demoted from seaman to ordinary seaman, and Black Listed for three months.

From the first Sunday after her commissioning, the *Carondelet* hosted Divine Services on her gun deck every Sabbath after muster. Officers and men, garbed in their best uniforms with their heads uncovered, stood in a circle around Capt. Wake, who served as minister and often read the Episcopal service. Other commanders, from Flag Officer Foote downwards, delivered sermons to shipboard assemblies and, occasionally, at churches ashore.[12]

Some free time in addition to the evening "skylark" was occasionally available to crewmen onboard the *Carondelet.* After days of cruising up and down the rivers or anchored duty as "station ship" at locations such as Helena or the mouth of the White River, even such a taskmaster as Capt. Walke sometimes ran out of "busy work" for the men. At such times, virtual holidays existed.

Checkers or whittling and carving were favorite pastimes when laundry and canvas (awnings) were not being mended or washed. There may have been a banjo, harmonica, or guitar player aboard who helped to while away leisure time. Many men engaged in active correspondence with loved ones at home, waiting, as sailors always did prior to the Internet, for the next mail steamer. Some bluejackets, however, were sadly without relations but enjoyed sharing the letters or newspapers of their messmates. Rowing and shooting con-

Taking the giant Dahlgren and other naval cannon into action without being destroyed was the principal reason for the creation of the *Carondelet* and her six sisters. Nearly every day, the men trained at the great guns, learning how to fire them as rapidly and accurately as possible. In this drawing by Rear Adm. Walke, the contemporary uniform of the Federal enlisted sailor is well depicted (*Battles and Leaders*).

Appearing nearly identical in wartime black and white photographs, the seven boats of the City Series were often misidentified. For many years, this photo was believed to represent the *Carondelet*, when, in fact, the vessel is the *Cairo*. Nevertheless, the portrait is remarkable for the size perspective and the crew activity depicted, including the men on the foredeck and in the small boat off the port bow. Note also the flag waving topside behind the wheelhouse (U.S. Army Military History Institute).

tests rivaled fishing. When anchored off a place occupied by U.S. troops or other gunboats some participated in pickup games of that new sport, baseball. Although drink was prohibited, smoking was not and it was pervasive, as was tobacco chewing. Used "plugs" were always disposed of "neatly" over the side of the black-painted ironclad.

Pets were not common, but were occasionally allowed, especially dogs. As with sailors everywhere, the enlisted men of the *Carondelet* (and perhaps some junior officers) always appreciated any chance to view members of the opposite sex — a rare treat as few were to be seen, even through spyglasses. At such time that ladies (Caucasian, not African American) were spotted, any men who were free "turned eager eyes to gaze upon the wondrous creatures."

On a different plane, officers and men regarded the visits of generals, from Maj. Gen. Ulysses S. Grant on down, and their own squadron commander, whichever admiral it might be, as important events. These were often accompanied by impromptu but formal reviews, complete with inspections.

Drawn largely from contemporary sources, these glimpses at the working and leisure lives of the *Carondelet*'s crew only scratch the surface. In the years since this writer first visited the ironclad's story, remarkable work concerning the sociology of gunboat crews has appeared and adds greatly to our understanding. That acknowledgment made, we note the comments of the famous British correspondent William "Bull Run" Russell when he first viewed the men of the Western Flotilla: "It will run hard against the Confederates when they [the Federal sailors] get such men at work on the rivers ... for they seem to understand their business thoroughly." The *Carondelet*'s crew would now have to prove that point in practice. The time had come to move into actual combat operations.[13]

4

Fort Henry

At the beginning of the Civil War, the economic value of Tennessee and the northern parts of Alabama and Georgia were underappreciated in many circles in the South. Although the value of sectional trade may have been understood, the politics of warfare in that time required that major attention be focused on the two perceived seats of power, Washington, D.C., and Richmond, VA; "On to Richmond" was both an all-absorbing battle cry and an approach to securing victory. Confederate military leaders from Robert E. Lee to Leonidas Polk, Gideon Pillow, and Albert Sidney Johnston all really failed "to grasp fully the importance of the munitions-producing area of Georgia, Tennessee, and Alabama" and failed, accordingly, to plan for its defense.

The resources of the rebellion's heartland area required protection. Failure to guard these assets would have a drastic and tragic impact upon the fortunes of the South if invasion did not come along the Mississippi River corridor below Cairo. While the Confederacy "was criticized and may have seem indifferent to forwarding the men and tools of war," as might have been expected, "it should be remembered," Douglas wrote in 1961, "that the Confederacy was an infant republic" as yet unable to defend its totality. Each southern state was initially responsible for its own protection as all of the seceding states were clinging "to the traditional doctrine of 'States Rights'"—which had many faults requiring time and patient to overcome.

The Scott-Eads plan for the Union's reduction of Confederate positions in the West and an associated great move south along the Mississippi River was not a secret. Indeed, when Tennessee became the last seceded southern state on June 8, 1861, the outline of the Yankee scheme was widely accepted as strategy on both sides of the Mason-Dixon Line and a guide to the way the western conflict would be fought.

At Nashville, Governor Isham G. Harris, following this logic, fully expected that his northern border was safe due to Kentucky's declared "neutrality." Not having any particular reason to think that northern generals would operate outside the perimeters of the Scott plan, Harris, together with his military advisors Maj. Gen. Leonidas Polk and Brig. Gen. Gideon J. Pillow, believed that most of the fighting involving Volunteer patriots, more of whom would bear Confederate arms from any other state save Virginia, would occur along the state's Mississippi River border. Indeed, Pillow went so far as to write one concerned citizen that "nothing of military importance [is] to be gained by [the Yankees] ascending [the] Tennessee River."

So it was that most available troops of Tennessee's provisional army, including engineers and artillery, were ordered west to help protect a chain of defenses running south from Island No. 10 (the 10th island in the Mississippi south of the Ohio) to Memphis. That noted Tennessee community, located 790 miles by the river from New Orleans and 240 from Cairo, stood on an elevated bluff on the left bank of the Mississippi River. It had to be kept out of the hands of Union troops as it was " a place of much business activity, being the distributing point for the produce of West Tennessee." Thus it was that only 4,000 soldiers guarded the Cumberland Pass and the vital economic areas of Middle Tennessee at the time James B. Eads was building ironclads near St. Louis.[1]

By its September 4 capture of Columbus on the Mississippi, the Confederacy violated Kentucky's so-called neutrality and threw the entire northern border of Tennessee open to invasion. Brig. Gen. Ulysses S. Grant, for his part, quickly seized two vital Kentucky communities on the Ohio River: Paducah, which sits at the mouth of the Tennessee River, and Smithland, at the mouth of the Cumberland River. As rivers in the region flow north, the two were, at those points, downstream from Tennessee.

After Gen. Albert Sidney Johnston took charge of Confederate western forces during the month, he chose to concentrate his defense on what Grant later described as "a line running from the Mississippi River at Columbus to Bowling Green and Mill Springs, Kentucky." This deployment would permit protection of the twin rivers, as well as the regional railroad network. It was Governor Harris who sent engineers down the Cumberland and Tennessee to look for places to erect forts. Work, which progressed only slowly, was begun on two main defensive positions: one named Fort Donelson (after West Point graduate Daniel S. Donelson, Tennessee's attorney general) on the Cumberland River and the other, 12 miles northwest on the Tennessee River, called Fort Henry (in honor of Gustavus A. Henry, the state's senior Confederate senator). Fort Donelson was mostly abandoned until October.[2]

Union supporters and a number of Yankee generals now believed that a strike into the heart of the western Confederacy, via the Tennessee and Cumberland rivers, would pay huge dividends. As famed Civil War authority Allan Nevins would write in 1960, "A mere glance at the map would seem to reveal that the Tennessee-Cumberland river system offered the North a heaven-sent opportunity to thrust a harpoon into the very bowels of the Confederacy." In early October, Lt. S. Ledyard Phelps by army request began a series of probing reconnaissance cruises to points above Forts Henry and Donelson with the timberclad *Conestoga.*

Posted to command of the Department of the Missouri in November 1861, Maj. Gen. Henry W. Halleck, "Old Brains" as he was known, quickly reviewed the strategic situation in the West. It did not take him long to determine that thrusting Nevins' harpoon into the area of Middle Tennessee between the rivers could be "the turning point of the war." Plagued by a case of the "slows" and in rivalry with Department of the Ohio commander Maj. Gen. Don Carlos Buell, he authorized no move against the twin river fortifications.[3]

Deep into the last quarter of 1861, Confederate generals Johnston and Polk finally realized the importance of the Nashville area economic contribution to the Rebel war effort. Consequently, they started to focus their attention upon improving the defenses of the Tennessee and Cumberland rivers. After all, as Johnston wrote to Polk on October 31, an enemy invasion down the two rivers "may turn your right with ease and rapidity."

At this time, Columbus, the "Gibraltar of the West," held 150 cannon and over 21,000 soldiers. This was the largest force anywhere in Gen. Johnston's entire department. As historian Thomas Connelly tells us, Maj. Gen. Polk's "fear of attack had become almost pathological." With Polk promising cooperation, work on strengthening Forts Henry and Donelson was stepped up. In November, Kentuckian Brig. Gen. Lloyd Tilghman was placed in charge and ordered to complete the two citadels as soon as possible.[4]

New Year's Day 1862 was just another day in the office for Flag Officer Andrew H. Foote and his officers. Last minute construction or outfitting details were addressed for the City Series ironclads, recruiting efforts were continued, and the timberclad gunboats maintained their patrols on the Mississippi and Ohio.

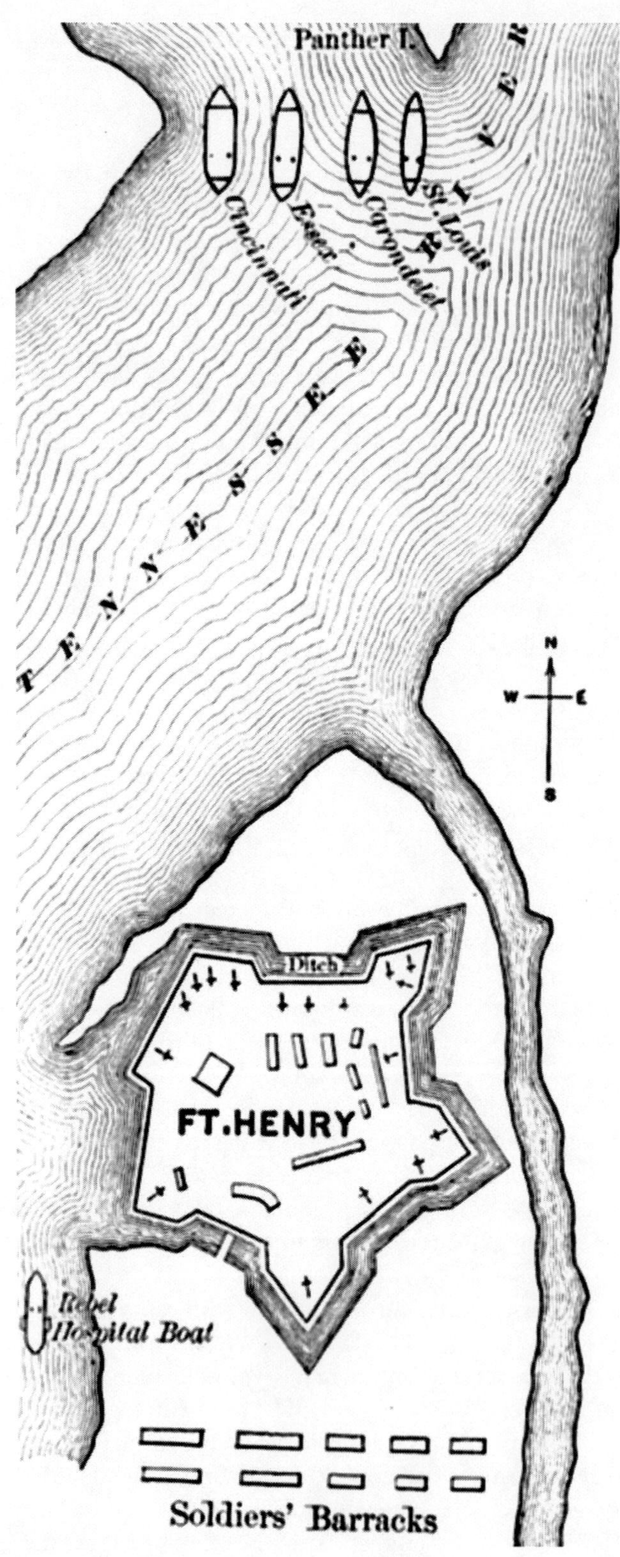

This map, from Hoppin's *Life of Andrew Hull Foote*, allows the reader to note the relative positions of Fort Henry and the attacking Federal ironclads at the beginning of the contest (Hoppin, *Life of Andrew Hull Foote*).

On a higher level, strategic planning on the Northern side in the West was still quite ineffective. Instead of Jefferson Davis' problems with a stubborn commander defending a city and the belated recognition of a threat to the entire central region, President Abraham Lincoln and Maj. Gen. George B. McClellan found themselves with two generals (Maj. Gens. Buell and Halleck) who prized control over their own territories and couldn't agree to attack anywhere. Both of these commanders made excuses about why they could not communicate, cooperate, or most important, advance.

On January 3, McClellan, ignorant of Polk's fundamental defensive principle, wrote to Halleck. It was "of the greatest importance," the U.S. Army's top general spelled out, that reinforcements from Columbus not be sent to aid Confederates elsewhere. To prevent a Rebel transfer, "Little Mac" suggested expeditions and demonstrations, supported by gunboats, up both the Tennessee and Cumberland rivers and against Columbus itself. If the latter place was vulnerable, it "should be taken." Also, whatever kind of mission(s) might be sent out "should be done speedily, within a few days."

On January 6, Lt. Phelps, just back from the Tennessee and Cumberland, observed, "It is now too late to move against the works on either river, except with a well-appointed and powerful naval force." That force became available on January 16 when Flag Officer Foote informed Washington that "the seven gunboats built by contract were put in commission today." If Halleck and Buell could determine their timing and objectives with regard to the forts, the navy finally had ironclad power to support whatever waterborne or combined assault mission might be chosen. Although there was ice in the water, the level of the Mississippi and its tributaries was rising.

Largely as a result of McClellan's directive, Federal soldiers and sailors from Cairo spent most of January executing mud-slogging "demonstrations" toward Columbus, and also up the Tennessee, designed to confuse Rebel commanders as to Union intentions. Cover was provided by the *St. Louis* and *Essex*, as well as the three timberclads, *Tyler*, *Lexington*, and *Conestoga*. The latter pair, in particular, were dispatched on several probing missions to spy out the new forts being completed up the Tennessee and Cumberland rivers. On January 17, they feigned an attack on Fort Henry. This demonstration caused Confederate general Johnston three days later to order the bolstering of the center and left of his line, including its weakest links, Henry and Donelson.[5]

As January ended, Maj. Gen. Halleck, Flag Officer Foote, and Brig. Gen. Grant perceived the possibilities offered by a trip up the Tennessee. Despite nasty, cold weather, there were advantages to such a move. Grant came to believe that a relatively small force could capture both the high ground across from Fort Henry and the main fortification itself. The roads and ground east of Columbus were rain soaked, making any reinforcement for (Confederate) Brig. Gen. Tilghman almost impossible. In addition, there was, as the *New York Times* correspondent "Tennessee" told his readers from Paducah, a "great freshet running out of the Tennessee and Cumberland Rivers." Although the rivers at flood-tide were "throwing out into the Ohio an immense quantity of drift[wood], which covers the face of the rivers, it also gave them sufficient depth not only for Foote's ironclads but to render inoperable any submarine batteries ['torpedoes,' or in modern terms, mines]."

With the Pook turtles available and a steamboat supply chain, too, Fort Henry appeared to be a far less dangerous—and possibly just as important—prize as Polk's citadel. With Henry and Fort Donelson in hand the map showed, Columbus was turned and rendered militarily useless. And of course, there would be the added plum of capturing defenseless Nashville. Both Foote and Grant now suggested the move and Halleck cautiously agreed.

Taking Columbus would be costly, the theater commander believed, and could not be taken "without an immense siege train and a terrible loss of life." On the other hand, he thought, the river forts might not be too difficult and could "be turned, paralyzed, and forced to surrender." "Old Brains" was encouraged in his thinking on the Tennessee River approach by other events. These included Lincoln's January 27 General War Order No. 1, which required all of his generals to show some kind of movement on or before February 22.

Two days later, Maj. Gen. McClellan telegraphed St. Louis to say that Gen. P.G.T. Beauregard, the Rebel hero of Fort Sumter and First Bull Run, had been ordered west with 15 regiments to assist Gen. Johnston in Kentucky. These developments, along with Foote's promise that he could take the fort with four ironclads, persuaded Henry Halleck to act irrespective of Maj. Gen. Buell.

The *New York Times* correspondent Frank B. Wilkie sent a prophetic article from Smithland, Kentucky, to his paper, also on January 29. "Galway" told subscribers that the "nearest points of any importance garrisoned by Rebels are Forts Donelson and Henry ... both distant from here some 60 miles." After describing what was commonly known of the citadels, he went on to predict that "It is more than probable that within the next ten days or fortnight, the occupancy of Fort Henry, and possibly that of the other, will change hands.... I hope in my next to inform you that the Federal flag floats over the ramparts of Fort Henry." Just 24 hours after Wilkie sent off his Smithland piece, Halleck wired Grant: "Make your preparations to take and hold Fort Henry." In his written confirmation of the telegram, he noted that "Flag Officer Foote will protect the transports with his Gun-boats."

At the start of 1862, land warfare had not changed much since Caesar's legions invaded Gaul. Due to often impassable roads and ground for large-scale troop movements, armies from December to March generally went into winter quarters. However, because the high waters of the winter freshets permitted ascent of the twin rivers, the Henry and Donelson campaigns became the only extensive operations of the Civil War deliberately planned and carried through under winter conditions.[6]

Fort Henry was the type of citadel known in engineering circles as a "regular bastioned" fort, enclosing a space of about five acres. Erected in a short time by several engineers, this five-sided hybrid earthwork lay low in a bend on the eastern riverbank. Trees above and behind the citadel bore watermarks that indicated the site was usually swept by the river's flood-wash. Close in, felled trees linked up the bogs, forming a secondary line of defense. From a swamp to the north down to a spot behind the fort a line of rifle pits was sited, about three quarters of a mile from the main work. Garrison quarters were situated just east of the fort and were protected by more rifle pits further east. A road was laid east to Fort Donelson and telegraph wire was strung to that bastion and Cumberland City. Work was begun on providing a redoubt atop a hill on the opposite side of the river, also commanding the fort.

The fort's commander, Brig. Gen. Tilghman, believed it was built in a very "unfortunate location." Later on in reporting upon its loss, he commented most forcefully on its configuration, concluding that "the history of military engineering records no parallel to this case." Still, it was armed with heavy cannon. There were 17 inside the fort, 12 being laid on the river. Most of that dozen pointed at the straight downstream river stretch below and enjoyed an unobstructed field of fire of about three miles. The angles and faces of the fort well commanded the main "chute" (channel) to the east of Panther Island, a mile and a quarter above. The chute to the west of the island was usually impassable — except at flood-tide.

Fort Henry's river guns included one 10-inch Columbiad, a rifled 62-pdr., two 42-pdrs.(not unlike that carried at the bow of the *Carondelet*), eight 32-pdrs. and five 18-pdrs., which latter types would have little effect on the ironclads. Those facing the river were all at water level, but only nine were combat ready, as the 42-pdrs. had no ammunition. Without the ability to drop plunging fire like the cannon lining the Iron Banks at Columbus, these cannon would prove a fairly easy target for Foote's ironclads.

There was a large force at Fort Henry, though it was uncertain to the Yankees just how many men were there or how they were armed. It later turned out that the answers were insufficient and poor. When Halleck ordered Grant to proceed, there were at Fort Henry roughly 2,600 men in six raw infantry regiments, two light artillery batteries, and some cavalry equipped with all manner of small arms, down to and including personal squirrel guns and shotguns. The best trained regiment, the 10th Tennessee, was outfitted with flintlock "Tower of London" muskets that Gen. Andrew Jackson had used in the Battle of New Orleans 57 years earlier!

A total of 12 (some sources say 20 or more) submarine batteries, also known as "torpedoes," or what we now call underwater mines, were anchored in the western chute where Panther Island divided Fort Henry from the unfinished Fort Heiman. Each of the sheet-iron cylinders was 5½ feet long with a 1 foot diameter and was loaded with 70 pounds of black powder. Anchored on the bottom and normal river flow level, each was outfitted with a prong or rod which extended upward and sought the bottom of a passing vessel. Any craft hitting a prong would trigger an explosion. A picture of one appears in Admiral Walke's *Battles and Leaders* article on Fort Henry. When the Tennessee began to flood, a significant number of these broke their moorings and sank; the remainder would prove ineffective. More were sent out and sailors from the steamer *Samuel Orr* attempted to plant them, but the operation was largely unsuccessful.[7]

At Cairo on February 1, Joseph B. "Mack" McCullagh, the correspondent of the *Cincinnati Daily Gazette,* sent the readership of his paper, three days after Wilkie, essentially the same prognostication as the *New Yorker*: "From certain indications, I had concluded that Fort Henry, on the Tennessee River ... was the point aimed at." The newsman "was not surprised to learn on Saturday ... that some 10 regiments of infantry, together with artillery and cavalry, then at Cairo, had received orders to be in readiness to embark next day."

Fort Henry as seen from the ground following its capture. By the time this drawing was made, the swollen Tennessee River had fallen significantly (*Leslie's Illustrated*, March 15, 1862).

"Steamboats," wrote Cumberland River historian Douglas a century later, "had been used for many various purposes, but never before in an amphibious military operation to transport an entire army."

Although their officers did not tell them, many of the enlisted bluecoats were, like the journalists, able to guess their objective. As Pvt. Allen Greer of the 20th Illinois noted, "Our destination appears to be Fort Henry on the Tenn. River." Brig. Gen. Lew Wallace remembered that "There was riding in hot haste from camp to camp. Tents went down, and the streets filled with troops in orderly march to the river." While troop preparation for the Fort Henry advance got underway, the flag officer issued his first operational orders for the campaign. Sailing orders were sent to Cmdr. Henry Walke. Fully coaled, the *Carondelet* would get underway the following morning (February 2) at 6:00 A.M. and steam down to Paducah. Similar orders were sent to the captains of the *Cincinnati* and *St. Louis*. The trio would follow Cmdr. William "Dirty Bill" Porter, who was to start out with his *Essex* at 1:00 A.M. Because of crew shortages, these were the only ironclads that could be fully manned for the Fort Henry expedition. Brig. Gen. Grant's troop boats were also scheduled to leave Cairo that morning.

Just after the appointed Sunday morning hour as rain splattered the pilothouse, Chief Pilot William Hinton pulled a cord swinging to the right of the *Carondelet*'s six-foot steering wheel. Deep in the engine room, a bell sounded, alerting Chief Engineer William D. Faulkner to ease open his throttles, setting the great paddle wheel to thrashing. Moving slowly ahead, the *Carondelet* churned to war. As the craft moved away from the tip of Illinois, several guns at Fort Defiance fired a salute. Whistles aboard the gunboats returned the compliment. Despite a nasty and damp beginning to the day, numerous Cairo townsfolk lined the shore and, together with mechanics, laborers, soldiers, waved, hollered, and cheered. They were joined by sailors and crewmen aboard anchored steamboats; several were nosed into the bank.

This voyage up the Ohio was the first time that any of the new Eads ironclads steamed together as a task unit on a war footing. The spaced-out procession, dimly perceived as it was through heavy weather, probably inspired citizens of Union heart witnessing it from shore and troubled those of Rebel persuasion.

Stiff, bitter, and cold winds pummeled and roiled the turgid river waters, grabbing and dispersing the great clouds of black, sooty smoke rising from the gunboat chimneys. The turtle-like monsters pushed steadily ahead, the flags on their staffs nearly stiff in the breeze. The poky *Carondelet* followed the lead boat *Cincinnati*, her pilots keeping her jackstaff, mounted directly in front of the pilothouse at the leading edge of the hurricane deck, lined up with the wheelhouse of the *St. Louis* just ahead. The slow Pook turtles were approaching Mound City when Foote left Cairo aboard the timberclad *Tyler*.

As her great paddle wheel splashed the cold Ohio, a variety of noises, strange-sounding to the uninitiated, emanated from the *Carondelet*'s exhaust pipes. These staccato cracking and popping reports were, however, normal and were heard from the power plants of almost every steamboat chugging along on the western waters. Early on it was recognized that Cmdr. Walke's boat would never be able to turn up much beyond 4–5 knots, no matter how much the firebox draughts were forced or how her exhaust pipes protested. Slow she might be, but the ironclad, like her sisters, vibrated and rattled noticeably whenever her engine impulses increased.

By early afternoon, the dancing mists, powerful wind, and sheeting rain nearly blotted out visibility, creating a dangerous situation. Not only were the sisters losing sight of one another, but also of dangers passing in the water. The great winter rise that washed the riverbanks of the Upper Mississippi Valley carried all manner of wreckage, debris, and snags, to say nothing of chucks of ice and even small drifting floes. Fence rails, wagons, privies, water-logged skiffs and boats, roofs and parts of buildings were commonly encountered in the swift current. Having tumbled in when banks collapsed in the flood, whole trees appeared in the water, regularly forcing the pilots to swerve sharply to avoid them.

Because the freeboard of the Pook turtles was less than three feet, avoiding the smaller flotsam as it bobbed past thick and fast was not always possible. Small snags, branches, and other kinds of junk rode over the prow of the *Carondelet* and occasionally lodged on her foredeck, sometimes forcing men to climb out in the bluster to push it off. No one aboard the boats knew whether or if they might be struck by sinister sunken trees, known as sawyers or deadheads, each capable of stoving in a boat's bottom.

Not all of the action was in the pilothouse and engine room during this first trip of the war. Although we do not have *Carondelet* logbooks for this period, it is reasonable to assume that much of the crew was involved in training exercises at various times during the passage, particularly gunnery drill. Being able to load and fire the cannon with speed and care was vital to the success of the upcoming enterprise. By the time his vessel reached Fort Henry — Walke later related — his gun captains, sent west from the Atlantic squadrons, "had their men well drilled."

The ironclads anchored inside the mouth of the Tennessee at Paducah toward dusk and were joined by the flotilla commander after dark. Both on his voyage up the Ohio and aboard the anchored *Tyler* that evening, Flag Officer Foote had considerable time to write out his battle plan and orders and to send letters and a telegraph. The grizzled veteran also wrote a report to Secretary Welles outlining his activities thus far and immediate hopes for the future once he moved to his new flagboat *Cincinnati.* That action would be slightly delayed as the transports were late and did not arrive Sunday night as expected.

Foote's Special Orders (SO) to his commanders, published in the Navy *Official Records*, demonstrate much thought and confidence. His seven gunboats were distributed in two divisions: "the four new armored boats and the old gunboats *Tyler*, *Conestoga*, and *Lexington.*" Each division received its own set of orders, No. 1 or No. 2. The heavy lifting would be accomplished by the *Essex*, *Carondelet*, *Cincinnati*, and *St. Louis*, directly under his command under terms of SO-1. The timberclads, led by Lt. Phelps, would take a supporting role and were governed by SO-2.

Basing SO-1 on operational intelligence gained from reconnaissance, from the fall activities of the timberclads in the waters off Columbus, and hours of professional discussion, Foote laid out a battle plan having as its "great objective" the dismounting of "the guns in the fort by the accuracy of our fire." It would be permissible to occasionally throw a shell "among a body of the enemy's troops," though caution was to be taken to make certain that none hit Federal soldiers.

SO-2 frankly admitted that the wooden-clad gunboats were not as able as the ironclad main division to withstand at close range the expected fire of Fort Henry. Thus they would "take a position astern and, if practicable, inshore on the right of the main division." Then they could throw shells into the fort — as opposed to directly at the water batteries — without too much exposure.[8]

In just three days, according to his biographer, Jean Smith, Brig. Gen. Grant put together the elements of this offensive, the largest so far in the Mississippi Valley. He "organized his command for battle, issued rations and ammunition, provided for resupply, procured river transportation, and coordinated the movement of seven Union gunboats." All of this was, in fact, "no slight labor."

The morning of February 3, Halleck received a slightly optimistic wire from Grant at Paducah: "Will be off up the Tennessee at six o'clock. Command 23 regiments in all." Several of these, part of what would form two divisions, faced long journeys and staggered departures. It was not until Monday afternoon that *Cincinnati Daily Gazette* journalist McCullagh, who first reported the military call-up on Saturday, was able to report "that the last of the transports left Cairo and steamed up the Ohio in the direction of Paducah. Franc B. Wilkie of the *New York Times* was at Paducah to welcome the first of the steamers, "laden with troops and stores," as they began coming in from Cairo. By evening, "the whole landing in front of the town was crowded with the arrivals."

Grant did not have sufficient steamer bottoms to take both of his divisions to the vicinity of Fort Henry in one lift. Thus it was decided to move by echelon; the 1st Division would proceed down first and when it was ashore, the contract boats would come back for the 2nd. Foote's craft would provide escort.

As many army boats continued to make their way to Paducah, trumpets, bells, and whistles marked the departure of Foote's four ironclads towards an advance point. By now, the flag officer had transferred to the *Cincinnati*, and the *Essex* was available. Carefully, the Western Flotilla boats steamed upstream, continuing to avoid the debris that made the swift current of the Tennessee as dangerous as the Ohio. Having trailed a long cloud of smoke for 13 miles, one visible to any curious eye, the black-painted gunboats dropped anchor at Patterson's Ferry to wait for Grant. At Paducah, Wilkie and the other correspondents found steamer berths. This was going to be a big show and men from the large newspapers in St. Louis, Chicago, and New York wished to be witnesses. One of the scribes, Albert H. Bodman of the *Chicago Daily Tribune*, sent a last minute wire home announcing that the transports were away.

A little before midnight, Grant and his staff boarded the *W.H. Brown*. Then, just minutes into February 4, the troop convoy was "ploughing up the muddy, swift waters of the Tennessee." Breasting a strong wind and heavy rain, the military armada continued upstream to Patterson's Ferry, where the four anchored ironclads were found: *Essex*, *St. Louis*, *Cincinnati*, and *Carondelet*. Here embarked cavalry regiments were sent ashore to march overland to Pine Bluff Landing, on the Kentucky side of the Tennessee seven miles north of Fort Henry.

While the steamers were unloading the horses and their riders, the *Essex*, *Cincinnati*, and *St. Louis* proceeded ahead to Itra Landing to await the troop boats. After the transports was re-formed, they were escorted by the *Carondelet* and the timberclads down toward the appointed debarkation point at Itra Landing, across from Pine Bluff. The dark night successfully cloaked the passage and, luckily, no spies at either Cairo or Paducah forwarded a warning.

Early in the morning the dispatch tug *Spitfire* distributed Grant's debarkation instructions. The transports were to come down as rapidly as possible, making sure to keep behind the forward gunboats, and land the landing force "where they may anchor." The procession was anything but rapid and, like many later Civil War river convoys, was spaced out over a great distance. Because the convoy was so stretched out, the escorts had to make their most protective dispositions.

About 4:30 A.M., the *W.H. Brown.* was the first to "run her nose against" Itra Landing on the Kentucky shore. The spot chosen was about five or six miles from Fort Henry, though

Abbott says nine. The Confederate picket at nearby Bailey's Landing sent up a rocket, which was immediately acknowledged by Fort Henry. Then three more rockets shot up "announcing the approach of three of the enemy's gunboats." Soon, correspondent Wilkie observed, four other transports arrived and the "work of debarking the troops commenced." Grant hoped this location would permit his soldiers to avoid the necessity of crossing swollen Panther Creek in the face of any determined enemy.

Alerted, the defenders of Fort Henry were ordered to their posts. Brig. Gen. Tilgham, then inspecting Fort Donelson, was recalled and requests were sent upstream for reinforcements. Just after daylight, reports came in from pickets on both sides of the river of "a large fleet coming up." Smoke from several gunboats was visible over Panther Island. It was, however, suspected that Itra Landing was within range of Fort Henry's guns. To find out, Grant and Foote elected to make an armorclad reconnaissance. Coming within range of the Rebel citadel, the big naval guns burst shells over Fort Henry. Confederates in the bastion, Peter Franklin Walker later observed, "watched as the solid and spherical shot skipped over the water and dug into the earthen walls of the fort."

The aroused Confederates turned their cannon on the intruders and cannonballs soon whizzed around the gunboats as they withdrew. Having obtained the answer, the Federal commanders now determined to remove the men to a safer location four or five miles below Fort Henry at Fisher's Landing. This point was near a clearing opposite the village of Buffalo. The order was passed and the five troop steamers at Itra Landing halted, unloading men and equipment and reembarking that portion of the force already ashore. Coming abreast of the new landing beaches, Foote's gunboats bombarded the picket quarters "and other buildings in the neighborhood" to chase away any lingering scouts or sharpshooters. Fleeing the naval guns, Confederate pickets reported that eight gunboats were in the river and 10 heavy transports were putting their men ashore.

On the Federal side, it took until 2:00 P.M. to get everyone and everything back aboard the army contract steamers, after which they were directed to their new destination. As they eased into the bank about an hour later, they were guarded by the Pook turtles. As the initial Northern troops went ashore at Fisher's Landing, some immediately went out on reconnaissance. The remainder were disposed in "line of battle" on a range of hills overlooking the river. Artillery was unlimbered and the "trains of the whole division" were appropriately disposed and the whole operation was carried out "under cover the Gun-boats." The remainder of the afternoon was spent on this disembarkation and in conferences. Aboard the *Carondelet*, the opportunity was taken to construct wooden barricades around the boilers in an effort to provide additional protection to the boat's most vulnerable spot.

The *New York Times*, in its February 8 issue, also reported that the *Carondelet* and her sisters were also equipped with "the most dreadfully savage contrivance ... to prevent boarding." Each boat was supposedly "supplied with a number of large hose-pipes for throwing hot water from the boilers, with a force of 200-pounds pressure to the square inch." Anyone so sprayed with "this terrible stream of hot water will be boiled in an instant."

The weather was cloudy, with heavy rains. The rampaging Tennessee reached an unusual height and its swift current continued to uproot trees and fences that hurled downstream. This rise gave Fort Henry problems aside from the invaders. A large force was necessarily assigned to keep floodwaters out. By this time, the lower magazine was awash in two feet of water, forcing the transfer of ammunition from it to a temporary aboveground magazine. A courier from Fort Henry reached the Cumberland River at 4:00 P.M. and informed Brig. Gen. Tilghman of developments. Escorted by cavalry, the citadel commander, with his chief engineer, Maj. Jeremy F. Gilmer, raced back, arriving about 11:30 P.M.

The U.S. troops and gunboats up the Tennessee passed a peaceful night. In some of his most artistic prose, "Galway" painted a far more positive picture 24 hours later than he had the night before. The gloom was gone and "the sky was as warm and tender as one that bends over the flowers of May." Looking about, he saw that the wooded hills were "highly silvered by a crescent moon that glittered in the western sky." Adding to the charm of the early evening, a half dozen regimental bands "roused the soul with patriotic strains" or "soothed it with some dreamy waltz."[9] "The 5th was a day of unwonted animation on the hitherto quiet waters of the Tennessee," Capt. Jesse Taylor observed from Fort Henry's batteries. "All day long the flood-tide of arriving and the ebb of returning transports continued ceaselessly."

Brig. Gen. Tilghman, like many 19th century generals, chose to rely on the strength of his fort rather than contest Grant's landing, despite the vulnerability of the Fisher's Landing beaches. When Maj. Gen. Polk offered some reinforcing cavalry, the defensive-minded commander wired in reply: "I'd rather have disciplined infantry." Such position "warfare ... would," confirms Grant's biographer Smith, "prove to be a mistake."

Foote's main unit remained anchored out on the Tennessee about four miles below Fort Henry, opposite the Union troops. The *Tyler* and *Conestoga*, steaming closer to Panther Island, sounded the west channel, then reconnoitered the riverbanks, of both the island and the Tennessee shore. These visits were designed to prevent Rebel troops from throwing up masked batteries or transferring troops. Brig. Gen. Tilghman later admitted that their activities "prevented any communication, except by a light barge, with the western bank."

The flooding Tennessee continued to wash debris upon the Union vessels, including the *Carondelet,* fouling their bows and anchor chains. Large quantities of driftwood lodged around the bow of Capt. Walke's craft. The weight and speed of the current forced her downstream over half a mile. Even with both anchors down, it was only by keeping her paddle wheel turning at half-speed that her officers and men were able to clear away the rubbish and return her to station. Also during the 5th, the *Essex* went forward to get a better view of Fort Henry's water batteries and received a shot in her steerage for her troubles. Upon her return, the flag officer assigned each of his boats a signal number. The *Carondelet* received No. 2 (the flagboat *Cincinnati* was, presumably, No. 1).

To help pep up his men, Foote was rowed around the flotilla aboard a cutter broken out from the *Cincinnati*. Anchored slightly in advance of her sisters, the *Carondelet* received his first visit. The grizzled flag officer climbed aboard via the fantail, saluted the National colors as they snapped in the breeze, and entered the ironclad through a stern gun port. In the semidarkness of the casemate, illuminated by weak light from the big gun ports, Foote's penetrating blue eyes inspected the officers and crew at quarters, paying particular attention to the demeanor of the men standing silently in their best blues.

The stumpy Foote and much-taller Walke, both resplendent in their best uniforms with gold braid, then moved smartly across the *Carondelet*'s gun deck. Both noticed how the brass glistened and every full ammunition locker was ready for review, how the tackle and ropes were coiled and ready, and how even the cannon tubes shone a dull gleam. In the course of daily routine, anything less than a smart appearance aboard Walke's command would have been unacceptable. Once the gun crews were inspected, Foote stopped near a bow cannon and, as a signal to all, removed his cap, tucking it under his arm. He then admonished the sailors to give brave service and offered a prayer. After a few words with Walke, he was gone.

As mentioned above, the Confederates in laying out Fort Henry's defenses planned to use "torpedoes" in the river near Panther Creek Island to block the movements of the Union gunboats. Many of these "infernal machines" were anchored to the river bottom during

Capt. Walke's drawing of the Battle of Fort Henry in early February 1862, as depicted in his memoir *Naval Scenes and Reminiscences*, clearly shows the gunboats advancing and an absence of plunging fire from the Confederate guns. Note also the clouds of gun smoke.

***Harper's Weekly*'s slightly inaccurate depiction of the Western Flotilla advancing up the Tennessee River toward Fort Henry, February 1862 (*Harper's Weekly*, February 22, 1862).**

Alexander Slimplot's depiction of the capture of Fort Henry formed a large panel in an issue of *Harper's Weekly*. Physical conditions at the Tennessee River citadel are striking to the viewer (*Harper's Weekly*, March 1, 1862).

the week before the Federals arrived. Sailors aboard the Yankee gunboats were aware that such mines existed and "this adversity," Walke later wrote, "appeared to dampen the ardor of our crews." During the foul weather of the last few days, a number of these torpedoes had broken their moorings and swum down on the Union anchorage. Several blew up en route and the Union sailors heard these explosions as mysterious, dull booms. Attentive lookouts on the *Carondelet* spotted several of the descending bombs, dirty-white in color, about five feet long, and looking like "polar bears." It was this menacing flow that Walke and Foote spoke about as the gunboat's inspection concluded. Foote ordered the small boats from the timberclads to catch as many as possible and drag them ashore. The *Carondelet*'s captain saw his men take heart, relieved that the hidden peril was discovered and addressed in daylight.

Continuing to reconnoiter in the west channel of Panther Island, the *Tyler* and *Conestoga* "discovered two ugly torpedoes." *New York Tribune* correspondent Albert D. Richardson and his *Boston Morning Journal* colleague Charles Carleton Coffin in their memoirs indicate that the resting place was given away by the "imprudent tongue of an angry Rebel woman." Prophesying earlier in the presence of bluecoated scouts visiting her farmhouse that Foote's fleet would soon be blown into atoms, "she was compelled to divulge what she knew, or be confined to the guard house. In mortal terror, the lady gave the desired information." Whether, as is probable, the submarine batteries were located by keen-eyed lookouts or Richardson and Coffin's loose-lipped Tennessee shrew, "Galway" notes, both were carefully swept out and towed out of the way. Rain of the past few days caused the river stage to stand at 25 feet above low water.

Rear Adm. Walke's depiction of the Battle of Fort Henry clearly illustrates the close-in nature of the engagement. As always, the artist ensured that his portrait was ringed by natural elements that helped convey a sense of the weather and scene (Hoppin, *Life of Andrew Hull Foote*).

Telling the same story, *Cincinnati Daily Gazette* reporter McCullagh, embedded aboard the *Cincinnati,* observed that the two gunboats "succeeded in removing six torpedoes ... without injury." At the time, Charles Carleton Coffin assured his Massachusetts audience that "Three were first taken up with grappling hooks, and all but one were found to be so moist that they would not have exploded."

Once Flag Officer Foote had completed his inspection tour and as the timberclads continued to sweep, final plans for the naval tactics to be employed in the next day's attack were completed and distributed. Augmenting his previously promulgated Special Orders, the flotilla commander directed that once the torpedoes were out of the chute between Panther Island and the shore, the ironclads could steam up the chute (rather than the main channel), taking advantage of cover from the island's timber. After that, they could form line of battle, advance toward the bastion, and, at the *Cincinnati*'s signal, open fire when the head of the island was passed. Foote also held a final prebattle conference with Brig. Gen. Grant, who was finishing his own battle plan for his commanders. It incorporated a key lesson learned from the latter's near encirclement at Belmont, Missouri, the previous November: naval coordination.

The Buckeye brigadier planned to surround Fort Henry. His men would make certain that no one got out of the bastion or reinforced it from Fort Donelson. Foote was to bombard the citadel and, if possible, drive the Rebels away from their cannon. The navy, in the recollection of Charles Coffin, would "shell the Rebels out just as you can pound rats from a barrel or a box." In order to give the soggy countryside time to dry out—at least a little—the advance would not start until almost noon. Foote asked his army counterpart, in light of the poor roads around the citadel, to move out his bluecoated soldiers earlier than scheduled. The confident general refused, whereupon the bearded sailor predicted: "I shall take it before you will get there with your forces!" According to Bearss, Grant did not know that, in order for the soldiers to have any chance of keeping abreast, the flag officer would intentionally hold down his gunboats' speed while moving upstream.

The brass bands resumed their concerts that evening after dinner. Around 8:00 P.M., as many listeners were enjoying the inspiring strains, a tremendous thunderstorm burst over the area. White-blue lightning streaked from the heavens and the thunder sounded like heavy cannon. "Everyone," the soggy journalist Frank Wilkie recorded, was sent "grumbling, wet, and disconsolate to the best shelter he could find."

Out on the river, the clay-colored current continued exceptionally swift and it was difficult to keep the gunboats and the transports securely anchored. Donald Davidson tells us that the "crews had to work constantly to fend off floating trees, driftwood, lumber, and fences." Many vessels kept their engine pressure up so that their huge paddle wheels could help keep them properly moored. Even the ironclads had difficulty maintaining station. "It required all the steam-power of the *Carondelet,* with both anchors down, and the most strenuous exertions of the officers and crew working day and night," Cmdr. Walke later recalled, "to prevent the boat from being dragged downstream."

The *Tribune*'s reporter was not too bothered, however. "The night was excessively rainy and severe upon our boys in blue in their forest bivouacs," Albert D. Richardson remembered later, "but in the well-furnished cabin of General Grant's steamer, we found 'going to war' an agreeable novelty."[10]

February 6 was a day of destiny and it dawned cloudy, but without fog or rain. The sun came out about 9:00 A.M. and the air began to warm. This was the day designated for the Federal attack.

Looking out from Fort Henry, Col. Adolphus Heiman was able to see "heavy volumes of black smoke" rising a mile or so away over Panther Island. To the officers of his 10th Tennessee and others, these ominous clouds manifested "that the fleet was not to remain idle long." The *Cincinnati* hoisted a general signal at 10:00 A.M., to which all of the gunboats, anchored with her across from the 1st Division camp, made answer. The captains were all rowed to the flagboat, where they received encouragement and handshakes from their commander.

Forty minutes later, after the skippers were back aboard their boats, Foote's signalman raised the general departure flag. Within a few short minutes, the warships weighed anchor and started to form their line of battle. "No one who witnessed the departure of the fleet," Wilkie later remarked, "had a moment's fear of the result — we were confident that Fort Henry was doomed."

It was increasingly warm and pleasant as the four ironclads, all beat to quarters, slowly wallowed up the shallow eastern channel of the Tennessee River protected by Panther Island, what Charles Coffin called "a long, narrow sand-bank, covered with a thicket of willows." The atoll covered the boats from the long-range cannon the Rebels were believed to possess. When the ironclads came to the foot of the island a mile and a quarter from the fort, they moved abreast of one another, with the *Essex* anchoring the line on the right and the *Cincinnati* on the left. For want of room on the interior, the *Carondelet* and *St. Louis* steamed almost in concert.

Coal heavers working deep in the engine rooms of the *Carondelet* and her consorts made certain that the fireboxes were fed, while the sound of the monotonous exhaust snaps and escape valve crackles grew constantly louder. The four craft churned slowly up the chute with great billows of choking smoke gushing from their chimneys. Not a sound could be heard from man or beast, save a pilot's occasional bell; the thick woodland was silent and not an object was seen.

As on the other boats, the gun crews of the *Carondelet* stood at their divisional posts, no doubt convinced that, as it would be a bows-on fight, the eleven cannon of the gunboats would be more than a match for those in the fort. It would be a "fair and square" fight and an important first test for the Eads casemates. Still, as casualties in a naval battle could always be expected, sand was spread to prevent busy feet from slipping on any spilled blood. With all hands at their battle stations, the "old boats" also ranged themselves abreast, but followed at least a half mile to the rear. As George W. Beaman of the *St. Louis Daily Missouri Democrat* later testified, the timberclads "remained behind, but within easy hail."

It was almost noon and still warm and pleasant, with a wind from the west. The timberclad captains watched both their ironclad colleagues and the menacing, increasingly more detailed Confederate fortress. To many, its embrasures appeared, in the words of Franc Wilkie, "simply a rim of new earth that appeared just above the edge of the water." The men aboard Foote's gunboats did not know that Brig. Gen. Tilghman had supposedly concluded the game was up and had elected to "merely stage a delaying action." In an effort to reinforce Fort Donelson, he had already evacuated most of the soldiers from his untenable location, sending them overland to the Cumberland river position.

As the flooding river continued to spill over soggy earth into Fort Henry, legend—repeated in Tilghman's after action report, in Capt. Jesse Taylor's *Battles and Leaders* account, in historian Mullen's article, and elsewhere—has it that 50 to 75 volunteers from Battery B, 1st Tennessee Heavy Artillery, agreed to stay behind and help their commander man the cannon. That this was a myth was noted by contemporary Yankee journalists and has recently been argued by Grant biographer Jean Edward Smith. What was not a story was a constant influx of ground and naval sightings. Most alarming were reports from men posted on the parapets that the ironclads had debouched from the Panther Island chute and were forming line of battle.

At noon, the bastion was visible to the men aboard the ironclads. Its flag waved steadily in the breeze from a ship-rigged flagstaff. According to the logbook of the *Lexington,* the giant 8-inch bow Dahlgren of the *Cincinnati* opened the attack on Fort Henry from about 1,700 yards out at precisely 12:27 P.M. That mark was three minutes before the time marked by Flag Officer Foote and 18 before that remembered by Brig. Gen. Tilghman. Blasts of flame and huge clouds of gray-white smoke now burst from the forward guns of all four gunboats. The thunderous booms resounded up and down the river and within moments, clouds of bad-smelling, dirty, hot gunsmoke temporarily obliterated vision.

Despite Foote's best efforts to slow the advance of his craft, Federal troops found that the mud made it difficult for them to scramble ahead. Most were only about halfway to their stepping off point when, in contemporary terms, "the ball was opened." Three minutes after the first cannon lanyard was yanked, the timberclads also opened their portion of the battle.

Brig. Gen. Tilghman and his staff hurried to their stations in the center battery. In accordance with earlier instructions, the Confederates held their fire until gunboat shells started to explode and their initial impact could be evaluated. At that point, Capt. Taylor received permission to return fire, initially with the 10-inch Columbiad and the 24-pdr. rifle. The 32-pdr. smoothbores and the 42-pdr. rifles followed. Just as the decks of the gunboats lurched upon the discharge of their guns, the ground near the Rebel cannon also shook.

Aboard the *Carondelet,* which began firing just after the *Cincinnati*, sailors were able to see the water batteries come alive, ablaze in fire and smoke. The ear-splitting action then became general, with each side firing as its cannon were served and aimed. "Galway," a witness, observed the following: "A thick veil of smoke soon enveloped all the boats, and hid them completely from view. About all that was visible was a dense white vapor, from out of which could be seen constantly, flashes of flame, and above which could be seen, rising, delicate, balloon-like forms of smoke, which an instant before were imprisoned in Rebel shells." The wild whistle of Confederate shells was heard on every side of the *Carondelet* and her consorts, flying overhead to raise geysers in the water or crash into the woods beyond. Simultaneously, the ironclads showed Tilghman and Taylor "one broad and leaping sheet of flame."

According to her captain, not a word was spoken aboard Walke's boat, save those required to complete necessary tasks. It is hard to imagine, however, that there might not have been a number of cries or expletives as shells hit and gun carriages rumbled. There was no panic aboard the *Carondelet,* though her new hands were probably petrified. "Our old men-of-war's men, captains of the guns, proud to show their worth in battle, infused life and courage into their young comrades," the vessel's commander later recalled. "When these experienced gunners saw a shot coming toward a port, they had the coolness and discretion to order their men to bow down, to save their heads."

Signal Quartermaster Matthew Arthur, the captain of the ironclad's starboard bow piece, sought and received permission to fire upon the steamboats retreating from the Rebel fort. In firing, however, his gun missed its targets and hit a Southern hospital steamer, the yellow flag of which could not be seen from the ironclad. Arthur quickly shifted targets as the mistake was realized. Fortunately, no one was hurt as the shot passed through an upper cabin. For his distinguished gun crew leadership during both this battle and the one at Fort Donelson, Arthur (who was born in Scotland in 1835 and had enlisted at Boston a few months earlier) would receive a Congressional Medal of Honor. The nation's top heroism award would also go to Cincinnati seaman John Henry Dorman (1843–1921), who refused to seek medical aid when wounded during both fights and continued at his post, inspiring his crewmates.

The gunboats churned steadily toward Fort Henry; however, before they reached a distance of 1,200 yards, the Confederates believed their fire was "very wild." After that point, the elevation of the Union cannon was steadily decreased and the shells were given shorter fuses. Aboard the *Carondelet,* elevation was eventually reduced from seven to six degrees while fuses were cut from 15 seconds to five. The Union fire had a punishing effect upon the earthen embrasures of the Southern post. As Coffin recalled, "Their huts were blown to pieces by the shells. You see the logs tossed like straws into the air. Their tents are torn into paper-rags. The hissing shells sink deep into the earth and then there are sudden upheavals of sand, with smoke and flames, as if volcanoes were bursting forth. Sand-bags are knocked about. The air is full of strange, hideous, mysterious, terrifying noises."

Yellow and red tongues of fire continued to escape from the muzzles of the flotilla's big guns, helping to create a huge cloud of smoke that obscured sight. Bolts and shells from both sides landed everywhere, crashing into boats, the fort, woods, and the river. Some exploded, others were duds. At one point, a 32-pdr. shot smashed into the *Essex*'s boiler; the ensuing explosion scalded a number of crewmen and forced the boat out of action with 38 casualties. The disaster was clearly visible to many aboard the *Carondelet,* particularly those in her starboard gun crews. The other ironclads also took some punishment, as shells clanged against their casemates, making them shudder. Indeed, one observer recalled that the heavy shot "broke and scattered our iron-plating as if it had been putty." Abbott colorfully noted afterwards that the Confederate shells fell "as harmless as rain-drops."

Not long after the *Essex* was hurt, the Confederate long-range 24-pdr. burst, killing one man and wounding most of the others. Capt. Taylor had taken personal charge of the piece and its loss had an impact on morale. By now, the range was reduced to 600 yards with the accuracy of the gunboats greatly increased, even as Rebel bolts regularly forced spray from the water between them. The river narrowed at this point, forcing the nearly adjacent *St. Louis* and *Carondelet* to become virtually interlocked. They would remain together until the close of action. About this time, a floating torpedo passed close inboard of the two, but with no effect.

Though her pounding was ferocious, Fort Henry still replied with, at times, effective fire. In his *Naval Scenes and Reminiscences*, Walke recalled that that the Rebel gunners had the range of the boats. Nearly every shot struck the iron plating. The *Times*' "Galway" noted how they "indented deeply the iron sheathing, and then glanced off, down the river." Regarding Rebel shots, the *Carondelet*'s captain continued, "They are like the strokes of sledge-hammers, indenting the sheets, starting the fastenings, breaking the tough bolts." Many other shots missed. "A perfect storm of the iron missiles whistled around above," Wilkie observed, and then "ploughed into the water on either side."

As the *Cincinnati*, *St. Louis*, and *Carondelet* pressed home the fight, Fort Henry's Columbiad was lost when a jammed priming wire closed its vent and could not be removed even by a blacksmith. Two 32-pounders were simultaneously put out of action. Five Confederate cannon were out of action by this time and the contest was now very unequal. The naval shells pummeled the earthworks, Capt. Taylor remembered, "as readily as a ball from a Navy Colt would pierce a pine board."

Very few of the Federal soldiers ashore were able to witness the fight, though almost all heard the heavy booming of the naval guns and some the reply of the fort's defenders. Years later Maj. Gen. Wallace remembered the "almost unintermittent thunder." Albert D. Richardson of the *New York Tribune* and several other correspondents tried to see the action from a riverbank tree located somewhere between the fortifications and the gunboats. "There was little to be seen," he confessed, "but smoke."

With exhausted gun crews and no reserves to replace them and with water continuously rising within the fort, Brig. Gen. Tilghman decided further effort was futile. At 1:30 P.M., with five dead and double that number wounded, Tilghman climbed a parapet and waved a white flag. This was not seen from the gunboats, shrouded as they were in gun smoke, and the uneven battle continued for five minutes more. After Tilgham lowered the Confederate flag, the firing ceased and the hour and half long contest was over. Seeing the Confederate banner lowered, the jack tars could hardly restraint themselves offering rousing cheers. "Wild excitement," wrote Bodman of the *Chicago Daily Tribune*, "seized the throats and arms and caps of the 400–500 sailors of the gunboats." He challenged his readers: "Well, imagine it."

At 1:35 P.M., Fort Henry surrendered and five minutes later, Foote's vessels, minus the badly damaged *Essex*, moved cautiously toward the enemy citadel, coming opposite the citadel about 45 minutes later. As the boats advanced, the *Cincinnati* and *Carondelet* steamed to a position where they flanked Fort Henry's batteries. The latter, unable to halt her forward momentum, went aground about 150 yards offshore, while the *Cincinnati* began to drift. The *Carondelet* thus appeared to be moving ahead of the flagboat. Unaware of the situation, Flag Officer Foote angrily hailed Cmdr. Walke, warning him to maintain his station. As the flagboat continued to drift and the *Carondelet* was stuck, the charade continued until, at last, Walke's boat slid off the bank into deeper water.

The *Cincinnati,* also severely pummeled during the fight, lost all of her cutters. Flag Officer Foote hailed one of the nearby timberclads. The *Conestoga*'s captain, Lt. S. Ledyard Phelps, was ordered to take the flagboat skipper, Cmdr. Roger Stembel, in one her longboats to see what Tilghman had in mind. Once Stembel and Phelps were rowed directly through Fort Henry's sallyport, Tilghman, via Capt. Taylor, wasted no time. At 2:30 P.M., the fort was promptly surrendered to the two sailors, along with its surrounding camps, the hospital boat *R.M. Patton* (hit by the *Carondelet*'s shell), her crew and patients, plus some 60 soldiers. Less than 10 minutes later, the Stars and Stripes was hoisted up the center flagpole (the bottom two feet of which were under water in the flooded fort). Brig. Gen. Tilghman was taken by Stembel aboard the Cincinnati where he met the flag officer. Later, he was introduced to the other ironclad captains as they came aboard the flagboat, including Cmdr. Walke, who was ordered to go ashore and hold Fort Henry until Grant arrived to take possession.

Good men died and others fled or were taken prisoner. Years later, however, Capt. Taylor confessed: "If the attack had been delayed 48 hours, there would hardly have been a hostile shot fired; the Tennessee would have accomplished the work by drowning the magazine."

The *Carondelet* was the least damaged of the Union ironclads. Even though she was struck at least nine or 10 times by Rebel projectiles, none of her officers or crew were killed or wounded. Five Confederate bolts hit the bow casemate within eight inches of the gun ports. Others hit the sides of casemates. During the engagement, her guns delivered 107 shot and shell upon the Confederate fortress.

Although the *Essex*, *Cincinnati*, and *St. Louis* fired nearly the same number of shells, they did not score nearly as many effective hits as the *Carondelet.* Moving among the prisoners next day, First Assistant Engineer Charles H. Caven and Paymaster George J.W. Nexsen received gratifying testimony, later printed in the Navy *Official Records.* One Confederate gunner went out of his way to say the following:

> The center boat, or the boat with the red stripes around the top of her smokestacks, was the boat which caused the greatest execution. It was one of her guns which threw a ball against the muzzle of one of our guns, disabling it for the remainder of the contest. The *Carondelet* (as I subsequently found her name to be) at each shot committed more damage than any other boat. She was the object of our hatred, and many a gun from the fort was level at her alone. To her I give more credit than any other boat in capturing one of our strongest places.

Believing his services indispensable at Cairo and wishing to get his damaged ironclads under repair as quickly as possible, Foote, with the *Cincinnati*, *Essex*, and *St. Louis*, departed the scene in early evening. After steaming all night up the Tennessee and down the Ohio, the three ironclads arrived off the tip of Illinois on the morning of February 8, the same day that Grant announced his next target: Fort Donelson on the left bank of the Cumberland River, 12 miles southeast of Fort Henry, north of the little town of Dover.

Interestingly, when the *Cincinnati* approached her Cairo anchorage, onlookers could see Fort Henry's Rebel flag flying upside down below the Stars and Stripes. Foote's victory propelled navy stock "to dizzying heights." No one seemed to realize that the swollen river and a poorly laid-out citadel were largely responsible for the victory, especially after the *Essex* was knocked out.[11]

Grant and his troops arrived at Fort Henry about 3:00 P.M. and relieved the navy of its responsibility for the captured post. The brigadier and his staff accompanied Capt. Walke aboard the *Carondelet,* tied up at the bank, all the while paying the flotilla high compliments and lamenting his inability to participate in the operation.

In accordance with earlier orders from Maj. Gen. Halleck, Grant was also ensure destruction of the important bridge of the Memphis and Ohio Railroad, upstream at Danville. Such an action would obstruct communications between Columbus and Bowling Green, Kentucky. The three timberclads, sent on a raid up the Tennessee, were to visit the structure, as was an army force sent aboard the transport *Illinois*. Both of those missions failed. When the *Illinois* returned, Grant learned that Mississippi cavalry was at Danville bridge and that it was not destroyed. About the same time, both he and Flag Officer Foote received new orders from Halleck: "Push the gunboats up the river to cut the railroad bridges. Troops to sustain the gunboats can follow in transports."

Certain that the timberclads had also left the bridge standing, and armed with Halleck's instructions, Grant turned to Cmdr. Walke to finish the job with the *Carondelet*. That Pook turtle, the only gunboat available, would now proceed to Danville and put the bridge out of commission. While the ironclad made ready to depart on the morning of February 7, two companies of sharpshooters from the 32nd Illinois were ordered aboard. They were joined by Cols. Joseph D. Webster and James B. McPherson and Capt. John A. Rawlins of Grant's staff. The *Carondelet* proceeded the 11 miles up to Danville where the troops were debarked near the bridge. No opposition was met because the Rebel horsemen were able to see and hear the noisy Pook turtle's approach. Only one family was left in the town at the bridge.

In their rapid departure, the Southerners abandoned the bridgehead camp, tents, wagons, some horses, and so forth, leaving all of it to fall into Union hands. Some of this booty Col. Webster ordered taken back to Fort Henry aboard the gunboat and the accompanying *W.H. Brown*. The soldiers then ripped up trestles and destroyed a major bridge pier, preventing the passage of trains. Such Confederate materiel as was not removed was then burned.

When the task was finished on Saturday morning, the *Carondelet* returned to Fort Henry where Grant and the waiting newspapermen were told of her trip and word was sent to Flag Officer Foote. Shortly thereafter, the *W.H. Brown* arrived from the bridge and offloaded captured horses, wagons, and commissary stores. Aboard the *Carondelet,* the remainder of February 8–9 was used to effect as much repair on the vessel as possible. The ironclad was nearly out of food and fuel and her magazine and shell rooms leaked badly.

During the evening of February 10, Capt. Walke again met with Brig. Gen. Grant. At this conference, the *Carondelet* was ordered to proceed to the Cumberland River. After coaling and taking aboard stores and ammunition at Paducah, she would have the opportunity for a larger part and to gain additional laurels for her performance in the investment and capture of Fort Donelson.[12]

5

Fort Donelson

For the Confederacy, the loss of Fort Henry was nothing short of a disaster. "The Yankees," wrote the editor of the *Atlanta Confederacy*, "have brought their gunboats and forces from Paducah, down the Tennessee River across the entire State of Kentucky, in the most populous and wealthy portion of it, to the Tennessee line." Then, they "captured a fortification which our people considered strong which was intended to keep them out of the State of Tennessee."

Elsewhere, on February 8, 1862, the *Nashville Union and American* told its readers that the evacuation of the fort was "inevitable from the high water of the Tennessee rising almost into it." The editors complained that it "was regarded as a weak fort," but had to be sited where it was because, at the time it was started, "Kentucky professed to occupy 'neutral ground.'" The *Memphis Daily Appeal* of the same date informed local citizens that Fort Henry "was purely an earthwork defence, though of considerable magnitude"; its armament "was very inferior" and the efforts to plant submarine batteries "were disturbed before fully perfected."

At Bowling Green, Kentucky, on the day after the victory of Flag Officer Andrew Hull Foote, Gen. Albert Sidney Johnston met with Gen. Pierre G.T. Beauregard and Maj. Gen. William J. Hardee to decide what next to do. "The plan finally adopted," writes Joseph H. Parks, biographer of Maj. Gen. Leonidas Polk, defender of Columbus, Kentucky, "defies explanation." Almost immediately, the three men concluded that Fort Donelson on the Cumberland River was no longer tenable. It was also determined that the two remaining Southern field armies—the one at Bowling Green and the one at Columbus—"must act independently of the other until a concentration could be effected at a later date." Fort Donelson would fight while these retreated. Most reviewing this strategic decision have concluded, with Parks, that "it was poor generalship to send in thousands of men to be crushed or captured by twice their number." While the shocked South recorded the Union triumph and continued planning to prevent a recurrence, the Pook turtle *Carondelet* was prepared to play a solitary role in further discomforting the South.[1]

Flush with victory at Fort Henry back on February 6, Brig. Gen. Ulysses S. Grant wrote out an after-action report for western theater commander Maj. Gen. Henry W. Halleck. Coming to Fort Donelson, he noted that he would take and destroy it two days later. "It seems clear," Bruce Catton later suggested, "that both he and Halleck looked upon this step as just part of a mopping-up process."

The next day, *New York Tribune* correspondent Albert D. Richardson stopped by Grant's Fort Henry headquarters to announce his departure for the East and wish the brigadier good luck. "You had better wait a day or two," Grant said, "Because I am going over to capture Fort Donelson tomorrow." "How strong is it?" the scribe inquired. "We have not been able to ascertain exactly," Grant replied, "but I think we can take it. At all events, we can try." "I was very impatient to get to Fort Donelson," Grant revealed in his memoirs, "because I knew the importance of the place to the enemy and supposed he [Gen. Albert Sidney Johnston] would reinforce it quickly." Far better to send 15,000 up against it now than 50,000 later. On February 9, Maj. Gen. Halleck told Brig. Gen. Grant that "some of the gunboats should be sent up the Cumberland with the least possible delay." It was now "of vital importance that Fort Donelson be reduced immediately.

At Cairo, Flag Officer Foote knew he had been in a scrape. Repairs needed to be effected soon if he was going to play a role in Grant's proposed Fort Donelson push. The old sea dog had no confidence any ironclad fix would be quickly done and, in a letter written to his wife, and quoted by Jay Slagle, promised "I never again will go out and fight half prepared."

The three Federal timberclads, dispatched by Flag Officer Foote three days earlier on a raid up the Tennessee River, returned in triumph to Fort Henry on February 10. About the same time, the wooden task group commander, Lt. S. Ledyard Phelps, was reporting to post commander Brig. Gen. Ulysses S. Grant, according to Cmdr. Walke's memoirs, Lt. William Gwin of the *Tyler* went aboard the *Carondelet* to pay his respects, on Phelps' behalf, to the senior naval officer present. Aboard the black ironclad, the junior officer was informed by Walke that Grant wanted the ironclad and the three timberclads to move over into the Cumberland as soon as possible. It was hoped that they could command the river below Fort Donelson, prevent the fort's reinforcement from the water, and perhaps mount a demonstration favoring the arriving Federal army. According to Walke, Gwin was then ordered to have the "old boats" follow as soon as possible.

Not long after the departure of her visitor, the *Carondelet* steamed down the Tennessee to its mouth at Paducah, to make modest repairs, to coal, to take on supplies and victuals, and to wait for her three wooden consorts. While halted, Walke, anticipating Foote's imminent arrival, left a letter for his superior reviewing the chain of events leading to his departure up the Ohio to the Cumberland. As Grant desired his presence at Fort Henry as soon as possible, the ironclad could not wait. She had to weigh anchor because, as her captain put it, "I am (or the *Carondelet* is) very slow." He also added that Grant would "send the *Tyler*, *Lexington*, and *Conestoga* after me."

At Cairo, Flag Officer Foote remained uncertain that his ironclads were ready for any such immediate expedition. To help push the sailor along, Halleck dispatched his chief of staff, Brig. Gen. George W. Cullum, to the tip of Illinois to do everything possible to get the flotilla started. Halleck also wrote to Foote imploring him to shove off. "Act quickly," he begged, "even though only half ready." Halleck, Cullum, and Grant badgered the flag officer until he finally agreed, against his better judgment, to weigh anchor with his ironclads. Leaving the damaged *Essex* and *Cincinnati* behind, Foote weighed for Paducah at 10:00 P.M. on February 11 aboard his flagship *St. Louis*, the *Louisville* and *Pittsburg* in company. The *St. Louis Daily Missouri Democrat* conjectured that the passage up the Ohio would be slow, "in consequence of the high water and the unusually rapid current in al the rivers."[2]

The evacuees from Fort Henry went approximately 12 miles southeast across a series of ridges that separated the land between the Tennessee and Cumberland rivers and straggled into Fort Donelson on February 6. By dark, the latter's garrison totaled some 3,000 men. Gen. Johnston now withdrew his right wing from Bowling Green and divided it between Donelson and Nashville. The same day Richardson was invited to remain, 12,000 troops from Kentucky arrived at the Cumberland River fortress.

Union forces were never able to make a full reconnaissance of Fort Donelson as they had Fort Henry. As a result, neither the Federal land nor nautical forces on the scene, let alone at Halleck's St. Louis headquarters, knew very much of anything about the defenses of the bastion east of the just-taken Henry. Indeed, they did not even possess accurate maps of the area. Col. Joseph D. Webster of Grant's staff was blunt: "Our army approached the place with very little knowledge of its topography." About all that was known for sure was that the Cumberland River, at this point, flowed almost due north.

Bigger than Fort Henry, Fort Donelson sat atop a hill on the west bank of the river approximately 1,400 yards southwest of the little Stewart County seat of Dover. Visiting it after the battle, *Chicago Daily Tribune* reporter Irving Carson found the community "a straggling place of 20 or 30 houses, with a brick court house, and a church which war has turned to its own use. Everything was dilapidated." "It was," confirmed Junius Henri Browne, "Junius," the scribe from the *Cincinnati Daily Times*, "a town of some eight or nine hundred inhabitants in ordinary times."

Just below Dover, the Cumberland swept west around a high bluff for several hundred yards before resuming its natural course north. It was this eminence that was chosen for fortification and the situation of batteries that gave the ridge-mounted cannon a clear mile and a half long field of fire. Reporter Carson, who inspected the area after it fell to the Union, noticed that the western banks of the river were quite elevated; hills were over a hundred feet high, just like those seen "in Egypt [Southern Illinois] or along the Ohio." It was from these bluffs that the Rebel guns frowned down on the fast-flowing river below.

Two nearby streams, Indian Creek at the elbow end of the curve and Hickman Creek 700 yards farther up, were prone to swell with backwater when the river rose, turning the adjacent ground into a quagmire. Great thickets of oak and ash stood in the water further screening the flanks. Unlike Fort Henry, Confederate engineers here well used the topography available to them.

An irregular, bastioned parapet, the main part of Fort Donelson was about 500 feet long at its greatest length and enclosed approximately a hundred acres. Its narrow ridge base slid into a slight neck in the west and the ground sloped away sharply toward the Cumberland and the two creeks. On another ridge about 700 yards west of the parapet and roughly perpendicular to it was a group of earthworks, coupled with abatis.

Fort Donelson — like Fort Henry — existed to mount cannon, hopefully screened from waterborne attack. Two water batteries were constructed on the river side of the fort, both protected by substantial breastworks. East of the fort, the crescent-shaped upper battery was 50 feet above the Cumberland immediately abreast of the earthworks and was armed with a 10-inch Columbiad built at the Tredegar Iron Works, Richmond, VA. It was rifled to fire a 6.5-inch conical 68-lb. shell and was, as newspaperman Irving Carson later told readers of the *Chicago Daily Tribune,* "a fair piece of workmanship." Also mounted in this "admirable position" were two limited-range 32-pdr. naval carronades, distinguishable by their short iron tubes.

Located north of the citadel, the lower battery was about 150 yards lower down from the upper battery and 20 feet above the river. It mounted one 10-inch Columbiad on a barbette carriage that fired a 128-lb. shell and eight 32-pdr. smoothbores. This straight line defense in fact "ran *en echelon* to the left over the point of a hill that made down obliquely from the earthworks to the river, with the right piece resting on the brink of the river bank, and the Columbiad over in the valley of the stream, emptying into the river some 150 yards lower down."

Nashville attorney and Mexican War veteran Col. Milton A. Haynes had been in charge of the post's heavy artillery for less than a month. Upon his arrival, he was dismayed to learn that most of the few soldiers detailed to the water batteries had little or no training.

Only days before the Western Flotilla arrived, 200 additional men from the Capt. Reuben R. Ross' Maury Artillery (part of the 1st Tennessee Heavy Artillery) reached Fort Donelson and were assigned to man the water batteries. Mississippian Lt. Hugh S. Bedford commanded the Columbiad, emplaced just the day before in the lower battery, with a detachment of 20 men, while Capt. Ross took charge of the 6.5-inch rifled Columbiad in the upper battery, with the heavy batteries all coordinated by Lt. Joseph Dixon. The new men were encouraged to look down the river and to imagine the destruction that could be visited upon any approaching gunboat. Any vessel approaching Fort Donelson could "be raked from stem to stern." Shot from the lower battery could be poured straight into the bow of any enemy. The most important feature of this bastion and its greatest advantage over Fort Henry was the ability of its high water batteries to deliver plunging fire onto targets below. Should the Pook turtles engage, their lightly armored decks and roofs would not be spared as they were at Henry.[3]

Their progress also retarded by the swift currents of the gray Cumberland River, the *Carondelet* and *Alps,* minus the timberclads, dropped their anchors around the bend below Fort Donelson during the morning of February 12. That Southern post, under the command of ex-president James Buchanan's secretary of war, Brig. Gen. John B. Floyd, was now defended by upwards of 25,000 graycoats and there was only one gunboat on the scene. The absence of the timberclads, which diverted to Cairo, left the ironclad and her consort as the only waterborne Federal representatives this far upriver. Determined to unmask the Confederate batteries while simultaneously announcing his arrival to Grant's arriving Federal forces, Capt. Walke ordered the ironclad to churn slowly upstream under her own power to within long range of the citadel. The *Alps* was released to return downstream, taking news of Walke's mission to Flag Officer Foote's fleet, which was advancing slowly up the Cumberland from Smithland, Kentucky.

The same morning, within Fort Donelson's defenses, as Lt. Bedford later reported, "the finishing touches were put on the Columbiad and the batteries were pronounced ready for gunboats." Few of the Tennessee soldiers assigned to the big 10-inch gun had ever seen a heavy battery prior to that morning and consequently, their drill began immediately.

As the *Carondelet* paddled ahead to within view of the Confederate citadel, observant crewmen noticed how the giant, leafless hardwoods on the Cumberland's west bank hills helped to conceal the enemy's defenses. Some of the forests had been cleared when work on Fort Donelson started back in the fall. The eastern shore largely comprised snow-covered hills and tall, ragged, dirty-yellow hued bluffs. From the water, the upper battery resembled, as correspondent Irving Carson reported, "a hole in the side of the hill." Overall, the fortifications built into the eastern embankment were "well constructed and, from the nature of the ground ... almost a casemate. A shot striking below or above would do no damage."

Observing the Confederate cannon through his spyglass, Cmdr. Walke was reminded of the "dismal-looking sepulchers cut in the rocky cliffs near Jerusalem, but far more repulsive." Perhaps the biggest worry was, as Carson put it, "that it would be next to an impossibility to reach the big gun at the upper end of the trench, for turn your bow's head on to avoid the shot, you would still be raked by some of the other Rebel guns."

No signs of life were visible in Fort Donelson as the *Carondelet* slowly obtained her firing position, 2¼ miles below. Determined to test the Confederate works, the gunboat opened fire at 11:20 A.M. with her three bow cannon. One giant shell was seen to fall short. The ironclad deposited seven additional 64- and 70-lb. bolts into the side of the bluff, eliciting no response other than echoes from the surrounding hills. As the Pook turtle had not come within effective range of the water batteries, the Confederates chose not to return fire.

At this point, the *Carondelet* withdrew four miles below and anchored near the eastern bank for the night. Extra armed sailors were posted on watch, as her captain feared that the isolated ironclad might be boarded. Steam was lightly maintained in case of emergency. Lt. Bedford was less than pleased when drill for his freshman gunners "was effectively interrupted by the appearance of a gunboat down the river." Although the red bands on her chimneys glistened in the early sun for all to see, the boat's identity was not immediately known, though it was subsequently "ascertained to be the *Carondelet*." Bedford admired the "remarkable precision" of her shot and her smooth retirement.

By the morning of February 13, Union field batteries were nearly all unlimbered as bluecoat troops continued to invest the perimeter of Fort Donelson. Early in the morning a small boat from shore brought Capt. Walke a dispatch from Brig. Gen. Grant asking that the *Carondelet* make another demonstration against the water batteries, thereby creating a distraction while his men completed their positioning. If it could begin at 10:00 A.M., the soldiers would be ready to take advantage. Bells jingled just before 9:00 A.M. asking Chief Engineer Faulkner to order up steam. The *Carondelet* noisily stood up the river generously spitting sparks and sooty smoke from her red chimney tops. Pushing against the current at approximately 4 knots, the ironclad hugged the river's outer edge, where the water was less swift. Upon reaching a forested point in a river bend about a mile below the water batteries, the Pook turtle came to, the anchors were cast overboard, and the crew was beat to quarters. Correspondent Coffin later recalled that the weather that Thursday morning was genial with "breezes from the southwest so mild and warm the spring birds came."

At the appointed hour, the ironclad's three bow guns, alternately poking out from the ports in her square forward casemate, started throwing out their big shells. With no need to rush, the experienced gun captains, employing fuses cut to 10- or 15-seconds, took care-

Drawn years later by Capt. Walke, this scene depicts the *Carondelet*'s lone bombardment of Fort Donelson on February 13 (*Battles and Leaders*).

ful aim along the primitive sights and pulled their lanyards with confidence. Once more, the Rebel gunners were caught at practice and forced to quit. As they scrambled to safety, shells began to burst yards short of the water battery and then directly over it. Others hit the parapet, while some excavated the hillside, in every case blowing up great dirt piles.

The *Carondelet* "was diabolically inspired," Lt. Bedford testified, "and knew the most

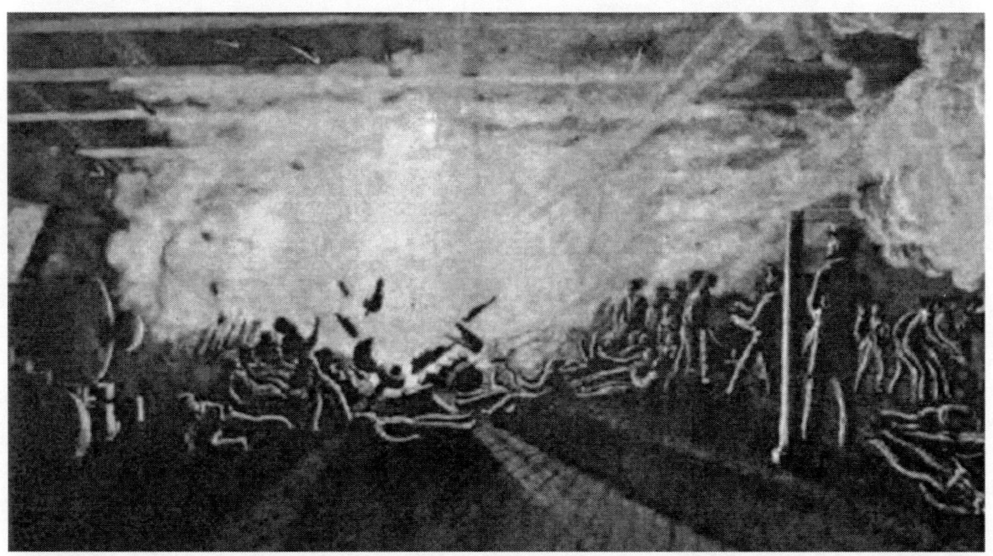

As depicted in two renderings by Capt. Walke, the *Carondelet*'s improperly loaded port bow 42-pdr. discharged prematurely during the attack on Fort Donelson in a great cloud of gunpowder, noise, and flame that rocked the boat. Although no one was killed in the thunderous explosion, over a dozen men were wounded and the cannon was broken into four pieces. Walke later learned that the reason no one was killed was that the crew realized their error in not properly seating a shell early on and were able to stand back (Walke, *Naval Scenes and Reminiscences*, in *Battles and Leaders*).

Capt. Walke's depiction of the Battle of Fort Donelson is filled with local color that conveys both the river and land engagements, and the weather as well. Local color fills the foreground (Hoppin, *Life of Andrew Hull Foote*).

opportune time to annoy us." Refusing to remain silent a second day, Capt. Dixon ordered the two Columbiads to respond. The lone gunboat and the big fort would duel for the next hour and a half. It probably did not please Cmdr. Walke or his men when they read, as they surely did, the observation of "Junius" in the *Cincinnati Daily Times* a few days later about "the sole gunboat taking part being the *Conestoga*."

The huge projectiles from the long-range Southern cannon arched high into the sky and flew downrange. The first passed over the *Carondelet* and brought up a huge geyser a quarter mile astern. The second splashed short, piercing the Cumberland with iron splinters. A third shot was heard by Confederate gunners to strike their antagonist. Amidst Rebel cheers, Capt. Dixon ordered the 32-pounders to join in the contest, even though most of their captains believed the low-slung gunboat too far away. At maximum elevation, these cannonballs missed.

Dozens of shot and shell were exchanged between ship and shore. Walke and his gunners quickly determined that the Confederate Columbiads were the fort's most dangerous guns. A shell from one of these suddenly burst abreast of the gunboat, but far enough out that only fragments rang against the broadside casemate.

One of the Dahlgren projectiles from the Pook turtle caused a serious Southern loss when it struck the left cheek of the sixth 32-pounder from the left in Fort Donelson's lower battery, dismounting the piece. Four men were wounded and two killed, including Capt. Dixon, who was hit in his left temple by a screw-tap torn off the carriage. Capt. Haynes now moved his command post to this location.

The *Carondelet*, meanwhile, continued to singly engage the batteries. Reporting to his readers, *New York Times* correspondent Franc "Galway" Wilkie noted how she was able to blaze away and receive "no great damage in the tremendous fire to which she was exposed — save in the case of a single shot." Historian John S.C. Abbott cheerfully informed his readers right after the war that the "heavy boom" of her guns "gave great joy, and cheer upon cheer rose from the troops encircling the beleaguered fort."

About 11:30 A.M., a 128-lb. projectile from the 6.5-inch rifled Columbiad hit the corner where the port side of the *Carondelet*'s casemate joined the bow protection. Tearing through the exterior, it ricocheted over the temporary log barricade Walke had placed around the boilers, jumped over the steam-drum, hit upper deck beams, carried away the railing around the engine room, and burst the steam-heater before bouncing back to rest in the engine room. One of the assistant engineers later remarked that the shot "seemed to bound after the men like a wild beast pursuing its prey." Twelve men were wounded by the Confederate gift, seven severely. Most of the injuries came from the wooden splinters knocked loose by the ball during its interior passage. Although a number of these were huge, many were small, like needles. Among the injured, some did not know they were hurt until they felt blood oozing into their shoes. Had the collapsible barrier not been erected before the boiler, the ironclad might very well have exploded and sunk right there.

In order to allow his wounded to be treated and the damage control parties to effect repairs, Capt. Walke ordered Pilot Hinton to drop the gunboat further down a few miles behind the point. As "Galway" noted: "she retired from the unequal contest, having covered herself with glory." During the course of the morning, the ironclad blasted 139 shells into the sides of Donelson's defensive embankment. The *Alps*, having returned, met the *Carondelet* and received her injured. Dinner was ordered served, it being long past lunchtime.

Each side scored one terrific blow upon the other during the course of the morning shoot. Capt. Ross, however, believed the gunboat's shooting the best. After the *Carondelet* withdrew, 14 cannonballs were collected within the confines of the upper battery "within the narrow radius of as many yards."

As the bluejackets cleared away their dinnerware, distant firing was heard from Federal artillery. The time had come to renew their diversion. When it appeared that the Yankee turtle would venture extremely close in, Capt. Haynes, hoping his 32-pdr. gunners could see some action, had them withhold fire. They did so in vain. Refusing to move within range of the 32s, the *Carondelet* assumed station about a mile from the water batteries. Because her ammunition was running low, Walke opened a much more deliberate and slower fire than sanctioned that morning. A frustrated Haynes ordered his two Columbiads to resume the contest.

All afternoon, Haynes and Walke played a game of chicken. First the gunboat would sneak closer to the batteries. Then the Columbiads would fire, sometimes coming close. The *Carondelet* would then drop downstream, out of range.

When the Eads craft retired downstream at dusk, 45 more of her shells lay in and about Fort Donelson and the boat's ammunition locker was nearly empty. George W. Beaman of the *St. Louis Daily Missouri Democrat*, writing later in February after the battle, indirectly quoted Capt. Haynes. "The fire of the *Carondelet* did more actual damage" to the Confederate defenses that day, he believed, "than the heavy bombardment" of all the gunboats on the next.

While the Federal gunboat and the Dixie gunners dueled, the weather began to turn, veering to the north with heavy developing clouds. As the afternoon passed, the balminess gave way to a fierce blow that "commenced to moan its dirges." The rain came toward dusk followed after dark by sleet and snow. It grew so cold that Col. Richard Oglesby, a future Illinois governor, observed that many of his huddled bluecoat soldiers became "nearly torpid from the intense cold." The usually overwarm casemate of Walke's ironclad was, however, now "just right." Here many jack tars, some with their ears still ringing after the shoot, made further preparations for additional action while carpenters made repairs. Inside Fort Donelson, the men at the heavy guns received cooked rations and a bit of Tennessee "sipping whiskey."

About 10:00 P.M., a lookout aboard the *Carondelet* spotted the chimney flashes of boats approaching from Smithland. Within a quarter hour, Lt. Egbert Thompson's leading *Pittsburg* anchored at the landing four miles below Fort Donelson where the *Carondelet* was already tied up.

According to "Try Again," a correspondent for the *St. Louis Daily Missouri Democrat*, the transports, with six new Ohio, Nebraska, and Illinois regiments, came in a little later. The night that followed was cold and noisy, as Rebel cannon fire toward the bluecoats west of the fort continued at intervals and an icy wind howled and spent its fury on every person for miles around.[4] When the sun rose on the morning of February 14, the temperature in Stewart County, Tennessee, was 10 degrees above zero Fahrenheit. There was about 2 inches of snow on the ground and it continued to fall. After a while, however, the sky became clear and bright. The Northern and Southern military participants in or around Fort Donelson, to say nothing of residents in homes around Dover and elsewhere in the twin rivers region, all shivered in the cold.

Maj. Gen. U.S. Grant (1822–1885) was well acquainted with the *Carondelet*. His troops saw her in action at Fort Henry, Fort Donelson, and Vicksburg and he was several times aboard. From his earlier work with Capt. Henry Walke aboard the *Tyler*, Grant developed a warm opinion of the navy. Later, at Fort Donelson, Grant called upon Walke's ironclad to occupy the attention of the Confederate defenders while his men invested the bastion and awaited the arrival of Flag Officer Foote's main fleet (National Archives).

When Capt. Charles Nott of the 5th Iowa Cavalry went on deck of his steamer, the *McGill*, he was struck by the snow and intense cold, as well as the high wooded hills on either bank. From his location on the western bank, he could see far down the river the other troop steamers tied to trees along the shore. Smoke trailed upwards from fleet chimneys and the great collective cloud was easily seen from Fort Donelson, tipping off the Confederates that the great convoy had arrived and was about to, if it had not already, begin unloading men and equipment. "The gunboats lay anchored in the middle of the stream," Nott remembered, "all signs of life hidden beneath their dark decks, save the white steam that slowly issued from their pipes and floated gracefully away."

At approximately 9:00 A.M., Brig. Gen. Grant arrived at the *Carondelet*'s landing to confer with Flag Officer Foote. Just after dismounting and as he prepared to climb aboard the *St. Louis,* which had recently nosed into the bank, he passed word to his aides to have the soldiers disembark from the newly arrived troop boats. No notes were kept during the Grant-Foote discussion. It is known that the flag officer was very reluctant to engage or run by the water batteries. Grant, who wished the naval magic of Fort Henry reapplied here, believed the ironclads could be successful not only in neutralizing the enemy's heavy ordnance, but also in cutting his communication with Nashville. As such an action was deemed a military necessity by generals from Halleck on down, Foote agreed to try.

According to Steven Woodworth, the strategy the two leaders doubtless agreed upon went like this. As at Fort Henry, Foote would, using a favorite Civil War phrase, "open the ball" by silencing Donelson's big guns. His boats would then steam up past Dover and assume a position blockading the Cumberland against Confederate reinforcement or retreat. With fleet gunfire support, the Union division on the right would drive the Rebels toward the two other U.S. divisions. Cornered, Floyd's men would see the light and surrender. Bruce Catton pointed out during the Civil War centennial that this plan had two major flaws. First, Fort Donelson was massively reinforced and its soldiers were not being evacuated. Second, and most important to our story, the plunging fire arcs from her water batteries, a cooperative river, and her excellent physical situation made this outpost much stronger than Fort Henry.

After the meeting, as the brigadier was jumping down to the bank from the ironclad's deck, he was approached by several Northern newsmen. Stopping to tamp his pipe, he informed the scribes "that, aided by the gunboats, he could capture every man in the fort." The writers had the opinion that the general believed Fort Donelson would be another "easy victory."

It took the remainder of the morning for the bluecoated soldiers to disembark from the steamers and assemble in the center between the units already present. During this time, a series of miscommunications and a foot-dragging decision process prevented the Confederates from opening on the transports with their 10-inch Columbiad. By noon, the wings of Grant's army arced around the Rebel citadel, with the Confederates occupying trenches and rifle pits from Hickman Creek to Indian Creek to Dover. Looking down from one of the fort's batteries, Confederate soldier Wesley Smith Dorris wrote in his diary: "Today the enemy's drums are within hearing distance.... At noon, the smoke of the enemy's gunboats were seen down the river."

As the troops deployed or stiffened their defenses, the north wind's chilly breath was still felt and the snow made land maneuver difficult. The warmest places for anyone in the Dover area this day were the engine rooms of the troop and war boats. While only scattered actions occurred ashore, the main event on the day's military calendar would be what Gen. Johnston's son labeled "The Battle of the Gunboats."

Once Brig. Gen. Grant had gone ashore from the *St. Louis,* the flotilla commander signaled all of the gunboat captains to repair aboard the flagboat for a conference. Noting that he was not happy with the role they must play, but play it they would, Foote laid out the battle plan, which was essentially the same one employed at Fort Henry. As they did a week earlier and on the next river over, the first division ironclads would move against the fort in line abreast, with the two timberclads of the 2nd Division following behind by a thousand yards. The turtles would get as close to the works as possible, without regard to the elevation of the defending batteries. Writing years later, Rebel Lt. Bedford observed of Foote that, "flushed with his victory at Fort Henry, his success there paved the way for his defeat at Donelson."

After the war council broke up, the gunboat captains took turns coaling their crafts from the barge brought up by the *Conestoga.* While waiting their turn, they tried to make certain that their crafts were as ready for action as possible by adding temporary protections. Hands could be seen sweating in the cold as they stacked extra lumber, bread bags filled with coal, spare anchors, lengths of chain, and heavy hausers, on the decks and down the sides of the boats. The river tars knew, from stories reinforced by the crew of the *Carondelet*, what plunging fire could do. Special attention was paid to the preparation of log barricades for the boilers. Coaled and protected with everything substantial not nailed down, the gunboats were as ready as possible by 1:45 P.M. when Flag Officer Foote signaled them to weigh. Within a half hour, all were proceeding up the river.

At a point about a quarter mile above the landing, a signal was hoisted to assume battle formation. Slowly and in this order, the *Louisville, St. Louis* (flag), *Pittsburg*, and *Carondelet* came into line abreast of one another. The *Conestoga* and *Tyler* fell in about a thousand yards behind. "All was silence onboard the gunboats," Irving Carson observed, "the dip of whose paddle wheels alone broke the stillness."

Brig. Gen. Grant found a shore location from which, as he later put it, "I could see the advancing navy." *Times*' correspondent Wilkie "secured a position about half-way between the boats and the fort, a little bit out of the line of fire." Beaman from the *Daily Missouri Democrat* and several others were with the troops ashore and so would see nothing. On the other hand, "Mack" McCullagh of the *Cincinnati Daily Gazette* was with Foote aboard the *St. Louis*, while Frank G. Chapman of the *New York Herald* was on the *Louisville.*

At Fort Donelson, meanwhile, the decision to open fire on the transports had finally been taken and the two largest cannon sent several shells screaming toward the clouds of smoke at about 2:00 P.M. Suddenly, the Rebel gunners saw the combined sooty puff begin to part. A large billow moved downriver while the other approached. The first turned out to be the transports and the second was Flag Officer Foote's gunboats.

It was approximately 2:35 P.M. when the lead gunboat *Carondelet* rounded a wooded point and spied the Confederate water batteries ahead. The *Pittsburg* and *Louisville* were lagging and Flag Officer Foote, hailing them from the *St. Louis*, demanded that they "steam up." The water aft their fantails frothed mightily as thrashing paddle wheel buckets dipped faster.

After a brief pause while the Confederates witnessed the naval formation taking shape, the 6.5-inch rifled Columbiad opened fire at 2:38 P.M. The range was 1.5 miles and her first ball was a ricochet that splashed the water just ahead of the *St. Louis.* Minutes later another from the same gun hit the water 150 yards ahead. While the gunboats entered their battle echelon and pushed ahead at roughly three miles per hour, soldiers and newsmen on both sides watched or wanted to, not all of them passively. As in a modern day Super Bowl, the visiting team headed toward the goal line and was cheered by its supporters while fans of the opponent remained largely silent. In this case, Grant's soldiers were the ones cheering first, "remembering the victory eight days before."

The Columbiad's greeting was answered by the *St. Louis* when she came within range of the 32-pdrs. at, Carson jotted in his notebook, "precisely 10 minutes to 3 P.M." Thus the "ball was opened." The ironclads paddled cautiously ahead, firing deliberately, though rapidly. The gun layers aboard the *Carondelet* and her sisters sighted their weapons as precisely as possible while each varied speed slightly to confuse the Rebel gunners. At one point, Flag Officer Foote noticed that the *Carondelet* was firing more rapidly than her consorts. Raising his speaking trumpet, the unit commander hailed Capt. Walke, ordering him to reduce his rate of fire. Initially, shell fuses were cut for 15 seconds; as the boats approached the fort, the time was reduced to 10 seconds, then five. Trailing behind, the wooden gunboats increased the elevation of their cannon and began long-range firing.

It must have been fascinating to the hundreds of witnesses, many of whom saw little through acrid clouds of gunsmoke. In addition to the cannon fire, which was loud enough in and of itself, there was the new and tremendous sound heard only once previously, at Fort Henry — heavy shells and cannonballs hitting the Pook turtle armor.

An ineffective water barrier was passed by the gunboats about 3:15 P.M., bringing them face to face with seven 32-pdrs. in the lower batteries. In an effort to neutralize the rapid fire from the Confederate guns, Foote granted permission to increase the rate of fire. Within three-quarters of an hour the ironclads had closed to a point some 400 yards from the lower batteries. The intensity of the bombardment increased on both sides as the booming intensified. Splashes from plumed geysers and shell fragments from the fort's cannon seemed to punch and wash the ironclads equally.

The decreasing range allowed the tempo and volume of gunboat fire to increase. The lower Southern battery was raked, as were parts of the fort. Several of the craft switched briefly from shell to grapeshot, and those deadly small balls supposedly encouraged several Confederate gun crews to abandon their pieces. At least that is how it appeared to the gunboat embedded newspapermen, though Lt. Bedford, for one, was later emphatic that the Rebel gunners showed no panic or cowardice. Though slow, the roar of his Columbiad "was almost as regular as the swinging of a pendulum." The fact of the shoot was, however, that the gunboats were actually now firing over the Confederates, landing shells with the lines of waiting Federal troops. If anything, the advancing boats now seemed to be exposed to far worse than they were dishing out, the terrible plunging fire pouring down from above. The heavy bolts from upon high were devastating.

The water batteries at Fort Donelson had a formidable view of the Cumberland River. Here conquering Union soldiers and others inspect the battlements, perhaps considering the fury of the battle in which the gunboats were repulsed (*Leslie's Illustrated*, March 15, 1862).

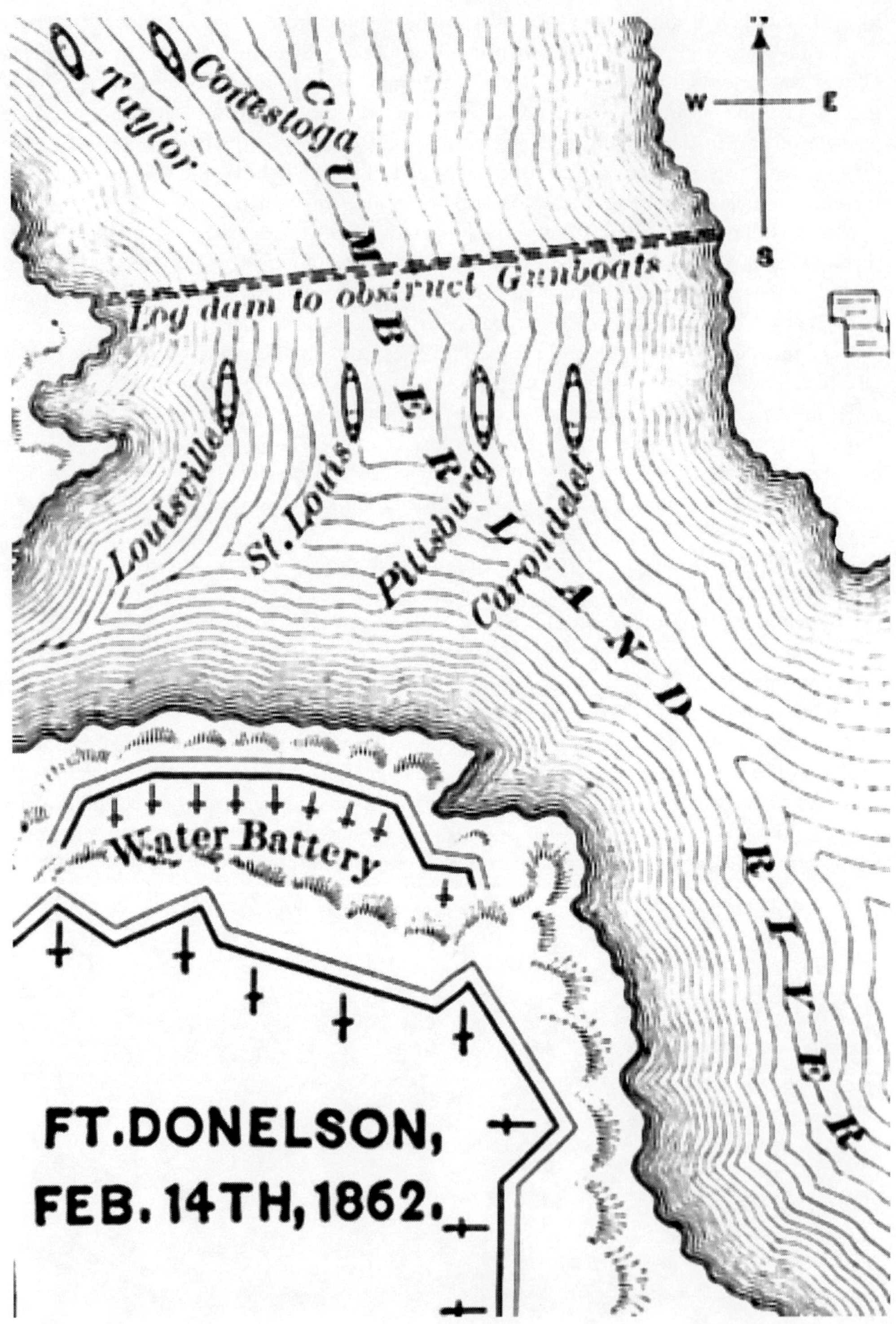

This map drawn from Hoppin's *Life of Andrew Hull Foote* conveys a sense of the fight between the gunboats and the batteries at Fort Donelson. The Federal ironclads are shown in the advance, with the timberclads behind (Hoppin, *Life of Andrew Hull Foote*).

The brains of the men within the turtle casemates must have been semi-paralyzed. The extreme noise and the pandemonium caused by the roar of the guns and shells hitting, smashing, or bouncing off the armor did not stifle the response as the bluejacket gun crews. Despite sheets of gun smoke drifting back into and through the stifling gun deck, the practiced bluejackets performed the load and shoot drills drilled into them since commissioning day. Still, for many, it must have been like standing inside a huge bell, with the enemy banging on it from the outside with giant sledges.

While the ironclads, having closed to 400 yards, were taking a beating and continuing to fire over their targets, the two timberclads remained well behind. They sent their shot, for the most part, toward the Rebel works from long range, and they, too, were not always accurate. "Rebel officers commanding the river batteries," interviewed by *St. Louis Daily Missouri Democrat* reporter George W. Beaman after the battle, were quoted as saying that "the practice of our gunners" in the excitement of the fight "was much inferior to that displayed in the reconnaissance [by the *Carondelet*]—where matters were conducted with more deliberation."

All of the ironclads were badly knocked about. Damage to the *Carondelet* and her consorts began to tell. Planking and plating were ripped away in many spots, "as lightning tears the bark from a tree." The flagstaffs, chimneys, and remaining boats and davits were damaged or shot away. Ashore not far from the river, Federal enlistee Jesse Bowman Young could not only hear the roar of the guns and the resounding noise of bolts and splinters hitting the casemates, but the cries of the wounded, the shots of the officers and gunners, and the hammering and banging of damage control parties.

Shortly after the general action started, the 6.5-inch Confederate Columbiad went down when a bent priming wire became lodged. After it was cleared, the crew, in loading it, jammed a shell in its barrel. Finally, that difficulty was resolved and the shot smashed one of the *Carondelet*'s anchors, sending fragments to bounce up and carry away parts of her chimneys. As the four boats closed the lower batteries, her red-banded chimneys offered a larger target. Lt. Bedford's gun continued to zero in on the closest ironclad, with the red-topped chimneys, and a lookout, Lt. J.M. Sparkman, reported that much of her armor was raked away.

After some difficulty with his piece, Pvt. John G. Frequa, gun captain of the 6.5-inch rifle, once more took on the *Carondelet.* Just before pulling the lanyard, he yelled to his gun crew, according to the *Battles and Leaders* piece by Maj. Gen. Lew Wallace, "Now boys, see me take a chimney!" The projectile flew down toward Walke's command, taking away her flag and one of her stacks. The men at the Rebel gun cheered, their leader adding, "Come on, you cowardly scoundrels; you are not at Fort Henry!"

Rebel shot snapped a set of Walke's boat davits, smashing a yawl and leaving it trailing in the river. One ripped open the iron plating and fell off; another went through and lodged in the wood of the casemate. With improving aim, the Rebel gunners succeeded in hitting the *Carondelet*'s pilothouse. The iron facing was knocked to pieces and one of the many iron splinters cast about mortally wounded Chief Pilot Hinton.

The gun crews on the Federal boats fought hard. Occasionally, orders were confused and mistakes were made. One such error had tragic consequences. Improperly loaded, the *Carondelet*'s port bow 42-pdr. discharged prematurely in a great cloud of gunpowder, noise, and flame that rocked the boat. Although no one was killed in the thunderous explosion, over a dozen men were wounded and the cannon was broken into four parts, the largest of which was projected outside the port and into the river. Capt. Walke himself joined First

Master Richard Wade and others in running to the disaster scene as the cry of "Fire!" rang through the boat. The *Carondelet*'s commander later revealed that the reason no one was killed was that the crew realized its error in not properly seating a shell early on and was able to stand back.

While men fought a fire in the debris and pulled the injured to safety, two more Rebel cannonballs snuck through the bow gun ports, killing four men and wounding others. As carpenter Donaldson and his men extinguished the blaze, another 32-pdr. solid shot hit the already-damaged pilothouse. The injured number two pilot, Daniel Weaver, slumped, and the huge 6-foot steering wheel was damaged. Down below, Walke personally encouraged the remaining gunners of the First Division to stand to their guns and maintain as rapid a rate of fire as possible. At one point, a giant ball stripped a lengthy chunk of boilerplate from his gunboat's thinly protected casemate further aft.

The *Louisville,* hit 59 times, was disabled by a shot that cut away her rudder chains. Another ball wounded the flag officer and killed the pilot of the *St. Louis* as it passed through her pilothouse. The flagboat was smashed three dozen more times. The *Pittsburg* was also touched almost 30 times. As damage control parties aboard all of the gunboats fought to keep their boats operable, all began to back out of line, increasing their distance from the intense Confederate cannonade. Looking out, Rebel Pvt. "Spot" F. Terrell noted that, "while the Iron and Wood was flying from them up in the air, tha sneaked down behind the bend badely tore to peasis."

During her effort to quickly get out of harm's way and cover herself while doing so, the stricken *Pittsburg*, hulled below the waterline and taking on water, turned to bring certain guns to bear. In the process, however, she smashed into the stern of the *Carondelet*, crushing her starboard rudder. As Walke attempted to maneuver his boat away from the collision with his rampaging consort and simultaneously avoid a rocky point jutting out from the right bank, he was forced to move forward and not back.

Capt. Walke's battle scene at Fort Donelson reveals the snow and misery of the day on which the *Carondelet* and her sisters were forced to retreated from the plunging fire of the Confederate defenses (Walke, *Naval Scenes and Reminiscences*).

By now, the wheel ropes of both the *Louisville* and *St. Louis* had been shot away and both were drifting out of action, followed by the *Pittsburg*. Occasionally, due to their poor steering qualities, the trio exposed their broadsides in unintentional swerving maneuvers commented upon in several Confederate reports. The *Carondelet* was left alone to face the wrath of Fort Donelson's gunners.

Walke and his men had only one hope of surviving in the narrow stream: back their vessel straight out of danger, keeping her two undamaged bow guns firing at the lower Rebel battery. As the ironclad reversed engines again, Confederate artillery, as could be expected, was sighted squarely upon her in an effort to sink their hated adversary. The gunners of the *Carondelet* responded as rapidly as possible in an effort to create a cloud of powder smoke to help cover her withdrawal. With smoke and steam escaping her ports, the ironclad's decks were now "so slippery with the blood" of shipmates that the survivors could hardly stand. Sand was spread about the gun deck to improve footing.

The Confederates now began to skip their balls over the water toward the Northern gunboat, much as a stone skipped across a pond has distance and sometimes effect. Meanwhile, having gained the attention of the forward gun crews, Acting Gunner John Hall, commanding the starboard bow cannon, ordered the tars to watch him closely. Whenever he spotted a shot coming, he would holler a warning and duck down. This was a signal for the tars to stand away from the gun ports. As she backed away firing, the *Carondelet* was continuously struck in the bow and casemate by Southern shot. Most of these were ricochets Hall warned the men about as he saw them skipping toward them over the water. A 32-pdr. smacked into the lower sill of the middle bow gun port just after Hall's warning. As the warned-off gunners watched, it glanced up into the upper sill, fell again to the lower, then entered, spinning on the deck like a top until it stopped.

Twice Walke's craft "was hit in the bow between wind and water" and only her watertight compartments kept her afloat. Three more 32-pdr. shots hit the starboard casemate and four the port, while one "struck on the starboard side, between the waterline and the plank-sheer, cutting through the planking." There are in every war a few who, through recklessness or bravado, fail to heed warnings. When another ball glanced off a bow gun, two who failed to drop down when the command "Down!" was given, lost their heads. Two others manning another piece also died.

Cmdr. Walke, whose experiences with the timberclads of late now left him no fan, was later very critical of their role at Fort Donelson. "The *Taylor* and *Conestoga* were so far astern that their shell fell short or exploded over our gunboats," he alleged. Their firing did "less damage, evidently, to their enemies than to their friends." Already, shells from the "stinkpots," as they were sometimes derisively known, had landed on the retreating *St. Louis* and *Louisville*. As she too backed off, the badly injured *Carondelet* was also struck. An 8-inch shell from the *Tyler* burst astern, showering the ironclad's casemate with shrapnel fragments. A part of the shell also lodged in the captain's cabin in the stern casemate and was dug out later by carpenters at Mound City. It was acquired by Cmdr. Walke as a souvenir.

After an hour and 10 minutes of Rebel pounding, Flag Officer Foote had been forced to withdraw. Aboard the ironclads, collectively hit 180 times, there were 9 dead and 45 wounded bluejackets. Hit 54 times, the *Carondelet* recorded 4 deaths and 29 injured. Although Foote's quartet was badly shot up, damages were not critical.

Covered by Walke's stalwart, the *St. Louis*, *Pittsburgh*, and *Louisville* drifted or proceeded under minimal power down around the point from behind which they had earlier emerged. The *Tyler* and *Conestoga* joined the retreat. One by one they dropped anchors (or tied to the shore). While the wooded hills now effectively protected them — at last — from Rebel guns, emergency crews swarmed aboard the mauled ironclads to plug shot holes and make every effort to keep them afloat. A few correspondents came to the bank seeking interviews. "Old man-of-war's men" told Irving Carson of the *Chicago Daily Tribune* that "the fight was the hottest they'd ever seen."

Taking on water, the *Carondelet*, meanwhile, was drifting toward a point just below Hickman Creek that was well within range of the Confederate big guns. To clear the jutting land, the gunboat steamed upstream under fire until, when just by it, her engines could be cut and she was once more allowed to ride the current downstream, her bow guns spitting defiance until she was out of range.

As her wounded were tended, a damage report was compiled. In addition to the serious blows already reported to him, Capt. Walke learned that, in addition to being hulled, not a mast, spar, or davit remained and his boats were all kindling; the port side of the casemate was sliced open for a distance of 15 feet, the hurricane and forward decks, and the fantail were splintered, and the chimneys looked like colanders. The *Carondelet* tied up to the shore near her consorts sometime after 5:00 P.M. She was the first and last Federal ironclad to draw Rebel fire at Fort Donelson. Counting the previous day's shoots, she was under fire longer than the others and certainly had the scars and casualties to prove it.

Somewhat stunned that they had defeated the vaunted "Linkum" gunboats, the Confederates were at least momentarily jubilant. After dropping 370 projectiles on their enemy, the victors looked around and found that not a single casualty had occurred within their ranks. Many, according to the *New York Herald* correspondent embedded aboard the *St. Louis*, "wild with enthusiasm," then "rushed down to the lower batteries" in celebration.

It was the Southern gun team and not the Yankees who had scored the big "touchdown." Rebel gunners and soldiers in the water batteries, joined by troops in the rifle pits all the way up and down the line, cheered until they were hoarse. Newsman Wilkie wrote bluntly in his memoirs what many Yankees must then have felt about their river ironclads: "They proved of no value." Indeed, he added, "they did more damage to the Federal right than to the batteries which they engaged."

"The shouts of triumph," Wesley Smith Dorris jotted in his diary, reverberated "through the hills and valleys, which doubtless went to the ears of the enemy, for they

Located north of Fort Donelson, the lower battery was about 150 yards lower down from the upper battery and 20 feet above the river. It mounted one 10-inch Columbiad (on a barbette carriage and that fired a 128-lb. shell) and eight 32-pdr. smoothbores. Alexander Simplot sketched the defense after its capture (*Harper's Weekly*, March 22, 1862).

seemed infuriated." Amidst the bastion's celebration, Lt. Col. Alfred Robb of the 49th Tennessee made certain that the day's best Dixie cannoneers received a well-deserved round of good Volunteer State whiskey. News of the victory over the gunboats was wired all over the South. The *Charleston Mercury*, the following Monday, was able to publish news from a February 15 telegraph which called the "Confederate victory, thus far, complete." It went on to point out that the Cumberland River was falling rapidly. With but 10 feet of water at Harpeth Shoals, it was doubted that the gunboats would be able to pass over if they did not leave soon.

Still, it has been argued that, while a tactical failure, Flag Officer Foote's attack did have one major operational result. Prior to the triumph of Donelson's water batteries, the Confederate leadership was mesmerized by the gunboats. This fixation caused them, in the view of Scott W. Stucky, to miss "the opportunity for strategic withdrawal and the saving of the 17,000 who eventually surrendered."

With the gunboats *hors de combat* and out of the picture, the battle became one between blue- and gray-clothed land forces, a frigid affair over whose participants the northern wind howled equally. On the morning after the gunboat attack, Capt. Walke read the Episcopal service as the *Carondelet* dead were buried in a lonely field back of the river bank.

When Flag Officer Foote returned to Cairo, he left the damaged *Carondelet* and *St. Louis* behind to provide Grant's army with whatever naval support would yet be required. Prior to the Confederate surrender on February 17, none was found necessary. After Divine Services that morning, the *Carondelet* returned to Cairo, bearing the initial firsthand news of the outpost's capture. Following her subsequent participation in a Columbus, Kentucky, reconnaissance, Cmdr. Walke's craft was sent up the Ohio River to Mound City for repairs that were completed in time for the start of her next campaign on March 14.[5]

6

Island No. 10

As part of a general defensive strategy adopted just before the battle at Fort Donelson, Gen. Pierre G.T. Beauregard, commander of the Confederate Army of the Mississippi, had recommended that Columbus, Kentucky, be rapidly evacuated, leaving only a small garrison as the rear guard. Most of the citadel's defenders would retreat, beginning on March 1, to New Madrid, Missouri, or to Jackson, Mississippi, as well as to Island No. 10, the 10th atoll in the Mississippi below its confluence with the Ohio River, which is now part of the Missouri shore.

The evacuation of Columbus would leave the Confederacy in the West with a defensive line that ran from Corinth, MS, across western Tennessee to Island No. 10. Included within this line lay such towns or posts as Humboldt, Union City, Paris, Jackson, and Fort Pillow. This strategic withdrawal was approved by the Confederate war department and President Jefferson Davis himself.

When Fort Donelson was captured on February 17, 1862, the fortifications at Columbus, Kentucky, guardian of the South's portion of the Mississippi River for the past six months, were, as Beauregard anticipated, outflanked and cut off. The great Confederate works on the Iron Banks were all but surrounded by Yankees in central Kentucky and across in Missouri. The reduction of Fort Henry by the *Carondelet* and her consorts began the North's penetration of the lower Mississippi Valley. The capture of Fort Donelson returned the Union to Nashville and, with some later argument, to central Tennessee.[1]

Her presence being "indispensable," the heavily-damaged *Carondelet* participated with other units of the Western Flotilla in a reconnaissance to Columbus on February 23. The next morning, she was dispatched from Cairo up to the Mound City Marine Railway and Shipyard, where her shot holes could be plugged, particularly those taken below the knuckle during the February 14 attack on Fort Donelson. Together, from a spot on the beach, Capt. Henry Walke, his crew, and the facility's supervisor, Capt. William L. Hambleton, watched as the *Carondelet* was pulled out of the water and put on the ways. The veteran boat builder promised the gunboat commander that his yard crews would quickly address the vessel's leaks. The laborers worked through the night, allowing the ironclad to come off the ways at 11:00 A.M. next morning. Once her cold machinery was fired up and steam raised, she returned to Cairo. Walke would later report that, while she was up on the ways, Hambleton's men failed to adequately caulk the engine room to halt the long-standing leaks.

Naval carpenters swarmed aboard the ironclad as soon as she hove to. Every effort was made to put her shipshape, with patched decking and armor, new chimneys, new staffs, davits, boats, and numerous other items. It would take a couple of weeks for the *Carondelet* to be made whole. Particular attention was paid to upgrading the pilothouse. *New York Times* reporter Franc B. "Galway" Wilkie, who stopped by to watch the gunboats "strengthening themselves," described the process. The armor on the pilothouse, so thin it would scarcely "turn a Minie ball," was temporarily removed and heavy oak timber was "spiked over the old frame" to improve its resistance. Another cannon was then brought aboard to replace the bow piece that exploded at Fort Donelson.

Fresh rumors about Columbus reached Cairo on the evening of March 1. The "Gibraltar of the Mississippi," as the Rebel redoubt was nicknamed, was being evacuated and the Rebels were retreating to make a stand at Island No. 10, which would become the most famous island in Civil War literature. Those making the claims suggested the new place was the strongest position on the entire Mississippi.

As the action started to move further south, the western waters experienced a ferocious rise. Upon her return to Cairo from Mound City, the crewmen of the *Carondelet* saw that the town streets were flooded (worse than usual). Capt. Walke received news that both banks of the Mississippi from the tip of Illinois to New Madrid were at and below the waterline. Indeed, the entire countryside 30 miles inland was submerged beneath from one to 10 feet of muddy liquid. Walke later remembered the current strength of the big river was more powerful than that encountered the previous month in the twin rivers. The Mississippi flow, he noted, "carried away every movable thing. Houses, trees, fences, and wrecks of all kinds were being swept rapidly down-stream."

On one sunny day during her refit, the *Carondelet* was sent on a shakedown cruise a short distance up the slate-hued Ohio River. Given the continuing strong current of the spring rise, it was necessary to know if she could, in fact, successfully go back upstream and execute turning maneuvers. Several unsuccessful trials were made, including the use of anchors to retard the way. As Capt. Walke put it in his memoirs, the gunboat "meandered over the wide-spread Ohio" "She looked like," he added, "a lame duck seeking a retreat from her unnatural task."

After the last of these unsuccessful experiments, the steam capstan was engaged to raise the anchor — which would not budge from the river bottom. Power was increased, but it "refused to show itself." After two hours, it was discovered that the *Carondelet* had hooked the main underwater Federal telegraph wire. Eventually, the telegraph line was cleared and the ironclad returned to base, where final repairs continued. During the afternoon of March 3, the *Carondelet* got up steam for a new mission. Backed by Walke's craft and her four sisters, U.S. troops and sailors from the Western Flotilla duly steamed downstream and occupied Columbus late on the morning of March 4. All of the Confederates were gone and the place was deserted.

Although theater commander Maj. Gen. Henry W. Halleck wished the gunboats to immediately push down to Island No. 10, Flag Officer Andrew Hull Foote observed on March 5 that his squadron could not immediately attack its Confederate defenses. Even as the troops of Maj. Gen. John Pope, commander of the Union Army of the Mississippi, moved down the Missouri west bank, the sickly flag officer, stung at both Fort Henry and Fort Donelson, refused to budge until his boats were completely ready.

Upon the approach of Pope's army, the Confederates at New Madrid retreated to Island No. 10. Although the western end of Beauregard's line was breached, as long as the Rebels under Brig. Gen. John P. McCowan and, later, his successor, Brig. Gen. William W. Mackall, held the island, the Mississippi River was blockaded.

The big naval adventure began promptly at 7:00 A.M., Friday, March 14, one month to the day following the attack on the water batteries at Fort Donelson. The *Benton* (flag) led elements of what *Chicago Daily Tribune* reporter George P. Upton, who wrote as "G.P.U.," called "The Naval Expedition" or "The Great Mississippi River Expedition," from Cairo for "down the river." At the same time, Maj. Gen. Pope occupied New Madrid. Its numbers slightly swelled en route, the Union naval parade continued on March 15, despite a low-lying fog, down to the vicinity of Island No. 10. It was, remembered *Tribune* reporter Upton, "a raw, cold morning." For safety, the transports and supply barges were left at Island No. 8, twelve miles above.

The great river continued to rise, its depth swollen by both local and distant rain and melting snow. Debris was everywhere in the water, pushed by wind and current and some-

The Pook turtle *Pittsburg* followed the *Carondelet* past the Island No. 10 batteries and together the two ironclads tackled Confederate gun emplacements below the atoll. Capt. Walke was visibly upset by the performance of the *Pittsburg* and verbally blasted her commander in front of visiting Federal army generals (*Battles and Leaders*, Walke, *Naval Scenes and Reminiscences*).

times hidden by fog. Occasionally, some of it was caught by the center paddle wheel buckets on the ironclads, hampering their rotation.

About 8:00 A.M., Henry Walke and the *Carondelet* rounded to above the head of Island No. 10 as it loomed into view on the other side of Phillips' Point. Although the captain and his boat would leave the scene famous, initially he, like the other commanders, was "greatly surprised" to see "on the bluffs a chain of forts extending for four miles along the crescent-formed shore, with the white tents of the enemy in the rear." Flag Officer Foote later reported, "The rain and dense fog prevented our getting the vessels in position [to launch a bombardment]. Most of the morning was spent in nautical reconnoitering, including, according to correspondent Upton, a scout by the *Carondelet* of "the Missouri shore for a long distance."

Watching from the island, Israel Gibbons of the 5th Louisiana, who was also a stringer for a New Orleans newspaper, observed Foote's craft "smoking and steaming back and forth plentifully." He could make out "five or six gunboats," auxiliary transports, and "little tugs or mortar beds." Several of the newly arrived Union gunboats moved up into spyglass range where it was soon determined that the bow-heavy ironclads were no better at holding their positions in the swift river than was the *Carondelet* during her earlier Ohio River experiment.

The gunboats were eventually moored to the shores on both sides of the river while the mortar boats were tied to trees along the Arkansas shore. Through stands of cottonwoods, shrubs, and dead trees, the men onboard the Federal armada could see Rebel activity on the island.

Located near the line separating Kentucky from Tennessee, Island No. 10 was approximately 240 miles below St. Louis, 26 below Hickman, 160 miles above Memphis, and 900 above New Orleans and just opposite the village of Obionville. Situated within an east-west channel that could control the river from three directions, it was a mile long and some 450 yards wide. The water depth here was between 90 and 120 feet. After passing the atoll, the "moderately fast" current of the Mississippi ran back north to New Madrid, where it suddenly turned south-southeast to the east bank hamlet of Tiptonville. At Island No. 10, read a March 3 dispatch in the *Philadelphia Inquirer*, the river was about 900 yards wide.

The S-shaped Madrid Bend, bordered on both sides by lakes and swamps, thus caused Tiptonville to be just five miles removed from New Madrid by land, but 27 by water. The Confederates protected their new bastion with 52 cannon, including 19 in four batteries on the north side and upper end of the island, 24 in five batteries on the Tennessee shore and abreast of the island, and nine on the floating battery *New Orleans*—all at or not too far above water level—as at Fort Henry—facing the Missouri swamps.

Of the five mainland batteries, the No. 1 battery, known as the Redan, with three 8-inch Columbiads and three 32-pdrs., was regarded as the most powerful. It was located on the Tennessee shore three miles east of the island in the river bend. The largest cannon, christened "Lady Polk Jr." and capable of throwing a 128-lb. projectile, was placed, along with an 8-inch Columbiad and four 32-pdrs., in Battery No. 1, the Belmont Battery, at the head of the island. Several other batteries were spaced down the Tennessee shore below the island's defenses and were aimed at Pope's army across the river.

The noisy bombardment of Island No. 10 began that Saturday afternoon when Mortar Boats Nos. 11 and 12 lofted the first 220-lb. shells toward the Rebel redoubt. From now until the position surrendered, thousands of shot would be hurled high into the sky to fall upon the besieged Confederate defenders.

"For several weeks," Junius Henri Browne of the *New York Tribune*, remembered, "life on the National Flotilla was dull enough." The *Times*' Wilkie, aboard the *Conestoga*, agreed. This was "a siege of intolerable length, and without any variety to break the everlasting monotony." There were, however, moments that elevated the despair of apparent inaction.[2]

At almost 1:00 P.M. on March 17, as Pope's soldiers moved south of New Madrid, the gun-and-mortar-boats of the Western Flotilla launched a spectacular long range bombardment of Island No. 10's defenses. Combining all their power against the swift current, the *Cincinnati* and *St. Louis*, with the *Benton* lashed between them, took a bows-on station in the center of the stream, forming an immense floating battery. The *Carondelet* and *Mound City* were tied up to the Missouri shore under cover of drooping cottonwood trees, while the *Pittsburg* was opposite on the Tennessee side.

Following a signal from Flag Officer Foote, the *Carondelet* and her consorts, already beat to quarters, opened a deliberate, once per minute bombardment of the Confederate redan and other Tennessee shore batteries over a range of approximately two miles. The ironclads could reach their principal target only by elevating their guns to the maximum of 8 to 9 degrees the gun ports allowed. Given the structural undependability of the 42-pdr. cannon, care was taken lest any of them explode. Writing under the pen name "F," William A. Fayel, the embedded *Daily Missouri Democrat* correspondent, drew an interesting verbal picture of Cmdr. Walke under fire. Standing near the ironclad's commander on the hurricane deck or in the pilothouse throughout the day, the scribe watched him spotting the shots of his gunners through a large spyglass.

All during the shoot, Walke, using the speaking trumpet he never seemed to be without, and called down aiming corrections to his gun captains. One of his bow cannon then succeeded in placing a round-shot in the water directly before the Rebel parapet. "You damned rebels," shouted the captain of the lucky piece, "put that in your pocket and never mind the change." "Look at 'em running," hollered a nearby gunner.

Shortly thereafter, as if in reply, the Confederates sent a huge 128-pdr. shell screaming up the river, seemingly directly at the *Carondelet.* Sighting it from the quarterdeck, the skipper shouted, "Get out of the way!" Impressed by the size of the shot as it streaked toward them, he added, "Let us pay our respects to that fellow. Lie close!" Thereupon, Walke, Fayel, the pilots, and all those within the sound of the captain's trumpet immediately dived behind the pilothouse. The shell, with a screech, flew over the turtle and landed in the turbulent river beyond, flinging up a gigantic geyser over toward the *Benton.*

As the *Carondelet* stood down from the morning session, one of her shells hit a large cottonwood overhanging the redan, causing it to splash into the water with such force that it was at first thought something had blown up. Cheers rang up from *Mound City* and the mortar boats anchored on the western river bank. "Well done, old *Carondelet*," they shouted.

Continuing to observe the fall of his shot, Capt. Walke was pleased to observe that "8 out of every 10" of the *Carondelet*'s rifled shells landed in or near the Confederate redan. The combined guns of the fleet caused repairable damage to the parapet and the gun platform, including the dismounting of one Columbiad. Many of the nearby trees were splintered or otherwise torn to pieces. Before she was ordered to cease firing just before 5:00 P.M., the *Carondelet* had fired 75 fifteen-second rifle shell, 18 eight-inch Dahlgren shells, 25 solid 8-inch balls, and two 10-second rifle shells. It was not known that many of the fuses employed in Foote's shells, manufactured before the Mexican War, actually caused premature detonations, lessening the effectiveness of the day's shoot. Rebel newspapers later reported the battle of St. Patrick's Day a great victory. That night, while Confederate soldiers labored to remount the redan's Columbiad, the *Carondelet* took a turn guarding the mortar boats, anchored on the Missouri shore.

After joining the *Mound City* for another ineffective shoot on March 18, the *Carondelet* had guard duty over the mortars during the next four days, which assignment allowed her gun crews to stand down. In mid-afternoon on March 20, Rebel return fire began to land near the ironclad, but neither she nor the mortars were hit. On the evening of March 22, she dropped down some 300 yards from her previous berth, taking up position under a clump of large overhanging trees at the end of Phillips' Point preparatory for a resumption next morning of her part in the bombardment. But Walke's command never had the opportunity to shoot on March 23. At about 8:00 A.M., two medium-sized cottonwood trees overlooking the boat gave way from the soft riverbank and fell squarely on the *Carondelet*'s bow. The foliage did no serious structural damage and damage control parties quickly climbed topside from the gun ports to begin hacking away at the tangled wooden mess.

While attempting thus to recover from the emergency, a third and much larger tree (four feet in diameter and of great weight) slammed down upon the port quarter decks and wheelhouse. Unfazed earlier, the ironclad now rocked heavily, "as if struck by a tropic squall." Four sailors were injured, one mortally. The ironclad's portside boats and their davits, the hog-chains, the hammock nettings, skylights, iron ventilators, signal masts and spars, and other exposed hardware, standing rigging, and fixtures were crushed and broken. The veteran of Forts Henry and Donelson was truly hors de combat, unable to free herself from the entanglements or make signals. Two hours into the emergency, a message concerning events aboard reached Flag Officer Foote, who sent the steamer *Alps* to assist. All the while, work parties sawed and cut the offending trunks and branches. Perceiving the commotion at the point, Confederate gunners at the head of Island No. 10 attempted to shell the craft. "As usual," wrote "Galway" to his *New York Times* readers, they "succeeded in only splashing up a good deal of water."

Confederates on the island witnessed the *Carondelet*'s plight, believing it was caused not by trees but by their cannonballs. One soldier later told a reporter from the *Memphis Daily Appeal* that the ironclad had been hit by a ricochet shot from the redan and then had run into the bank in sinking condition.

Alexander Simplot drew the *Carondelet* passing the batteries at Island No. 10 in somewhat more detail than Capt. Walke did, but changed the lighting from night to day. His location of the coal barge and insertion of other vessels is interesting and inaccurate (*Harper's Weekly*, April 26, 1862).

This depiction of the *Carondelet*'s run by Island No. 10 is the most contemporary of several drawn by Rear Adm. Walke and was published in James M. Hoppin's *Life of Andrew Hull Foote, Rear Admiral, United States Navy*, in 1874. The direction of the bullet and shell splashes in the water conveys the impression that the boat was nearly out of danger.

The *Alps* towed the *Carondelet* free and took her a distance upstream to another location. There, after a day or so in transit down from above, a gang of carpenters arrived and made repairs. Over a week was required to put the *Carondelet* right.[3]

In spite of a change in Confederate command on Island No. 10, the digging of an innovative but unsuccessful U.S. Army bypass canal, and continued shelling by gunboats and mortars, the situation in this theater remained largely unchanged over the next two weeks. All this time, Maj. Gen Pope chaffed to cross the river below New Madrid and move on the Southern position from the Tennessee shore. What was needed was naval support, and time and again the ground commander wrote Flag Officer Foote and area commander Maj. Gen. Halleck requesting that a gunboat be sent down. Pope suggested that a boat could survive such an adventure if it were sent down by night. Personally believing such a gambit unwise, the naval boss, his Fort Donelson injury and the recent death of his son probably giving him "the slows," continued to balk.

Writing his counterpart at New Madrid, Foote confessed his belief that, should he attempt to send an ironclad past the island, the Rebel gunners would shoot it out of the water — "a sacrifice I would not be justified in making." Exasperated, Pope finally suggested to Halleck that, if the sailors could be removed, he would put soldiers onboard one of the gunboats and sail it by himself.

No one on the Union side knew that Gen. Beauregard, on March 15, had ordered a general withdrawal of his forces from the Madrid Bend down to Fort Pillow. A significant part of that evacuation was completed within four days.

As the year's first quarter drew toward a close, Flag Officer Foote began to entertain Pope's idea a little more favorably. The lack of naval success against the island had reached a point where the gunboats were fast becoming a source of ridicule among army officers. One military man from Cmdr. Walke's adopted home town of Chillicothe, Ohio, was

This 1874 drawing of the March 17, 1862, bombardment of Island No. 10 was drawn by Rear Adm. Walke not long after his retirement. As in all Walke renderings, the drama and noise of the shoot is suggested by the smoke and sky (Hoppin, *Life of Andrew Hull Foote*).

reported to have commented to a friend making inquiry concerning campaign progress that the fleet was still busily "bombarding the state of Tennessee at long range."

While visiting the many Union war craft to alleviate his boredom, *New York Times* ace reporter Franc B. "Galway" Wilkie heard talk around the flotilla that "the Rebels appear to be very fearful that some attempt will be made to run the blockade." Wondering why anyone would ever want to rush past all those guns on Island No. 10 save in an act of bravado, Wilkie penned his belief that there was "probably no danger of any boat being called on for any such purpose." The fleet-wide discussion on breaking the blockade continued over the next several days. Perhaps it was based on leaks from a supposed meeting between the ironclad captains on March 18 or on idle rumor and "scuttlebutt." "It has been suggested that, by placing flatboats alongside and filling them with bales of pressed hay," Wilkie recorded on March 20, "the thing might be done."

Naval officers of any age hate to be made out as fools by army men. Foote was under growing pressure from his ground-pounding counterparts, including assistant secretary of war Thomas Scott, who was on the scene as something of an inspector. So, that very evening of March 20, Flag Officer Foote, according to Cmdr. Walke, sent Cmdr. Roger Stembel around to consult the captains of his ironclads. Each gunboat commander was asked to submit his views on the feasibility of running past the Rebel guns to New Madrid. All except Walke and Capt. Phelps of the *Benton* gave assurances that the kind of plan correspondent Wilkie wrote of was crazy and prophesized the destruction of any boat making the attempt.

A few days later, Maj. Gen. Halleck, responding to repeated requests from Maj. Gen. Pope, once more wrote to Flag Officer Foote asking that he find a way for his ironclads to support the New Madrid Federals who wanted over the river. "One or two gunboats are very necessary," he indicated, "to protect his crossing."

A week later, just after the *Carondelet* completed her cottonwood-required repairs, several newspapers erroneously published reports that Island No. 10 was already captured. Carrying the story "Island No. 10 Is Ours," several copies of the *St. Louis Daily Missouri Democrat* made their way to Foote's gunboats via dispatch vessels and caused quite a stir. A number of bluejackets aboard the *Carondelet* obtained a copy and immediately took it to Capt. Walke. As they handed it over, they also asked if liberty would soon be possible. As he read the headlines, the commander inquired why the men wanted to go ashore. "For fresh grub," was their reply. As the men with their hats off addressed their superior, a Confederate cannonball skipped across the water not too far from the boat and ploughed into the bank off her port quarter. Walke suggested that this latest gift from the island did not

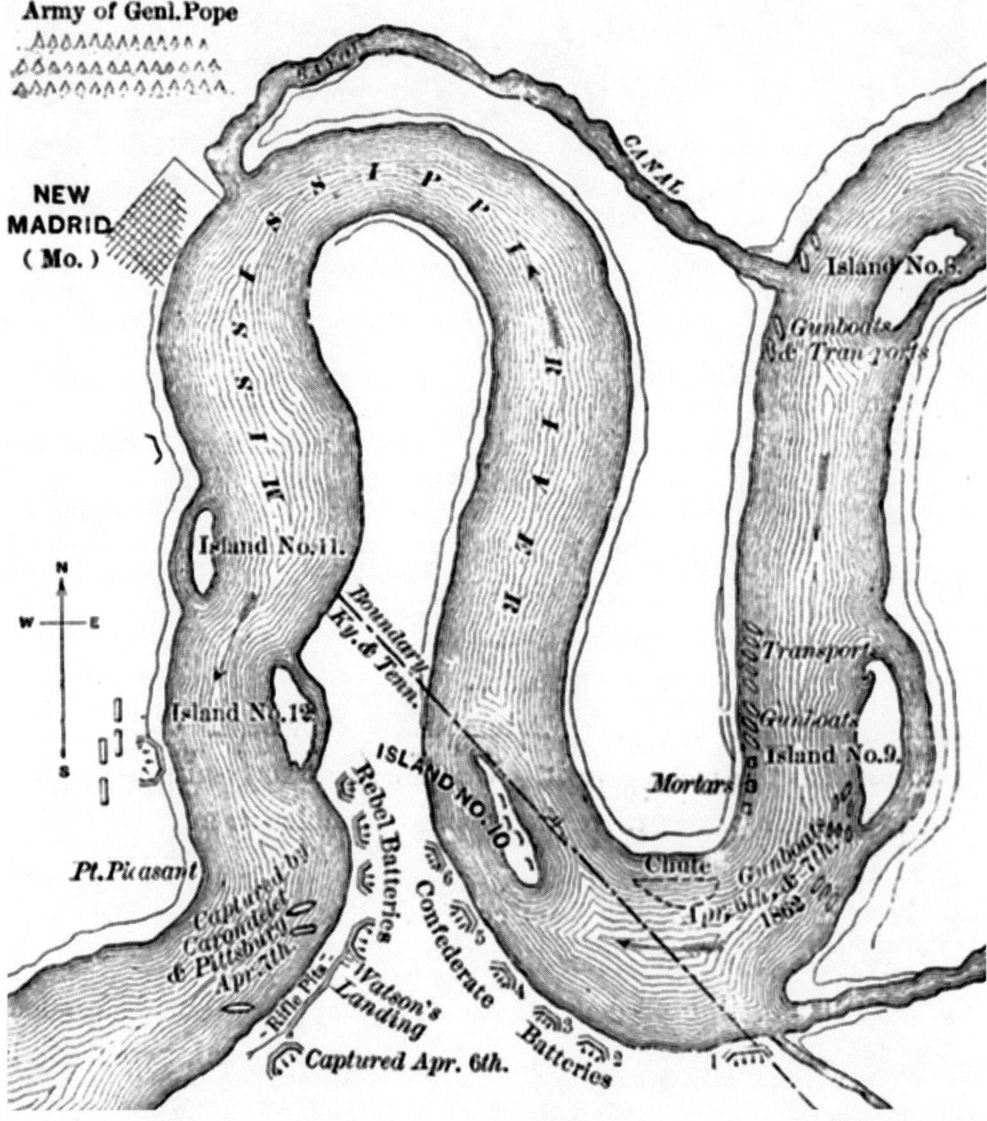

One of the more helpful — and earliest — maps of the Island No. 10 region gives a clear sense of the accomplishments of the *Carondelet* here as April began in 1862 (Hoppin, *Life of Andrew Hull Foote*).

suggest its surrender, but his men remained unconvinced. Pointing at the newspaper, one suggested that it had to be true because the theater commander was quoted as say so. "General Halleck says they've quit," the man protested, "and he ought to know, being he's right at headquarters." As the losing appeal continued, another round from Island No. 10 splashed into the water, even closer to the *Carondelet* than the last.

The demands for action emanating from the army field officers and War Department officials were now so great that the flag officer once more sought the counsel of his captains. A formal council of war was called, "on the 28th or 29th of March," in the great stern cabin of the flagboat *Benton* to go over the "suicidal" run-by idea once more. After reading the latest communications from Pope, Foote put all his cards on the table. It was, he admitted again, a grave, if not impossible, risk for an ironclad to steam past the Confederate batteries. As his officers looked at one another, Foote announced that he would take their verbal opinions, one by one, in another cabin. There would be no hard feelings or disdain for any man refusing to go. Seniority caused Henry Walke to be the second man interviewed. Foote bluntly asked him if an ironclad passage down the river past the Rebel guns was possible. The taciturn Walke replied that it was and recommended compliance with Pope's urgent request. Seeking to take advantage of this advice, Foote inquired whether or not Walke would be willing to make the attempt. The *Carondelet*'s captain immediately "replied in the affirmative."

When the captains reassembled, Foote announced that Walke would make the run. None of the others had signed on to the idea. Foote later told the *Carondelet*'s skipper that his stepping forward gave him great relief from a heavy responsibility because he still believed such an expedition to be overly perilous and of doubtful success and "had determined to send none but volunteers." Walke received his written orders on March 30. In them, Foote ordered that the mission go "on the first foggy or rainy night." If all were lost, the boat was to be destroyed to prevent her capture. The message ended with the flag officer commending Walke's boat "to the care and protection of God."[4]

The kind of weather Foote recommended was not in the forecast, but April is a time of fierce storms in the Mississippi Valley. On the evening of April 1, a great thunderstorm passed through the Madrid Bend area, spawning a tornado that swept the waters near Island No. 10, sinking one Confederate transport and damaging two Union vessels. Maj. Gen. Pope, who knew of the Foote/Walke plan, thought that an ironclad might use the storm's coverage for her passage and was disappointed when it did not occur. Although the night's bad weather brought no gunboat, it did provide cover for a boat expedition to spike those guns in the redan expected to pose the greatest danger to any passage. Led by Col. George W. Roberts, a combined force of soldiers from his 42nd Illinois and sailors from the gunboats snuck over the parapet and disabled the cannon. All of the raiders escaped safely.

Next day, Flag Officer Foote elected to disable the floating battery *New Orleans*, which was menacing the mortar boats tied to the Missouri riverbank. Converted from a Crescent City floating dry dock named *Pelican*, she helped to guard Columbus from December 23 through her transfer down the river on March 1. The unique craft was already the victim of several near misses between March 22 and 29.

On the morning of April 3, the *Benton*, *Cincinnati*, and *Pittsburg* tied to the shore, joined the mortar boats in a fearsome bombardment of the *New Orleans*, which caused her additional damage, cut her cable, and forced the craft to drift two miles below Island No. 10. With this preliminary work out of the way, Capt. Walke began to prepare for the upcoming dash. The first step was to make certain that his officers wished to go. Most readily agreed to join his volunteer venture, though at least one wished to be excused.

The captain also granted permission for a reporter from his favorite western newspaper, the *St. Louis Daily Missouri Democrat,* to come along, later referring to the man as "Tip." We do not know for certain who the man was but we have a suspect. George W. Beaman, who always signed his stories "G.W.B.," was the senior *Democrat* man on the scene and spent much time aboard the *Benton.* William A. "F" Fayel, already aboard to write about Walke during the March 17 bombardment, likely remained to cover the passage.

Next in importance was improved protection against plunging shot for the *Carondelet*'s light hurricane deck. A damaged barge was secured and stripped of planking that was immediately secured atop the upper deck. Once it was nailed down, the heaviest chains available in the flotilla were handed topside and coiled around on top. Next, stout hawsers and lighter chains were wound around the pilothouse, round and round to a depth of between 11 and 18 inches. Only the peephole windows were exposed now. Chains were also hung down the more vulnerable aft sides of the casemate.

The barrier around the boilers and engines that proved so helpful at Fort Donelson was strengthened with additional cordwood brought up from the hold and with iron kept aboard for casemate repairs. Meanwhile, the engineers rerouted the escape steam from the pipes into the wheelhouse to lessen the loud puffing sound made when it was blown out of the chimneys. Several large hoses were also connected to the boilers and snaked topside, where they were coiled for possible use in repelling boarders.

Col. Napoleon B. Buford of the 27th Illinois, who had known Walke since the two of them participated in the November 1861 Battle of Belmont, was in command of the brigade of troops assigned to the flotilla. During the waterborne siege of Island No. 10, the soldier's men had little to do save sit on their transports near Island No. 8. To gain some relief from boredom and provide exercise, Buford led his men on a successful March 31 raid on Confederate positions at nearby Hickman, Tennessee. Upon his return, the colonel met his naval colleague and learned of his upcoming mission. Upon Walke's request made following hearty congratulations, Buford readily agreed to provide some men to act as marines. Twenty men from Capt. John A. Hottenstein's Company H, 42nd Illinois, were assigned to wait onshore near the *Carondelet*, from where they could be quickly summoned when she was ready to depart. Among the bluecoats was Private Charles P. Swigert, who later wrote down his impressions of the mission.

Nearly Walke's age, Buford was described by a contemporary as a "fussy old gentleman." With nothing to do more pressing, he decided to help the *Carondelet*'s captain obtain a coal barge for use in the mission. As the gunboat would have no fuel below, it would have to come with a goodly supply. While Foote's gunboats blasted away at the *New Orleans* on April 3 and Walke's crewmen worked on the *Carondelet,* Buford "was with the captain ... on the *Rob Roy* searching for the suitable barges."

The idea, bandied about by Franc Wilkie and others earlier, regarding the possible use of hay-filled flatboats as protection, was taken seriously by Capt. Walke, who, when the opportunity came, seized upon it. As a result of his collective scout with Col. Buford, a loaded coal barge was located. It was ordered brought down by two steamers from its location with the transport fleet at Island No. 8. At Walke's request, hay bales, originally slated for Buford's cavalry mounts, sat atop the coal in the barge when it was tied to a cottonwood on the Missouri shore that night. Next day, when the barge was lashed to the port quarter of the gunboat just before her departure, these would be moved by the crew to the inboard side. Some of the hay was stacked up to the top of the broadside gun port top sills, forming another layer of protection for the magazine and shell rooms. One course of bales was laid over the fantail and casemate astern in anticipation of a vulnerable period of exposure once the island was passed. At that point, the skipper later remarked, the *Carondelet* would have the appearance of "a farmer's wagon prepared for market."

Work on readying the gunboat for her run, meanwhile, continued. On the very day of departure, Wilkie informs us, two of the old army 42s were removed from the bow and tossed into the river. They were replaced with one each 30-pdr. and 50-pdr. Dahlgren rifles. The presence of these short pieces was noted, with a later date, in the *Official Records.*

Belowdecks, ammunition for the new guns and old was stored in the magazine. It was also made certain that a generous supply of small arms was readily available. Pistols, cutlasses, boarding pikes, grenades, and muskets were all checked and readied. If swarms of graycoats made it aboard past the scalding water hose, they would receive a warm welcome from the crew before the boat was scuttled.

On this later idea, Pvt. Swigert later recalled that few onboard knew at the time that "the captain had the magazine laid ready to blow up the boat (with all onboard) rather than surrender." Had they known, he added, "some of us might have been less enthusiastic than we were." In fact, as reporter Fayel told his readers, Chief Engineer William H. Faulkner, in the event of terminal danger, did not plan to fire the vessel. Instead, he would cut the cold-water supply and the injector pipe. This action would, it was believed, not only avert a terrible loss of life that would "inevitably have resulted" if the boat were torched and her magazine exploded, but give the crew a better chance to escape.

Much depended upon the weather. It was picture perfect on April 2 and 3, without rain or even fog. The river level was now falling, as were Maj. Gen. Pope's hopes that a timely passage could be made. April 4 was another beautiful day; it initially appeared unlikely that the required precipitation would develop. Still, Walke determined to go that night, as soon as the moon went down, "whatever the chances." The captain sent a mes-

On March 17, 1862, the Western Flotilla launched a spectacular bombardment of the defenses of Island No. 10. In this drawing by Capt. Walke, the *Carondelet* is one of the two Pook turtles center right (Walke, *Naval Scenes and Reminiscences*).

The defenses of Island No. 10 are shown in this Alexander Simplot drawing that appeared in *Harper's Weekly* on May 3, 1862.

senger to Flag Officer Foote about 8:00 A.M. with the news that he would go that night, if that met "his approbation." An affirmative response was quickly rowed back.

Two chutes allowed the Mississippi to flow past Island No. 10. The Rebels had blocked the smaller passageway next to the Tennessee shore. Access via the Missouri side was partially obstructed by a sandbar and required steaming through tricky turns. A good pilot was required and fortunately, one was available. When First Master Richard Wade earlier expressed his desire to withdraw, Cmdr. Stembel of the *Cincinnati* suggested as a replacement his own first master, William R. Hoel, who had just returned to duty following his wounding at Fort Donelson. When interviewed, the 21-year veteran pilot agreed to accompany the daring enterprise and chart its course. Wounded at Fort Henry, Hoel boasted of having already completed 193 round-trips to and from New Orleans and he looked forward to another downstream run.

Hoel came aboard the *Carondelet* about 9:00 A.M. that Friday morning, at which point his predecessor was relieved. His arrival was undoubtedly noted by many crewmen, who were busily packing their bedding into the hammock nettings that surrounded the upper deck. The new executive officer immediately summoned the boat's two pilots, Daniel Weaver and John Deming, and went into a lengthy conference. Everything that was known about the waters between their anchorage and New Madrid was reviewed by the three men, including each wreck, sandbar, and channel course.[5]

About 5:00 P.M., the skies changed color, as dark clouds, increasing in width, loomed closer. A storm was brewing and Capt. Walke now determined to make his run. Col. Buford signaled his men, who were brought down through growing haze in the gunboat's cutters. Once aboard, the bluecoat marines were mustered on deck, inspected, and assigned to stations around the boat from which they could harass Confederate gunners or, if necessary, repel boarders.

As the winds shifted and grew stronger about 8:00 P.M., the *Carondelet* moved upstream a mile from her Missouri shore anchorage to tie on the protective coal barge, then partially hidden between two transports. By now, the moon had set and the arriving clouds intensified the darkness. As that task was completed and the last of the hay was distributed, Hoel returned from the *Cincinnati* and took his place in the pilothouse. As the Pook turtles were sisters, he needed no familiarization with its layout. The boat was buttoned up; its guns were drawn in and its gun ports closed. The boat howitzer topside was made ready for use as a signal gun. No lights, John Fiske tells us, were to be shown save a single lantern in the engine room.

The appointed departure hour approached, even as a tremendous storm came roaring up the river. Other than Capt. Walke's guest, Col. Buford, who had remained to encourage the sailors and his own riflemen, no other officers from the flotilla were on hand as she made ready to leave. Down on the gun deck by light of the last unextinguished lanterns, the ironclad commander briefly addressed his crew, outlining the importance of the job ahead. The men were cautioned not to make any loud noises and to talk in low voices or whispers.

With handshakes all round, Col. Buford took his leave of Walke, Hoel, and Hottendorff, and stepped ashore. At 10:00 P.M., as a heavy rain squall hit, the skipper ordered "cast off the hawsers." As the lines snapped aboard, the black boat moved almost noiselessly into the dark. "[S]ome of the officers were almost unbelievers," Fayel recorded, "when they asked the engineer, through the speaking pipes, if he was "going ahead on her." "Her bow was slowly turned to the westward," Walke later remembered. Word of the departure spread quickly on the other gunboats and transports and, despite the rain, hundreds crowded their decks to get a view of the *Carondelet,* through what Franc Wilkie called "the almost blinding flashes."

Not privy to the departure, Confederate troops on the island sought safety from the howling storm. As J.M. Grace of the 1st Tennessee later remembered, "The wind was blowing so hard that I had to hold to a sapling to keep from being blown in the River. It was a raining torrent."

Upstream, the *New York Herald* reporter with the Western Flotilla attempted to draw a word picture for his Atlantic coast readers. "You people in the East may imagine that you have heard thunder and seen lightning, witnessed storms, and beheld majesty," he suggested. "But allow me to say," the scribe continued, "that I have seen your choicest samples in that line and can safely assert that an Eastern thunderstorm bears about the same relation to a Western one that a Berkshire county mill stream does to the Mississippi River."

Silently, the iron mountain slid downstream in sheets of rain. Difficult to manage at the best of times, the attached coal barge made the 500-ton gunboat very hard to steer and turn. More silent than usual, the *Carondelet* passed down beyond the advance elements of the flotilla. The *New York Times* man noted that she was visible to the Union seamen left behind: "We could see her almost every second; every brace, port, and outline could be seen with startling distinctness, enshrouded by a bluish-white glare of light, and then her form for the next instant would become merged into the intense backness." Still visible above to men "with beating hearts," the turtle was soon past Donaldson Point, and then beyond the Confederate redan, still out of order following Col. Roberts' raid. The first half mile went surprisingly well, too well to last.

Because the thunderstorm was becoming more violent, the lightning flashes that increasingly lit the sky did not give her away to sheltered eyes ashore and no Southerner spotted her. The bolts from the sky did however "show us the perilous way we were to take." Once in a while, "the dim outline of the landscape could be seen ... the forest bending under the roaring storm." A tempest of lightning and rain continued to sweep the area as the ironclad plodded abreast the No. 2 shore battery. Doubtless anxious to get to New Madrid as quickly as possible, the coal heavers working for Chief Engineer Faulkner shoveled fuel more rapidly into the furnaces than was necessary for the maintenance of the required moderate head of steam.

Suddenly, a five-foot flame shot up from the gunboat's chimneys. Dried soot, normally kept wet by boiler steam, had been ignited when flames ascended from the firebox. Fortunately, the hunkered-down Confederate sentries did not see it before the flue caps were opened, causing the flames to subside. The problem was not solved, even as the *Carondelet* swept ahead. Once again, after the flue caps were closed, the chimneys took fire. This time, the Rebels were not caught napping. Sentinels sounded the alarm by shooting up rockets from both the island and the Tennessee shore, while "a broad blaze of flame burst" (at nothing) from the cannon in mainland No. 2 battery.

Walke was furious. It was not the lightning that gave them away, but his own boat. With no other choice, the captain ordered "full speed ahead." First Master Hoel pulled the bell cord and when Chief Engineer Faulkner below heard the clanging command, the throttles were opened wide.

Years later, though largely ignored by historians of the dash, Henry Walke suggested the closed flue cap incidents were blown out of perspective and constituted little more than a "blunder." "The gunboat was far more distinctly seen by the lightning than by a dull-flaze from her smoke-pipes," he affirmed. Additionally, the enemy could more easily see his boat than crewmen aboard her could see them.

Thunder crashed and lightning created "checquers of darkness" that occasionally illuminated the oncoming gunboat. Simultaneously, dozens of soldiers shot off their muskets, their volleys plinking off the gunboat's armor. As the *Carondelet* shot slowly forward, the attached barge further detracting from her speed, the cannon at Nos. 3 and 4 batteries on the mainland roared. Again, the Eads creation was favored, as the Confederates shot anywhere from five to 35 yards high. Although bolts hit the water all around, only one registered, and that on the barge.

To help distract the Rebel gunners, the *Benton, Pittsburg,* and several mortars fired supporting rounds in their direction. Everyone aboard the Union flotilla remained anxious. As *Cincinnati Daily Commercial* reporter Joseph P. "Mack" McCallagh confessed, "Flash after flash, boom after boom, in concert with the lightning and thunder of nature, made us almost despair of the safe passage of the brave men."

Meanwhile, perhaps at Hoel's suggestion, Walke ordered the *Carondelet* steered closer toward the island, so that his borrowed XO could maneuver her around the shoals. With the water ahead visible only when lightning flashed, Hoel left the wheel to the boat's regular pilot, Daniel Weaver, and climbed out, through a briefly opened gun port, making his way to the hurricane deck in front of the pilothouse within easy communication distance of the man at the wheel.

Boatswain's mate Charles Wilson was simultaneously sent to the forecastle to take soundings with a lead line. His findings were called up to Master's Mate Theodore S. Gilmore — standing on the forward end of the hurricane deck — who shouted them back to Hoel, who passed steering directions to Weaver.

Inching along as the result of caution and the drag of the barge, the ironclad, "the sky all ablaze around her, approached the head of the island. Here, while "the thunders of the storm and the roar of the rebel artillery commingled," the frothing current shoved her dangerously close to the bank. "Hard-a-port," shouted Hoel. As Weaver spun her 6-foot wheel, the *Carondelet* passed so near shore as to briefly touch. Indeed, she came so close to the Belmont Battery that Cmdr. Walke could hear the Rebel gun captains ordering their men to elevate their pieces, depressed earlier to keep the rain out. These, too, were thus aimed too high and that action was, the captain believed, "the cause of our remarkable escape."

Dragging the awkward but protective barge, the *Carondelet* chugged on hugging the island shore, with Confederate cannonballs splashing everywhere nearby, but providentially, not aboard. Many rifle balls struck the boat, but with all hands below, no one was hurt. As her gun ports remained sealed, the turtle could not return fire. That was probably just as well as her cannon flashes would have further illuminated her location.

Several Southerners watched the gunboat, buffeted by high winds and rain, continue her run, which would take another half hour to complete. Seeing her passage, Lt. Col. W.D.S. Cook of the 12th Arkansas was disappointed that the darkness and weather made it impossible for the guns, fired from almost every island battery, to "be pointed as to disable her." Grace, of the 1st Alabama, looked up from his location and "saw a huge monster coming down the river."

Commander of the Federal Army of the Mississippi, Brig. Gen. John Pope (1822–1892), in cooperation with Flag Officer Foote, orchestrated the campaigns that resulted in the surrender of New Madrid, MO (March 14, 1862), and Island No. 10 (April 7, 1862) (Signal Corps Collection, National Archives).

Once past Island No. 10, Mate Wilson was able to shout "Deep Water!" and the *Carondelet* crossed back into the main channel. She still faced potential opposition from the floating battery *New Orleans.*

After her pounding the previous day, the one-time *Pelican* floating dry dock brought up from the Crescent City had drifted down to be tied up three miles below on the Tennessee shore. Under repair, she was only able to get off about half a dozen shots. Still, she scored more often than all of the island batteries; one of her bolts hit the barge and another demolished a hay bale.

Walke and Hoel had done it. The *Carondelet* was out of danger and past the last obstacle an hour after leaving the fleet, heading for the New Madrid landing. All aboard were exceedingly relieved, including Pvt. Swigert of the 42nd Illinois, who noted that they luckily escaped harm, even though the Confederates fired their cannon 56 times, "besides several volleys of musketry."

There remained the matter of the Union guns at New Madrid. Although messages were earlier sent regarding the firing of the signal howitzer, it was possible, Walke reasoned, that the thunder of the great storm and the firing of the Confederate defenses may have raised either false hopes or increased fears that the boat was taken and being used in an attack.

With the storm of metal having ceased after the passage and the storm of nature dying, there remained keen suspense in the upper flotilla, as no one knew immediately the fate of Walke's command. "Had she gone down," wondered Wilkie, "or was she drifting helpless in the swift current?" The prearranged signal was executed: three cannon shots a minute apart and then repeated after a five minute lull. Then the prearranged roar of the signal cannon "came up faintly from below, and then another and another." Knowing that the

Carondelet was safe, "there went up such thunders of cheers and hurricanes of shouts from the watching crowds that even the storm itself was outroared."

Suddenly, when 50 yards off the beach, the gunboat ran hard aground due to a misunderstanding between the pilothouse and the engine room. The remedy to this embarrassment was to move the forward guns and the crew aft to lighten ship.

It was about 1:00 A.M. on April 5 when the ironclad backed off and put in toward shore. Seeing a group of soldiers, Capt. Walke informed them through his ever-ready speaking trumpet that the vessel was the U.S. gunboat *Carondelet.* Overjoyed, the men quickly pointed out the best landing place and kindled a fire to mark its spot.

After the three hour ordeal — more stressful than damaging — Purser George Wilson asked Capt. Walke for permission to "splice the main brace." Flag Officer Foote's squadron-wide prohibitionist stance not withstanding, the relieved skipper ordered a round of spirits for every man aboard. For the first time since Andrew Foote took over the flotilla the previous October, a Western Flotilla boatswain's mate whistled "Grog, Oh!"

The arrival of the Eads ironclad was heralded through all of the U.S. Army camps in the vicinity of New Madrid, and by dawn Federal soldiers and their officers began to crowd the bank to see the famous *Carondelet.* Pvt. Swigert saw Maj. Gen. Pope, who arrived on the scene with assistant secretary of war Thomas Scott at 8:00 A.M. The bluecoats along the shore "howled with delight." Cheers echoed all along the waterfront "for Commodore Foote, Captain Walke, the Navy, the *Carondelet,* the tars, and even for the colored cabin boy." When Walke's gig touched the beach, Pope and Scott received the captain "warmly." While stretching their legs, Frank Chapman heard, members of the gig's crew were caught up by the soldiers "in their arms and passed from one to another, with accompanying embraces more heartfelt than agreeable."

All morning and into the afternoon, pleased military visitors viewed the ironclad from shore, pronouncing her formidable and their relief that she and her bluejackets had come. The *Carondelet,* whose reputation from earlier exploits was already somewhat legendary, was described by an army artillerist. "She is of course ironplated and painted black," he wrote. Members of her "jolly crew" were "hardy-looking fellows with the regular dress of a tar — the usual blue-round about and breeches, and a cap without a brim, and with a broad top."

As the sun rose, Maj. Gen. Pope sent a messenger to Flag Officer Foote notifying him of the *Carondelet*'s safe arrival. He simultaneously requested that a second ironclad be sent down to provide support, pointing out that the Rebels could not hit a moving target in the dark. The success of the entire campaign, Pope concluded, "hangs upon your decision."[6]

The passage of the ironclad by the island's guns was one of the most dramatic events of the Civil War. Every account mentions it somewhere, if only by a sentence. John Fiske wrote that "in the matter of Island No. 10, the decisive blow was struck by the *Carondelet.*" In the years immediately after the event, the drama was not so much appreciated. As the war progressed, the passage of vessels under the guns of fortresses was thought less dangerous, and the glory which the two hours gained the *Carondelet* was modified. William Fowler wrote in 1990 that this tactic soon "became almost commonplace on the western rivers."

In his memoirs, Henry Walke railed against this view, but it was not until Alfred T. Mahan, later one of America's foremost naval strategists and historians, wrote his *Gulf and Inland Waters* in 1883 that her daring was given full credit:

> The passage of the *Carondelet* was not only one of the most daring and dramatic events of the war; it was also the death-blow to the Confederate defense of this position. To do full justice to the great gallantry shown by Walke, it should be remembered that this running of the batteries was done by a single vessel, three weeks before Farragut passed the forts down the river at New Orleans with a fleet, among the members of which the enemy's fire was distracted and divided. The daring displayed in this deed ... must be measured by the then-prevalent opinion and not in the light of subsequent experience. Subsequent experience, indeed, showed that the danger, if overestimated, was still sufficiently great.

The magnitude of the stroke was summed up years later by Eliot Callender. The "direct result" of Walke's "dare-devil act," he wrote, was the capture of "five thousand prisoners, three general officers, and an immense amount of ammunition and provisions. In later reports to the War Department after the Carondelet and another gunboat had finished Southern hopes by knocking out Rebel shore batteries below the island and guarding the Union Army's landing, Maj. Gen. Pope added the following: "I cannot speak too highly of the conduct of Captain Walke.... Prompt, gallant, and cheerful, he performed the hazardous service assigned to him with signal skill and success. I here bear testimony to [his] thorough and brilliant manner ... and [his] hearty and earnest seal."

For their part, the Confederates on Island No. 10 and some of those attached to the small CSN gunboat fleet below it were aware of the danger the *Carondelet* posed. Brig. Gen. William W. Mackall, the atoll commander, wrote to Com. George N. Hollins begging that his vessels attack Walke's craft before it could cover Pope's river crossing. The commanders of the Rebel gunboats *General Polk*, *Maurapas*, and *Pontchartrain* all volunteered to take on the Federal gunboat, believing that they could sink her or at least put her out of action. Hollins, according to Lt. Charles W. Read, a CSN eyewitness, firmly declined, "saying that as the *Carondelet* was iron-clad and his fleet were all wooden, he did not think he could successfully combat her."[7]

Despite Foote's reluctance to hazard a second boat, the flag officer agreed to send the *Pittsburg* down after dark. Lt. Egbert Thompson was ordered to make ready and spent the daylight hours readying his boat. Alerted that another ironclad would soon be en route, Maj. Gen. Pope elected to postpone his trans-river crossing for a day. At the same time, he took the opportunity to ask Capt. Walke to make a downstream reconnaissance. Brig. Gen. Gordon Granger, commander of the cavalry brigade, and Col. J.L. Kirby Smith of the 43rd Ohio would go as observers.

"After divine services at the usual hour," wrote the *Pittsburgh Evening Chronicle* witness, the hawsers were pulled in again. The *Carondelet* eased out from the bank, gathering steam away from the many soldiers still gathered in admiration. En route toward Tiptonville, the boat exchanged shots in passing with the Confederate battery opposite New Madrid before reaching Riddle's Point. There she put into the bank near the Federal military camp.

Brig. Gen. John M. Palmer (1817–1900), who would serve as Illinois governor from 1869 to 1873, and his officers came to the shore to greet the ironclad, whose captain welcomed them aboard. Once the handshakes and obligatory tour were completed, Palmer was invited to take a short river excursion, with the captain pointing out details of the enemy batteries en route.

Not far below lay a small battery at Meriweather's Landing. A few 42-pdr. broadside shells into it failed to elicit any response. It was decided to round to and go back upriver approximately three miles for an attack on the battery mounted on the Tennessee bank opposite Point Pleasant. As the *Carondelet* addressed the still-strong spring current, Walke decided this would be an excellent opportunity for his gun crews to test the 30- and 50-pdr. Dahlgrens recently mounted in the bow. After the ironclad came to abreast the Confederate position, she turned and fired her three forward pieces directly at the earthworks, Fort Henry–style.

There was only a small contingent of Southern Guards, from Memphis, at the battery, manning a pair of 24-pdrs. It was devastated by the initial Dahlgren rounds; several men

Both of these Currier and Ives prints depict the bombardment of Island No. 10 by the units of the Western Flotilla in March 1862. The top version was sold commercially, while the bottom was employed by Capt. Walke to illustrate his memoirs. Therein he took the time to identify the vessels shown (Currier and Ives, Naval Historical Center, Currier and Ives, Walke, *Naval Scenes and Reminiscences*).

This dramatic depiction of the *Carondelet*'s stormy run past the batteries at Island No. 10 was painted by Capt. Walke for use in his memoirs (Walke, *Naval Scenes and Reminiscences*).

were killed and the rest fled. Capt. Hottenstein led a detail of 42nd Illinois soldiers ashore to spike the guns and throw their ammunition and ordnance supplies into the river. Palmer was impressed. The gunboat, he later remembered, "made quick work of it."

Tennessee has long been famous for its sharpshooters, Sgt. Alvin York being the modern reminder. There were numerous Confederate marksmen at this time and one of these unnamed Volunteers now stepped forward to fight the *Carondelet* single-handedly. When Hottenstein and his men undertook to spike and dismantle the battery, the Rebel sniper, secreted with a pair of muskets behind a large cottonwood, drew a bead and started shooting. For 15 minutes, he fired away at the Illini soldiers and the gunboat. The Federal riflemen, naturally, returned the compliment many fold, while the *Carondelet* blasted his position and the woods around him with grape and canister from almost point-blank range. Eventually, the man was seen to throw down his muskets and run into the woods. It would be discovered next day when the shooter was captured that he had fled only because a bullet had clipped off a part of his nose.

The *Carondelet* continued on to the next battery, where it was believed one of the Confederate guns was dismounted. The emplacement could not be fully silenced as it was growing so dark that the position of the Rebel cannon could not be distinguished.

The gunboat scouting trip, including the 25-minute episode with the Southern Guards battery, took most of the day and it was not until approximately 9:00 P.M. that the *Carondelet* returned to New Madrid. There, Maj. Gen. Pope told the ironclad captain and his guests that a sister boat would be running past the island within hours. Instructions were given to Walke as task group commander pro tem to take the two downriver early next morning and destroy the remaining Confederate emplacements. The *Pittsburgh* followed down in another thunderstorm and safely docked at New Madrid at 5:00 A.M. on April 7. Pope now had two ironclads with which to cover the crossing of his men from the Missouri shore to Tennessee and to block the Confederate escape route at the base of the Reelfoot peninsula.[8]

As the first rays of dawn lightened the eastern horizon on Monday morning, April 7, Cmdr. Walke, the naval officer at New Madrid, sent a messenger to Lt. Thompson ordering that the newly arrived *Pittsburg* ready itself for action. Word was returned that the craft was not ready for service, though no reason for her unfitness was provided.

Knowing that the newcomer was not damaged, Walke, experienced in task group command from his days with the timberclads, could not fathom what might be causing Thompson's delay. At 6:30 A.M., with Pope's transports beginning to shove off for their crossing, *Carondelet*'s captain could wait no longer and ordered his lines hauled in. As the ironclad moved out into the stream, a "follow me" signal was hoisted for the *Pittsburg*. The *Carondelet* chugged down along the western bank of the river, her port broadside battery bombarding enemy positions as she passed. Her intended goal was to round to and face the Confederate's lower battery at Watson's Landing. This earthen Rebel emplacement, about an acre in size, held two 8-inch siege howitzers and a 32-pounder.

Standing off as he had at Fort Donelson, Walke began to slowly pound the little fort from a quarter mile distance. The deliberate turtle shoot was frequently interrupted to allow the clouds of gunsmoke to dissipate. Return fire ineffectively bounced off the bow casemate, but played havoc with the lifeboats. As she continued her shoot, the *Carondelet* drifted bows-on to the Tennessee river bank. To avoid grounding, Pilot Robert Deming headed her upstream, but this maneuver prevented her bow batteries from taking true aim. To continue firing while the vessel veered away under a hail of Southern musketry, Capt. Walke ordered Deming to sheer off to the northwest, allowing her broadside battery to bear on the enemy until the ironclad was in position to resume her bows-on attack.

Maj. Gen. Henry W. Halleck (1815–1872) was the U.S. Army Western theater commander until July 1862. While the gunboats were being repaired after Forts Henry and Donelson, Halleck pushed Flag Officer Foote to advance upon Island No. 10 (*Battles and Leaders*).

At this point, the starboard wheel rope was shot away, disabling the gunboat's steering gear and forcing her to come to briefly in order to make repairs. One 64-pdr. Confederate bolt now struck the *Carondelet*, smashed her fourth quarter, went starboard and quarter into the cabin, struck the stern gun, and bounced overboard. A half hour into the duel, as the *Carondelet* returned to action and dismounted the Confederate 32-pdr., causing its surviving gunners to flee.

At this point, the *Pittsburg* unexpectedly arrived from New Madrid. Approaching the ship-vs-shore duel from behind, she began long-range firing . A number of her shells passed dangerously close over Walke's hurricane deck and the bow, causing the veteran commander to wave his speaking trumpet at the latecomer in anger.

Having observed rifle pits and other infantry entrenchments from which grayclad soldiers were shooting, the *Carondelet* elected to neutralize these as well. Moving closer, the ironclad spat out 5-second shell and grapeshot that quickly cleansed the area of all resistance. Once the shooting ceased, the *Carondelet* ordered the *Pittsburg* to cease firing. By dipping and raising his ensign three times, Walke informed Maj. Gen. Pope that the battery was captured and clear of the enemy. The single remaining boat was lowered and three sailors were rowed ashore to spike the abandoned 8-inchers. While the bluejackets completed their tasks, the boat returned to the *Carondelet* with a spy from the 11th Missouri, who informed the gunboat's captain that the other batteries were all being evacuated.

With the Watson's Landing battery neutralized, the *Carondelet* and *Pittsburg* moved upstream about a half a mile to destroy the next Southern battery in line, this one mounting two 8-inch siege howitzers. Again, one of the pieces was dismounted, with the small fort's survivors all abandoning the place, chased by the gunboat cannon.

The Water's Point battery, approximately a quarter mile above, was the northernmost Confederate water barrier, mounting a single 8-inch Columbiad on a naval pivot carriage. As the Union vessels approached, it opened the exchange, but was only able to fire once before blowing up. As her crew and supporting soldiers retreated, Walke remembered, "we fired on them as they ran."

The Federal ironclads required approximately two hours to dispose of the three Confederate river batteries. The entire action was visible to spectators at New Madrid and along the Missouri shore. From a vantage point 10 miles away, one Union soldier later recalled that the pair were "in plain sight. We could see the bright flame and white smoke leap from the cannon's mouth."

As the *Carondelet* and *Pittsburg* retired, a message was sent to Maj. Gen. Pope advising him that the opposite shores were cleared and the two boats were ready to cover his crossing and landings. The Federal troop boats pulled out from New Madrid about 11:00 A.M. and headed over to Watson's Landing. Once the first units were ashore, the steamers returned for a second wave, 3,000 men under the command of Brig. Gen. David S. Stanley. While Stanley's men formed up at the beach and awaited the third wave, the *Carondelet* arrived, taking a hearty salute of congratulation from the brigadier and his officers. As he had with Brig. Gen. Palmer, the affable Walke quickly invited Stanley and his staff aboard.

The army officers were barely aboard the black ironclad when the *Pittsburg* pulled abreast. Lt. Thompson, standing in front of the pilothouse, shouted to his senior, offering praise for their combined work. Walke had had it with Thompson, the same man whose boat had rammed him at Fort Donelson. Not only had he failed to follow his commands with alacrity, he had nearly caused damage again, endangering the lives of every tar aboard the *Carondelet*. Grabbing up his ever-present trumpet, Walke hollered back: "Damn you, I don't congratulate you."

Before his surprised visitors and anyone (jack tar, bluecoat, or steamboatman) else within earshot, Capt. Walke blasted his subordinate. "You sulked behind my boat and fired shots over my deck," he accused Thompson. "Damn you, if you ever do such a thing again, I will turn my batteries on you and blow you out of the water." As Stanley remembered it, he considered this outburst an intraservice dispute and just "turned away."

The Confederates opposing Pope were cut off by lunchtime on April 7, the same day Grant counterattacked at Shiloh. Island No. 10 was surrendered to Flag Officer Foote on the evening of April 8 and the Mississippi was opened down to Fort Pillow. Three Confederate generals, 4,500 soldiers, and 109 artillery pieces were now taken off the table. "The circumstances as connected with the surrender of this position, with all its guns, ammunition, &c., are," wrote an editorialist for the *Richmond Press* on April 14, "humiliating in the extreme."[9]

7

Fort Pillow and Memphis

After the fall of Island No. 10, Western Flotilla Flag Officer Andrew H. Foote met at New Madrid with Maj. Gen. John Pope, commander of the Army of the Mississippi, to review plans for the capture of Fort Pillow (sometimes called Fort Wright), the next position of Confederate strength on the Mississippi River, approximately 80 miles above Memphis. From army intelligence, the squadron leader learned that a number of Confederate navy vessels, some escaped from the defense of Columbus and Island No. 10, were anchored in waters some 15 miles away.

The main elements of the Western Flotilla began downstream on April 12 and were joined at Tiptonville by the *Carondelet.* These warships would be followed sometime later by Pope's troop transports and support vessels, including the mortar boats. After spending the night at anchor off Hale's Point, 50 miles below New Madrid, the ironclads resumed their voyage about 8:00 A.M. next morning. They were hardly underway in the swift current when five Confederate gunboats, led by the *General Sterling Price* and *Maurepas*, came around the bend, intent on offering battle. After an exchange of long-range greetings between the two vanguard Rebel vessels and the *Benton* and the *Carondelet*, the challengers rounded to and retreated down the river. Although it was impossible to catch the speedy Southerners, Foote ordered a pursuit, which ended three hours later in the vicinity of Fort Pillow.

Just before lunch, the *Benton*, *Carondelet*, *Mound City*, and *Cincinnati* moved to within a mile of the fort to examine the citadel. Peering up through their spyglasses, the boat captains were unable to determine specific detail, but appreciated what a large obstacle they faced. Just as a welcome was fired from several heavy Rebel guns, the ironclads rounded to and returned up the river three miles, dropping anchor out of range at Plum Point on the Tennessee shore, directly across from Osceola, Arkansas. "At Plum Point," wrote John Abbott just after the war, "the Mississippi turns sharply from its southern course and flows almost directly east." After a few miles, "it strikes the first Chickasaw Bluffs," on the Tennessee shore, upon the summit of which was Fort Pillow (Wright). The stream was then "thrown abruptly back again in a southwestern direction."

Across the Mississippi, the Arkansas shore juts out sharply as the river changes direction at a spot called Craighead Point. The great stream then "continues below Island No. 34, where it again bends in a majestic curve. At the point are found the Second Chickasaw Bluffs, surmounted by Fort Randolph." This defensive position was 12 miles below Fort Pillow, back on the First Chickasaw Bluffs.

The army transports and support craft arrived in mid-afternoon. The military steamers headed for the Tennessee shore while the mortar boats were tied to the Arkansas shore in the bend above Craighead Point, more or less across the river from Plum Point.[1]

Between April 14 and 16, the Federal mortar boats launched their attack, tossing their 13-inch shells 3,800 yards downstream into and around Fort Pillow. On occasion, the big Confederate guns returned fire. The Confederate vessels huddled below were not hit.

The *Carondelet* and one or more of her sisters drew the daily assignment of guarding the mortars as they continued to "soften up" the area for an attack by Pope's bluecoats. Capt. Walke later recalled that on at least two occasions during these opening rounds, Foote made inquiry as to whether he would run past these batteries in order to render assistance to a military attack from below. Twice the gunboat commander affirmatively replied, but no action was taken.

Around noon on April 16, as three ironclads stood guard over the mortars, Confederate 10-inch Columbiads at Fort Pillow refined their targeting. A 128-pdr. shot plunged down toward the *Carondelet,* grazing her hammock nettings before continuing on into the river. The *St. Louis* and *Cairo* also suffered slight damage.

That evening, Foote and Pope received an order from Maj. Gen. Henry W. Halleck transferring Pope's army to the Tennessee River. The Union theater commander was then beginning a campaign against the key railroad center of Corinth, Mississippi. The siege of Fort Pillow was to continue and, if the opportunity allowed or the enemy withdrew, a brigade of Indiana troops (1,500 men) left with the flotilla was to land and secure it.

Without a field army to assault the Rebel river defenses, the attack on Fort Pillow settled down into a siege reminiscent of that at Island No. 10 a month earlier. Every day, two or three mortar boats, protected by one or two ironclads, would shell the enemy. When not on guard duty, the ironclads were anchored in two upstream divisions: the *Benton*, *Carondelet*, and *Pittsburg* off Plum Point and the others across the river opposite on the Arkansas shore. Occasionally, the Confederates fired back, sometimes dropping their bombs relatively near. Thunder from the less-than-hurtful explosions reverberated up and down the Mississippi, while the geysers raised in the flood-swollen waters were sometimes quite spectacular.[2]

On the morning of May 8, the same day Capt. Davis reported aboard the *Benton,* Confederate Com. J.E. Montgomery expected that, as usual, Union mortar boats would descend to their Craighead Point bombardment positions. Expecting to catch the Federals off guard, he led the *General Bragg*, *General Sumter*, and *General Earl Van Dorn* around the bend and behind a projecting point, prepared to strike.

The eager Confederates arrived too early; there were no mortar boats present as yet. Disappointed, the trio rounded to and returned to base. Tactically for the Confederate River Defense Fleet (CRDF), the Battle of Plum Point Bend got off to a false start. Strategically, the abortive run made little difference. The Union flotilla remained dispersed. Guarded by but one slow ironclad, the mortar boats continued to fire during the next three days from an exposed position beyond immediate squadron support. No picket boats patrolled to provide early warning, not even a cutter.

To make certain his boat at least was not surprised, the *Carondelet*'s captain ordered "watch on watch" be maintained, both day and night. Steam was up and her lines were singled and ready for slipping. At night, the crew lay on their arms, while sentinels and watchmen kept close watch, anticipating an attack. Although Flag Officer Foote had ordered all of his gunboats to remain vigilant, not all were.

The following afternoon, a flag-of-truce steamer from Fort Pillow paddled up to the Union anchorage, signaling a desire to parlay. Following a brief conversation between the two sides, two Union surgeons, captured during the Battle of Belmont, were returned. Watching the proceedings through his spyglass, Cmdr. Walke was convinced that the Confederate action was a *ruse de guerre* designed to learn the deployment of the ironclads and support vessels, including the mortar boats.[3]

It was dark, cool, calm, and foggy at 4:00 A.M. on May 10 when a steamer towed Mortar Boat No. 16 down to her usual firing position below Craighead Point. She was accompanied by the Pook turtle *Cincinnati*, whose turn it was in the rotation to provide cover. Once the transport had cast off and the bomb vessel was secured to the bank, the ironclad moved a short distance up the river. She dropped anchor off a suitable beach with her bow pointing north.

The *Cincinnati*'s veteran captain, Cmdr. Roger Stembel, had drawn the same conclusion from the previous day's POW exchange as Cmdr. Walke. Consequently, he kept steam up, his great paddle wheel revolving very slowly helping to keep the vessel steady in the swift current. His command was readied for any eventuality, even as the mortar boat opened fire on Fort Pillow at 5:00 A.M.

The river was still swollen, overflowing its banks for many miles through the forest and beyond. It was also clogged with large amounts of driftwood. Some of this debris accumulated in the 5 mph current on the bow of the *Cincinnati* and became heavily tangled before deck hands could cast it off.

Meanwhile, about an hour later, after five 13-inch mortar bombs were launched, lookouts aboard the *Carondelet* spotted a huge cloud of smoke advancing north from the direction of Fort Pillow. Word was passed below and soon Capt. Walke was up the chartroom ladder leading into the pilothouse.

At approximately 6:00 A.M., eight CRDF rams, led by the rakish, former side-wheel Gulf steamer *General Bragg* so easily distinguishable by her large walking-beam engine, departed the waters of Fort Pillow and paddled up the west bank of the river in formation toward the Union mortar raft and the picket ironclad. As the rebel boats moved up around Craighead Point, they were spotted aboard the flagboat *Benton*, according to her log, at 7:25 A.M. Fifteen minutes later, the enemy "ran into the *Cincinnati* and commenced the engagement."

Rear Adm. Davis later called the Battle of Plum Point Bend "a smart affair." It was the

Battle of Plum Point Bend—first position. Drawn by Capt. Walke for his memoirs, *Naval Scenes and Reminiscences.*

first Civil War engagement between naval squadrons and would be one of the few in which the Federals would be outshone. The *Carondelet* played a significant supporting role, but was fortunately not one of the Union ironclads made to suffer. According to a lost portion of the deck log, attentive lookouts aboard the *Carondelet* saw the heavy volume of smoke below and sounded the alarm. When Capt. Walke reached the pilothouse from below, he,

This depiction of the Battle of Plum Point Bend, a follow-up drawing to the first position, was labeled "Final Position" by Capt. Walke (*Naval Scenes and Reminiscences*).

This ***Battles and Leaders*** depiction drawn by Capt. Walke is entitled ***The Close of the Battle of Memphis June 6, 1862 (Looking North).*** In it, he kindly provided the names of the vessels he observed from this vantage point.

This rendering of the Battle of Plum Point Bend was drawn by Rear Adm. Walke in retirement for the Century series *Battles and Leaders.*

together with all hands topside, watched as the CRDF craft headed toward the *Cincinnati,* about four miles below. Even before the drum could "beat to quarters," the jack tars caught the shouted alarms, sprang to their guns, and cleared the ship for action. Looking back years later, the boat's skipper was proud to note his gunboat "all ready for battle in three or four minutes."

Capt. Davis was below in his cabin when the *Benton*'s officer of the deck, pilot Richard Birch, seeing the drifting cloud of Rebel smoke, sounded the alarm aboard the flagboat, hoisted the general battle signal, and sent word down below to the flotilla's acting commander. Before Davis could get topside up the ladder, Birch, seeing that the *Carondelet* was ready, passed verbal orders through his trumpet for Walke to proceed independently and to act on his own initiative, not waiting for either the flagboat or orders. In the rigid formality of the 19th century USN, this act by a noncommissioned officer, Walke later agreed, "deserves great credit, as time was precious." The *Carondelet* immediately slipped her hawser and started sheering downstream across the river, as her coal heavers fed more fuel into the engine fires. Walke's gunboat passed the *Benton* as Davis reached his quarterdeck and the new unit leader grabbed Birch's trumpet and shouted across to the Pook turtle to "go ahead and not wait for the *Benton.*"

Neither the approach of the CRDF nor the *Benton*'s general signal, owing to the haze, was not seen aboard the other Union ironclads, including all of those anchored off the west bank. Capt. Augustus Kilty of the *Mound City,* like Walke a veteran officer, also did not wait for a signal. About the time the *Carondelet* was slipping her hawser, Kilty saw the enemy and, as Walke passed the *Benton,* the *Mound City* also started down parallel to the Arkansas shore. Both turtles flew at the top of their pitifully slow speed. The other Federal vessels followed as their steam and general readiness permitted. The *Benton* herself was cut loose and allowed to drift down as steam built up in her boilers. Initially, she too steered across the river, about a mile behind the *Carondelet.*

At a distance of approximately ⅜ mile from the *General Bragg*, the *Carondelet* and *Mound City* opened fire on Capt. N.H.H. Leonard's Rebel ram from their bow guns. Unhappily, the gunners all aimed poorly and every shot missed. Soon, the hard-charging turtles were forced to cease shooting as the two-masted *General Bragg* closed upon the *Cincinnati.* As the latter frantically attempted to swing her bow around, everyone aboard knew that she would be hit; the only question was how serious the damage would be from the collision.

As a result of the *Cincinnati*'s shift, the *General Bragg* managed to strike only a glancing blow on her opponent's starboard quarter. Nevertheless, it was quite serious, tearing a 12-foot long midships hole six feet deep that allowed the river to rush inside. The whole ironclad was rocked and the forward shell room was flooded. The force of the crash was so strong that the *Bragg*'s starboard wheelhouse and paddle wheel climbed right up the side of the ironclad's sloping casemate.

As soon as the two vessels parted, the *Carondelet* and *Mound City* resumed shelling the *Bragg*. Even now, however, two more craft, the *General Sterling Price* and the *Sumter*, made for the *Cincinnati*, then retreating at her best (very slow) speed upstream. Gun captains aboard the two Pook turtles desperately called upon their men to divide their fire, concentrating any gun that would bear upon the new threats. Entering the arena, the *Benton* added her heavy guns to the noisy cannonade. In the flagboat pilothouse for his first action, Capt. Davis calmly smoked a cigar. As the two Rebel rams closed on the *Cincinnati*, all three Federal boats were forced to hold their fire.

The *General Sterling Price* was the first to strike the *Cincinnati*, hitting her starboard beam and carrying away the rudder, sternpost, and, indeed, a large part of the stern itself. More water entered. The *Sumter* followed up, striking the *Cincinnati* so hard in the stern that her bows went under water. Her fires were extinguished, her magazines and shell rooms were all flooded now, and sharpshooters, in sweeping the decks, gave Cmdr. Stembel a serious but non-mortal wound.

Once the *Price* and *Sumter* retreated, the *Carondelet*, *Mound City*, and *Benton* walked their shells after them. At Capt. Walke's behest, Pilot Deming maneuvered their ironclad to bring her port broadside guns into action as well. The *Sumter* became a target for the turtle's new 50-pdr. Dahlgren. A shell from the *Carondelet* hit the Rebel craft forward, sending clouds of white steam from her ports. It was believed at the time that a shell from the *Carondelet* cut her steam pipe. She drifted out of action and was carried by the current to safety, badly damaged. The thick gun smoke lying atop the morning haze made observation at any distance difficult. It also contributed to the unreported passage by the *Carondelet* of two other CRDF rams, the *General Earl Van Dorn* and the Confederate flagboat *Little Rebel.*

Fourth in line of attack, Capt. Isaac D. Fulkerson elected to go after the *Mound City.* Bearing down on a collision course, the *General Earl Van Dorn* was subjected to skipped shot sent skimming through the haze along the river by Cmdr Kilty's gunners. Neither the *Carondelet* nor the *Benton* could help, again having to hold fire, as the Southern ram ploughed directly toward the *Mound City*, midships. At the last moment, the ironclad's pilot swung hard aport, causing the *Van Dorn* to land a glancing blow. The strike on the starboard forward quarter was, however, sufficiently hard to punch a four foot hole in the hull. Despite help from the crews of at least two ironclads that did not make it into the fight, the *Mound City* was nearly lost.

With the *Cincinnati* and *Mound City* both out of action, the *Carondelet* was left alone between the oncoming Federals and the three remaining Confederate rams, the *General Jeff Thompson*, *General Lovell*, and *General Beauregard*. Attempting to avoid a shoal by rounding to, Walke's boat became a target for both sides as she headed for the enemy. Passing the *Cincinnati*, the men aboard the *Carondelet* could clearly see steam escaping from the ports of their sister turtle and her sinking condition — but not for long. Immediately, Walke's command was taken under fire by the three Rebel rams. Southern cannonballs bounced off her casemate, which reverberated inside like a gong.

Not only was she shot at by the three Southern craft, but the *Carondelet* also "received a discharge or two of grape shot, that swept across her decks, from the *Pittsburg*." A number of the army sharpshooters, stationed on the hurricane deck behind temporary barricades, "were obliged to lie down under shelter to save themselves from the grape" as well as from shell fragments. For the third time in three months, Lt. Thompson's vessel had harmed or nearly harmed Walke's. Seeing the plight of the *Cincinnati*, Thompson, to his credit, returned upstream to render her aid. This time, Walke attributed the *Pittsburg*'s mistake to a dense smoke of battle that prevented the determination of vessel movements "within a quarter of a mile."

With "her bow pretty much wrenched off," Cmdr. Kilty's boat was run onto a shoal opposite Plum Point, where she sank. The *Cincinnati* stood afloat only a little longer than the *Mound City*. Assisted by a tug and the *Pittsburg*, Cmdr. Stembel's vessel pushed toward the Tennessee shore, water pouring in rapidly. Before she could make it, the turtle went down bow-first, coming to rest on the bottom in 11 feet of water.

About the time the *General Earl Van Dorn* withdrew, Rebel commander Montgomery noticed that the surviving Federal ironclads were coming on but remaining in water too shallow for his rams to follow. The signal to withdraw was hoisted and the Confederates retreated toward Fort Pillow. As the Rebel rams departed, the *Carondelet* pushed down to within half a mile of Craighead Point, her bow guns continuing to fire upon Montgomery's boats. Just as the fleet Confederates were moving out of range, the *Benton*, with a full head of steam, came along, her guns thundering, to pass the *Carondelet*. A reporter for the *Cincinnati Times* remarked, in fact, that had it not been for this timely arrival, "the *Carondelet*, Captain Walke, which was moving down to the foe, would have been cut off from the fleet and possibly captured, if her gallant commander had not blown up his ship, which is very probable, rather than let her fall into the hands of the enemy."

The two ironclads continued their pursuit until they came within range of Fort Pillow's guns, at which point both ceased firing and rounded to. Voluntarily, Walke positioned his boat as a "guard or picket boat" for the fleet and for Mortar Boat 16, which continued to lob shells at Fort Pillow after the fight.

Both sides claimed victory in the 1 hour, 10 minute engagement. Casualties were light (2 Confederate and 1 Union dead), but, in the end, the blow to Federal prestige would be significant. In one of the few "fleet actions" of the Civil War, the ready Rebel rams sank two of their ill-prepared and superior Union opponents (quickly repaired and returned to service) and, though damaged, all managed to withdraw as planned. Memphis was spared for the moment.

In addition to the lessons of vigilance driven home by Com. Montgomery, the captains of the Federal flotilla also learned, if they did not already know, that their vessels required additional waterline protection. Capt. Davis immediately ordered that each ironclad be strengthened with additional wood and iron protection.

Like those aboard several of the other Pook turtles, Capt. Walke's crew, led by carpenter Donaldson, secured a number of heavy logs from shore. These were duly suspended and lashed at the waterline, port and starboard, rendering the gunboats invulnerable to Confederate rams. This additional buttressing, however, caused a serious decline in available speed. Indeed, the problem was so bad that, during and after the upcoming Battle of Memphis, the scheme was abandoned by the Western Flotilla in favor of fortification, fore and aft, with railroad iron and heavy timbers.

"Another month passed away," wrote John Abbott, "of languid, monotonous, ineffective bombardment on both sides." Most of the time, the shells went south from the Federal mortar boats; but occasionally, they were dispatched north from the citadel. On one occasion, two 128-pdr. bolts nearly hit the *Carondelet.* The first fell very close by, throwing a huge geyser of water on her deck. Not wishing for another bath — or worse — Capt. Walke ordered the ironclad to weigh anchor and move upriver a short distance. She had barely dropped anchor at the new location when a second shell hit the water exactly where she was anchored previously. Had it hit, the *Carondelet*'s story might very well have ended right then and there.

Maj. Gen. Henry Halleck's command, including soldiers under Maj. Gen. Pope, captured Corinth, Mississippi, on May 30. This success forced Gen. Beauregard, as part of a strategic Confederate withdrawal, to abandon all Mississippi River positions north of Vicksburg. The evacuation of Fort Pillow and Memphis was ordered on June 4 and next day, the CRDF withdrew to Memphis. Once the Federals discovered the retreat, the ironclads followed.[4]

Rear Adm. Charles H. Davis (1807–1877) commanded the Western Flotilla between May and October 1862. During his tenure on the Mississippi River, the *Carondelet* participated in the battles of Plum Point Bend and Memphis. Having taken his vessels downstream to meet Flag Officer David G. Farragut above Vicksburg, Davis sent the *Carondelet* and two other craft up the Yazoo to investigate reports of a Confederate ram called the *Arkansas* (Library of Congress).

At dawn on Friday June 6, CSS *Earl Van Dorn*, *General Beauregard*, *General M. Jeff Thompson*, *General Bragg*, *General Sumter*, *General Sterling Price*, and *Little Rebel* of Com. Montgomery's CRDF cast off, dropped below Railroad Point, and were drawn up in a double line in front of Memphis. There they were seen through Federal spyglasses and, at 4:20 A.M., the Western Flotilla flagship *Benton* and the Pook turtles *Louisville*, *Carondelet*, *St Louis*, and *Cairo* headed downstream toward the Rebel warships, that had, meanwhile, opened fire. As the two squadrons approached, Col. Charles Ellet, Jr., who was charging to the sound of the guns, suddenly appeared with the rams *Monarch* and *Queen of the West* from his independent Mississippi Marine Brigade and attacked at full steam.

Tiptonville following the surrender of Island No. 10. From here the *Carondelet* (perhaps pictured) was joined by other units of the Western Flotilla from New Madrid above on April 12 and steamed downstream toward Fort Pillow (*Battles and Leaders*).

Having pursued five Confederate gunboats, the *Carondelet* and three other Western Flotilla ironclads steamed within a mile of Fort Pillow on April 13, 1862, examining its defenses (*Battles and Leaders*).

The close action which followed the appearance of the U.S. Army rams was dramatic, with fast-paced give-and-take fighting between the ships of Ellet and Montgomery ensuing before the heavier ironclads could come up. After smashing into the *Lovell*, the *Queen of the West* was rammed by the *Beauregard* and disabled; Colonel Ellet received a mortal wound. The *Beauregard* and *General Sterling Price* then aimed at the *Monarch*, missed, and collided, with the *General Sterling Price* the worse for the assault. The *Beauregard* was rammed by the *Monarch* and sunk by a shot from the *Benton* as Davis' boats came closer.

This idealized view of the Battle of Memphis accurately depicts the position of the *Carondelet* and a sister after the Ellet rams rushed past them to tackle the Confederate River Defense Fleet (***Illustrated London News***, July 19, 1862).

Little more than scows equipped with 13-inch mortars, the little mortar boats played an important role at Island No. 10, at Plum Point Bend, and at Vicksburg. An attempt to destroy one of them led directly to the confrontation at Plum Point Bend (Lossing, ***Pictorial Field Book of the Civil War: Journeys Through the Battlefields in the Wake of Conflict, 1874***).

The role of the *Carondelet* and her consorts was now one of support as the surviving Rebels fled. The ironclads pursued the Confederate craft that Ellet had dispersed. An hour-long running duel ensued that carried the opposing units 10 miles downstream past President's Island. In the end, only the *Van Dorn* escaped, with all the others captured, sunk, or grounded on the riverbank to avoid sinking. Com. Montgomery and Brig. Gen. M. Jeff Thompson, who had both promised better results, "were hurried," as the latter subsequently reported to Gen. Beauregard, in their "retirement from Memphis." By lunchtime, Union soldiers were being landed at the Memphis docks.[5]

8

The Arkansas

As Union forces slowly snaked their way down the Mississippi from Island No. 10 to Memphis in the weeks of March–June 1862, the Confederacy struggled to prepare a special river warship strong enough to mount an effective opposition. On May 26 Lt. Isaac N. Brown, CSN, who had lost a similar project, the *Eastport*, to the U.S. timberclads earlier in the year, was ordered to take command of C.S.S. *Arkansas* and "finish the vessel without regard to expenditure of men or money." Progress on completing the vessel was spotty after her removal from Memphis to the Yazoo River.

Lt. Brown's superior, Flag Officer William F. Lynch, CSN, after inspecting the unfinished ram reported to secretary of the navy Stephen R. Mallory that "the *Arkansas* is very inferior to the *Merrimac[k]* in every particular. The iron with which she is covered is worn and indifferent, taken from a railroad track, and is poorly secured to the vessel; boiler iron on stern and counter; her smoke-stack is sheet iron."

Nevertheless, exhibiting great energy that he used to overcome shortages and difficulties of every nature, Lt. Brown completed *Arkansas*. Not only did he secure a workforce under the most difficult circumstances, he was able to finish her in a backwater only a few miles from the Federal fleet. The armorclad, according to her commander, "appeared as if a small seagoing vessel had been cut down to the water's edge at both ends, leaving a box for guns amidships." Ready just five weeks after Brown's arrival, the *Arkansas* mounted a formidable armament of 10 guns on locally constructed carriages: two 9-inch smoothbores, two 8-inch 64-pdr. smoothbores, two 6-inch rifles, and two 32-pdrs. These protruded through small portholes with heavy iron shutters.

Such was her captain's charisma that a number of Southern army artillerists volunteered to act as her gunners and part of a 200-man ship's company. In addition to Brown's impressions of the ship, future lucky readers would learn of the vessel from several other officers, including Executive Officer Lt. Henry Kennedy Stevens; Tennessean George W. Gift, commander of the portside 8-inch Columbiad; Lt. John Grimball, commander of the starboard Columbiad; and Charles W. Read from Mississippi, who oversaw the two stern chasers. Lt. Brown, was, however, the human force behind the *Arkansas*. Cmdr. Henry Walke, a messmate in years gone by, admitted she was "commanded by one of the best of the Confederate officers." Not having been to sea in some time, he was, however, confused by Philadelphia newsman Bentley for "an old steamboat man, resident of Memphis."[1]

As a result of the great Northern victories at Memphis and New Orleans, the latter captured by forces under Flag Officer David G. Farragut in late April, vessels from the Union's Western Flotilla and West Gulf Coast Blockading Squadron were able to meet above the Confederate citadel at Vicksburg on July 1. Preparations were made to attack the city's upper batteries.

The weather was hot throughout the Mississippi Valley and sickness (primarily malaria) plagued Northern and Southern forces, afloat and ashore, in the Vicksburg vicinity. During this hot period, the fighting ability of entire crews was often endangered. A variety of measures were adopted to combat prickly heat, another bothersome irritation, including, according to the *Cincinnati Daily Commercial*, vinegar baths. The summer sun beat down unmercifully from Cairo to New Orleans and, as happened every year, the rivers fell. The 4th of July at St. Louis, for example, "passed tamely" due largely to the fact that the "day was intensely hot," causing a "want of spirit."

On the Mississippi before Vicksburg, Farragut and Flag Officer Charles H. Davis grew concerned that the former would be forced to come about and run back down past the Rebel batteries to New Orleans. Soundings revealed the channel was becoming worrisomely shallow for Farragut's oceangoing vessels, many of which had drafts around 16 feet. In less than a fortnight, the "Father of Waters" was down to 18 feet. How much longer Farragut could remain on station was unknown.

As July deepened, the weather grew even warmer, the disease rate climbed higher, and the fuel situation for the two flotillas became questionable. To preserve the precious amounts of coal received by barge all the way from Memphis, many vessels banked their fires and some even took advantage of this opportunity to clean their boilers.

While the two fleets lay together, Cmdr. Henry Walke, captain of the *Carondelet*, took this opportunity to have "a heavy timber casemate built over the boilers of his vessel." This bulwark, an improvement upon earlier efforts, would protect the boat's power plant "from the enemy's shot and shell in her subsequent career."

In these days, refugees and Rebel deserters brought Davis a steady stream of details concerning the building of "this devil, the *Arkansas*," up the Yazoo, the mouth of which was only six miles from his anchorage. Many of their details differed. Even as Farragut sought Secretary Welles' permission to leave and continued to discuss the possibility of a downriver departure with Davis, the commander of the Western Flotilla knew that some sort of Confederate naval threat loomed. Davis and his colleagues believed that the ram "was unfinished and aground." "Delta," the imbedded correspondent of the *New Orleans Daily Delta*, a reborn Southern newspaper, told his readers that "The great terror of modern times, 'the Ram,' was discussed in all its ramifications." He went on to agree with others that "there was a good deal of bugaboo in Ram fears."

At the beginning of the month, Lt. Col. Alfred W. Ellet, commander of the experimental War Department unit known as the Mississippi Ram Brigade, scouted the Yazoo River for Flag Officer Farragut. Two fast rams, the *Monarch* and the *Lancaster*, traveled the winding, twisting tributary for a distance of 65 miles. The stream was found to be shallow in places and too narrow for any of the seagoing warships to turn. The Confederate ram was reported at Liverpool, not yet ready to sortie. Additionally, a giant raft was reported blocking the stream. Upon his return, Ellet recommended to Farragut that Flag Officer Davis be approached. His vessels drew less water than Farragut's and might be able to ascend further.

On July 7, Henry Bentley, a noted correspondent of the *Philadelphia Inquirer*, wrote for subscribers: "the ram and gun-boat *Arkansas* is finished and ready for active service." He went on to opine that "If the *Arkansas* is anything like what those who have seen her represent her to be, she will give our flotilla a good deal of trouble."

Until he knew for certain what blue-water sailor Farragut intended, however, the Western Flotilla commander had to be prepared to cover his departure as well as defend against any nautical surprises. Plans were made to send a gunboat or two "up the Yazoo to reconnoiter and prepare the way for an expedition, which will go up in considerable force if necessary."

The same heat, sickness, and water level issues which faced Farragut and Davis on the Mississippi also concerned Lt. Brown up the Yazoo. By the second week of July, as his sailors and work crews placed the finishing touches on the *Arkansas*, the determined sailor noted that "the now rapid fall of the river rendered it necessary for us to assume the offensive." Confederate military authorities," noted Michael B. Ballard a century later, "counted on Brown to break up the enemy naval presence in front of Vicksburg." If the ram did not sortie out soon, it would be stranded. In that event, she would be of no use and would probably, like the *Merrimack-Virginia*, have to be destroyed.

Fully loaded, the *Arkansas* drew nearly 13 feet (seven more than any of the Pook turtles) and could be trapped behind the Satartia Bar if it did not leave in a timely fashion. Two days earlier, Maj. Gen. Earl Van Dorn, Vicksburg's new commander as of June 20 (arrived June 23), sent a note to Brown telling him that the combined Union fleet off his city numbered at least 37 men-of-war. The city commandant wanted the armorclad to steam forth and smite the enemy. "It would," Van Dorn wrote, "be better to die in action than be buried up in Yazoo City."

On July 12, the ram sortied Yazoo City on the first leg of her desperate mission and dropped below Satartia Bar to within five hours steaming time of the Mississippi. Lt. Steven was given the next day to whip the new crew into shape and test the big guns. The "breakout" of the *Arkansas* began after breakfast on Monday morning, July 14. It ground to a halt at the mouth of the Sunflower River 15 miles below when it was discovered that leaky boilers had dampened all of the powder in the forward magazine. The armorclad came to off an old Yazoo River sawmill and made fast to the bank. The crew then painstakingly hauled all of the powder ashore and dried it in the sun on tarpaulins. By dusk, it was stored aboard once more, this time in the aft magazine. The vessel anchored near Hayne's Bluff at midnight.

Kentuckian Lt. Isaac N. Brown (1817–1889), a 28-year prewar veteran of the U.S. Navy and a one-time messmate of Capt. Henry Walke, was the driving force behind the completion and operation of the Confederate armorclad *Arkansas*. On July 15, 1862, Brown took his ram from its lair up the Yazoo River and headed for Vicksburg on the Mississippi. En route, he fought a running duel with his old colleague's *Carondelet*, very nearly destroying her in one of the great ship-to-ship duels of the entire conflict (*Battles and Leaders*).

All hands turned to aboard the *Arkansas* about 3:00 A.M. on Tuesday morning. True to deserter tales, the ram now weighed anchor, hoping to surprise the Federal fleet at sunrise. Unhappily, just as she gathered way, the big warship ran aground in the darkness. An hour was lost getting free. As the first rays of another hot day glowed in the east, the pride of the Confederacy entered Old River, a lake or "old channel" 12 miles north of Vicksburg. A cut-off from the Mississippi formed at the north curve of the Yazoo, it flows into the main river three miles below the mouth of the Yazoo. There was a light mist, but nothing that really interfered with visibility.

Steaming along Old River's expanse, *Arkansas* lookouts peering to the left at about 7:00 A.M. suddenly saw "a few miles ahead, under full steam, three Federal vessels in line approaching." Peering out his porthole, Lt. Gift saw them "round a point in full view, steaming towards us gallantly and saucily, with colors streaming in the wind." Standing atop the casemate just behind the pilothouse, Lt. Brown and Lt. Stevens also saw the three Yankees. Descending to the gun deck and summoning his officers, the skipper offered a quick pep talk: "Gentlemen, in seeking the combat as we now do, we must win or perish. Should I fall, whoever succeeds to the command will do so with the resolution to go through the enemy's fleet, or go to the bottom." If there was a close action that went poorly, the armorclad was to be blown up rather than surrendered. His comments finished, the peppery leader barked, "Go to your guns!" He then returned to the casemate roof, leaving Stevens to command the gun deck.[2]

On the evening of July 13, two men were allowed to go onboard the War Department ram *Lancaster* from a skiff; they reported that the *Arkansas* would depart her anchorage the next evening. The pair, deserters from Confederate Gen. Pierre G.T. Beauregard's army, were sent to Lt. Col. Alfred Ellet as POWs. Scharf and Cmdr. William D. "Dirty Bill" Porter reported that, on the following night, two other deserters from Vicksburg went aboard the latter's *Essex* and reported that the *Arkansas* would assault the Union anchorage within hours or just after dawn on July 15. Porter immediately had the men transferred to the *Benton*, where they repeated their story for Flag Officer Davis and later for Flag Officer Farragut. The two squadron leaders, who may not have heard about or from the men taken aboard the *Lancaster*, were reportedly skeptical of the tale told by the Vicksburg men, preferring to believe it "Ram bugaboo." Conserving coal at anchor seemed a far more pressing concern.

As noted, stories had been circulating for some time that a powerful warship was abuilding up the Yazoo "equal to the 'cleaning out' of the Mississippi River, the recapture of New Orleans, and perhaps an excursion to New York and the destruction of that city." Thus historian John D. Milligan reminds us, they were "perfectly aware that the enemy was finishing the *Arkansas* up the Yazoo, but refused to believe that he would dare to bring her out."

However, the two commanders were, according to Scharf, "moved by the persistency of the two deserters." They agreed to send an exploring expedition to make certain, as New Orleans newspaper correspondent "Delta" put it, "that floating Rams ought to be tied up." Davis, the more concerned of the Union flag officers, undoubtedly took the testimony of the Rebel sailors as confirmation of the necessity for a reconnaissance.

Final preparations for Davis' examination of the Yazoo began in earnest on the morning of July 14. Just before 9:00 A.M., Lt. William Gwin, commander of the timberclad *Tyler*, was summoned aboard the Western Flotilla flagboat *Benton* for a strategy session with Davis and Farragut, plus Brig. Gen. Thomas Williams, who had come up the Mississippi with Farragut. The two fleet commanders rather quickly resolved to order a Yazoo River reconnaissance. "The shoalness and narrowness of the stream," wrote Prof. James R. Soley for the *Battles and Leaders* series, "led them to take vessels of the upper squadron in preference to those of the lower."

The general's men were presently attempting to build a canal nearby at De Soto Point on the peninsula of that name (also known as "Swampy Toe") across from the city. When completed, it would link Tuscumbia Bend with the Mississippi south of the citadel. The latest intelligence available to the Federals indicated that there was, indeed, a raft obstructing passage of the Yazoo about 80 miles from its mouth, with a battery below as additional protection. The *Arkansas* was above the raft and was said to be very well protected with a heavy battery of her own.

When the planning team broke for lunch at noon, Lt. Gwin returned to the *Tyler*. There he informed his lieutenants their craft would soon weigh on a new and special mission. Twenty 4th Wisconsin sharpshooters that Brig. Gen. Williams had offered to provide would be coming aboard shortly.

Davis and Farragut, with others from the morning team and without, including Davis' assistant and acting fleet captain, Lt. S. Ledyard Phelps, resumed their meeting in early afternoon. It was now agreed that the *Tyler*, strengthened by U.S. Army riflemen, would carry out the reconnaissance. Backup would be provided by one of the Ellet rams, with a 20-man marksman detail from the 13th Massachusetts, as well as an Eads ironclad that would take station at the mouth of Old River about seven miles from the Mississippi. Gwin's instruction — as he later told his aide and the boat's signal officer, Paymaster Silas B. Coleman — was to take the *Tyler* and *Queen* up the Yazoo looking for the *Arkansas*. If she were underway as the deserters had warned, he was to bring her to action and destroy her with the assistance of the *Queen* and, if need be, the *Carondelet*.

Once the meeting concluded, practical and logistical matters continued to occupy the planners. Davis got off a dispatch outlining his scheme to navy secretary Welles. In it, he announced that he was sending the *Tyler* on a reconnaissance up the Yazoo River "preparatory to an expedition in that direction." Sometime after writing his superior, the flag officer also wrote out orders for Cmdr. Walke, commander of the *Carondelet*, then anchored four miles upstream from the *Benton*. It is uncertain why the hero of Island No. 10 was not involved in the Farragut-Williams-Gwin discussions. It is probable that someone, after the meeting broke up, suggested that the timberclad might require support.

Walke, the flotilla's senior operational captain, was not then expecting movement because his ship was "so reduced and debilitated by sickness that she could not fight more than one division of guns." He himself came down with a fever, most likely malaria, during July.

The medical situation notwithstanding, Lt. Phelps, "suddenly delivered" Davis' "formal, brief, and verbal" orders via steam tug late in the evening. Phelps and Walke, the "restored officer" and *Tyler*'s former commander, were not the best of friends, having been on the outs since early February. Phelps may or may not have elaborated on the Davis instructions. Walke, according to his memoirs, "was induced to think" his ship would cruise alone up the Yazoo next morning. Nothing was intimated "that any other gunboats were to join him." In short, even though Walke would be the ranking officer on scene, he was either not given or did not fully understand the plan Davis and Farragut had worked out with Lt. Gwin.

For his part, Flag Officer Farragut contacted Lt. Col. Alfred Ellet, with whom he got on better than he did with Davis, and asked that he contribute one of his rams to the expedition. Davis and the Ellets had quarreled over possession of salvageable Confederate vessels after the Battle of Memphis, as well as later expeditions. Responding to Farragut's request, Ellet agreed to sent his fastest vessel, the *Queen of the West*, skippered by Lt. James M. Hunter of the 63rd Illinois.

A hero of the Memphis engagement a month earlier, Hunter had commanded the *Queen*'s marines during the big fight; the late Col. Charles Ellet had been the ram's commanding officer. After the victory was secured, Hunter took the steamer to Cairo for repairs and, upon her return to the waters off Vicksburg, remained in charge.

Ellet told Hunter to follow Lt. Gwin of the *Tyler* next morning "as far as the officer of that boat deems it necessary to proceed for the purposes he has in view." Hunter was to take care that his guns were loaded and his men ready. If Gwin were attacked by the *Arkansas*, the *Queen* was to "dash to her rescue" and sink the armorclad "by running full speed right head on into her." It appears that Hunter did not know that the *Carondelet* would be in the vicinity.

It was still dark and as cool as the day would get when the gunboatmen assigned to the reconnaissance prepared to cast off on July 15. Lookouts aboard the craft had to keep a close eye for other units of the combined fleet, anchored as they were in a mixed order. Steam was down on every vessel except those of Gwin, Hunter, and Walke. At 3:55 A.M. that Tuesday, observed the officer of the deck of the U.S.S. *Hartford*, the *Tyler* got underway a short distance up the river. Going alongside the *Lancaster*, she requested the services of an experienced Yazoo River pilot and, after an hour's delay, one was provided.

It being the middle of the night when the reconnaissance kicked off, it is perhaps understandable that several of the imbedded correspondents, sleeping on civilian steamers, thought the advance units had departed earlier. Frank Knox from the *New York Herald* actually told his readers that the *Tyler* and *Carondelet* had arrived at the mouth of the Yazoo "about 7 P.M. on the 14th and lay to until morning."

While Lt. Gwin sought a guide, the pokey *Carondelet* actually tripped her anchor at 4:00 A.M. and began slowly steaming up the Mississippi. A half hour later, the ironclad entered the Yazoo. Capt. Walke, an artist ever alert to color and aura, recorded the following: "All was calm, bright and beautiful. The majestic forest echoed with the sweet warbling of its wild birds, and its dewy leaves sparkled in the sunbeams." Finally, at 5:00 A.M., the *Tyler* was also able to depart the fleet anchorage, trailed by the *Queen of the West*. The two arrived at the mouth of the Yazoo 45 minutes later and stood on up, soon catching up with the *Carondelet*.[3]

As reported by newsman Knox, the initial miles covered by the three Union vessels were peaceful, with nothing out of the ordinary sighted, even though there was at this time a number of Rebel-employed civilian steamboats up the Yazoo River in addition to the *Arkansas*. The occasional local youth or old man "gazed wonderingly at the 'Linkum gunboats' until they disappeared from sight." A number of African Americans, having first made certain that they could not be seen by their Caucasian masters, came to the bank and "waved hats and branches of trees in token of their delight at our appearance." Knox also reported that one "butternut hero" shouted to the three boats as they passed near him in the river that "the *Arkansas* was coming and would meet them soon." He then retired from sight into "a neighboring canebrake." Whether true or not, the bluejackets dismissed the Southerner's message as a Rebel canard.

Between 6:00 A.M. (Brown) and 7:00 A.M. (Gwin), the *Tyler* and the *Queen of the West*, paralleling the sides of the river right and left respectively, came within three miles of the mouth of the stream. The *Carondelet*, plodding along roughly in the middle between the two, was a mile and a half further back. Having reached her assigned holding area, the *Carondelet* came to, as her two companions churned slowly on. Despite Cmdr. Walke's joyful observation on the morning's wonder, there was a slight haze that prevented full forward visibility. This was a good time to pipe the crew to breakfast.

This drawing of the duel between the *Carondelet* (left) and *Arkansas* (right) was "drawn by an officer" and originally appeared in *Frank Leslie's Illustrated Newspaper* (Frank Leslie, *Famous Leaders and Battle Scenes of the Civil War*, New York: Mrs. Frank Leslie, 1896).

At this point, the officer of the deck aboard the *Tyler* saw what he thought was smoke from one of those fugitive transports— or what Knox called a "foraging tug"—coming down the river about 500 yards ahead. Most of the officers and men were at breakfast, but Lt. Gwin, fastidiously attired as usual in his full uniform, was summoned on deck. The same puffs were seen across a point of land aboard the *Carondelet.* Captain Walke, as correspondent Knox later learned, was told by Pilot John Deming that the billowing "was caused by wood smoke and not by the bituminous coal used exclusively by the boats of our fleet." As the small cloud could be from any of the civilian boats known to be operating in the area, no special attention was paid to the distant craft.

As soon as the interloper was seen rounding a bend above about half a mile away, the timberclad commander ordered Gunner Herman Peters to fire a shot across her bow with the 12-lb. howitzer. The unusual *tout ensemble* of the mysterious craft was very suspicious. "Surely," wrote Junius Henri Browne, "there never was such a queer tug before." If this were a civilian vessel, its captain would know to heave to and await boarding or would round to and make a run for it. In the worst case, it would fight.

The little shell made absolutely no difference to the oncoming stranger. With the haze lifting, the officers assembled on the old gunboat's deck were clearly able to see her house-like shape, her rust brown color, one giant chimney belching forth sparks and black soot, and, most ominously, a sudden puff of smoke at her bow, accompanied by a loud roar. Within seconds, a giant projectile passed overhead. This was not a complimentary missile across her bow, but a cannonball that whizzed between the *Tyler*'s tall chimneys, just above the pilothouse, and splashed into the water far astern.

Neither of the veterans Lt. Brown or Cmdr. Walke, to say nothing of Lt Gwin or Hunter, had ever fought an ironclad before. Indeed, "Delta" tells us that the Union boats were as surprised to actually find the *Arkansas* as she was to find them. "There was common astonishment." Undeterred, the Confederate commander, also garbed "in full-dress uniform," according to Carter, "his tawny beard parted by the wind," ordered colors shown and the *Arkansas* to stand for the *Carondelet.* "I had determined," Brown later revealed, "to try the ram on our iron prow upon the foe, who was so gallantly approaching."

Belowdecks, Lt. Gift observed the scene of his man-of-war cleared for action this warming morning, one shared in common with the Federals downstream as well. As he later recalled:

> Many of the men had stripped off their shirts and were bare to the waists, with handkerchiefs bound round their heads, and some of the officers had removed their coats and stood in their undershirts. The decks had been thoroughly sanded to prevent slipping after the blood should become plentiful. Tourniquets were served out to division officers by the surgeons, with directions for use. The division tubs were filled with water to drink; fire buckets were in place; cutlasses and pistols strapped on; rifles loaded and bayonets fixed; spare breechings for the guns and other implements made ready. The magazines and shell rooms forward and aft were open and the men inspected in their places.

To avoid any loss of speed, the *Arkansas*' forward gunners were ordered to hold their fire. The armorclad would yaw back and forth from side to side as she came on, firing her broadside guns as they bore. Brown knew that the ensuing concussion from the guns when fired in this manner would not arrest her progress as significantly as would otherwise have been the case.

This zigzag tactic would permit the *Arkansas* to gain on the Eads boat. All of them were slow, although Lt. Brown, exercising command from an exposed position outside of the pilothouse, did not immediately know that he was facing his old friend Walke in the *Carondelet,* the pokiest of the seven sister-ironclads. Brown and Walke had been messmates aboard the *Boston* of Com. Lawrence Kearney's prewar Chinca squadron.

Her crab-like maneuvers would also permit the *Arkansas* to keep the *Tyler* and the ram *Queen of the West* occupied and away from her own quarter. From the beginning, however, they were regarded as distractions— Brown's primary goal was to "stand for" the *Carondelet.* When he caught up with the Federal ironclad, the Confederate intended to ram her just as the cotton-clads had struck the *Cincinnati* and *Mound City* at Plum Point Bend.

Lookouts aboard the Union vessels could not immediately discern a flag flying aboard the oncoming enemy. Still, when they saw the huge black guns protruding from the two forward gun ports, everyone from commander to cabin boy quickly figured out that this was, indeed, the "celebrated ram *Arkansas.*" Many Northern sailors doubtless reflected that the refugees and deserters were correct after all. Paymaster Coleman later remembered that, onboard the *Tyler*: "The men sprang to the guns without waiting for the boatswain's whistle; the breakfast things were hastily brushed aside." There would be ship-to-ship action this day. A signal was made to the *Carondelet,* two miles away, that the *Arkansas* was breaking out.

Once the armorclad opened fire, Lt. Gwin immediately returned fire with his bow guns. The *Tyler,* too, had to yaw to accomplish this maneuver. This was not a matter of choice, however, as his most forward guns still had to be angled out of broadside ports. Gwin's courage (and his forward location in the river) brought the initial Southern armorclad wrath down upon the *Tyler.* As soon as the Confederate pilot knew he was safe from grounding, the *Arkansas* steered directly for the one-time Ohio River packet. Upwards of the maximum 120 pounds of steam pressure powered her engines and screws as she launched her pursuit.

Almost immediately, two of the *Tyler*'s 8-inch shells struck the armorclad's bow shield. "The gunnery of the enemy was excellent," remembered Lt. Gift, captain of the *Arkansas*' port side bow and broadside Columbiads. "His rifle bolts soon began to ring on our iron front, digging into and warping up the bars, but not penetrating." Coming to a stop, the *Tyler* reversed engines and began to slowly drop back down, maintaining a continuous fire. "'Stinkpot' against ironclad ram was suicide," as Ivan Musicant put it in 1995.

Every effort was made to maintain enough speed to remain ahead of the enemy, now only 150–200 yards behind. Gwin hoped to reach the "protection" of the *Carondelet* before Mr. Brown smashed his unarmored boat into kindling. Lt. Gift, however, soon got in an opportune and telling shot at Gwin's boat from his huge, black bow Columbiad. An 8-inch shell with a five-second fuse smashed through the *Tyler*'s wooden bulwark, sending up showers of splinters over the decks, and struck in her engine room "fair and square."

Rebel gunner Gift later wrote that, when it exploded, the Confederate projectile killed a pilot in its flight, burst in the engine room, and killed 17, while wounding 14 others. "I think this shell did the better part of the day's work on him," he later opined.

While the *Arkansas* and *Tyler* were paying their mutual respects to one another, Capt. Walke paced the hurricane deck of the *Carondelet* in front of her pilothouse studying the Confederate's approach with his spy glass. Convinced that he faced "a powerful gunboat and ram," he shouted orders for his bow gunners to open fire. Unhappily, the initial shot from his three cannon went wide. As the bolts gained accuracy and hit, they just bounced off the Southern monster's casemate.

The revolutions of the *Arkansas*' twin screws in the fast current soon made it evident to the *Tyler*'s captain that his initial evasion plan was not working. The armorclad, steaming slowly but with determination, was nearly on top of him. Now less than 200 yards from the Rebel, Lt. Gwin ordered the *Tyler* to round to and follow Lt. Hunter's *Queen of the West,* already retreating. As the timberclad yawed, Gunner Peters' men replied with a broadside, but all of their shot seemed to bounce off. The timberclad would remain within 200–300 yards of the *Arkansas* for the next six miles.

As the *Queen of the West* and *Tyler* paddled furiously toward him in retreat, Capt. Walke's gunners continued their effort to halt the oncoming armorclad. Their efforts were in vain. Shells from the *Carondelet*'s three forward guns, and all of her starboard broadside, threw up huge geysers around the enemy; others clanked harmlessly off her armored forecastle.

The *Arkansas* returned fire. Walke later told Prof. Soley that his command was "raked from stem to stern," being hit forward at least three times. "One shot," he remembered, "glanced on the forward plating, passed through the officers' rooms on the starboard side, and through the captain's cabin." As the fireworks continued, the *Tyler* came within "about 100 yards distant on the port bow of the *Carondelet*." When his consort achieved hailing distance, Cmdr. Walke, shouting through his speaking trumpet, ordered Lt. Gwin to speed on down and warn the fleet. Prof. Soley reveals the dilemma Walke now faced: "It now became a question for Walke of the *Carondelet* to decide whether he would advance to meet the *Arkansas* bows-on, trusting to the skillful management of the helm to avoid a ram-thrust, or would he retreat, engaging her with his stern guns. He chose the latter course."

Often criticized in the weeks and years after for the decision he took next, Cmdr. Walke, sensing that he was, indeed, a potential ramming target for the *Arkansas*, also swung about. Being a stern wheeler, the *Carondelet* "required room and time to turn around," and so now rounded to and retreated "to avoid being sunk immediately." As the helmsman spun his huge wheel, the turtle's gunners were able to bring their pieces into play "bow, broadside, and stern." Given that the *Arkansas* was twice as fast as his boat, Walke was convinced she would come up with him as he was fighting bows-on and maneuver around until she could thrust her beak into his side. If that happened, his proud vessel would be "sunk in a few minutes." Taking increasingly serious punishment, the *Carondelet* stood down the Yazoo, trying to stay ahead of the Confederate's dangerous ram.

Even though he knew, in the words of historian Chester Hearn, that he "had no business fighting an ironclad with his flimsy wooden gunboat," Lt. Gwin refused to leave Cmdr. Walke to his fate. Even as the *Arkansas* relentlessly bore down on the *Carondelet*, the *Tyler* stood by her, firing as her guns bore. This did not go unnoticed aboard the *Arkansas*, where Lt. Brown acknowledged that "the stern guns of the *Carondelet* and the *Tyler* were briskly served on us."

For the better part of an hour, the Confederate vessel pursued her Northern enemies in a zigzag fashion designed, wrote Brown, to keep them "from inspecting my boiler plate armor." At one point, the armorclad captain, who continued to fight his ship from an exposed position on the hurricane deck, received a severe head contusion, but upon examining the clotted blood was most relieved not to see any "brains mixed with" it.

The Pook turtle, the principal target of the *Arkansas*, was hit repeatedly. Many shells from the Columbiads of Lts. Gift and Grimball smashed into the *Carondelet*; Capt. Brown thought he could see "the white wood under her armor," not knowing she had no armor aft. Satisfied, the Rebel captain knew, as he wrote years later, that it was only a matter of time until he overtook the Eads creation: "no vessel afloat could long stand rapid raking by 8-inch shot at such short range."

While the armorclad's bullets repeatedly ploughed into the *Carondelet*'s stern, her missiles and those of the timberclad struck the inclined shield of the *Arkansas* and disappeared. Watching the fall of shot through his glasses, Lt. Gwin could not see that those from either vessel were doing much good, "though one of them raised the iron on her bow."

As Cmdr. Walke's boat began to lose headway, Lt. Brown doubtless rubbed his hands together believing that his original plan was coming together. "There was a near prospect of carrying out my first intention of using the ram." The stern of the Eads boat was the "objective point" for the prow of the *Arkansas* as the distance between the major combatants steadily shrank from 500 to 50 yards. The single-minded approach of the *Arkansas* was not made without cost. Aboard the *Tyler,* Gunner Peters and his men were able to blast away at the armorclad, the guns of which remained focused on the *Carondelet.* A moment or so after Lt. Brown escaped the feared loss of his gray matter, a shell from the timberclad hit the hurricane deck at his feet.

The *Tyler*'s shell penetrated into the pilothouse, cut away the forward rim of the steering wheel, and mortally wounded Chief Pilot John G. Hodges, the one guide aboard familiar with Old River. The second pilot was also wounded, leaving only a Missouri volunteer to take over. As they were moved below, the wounded pilots screamed for the captain to remain in the middle of the channel. Lt. Brown, still wanting to smash Walke's boat, told the new man at the wheel to "keep the iron-clad ahead."

Within approximately half an hour of mutual sighting, the *Arkansas* overtook the *Carondelet.* The *Tyler*, keeping pace with the turtle, was now able to intervene again. By this time, the Confederate armorclad was within easy range of the 4th Wisconsin riflemen. The Yankee sharpshooters began rapid volley fire at the *Arkansas,* aiming at her gun ports, portholes— and Lt. Brown, the only human target outside the casemate. Although Lt. Gwin was unable to see a single man "on her upper deck during the entire engagement," a Wisconsin minie ball found his opposite number. Brown's left temple was grazed and he was knocked down the hatchway to the gun deck below. Lts. Stevens and Gift thought their valiant commander a casualty and ordered several sailors to carry him to the sick bay. En route, Brown awoke and, brushing aside worried hands, climbed back up the ladder to his topside post. At this point, the flagstaff of the *Arkansas* was shot away and no effort was made to rehoist the colors.

"I ought to have told Stevens to hold off" the gunners "from the iron-clad," the Rebel captain later confessed, "'till they could finish the *Tyler*, but neither in nor out of battle does one always do the right thing." If Brown had done "the right thing," there is little doubt that the timberclad's story would have ended in the Yazoo right then.

The *Arkansas* now closed the range on the Pook turtle. Aboard the *Carondelet*, now seriously hurt by Rebel fire, her stern gunners gamely kept up the pace with a pair of old 32-pdrs. Their aim was "excellent" and many hits were scored on the enemy's bow casemate. Lt. Gift recorded a part of his opponent's agony: "The *Carondelet* was right ahead of us, distant about 100 yards, and paddling downstream for dear life. Her armor had been pierced four times by [Lt.] Grimball, and we were running after her to use our ram, having the advantage of speed. Opposite to me a man was standing outside on the port-sill loading the stern chaser. He was so near that I could readily have recognized him had he been an acquaintance. I pointed the Columbiad for that port and pulled the lock-string. I have seen nothing of the man or gun since."

Unfortunately for the Yankees, the shots from the lone remaining gun all "seemed to glance off." When less than 50 yards apart, the two armored protagonists departed the main channel and entered a shallow area near the eastern bank where a great number of willows, broken stumps, and reeds protruded above the dark but more shallow water. "The crippled duck," crowed the refugee *Granada Appeal* about the Federal gunboat a few days later on July 23, "commenced his favorite dodge of hunting for shallow water, and for this purpose sheered to the left bank of the river." Still, the Confederate commander ordered his craft as close as possible, even as he watched the *Tyler* and the *Queen*, out in deeper water, looking as thought they were "awaiting our entanglement."

The *Arkansas*, one of the most successful of all the Confederate armorclads, fought a running battle with the *Carondelet* in the Yazoo River on July 15, 1862, before coming out on the Mississippi River to engage the combined Federal fleets. Underpowered, the Confederate craft, nevertheless, crushed the Pook turtle, forcing her into shallow water where the ram could not follow. This is a noted 1904 rendering by the naval artist Robert Skerrett (Naval History and Heritage Command).

As the Confederate armorclad rushed toward the *Carondelet*, there was a momentary thought aboard the Federal craft that a boarding situation might be at hand. Capt. Walke called for boarders and a number of crewmen, led by Coxswain John G. Morrison (1842–1897), climbed to the hurricane deck, via the gun ports, prepared for attack or defense as warranted.

In an entirely fictitious report, the *Philadelphia Inquirer* (and several other Northern newspapers), boldly stated on July 22 that the gunboat's seamen almost succeeded: "Just as the latter [*Arkansas*] was passing over the bar, the *Carondelet* closed with her, intending to board. She succeeded in throwing a grapnel aboard and getting out a plank, when the *Arkansas* opened her steam pipe, throwing hot water across the plank. The *Carondelet* replied in the same manner. While thus engaged, both vessels grounded, and the shock separated them." The *Chicago Daily Tribune* story published next day is even more heroic and fantastic:

> Finding his guns were doing no service, Capt. Walke had his boarders called away, and into the Rebel craft they poured; but not a man or a passage could be found. The boarders now returned and the guns set to work, but it was so much powder wasted. The *Carondelet*'s stern was now perfectly riddled.... At this juncture, Capt. Walke led a party on the Rebels' deck, but could find no possible way of getting below. The hatches were all secured underneath and the smallest kind of an aperture or hole was nowhere to be found. This discovered, the party returned to give up their boat only when the bottom of the river called for her.

When the actual and momentary opportunity passed, Morrison led his volunteers back to their guns. A native of Ireland, Morrison received the Congressional Medal of Honor for his bravery under fire.

Brown of the *Arkansas*, who had been, as Walke feared, hoping all along for a chance to ram the Union ironclad, now saw the *Carondelet*'s course becoming quite erratic. One of his shells shot away the Federal's steering ropes and despite all Walke's damage-control people could do, the turtle became unmanageable. Rebel balls also cut away a number of the Union craft's steam and water pipes and the steam gauge, while others smashed directly through the captain's cabin, continuing on to clear the steerage cabin and lodge in a makeshift bulkhead completed around the boilers just since the 4th of July. Additionally, one of the two 32-pdr. stern chasers was now knocked out. With a brief cloud of steam escaping from her gun ports and losing speed rapidly, the *Carondelet* ran inshore among the trees. A number of the crew, perhaps fearing a boiler would explode, jumped overboard to escape the steam and two men were drowned.

Unable to ram his opponent and advised by the pilot that he could not follow her into the shallow water near the bank, Lt. Brown avoided grounding at the last moment when he screamed "Hard-a-starboard!" This order brought the *Arkansas* sliding alongside within 30 feet of the *Carondelet* and, in passing, she loosed a terrible broadside. The Confederate crew followed it up with "three hearty cheers" and then continued firing from her stern chasers.

Over a century later, Kevin Carson pointed out how fortunate it was for the hopes of the South that the *Arkansas*, in fact, turned away. "Had the Confederate ironclad followed the Union ship," he wrote in 2006, "they both would have run onto the shoals. That would have ended things for the Confederates right there, but such was not the case."

The blast of the *Arkansas*'s full port broadside was so powerful that her gunners were able to see the *Carondelet* "heel to port and then roll back so deeply as to take water over her deck forward of the shield [casemate]." Despite this blast, Walke's starboard gunners were able to send a partial broadside into the ram as she passed ahead. Some of these cannonballs were seen by Yankee bluejackets to take effect, as a pair of holes opened on the enemy's port beam.

As the *Arkansas* continued to move off, the bow guns of the Eads boat, silent for some time, were able to open up once more. However, at the same time they detonated, the *Carondelet* hit a small stump, causing all three shots to fly wild. Turning his own stern 32-

pdrs. on the grounded Pook turtle, Capt. Brown ordered his craft to continue downriver, leaving Walke's boat, as he put it to Flag Officer Lynch later in the day, "hanging on to the willows."

The captain and crew of the *Arkansas* believed and later testified that they had defeated the vaunted *Carondelet*, both actually and formally. "The rascal," boasted the *Granada Appeal* editor, was seen to "haul down his colors, set a white flag, and desert his vessel." Indeed, after the armorclad reached Vicksburg, the story was magnified. Walke's vessel became the Western Flotilla flagboat *Benton* and she, in the hurried prose of *Jackson Mississippian* correspondent "Subaltern," "was on the bottom of the river near the shore, careened to one side, and her career ended forever!" Robert G. Hartje, biographer of Vicksburg commander Maj. Gen. Van Dorn, later opined that the *Carondelet* "should have been forced to surrender except that the ironclad [*Arkansas*] could not risk delay."

When the armorclad captain announced to the sweating crew the victory the *Arkansas* had achieved, there was, according to Lt. Gift, considerable "yelling and cheering" all over the boat. In 15 minutes, the Confederate seamen had "thrashed three of the enemy's vessels— one carrying arms as good as ours."

Although Cmdr. Walke vehemently protested that he did return fire and that his flag was not down as all of the *Arkansas*' officers later testified, two facts stood out. The heaviest of the three reconnoitering Northern craft was out of action, steam escaping from her as she lay on the bank a mile and a half from the mouth of the Yazoo. Four men aboard were killed, 16 wounded, and 10 missing. "Walke had fired 90 rounds," Jim Miles points out. "He thought he had accomplished everything that could have been expected of him."[4]

The entire close quarters engagement between the *Arkansas* and *Carondelet* was witnessed with uncertainty and alarm from the *Tyler* and the *Queen*. It was difficult for their officers and men to tell exactly what was happening, though the Pook boat did suddenly seem to run into the bank. At that point, the *Arkansas* moved toward Walke, coming almost abreast, and fired every gun brought to bear. "Until it was evident that the ram was intent upon continuing her journey down the river," Paymaster Coleman remembered, "we considered the capture of *Carondelet* certain." Once the Yankee ironclad was disabled in the weeds of a riverbank sandbar, the *Arkansas* "turned toward the spiteful *Tyler* and the wary ram." Lt. Brown now determined "to do the right thing" and get the timberclad.

The boats of Gwin or Hunter were never a match for the armorclad and now both "very properly" took advantage of a speed double Brown's to seek the safety of the combined fleet. "Our last view of *Carondelet*," Coleman confessed as *Tyler* and *Queen* left the scene, "was through a cloud of enveloping smoke with steam escaping from her ports and of her men jumping overboard."

Watching the rust-colored enemy plough back into the channel, Lt. Gwin knew that he dare not linger or he would die. As the *Tyler*'s commander unashamedly later confessed, "I stood down the river with all speed." Running like an energized paddle-wheel bunny, though nowhere near as fast, the *Tyler* set course to warn the fleet. Over the next hour, she took a pounding from the Confederate guns, but it was not all one-sided. As the *Arkansas* neared the Mississippi, the effectiveness of the *Tyler*'s shot began to tell. With her chimney "shot through and through" and smoke pouring out the shrapnel and minie ball perforations, the draft for her fires was lessened. The steam pressure so necessary to propulsion now dropped steadily from 120 pounds to about 20 pounds, which was barely enough to keep the engines turning. Using the ram fell completely out of the question as the speed of the *Arkansas* approached just 3 mph.

At long last — 8:30 A.M., according to the timberclad's logbook — the *Tyler* was able to turn out of Tuscumbia Bend into the broad Mississippi around De Soto Point, with the *Arkansas* snapping at her heels. Aided by the current, the two boats rapidly approached the Farragut-Davis fleet. Scharf says the timberclad was actually a half hour ahead of the armorclad, which gave the Federal fleet "sufficient time to prepare for the reception of the unwelcome visitor."

Aboard the units of the Federal fleet, the thunder back up the Yazoo had been heard for some time. The officer of the deck aboard Flag Officer Farragut's flagship, U.S.S. *Hartford*, wrote in her log at 7:00 A.M.: "heavy firing heard up the river, supposed to be artillery on shore." The noisy commotion was noticed in Vicksburg. Hundreds of civilians hurried to rooftops, the bluffs, and the levee to watch and cheer. A century later, the town newspaper opined that "Probably no vessel in history had the hopes of so many people riding with her."

Lt. Brown warned his pilot to steer as close to Farragut's wooden ships as possible in order that Ellet's rams could not strike. Thus it was that the *Arkansas* fought her way "within pistol shot" right through an intense bombardment by the vessels of the stationary Union fleet. Easily visible throughout the fight was "the smoke from the heavy guns in the still air" as it "began to settle on the water." Surviving this fiery gauntlet, the Rebel armorclad reached the protection of Vicksburg's batteries and received a rousing Rebel reception. Years later, Lt. Gift reflected that their day's work represented "the first and *only* square, fair, *equal* stand-up and knock-down fight between the two navies in which the Confederates came out first best." Flag Officer Davis himself observed that Brown's passage "was certainly a very exciting and pleasing sight so far as the gallantry of the thing was concerned."

"Much of Brown's spectacular success against the Federal Fleet was due to the fact," Jack D. Coombe opines, "that his enemy was asleep on the watch, with its steam down to conserve fuel." Writing immediately after the war, Northern naval historian Charles Boynton was straightforward in his review. "Her appearance was so sudden, our officers were so conscious of having been caught unprepared, and the success of the bold maneuver was so complete that, for a time," he revealed, "the prevailing feeling was simply astonishment."

Flag Officer Farragut in particular has been roundly criticized over the years for not being more fully prepared, knowing as he did that a sortie by the *Arkansas* was a distinct possibility. In all honesty, as Musicant reminds us, "For both Davis and Farragut, it was an inexcusable lapse." "Delta" told readers in the Crescent City that they could surely believe "our folks were chagrined and chopfallen for a moment." To paraphrase and continue Coombe's thought, both flag officers, however, "should have been more prepared for the much anticipated sortie by the Confederate ram down the Yazoo." They "should have alerted the entire fleet, instead of just several vessels — even if one of them was the legendary *Carondelet*."

Northern newspapers, unlike those in the South, downplayed the success of the armorclad and, as reported in a headline of the *Philadelphia Inquirer* on July 22, dwelt on the "desperate encounter" fought against her. Henry Bentley, the paper's correspondent, wrote three days later that the contest between the *Carondelet* and the *Arkansas* "was a brilliant affair, and had it not been that the former ran aground and could not free herself, the Rebel craft would never have passed into the Mississippi River." "A few more shots were exchanged," wrote Junius Henri Browne, "when the *Arkansas* made off and hastened so rapidly down the river that the *Carondelet*, in her crippled condition, could not follow her."

When the embarrassed U.S. navy secretary, Gideon Welles, heard and digested the full story of the Rebel armorclad's achievement, he wrote to both Farragut and Davis on July 25 stating the department's "regret" that the *Arkansas* had slipped through the fleet "owing to the unprepared condition of the naval vessels." That vessel, he ordered, "must be destroyed at all hazards."[5]

Although out of action, *Carondelet* could be repaired. There would be no need, as Walke frankly feared during the heat of battle, for her to be salvaged from the bottom of the channel. As the *Tyler*, *Queen*, and *Arkansas* passed out of sight, the wounded aboard the Eads ironclad were, as possible, brought up to the hurricane deck to escape the heat and steam belowdecks. During the remainder of the morning, as the Rebel armorclad reached and passed through the combined Union fleet, crewmen aboard the damaged craft were mustered and accounted for and then labored mightily to get her back to base.

In these hours, damage control parties made repairs and surveyed the situation. It was found that the gunboat had received 13 "effective shots" and her hull and machinery took "extensive damage." The carpenter reported that 19 beams were cut away along with 30 timbers; three small boats were cut up; the deck pumps were cut away; and davits, pieces of the chimneys, hammock netting, and chunks of the casemate were missing. Three escape pipes were cut away, the engineer added, along with the steam gauge and two water pipes.

With the most important shot holes patched and the turtle able to get up steam, the *Carondelet* slowly pulled out of the willows and returned to the main channel. She had not been forgotten. Just after the *Tyler* had anchored and even as the *Arkansas* was passing through the fleet, Lt. Gwin sought aid for the *Carondelet.* The newly arrived *General Bragg* was ordered to steam immediately to the Yazoo and provide help. The assistance of the onetime Confederate warship was not required, as the *Carondelet*, her immediate injuries addressed, was able to rejoin the fleet not long after the *Arkansas* reached Vicksburg. Shortly after the *Carondelet*'s arrival, about 8:30 A.M., the hospital boat *Red Rover* tied up alongside and took off the wounded.

The debate over Cmdr. Walke's handling of the *Carondelet* during her encounter with the *Arkansas* began to rage within days of its occurrence and has continued ever since. Most of the initial indictment came, naturally enough, from the Southern press and Confederate navy officers, who continued it on into the postwar memoir-writing period. It was whispered throughout the Western Flotilla at the time that the commander was ill or, at age 55, no longer in fighting trim. He was, as Ivan Musicant put it, "faulted for 'running away,' as some ignorantly thought." As late as 2003, William L. Shea and Terrence J. Winschel wrote that "Walke panicked and lost control of his flotilla."

The former point may certainly have had some impact upon the manner in which Walke chose to engage the *Arkansas.* The *Carondelet*'s captain, a man stung earlier by the navy's retiring board and a court-martial, could admit no error in a third case, even if it might have been caused by illness. What is not commonly taken into account in judgments of his actions during this encounter was the fact that Walke was probably sick. On July 20, he was confined for a fever — doubtless malaria — aboard the *Red Rover* for a period of two days. This disease would continue to haunt him as long as he served on the inland waters. Just how bad this fever was at the time of the *Arkansas* battle or what effect it might have had upon his tactical decisions is impossible to say precisely. This writer believes, however, that it may have been considerable.

Capt. Walke's nemesis, Lt. Cmdr. Seth Ledyard Phelps, failing to acknowledge the possibility of sickness, believed the *Carondelet*'s captain was too old and unfit for his position:

"Walke is a brave man and a reliable one when minutely directed as to what is expected of him. He made a fatal error in judgment in the Yazoo when he met the *Arkansas.* Had he kept head to the enemy, the *Carondelet* and *Tyler* would have destroyed him where they met. It was no lack of determination on Walke's part. Younger men are wanted who have the physical energy and habit which will lead them to drill & exercise and discipline their officers and men personally and constantly." The state of his health (and age) aside, two fighting questions are usually raised: (1) Was it a mistake for Walke to avoid fighting the Rebel ram bows-on; and (2) Was the *Carondelet*'s flag struck in surrender? Let us revisit these points.

In respect to the decision to round to, it is now generally conceded that Capt. Walke erred in judgment. It has been suggested that, had Walke elected to engage Brown bows-on, he might have stopped the ram — or at least not have been badly damaged. This view is based on the knowledge that the Federal's shot outweighed the Rebel's by 44 pounds, 150 to 106. Additionally, the thick, specially built armor plating on the forward casemate of the *Carondelet,* designed to battle the heavy guns of land forts, should have proven superior to the old railroad tracks covering the sides of the *Arkansas.*

There is no question that the surprise appearance of the Confederate armorclad — the ram all the newspapers had been speculating upon for some time — and her offensive gunnery were effective. As soon as the *Arkansas* was within range, her shot began raking the *Carondelet* "from stem to stern." The retreat of the *Tyler* and the *Queen of the West* could not have been reassuring.

It was, however, the unknown size and shape of ram at the *Arkansas*' bow that concerned Capt. Walke. Early in the fight, before her chimney was perforated, causing her progress to be slowed, the twin-screwed enemy was descending upon him at a speed difficult to determine. It was not fast, but it was steady. Having seen the effectiveness of rams at Plum Point Bend and Memphis, Walke was concerned that he not become the victim of one, his proud ironclad sacrificed to the ooze of the Yazoo.

Considerable debate on the captain's decision to round to occupied space on the *Civil War Navy Messageboard* in March 2006. One contributor, George Wright, pointed out that, compared to the *Arkansas,* the Union vessel "and her sisters were pigs to steer." Warming to his subject, he continued: "Her rudders were normally 'blown' by the current coming out of the wheel. When being backed, you lost this additional flow over the rudders and steering suffered." Not only that, but "speed backing was also penalized."

What Walke may have failed to fully consider, either on July 15 or in later years, was what the actual effect a collision between the two boats would have been "in that narrow river." The *Arkansas,* though smaller than the *Carondelet,* was no swift cotton-clad like those fleet Confederate boats at Plum Point Bend or even the somewhat heavier Ellet rams employed at Memphis. Although twice as fast as the *Carondelet* at top speed, the *Arkansas* was still awfully slow and zigzagging to boot. Even had she managed to run into the bow of the *Carondelet,* it would have taken a fairly direct hit to sink the Eads craft. In all probability, the Rebel would only have succeeded in shoving the broad-beamed *Carondelet* aside.

In any event, Walke was not prepared, for whatever reason, to accept the enemy's blow, believing it better to join his consorts in withdrawal, perhaps drawing — as he certainly succeeded in doing — the full attention of the *Arkansas* while the *Queen* and *Tyler,* as he ordered, steamed to warn the fleet. On the other hand, as George Wright contends, Walke's first instinct was to keep his command intact. "Logically, the *Carondelet*'s only hope was to run for it and hope that the presence of other Union steamers would cause the *Arkansas* to split her fire."

Despite a ferocious defense of his actions in his memoirs, the hero of Island No. 10 lived long enough to read unfavorable reviews by impartial critics. In 1882, Alfred T. Mahan, whom Walke knew and who had praised so highly his action at Island No. 10, weighed in

Capt. Walke's artistic depictions of the *Carondelet*'s encounter with the *Arkansas* were both published in his memoirs. Neither is wholly accurate (Walke, *Naval Scenes and Reminiscences*).

Tied to shore, the *Carondelet* here shows us her stern. This vulnerable area, home to two 32-pounders, was badly damaged by the *Arkansas* as she engaged. Note the awnings designed to help keep away the fearsome summer heat and the ladder leading from the fantail to the hurricane deck (Naval History and Heritage Command).

on the debate. In his still-quoted history of the war on Western Waters, the future strategic thinker bluntly stated that the loyal Virginian's tactics were "not judicious" because they exposed the weakest part of his craft. "Besides," Mahan continued, "when two vessels are approaching on parallel courses, the one that wishes to avoid the ram, may perhaps do so by a maneuver of her helm." But when the slowest ship, in this case the *Carondelet,* "has presented her stern to the enemy, she has thrown up the game, barring some fortunate accident."

Just after Mahan, Prof. James R. Soley published a more concise review in his piece "Naval Operations in the Vicksburg Campaign" for the Century Company's *Battles and Leaders* series. The naval academy academic readily admitted that the *Arkansas* "was decidedly the superior vessel," better armed and armored. The *Carondelet* was only partially protected and her stern "was not armored at all." He then crushed her commander. "The position adopted by Walke was the one," he concluded, "which, by exposing his weakest point, gave the enemy the benefit of his superiority." When the *Carondelet* presented her unarmored stern armed with two ancient 32-pdrs. and then engaged in an hour-long running fight with the two 8-inch guns carried forward by the *Arkansas,* it was "little short of a miracle ... that she escaped total destruction." To perhaps soften the blow, Soley tells his readers that once the decision was taken, "Walke made a very good fight of it."

Today, most Civil War writers accept the views of Mahan and Soley and kindly refrain from mention of the controversy over the *Carondelet*'s maneuver even in books or articles in which the armorclad's breakout is featured. They prefer to heap well-deserved accolades upon both boats, forgiving the temporary failures of captains who gave exemplary service.

There are many sides taken on the truth of our second question concerning the striking of the *Carondelet*'s flag, and Adm. Mahan found it impossible to resolve them in the

1880s. In his account of the battle, Cmdr. Brown contended that, in passing the grounded Union vessel, he saw "their ports were closed, no flag was flying, not a man or officer was in view, [and] not a sound or shot was heard." Confederate Acting Masters Mate John A. Wilson saw the Federal boat was "compelled to strike her colors," while Lt. Gift noted "the enemy hauled down his colors." Neither Capt. Walke or Gwin corroborated this signaling of surrender in their reports to Flag Officer Davis— or even mentioned it. In their story of July 23, the correspondent of the *Chicago Daily Tribune* wrote in passing: "The flag which still floated from her stern was never to be struck to the Rebels as so long as one board floated to hold it up."

Later, when the subject became an item of controversy, Walke flatly stated: "The flag of the *Carondelet* waved undisturbed during the battle." It was not until 67 years later that the actual events of this controversy may have been resolved in an obscure personal letter forgotten in a filebox. In 1929, Mr. A.B. Donaldson of Cleveland, OH, wrote a letter to secretary of the navy Charles F. Adams. His uncle, Oliver Donaldson, was a mate and chief carpenter aboard the *Carondelet* in July 1862. According to a testimonial which accompanied his nephew's letter, the late ironclad sailor claimed that the gunboat's colors were shot away during the engagement with the *Arkansas.* When the flag fluttered into the muddy Yazoo, he dived in to retrieve it. Once the Southern monster had passed down and the *Carondelet* was alone in the willows, the rescued bunting was again hoisted to the main and was waving there when the turtle rejoined the fleet. The disputed flag, given to Donaldson after the war, is today at the U.S. Naval Academy Museum. Interestingly, the deck log of the *Carondelet* notes, among its record of carnage aboard on July 15, that when the *Arkansas* passed the grounded Eads craft, her "flag was down and not hoisted again while in sight." No debate ever surrounded its absence.

Cmdr. Walke's reputation did not suffer as a result of this event until years later when Civil War officers wrote their memoirs or offered comments before patriotic groups. The captain's encounter with "the Ram" was written up at the time as "a most gallant exploit" against overwhelming odds. Luckily for him, as a result of the *Arkansas*' escape from the combined Union fleet, official heat fell not on him, but upon Davis and Farragut.

At the same time, doubtless intrigued by the pile of documents, petitions, and reports taking up space supporting Walke's good works with the Western Flotilla since the time after his court-martial when he was posted west, Secretary Welles decided to include the *Carondelet*'s skipper on the list for advancement. On July 16, Welles mailed Walke word of his promotion to the rank of captain.

Had Welles suspected that Walke had displayed faulty judgment in combat the day before, one might reasonably speculate that the one-time lighthouse inspector's enhanced credentials never would have left his desk. Fortunately for the *Carondelet*'s captain, the same fate that robbed him of glory at Island No. 10 spared him shame in the Yazoo. There was no 24-hour news, the mails moved slowly, Washington offices, often noted for political intrigue, rapidly filled with intelligence of important defeats and advances, and those newspapers that filed dispatches to the Federal city all masked Walke's decision not to fight bows-on, with several actually making him a dime-novel type hero for his supposed boarding exploits.

After rejoining the flotilla, the tars of the *Carondelet* continued to make repairs to their boat. In what was by now a long-standing practice, as one of the newcomers would later remark, many of the musket balls were not dug out, but were simply allowed to remain "in the timber and upper works where it is not iron plated" as visible reminders of combat.

With Capt. Walke returned from the *Red Rover*, Flag Officer Davis was piped aboard on the morning of July 22 to examine the ironclad's state. Moving around the decks with the visibly weakened Walke, the flotilla leader was aghast at the terrible personnel conditions aboard. As a result of the fever epidemic sweeping the area, one of every two sailors aboard the gunboat was ill.

At noon, a tug came alongside the *Carondelet* with orders that she return upriver for professional repairs, making stops en route at Carlton Landing and Memphis to review matters and communicate with local commanders. At Mound City, her officers and men would be granted personal and sick leave.

Due to illness and the falling river level, the blue-water fleet of Flag Officer Farragut, in Vicksburg waters since the end of June, departed its station below the Southern citadel on July 24 and headed back down to Baton Rouge and New Orleans. Farragut's withdrawal from Vicksburg forced Flag Officer Davis to also abandon the month long close-in nautical presence off Vicksburg and, initially, move upstream to the mouth of the Yazoo River. On July 30, the lower anchorage of the Western Flotilla was shifted to Helena, Arkansas.

Stopping only to rescue survivors from a sunken dispatch boat, the *Sallie Wood*, the *Carondelet* arrived at Mound City on August 5. Here she would remain in the hands of the carpenters for the next 70 days.[6] Returning from leave on August 24, 1862, Capt. Walke was extremely disappointed to find that repairs being made to the *Carondelet* after her bout with the *Arkansas* were far from completed. On September 4, he wrote to Flag Officer Davis, commander of the Western Flotilla, that "she will be detained longer than was expected, I fear."

Taking advantage of a continuing lull in riverine operations and not knowing when his Pook turtle would be ready, Walke sought a transfer to one of the new ironclads James Eads was building at the Carondelet yards near St. Louis. No answer was received. A general shakeup was about to take place in the western navy and Davis chose not to make any promises concerning new appointments.

In July, the Western Flotilla was ordered transferred from the War Department to the Navy Department and redesignated the Mississippi Squadron. Flag Officer Davis would be rotated back to Washington, D.C., and his place taken by the colorful David Dixon Porter. The official date for the reconfiguration was October 1, but the actual changeover would come in mid–October.[7]

The *Carondelet* was at the fleet operational base at Cairo, Illinois, by the second week of September, where carpenters continued to make final repairs. On September 25, Fleet Capt. Alexander M. Pennock, the facility commander and the officer charged with vessel overhauls, wrote to now Acting Rear Adm. Davis to say, among other things, "that the *Carondelet* would probably be ready early next week." Pennock had received requests from the Federal army for support in the Fort Pillow area and promised to "communicate with Capt. Walke upon the subject."

The extensive rebuilding and refurbishment of the hero vessel of Island No. 10 was finally completed at the beginning of October. In anticipation of the arrival of the new squadron commander, Acting Rear Adm. Porter, Davis asked Walke on October 7 to hoist his flag onboard the *Carondelet* on the morning of October 9. At that point, Walke's craft was the flotilla flagboat.

The new squadron commander arrived at Cairo on October 15 following an inspection tour of Ohio River and St. Louis boatbuilding and facilities. A change of command ceremony was duly held. Davis' flag was lowered from the main yard of the *Carondelet* and

Porter's was hoisted; the customary salute was then fired by the boat's howitzer. Porter remembered the event in a letter to navy assistant secretary Gustavus Vasa Fox on October 17: "I have been much pleased with my reception here by ... Pennock and Walke, who met me with open arms." The new leader was very pleased to have the counsel of the *Carondelet*'s skipper. As his latest biographer put it in 1996, "Nobody knew conditions on the river better than Walke."

As Porter familiarized himself with squadron details and conditions, he often exchanged visits with Walke, whose experience made him an excellent source of information. The *Carondelet*'s captain, whom Lt. George Gift of the *Arkansas* styled "a renegade Virginian," appealed to the much-younger Porter. Working in a frenzy to beef up his new command, the admiral soon chose Walke to lead the squadron's lower division.

On October 18, Walke received orders to take the *Carondelet* to Helena, Arkansas, to assume command of the gunboats in that quarter, to defend the town against a rumored attack, and to aid in a contemplated army advance up the White River. If any hostility was met, Porter instructed his southern troubleshooter to "leave your mark wherever you go."[8] The *Carondelet* arrived off Helena five days later. Unhappily, it was quickly learned that the level of the White River was so low that no Federal force could ascend. Although a Confederate attack on the Arkansas coastal community was expected "at any moment," it never occurred.

It was not until the middle of November that the Federal army sounded the "all clear" for Helena. Walke now agreed, per Porter's earlier directive, to provide support while forces under Brig. Gen. Alvin P. Hovey steamed up the White toward the Post of Arkansas. This planned expedition was also doomed by low water. After the *Carondelet* returned to Helena, her captain had a mild recurrence of his old illness, characterized by a "couple of shakes." By November 20, Walke was apparently better.

Toward the end of November, rumors began circulating concerning a new Federal move on Vicksburg. On November 21, Acting Rear Adm. Porter confirmed these in an order sending his "Lower Division" down to the Yazoo. There Capt. Walke was to clear Rebel batteries from the river's entrance "as far as your guns will reach." The navy had to create one or more landing sites "for the army at all events." The *Carondelet*, with a small supporting squadron, arrived above the Rebel fortress town on November 28 and anchored off Milliken's Bend, Louisiana. Unhappily, the Yazoo, like the White, was down and only the smallest steamers could ascend it for another two plus weeks.

When, on December 11, the Yazoo finally began to rise, a number of expeditions were sent in to ascertain the level of Confederate riverbank defenses. The steaming was made difficult by the placement of large numbers of underwater mines, called "torpedoes" in those days, one of which claimed the *Carondelet*'s sister boat, the *Cairo*. During this period, Capt. Walke was again often down with recurring malaria attacks, though these seemed to clear again by mid-month.

By Christmas, Acting Rear Adm. Porter had arrived to take over command of local operations and aid what turned out to be Maj. Gen. William T. Sherman's ill-fated advance to Chickasaw Bayou. During the attack, the *Carondelet*, and Henry Walke, who was still seeing a doctor daily as he would for some time, remained guarding the squadron's support vessels at the mouth of the Yazoo.

On December 30, Capt. Walke received an invitation to come upstream and breakfast with the admiral. "I have some plans to arrange with you," Porter teased. Accordingly, the *Carondelet* tied up to the flagboat *Black Hawk* early on New Year's Eve. Over coffee at the

As a result of the great Northern victories at Memphis and New Orleans, the latter captured by forces under Flag Officer David G. Farragut in late April, vessels from the Union's Western Flotilla and West Gulf Coast Blockading Squadron were able to meet above the Confederate citadel at Vicksburg on July 1. Preparations were made to attack the city's upper batteries (*Harper's Weekly*, July 26, 1862).

squadron commander's sumptuous table, Walke received some of the best news a sick but determined naval officer could have. His September request for command of a larger ironclad was being granted. First, however, Porter had a little job for him to perform further up the Mississippi.

While Sherman's men were failing against the entrenched Confederates in Chickasaw Bayou, intelligence was being received that Rebel Brig. Gen. Nathan B. Forrest was planning an attack upon New Madrid and Island No. 10. Alarmed, Porter wanted the *Carondelet* to go up and hold the place "against any force that may be sent there." Taking his leave, Capt. Walke returned aboard his turtle and began preparations for a return to the scene of his greatest professional success.[9]

9

Transition, January–March 1863

During the afternoon of January 1, 1863, a tug came down the Yazoo River and made fast alongside the *Carondelet*, now lying at the bank near Johnson's Plantation. Orders were passed aboard for the ironclad's commander, Capt. Henry Walke, from the squadron commander, Acting Rear Adm. David Dixon Porter. Once this written directive, based upon discussions between the two officers aboard the *Black Hawk* on the last day of 1862, was delivered, the little messenger returned upstream.

Porter, concerned about rumored activities by Confederate Brig. Gen. Nathan B. Forrest across the Mississippi from New Madrid, Missouri, wanted the *Carondelet* moved up to Island No. 10 and anchored in a position that would enable the Eads-built turtle to hold the island. As news traveled slowly in those days, he did not know that the town and island were reoccupied by the 30th Missouri (U.S.) the day before.[1]

At sundown, Acting Ensign Walter E.H. Fentress and Acting Master's Mate John Bath, both of whom had been serving on detached duty aboard the flagboat *Black Hawk* due to their expert knowledge of mortars, returned aboard the turtle. Toward 8:30 P.M., the *Carondelet* cast off from the bank and gathered speed down the swollen Yazoo toward its mouth. An hour and a half later, she began her journey up the Mississippi, joined by her tender, the tug *Laurel*.[2]

Coal for ironclad steaming was scarce at this time, and even though Porter had indicated to Walke that towage was available, none could be found, the *Laurel* being too small to do the job alone. Thus, the *Carondelet* used her own meager supply of coal — in addition to supplying 20 to 30 bushels at a time to the tender. On the morning of January 4, the captain ordered his pilot to steer the boat into the bank at Island No. 89. Once she was tied up, a party, accompanied by pickets, was dispatched ashore to bring off some wooden fence rails for use as fuel. This common procedure, known as "railing" throughout the squadron, would be repeated twice more this day and occasionally in the days ahead.[3]

The ironclad received her first tow on January 7. At 6:00 A.M., in response to the red flag that Capt. Walke had ordered his signalman to hoist, Capt. Robert Getty — the first to see the bunting — ordered his tinclad, the *Marmora*, to go alongside. A hawser was passed and the light draught began pulling the squat, black *Carondelet* up the river toward Helena. During the middle of the afternoon, the tinclad *Juliet* came in sight and also took a hawser. The veteran crusader, pulled by two light draughts, began to make some speed. About 6:30 P.M., the hawsers were cast off and a half hour later, the *Carondelet* was tied to one of the coal barges moored off the Arkansas town.[4]

After reviewing the local military situation with Federal army officers, Capt. Walke ordered the *Carondelet* and the *Laurel*, newly coaled, to resume their march upstream on the afternoon of January 9, with the former under tow by the steamer *V.F. Wilson*. Halted by heavy rain and fog, the trio reached Memphis on the afternoon of January 10. Once again, consultations with local officials were held prior to Walke's departure at dusk.

The passage up the river was proving anything but swift. To compensate, orders were passed for the group to continue upriver regardless of time or the elements. Although this decision would help the gunboat reach her destination hours earlier, it was not without risk. During mid-watch (12:00 A.M.–4:00 A.M.) on January 11, a collision was narrowly averted with another vessel coming downstream. According to diarist Lyons, Capt. Walke then supposedly came on deck in a towering rage and, after surveying the situation, ordered the officer of the deck, Oliver Donaldson, arrested and confined to quarters immediately. Although the *Carondelet*'s logbook does not note the incident and there is no other supporting evidence that it actually happened, Donaldson did not again sign the log as OOD until January 18.

Collision, however, was not the most dangerous navigational hazard a gunboat sailor faced. In number one rank among nonmilitary disasters was a longstanding plague of steamboatmen, the snag or its cousin, the bobbing "sawyer." The *Carondelet* was en route above Fort Pillow not long before midnight on January 11 when a sawyer smashed into her port side. Crewmen raced on deck as the vessel's whistle signaled the *V.F. Wilson* to stop. The snag rose up and continued aft, sweeping away all of the awning stanchions and hammock nettings as far back as the boat davits of the first cutter, the bow of which was stove in. Additionally, the large hog chain with both its stanchions was broken; the midship stanchions, ridgepole, and the mainmast came down; and a number of skylights were smashed. After the sawyer was pushed off, the vessel was cleared and repairs begun. The mainmast and heavy stanchions would have to come from the Cairo base, but all else could be fixed by the carpenters. The *Wilson* was signaled to resume her tow; and about 8:00 P.M. on Monday, January 12, the *Carondelet* and her consorts tied up to a quay at New Madrid.

On Tuesday, Walke conferred with military forces ashore, where he learned the Confederates had abandoned plans to attack either New Madrid or nearby Island No. 10. A little after 2:30 P.M., his ironclad anchored off the upper end of the island on the Kentucky side.[5]

On Saturday evening, January 17, the tinclad *New Era* hove around Island No. 10, making herself known by signal to Acting Ensign Fentress, the *Carondelet*'s OOD. Capt. Walke was summoned topside as the light draught anchored. Messages and orders were sent aboard, including news of the Union victory in the Battle of Arkansas Post. Later, one communication from Acting Rear Adm. Porter was savored by the ironclad's commander.

During the last days of 1862, James B. Eads, father of the City Series gunboats, was completing work on one of several large ironclads that Cmdr. William D. "Dirty Bill" Porter — the admiral's brother — had sanctioned on behalf of the War Department the previous June. Fearing rumors that, like the *Arkansas*, Rebel gunboats abuilding up the Yazoo might turn out to be real, the squadron commander wrote to Fleet Capt. Pennock at the Cairo naval station authorizing him to send a message down to Island No. 10 ordering Walke to come on up immediately. Upon his arrival, he was to take command of the *Lafayette*, as she was christened, and supervise her "fitting out." When ready, she was to steam down to Porter's lower fleet anchorage.

At exactly 8:00 A.M. Sunday morning, January 18, the entire crew of the *Carondelet* was mustered on the spar deck to bid farewell to their skipper. Down on the fantail, an honor guard was drawn up in line to present arms as a drummer stood nearby ready to beat the retreat. A few minutes later, Capt. Henry Walke appeared, offered a little speech of thanks to the assemblage, and then shook hands with his officers. As the drummer took up the beat, the veteran commander saluted the flag and deck and, followed by his coxswain, steward, cook, cabinboy Maurice Phillips, and clerk Thomas Lyons, boarded the *Dahlia* for the quick hop over to the *New Era.* While the tug steamed across the smooth water, the turtle's bluejackets gave three cheers for the departing men.

Interestingly, captain's clerk Thomas Lyons, the man who kept the *Anonymous Journal* we have been citing, continued his diary — with the same title save a change in the warship's name — aboard the *Lafayette* from January 20 to June 25. Pilot John Deming would join the group a few days later, along with several other men. Capt. Walke had permission to take up to 25 men from his former vessel to help make up for the lack of new recruits available from the Cairo receiving ship.

Following Walke's departure, the *Carondelet*'s executive officer, Acting Volunteer Lt. Edward E. Brennand, read himself into command and inspected the still-mustered crew before dismissing it for Divine Services. Walke had met with Brennand shortly before the ceremony to inform him of Porter's orders and the fact that his tenure as boat commander would be temporary. Shortly thereafter, the *V.F. Wilson* arrived from Cairo. Coming alongside, she left a coal barge, various provisions, and several replacements.

In the days following the command change, Capt. Brennand, whom Lt. Cmdr. Selfridge would judge "one of the most capable of our volunteer officers," kept his men hard at work finishing the ironclad's repairs, drilling constantly and keeping a close watch on river traffic. The *New Era* relieved the *Carondelet* as the island's guardian on January 25 and, at 6:00 P.M., Brennand's boat cast off and started downriver toward the Yazoo.

While Brennand refreshed his command, Capt. Walke's full-time replacement was coming west as a result of a December 21, 1862 telegram. Unfortunately for him, he would be too late to reach the ironclad, as originally intended, before she left Island No. 10. The *Carondelet*'s rapid departure also interfered with the plans of her former commander, who had not figured on the speed with which his successor would have repairs completed. On January 22, Walke had written to Porter asking that the *Carondelet* be sent to Cairo, where she could be repaired, receive new guns, and transfer a portion of her officers and crew to the *Lafayette.* Before Acting Rear Adm. Porter could receive and reply to the message, the volunteer captain had the ironclad steaming down the Mississippi. Such efficiency would soon win Brennand command of the tinclad *Prairie Bird.*[6]

Composing a telegram to Acting Rear Adm. Porter shortly before Christmas 1862, former colonel of New York Engineers, John McLeod Murphy indicated a preference to return to his "first love — the Navy." As a result of the "fiasco at Fredericksburg," the 32-year-old Murphy had quit the Army of the Potomac in hopes of serving under the Mississippi Squadron commander — an old acquaintance, "one upon whom the hearts and hopes of our people are centered." The ex-army man, who planned to bring with him some 50 men from his old regiment, confessed that it might take some time to get secretary of war Edwin Stanton to approve the transfers and get his company entrained. "In the meantime," Murphy continued, "I hope you will reserve a command that may in some measure assimilate with the one I have resigned." Fleet Capt. Pennock sent the wire down with other messages aboard the December 23 mail boat. In his reply a few days later, Porter told both the Cairo station chief and Capt. Walke that he intended to give *Carondelet* to Murphy.[7]

As Col. Murphy, who would have the rank of acting volunteer lt. in the navy, hurried about Washington attempting to get his men transferred to the navy, the *Carondelet* continued her unexciting passage down the Mississippi. Memphis was visited on January 27 and Helena the next day. As the *Carondelet* continued down in cold, wet weather, Porter, from the flagboat *Black Hawk*, issued orders dividing his lower squadron into two divisions of heavy vessels and one or two of light draughts. In mid-afternoon on January 30, the gunboat dropped anchor off the mouth of the Yazoo. She was now part of the First Division with the *Louisville*, *Cincinnati*, *Baron de Kalb*, *Chillicothe*, *Lexington*, and *Conestoga*. The unit would be commanded by Capt. Henry Walke when he arrived with the *Lafayette*.[8]

Crisscrossed with various lakes, small rivers, and bayous, the Yazoo Delta lies on the eastern side of the Mississippi River between Vicksburg, Mississippi, and Memphis, Tennessee. Much of the land is rich, black farming soil, but due to faulty drainage in Civil War times, most of it was either swamp or flooded land. As Maj. Gen. William T. Sherman and Acting Rear Adm. Porter had discovered the previous December during their adventure to Chickasaw Bayou, it would be a difficult, if not impossible, task to take the route up the Yazoo River to the high ground northeast of Vicksburg.

Across the Mississippi, the situation for an invader was no better. The land there was also low and overly wet. It would be suicidal for any Union army to try to cross the river and attack the high batteries defending the city and eastern banks. Perhaps the geography of the area is best summed up by quoting that old observer T.B. Thrope: "The country through which [the Mississippi] flows is almost entirely alluvial."

As naval forces congregated off the mouth of the Yazoo toward the end of January, Federal maj. gen. Ulysses S. Grant arrived on scene to restart the dormant Yankee advance upon Vicksburg. There would be no more direct attack upon water defenses, like those at Haynes Bluff or Chickasaw Bayou. Grant believed that, with the aid of Porter's vessels, it was time to find a way of getting behind the town's defenses. Schemes to that end would begin to unfold within days.

On January 30, Acting Rear Adm. Porter issued a General Order concerning the duties of the ironclads anchored on the Yazoo station. Their main function, it specified, would be to serve as guard vessels, closely checking the identity of all vessels in the area and covering the Union amphibious force at night. The *Carondelet* was tasked to join four other First Division craft in alternating positions as the advance guard boat, the one stationed furthest up the Yazoo. Lt. Brennand's vessel had not yet taken her turn on this duty when, on February 3, he was succeeded in command by squadron newcomer Lt. Cmdr. James A. Greer,

Many joining the vessel as new officers had the same idealized view of the *Carondelet* as did readers who saw her depicted in a July 1862 issue of the *Illustrated London News* (*Illustrated London News*, July 19, 1862).

a regular USN officer in need of a temporary berth. The volunteer remained with the ironclad for most of the month as executive officer until he could take over the *Prairie Bird.* Two days later, the *Carondelet* had her first turn at night picket duty.

The initial duty passed uneventfully. As the ironclad secured from her night duty, a task group under Lt. Cmdr. Watson Smith, led by the *Chillicothe* and *Baron de Kalb,* departed upriver. Acting Rear Adm. Porter hoped that the group could outflank Vicksburg via the Yazoo Pass. Although Greer's command was too far up the Yazoo to see Smith's departure, the tars aboard knew, even as they started to give their boat a new coat of black paint, that something important was afoot. Unfortunately, this expedition would fail, causing Maj. Gen. Grant to call it off on March 23.

Left: An Atlantic Ocean mariner from 1847 to 1852 and a farmer until Fort Sumter, Scott D. Jordan (1825–1899) of Cape Elizabeth, ME, was appointed an acting ensign effective April 22, 1863. Like many Civil War gunboatmen, he would maintain an active correspondence with his family (primarily his wife, Judith) at home through his honorable discharge on November 22, 1865. After the Civil War he returned to farming and, in the 1870s, patented a pie rack that he sold around New England. His gunboat letters, written mostly aboard the _Carondelet,_ were saved by the family and collected by his great-granddaughter, Eleanor Jordan West, transcribed and with the help of Ensign Jordan's great-great-grandson Douglas Bell, were made available to scholars. The work in hand is the first to make extensive use of this collection (courtesy Eleanor Jordan West and Douglas Bell). _Right:_ Acting Volunteer Lt. John McLeod Murphy (1827–1871) was the _Carondelet_'s second appointed captain. A U.S. Naval Academy graduate who quit the service to work as a civilian engineer, surveyor, and New York state politician, he had previously served as Col. of the 15th Regiment, New York Volunteer Engineers. After the December 1862 Union disaster at Fredericksburg, Rear Adm. Porter, an old acquaintance, arranged his transfer to the ironclad. The _Carondelet_'s new skipper would take a prominent role in the Steele's Bayou expedition and served aboard until illness forced his resignation. Extremely well regarded by the gunboat's crew, he was found wanting in almost every respect by his predecessor, Capt. Walke, who believed him a political hack (Library of Congress).

Two days after Smith steamed away from the Yazoo, Second Lt. Lewis Keller arrived onboard with 24 bluecoats from the 58th Ohio. These men would be the *Carondelet*'s new company of marines, the first sea soldiers berthed aboard since Company D, 42nd Illinois, departed following the July battle with the *Arkansas*.[9]

During the week of February 15, a number of boats in the lower squadron received efficiency examinations. A few minutes after noon on February 18, Lt. George M. Bach and Lt. Byron Wilson, skippers of the City Series boats *Cincinnati* and *Mound City* respectively, went onboard the *Carondelet* to conduct her review. They were received by Lt. Cmdr. Greer, after which the turtle's crew was sent to general quarters. From GQ, the tars moved to their fire and boat stations, after which the gunboat's First Division demonstrated its proficiency at the great guns and the Second Division at small arms. The two visitors completed their examination by 3:00 P.M. and left the boat well pleased.

Meanwhile, upriver, John McLeod Murphy, the *Carondelet*'s full-time commander designate, had by this time arrived at Cairo with his men, all duly transferred over from War Department control. Late on February 27, Fleet Capt. Pennock ordered Murphy to take passage with Capt. Walke aboard the *Lafayette*, which was leaving that night for "down the river." The big new gunboat arrived at the lower fleet anchorage four days later.[10]

At noon on Wednesday, March 4, Acting Volunteer Lt. John McLeod Murphy stepped aboard the fantail of the *Carondelet*, where he was received by Lt. Cmdr. Greer. After three months of waiting, the new skipper and the old entered into the deck where the crew was assembled. With Greer at his side, Murphy read himself aboard before the mustered men. After shaking hands with the turtle's new commander, doubtless offering an expression of "good luck," Lt. Cmdr. Greer boarded and head downriver on the same tug that brought Murphy over from the *Lafayette*. After his predecessor left, Capt. Murphy greeted his officers and inspected the assembled bluejackets. Then, before descending below to his new quarters in the captain's cabin to review standing squadron orders, he sent the men to lunch. As soon as his gear was situated, he toured the vessel from stem to stern, becoming familiar with the famous old gunboat. During the afternoon, two new 9-inch guns, together with 200 rounds of ammunition for them, were manhandled aboard from the *Lafayette* under the watchful eyes of both Walke and Murphy, the *Carondelet*'s first and second captains.

Many changes occurred in the ranks of the gunboat's officer corps about the time Murphy assumed command. Transfer, death, or the expiration of service time eliminated many of those who had seen action aboard earlier. Among the new officers were Acting Ensigns Scott D. Jordan and Thomas A. Quinn, who came aboard with the new captain, and Charles H. Amerman. Other new men included Acting Assistant Surgeon Douglas R. Bannon and Acting Assistant Paymaster (commonly known as Purser) L.C. Worden. In the engine room, Acting Ensign Caven was joined by Acting First Assistant Engineer George N. Athinson, Acting Second Assistant Engineer Michael Norton, and Acting Third Assistant Engineer John McWilliams. Former Acting Master's Mate James C. Gibson, newly promoted to the rank of master, was succeeded by Acting Masters Mate Charles W. Miller. The other acting masters mates, Lauren W. Hastings and William H.H. DeGroot, were newcomers.

Topside in the pilothouse, the new pilots were John Murray and William Kantz. The man who, by naval law, was Murphy's number one subordinate, executive officer, and the boat's second in command was now, after the departure of Acting Volunteer Lt. Brennand, none other than Acting Ensign Oliver Donaldson, the former carpenter whom Capt. Walke had promoted then confined in a fit of rage nearly two months earlier.

After a brief tour of the *Carondelet*, new Acting Ensign Jordan pronounced himself "well satisfied with the appearance of the vessel." In a letter home to his wife, Judith, he proudly reported that "she is well calculated to take care of herself, I should think being heavily ironclad." He was also relieved to note that "the health of the men is good." There were only two hands on the sick list, which was "first rate."

The Mississippi River began its annual rise in December and, aided by the January rains, continued to gain height during February. By early March, the water was so high that many of its tributaries overran their banks, flooding the surrounding countryside. This was true in the Yazoo Delta where, it must be admitted, when Watson Smith cut the levee to gain entrance into the Yazoo Pass, the situation was greatly aggravated.

At the middle of the month, with Smith's effort to flank Vicksburg in doubt, a new thrust would be attempted via Deer Creek. "This was one of the most remarkable military and naval expeditions that ever set out in any country," Porter recalled after the war, "and it will be so ranked by those who read of it in future times."[11]

10

Vicksburg

In the months after the capture of Arkansas Post in January 1863, the Federal military effort against Vicksburg, Mississippi, bogged down, both as to strategy and because of the unusually widespread floods of late winter. To quench the North's thirst for action and to ease the boredom of his men, quartered mostly upon river steamers, local theater commander Maj. Gen. Ulysses S. Grant sanctioned several alternatives preliminary to any full-scale attack. Two canals and the Lake Providence route were explored on the Louisiana side of the Mississippi — all doomed to failure.

On the opposite shore, the Yazoo Pass Expedition, an effort to outflank the fortress town via the northern Yazoo River Delta, also came to naught. Of it, Acting Rear Adm. David Dixon Porter later wrote of his frustration indicating that "I never wanted to hear of the Yazoo expedition again."

In a March 26 first quarter summary to navy secretary Gideon Welles, Porter, commander of the Mississippi Squadron and the navy's chief liaison with Grant, reported on the possibilities of a trek through the waterways of the lower delta. On the basis of information supplied by a friendly African American, such a thrust was deemed most encouraging.[1] When the idea of a different flanking route began to receive wider circulation, an attentive Union newspaper reporter jotted down for his readers a mileage estimate of such an operation: "From the mouth of Steele's or Cypress Bayou to Big Black Bayou, thirty miles; from Big Black Bayou to Big Deer Creek, six miles; Big Deer Creek to Rolling Fork, eighteen miles; Rolling Fork to Sunflower [River], ten miles; Sunflower to Yazoo, forty-one miles— sixty miles from its mouth. Total, one hundred and five miles." Area flooding almost made the route attractive. Channels now appeared, some as deep as 17 feet, where forests commanded in the dry season. It should be possible to pass an Eads-built turtle through these passages to a point back of the citadel.[2]

Regardless of the distance involved, the immediate objectives of this new program were twofold. Paramount was the need to link up with the remnants of the Yazoo Pass Expedition before current reports of an enemy effort to encircle it turned out to be true. If this combined Northern force would next blast an entrance onto the Yazoo somewhere between Haynes' Bluff and Yazoo City, it would control the navigable, upper reaches of that stream. The high, dry ground behind Vicksburg would thus be attained and the labor of canal-building in the flooded regional below could cease. The acquisition of Yazoo City would be a fine bonus, as its shipyards and other facilities would provide the Union with an excellent base from which Grant might launch a final advance.

Reading over his newly received data, including further reports of failure from Lt. Cmdr. Watson Smith's northern venture, and dreaming of these possibilities, Acting Rear Adm. Porter decided to act. Success in this new direction, he later wrote, would make the subsequent attack on the Confederate citadel "a sure thing."[3] In need of further information and not altogether satisfied with the report of the "truthful contraband," Porter decided to reconnoiter a part of the route himself. Taking a detachment of 41 marines from the

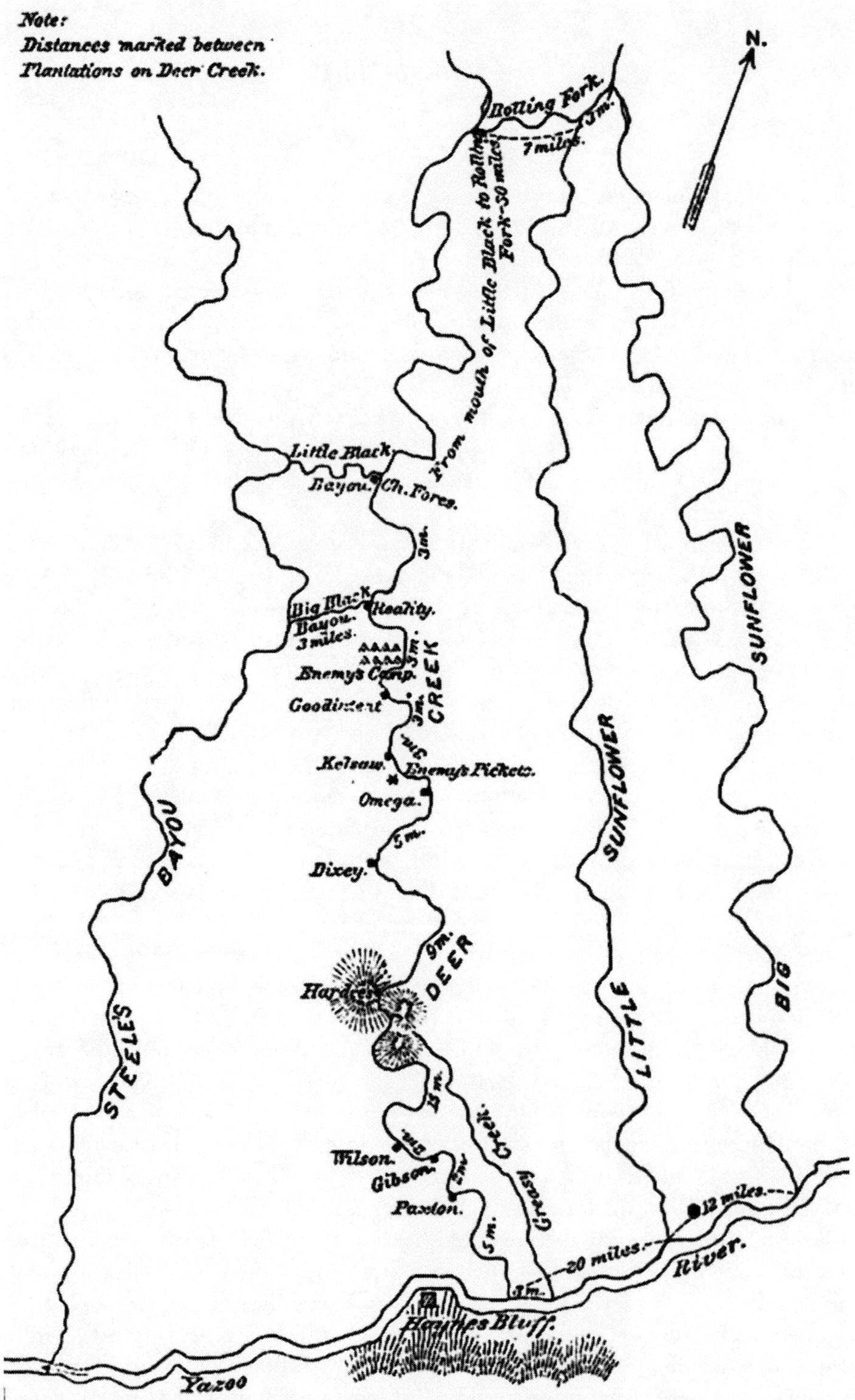

The reader can readily imagine the convoluted Steele's Bayou route from this map, but never the natural difficulties of the trek (OR Series I, Vol. 36).

giant gunboat *Benton*, the naval chief went aboard the *Carondelet* on the morning of March 12 and signaled the timberclad *Tyler*, together with a transport and two tugboats, to join her in steaming up the Yazoo. At noon, the group hauled up at Johnson's Plantation, where the ironclad eased into the bank astern of the transport.

Having signaled his intention, the squadron commander — accompanied by the *Carondelet*'s new skipper, Acting Volunteer Lt. John McLeod Murphy — boarded a tug and set off up the bayou a half hour later. The second tug, transporting the marines, came along to provide cover. As the tiny craft steamed out of sight, Acting Ensign Symmes Brown, aboard *Tyler*, performing picket duty at the mouth of Steele's Bayou, noted as follows: "It is strange too what an effect the slightest move has on our forces. Every man puts on a bright face and his spirits rise in proportion to the importance of a move or the prospects of a fight."

Ordinarily, Steele's Bayou was rather shallow, little more than what Porter later colorfully called "a ditch." Now, with the entire countryside flooded, the going was quick and simple. Soundings revealed a depth of water to 5½ fathoms over 30 miles up to Big Black Bayou. At this junction, the admiral, in conversation no doubt with Murphy the engineer, considered the forest sprouting from the water and the narrow, twisting shape of the creek. Even though there was not much water between the banks, it should be possible, it was reasoned, to "heave the vessels" around the many small bends of the bayou. Odds for success appeared to favor the bold.

The tugs returned to Johnson's later that afternoon. Porter and his marines returned downriver to cut orders for the operation. Capt. Murphy, returning aboard his gunboat, guided her into Steele's Bayou. By previous arrangement with the admiral, the *Carondelet* would steam upstream about five miles and then make fast to the trees overnight. En route, she would continue to gather information and, as necessary, break down obstructing trees — a duty far less glamorous than her dash by Island No. 10 a year earlier.

Hopeful of an early triumph, Acting Rear Adm. Porter also met with Maj. Gen. Grant at the latter's Young's Point headquarters. After both hearing the fine results of the day's upstream scout and pouring over a number of area maps, the military commander agreed that the sailor's idea had merit. Army troops, he promised, would be committed as necessary to insure the endeavor.[4]

Having gathered his data and secured army blessing, the Mississippi Squadron boss signaled the Pook turtles *Louisville*, *Cincinnati*, *Mound City*, and *Pittsburg* to coal and assemble off Johnson's place the following morning. Four tugs were each instructed to take a mortar boat in tow and also report. "Engineering tools," including axes and saws, were broken out and made ready for distribution to the various vessels next day. Finally, a large coal barge was ordered topped off and prepared for towing — later, she would almost prove the task group's undoing.

All was in readiness by an early hour on March 14. About 6:00 A.M., Porter and Grant arrived at Johnson's aboard the former Confederate ram *Sterling Price*, which had been taken into the USN some months before. So anxious had the general become for the mission that he wished to accompany the gunboats upstream for a short distance to see just how difficult their task would be. Two hours later, the group cast off the banks near Johnson's and angled across the Yazoo toward the entrance of the intended waterway, with the tugs and the ironclads in the lead and the *Price* bringing up the rear. While they were away, the *Tyler* would remain off the mouth of the Yazoo, acting as picket and liaison with the remainder of the squadron.

The weather was cool, with a slight northeasterly wind. During much of the first day, the tug *Thistle*, with Murphy, two officers, and a howitzer crew from the *Carondelet*, proceeded ahead. As they advanced, leadsmen found the current changed by water from Muddy Creek. About 7:00 P.M., the *Carondelet* tied up to the trees near that Mississippi River outlet, only about a mile off, to await the arrival of the trailing gunboats. Progress so far was good.

Maj. Gen. Grant, who came with the Federal task group on its inaugural day, remained with the navy throughout much of the 15th. Again the weather was clear, but easy steaming was over. Although great clouds of startled birds took wing, apparently no local human inhabitants saw the armada.

It is difficult for the modern reader to imagine the landscape the Northern gunboatmen now encountered. The entire scene, save for a narrow strip along the banks, seemed to be submerged. Embedded newsman Wilkie recorded the sight:

> We turned up the Bayou, since which land and in fact everything but swamp has disappeared. For ten miles or so, the Bayou was straight and broad, and we drove along most merrily. Suddenly, however, it grew narrower and crooked, 'till it resembled more the course taken by some erratic meadow brook. The willows approached us closer on either side, and the gloomy cypresses began to thrust long branches across our decks, as if anxious to impede our further progress. As the way narrowed, our advance became excessively slow and tedious.

On top of this, as the ships moved deeper into this web of trees, assorted mosses, briar, wild eglantine, and wild grapevines, the bluejackets found the area literally crawling with poisonous snakes, alligators, huge snapping turtles, and millions of cockroaches and stinging insects. Nevertheless, the ironclads steamed ahead, everyone hoping the terrain would improve.

Shortly after 2:00 P.M., the fleet overtook the *Carondelet*, still tied to the bank above Muddy Creek where she had arrived the day before. Casting off, she now took the lead in a procession that included, in order, the *Cincinnati*, *Pittsburg*, *Mound City*, *Louisville*, mortar boats, and *Price*. Throughout the remainder of afternoon, the Federal vessels, spaced about a quarter of a mile apart, found steaming relatively easy with little interference from the swamp. The leadsmen consistently called out, "quarter less three." About 6:00 P.M., the vessels entered Big Black Bayou and a little later tied up for the night. Lookouts were posted in the usual manner and pickets were sent ashore.

That night, Maj. Gen. Grant bade the admiral farewell and returned aboard the *Price* to Young's Point. The army man, impressed with the gunboats' progress, was now convinced of the route. "This one," he wrote, "to get all our forces in one place, and that, where it will be in striking distance of the enemy's lines of communication north, is the most important until firm foothold is secured on the side with the enemy."

Toward 11:00 A.M. on March 16, Porter went aboard the *Carondelet* to assume control of the advance. Forward progress up Black Bayou slowed as the gunboat, still in the lead, was forced to butt down trees, the water-soaked roots of which easily (in most cases) gave way before the ironclad. Crewmen often had to saw off or haul out the smaller or more unyielding timber, while overhead the foliage began to intertwine regularly with great risk to the boat's chimneys.

Ten miles were traversed that Monday. All of the ironclads were now in the tree removal business. Like trained elephants in a rain forest, they smashed into obstructing century-old trees as hard as possible to knock them over and off their roots. Sometimes they tied hawsers to them and pulled them out of the way. Many did not go easily, tearing at chimneys, crunching cutters, and smashing skylights. While the ironclads battled the trees in their path, foraging parties were sent ashore into the still largely unsuspecting countryside. Fresh provisions, including hams, chickens, eggs, and butter were easily secured.

At 6:00 P.M., the *Carondelet* was trapped by the vines and "struck hard." Only a mile or so from Hill's plantation and with dusk falling, Porter decided to lay by. When the remaining vessels came up and tied to, a combined picket force was sent ashore. Later that evening, a letter from the task group arrived at Grant's headquarters requesting that troops be sent to help maintain its position and protect the passage already cleared. The commanding general was, however, ahead of Porter. No sooner had the *Price* hauled up at the bank that afternoon than Grant was sending instructions to Maj. Gen. William Tecumseh Sherman for a link-up with the gunboats. By the time the admiral's message came in, Sherman was pushing the pioneers of Col. Giles A. Smith's 8th Missouri to Johnson's plantation.[5]

Tuesday was St. Patrick's Day, but there was little celebration for the Federal tars, Irish or otherwise. By 8:00 A.M., they were again hewing their way forward. The struggle to push through the remainder of four-mile-long Black Bayou soon slowed to about half a mile per hour. Hundreds of logs, standing trees, and snags blocked the route. The willow saplings proved to be the worst offenders. Their thousands of tiny branches clung so tightly to the flat bottoms of the Eads-made craft that the bluejackets were forced to cut them off one by one. The effort was horrendous.

The USN arrived off Hill's plantation sometime after 11:00 A.M. The layout was clearly visible as the boats passed through the "artificial water course" in front of the farm. About an hour later, the Yankee turtles rounded the point from Black Bayou into Deer Creek. Just as the *Carondelet* was making the turn, Maj. Gen. Sherman, riding the *Fern*, caught up with the flotilla. While his men downstream launched the painstaking task of making the bayou navigable for troop boats, the redheaded Buckeye soldier wanted to view the ironclads' progress and determine if unarmored steamers could do as well. Acting Rear Adm. Porter obliged him and, going aboard his tug, conducted him on a scout upstream, explaining his ideas as they steamed.

Despite the squadron commander's optimistic statements that the worst was past and even though he could view the "ease" with which the gunboats seemed to push aside the vegetation, Sherman was not convinced. He believed, correctly, that only the smallest steamers (carrying consequently fewer troops) could follow Porter's route — and then only with the probability of substantial damage to their superstructures. Even with his reservations in mind, the general agreed to push some men up to relieve the *Louisville*, which had drawn the assignment of guarding the junction before Hill's. These men were already being ferried to the Mississippi shore near Muddy Fork, down which they were expected to take passage to Steele's Bayou via "small-class boats."

For a while, Deer Creek proved somewhat more tree-free than Black Bayou. Leaving Sherman, the fleet steamed ahead. The tug *Thistle*, towing a mortar boat, took the lead. About mid-afternoon, the Union warships came abreast of Fore's plantation. The outpost was quite peaceful, as slave women were seen quietly working the fields. Unbeknownst to the sailors, the element of surprise was gone; local inhabitants knew the black gunboats were in the area and would soon begin taking appropriate measures to oppose them.

Two and a half hours after passing Fore's, the *Carondelet*-led task group halted off the Watson plantation. As the pickets were ordered out and the day's business concluded, the *Louisville*, replaced by Sherman's soldiers, came up from Black Bayou and assumed a position at the bank last in line.

As the men onboard the ironclads fell asleep in their hammocks, excited local citizens

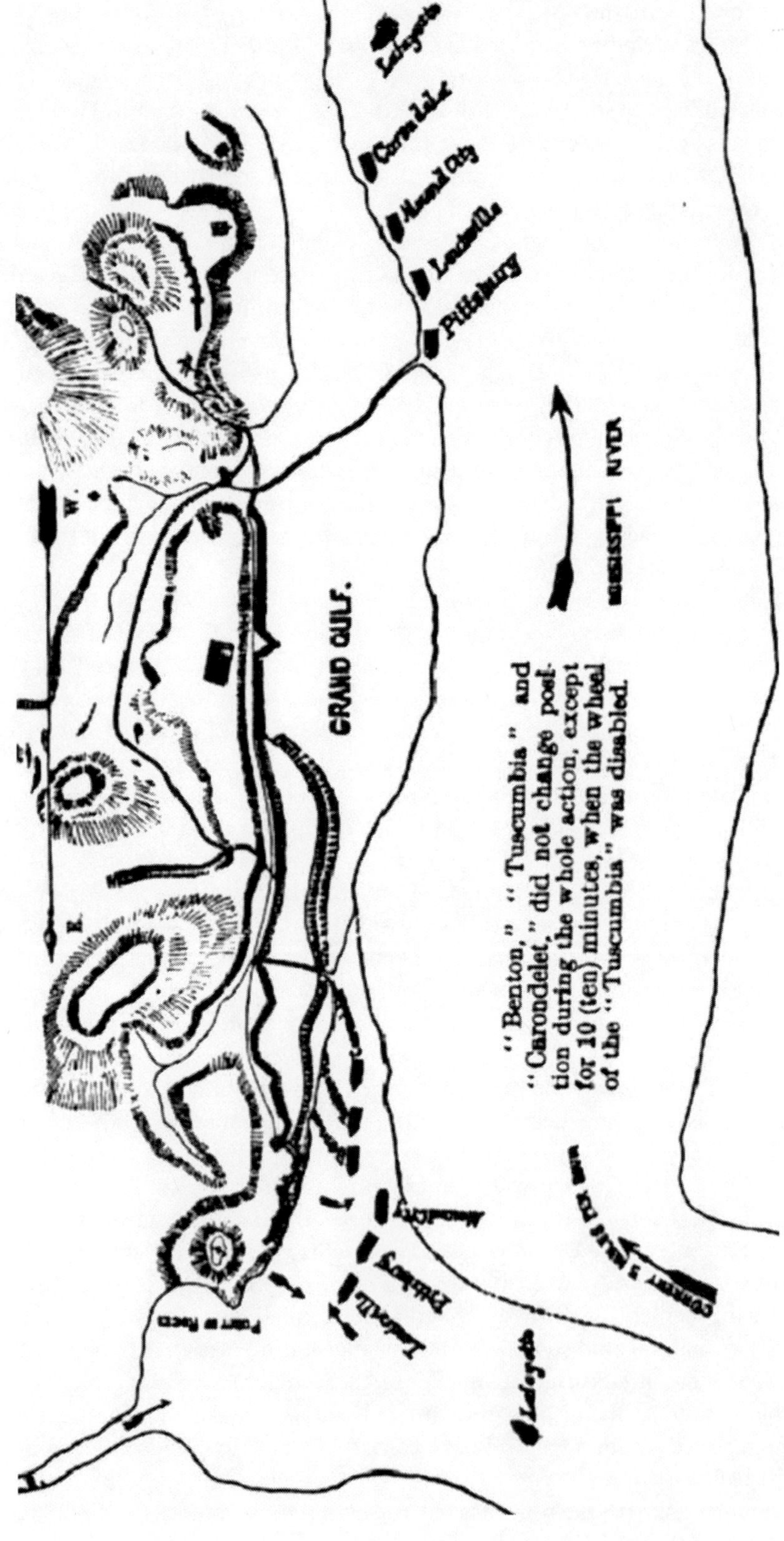
GRAND GULF.
MISSISSIPPI RIVER
"Benton," "Tuscumbia" and "Carondelet," did not change position during the whole action, except for 10 (ten) minutes, when the wheel of the "Tuscumbia" was disabled.
Lafayette
Carondelet
Mound City
Louisville
Pittsburg
Point of Rocks

broke upon the camp of Confederate Col. Samuel W. Ferguson with news of Porter's movements. The Southern position, 40 miles above Rolling Fork, had received some intelligence of Federal activity below, but nothing so immense as the commitment of ironclads. After getting off a quick wire to Vicksburg, the colonel took the infantry and cavalry detachments at hand, together with half a dozen artillery pieces, placed them all aboard a steamer, and moved off toward the enemy "with all dispatch."

Wednesday, March 18, began for the Federals like most thus far. None knew that it marked the beginning of the end of the Steele's Bayou expedition. On that day, the Confederacy took official notice of the Yankee's lunchbox invasion, one which would not be tolerated.

As the Federal boats pushed on, a new and ominous sign was everywhere noted—clouds of smoke. During the day as they passed Wright's, Clark's, Williams' and Messenger's plantations, the scenes of destruction multiplied. The *New York Times*' "Galway" wrote in his notebook: "As the gunboats approached the different plantations, the cotton was set on fire and burned; cotton and ginhouses were everywhere in a blaze, to prevent it from falling into our hands. Men were now frequently seen on horseback, fleeing to give information of our approach." Other men placed cotton bales on the levees and set them afire to stop the gunboats as they squeezed by in the narrow streams. Acting Rear Adm. Porter, visiting aboard the *Cincinnati* for a conversation with her commander, Lt. George Bache, suddenly saw two stacks of cotton, across from each other on opposite sides of the stream, burst into flame. The *Carondelet*, ahead, entered the conflagration and disappeared.

Rather than wait for the obstruction to burn out, the admiral, refusing to stop, ordered the gunboat's ports closed and her exposed sides wetted down. When the heat on deck became too great, he and Bache retreated into the pilothouse, where they found the helmsman had covered himself with a wet old flag. "It was a red-hot undertaking," remarked one participant, "but the warships passed through only slightly scorched and with no injuries."

Confederate incendiaries, who like the populace at large at first could not "believe that anything the shape of a vessel could get through Black Bayou or anywhere on the route," speedily set fire to everything they imagined the Yankees might want, especially cotton and outbuildings holding grain or livestock. The ironclads occasionally fired on torchbearers; and, suggesting it a way to help defray expenses, the admiral sent several landing parties out to harvest loose cotton bales. (This routine continued for at least three more days.)

Around 4:00 P.M., the *Carondelet* ran fast upon a log, two hours' work being necessary to free her. By late afternoon, she was within seven miles of the next connecting streak, Rolling Fork. Porter was pleased until he received a report that trees were being cut down in his path. Quickly reacting to this threat, the squadron boss ordered Capt. Murphy to board the *Thistle* and steam off to the attack. As the sluggish ironclad followed, the admiral heard rapid 12-pdr. boat howitzer fire ahead and then three blasts from the tug's whistle indicating "all's well."

When Murphy returned, he reported a number of trees were being axed when he came upon the activity. A few shells from his gun, he continued, were sufficient to chase the Rebel horsemen away before more mischief was done. Once the *Carondelet* and her men, working now by torchlight, pulled away these snags, the fleet, having come together, was ordered to for the night.

Opposite: **A stickler for detail, Capt. Walke drew this chart of the fighting at Grand Gulf to prove a point made in his memoirs. It is generally accurate (Walke, *Naval Scenes and Reminiscences*).**

In the small hours of March 19, Confederate Maj. Gen. Carter L. Stevenson in Vicksburg received Col. Ferguson's telegram. He immediately advised area commander Maj. Gen. John C. Pemberton, then in Jackson, "several gunboats have gone up Steele's Bayou, thence through Black Bayou to Deer Creek." He continued: "The citizens of Vicksburg and of that section told me it was absolutely impracticable. I will send at once a force to Rolling Fork."

As the bluejackets, up and working early, moved deeper into Deer Creek, the stream narrowed and the going became worse than Black Bayou. Presently, the leading *Carondelet* and her following sisters could just barely wedge through. Decks were showered with falling tree limbs, rotting vines, mosses, and assorted animals like raccoons, mice, snakes, and possums driven into the trees by the floodwaters. An added natural danger now manifested itself. The bayou banks, aided by their man-made levees, grew higher. Within a short time, they were some three feet above the stream, making it difficult, and sometimes impossible, for the gunboat cannon to be sufficiently elevated to fire over them. With all these problems, the men became increasingly tired. One officer recalled years later: "Pirouetting through the woods with ironclads, tugs, and mortar boats, while rich in novelty ... had ... grown tedious and depressing."[6]

As the sailors continued their labors, Capt. Murphy went ahead again with the *Thistle.* When they were within some three miles of Rolling Fork, an immense cloud of smoke was seen in the direction of its junction with the Sunflower. Sensing that the enemy might now be moving upon him in force, Porter, aboard the *Carondelet,* signaled the tug to reconnoiter the area near Dr. Butt's farm.

Near the plantation, bordering the confluence of Deer Creek and Rolling Fork, there was at this time several Native American burial mounds on the eastern side of the bayou. When Murphy saw these from the tug, he believed they might be made to serve as inland outposts. Returning to the *Carondelet,* he told Porter of his find and asked to have some tars set up camp atop them. The admiral was not so sure, but the ex-engineer, pressing his case against Porter's reluctance, won his point. Exasperated by the New Yorker's determination, the naval chief gave his permission. "Go ahead and fortify it," he told the lieutenant, "it will keep you employed."

Taking a pair of howitzers and 300 men, Murphy set off upstream. The tallest mound, lifting about 60 feet, was selected and the little wheeled cannon were mounted on its summit covering Rolling Fork. As the sailors secured their positions ashore, the *Carondelet* reached a point less than three miles from the junction by 2:00 P.M.

As cotton smoke continued to billow into the spring sky, "the indications now began to increase, that the country had been aroused, and that the rebels were congregating to oppose the advance of the Union forces." Franc Wilkie's observation was correct; that afternoon, Col. Ferguson's transport arrived at the mouth (upper end) of Rolling Fork. There he was joined by men responsible for placing obstructions before the advancing gunboats.

With Murphy's guns protecting, Acting Rear Adm. Porter directed his commanders to push on as quickly as possible. "The labor of clearing out these obstructions was very great," he explained a few days later. But by dusk, the *Carondelet* was within 800 yards of the junction. With only a few large trees and an apparently "easy" stand of willows ahead, the task group commander called a halt. Certain these willows could be easily lifted the following morning, he sent pickets ashore and allowed his exhausted men to sleep until sunrise.[7]

Porter's timber-removal decision was incorrect. When the *Carondelet*'s bluejackets launched into the willows on Friday morning, March 20, they found these trees the toughest growth yet encountered. As nowhere earlier, the little underwater limbs here seemed determined to grip the monstrous boats in their embrace. Saws and axes plied endlessly in an effort to move forward, but only a mile and a half was gained all morning. Into the afternoon, the work, wet and dangerous, cut on and, inch by tedious inch, the ironclads moved ahead. The determination of the underbrush was proving to be nature's gift to the Confederacy.

Shortly after daylight, Capt. Murphy returned to his hill and ordered his scouts forward. If these established enemy contact (and there is no record they did), the findings would have been most disturbing. Col. Ferguson was now on the dry ground of the Chaney farm, about a mile north of the fleet, positioning his artillery. Truly, it would be "the most exciting and decisive day experienced by the expedition."

As soon as their guns were pointed, the Confederates opened fire upon Murphy's short hill. It was no contest. The Rebel battery, directed by Lt. R.L. Wood, had greater range and could not be touched by the boat howitzers. "Suddenly," the admiral recalled in his memoirs, "I saw the sides [of the mound] crowded with officers and men. They were tumbling down as best they could; the guns were tumbled down ahead of them; there was a regular stampede."

Unable to elevate the *Carondelet*'s big guns to reply, Porter sent Murphy and a number of the retreating sailors over to a nearby mortar boat. The distance from it to the estimated location of the Rebels was audibly measured. Soon, giant 13-inch shells were sent streaking on their way 2,600–2,800 yards northward. The Confederate barrage, "which was pushed with success until the ammunition failed," was lifted shortly after the bombs began to drop.

There was a lull in warlike activities through most of the afternoon. The only sounds heard on the water were those of axes, saws, and grunting tars. The rear gunboats had by now made their way up behind the *Carondelet.* At the same time, Brig. Gen. Winfield S. Featherston arrived by Col. Ferguson's side to estimate the field situation.

The Southerners were in a good position. The boats were neatly bottled up and Sher-

Hopeful of an early triumph, Acting Rear Adm. Porter met with Maj. Gen. Ulysses S. Grant at the latter's Young's Point headquarters in mid–March. After hearing results of an upstream scout and pouring over a number of area maps, the military commander agreed that the sailor's idea of flanking Vicksburg via Steele's Bayou had merit. Army troops, he promised, would be committed as necessary to insure the endeavor succeeded (Naval Historical Center).

man's troops were nowhere to be seen. Seizing his opportunity, Featherston placed an infantry battalion on the right extending down to Deer Creek. The left, in a strip of timber near the ironclads, was assigned to the 22nd and 23rd Mississippi Regiments for a distance down the creek below the Federals. The men, with luck, would be able to place substantial obstructions in the path of any naval retreat. The open field extending northeast of the boats for an estimated distance of a mile and a half was left unoccupied.

As the Rebels moved to their positions, most realized the importance of one order from their brigadier. With most of his men crack shots, Featherston had directed them to shoot at "every man who made his appearance on the boats." As will be seen, this would have the effect of pinning most of the sailors down inside their casemates.

Meanwhile, Porter, aboard the *Carondelet*, learned of the men sent to fell trees in the rear. "This looked unpleasant," was his later understatement. If this Confederate effort was successful, the boats might be unable to escape and Sherman's soldiers, whom it was hoped were en route, would be delayed.

Ferguson's guns, aided by additional pieces brought by Featherston, were ordered to open fire once more. This time, by jacking their cannon to extreme elevation, the USN gunners were able to reply. As the cannonade thundered on, the task group commander continued to receive reports of Southern activity behind him. Growing fearful for the safety of his boats and people in a stream too narrow to round in, Porter concluded that further forward progress was impossible. When the Rebels ceased fire at sunset, he ordered the rudders of the ironclads unshipped and a retreat begun. Rebounding "from tree to tree" with the *Louisville* now in the lead, the Federals backed slowly downstream to lay by Butler's plantation for the night.

Maj. Gen. William Tecumseh Sherman (1829–1891) was always appreciative of the supportive effort of Union gunboats and called upon them for assistance on numerous occasions. During Rear Adm. Porter's Deer Creek expedition in March 1863, when it appeared that the *Carondelet* and several other Pook turtles might be lost, he and his men went literally to their relief (Library of Congress).

Instead of tying up to the trees as usual, the Federal gunboats were kept anchored in midstream. The Confederates could not board them without crossing water in some places up to 20 feet deep. Southern forces maintained their positions with orders to attack only if the Yankees attempted a landing on the eastern side of the bayou. As this did not occur, the evening passed bloodlessly.[8]

March 21 marked a week the fleet had been in Porter's ditch. As soon as it was light, the Confederates renewed their attack. Artillery shells from the mound and elsewhere rained down upon the flotilla. These were answered by the *Carondelet* and the *Cincinnati* as they moved up to mask the retreat of the others. The soldiers manning Murphy's ex-mound location were dislodged and the remainder of the Southern artillery, out of ammunition, ceased fire. "After all," quipped the admiral, "Murphy was right; it [the mound] was a strategic point! But only for Whitworth rifles, not smoothbores."

Unable to employ his guns further, Col. Ferguson expected his superior to order an infantry attack. Cautious against the big floating guns, he, however, only ordered his regiments to new positions in the woods running on both sides of the stream. Featherston was content to wait until the vessels were completely blockaded. Rebel snipers, perched in trees or along the banks, harassed the turtles for the remainder of the day. Every time a bluejacket emerged on deck or tried to use a pole to fend his boat off from the bank, he became a target. All the while, the noose of encirclement was drawn steadily tighter about the Northern gunboats.

The officers and men of the fleet kept below as much as possible. Rebel small-arms fire was particularly effective against the tugs and the gun ports left open on the ironclads. No one knew how much longer it would be before — or even if — they would escape from this nightmare. Acting Rear Adm. Porter, whose flag now flew from the *Louisville,* had no word from Sherman and prepared for the worst. In an effort to combat the Confederate sharpshooters, the Union skippers posted their best riflemen in the gunboats' pilothouses with instructions to shoot out of the little slits at whatever target of opportunity was seen. For psychological and defensive reasons, the mortars and heavy guns were discharged whenever a sniper nest was reported or suspected.

All of this had little effect on the well-hidden Southerners. Col. Ferguson, watching the exchanges through his field glasses, was mildly pleased and noted that "the expenditure of al kinds of missiles, from a 13-inch shell to a minie ball, on every point where it was thought they [the snipers] might be hit, showed the estimation the enemy had of them." In all, he dismissed the Yankees' firing as "an amusing display of pyrotechnics."

As the day passed, Porter forwarded further defensive orders. The gun ports aboard the *Carondelet* and her sisters were to be closed and sealed. As a result, the men were forced to sleep on the hot, stuffy gun decks. No hammocks would be "piped down" until the boats were safe. Cooks were to serve only half rations until further notice. Should night come without relief, no lights would be shown, save single small lamps at the after ends of the gun decks. If worse came to worse, the boats would be ordered scuttled and destroyed, with their crews forced to seek their way to safety afoot through the marsh.

Maj. Gen. Sherman continued his efforts to get men up to the gunboat task group. About 3:00 A.M. on Saturday morning, an African American contraband arrived with another letter, which he had hidden in a tobacco pouch. Written in the clearest language, it stated frankly that relief soldiers needed to reach the gunboats now. "My own impression, " the general gloomily wrote headquarters, "is that the enemy have so obstructed Rolling Fork Bayou that it will be absolutely impassable to the admiral's fleet." He added, "It will be a difficult and dangerous task to withdraw it safely back."

Before dawn, orders flashed from Sherman's tent and, at first light, the 8th Missouri set off over a recently repaired bridge and up the east bank of Deer Creek toward the trapped gunboats. As the three pioneer regiments marched along as quickly as possible, all of the general's steamboats were put in motion "to bring forward more troops." Smith reached the gunboats about 4:00 P.M. and Porter was overjoyed to see him. "I never knew before," he later confessed, "how much the comfort and safety of ironclads, situated as we were, depended on the soldiers." Almost before the handshakes were over, the sailor gave the colonel his entire 150-man land force and the *Carondelet*'s two wheeled howitzers. Enough of the joint force was kept together to clear out the Confederate snipers, while the rest were posted downstream six or seven miles to prevent further obstructions being placed that night. A protected force quickly travelled up to remove the obstructions blocking the lead boat.

The most immediate snag was self-created. As she backed down that morning, the *Louisville* had the misfortune to ram the task group's coal barge, which quickly sank on an even keel, bottling up the gunboats as successfully as a million downed trees. Porter's people could not work on refloating it under fire. Once Smith arrived, coal heavers from the *Carondelet* and the other boats were sent to shovel the black knobs into the stream, making certain to spread them out evenly along the bottom. Well after dark, charges were placed on the hulk and it was blown to smithereens, pun intended.

Although Porter was temporarily safe, the uncertain task of extricating the ironclads was not yet accomplished. Even as they got underway backing down at first light on March 23, Confederate troops, reinforced by the arrival of the 40th Alabama, continued their harassment.

After bouncing downstream about half a mile, the *Louisville* came upon a river bend near Egremont's plantation, some 14 miles above Hill's, completely blocked by felled trees. This was the acid test, and a correspondent from the *Chicago Daily Tribune* noted the fear sweeping through the casemates: "The creek was barely the width of a gunboat — the boats were so closed up that only one bow gun apiece of four could be used, and then at an inconvenient angle — in fact, in only one position — and the broadsides of several [those in the center] were useless on account of the bank. If the rear was gained, their [the Confederates] numbers could board the first or the last boat, and, having captured her, use her guns with fearful effect on the others." The bluejackets were advised that they were facing a last-ditch battle. Their commander, anticipating the worst, passed fresh instructions to Capt. Murphy and his other skippers: "Every precaution must be taken to defend the vessels to the last, and when we can do no better, we will blow them up."

With the ironclads caught upon the obstructions, Brig. Gen. Featherston had his moment and ordered an attack. With sharpshooters pressing on the right, the 40th Alabama opened fire from the left, leaving the Mississippi boys to go below the boats. The giant naval cannon returned the compliment and, as Col. Smith later testified, "poured a destructive fire into their lines."

The battle continued into the afternoon. Downstream, three transports loaded with fresh Federal troops arrived at the foot of Black Bayou on Saturday night. Maj. Gen. Sherman personally guided these men by candlelight through the canebrake to Hill's. At sunrise, he took them on a fast march up the same road the Missouri men had trekked the day before. Soon Porter's great guns were heard and the general knew that "moments were precious."

Aboard the gunboats, the distinct sounds of skirmishing were heard below. Thinking three of the companies sent out as pickets the night before were stranded, Col. Smith ordered a major to take four companies to their relief. The soldiers below appeared doomed. There were no lost companies. Rather, after a brief contest with the Yankee newcomers, the surprised Mississippians were routed and retreated up Deer Creek and faded into the woods at the rear of Egremont's place.

Riding bareback on a borrowed steed, Maj. Gen. Sherman, to the huzzas of the men emerging from the ironclad casemates, found Acting Rear Adm. Porter on the deck of the *Louisville* "with a shield made of the section of a smokestack." For his part, Porter offered, "I do not know when I felt more pleased to see that gallant officer."

Once the area was secured, Sherman's soldiers formed a cordon around the boats and marched along the shore as they slowly backed down. The "slow and tedious process" was continued through almost continuous rain until mid-afternoon on March 24 when wider water was entered for the first time in nearly a week. During that morning, the *Carondelet* halted at the lower Foster's plantation and took onboard 125 of Sherman's ill soldiers. Sometime after 8:00 P.M., Murphy's command, still "tail-end Charlie," came to for the night at the mouth of Black Bayou.

Having suffered Confederate gunshot and much light-hearted joshing from the bluecoat soldiers, the jack tars aboard the ironclads were delighted to reship their rudders and finally round to. Moving bows-on, the vessels gathered speed, passed down Black Bayou, cruised Steele's Bayou, and finally reached their original positions off Johnson's plantation on the afternoon of March 27.

That night the *Carondelet* returned to the Mississippi, anchoring near the *Black Hawk*. Although she suffered no casualties, the exterior of the veteran Eads-built gunboat was badly harassed. Worse still, her knuckle suffered a number of jams, while a beam in her engine room had parted. Thereafter, she was in such a leaky condition that her pump had to be worked constantly.

What some called the most romantically colored adventure of the Vicksburg campaign was over. Although regretting its collapse, Prof. James R. Soley, Porter's earlier biographer, considered the mission "brilliantly conceived and boldly and firmly executed." With the nearly simultaneous failure of the Yazoo Pass expedition, the North realized that advances upon the Confederate citadel via the Yazoo Delta were impossible. The next question was how best the 60,000 bluecoats could now, in camps stretching 60 miles from Young's Point to Lake Providence, get into action against the Rebels across the Mississippi.

The Grant-Porter team was nothing if not innovative. Only two days after the ironclads returned to their anchorage, the former was penning the latter proposing that "one or two vessels be put below Vicksburg" in order to "insure a landing on the east bank for our forces." Checking his maps for a way to pass Vicksburg that did not involve the Yazoo, Maj. Gen. Grant saw that it would be possible to march his Army of the Tennessee down the west bank of the Mississippi from Milliken's Bend to New Carthage, 15 miles below the Rebel batteries at Warrenton. Going another 15 miles down, they could come to a point opposite Grand Gulf, which was strategically located between Vicksburg and another fortress city, Port Hudson. Once the USN had silenced the batteries atop the Grand Gulf bluffs, the military could be ferried across, take the fortifications, and march on Vicksburg from the south.

Acting Rear Adm. Porter took some heat from the Navy Department for the naval failures in the Yazoo Delta, as well as the loss of an ironclad and several rams sent past the Vicksburg batteries. Still, he was ready to support Grant's next plan. When the general wrote him on March 29 asking for several ironclads to support transports he planned to run by the city's guns, the squadron chief, though reluctant, promised to help.[9]

The naval captains of the Mississippi Squadron all knew that it would not be possible to steam past Vicksburg and adequately cover Grant's army, let alone battle the Grand Gulf fortifications, with only the one or two gunboats requested. Rather, such a move would require taking the heaviest ironclads. Vicksburg mounted 34 big guns and 16 fieldpieces along a 3.5 mile stretch before the town, and the fortifications at Grand Gulf were no less a tough nut to crack than those faced at Fort Donelson almost at the war's beginning.

On April 2, Maj. Gen. Grant set in motion his new plan to capture Vicksburg from below. Requests were sent to St. Louis and Cairo for additional tugboats and transports, while engineers began widening the road down the Louisiana shore leading to New Carthage. Some 20,000 XIII Corps men would soon begin marching over it.

While the army started its land preparations, the navy off the mouth of the Yazoo did the same for a dangerous river descent. The eventual component chosen would comprise both naval gunboats and army transports. Acting Rear Adm. Porter issued written orders concerning preparations on April 10. A night passage would be made past the Vicksburg and Warrenton batteries as soon as bad weather abated.

Grant originally wanted to have six USQD steamers run the gauntlet accompanied by,

The Battle of Grand Gulf is depicted in these two scenes drawn by Capt. Walke. The upper illustration shows the following gunboats in action left to right: *Benton, Tuscumbia, Louisville, Carondelet, Pittsburg, Mound City,* and *Lafayette.* At the bottom, the *Carondelet* is seen inboard and astern of the *Lafayette* (Walke, *Naval Scenes and Reminiscences*).

at most, two gunboats. Reason prevailed as the initial scheme was deemed too dangerous. The number of transports was halved. Only supplies such as rations and forage would be carried aboard the trio, no fighting soldiers. A number of barges would also accompany the fleet; those loaded with coal would be lashed to gunboats and steamers, while one, with ammunition, would be started later and allowed to drift separately with the current.

The vessels of the lower Mississippi Squadron were divided into two task forces. The flagboat *Black Hawk*, the powerful new *Choctaw*, two Pook turtles, and all of the available tinclads and other auxiliaries were left above. Accompanying Porter in the second group, spaced 50 yards apart, would be his flagboat for this operation, the *Benton*, followed by, in order, Capt. Walke's new *Lafayette* and the turtles *Louisville*, *Mound City*, *Pittsburg*, and *Carondelet*.

The tug *Ivy* would be tied to the starboard beam of the *Benton*, while the ram *General Price* was added as a counterweight to the side of the *Lafayette* and coal barges would be lashed to the starboard sides of the other gunboats. The ironclad *Tuscumbia* would bring up the rear following the three army steamers to make certain they did not turn about once the shooting started.

The order of sailing determined, the bluejackets, and their civilian counterparts on the contract military steamers, set to attempting to make their boats as safe as possible, particularly their vulnerable machinery spaces. Hundreds of cotton bales (some captured up Steele's Bayou) and numerous heavy logs were placed around the boilers and other dangerous spots. Hay bales (useful later as animal feed) were also stacked about engines, steamboat decks, and gunboat casemates; sandbags were also stuffed around magazines and into spaces too small for cotton or hay.

Getting by the batteries undetected for as long as possible required a minimum noise level — something steamboats, with their high-pressure engines, were not noted for at the time. Capt. Walke pointed out that, during his run by Island No. 10 a year earlier, he had successfully muffled the *Carondelet* by diverting the exhaust steam from her engines into her wheelhouse. Porter ordered all captains to adopt this measure and added to it by directing that all livestock and pet dogs be sent ashore.

While the Northern tars made ready, the commanders in Vicksburg, grown comfortable since the defeat of the Steele's Bayou enterprise, chose to concentrate their attentions upon preparations for an upcoming grand ball. The weather was spotty, with much rain and some thunderstorms. Even after a spy warned Maj. Gen. Stevenson that the Federals were planning to run boats past the city's batteries, no enhanced defensive action was taken. Earlier orders to torch a number of tar barrels and old buildings on the riverbank opposite in the event of a Northern night passage continued in effect.[10]

All was in readiness by Wednesday morning, April 16. According to earlier orders, the boiler fires aboard the designated gunboats and steamers were lit early in order that, by evening, the hot power plants would be producing very little black exhaust smoke.

As the day progressed, finishing touches were made to shipboard defenses, and the last barges were secured. Around 6:30 P.M., the *Carondelet*'s crew, as well as those aboard her consorts, were beat to quarters and final preparations for running the blockade were completed. Fifteen minutes after the departure signal was hoisted aboard the flagboat *Benton*, at 9:00 P.M., the vessels of Porter's downriver task force cast off from shore. William L. Shea and Terrence J. Winschel called the forthcoming adventure "the most dramatic episode in the long struggle for Vicksburg, and one of the most spectacular episodes of the entire Civil War."

In the dark, two hours after sunset, the Federal line was quickly established, each boat separated from the next by 50 yards (give or take a few). To help avoid collisions, everyone steered a course in the wide river just slightly aport of the boat ahead. According to Acting Master's Mate Charles Heckman "Heck" Gulick, captain of the tug *Ivy*, the gunboats steadily passed ahead, with their engines "worked slow." As they began to turn into De Soto Point, all lanterns on each vessel were extinguished (save a red one at the stern) and the gun ports were closed to keep light from escaping the interiors. The way of the craft was now greatly reduced and their speed was at the minimum needed by helmsmen for control, or a little more than that of the current.

In Vicksburg, the grand Rebel ball was in full, happy progress about the same hour. The lights of the town were clearly in sight to men aboard the approaching gunboats. Even though the Confederate high command were not particularly vigilant, a number of pickets assigned to the river defenses of Col. Edward Higgins were. As the gunboats came down, these men went across the Mississippi and, about 11:10 P.M., lit the incendiary materials and buildings on its western bank. Maj. Gen. Grant, with his son and staff, watched from the hurricane deck of his headquarters transport. In an 1887 newspaper article, Fred Grant remembered how "suddenly a rocket went up from the shore. Then a cannon burst forth from Warrenton.... [S]oon fires were burning all along the shore, in front of the city, and the water was illuminated as by day's brightest sun."

The huge blaze backlit Porter's approaching fleet as it doubled De Soto Point, while signal rockets alerted Vicksburg's batteries to commence firing. The resultant excitement quickly ended the Confederate dance as participants ran to their stations—or for cover. As the long roll sounded, many hundreds of curious citizens found viewing seats atop Sky Harbor Hill and Court House Hill. The Federal craft were seen by hundreds in light and shadow creeping downstream close to the Louisiana shoreline. Fred Grant continued: "There in front of us, steaming down the river, were six gunboats, which looked to me like great black turtles, followed closely by three fragile transports, moving directly toward the batteries of the doomed city."

The ironclads and USQM steamers were targeted by Southern guns as they came to bear, six minutes after the lead vessels crept by the silent batteries opposite De Soto Point. Out on the *Lafayette*, Capt. Walke pictured the gun flashes as "a thunderstorm along the river as far as the eye could see." Confederate Maj. James T. Hogane later remembered seeing "Yankee gun boats slowly steaming down the river; nearer they came with almost a death-like motion, slow, and in harmony with the black, lithe, sinuous gliding of the river."

The noise of the cannon fire was so loud it could be heard 60 miles away. The noise of musket balls rattling off the casemates and superstructures was far more intimate. Added to the din was the sound of Federal cannon, firing toward the Confederate bastion from batteries on De Soto Point.

With their casemate interiors dark, it was arranged that Union gunners would pre-elevate their cannon for ranges of about 900 yards and return fire with grape and canister. Power to the gunboat engines was now increased and the gun ports were opened. All the while, musket balls could be heard plinking into and off the sides. As the Federals launched a return bombardment, their nice staggered steaming formation was jumbled. Blinding light flashes and thick clouds of smoke from cannon and burning buildings confused the pilots but serious collisions were avoided.

Even as they hugged the Louisiana shore, the gunboats first in line took a number of hits. The *Carondelet*, much further back, was not initially as exposed as, say, the *Lafayette*

Rear Adm. Walke's depiction of the gunboats, led by the ***Benton***, passing the Vicksburg batteries on the night of April 15, 1863 (***Battles and Leaders***).

Rear Adm. Porter's gunboats passing the batteries at Vicksburg on the night of April 15, 1863. In the dark two hours after sunset, the Federal line was quickly established, each boat being separated from the next by 50 yards (give or take a few). To help avoid collisions, everyone steered a course in the wide river just slightly aport of the boat ahead (Abbot's ***Bluejackets of '61***).

This sketch of Porter's run past the Vicksburg batteries was sketched by Confederate colonel S.H. Locket and gives the reader a vivid sense of the scene as seen from shore (*Battles and Leaders*).

or the *Pittsburg*. Still, Murphy's boat was hit twice. At the bend of the river opposite the upper Water battery, a 32-pdr. rifled percussion shell struck the *Carondelet*'s iron plates on the port side, bending two of them and cutting down a deck stanchion. Pieces from the shell entered one of the gun ports, slightly injuring four crewmen.

As the *Carondelet* approached the lower end of the Wyman Hill battery, an 8-inch Columbiad cannonball smashed through her signal locker, destroyed a couple of signal flags, and continued through the wheelhouse, landing in the river beyond.

To some extent, the frightful river eddies played havoc with each of the craft and the barges tied to them. The *Carondelet*'s pilots, John Murray and William Kautz, report what happened when — after passing the upper battery — the river took hold of their boat opposite the burning house on the right bank: "[O]wing to our being so close upon the *Pittsburg*, together with our want of speed, we drifted under these batteries near a point above Vicksburg. We immediately headed the *Carondelet* pretty well across the river, but the coal barge, on the one hand and the proximity of the *Pittsburg* on the other, prevented her from coming to as we designed, and we were compelled to turn her completely around before proceeding farther, during which time we were under heavy fire." The lights from the burning buildings was a significant factor in what occurred. In a letter home to the editor of the *Peoria Daily Mail*, Acting Master's Mate Gulick remembered that "one of the pilots of the *Carondelet* said that it bothered or blinded him so that he came near going ashore."

The *Carondelet,* according to Capt. Murphy, was under concentrated fire for about an hour. The fact that she got through without the Confederates getting her range was entirely due "to this fortunate pirouette." Coming abreast of the Warrenton battery sometime after 1:00 A.M., the *Carondelet*'s Second Division portside battery, two 8-inch Dahlgrens and a 42-pdr. under Acting Ensign Charles Amerman, fired three rounds without visible effect. The Eads-built ironclad rounded to two miles below the battery and subsequently anchored with the other gunboats about 2:30 A.M. Thursday morning on the outside of Diamond Island in Diamond Bend, 12 miles above New Carthage. The coal barge she was towing was moored to the bank "in good order."

About 10:15 A.M., the squadron got underway and continued down to New Carthage, where waiting soldiers gave it much the same sort of frenzied joyous greeting Capt. Walke and the *Carondelet* had received at New Madrid a year earlier. During the entire passage, only the transport *Henry Clay* was sunk. At Confederate army headquarters in the city, Maj. Gen. Pemberton wired President Jefferson Davis seeking additional support and adding, "I regard the navigation of the Mississippi River as shut out from us now."

On Saturday, April 19, the ironclads and barges were assembled off the Ion plantation at New Carthage within sight of the "Hurricane" plantation of Col. Joseph Davis, brother of Rebel president Jefferson Davis, that were three miles below on the Mississippi side. Tars aboard the *Carondelet* and her consorts were also able to clearly view the wreck of the former Federal ironclad *Indianola,* lost a month earlier, resting on a high bar with her forecastle out of the water. Many gave thanks that the terrific thunderstorm of the previous evening did not occur during their recent passage. A few days later, six Federal transports ran the batteries at night, with one lost.[11]

A "southern extremity of the Vicksburg forts," as Prof. Soley put it, the unfinished Confederate fortifications at Grand Gulf, Mississippi, 30 miles south of Vicksburg by road and double that south of Milliken's Bend, would be next to feel the wrath of the *Carondelet* and her consorts. It was unknown before the assault, but these defenses would not be conquered by the fleet.

By April 18, when Maj. Gen. Grant arrived at New Carthage, the four divisions of the XIII were already present . The location was inadequate as a staging area for a cross-river amphibious assault and so the men moved down along the shore first to Somerset (also unsuitable) and then to Hard Times, opposite the mouth of the Big Black River and three miles north of Grand Gulf. Troops from the XVII and XV Corps, north of Vicksburg, now began to follow.

While the Union's Army of the Tennessee came to Hard Times, the lower division of the Mississippi Squadron was not idle. For any assault crossing to be effective, the guns of Grand Gulf would have to be silenced. The *Carondelet* and several other vessels moved down to Brown's plantation, on the Louisiana shore about four miles above and across from Grand Gulf, on the afternoon of April 22.

Cautious at the prospect of facing heavy plunging fire, Acting Rear Adm. Porter determined to find out exactly what he faced. A week was spent by the gunboats, primarily the *Lafayette* and the *General Price,* reconnoitering and mapping Grand Gulf's artillery positions. What the sailors saw with their spyglasses was ominous. As was the case at Vicksburg (and Columbus, Fort Donelson, and Fort Pillow before), the defenses at Grand Gulf, under the command of Confederate Col. John S. Bowen, covered bluffs well above the water. Porter noted that "Grand Gulf is the strongest place on the Mississippi."

Dug into the side of Point of Rock, Fort Cobun was 40 feet above the river and protected by a parapet almost 40 feet thick. This upper battery mounted a pair of 32-pdrs., one 30-pdr. Parrott rifle, and an 8-inch Dahlgren smoothbore. The river formed a bend here, with difficult eddies.

Under a covered way, two parallel rifle pits stretched three quarters of a mile from Point of Rock to Fort Wade (named for artillery chief Col. William B. Wade). This lower fort, just behind the little town of Grand Gulf, was positioned on an abutment 20 feet above and a quarter mile back from the Mississippi; it was also armed with two 32-pdrs. and an 8-inch Dahlgren, as well as a huge 100-pdr. Blakely rifle. A number of fieldpieces were mounted at key points along the ridgeline at the top of the bluffs.

Aboard his lower flagship, the *Benton*, on April 27, Acting Rear Adm. Porter wrote out and dispatched to his ironclad captains specific general orders for the forthcoming assault they would make upon the Grand Gulf forts. In essence, the seven available boats would divide their attention between the two Rebel emplacements: *Benton*, *Tuscumbia*, and *Lafayette* versus the upper batteries at Fort Cobun and the four Pook turtles versus the lower at Fort Wade. Every captain was to explain Porter's plans to all officers, who would share the plans with their subordinates. In continuing deference to his skills as a pilot and his knowledge of local waters, Acting Volunteer Lt. William R. Hoel, commander of the *Pittsburg*, was "cheerfully," as Capt. Walke put it, chosen to lead the squadron into action.

Rear Adm. David Dixon Porter (1813–1891) commanded the Mississippi Squadron from October 1862 to October 1864. Working closely with the U.S. Army, Porter most notably participated in the capture of Vicksburg in 1862–1863 and the Red River expedition of 1864. During the former adventure, he briefly rode the *Carondelet* on an expedition up Steele's Bayou. When that failed, he led her and other ironclads in a run past the main riverfront batteries and into battle with guns at Grand Gulf that provided cover for Grant's army to cross the Mississippi (Library of Congress).

The next two days were spent in preparing the vessels for combat. Arrangements were the same as those made to pass the Vicksburg batteries, though Porter offered additional suggestions. For example, he recommended that each gunboat "should be well packed with hammocks, bags, and awnings around the pitmans." To guard against deckhouse fires, "water buckets and tubs should be kept filled all about the spar deck." Following the example first shown aboard the *Carondelet* at Fort Donelson, members of the gun crews were to be "cautioned about sticking themselves out of the ports when loading."

Maj. Gen. Grant was convinced that his naval colleagues could destroy the opposing guns, making it possible for his assault landing to proceed. To that end, 10,000 XIII Corps soldiers embarked upon their transports and a number of barges early on the morning of April 29 and were paddled down to a holding area behind the Coffee's Point peninsula. Once the "all clear" was signaled from the *Benton*, these would dash across the Mississippi, unload their charges, and return for others. Watching from crowded decks, the bluecoats, covered by the gunboat *General Price*, would have a ringside seat for the great bombardment show; Grant himself would see it from a tug.[12]

Having assembled in the waters off Grand Gulf between 6:00 A.M. and 7:00 A.M. on April 29, the seven available Federal ironclads, their colors flying bravely, advanced slowly in the six-knot current down upon their opponent's batteries. Led by the *Pittsburg*, the gunboats *Louisville*, *Carondelet*, and *Mound City*, at 150-yard intervals, came within about 1,500 yards of Fort Cobun around 8:00 A.M. As they passed, each unloaded from her bow guns a mix of grape, canister, and shrapnel (cut to ½ second) and percussion shells.

While the larger ironclads entertained this position, the turtles continued toward Fort Wade. A few minutes after the Union bombardment began, the Rebel guns returned the Northern compliment. The last big, loud ship vs. shore engagement of the western riverine war was underway—those to follow on the Red River and at Nashville would be small potatoes in comparison.

As the four Eads-built gunboats approached Fort Wade with portside guns blazing, the *Pittsburg* rounded to, taking a position close to the bank with her bows upstream. The maneuver was repeated by the *Louisville*. The *Carondelet* and *Mound City* successively performed the same evolution so that all available guns were blasting the defenders of the lower Confederate batteries.

A soldier from the 6th Missouri remembered in 1910 that "Many projectiles were seen to hit the iron sides of the gunboats, then glance off and go shrieking across to the Louisiana shore." Musket volleys from the rifle pits rained down upon the Federal boats and, occasionally, the eddies caused navigational difficulty for the Pook-designed craft.

The contest between the four Union ironclads, later backed by the *Lafayette*, and the Fort Wade cannon consumed some five hours before it was broken off. At this point, the turtles rounded to and moved up to support their heavier consorts, which were being roughly handled by Fort Cobun.

With the *Benton* temporarily out of action and the *Lafayette* and *Tuscumbia* holding previous station, the *Pittsburg*, *Louisville*, *Carondelet*, and *Mound City* steamed in circles, firing as their guns came to bear on Fort Cobun. A number of passes came as close to the enemy as 300 yards. Unhappily, owing to the "skillful and scientific arrangement of the embrasurers," the quartet scored few hits.

The fight with Cobun continued until Confederate resistance seemed to abate, somewhere around 1:00 P.M. During this time, according to Acting Ensign Scott D. Jordan, the *Carondelet* expended some 20 tons of powder, shot and shell. The guns atop the bluff were not silenced, but largely out of ammunition, despite the fact that nearly 2,500 Yankee shells had dropped into their works. When the guns were resupplied, they would be able to resume the contest almost as fresh as at its beginning.

Aware that the Rebel guns were still viable, but wanting to rest his men and confer with the military, Porter ordered his ironclads to cease firing at about 1:15 P.M. The ironclads withdrew to Hard Times, where the *Carondelet*, among them, dropped anchor at 2:00 P.M. Lunch was served and repair crews mended, as possible, the battle damages received. Capt. Murphy later reported his command received no major hits and suffered no casualties. The other six lost at least two dozen bluejackets between them. Three Confederates were killed, including Col. Wade.

Following a conference with Acting Rear Adm. Porter, Maj. Gen. Grant now determined to execute Plan B. The troops, who had witnessed the ironclad-gun battery duel, were debarked and marched three miles across the base of Coffee's Point peninsula to Disharoon's plantation. The *Lafayette*, meanwhile, amused the work parties at Fort Cobun, successfully keeping them from completing some repairs.

As part of the new Federal strategy, the gunboats cast off after dark and steamed down upon Grand Gulf. Just after 9:00 P.M., the morning contest was resumed. It was "as fine a display of fireworks as I had ever witnessed," remembered one 6th Missouri soldier years later. This assault was, however, a ruse. Blending into the shadows while hugging the Louisiana shore, five unarmed Northern troop transports passed down unscathed while the ironclads kept the Confederate gunners occupied. The gun smoke from the engagement completed the camouflage and within an hour, the contract steamers were tied to the west bank at Disharoon, four miles below Grand Gulf. That bypass mission accomplished, the gunboats also withdrew, making their landing at a point a mile above the military's vessels.

Later in the evening, Maj. Gen. Grant completed plans for his next move as the tired bluejackets retired to their hammocks. Capt. Murphy, with his colleagues, wrote out their after action reports. The *Carondelet* was hit only five times during the two attacks, suffering little damage. Acting Rear Adm. Porter closed his report of the day's fight to navy secretary Gideon Welles: "We land the army in the morning on the other side and march to Vicksburg."[13]

The USN gunboats, in addition to the USQM transports, undertook to transfer the XIII Corps across the Mississippi to the little unguarded town of Bruinsburg, south of Grand Gulf, beginning on April 30. The *Carondelet*'s contribution began at 6:30 A.M. when, once her decks were cleared, she boarded a portion of Brig. Gen. George F. McGinnis' arriving 1st Brigade (12th Division). Over the next several hours, these men were carried down to the main embarkation point.

Returning to her earlier anchorage off Disharoon's plantation in clear and pleasant weather at approximately 1:00 P.M., the veteran ironclad embarked two more regiments from McGinnis' command and, an hour and a half later, serving as an assault transport, once more steamed downstream. After passing the lower Grand Gulf batteries, she made directly for the levee at Bruinsburg, where she landed. Once her bluecoated passengers were aboard, they "marched up the river."

The *Carondelet* lay at the Bruinsburg landing until orders were received at 3:50 A.M. on May 1 for her to make another transport run. Arriving at Disharoon's plantation two hours later, she once more cleared her decks and made ready to receive troops. At 7:00 A.M., much artillery fire was heard on the Mississippi shore. The Confederates, unable to recover from the adroitness of Grant's maneuver, were facing defeat in the Battle of Port Gibson.

As that fight ashore matured, Capt. Murphy welcomed aboard 360 men from the 10th Missouri Volunteers and 450 from the 80th Ohio Volunteers. The lines were cast off at 8:45 A.M. and in an hour the craft arrived at Bruinsburg where the men were sent ashore and off to join the day's fighting. Another round-trip troop lift was completed during the afternoon.

In the hours after midnight on May 3, large explosions were heard from the Grand Gulf bluff and bright lights seen at the Mississippi Squadron anchorage at Bruinsburg. With the rising of the sun, about 4:30 A.M., Acting Rear Adm. Porter ordered several ironclads, led by the *Lafayette*, to go up, reconnoiter and, if warranted, resume the bombardment.

Fort Wade was abandoned when Capt. Walke arrived. Thereafter, according to his memoirs, a spirited race developed between the *Lafayette* and the remainder of Porter's vessels to see which could arrive first and take possession of the guns above Point of Rock:

> The *Lafayette* got the lead again, though only by a few feet, when the *Carondelet*, then commanded by Acting Volunteer Lieutenant J. McLeod Murphy, of political fame, blocked the way.

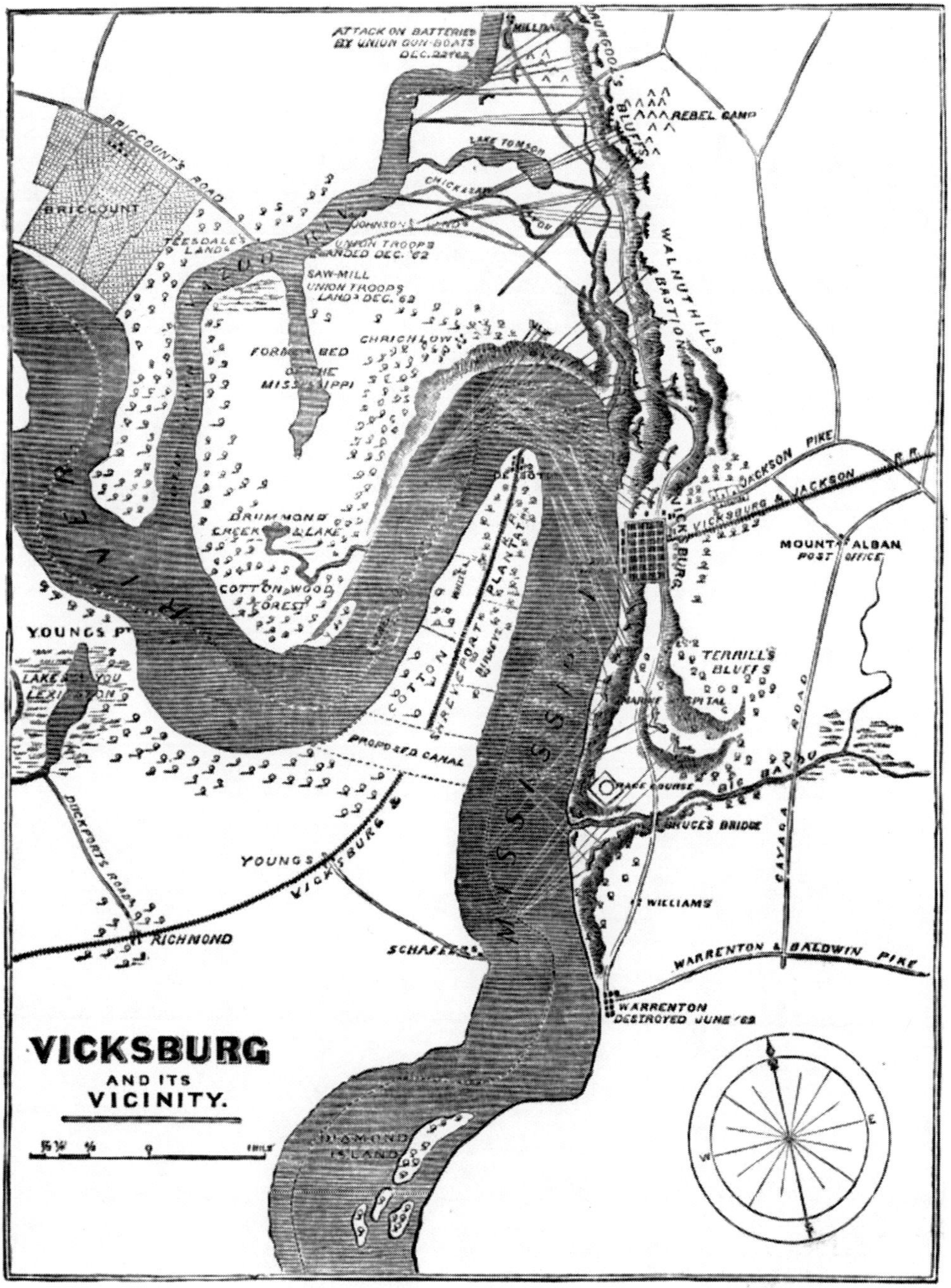

This map of Vicksburg and its vicinity appeared in the March 7, 1863, issue of *Harper's Weekly*.

> Her commander, taking advantage of the position of his gunboat on the start, ran her in the way of the *Lafayette*, and lodged the *Carondelet* against her port wheelhouse or guards, preventing her from passing ahead. Amidst the noise and confusion caused by the warning voices of the pilots, the orders or signals of Captain Walke to keep off were unavailing, and the *Carondelet* seeming to take it to be a scrub race, resorted to this ruse de guerre to keep ahead, and gain the honor of first raising our flag over the enemy's works. But just then the admiral came up in the *Benton* (the old war-horse!) and all had to give place to the flag [of his rank].

All of the racing ironclads came to anchor below Fort Cobun about 6:00 A.M., finding that bastion abandoned as well. Led by Acting Ensign Donaldson, a work party from the *Carondelet* joined several from other boats during the remainder of the day in "bringing guns from the Rebel works to the landing."

For most of the next week, Capt. Murphy's boat participated, with her consorts and USQM transports, in the transfer of follow-on troops sent down from Young's Point. These were embarked at Hard Times Landing and taken across the river to Grand Gulf, which had replaced the Bruinsburg beachhead. On the morning of May 7, the *Carondelet* undertook her greatest single trip lift: 850 men from three infantry regiments, plus seven wagons and three horses. Established on the eastern side of the river, Maj. Gen. Grant's Federals made relatively short work of the Southern defenders below Vicksburg. Following the May 16 Battle of Champion's Hill, Pemberton's men retreated within the citadel's perimeter, where a six week siege began.

The Mississippi Squadron participated in the encirclement and siege of Vicksburg by bombarding it from the river, while the U.S. Army cannonaded it from positions inland. Although the *Carondelet* was several times called upon to drop heavy shells upon the Confederate defenders, most of her time prior to the July 4 surrender was spent working the *Indianola* salvage site. Acting Rear Adm. Porter was determined to raise the sunken ironclad and engineer Capt. Murphy was placed in charge of the project. It would not be completed before the capitulation.[14]

11

From Vicksburg to Red River

Life aboard the *Carondelet* was not without its pleasantries even during the noisy investment of Vicksburg. In a letter home, Acting Ensign Scott D. Jordan reported that, on May 16, 1863, Capt. Murphy detailed an officer and 25 sailors to go ashore at James plantation and pick as many blackberries as possible. Three times larger than the junior Maine-born officer had ever seen, the blackberries came aboard by the bushel. As they were viewed as an excellent anti-scurvy source and an additional source of liquid in the hot climate, the men were encouraged to "eat as many of them as we wish at any time of day or night."

As the days of spring lengthened, so too did the siege. The opportunities for Confederate attacks upon Federal shipping up and down the western rivers also increased, some not far from the scene of the titanic struggle itself. On May 20, Acting Rear Adm. David Dixon Porter, "with characteristic energy," issued General Order No. 20, the inaugural outline of his divisional administrative plan for the U.S. Mississippi Squadron. This blueprint created six geographical sections, each, as the admiral later wrote, "extending between specified points." The admiral's divisions were "filled up with light-draft or "tinclad" vessels, to cruise up and down the river and carry dispatches." The light draughts in this chain were intended to be "strung along the river between ironclads." Lookouts aboard were "to watch the shore very close and capture every strolling party they may come across." Boats and skiffs encountered along the banks were to be taken and "every available method" taken to break up and disperse guerrillas.

The new geographical units, initially called "sections," were led by divisional officers, all trusted regular navy officers who commanded a certain number of named vessels. For example, Division Four from Natchez to Vicksburg was led from the *Benton* by Lt. Cmdr. James A. Greer. It also included four tinclads, as well as the *Carondelet* and *Pittsburg*. These leaders were also charged with the maintenance of "strict discipline" and cooperation with various U.S. Army officers, and were to employ all of their spare time directly or by mandate to their subordinates "exercising the men with the great guns and small arms."

The vessels in these new districts were responsible for patrol, convoy, and other work within the assigned boundaries. It was understood that vessels within a district could not leave station without the authority of the district leader, who would also approve all acquisitions (except money) and forward all communications from his subordinates to Cairo. As additional light draughts became available to the districts in 1864, it was common for the ironclads to remain all but stationary. For speed, district commanders oversaw activities within their commands, if they did not already do so, from the deck of a tinclad.

This decentralized district plan worked well, particularly in the months following the surrender of Vicksburg. From time to time over the next year as the squadron grew in size, it was amplified by later General Orders, all of which are printed in the Navy *Official Records*.

Having provided these general rules, Rear Adm. Porter did not often interfere with the routine work of his district commanders. All of his officers— particularly battle-tested leaders—were given the necessary authority to carry out their duties, were supported in their actions, and, for the most part, were not second-guessed.

"It is difficult to determine the importance of Porter's district policy in Union naval control of the rivers," wrote a group of distinguished scholars in 1986, "but the evidence strongly suggests that it was effective and efficient." Writing in 2007, Gary D. Joiner stated that this "district system worked as planned." He continued: "The rivers were never without a well-armed patrol, and the gunboats appeared along the same stretch of river often, but at irregular intervals."[1]

Having participated in the bombardments of Vicksburg on May 22, the *Carondelet*'s principal duty was now salvage of the sunken gunboat *Indianola*, a project her engineer-trained captain, Acting Volunteer Lt. John McLeod Murphy, initially undertook shortly after the Battle of Grand Gulf. Blown up by retreating Confederates, the broken vessel sat up straight in three fathoms of water about 20 yards from shore.

When the *Carondelet* dropped anchor off the *Indianaola*'s Hurricane Island wreck site on May 23, she was very nearly sinking herself. Twice hit during the previous day's encounter with Vicksburg's water batteries, she required extensive pumping just to keep her afloat. In addition, the gunboat's boilers had not been cleaned for 41 days. Engineer Caven reported that it was unsafe to employ them longer. When an order was received from Porter for the ironclad to join her sisters in the continuing bombardment of Vicksburg, Capt. Murphy sent word of her precarious condition to his superior. Ardently desiring to participate in the city's capture, the one-time army colonel had an even greater wish "not to suffer the well-earned reputation of the *Carondelet* to be diminished while in my hands."

With other ironclads available and wishing no harm to come to the famous boat, Porter unofficially withdrew her from further bombardment duties. Stationed as she was at the salvage site off the head of Diamond Island, at New Carthage, the *Carondelet* was able to obtain pumps and make some of her own repairs, while refreshing her power plant. Work on the *Indianola* was, meanwhile, expedited while the fleet's construction chief, Com. James B. Hull at St. Louis, completed arrangements with a private firm to raise her.

As Maj. Gen. Ulysses S. Grant's ground-pounding advance shoved around the Confederate fortress via the Big Black River, the supply, garrison and staging locations on the northwest side of the Mississippi River above Vicksburg were largely transformed into training and assembly points. A number of depots and hospitals were located close to the Louisiana shoreline.

Confederate leaders did not realize just how dramatically Grant's line of logistical support was shifting. They continued to believe that his supply route remained down the west bank of the river across from Vicksburg and that it was vulnerable to attack. As a result of this misperception, President Davis passed orders for Lt. Gen. Edmund Kirby Smith, commander of the Confederate Trans-Mississippi Department, to break up what was now a nonexistent supply line. Smith, in turn, ordered Maj. Gen. Richard "Dick" Taylor to mount this attack, to provide succor to Vicksburg, and to cooperate in every way with Lt. Gen. John C. Pemberton. To help carry off the assignment, Maj. Gen. John George Walker's Texas Division ("Walker's Greyhounds") was assigned to Taylor's command.

As Taylor and Walker approached the Mississippi from the Tensas River, they learned that the Yankee supply line from Milliken's Bend was largely history. Still, it was reasoned, if a portion of the Louisiana shore could be captured and held, it might somehow be possible to herd cattle and send other supplies across to Vicksburg's beleaguered garrison.

Shortly before 11:00 P.M. on May 30, War Department special envoy Charles A. Dana, armed with orders from Acting Rear Adm. Porter, came aboard the *Carondelet* seeking transport to a meeting with Maj. Gen Nathaniel Banks. After making a mid-river rendezvous with the steamer taking Dana south, the ironclad continued down to Perkin's Landing, MS, about five miles below James plantation at New Carthage. Just after she dropped anchor, about 3:00 A.M. on May 31, Col. Richard Owen, commanding the position with a 300-man detachment, was granted permission to come aboard. While shaking hands with Capt. Murphy, he breathlessly explained that an attack from a large Confederate force was anticipated and that his communications were cut off. Owen went on to say that he had destroyed as much of the local depot's stores as possible and built an improvised but very light defense behind cotton bales at the river's edge . Although an evacuation steamer, the *Forrest Queen*, was anticipated, the protection of an ironclad could be lifesaving.

The *Carondelet*'s captain agreed to move toward shore and provide cover until the transport arrived. After dawn, the gunboat shelled the woods in the lower vicinity, hoping to prevent the Rebels from enfilading the colonel's men. About 9:00 A.M., the *Forrest Queen* put into the bank and Owen's men started to embark.

Loading the Union troops was far from finished when, 15 minutes later, a Confederate brigade from Walker's Texas Division, estimated at 1,400 men and under the command of Brig. Gen. Henry E. McCulloch, "took the field and approached rapidly." The butternuts did not expect to find an ironclad that quickly opened upon them "with such guns as could be brought to bear." The *Carondelet* bombarded the Southerners for an hour until they retreated.

Lt. Gen. Richard "Dick" Taylor commanded the Confederate District of Western Louisiana from July 1862. He was the Southern general most directly responsible for the defense of the Red River against the combined Federal army and navy expedition in the spring of 1864 (U.S. Army Military History Institute).

After the Rebels withdrew, Col. Owens' soldiers resumed destroying the remaining abandoned Federal property at their former post. The troops soon reembarked aboard the *Forrest Queen*, and were convoyed by the *Carondelet* up to the James plantation. That place was also found evacuated, with "most of the negro quarters and outbuildings burning." A number of bluecoats who had contracted smallpox were found abandoned in the big farm's hospital. Believing he could not bring them off without endangering his crew, Capt. Murphy left them with stores. The *Carondelet* and her charge proceeded up the river, arriving at the Mississippi Squadron anchorage below Vicksburg about 10:00 P.M.

After making his preliminary report, Capt. Murphy was ordered by Fourth District commander Greer to communicate personally with the admiral, delivering a full account of his engagement. During the course of his interview, the ironclad's commander recommended to Porter the initiation of a gunboat patrol between Warrenton and Grand Gulf to halt any trans-river activity. Taylor and Walker, meanwhile, continued their riverbank attacks for a week. Their most spectacular assault occurred on June 7 when they attacked African American troops defending Milliken's Bend and were beaten back with the aid of two Navy gunboats.[2]

After her June 1 return to Palmyra Island, the *Carondelet* took no further direct part in the Vicksburg operation. She continued to guard and prepare the *Indianaola* wreck site for the remainder of the month. Acting Volunteer Lt. Murphy obtained the services of a group of 37 African American laborers from Turner's plantation at Point Pleasant, as well as the James place. They, with his bluejackets, were all, to one degree or another, busily engaged in the salvage work.

With Acting Ensign Donaldson, the on-scene superintendent, the sailors and day laborers were able to remove the mud from the *Indianola*'s interior, clean existing machinery, exhume a 9-inch cannon, making it ready for transport, and collect great piles of refuse. Considerable amounts of coal were identified for reclamation from the ironclad's bunkers, as well as a coal barge sunk opposite James plantation.

On June 18, Murphy reported to Acting Rear Adm. Porter that a clear trench was under construction around the hull of the *Indianola* and the African Americans were removing all portable weight. The New Yorker believed it possible to wait for the river to rise toward fall and refloat it. Toward the end of the month, Capt. Ed R. Nelson of the Missouri Wrecking Company visited the *Black Hawk*. There he learned that the *Carondelet* workmen had calked the *Indianola* hulk and had her ready to float into the river as soon as it rose. When he returned to St. Louis, Nelson informed Com. Hull that, in his opinion, the gunboat could not be saved by waiting for her to float off.

The death throes of Vicksburg continued through what remained of June and into the first days of July. Aboard the *Carondelet*, carpenters continued to make what repairs to the boat were possible. The weather was extremely hot and upwards of 25 crewmen were put on the sick list as the month ended. Taking advantage of good drying weather, the tars completely repainted of the vessel. There were, however, many scars on her that paint would not cover.

On the fittingly symbolic date of July 4, after a 45-day siege, the fortress city was surrendered. The event, coming with the equally vital retreat of Gen. Robert E. Lee from Gettysburg in Pennsylvania, marked for all to see the receding of the political tide that was the Confederacy. Like other vessels in the squadron up and down the rivers, Capt. Murphy's command fired a 21-gun National salute at high noon.

The following day, the *Carondelet* joined six other gunboats in anchoring off Vicksburg. Two days later, 100 of her bluejackets were given liberty ashore and all of the officers, the first for most in 10 months. Only Capt. Murphy and Ensigns Donaldson and Jordan remained behind, with a skeleton crew.[3]

Just before and immediately after the fall of Vicksburg, Confederate mounted raiders stepped up attacks on Mississippi River shipping in the area below the former Confederate citadel. Particular efforts were made to interfere with transports bearing supplies for Union posts or troops headed southward, including those bearing livestock ("cattle steamers").

On July 14, Porter wrote to Maj. Gen. Grant informing him that he had received intelligence of a large party of Confederate irregulars (nearly always called "guerrillas" in such Federal communications) in the Ashwood area, below New Carthage. They were preparing to assault shipping with masked batteries. Orders were sent to the *Carondelet*, whose anchorage was within two miles of Ashwood, to move closer down and Grant was advised that, if he wanted to send a force to investigate, Murphy's ironclad could provide cover.

As the admiral had requested, the *Carondelet* got underway and steamed down as far as possible without losing sight of the *Indianola.* It would not do for the suspected Confederates horsemen to double back and attack the sunken gunboat. No enemy was found.

On the other hand, there was at this time no lack of beef for the sailors of the Mississippi Squadron. Forage crews were sent ashore every Monday, Wednesday, and Saturday to find and slaughter oxen, which were then distributed to all Federal naval vessels. On August 7, a landing party from the *Carondelet* returned with 23 head, which were distributed to waiting boats from other craft, including two for the *Black Hawk.* Murphy's men brought one aboard that was cooked and handed out immediately. "We serve out a whole ox at once," remembered one officer, "as we cannot keep beef overnight." Three days a week, the jack tars ate as much steak as they wished.

The summer continued quietly. The heat remained ferocious and the water level declined. Although the *Carondelet* sailors were able to obtain fresh fruit and poultry from markets and peddlers ashore, it was extremely hot. Bugs were everywhere. In a letter home, Acting Ensign Jordan confided that flies and mosquitoes were a problem, but not nearly the one created by roaches:

> We have enough of them — I should come about as near to the number as a million years is to eternity. As I am writing this letter, if I raise my eyes from the paper, I see roaches in hundreds in any direction which I may look. The table on which I am writing is alive with them. They are continually running over the paper getting in the way of the pen, large and small. If we lay our caps down, they are inhabited immediately.... Our clothes are full of them. Our bunks are full of them. When our table is set and the food is put on, they are continually running over it. Our bunks are full & the floor of all the state rooms are covered with them. They annoy us a great deal though they bite but little. They eat all crumbs of food or pieces of fruit dropped on the floor. No bed bugs are found where the roach is as they are of all sizes from one inch in length to the 16th of an inch so they can go in to all of the cracks & crevices however small. Well, what I have said about roaches is true every word and will bear multiplying by 20 — without getting beyond the truth.

By early August, the gunboat's sick list was down to nine. Unhappily, one of those was Capt. Murphy, who was so ill on Sunday, August 2, that Divine Services, over which he always presided as did Capt. Walke before him, had to be cancelled. Fortunately, his bout of illness was passing.

On August 11, an unidentified party of riders, believed to be "guerrillas," approached the shore. As it was anticipated that they would attack the camp of the African American workers at the Davis plantation (referred to aboard the *Carondelet* as their "colony"), Capt. Murphy ordered his guns to fire on the men. Simultaneously, a 20-man landing party was sent ashore to see if it could capture any of the graycoats. Two men were taken and subsequently sent up the river.[4]

Late in August, Acting Volunteer Lt. Murphy became ill again. Evacuated to Memphis, he was treated aboard the *Benton* by that vessel's medical staff. There was great concern for Murphy's life and, on September 1, he was comforted by the Roman Catholic bishop of Natchez, William Henry Elder, who was visiting in the Tennessee city. The *Carondelet*'s captain received the Eucharist under the special administration of communion to the dying (viaticum). The last rites were not administered; however, Elder promised to return if that necessity arose. Whatever his illness, Murphy soon appeared stronger. On September 6, he returned to the *Carondelet* onboard the tinclad *Forest Rose.* Unhappily, his improvement did not last and within two weeks, he was forced to go on medical leave, this time returning home to recover. Acting Rear Adm. Porter retained Murphy as commander of the *Carondelet* "on the books" through October. The gunboat's officers did not know the extent of his illness; most expected him back "pretty soon."

Acting Ensign James C. Gipson took over the boat pending the skipper's return. Gipson, like Murphy, was popular with the *Carondelet*'s crew. Scott Jordan told his wife that his new captain was a very talented musician: "he can play or sing anything if he can hear it once — and he is always at one or the other unless when asleep." If he had a fault, Jordan confided later, it "is lack of education, which is quite a misfortune to anyone."

Temperatures off Hurricane Island moderated through the fall and the river slowly began to rise. Frost touched the wreck site on the night of October 25. Executive Officer Donaldson was also ill during much of this period, though he did not need to leave the ship. Ensign Jordan was his relief and conducted the gunnery divisions at practice every few days until early December.

Due to the increasing partisan threat, orders were received restricting the men to the *Carondelet* or the *Indianola* work site. Beef was still acquired, though now largely alive and by purchase from passing steamers. The animals were kept on a small mid-river atoll and slaughtered only when needed.

When, in November, it became clear that that Capt. Murphy would not be back, Acting Master Gipson was elevated. He would command the boat through January 1864. His popularity with his officers continually increased and he spent much time in the wardroom with them. Gipson often accepted the kind invitation of his subordinates to meals. He informed them that the pleasure of their company was a much happier arrangement than continuously eating alone in the captain's cabin as Walke, Murphy, and most other gunboat commanders did. On December 6, their repast included roast raccoon, roast beef, Irish mashed potatoes with butter, boiled onions, canned peaches, bread, various sauces, and pumpkin pie.[5]

Minor work on and protection of the *Indianola* continued without event under Gipson's eye. As Confederate cavalry and guerrilla attacks intensified along the Mississippi in the fall, Acting Rear Adm. Porter cautioned that every protection be taken to prevent a raid upon the sunken gunboat. Gipson, in a November 23 report, noted the removal of everything wooden from within a quarter of a mile of the wreck. Daily scouting parties went ashore to examine all possible approaches and "two negro scouts, mounted, rode backward and forward all the time between here [Hurricane Island] and the cut-off above."

Despite Gipson's precautions, 60 irregular horsemen approached the shore at the Davis plantation on December 11, intent upon destroying the wreck. The *Carondelet* opened fire, causing the Rebels to fade out of sight. To make certain they were gone, the gunboat captain led 30 men ashore toward the spot where the Confederates had been seen. As the boat party approached, the riders, visible again, withdrew once more, this time for good.

On December 19, the *Carondelet* was transferred to the Fifth District (Vicksburg to White River), then under Lt. Cmdr. Robert K. Owen of the *Louisville.* With his support, the veteran ironclad received new ordnance. A pair of 100-pdr. Parrott rifles were mounted forward, with two 50-pdrs. in the stern. During the month, upwards of two dozen men were on the sick list, some with fevers lasting as long as five days.

Her work with the *Indianola* completed, the *Carondelet* steamed to Skipwith's Landing on December 29 where, according to Owen, the locals "appear in constant dread of being attacked." When it was determined that no irregular assaults were about to materialize, the *Carondelet* was sent to Milliken's Bend, 70 miles further south, on the last day of the year.[6]

For some months now, Federal forces from Washington to the West had been involved in planning an incursion into the Trans-Mississippi theater. By the beginning of the new year, generals as diverse as Grant, Sherman, and Nathaniel Banks, the eventual expedition ground leader, were onboard with a plan to move up the Red River through Louisiana, via Alexandria and Shreveport, toward Texas.

The forthcoming operation would, in actuality, be a "rather grand undertaking," in the words of historian William Riley Brookshire. In the end, however, it would really consist of a "loosely connected joint land and naval exercise," with, as its ultimate military objective, the "completion of the subjugation of Louisiana and Arkansas." If this thrust was successful, it "would effectively remove the Confederate Trans-Mississippi Department from an active role in the conflict."

In addition to the purely military benefits of such a gambit, a big Red River offensive could disrupt Confederate commerce and have some hope of dissuading a northward view by French forces then trying to subdue Mexico. Naturally, the Mississippi Squadron would be invited along to provide support and guard the many necessary transports. Scuttlebutt, the sailors' rumor mill, had it that the fleet would "go into the Red River and clean the Rebels out at once when they got ready."

While the political, military, and logistical difficulties of a Red River campaign were reviewed and resolved (details far outside the scope of our story), the work of the *Carondelet* continued apace into 1864. Guerrilla and irregular force suppression remained a constant concern, as was the maintenance of an effective blockade against contraband goods and produce and the succor of loyal sentiment.

To combat the irregular threat, the *Carondelet* steamed slowly up and down the river as much as 60 miles from her anchorage, attempting to make certain that Confederate cross-river activity was stifled. Towns or locales passed or visited included Choctaw Bend, Eunice, and Port Anderson. Like all riverboats, the sounds of the approaching gunboat could be heard long before she was actually seen. Occasionally, large armed parties were sent ashore to forage or shoot beef. Small squads of Confederates were seen on shore from time to time, but they were "always hurried off by sending a few shells among them."

On February 16, a woman was brought aboard from shore near Gaines Landing claiming to be a refugee from a group of Rebel ruffians who intended to harm her. A widow, she supposedly was in the area under a Treasury Department permit that permitted her to move up to 5,000 bales of cotton from a plantation in which she held an interest. Aboard for two days as the vessel returned to port, the lady was entertained by Capt. Gipson and his officers and, in turn, charmed them with song and verse. Not long after she went ashore and the vessel returned to patrol, the skipper found that one of the official signal books was missing. It was immediately concluded that the woman was a spy intent upon delivering the weighted handbook to the enemy. Immediately rounding to, the *Carondelet* made her best speed back to Gaines. There, a lone house was quickly surrounded by 40 sailors and the lady was captured and returned aboard. The prisoner claimed innocence and the signal book was not immediately recovered, though it would turn up some days later.

Fresh from the Washington Navy Yard, Lt. Cmdr. John G. Mitchell, the *Carondelet*'s second full-time regular Navy captain, came aboard from a passing steamer on February 19. Once he had read himself into command, Ensign Gibson resumed the post of executive officer.[7]

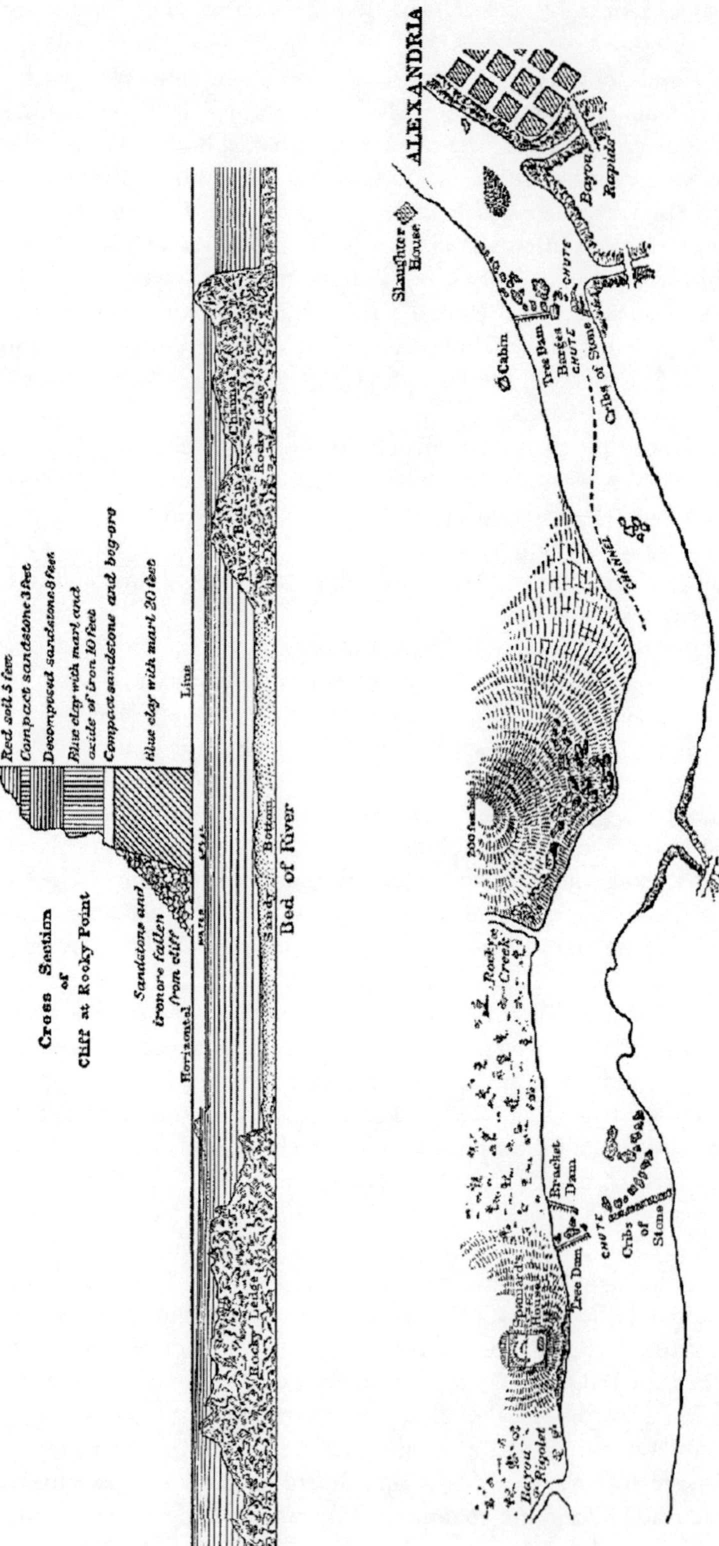

MAP AND SECTIONS OF THE RED RIVER DAMS ABOVE ALEXANDRIA.

This photograph of the *Pittsburg* on the Red River conveys a sense not only of the width of the river, but also of the configuration of one of the more active Pook turtles, albeit one that occasionally ran afoul of the *Carondelet* (Miller's *Photographic History of the Civil War*).

The water level in the Red River was quite low during the first weeks of the new year, contributing to a delay in the start of the planned Federal campaign. Still, once he had signed on, Rear Adm. Porter promised to obtain all of the hulls and guns needed. Indeed, he boasted to Sherman that he would ascend the Red "with every ironclad vessel in the fleet."

Gary D. Joiner reports that a crucial piece of evidence received by Rear Adm. Porter back on February 14 was a chart of Shreveport and vicinity drawn on the back of the death certificate of a Federal seaman, James O'Leary. The detail on this map was "perhaps the greatest influence of Admiral Porter's decision of which vessels should be included in the expedition."

Most of the USN ironclads, a ram, several support vessels, plus two large and nine standard tinclads chosen on the basis of the O'Leary document received orders over the remainder of the month to assemble for the upcoming Trans-Mississippi campaign. Porter himself arrived off the mouth of the Red River during the last week of February.

Wishing to know the state of Confederate defenses and preparedness in the adjacent area, the squadron commander ordered that a naval reconnaissance expedition ascend Louisiana's Black and Ouachita (pronounced Washitaw) rivers. A force of light draught gunboats and monitors was away for about a week, during which time it battled both regular and irregular troops, recovered several cannon, and gained information of less than immediate value. When the craft returned on March 5, few were surprised to also see their decks loaded with captured cotton.[8]

Opposite: **Red River dams above Alexandria, Louisiana, in May 1864. The top drawing shows the construction of the dams, while that on the bottom depicts their placement (*Battles and Leaders*).**

By the beginning of March, Confederate Maj. Gen. Taylor also knew that a large Federal force would soon be headed his way. To meet it, he had just 25,000 men. Maj. Gen. Nathaniel Banks and Rear Adm. Porter, coequal commanders of the Union expedition, enjoyed a force superiority of 42,000 men, including 10,000 on loan from the Army of the Tennessee. Arkansas area commander Maj Gen. Frederick Steele was also to participate.

The *Carondelet* received orders to join the expedition on March 5. With rumors of the upcoming adventure circulating widely, everyone aboard suspected that the boat was headed for the Red River, even though the initial instructions simply called for her to steam down to Natchez. The scuttlebutt was correct. The Eads-built craft dropped anchor off the mouth of the Red River at 6:00 P.M. on March 7. Fourteen other vessels were already present.

Maj. Gen. A.J. "Whiskey" Smith and his 10,000 men arrived at the mouth of the Red River on March 11 aboard 21 transports. Maj. Gen. Sherman, who had agreed to allow them to participate, wanted his men back by April 15. These soldiers and their munitions and supplies would be guarded up the Louisiana river by the Mississippi Squadron of the U.S. Navy.

Promptly at 1:00 P.M., Capt. Mitchell led all the boat's small arms crews ashore for battalion drill. They were joined by similar contingents from all of the assembled warships. Practice was also taken with a number of wheeled boat howitzers, just like those employed by Capt. Murphy atop his mound near Deer Creek the year before. In a pinch, Porter could support amphibious requirements with additional lightly drilled men.

In addition to the civil steamers chartered by the U.S. Quartermaster Department to transport the Union army, Rear Adm. Porter, over the previous few days, had finished assembling what Lt. Cmdr. Thomas Selfridge later called "the most formidable force that had ever been collected in the western waters." As noted earlier, it drew from every flotilla in the squadron. The admiral was "determined there should be no want of floating batteries for the troops to fall back on in case of disaster." The naval and quartermaster transport force assigned to the operation was thus 104 vessels, mounting 300 guns (210 naval).

In reviewing this naval strength, the embedded *Philadelphia Inquirer* reporter was moved to observe that "a more formidable fleet was never under single command than that now on the Western rivers under Admiral Porter." On the other hand, he continued, "it might be said, also, never to less purpose. At the time of departure, the strength of the Rebellion in the inland waters had been crushed."

As March continued to advance, the river stage of the Red, further south, did not. The gung-ho Porter knew from recent surveys that this was "the most treacherous of all rivers; there is no counting on it, according to the rules which govern other streams." Writing for *Battles and Leaders* after the war, Lt. Cmdr. Selfridge explained that the whole expedition hinged upon "the usual spring rise; but this year, the rise did not come." Indeed in looking back, it was his opinion that "Had the river been bank full, no force that the Confederates could have controlled could have stood for a moment against the fleet."

Just before Smith's arrival, Porter received the news that heavy rains were delaying Banks. He could not possibly reach Alexandria, one of the principal targets, before March 21. Additionally, the sailor found that work on the completion of the unfinished Fort De Russy, 30 miles south of Alexandria, was being pushed hard by the Rebels.

While the naval and military men bobbed on their vessels observing the overgrown marshlands ashore, Rear Adm. Porter and Maj. Gen. Smith held a meeting to decide what to do next in light of Banks' delay. The two men decided to capture Alexandria, taking Fort De Russy while en route. Their invasion armada started up the Red River at 8:30 A.M. on

March 12.[9] Advance Federal naval vessels and military forces captured Fort De Russy before sundown on March 14. News of the capitulation was taken down by tug to the *Carondelet* and her consorts, tied up to the bank 10 miles below, at 9:30 that evening. The following morning, in weather cool and pleasant, the main fleet continued toward Alexandria. Maj. Gen. Taylor, who had decided not to contest the Federal occupation, passed orders for his units to rendezvous at Natchitoches.

The *Carondelet* passed Fort De Russy just after noon, steaming easily. Her men, like those aboard the *Pittsburg* ahead and the *Mound City* astern, were quite interested in liberating some of the Confederate cotton seen along the shore. After all, in the opinion of the squadron commander, the law which gave sailors a third of the value of captured items applied to cotton as well as to ships. The gunboat halted at 4:00 P.M. and tied to the bank to wait for the grounded *Ozark*, in the lead, to be freed. Meanwhile, Capt. Mitchell sent a party to bring back aboard 40 bales of cotton near the bank, giving his boat a total of 96 bales seized at opportune times in the three days since the expedition began.

Just before 6:00 A.M. Tuesday morning, the ironclads cast off. With great plumes of grey smoke rising over their black hulls, the *Carondelet* and her consorts paddled up the Red, stopping from time to time to capture more cotton. Mitchell's bluejackets brought off another 50 bales.

Nine Union vessels arrived at Alexandria by late afternoon of March 16 and a pair of landing parties secured the levee. Happily for the gunboatmen, Maj. Gen. Smith's troop transports arrived earlier in the day, saving the sailors from performing occupation duties across town.

So far, the arriving soldiers, many of them from places like Wisconsin, New York, and Rhode Island, were not impressed with the Red River. "It is a dirty, sluggish stream, about an eighth of a mile wide," wrote Harris Beecher of the 114th New York, "flowing in an extremely crooked channel." He added, "Its ends and curves are so exaggerated that they seem almost unnatural."

Rear Adm. Porter was not at all pleased that Maj. Gen. Banks, plagued as he was by heavy rains, remained absent. The campaign seemed to be at a standstill. Shreveport, the principal objective, was still 350 miles up the Red.

Even though the Confederates had an active policy of burning cotton to prevent its capture by the Northerners, there was just too much for all of it to be fired. Some of it had already been picked up by the *Carondelet* and her sisters on their way to Alexandria. Until Banks arrived, Porter elected to use his men to capture even more. The bluejackets on this big outing enthusiastically sought out and gathered as much undestroyed cotton as possible. In the three days before Banks finally turned up, Federal sailors seized in excess of 3,000 bales. This booty was sent by trading steamers to a prize court at Cairo along with that picked up by individual warships earlier. It goes without saying that Union soldiers, who could not participate in the rewards of these spoils, were displeased. Maj. David C. Houston later told the War Conduct Committee that it "was rather demoralizing to the soldiers to see the navy seizing the cotton for prize on land, while they did not get any."

The last of Maj. Gen. Banks' troops trekked into Alexandria on March 26 and the Federals finally had what Ludwell Johnson called "an impressive display of military might—the greatest in the history of the Southwest." The same day, Lt. Gen. Grant called for the return of Maj. Gen. Smith's command.

The required spring rise on the Red simply failed to materialize—for the first time in nine years. Indeed, instead of rising, the water level in the Red was declining at the rate of an inch an hour. As the river stage dropped, channel bottom irregularities increased the number of dangerous rapids and exposed countless rocks, sandbars, snags, and other obstructions. At this point, Smith's corps undertook a march to Bayou Rapides, 21 miles above Alexandria. Despite the tardy rise in the water, elements of the Mississippi Squadron were needed to provide support.[10]

Having decided to continue on, Rear Adm. Porter was faced with the problem of getting his fleet over the double set of rapids just north of Alexandria. "The rapids of Alexandria," wrote Steven D. Smith and George J. Castille III in 1986, "were composed of rocky outcroppings of sandstone and siltstone forming shoals along a mile stretch of the Red River, even at times of high water." They continued: "At low water, the upper and lower ends of the rapids were exposed."

Electing to keep a number of vessels below, Porter sent others ahead into the danger zone early on March 28. The river looked passable for some of the lighter vessels, though questionable for others. Almost as soon as this effort began, the army hospital boat *Woodford* crashed on the rocks, swinging around in a sinking condition. A towboat and the *Carondelet*'s second cutter went to the rescue. Although no lives were lost, the craft sank at 6:00 P.M.

A few days later, navy secretary Gideon Welles received a letter from Porter, dated March 29, announcing that he was about to depart for Shreveport "or as high up the river as I can get." The *Carondelet*, with the assistance of a towboat, made it safely over the rapids early that morning, though not without "rubbing considerably on the bottom."

The low level of the Red River continued to hinder efforts to get other gunboats above the rapids at Alexandria. The giant ironclad *Eastport*, in the lead, grounded, requiring much effort to free her. With the *Eastport* finally available, the Porter-Smith expedition resumed its trek up the Red River on April 2. Maj. Gen. Banks, meanwhile, marched overland. All along the way, sailors on the gunboats and soldiers on the transports saw "large numbers of slaves of every age and sex on the banks of the river." Acting Ensign Jordan told his wife that they all waved "their handkerchiefs, aprons, hats, or anything else they can get hold of in welcome of the Gun Boats and Abe Lincoln's Flag."

In moving upstream, the vessels kept their guns "run out in case we should need them in a hurry." They also made every effort to remain away from the effects of the strong current. As the *Carondelet* steamed ahead, she, at one point, ran into a swirling current while doubling a sharp point in the river. Forced into the bank, it required a half hour's assistance from the steamer *Rob Roy* to work free.

The last of 26 civilian charter steamers with Maj. Gen. Smith's men and supplies passed the Alexandria obstructions early on April 3. By noon, the task force reached Grand Ecore, a little west bank town four miles north of Natchitoches, where Maj. Gen. Banks' soldiers started to walk in overland almost simultaneously. Here the bluffs were 120 feet high and contained fortifications dating back to the Mexican War. Rear Adm. Porter and Maj. Gen. Smith expected Banks to join them at the little river community later in the day. While they waited for the expedition commander, Maj. Gen. "Whiskey" Smith's soldiers disembarked, save for the XVII Corps Provisional Division, under Brig. Gen. T. Kilby Smith, which was detailed to remain with the transports.

Just before 5:00 P.M., Lt. Cmdr. George Bache's *Lexington* led a small task unit up the river to search for Rebel torpedoes that may have been laid in the Red. The river narrowed above Grand Encore as the speed of its current grew more swift. The banks were elevated at a number of points from the surrounding countryside.

A large fleet of Federal transports and gunboats assembled off the mouth of the Red River in late February and early March 1864. The *Carondelet* was among the vessels assigned by Rear Adm. David D. Porter to the enterprise. The expedition actually started out before its land commander, Maj. Gen. Nathaniel Banks, arrived and made its way up to Alexandria, Louisiana, where he joined it (*Battles and Leaders*).

Banks arrived at Grand Ecore during the evening and there the Federal generals agreed to a new plan for the rapid capture of Shreveport. The National expeditionary corps, comprising Banks' corps and most of A.J. Smith's, both of which thus far had moved mainly along the Red River, would strike inland away from water. They would proceed along the Shreveport road on April 6–7 headed toward Mansfield. Under escort of navy gunboats, Brig. Gen. Smith's 2,000 Provisionals, aboard 20 transports also carrying "many hundred thousand rations," would steam up to Springfield Landing, opposite Loggy Bayou, six miles northeast of Mansfield and about 30 miles south of Shreveport. It was expected that Banks and Porter would communicate at Springfield Landing in three days as the soldiers and sailors linked up.

The naval portion of the Banks grand scheme did not unfold immediately. As preparations for departure continued, several of the ironclads undertook a torpedo sweep on April 4. Armed cutters were called away near Madame De Roe's plantation, not far from Campti, and dragged for the nefarious mines. During the process, they sounded the channel's depth. At the same time, Federal forces, backed up by squadron units far upstream from the *Carondelet*, engaged a force of Confederate riders at Campti. As the Confederates retreated from the town, it was set alight.

Meanwhile, below, the *Carondelet* and her consorts steamed ahead. About 12:40 P.M., the old Eads-built gunboat came in sight of the *Louisville* and *Eastport*, both aground. An hour later, as her cutters sounded the area, Capt. Mitchell's craft sent a line to the *Louisville* and pulled her off.

That evening, after witnessing several POW columns headed toward the rear, the slower ironclads passed Campti, where numerous buildings remained on fire and citizens reported the morning battle. By virtue of the groundings of consorts, the *Carondelet* was able to pass several of those stuck and move up, eventually becoming the number two ironclad in line, four miles behind the lead boat.

The waters above Grand Encore continued to present significant navigational challenges for the Union gunboats. On top of this, Confederate sharpshooters were becoming quite bothersome, acting not unlike those who had harassed the ironclads up Steele's Bayou a year earlier.

By April 6, the *Carondelet* was 85 miles above Grand Ecore when Porter determined that the City Series ironclads, together with the *Eastport,* should return downstream. It being impossible to round to, the vessels backed down. The rudders of four boats were carried away and the *Carondelet* came close to losing hers as well. When her upper rudder brace and tiller carried away, Mitchell's command was detained making repairs for an hour and a half. Still, the *Carondelet* returned to Grand Ecore before four other boats less fortunate than she.

By the morning of April 7, the bluecoat soldiers of Maj. Gen. Banks and Smith, save for those of the latter detailed to remain with the transports, were disappearing into the distance ashore. It was now time for a leaner, light-draught nautical force to steam ahead. Leaving fleet captain and *Eastport* skipper Lt. Cmdr. S Ledyard Phelps behind off the town in overall command of the heavier gunboats, Rear Adm. Porter personally led his specialized task group up the Red River toward Shreveport. If the water level would only begin to rise, the remaining gunboats could be brought up. Those with the admiral were deemed sufficient, for the moment, to protect the U.S. Army convoy.

Porter's gunboats and the army transports of Brig. Gen. Smith slowly steamed towards Shreveport for three days, during which time Rebel sharpshooters treated them to regular lead greetings. Very few men on either side were actually badly hurt during the trip, but many Northern nerves were undoubtedly frayed. "The river was exceedingly narrow and torturous," remembered Smith, "the bottom covered with logs and snags and the banks full of drift, rendering the navigation most difficult and dangerous." On top of that, the banks in some stretches were even taller than the pilothouses of the boats, a situation which greatly favored the Rebel defenders.

The boats arrived as scheduled at Springfield Landing on April 10. Here, nearly 100 miles in the rear of Banks' army, they were stopped cold by Confederate ingenuity. The large steamer *New Falls City* was scuttled and her hull, stretched end to beached end, was sunk directly across the Red River, one mile above Loggy Bayou. An invitation writ large to a Shreveport ball, Porter later told Maj. Gen. Sherman, "was kindly left stuck up by the rebels, which invitation we were never able to accept."

Before the bluejackets could manhandle the broken packet out of the way, terrible news arrived by courier. The Federal Army of the Gulf was defeated at the Battle of Sabine Cross-Roads—near Grand Ecore—and in retreat. In the river off Grand Ecore, the *Carondelet*'s OOD wrote in the deck log: "Heard heavy firing upriver." As many of her crewmen provided assistance in hospitals ashore, none knew the exact significance of the noises they heard. Though not fully realized by all at that moment, the Union's Red River campaign had reached its zenith. Porter and Brig. Gen. Smith elected to quickly retreat south.

"The confusion which immediately followed" the revelation of Banks' defeat "was frightful," remembered Nicholas Smith, an officer aboard the steamer *John Warner*. Interviewed by the *Columbus* (WI) *Democrat* in 1895, Smith recalled that the quartermaster transport "captains became frantic and disorder seemed to control every movement." From this point on, Porter, his gunboats and the military transports faced a desperate battle against falling water and Confederate riflemen to avoid entrapment above the Alexandria rapids.[11]

Although many of the vessels that escaped Springfield Landing to reach Grand Ecore on April 14 bore the marks of Rebel sharpshooters, they were, in fact, little the worse for their ordeal. Still, the *St. Louis Daily Missouri Democrat* newsman embedded with Brig. Gen. Smith's transports called the fleet's escape "one of the most daring, as well as one of the most successful ... feats of the whole war."

The reader will recall that while the light draught task group was away upstream a number of deep-draft vessels were behind at Grand Ecore. Determined that these units should now retire from the river regardless of whether or not the Army of the Gulf returned to the offensive, Porter now ordered them to steam for Alexandria.

As the water level continued to fall, navigation was increasingly difficult. At 1:45 P.M., the *Eastport,* in line not far from the *Carondelet,* grounded while crossing the bar below the town. Capt. Phelps called upon Lt. Cmdr. Mitchell for assistance and, at 5:00 A.M. on April 15, pilots from his gunboat sounded the channel at the stern of the *Eastport.* By 9:30, the big ironclad succeeded in getting off the bar. The *Carondelet* dropped to the bank, allowing her to pass on down ahead of her. Following the *Ozark*, the giant *Eastport* was about eight miles below Grand Ecore at 4:00 P.M. that Friday when her bow struck a torpedo. This time she was hurt far more seriously than the bottom scraping experienced while crossing the Grand Ecore bar. While damage control parties scrambled, Phelps ordered the whistle blown five times in a prearranged distress signal.

Moving ahead, the *Carondelet* was one of several nearby gunboats that responded to the *Eastport's* signal. Coming upon the sunken behemoth, Capt. Mitchell immediately ordered a boat sent to her assistance. At 6:15 P.M., the Eads-built craft made fast to the bank just above the *Eastport* and dispatched additional cutters to Phelps' vessel. These joined boats from other gunboats in attempting to lighten the stricken giant by withdrawing ammunition and stores.

All efforts by men from several craft to help save the *Eastport* failed. At 11:00 P.M., her bow struck bottom and water covered the forward end. As soon as Rear Adm. Porter arrived alongside, he ordered that the *Eastport*'s battery also be removed. He then steamed down to Alexandria to order up additional aid. As the sun rose on April 16, crews from the *Eastport*, *Carondelet*, and *Lexington* set to work passing ammunition to the nearby monitor *Ozark*. When that task was completed, parties dismounted the aft 9-inch guns, which were manhandled through the gun ports to the waiting *Ozark.*

At approximately 8:00 A.M., Capt. Phelps boarded the *Carondelet.* After thanking Capt. Mitchell for his assistance, he confirmed that pump boats were en route and that there was no further need for the veteran ironclad to remain on the scene. She was ordered to continue her retreat to Alexandria forthwith.

The *Carondelet* tied up to the bank below Calhoun's plantation about 6:00 P.M. There she remained until April 24 when she arrived at a point near the Alexandria falls. On April 26, the gunboat moved up to Meade's plantation, where a landing party was sent ashore for fresh water. The barrels filled, the men returned aboard the *Carondelet* about 10:00 A.M., accompanied by an African American contraband. The refugee reported to Capt. Mitchell that a company of Rebels was approaching the bank intent upon attack. When the butternut soldiers appeared, the ironclad was ready and they were dispersed with 19 shots, includ-

Units of the Mississippi Squadron, including the *Carondelet*, grouped together above Alexandria, Louisiana, at the end of April 1864. Many of the naval vessels were, in actuality, tied to the bank and not spread out as depicted. Nevertheless, the drawing conveys the sense of urgency that faced every Federal sailor present in the days before the success of Lt. Col. Bailey's innovative dam (*Harper's Weekly*, April 30, 1864).

ing one 100-pdr., five 9-inch, and four from the boat howitzers. These were the most rounds fired by the boat during the campaign.

Unhappily, all efforts to save and move the *Eastport* failed during the day and she was blown up to prevent her capture.[12]

On April 28, Rear Adm. Porter, stranded above the rapids at Alexandria, advised navy secretary Welles of his precarious position, due to the falling water level of the Red River as well as Maj. Gen. Banks' withdrawal. "I find myself blockaded," he wrote, "by a fall of 3 feet of water, 3 feet 4 inches being the amount now on the falls; 7 feet being required to get over." Facing the distinct possibility that he would need to destroy his entire $3 million squadron, as he had the *Eastport,* to keep it out of Confederate hands, he lamented to his superior: "[Y]ou may judge of my feelings at having to perform so painful a duty."

Porter initially had some success in getting at least a portion of the transports and his flotilla through a little 20-foot-wide channel through the rapids. Led by the admiral aboard the *Cricket,* a number of quartermaster boats and tinclads thumped their bottoms along to safety in the deeper waters south of Alexandria caused by a growing back swell from the Mississippi.

Working with Maj. Gen. Banks and his officers, the Mississippi Squadron chief fortunately came up with the correct solution and the right man to carry it out, XIX Corps staff engineer Lt. Col. Joseph Bailey, who Nicholas Smith years later called "the Moses of Porter's fleet." For years, the story of Bailey's dam was the most celebrated single event of the entire Federal Red River fiasco.

The presence of the one-time 4th Wisconsin Cavalry officer with Banks' expedition was, wrote Smith and Castille in 1986, "one of those coincidences of history that sometimes result in turning the course of events." So it was that, on April 29, Bailey was tasked by Banks and Porter with constructing a dam that would raise the water sufficiently to allow the fleet to escape. Straightaway, Maj. Gen. Banks set over 3,000 men to work chopping down trees or dismantling whole buildings, finding stone and rock, and hauling the materials to the sites on either bank where the dam would be constructed. Interestingly, African American troops worked the Alexandria side, while soldiers from Wisconsin, Maine, and New York labored on the Pineville shore.

Around the clock for eight days the men strained without cessation, beginning the initial dam not far above the lower, downstream, rapids where the river was about 758 feet wide. It was hoped that, when the project was finished, the water behind the structure would have risen enough to float the gunboats over the upper rapids. Then when the time was just right, the dam could be broken and the gunboats could rush free over the lower rapids, carried by the force of the released water.

Despite a 9 mph current, the work continued and gradually the water level began to rise. On May 8, the stage on the upper falls was up sufficiently to allow the lighter gunboats and monitors to move down and make ready to pass the main dam the instant it was ready.

Early the next morning, great crashing sounds were heard in the vicinity of the dam. The tremendous water pressure against the dam forced two of the barges employed in its construction to burst loose, swinging in below the dam on one side. The *Lexington*, the only one of the gunboats with steam up fully ready to go, immediately passed the upper falls, ran down over the rocky stretch before the level fell, and exited to safety through the dam. Anchoring below the town, her crew observed the monitors and the big tinclad *Fort Hindman* come down a short time later.

The success of these boats proved Lt. Col. Bailey's dam would work and he resumed his work on it with spirit. Still, as the dam was mended, strengthened, and completed, the *Carondelet* and her consorts remained stranded, "locked in by a reef of rocks across the river just below."

About 11:00 A.M., Rear Adm. Porter sent orders to the remaining boats to remove their cannon and side armor. Capt. Mitchell pushed his crew to lighten ship. Tons of shot and shell, powder and stores were sent ashore along with four 9-inch broadside guns. As dark fell, a line was gotten up to the gunboat from the dam and plans were made to utilize it in pulling her agonizingly ahead.

By late evening, the *Carondelet*, which continued to lie in the channel at the head of the falls, had about 4 inches more water than when she first grounded, and her draft was now 6 feet, 1 inch, with another four inches required. Over 125 tons of iron plating were loosened by midnight and would be ready for disposal the next night.

Utilizing heavy lines, the crew of the *Carondelet*, working with hundreds of soldiers ashore, were able to haul their boat some 45 feet ahead on May 10, "nearly across the lumps in the channel." That night, the iron plating was thrown overboard. Darkness was chosen for two reasons. It was hoped that the Rebels would not know that the plating was missing and, if they did, would not be able to find it. Ensign Jordan was not much concerned on the latter point. "The water is so thick with mud," he wrote his wife, "I think they never will find it."

May 11 was the day appointed for the departure of the *Carondelet* and her consorts over the fall. That morning Capt. Mitchell's command got up steam, battened hatches and ports, and cast off from the bank, making "a fine start." Because she had no checking line, however, the ironclad went hard and fast up on the left-hand reef. There she was stuck with only 5 feet, 6 inches of water under her for 20 feet abaft her bow.

While a tremendous effort was made to free the *Carondelet*, several other boats passed her and continued to safety. By early next day, she, too, completed passage of the upper falls and made it through the dam at the lower falls, coming to anchor below the rapids. During the remainder of May 12 and the next day, the ironclad and her consorts reloaded their provisions and ammunition.

Union forces exited Alexandria on the afternoon of May 13, leaving the city in flames. They reached the mouth of the river eight days later. "And thus ended the 69-day Red River expedition," Lt. Cmdr. Thomas Selfridge wrote in his *Battles and Leaders* contribution, "one of the most humiliating and disastrous that had been recorded during the war."[13]

On May 27, Lt. Cmdr. Mitchell was named unit commander of the Eighth District of the Mississippi Squadron (Memphis to Columbus, Kentucky). In addition to the *Carondelet*, then at Hickman, his work would be supported by the monitor *Osage* and two tinclads, the *New Era* and the *Huntress*. Headquartered at Memphis, from which the turret-vessel seldom moved, the *Carondelet* patrolled the rapidly falling river from Memphis to Osceola, including those off Fort Pillow. Her job was to regulate commercial riverboat traffic, capture contraband, suppress "guerrilla" operations, and prevent unauthorized river crossings.

The *New Era* worked between Osceola and Tiptonville and the *Huntress* from Tiptonville to Columbus. The weather was hot (over 100 degrees daily at the end of June), mosquitoes appeared in clouds, and the duty was routine. Many steamers passed up and down every day, laden with troops, wagons, horses, etc. A few of the larger packets were equipped with calliopes and usually played a jaunty tune when passing the ironclad.

Although her casemate had received a touchup paint job, the armor plating discarded from the *Carondelet* during the Red River exodus remained off and "their vulnerable sides [were] exposed to field artillery," as one officer confided to the admiral on July 7.

In the face of Confederate irregulars, the need for additional craft was considered urgent. Still, as Mitchell put it in a letter to Porter on June 8, all that "two slow vessels [*Osage* and *Carondelet*] can do to break the guerrilla firing will be done."

In order to increase his mobility, Lt. Cmdr. Mitchell in mid–June transferred his divisional flag from the *Carondelet* to the *Huntress*. The new light draught, under Acting Master John S. Dennis, was able to rapidly cover not only the watery limits of her own geography, but also to check on the activities of the other units below Tiptonville. From this point until her transfer out of the district in November, Mitchell never returned aboard the *Carondelet* as active skipper, leaving daily command of the vessel to Acting Master Miller.

The activities of various Confederate cavalrymen, such Brig. Gen. John S. Marmaduke, Col. Colton Greene, and Brig. Gen. Joseph O. "Jo" Shelby, who were riding through Arkansas in June did not occur without some rumor or intelligence concerning them reaching Federal ears. While on a reconnaissance up the White River to DeVall's Bluff, Federal naval forces learned that the latter Rebel horseman was nearby.

Lt. Cmdr. Phelps, commander of the Mississippi Squadron's Seventh District, took precautions to protect river shipping and local shore bases or communities from the Rebel horsemen. The tinclads *Queen City*, *Naumkeag*, and *Fawn* were spaced out between Clarendon and St. Charles, while the old timberclad *Tyler* was tasked to directly protect the former town. And then these preparations were knocked into a cocked hat.

Brig. Gen. Shelby paused on June 20 to review his options. DeVall's Bluff, he knew, was the closest point to Little Rock on the White River and its railroad to the capital was the only train system then working in Arkansas. The Federal logistical hub at the Bluff was fortified, contained a good-sized garrison, and was constantly watched by gunboats. Attacking it directly would be difficult. On the other hand, this heart in the Union supply chain could be killed if the vital watery artery to it could be cut below. It was obvious from the map that the *point d'appui* should be the town of Clarendon, 14 miles downstream. Easy to reach or escape from, the largely deserted community offered a good position at which to plant cannon and to conduct blockade movement up or down the river.

In the months following the end of the Red River campaign, Confederate leaders in the Trans-Mississippi Department, including Brig. Gen. Joseph O. "Jo" Shelby (1830–1897), believed that Federal control of Arkansas could be significantly hampered if he could interdict Union convoys on the White River. In a night attack on June 24, 1864, he personally led a force to Clarendon and sank the tinclad *Queen City.* Within hours, he fought and withdrew from a U.S. Navy counterattack and within days the *Carondelet* was sent to Clarendon to protect Union interests (U.S. Army Military History Research Institute).

Having stealthily encircled Clarendon, Shelby's riflemen, supported by four artillery pieces, attacked the *Queen City* on June 24 and compelled her surrender, after which she was looted and burned. Hearing of the attack, Lt. George M. Bache led the *Tyler*, *Naumkeag*, and *Fawn* to Clarendon several hours later and drove Shelby back. Next day, the two tinclads, patrolling off the town, again shelled the Rebel horsemen. Destruction of the town, begun during the naval encounters, was completed when steamers from DeVall's Bluff arrived and disembarked 4,000 bluecoat soldiers.

The situation on the White River remained explosive and no traffic was able to operate on it for a week. Seventh District commander Lt. Cmdr. Phelps wrote to Rear Adm. Porter on June 27 asking that a tinclad from Cairo be sent to Memphis for Mitchell's use while the *Carondelet* was sent to the White River for a short period.

Taking advantage of the presence of the able Lt. Bache and the availability of a fast steamer, Phelps rushed to Memphis in person two days later. There he made arrangements for the *Essex* to cover for the *Carondelet* and for the Eads-built craft to return with him. He also sent a message to Rear Adm. Porter assuming responsibility, against standing orders, of moving a vessel from one district to another without authorization.

Even as the former *Eastport* captain was rearranging the heavy pieces of two districts, Porter confirmed Phelps' action in a June 30 order to Mitchell. Although the Eighth District commander was ill, the *Carondelet*, under Capt. Miller with Mr. Jordan as XO, was ordered immediately to the White River.

Rebel attacks on transport steamers passing up and down the White and Arkansas continued as Marmaduke and Greene joined Shelby in haunting their banks. Also on June 30, Rear Adm. Porter ordered Phelps to remove his gunboats from the latter; otherwise, "we will lose them all." Efforts would, for now, be concentrated on the White. In a letter to Porter, written on July 1 even as the *Carondelet* paddled upstream about 180 miles to Clarendon, Phelps himself suspected the declining river stage would soon force her to leave it.

The big gunboat ascended without incident and anchored in mid-stream off Clarendon. Observers aboard the *Carondelet* remarked that only one building was now standing on shore, though hundreds of chimneys gave evidence of a nice larger city days earlier. She was accompanied and supported by the tinclads *Silver Cloud* and *Naumkeag*, the latter under Acting Vol. Lt. John Rogers, who would one day command Mitchell's turtle.

The ironclad was located in "a good position to work our guns advantageously," wrote Ensign Jordan, "if it becomes necessary." The big cannon were loaded with ½ second shell and shrapnel; it was expected that any fight would be at very short range (about 200 yards) and this shotgun approach would ensure the enemy was not "overreached."

The local Union Army theater commander, Maj. Gen. Frederic Steele, at Little Rock was assured that the ironclad would remain off the town as long as possible. "I fancy Shelby will have a good time," Lt. Cmdr. Phelps confided, "if he runs against her."

The *Carondelet* remained at Clarendon four days; no Rebels tested her mettle. In the calm, the crew celebrated the country's independence and painted the boat's exterior. The officer's mess now included roast beef, fish chowder, bacon, applesauce, Irish potatoes, stewed beams, and prune pie.

On July 6, the ironclad, accompanied by the two tinclads, steamed up the river about 42 miles to DeVall's Bluff. Unlike the Mississippi, the White was narrow and crooked, and forests descended to its banks on both sides. Here the group found a large Federal army outpost, manned by hundreds of soldiers. The next day, the trio convoyed three transports back down to Clarendon. Much to some Rebel surprise, no opposition was encountered, not even snipers. One of the *Carondelet*'s rudders was, however, carried away.

After falling for a week, the river level reached a prearranged depth at which the Eads-built craft was to withdraw back down to the river's mouth. At 4:00 A.M. on July 7, *Carondelet* got underway. Having lamented not having a fight in 49 days, the gunboatmen would not be disappointed on their way out.

It was 9:00 A.M., just after the crew of the ironclad had been beat to quarters for gunnery drill. Timing could not have been better for the bluejackets. Lurking in a canebrake on the side of the river, hidden from the *Carondelet* about 30 yards distance, 25 Confederate riflemen opened up on her as she passed.

Aiming at the canebrake where the smoke of the Rebel rifles rose, the *Carondelet*'s gunners cut swaths with ½ second shrapnel. One 100-pdr. Parrot shell with a 2½ fuse was sent in the general direction, though no one knew what, if any, result the ensuing explosion occasioned. There was no second volley.

Upon the return of the *Carondelet* to her Memphis station, Lt. Cmdr. Mitchell departed on a leave of absence. Acting Master Dennis, the senior district officer, was left in charge of the Eighth District pending his return.[14]

12

Nashville

Following Maj. Gen. William Tecumseh Sherman's triumph at Atlanta at the beginning of September 1864, the Union high command had next to decide in which direction to send the scrappy redhead. Sherman himself favored a "scorched-earth" ride east destroying Confederate logistics between the Georgia capital and the Carolina seacoast. It would be his intention to emulate his greatest communications foe, Maj. Gen. Nathan Beford Forrest, by encouraging his Army of the Tennessee, made lean, to live off the countryside. "I can make this march and make Georgia howl!" he promised Lt. Gen. Ulysses S. Grant. Maj. Gen. George Thomas and 60,000 men could be sent to guard the Tennessee rear.[1]

Confederate general John Bell Hood now contemplated a visit north in a move historian Bruce Catton called a "strategy of despair, verging on the wholly fantastic, based on the belief that the way to counter Sherman's thrust into the deepest South was to march off in the opposite direction." The Rebel field commander believed that, if lucky, he could move "smartly" enough in western and middle Tennessee to defeat General Thomas and capture Nashville. Taking the Tennessee capital would not only destroy a major Northern supply depot, but could force Sherman to return to the Volunteer State.

During September and early October, Sherman and Hood took advantage of fine weather to reorganize their commands for what Benson J. Lossing later called the "vigorous work" ahead. As the great western field armies maneuvered, the *Carondelet* made her way from Fulton to Memphis between September 23 and October 2. A lengthy series of repairs were started at the navy yard, with serious attention paid to the gunboat's worn engines.

As a precaution against any Southern gambit, Sherman sent Maj. Gen. Thomas to Nashville on October 3. He also arranged for Maj. Gen. A.J. Smith to join him from Missouri. Meanwhile, over the next two weeks, Hood marched to the west of the Chattahoochee, trying to lure his opponent out of Georgia while avoiding a decisive battle.

Sherman was contemptuous of Hood's wild-goose chase northern goal and remained supremely confident in his own mission and men. Consequently, he determined to quit the Hood chase, go the other way, and march toward the sea. Lt. Gen. Grant approved his subordinate's Savannah strategy on October 13. Seven days later, Sherman gave Thomas full authority to deal with any northern Confederate incursion and started reinforcements to Nashville.

In Washington, D.C., U.S. Navy secretary Gideon Welles took the opportunity to infuse his Mississippi Squadron with new leadership. On October 19, he turned the unit over to Acting Rear Adm. Samuel Phillips Lee. Lee had recently been relieved from command of the North Atlantic Blockading Squadron, which Welles gave to Rear Adm. Porter.

Unable to gain any advantage in Northwest Georgia, Hood turned to cross the Tennessee River, first at Guntersville and then at Decatur, Alabama, where a key railroad terminus could deliver supplies from northern Mississippi. So it was that the Army of Tennessee headed for Decatur and points above.[2] Gen. Hood in the meantime called upon his cavalry to aid in his grand endeavor by smashing up the Union supply line from the north. In particular, he needed Maj. Gen. Forrest, the man whom Sherman himself had named "the very devil." It was widely hoped that the famous cavalry leader could divert the Yankees while the Confederate Army of Tennessee strode into the Volunteer State.

Swiftly, the Confederate horseman, who had already raided Memphis during August, led his men on a swing into middle Tennessee. Federal defenders of Memphis anticipated another assault in mid–October.

Just after 11:00 P.M. on October 16, alarm bells sounded all over Memphis. Pickets on both sides of the Mississippi began firing wildly, encouraging a belief that Forrest was headed back toward the city and a general engagement would quickly ensure. Union army commanders at Memphis informed Cmdr. Robert Townsend of the pending danger a few minutes after midnight, October 17, and that officer immediately alerted the captains of all of the naval vessels in port. In return, Townsend assured his military colleagues that, in case of an attack, the *Carondelet* would be towed into position to act as circumstances dictated. Her heavy guns would be supplemented by those of the *Essex* and several tinclads. No actual combat was expected before morning or even later, but the jack tars aboard that night could sleep little.

Throughout October 17, sailors aboard the *Carondelet* remained near their guns anticipating an attack. Down from Cairo, fleet captain and acting squadron commander Alexander M. Pennock came aboard during the morning. In meetings with Acting Master Charles Miller and Ensign Jordan, he proclaimed his belief that any assault would come the next day. Ashore, all of the stores were closed, streets were barricaded, business was suspended, and arms were made ready for distribution to civilian volunteers. While aboard the ironclad, Pennock took the opportunity to inspect the crew at battle stations and return Ensign Oliver Donaldson to duty. The one-time carpenter, who had incurred the wrath of both Capt. Walke and Capt. Mitchell, had been under arrest by the latter's command for the past five months.

Forrest skirted the area and appeared elsewhere; the Memphis alert ended uneventfully. Repairs on the *Carondelet*, which had not moved from her anchorage, continued apace. On November 7, the government towboat *Volunteer* anchored at the navy yard with orders from newly arrived Acting Rear Adm. Lee. She was to tow the ironclad to Mound City where her upgrade could be completed.

With her repairs approximately half finished, the *Carondelet* departed Memphis under tow on the afternoon of November 11. Her trip upriver was initially uneventful. The following morning, as an African American sailor was attempting to retrieve a pail of water, the ironclad lurched, throwing him into the Mississippi. A cutter was manned within a minute and went to pick him up, but the bluejacket did not surface. Although not the first of the gunboat's crew to fall overboard, he was the first not rescued. After passing Cairo, the gunboat turned into the Ohio and dropped anchor off Mound City on November 15. It would rain steadily for the next four days.[3]

As workmen from the yard came aboard to complete the ironclad's repairs, crew changes were effected. Some 35 sailors whose terms of enlistment had expired were discharged on November 18. They were replaced by 40 new men from the Cairo-based receiving ship *Great Western* the following day. A number of the men arrived noisy and drunk. Five were so disorderedly that they were placed in irons. Among the less-rowdy new arrivals was Irish fireman John Hagerty, who had enlisted in Pennsylvania to avoid the army draft. Hagerty's letters, like those of Ensign Jordan, would be preserved, though not in such volume.[4]

The convergence of the blue- and gray-uniformed soldiers in middle Tennessee, though occurring in late fall and early winter, was not unlike the coming of a summer thunderstorm to areas of the Volunteer State. Even today, the threatening clouds of such a local tempest can be seen well ahead of time by any attentive person and most folks, after some residence, can almost tell how long it will be from the first sightings of various thunderheads until the wind and rain arrives. Unlike the rapid thrust of a raider or guerrilla squall, the movement of the armies of Hood and Thomas was as ominous as such a gathering storm. Telegraph wires, scouts, patrols, shippers, journalists and civilians, like modern day electronic and communications media, all contributed to the pool of threat intelligence and assessment available for review.

As Hood, Thomas, their lieutenants, and others near and far made and remade their observations and preparations for the military deluge on land, the sailors of the Mississippi Squadron, led by Acting Rear Adm. Lee, made every effort to control the two biggest streams in the center of the Volunteer State, the Cumberland and Tennessee rivers. The seamen knew a gale of Confederate iron was blowing and that it was their duty to help protect against it. Mound City navy yard workmen continued to effect repairs aboard the *Carondelet,* though the pace was slow. On November 23, Acting Ensign Jordan confided, in a letter home, that they would not be completed for "at least another week."

Through close coordination with the army, the navy could best accomplish its duty by blockading the use of the twin rivers to Union purpose. Specifically, gunboats were tasked to prohibit their crossing or other use by Southern forces, to detect and, whenever possible, defeat Rebel movements, and to guard and facilitate the continuing transfer of Northern men and supplies. The last named goal included the protection of key ports and rendezvous as well as coordination with army quartermasters and railroad chiefs.

Through November the Union divisions of Maj. Gen. Smith, fresh from their victory over Maj Gen. Sterling Price at Westport on October 23, marched across Missouri to St. Louis. Early on November 24, Smith wired Paducah advising that lead elements of his corps were embarking for departure next day. Hood was now threatening Columbia and, according to Col. Henry Stone of Thomas' staff, it now became "an open question whether he would not reach Nashville before the reinforcements from Missouri."

While the month advanced, the riverine navy's mission intensified. As historian Byrd Douglas later commented, the arrival of Smith's army from Missouri remained "of utmost importance." Nearly every steamer coming up the Cumberland brought a few advance units of Smith's force. It now became obvious at both army and navy headquarters that a blocking assault on the Cumberland could be disastrous. If Maj. Gen. Forrest or one of his lieutenants could blockade transportation there as he had weeks earlier at Johnsonville on the Tennessee, "it might result in the loss of the impending battle with Hood before it was fought."

The on-scene Mississippi Squadron operational commanders and their army counterparts continued to push, directly and indirectly, the buildup of the Cumberland escort flotilla; "above all," this growth "indicates the respect that Thomas, Sherman and Admiral Lee had for Forrest." In order to cope with powerful rifled batteries the Confederates could be expected to erect along the Cumberland River, Acting Rear Adm. Lee wisely strengthened with ironclads the light draught force of Tenth District boss Lt. Cmdr. Le Roy Fitch.[5] One of the two sent to the waters near Nashville would be the *Carondelet.*[6]

None of the local Union leadership could, however, know that the "devil's role would be confined to support of Hood's main force inland of the rivers." Only a small portion of

Earlier a portion of a larger 60-acre tract (now home to Lowe's and Wal-Mart stores along with forested river frontage) the 6-acre Kelley's Point Battlefield (squared-off in white above) is nine miles west of Nashville in the Bellvue community. Confederate Col. David C. Kelley stationed his cannon and battled the *Carondelet* and *Neosho* during the December 1864 Battle of Nashville on this tract of land (courtesy Robert Henderson).

Forrest's command would threaten Cumberland transportation during the upcoming battle, and it was captained by a parson, Lt. Col. David C. "Parson" Kelley.[7]

The first of Maj. Gen. Smith's divisions left St. Louis for Cairo on November 24, with others following the next day. Smith's late departure prevented Thomas from implementing an earlier plan to place the soldier's men at Eastport, Mississippi.

Just after dawn on November 27, Acting Rear Adm. Lee, unhappy with the pace of repairs to the *Carondelet,* sent a messenger over to her commander, Acting Master Charles W. Miller, ordering that, Sunday or not, final preparations be speeded up and that the bearer return with an estimate of when she would be ready. Fully expecting that the carpenters, painters, and caulkers would be off the boat in a matter of hours and that she would have shipped her ammunition, the admiral signaled the auxiliary *Volunteer.* She was to coal and ready herself to tow the famous old fighting ship to Paducah.

Nicknamed "The Parson" from his days as a Methodist minister, Col. David C. Kelley (1833–1909), a confidant of Maj. Gen. Nathan Bedford Forrest, led the 26th Tennessee Cavalry (CSA) during the fall of 1864. Cannoneers under his command would deny Federals the use of the Cumberland River during the December Battle of Nashville. During that blockade, the Southern gunners beat off attacks by the Union navy ironclads *Carondelet* and *Neosho.* When their army retreated, the ironclads escaped as well (courtesy Robert Henderson).

As repairs were pushed onboard the *Carondelet,* Acting Ensign Jordan, the executive officer, spent every available minute drilling her crew. Meanwhile, Maj. Gen. Smith's fleet reached Paducah from St. Louis. Thomas' headquarters was notified that the transports would steam to Smithland next morning as soon as they had coaled. At 6:15 P.M., the squadron chief sent a wire to Smithland ordering Lt. Cmdr. Fitch, then returning from Nashville, to proceed to Paducah, where he would find new orders. At 9:00 P.M., Acting Master Miller of the *Carondelet,* which had anchored abreast the *Black Hawk* three hours earlier, met with Lee aboard the flagboat to report his ironclad ready, to receive his orders and to pick up packets for the Tenth District commander. The veteran gunboat "came away from Mound City very suddenly and very unexpectedly" at 11:30 P.M. Most of the crew had no idea where they were headed when the craft departed upriver under tow of the *Volunteer.*

The orders prepared for Fitch did not immediately reach the Indiana-born sailor and it would be another day or so before he would learn that, due to an illness, he now commanded both the Ninth and Tenth Districts. So it was that, unbeknownst to him at the moment, the 29-year-old Fitch now assumed tactical command of the USN ironclads *Carondelet* and *Neosho,* as well as the heavy gunboat *Peosta,* the tinclads *Moose* (flagboat), *Fairplay, Silver Lake, Brilliant, Springfield, Reindeer,* and *Victory,* plus at least one auxiliary.

As the river's historian Douglas confirmed, "these constituted the greatest fleet of gunboats ever to appear on the Cumberland during the War." Although it is not generally recognized, Fitch could, if desired, also call upon available army gunboats, such as the *Silver Lake No. 2* and *Newsboy*. Although holding no elevated rank, Fitch now had more operational authority over more heavy vessels than any Mississippi Squadron junior officer since Capt. Henry Walke had commanded the squadron's lower division at Vicksburg the previous year.

The *Carondelet* and *Volunteer* arrived at Paducah at 9:30 A.M. on November 28, where they joined the big tinclad *Peosta* and the *Neosho*. The captains of the three warships conferred throughout the morning, while their crews continued drilling, mostly at the great guns. Officers aboard the turtle believed they had at least another two days to get their men ready "to give an exhibition of the old *Carondelet*'s fighting qualities."

While the heavy units assembled at the Kentucky port and just before his own departure, Lee received a telegram from Thomas asking that he provide escort to Smith's troop fleet. The job was Immediately accepted. The *Black Hawk* landed at the Paducah levee just after noon and the admiral went to army headquarters to meet with local military commanders. A half hour later, the squadron boss wired Smithland asking that the junior officer on duty there notify Fitch that Lee was waiting for him Paducah. When by 2:30 P.M. the Tenth District commander had still not arrived, Lee penned new orders for the Hoosier sailor. After conferring with the skippers of the *Carondelet*, *Neosho*, and *Volunteer*, Lee ordered them on to Smithland, putting aboard the latter vessel his messages for Fitch. He then returned to Mound City.

Leaving in the darkness at 4:30 A.M. on November 29, the *Carondelet* and *Neosho*, together with the last of Smith's transports, arrived at Smithland three hours later. Lt. Cmdr. Fitch and his subordinate captains, in accordance with orders from Acting Rear Adm. Lee, quickly organized a water advance to the Tennessee capital and communicated the sailing order to the transport captains and affected military personnel. At 10:00 A.M., the flagboat *Moose* started up the Cumberland leading the grand parade of nearly 60 troop steamers. Interspersed among the transports were the other tinclad gunboats, acting as both shepherds and, on occasion, towboats.

Every available light draught of the Ninth and Tenth District was assigned to this expedition, except the *Paw Paw* and *Peosta*. As might be imagined, the departure was staggered. The *Carondelet* did not weigh anchor until 1:00 P.M.

The leading *Neosho* and the *Carondelet*, which brought up the rear, made their best speed; the sureness of their size and armament, if not their immediate proximity to the steamers, made them a viable "distant cover," a term later used for Allied battleship protection of convoys in the Atlantic during World War II.

Trailing huge clouds of smoke from over 100 chimneys, the steamboat armada, stretched out over miles of river length, proceeded without incident throughout the day and into the evening. Numerous steamers were passed moving downstream and for the most part the weather was pleasant. The first difficulty did not occur until 9:30 P.M. when an overhanging tree carried away and destroyed the *Carondelet*'s gig. The tiller rope of the gallant ironclad broke two hours later, forcing her to stop for three hours to effect repairs.[8]

On November 30, Gen. Hood's army, numbering something less than 16,000 effectives, attacked the 22,000 entrenched Union defenders of Franklin, losing 6,252 men, including six general officers killed. The five-hour battle cost the Northerners approximately 2,300 soldiers. Writing on "the five tragic hours" years later, historian Fisher opined that "Hood had virtually destroyed his [own] army."

Before midnight, all in the Union XXIII Corps who were able set off for Nashville, 18 miles away, arriving by noon the next day. There behind fortified lines they were joined by the IV Army Corps. As the day wore on, more men arrived from various Tennessee locations, including the Provisional Detachment of the District of the Etowah from Chattanooga.

As the Franklin bloodbath continued, the stretched-out Smith convoy continued up the Cumberland. The heavier vessels steamed more slowly and were often overtaken by lighter units; all were regularly passed by vessels traveling in the other direction. An officer aboard the *Carondelet* observed that "the country on both sides of the river is covered with white oak timber, except here and there small cleared spots have log houses upon them." Another surprise was a total absence of "annoyance" from guerrillas or Rebel masked batteries.

In Nashville, Thomas wondered, "was there news of Smith"? "No," replied, Col. James F. Rusling, acting chief quartermaster of the Department of the Cumberland, though he had sent a steamer (probably the army gunboat *Newsboy*) down the Cumberland earlier in the afternoon to hurry the fleet. "Well," the commanding general replied, "if Smith does not get up here tonight, he will not get here at all; for tomorrow, Hood will strike the Cumberland and close it against all transports."

Out on the Cumberland, the plodding convoy passed Fort Donelson at noon and Clarksville was reached at 10:45 P.M. Here the *Carondelet* dropped anchor to review her shaky tiller situation, but her respite was brief. An hour later, the *Moose*, with another steamer lashed alongside, came up with the final convoy elements and signaled the ironclad to get underway and follow her up.

It was around midnight when the first couple of troop transports, encouraged ahead by Rusling's steamer and speeding in advance, came to off the city levee. Also around 1:00 A.M. on December 1, the tinclad *Brilliant* was assigned the duty of towing the gallant *Carondelet* up the Cumberland. Thereafter the old turtle and the *Neosho* continued to plod upstream in pleasant, if cool, weather with various units of the "mosquito fleet" occasionally providing a tow. Moving on ahead, the steamers of the Smith convoy tied up or dropped anchor at Nashville all night long and throughout the morning.

As troop boats and their guardians headed up the final leg of the Cumberland River toward the state capital, the scenery seen by the bluejackets became even more spectacular, despite a violent rain storm. Ensign Jordan wrote to his wife Judith far off in Maine: "All day today we have been passing lofty ridges of solid rock, several of the peaks being from 500 to 1,000 feet above the bed of the river, and the side next to the river in many instances perpendicular from the water to the top, and as smooth as marble. The rock is genuine Limestone. We run so near the rocks that we cannot carry our quarter boats at the davits, but tow them astern of the ship, and are obliged to keep our guns run in to prevent them from striking the rocks."

The *Moose* escorted in the final boats with 5,000 men just before late afternoon darkness. Most had to anchor in midstream, as the levees were packed. The ironclads *Neosho* and *Carondelet* tied up to the bank below Fitch's tinclad about 8:00 P.M.

Relieved, the Nashville chief telegraphed Maj. Gen. Henry Halleck at Washington, D.C.: "I have two ironclads here, with several gunboats, and Commander Fitch assures me that Hood can neither cross the Cumberland or blockade it. I therefore think it best to wait here until Wilson can equip all his cavalry." In one of the more famous quotes of the campaign, Thomas went on to size up his enemy's chances: "If Hood attacks me here, he will be more seriously damaged than he was yesterday; if he remains ... I can whip him and will move against him at once."[9]

The Cumberland River leading into Nashville remained busy over the next two days as steamers brought in additional goods, men and horses. When not themselves being replenished in supplies or coal, Fitch's light draughts were constantly in motion. The *Neosho* and *Carondelet* remained tied to the bank, their watch officers duly noting every witnessed activity in their logbooks.

Meanwhile, Gen. Hood's 25,000 men were almost at Nashville. Thinking he might draw Thomas into battle, the Southern commander considered that the possibility of a demonstration against the Union garrison at Murfreesboro was in order. This Rebel compulsion would remove one infantry division and all but a few of the men Thomas feared most — those from Forrest's Cavalry Corps.

The rest of the Southern army soon began establishing its line. Unhappily for the Rebels, when in place Hood's four-mile line was three miles shorter than the outer defenses built by the Nationals around the Tennessee capital. Specifically, it halted two miles from the Cumberland River in the east and four in the west, leaving four of the eight roads into the city wide open. To help alleviate this deficiency, Forrest left the 1,500 men of Brig. Gen. James Chalmers' division to operate in the unclaimed spaces that ran about four miles south between the Cumberland River below Nashville and Hood's anchor on the Hillsboro Pike. As part of this deployment, Chalmers now made one of the most important dispositions of any Rebel commander in the Nashville campaign.

Late in the afternoon, Col. David C. Kelley was sent to blockade the Cumberland. Kelley, who had bombarded Tennessee River traffic twice in the last two months, positioned 300 men of Col. Edmund W. Rucker's brigade and two Parrott rifles of Lt. H.H. Brigg's section of Capt. T.W. Rice's artillery near Davidson's house on a ridge beyond a little creek that emptied at Davidson's Landing into the Cumberland opposite Bell's Mills. The Mills and Bell's Landing lay four miles below the town by land. By river, they were, depending upon who is providing directions, anywhere from 12 to 18 below. The spots were (and still are) located at the nearest point to the city in the large bend in the Cumberland that comes nearly back of Nashville.

Soon reinforced with another two guns, Kelley had a pair in a lower battery and two in an upper emplacement. Marksmen were detailed in support from points in the hills above and below the artillery. This arrangement allowed the "fighting parson" to be largely successful in his mission, even though he had already missed the biggest target of all — A.J. Smith's troop convoy. Still, as historian Byrd Douglas noted, Kelley in the days ahead proved "what even a small force in gifted hands could do to supply lines and all the fine gunboats sent up the Cumberland."

In a wire to Maj. Gen. Halleck, "Old Pap" Thomas outlined his defensive plans for Nashville. As part of that arrangement, the ironclads and gunboats were so disposed as to prevent Hood from crossing the Cumberland. "Captain Fitch," he added, "assures me that he can safely convoy steamers up and down the river." According to Durham, Thomas had two major concerns about the river: that Confederates be neither able to cross it nor cut off his supplies from below with mobile artillery. Neither the general nor his top local navy man knew for certain that old foe Kelley was even then endeavoring to ensure the latter, though rumors were beginning to come in that the Confederates were putting up cannon along the river in preparation for a night attack.

The vigilant Fitch had one last matter to deal with that evening. At 10:30 P.M., he called Acting Master Miller of the *Carondelet*, together with his Cumberland pilot, to a conference aboard the *Moose*. There the ironclad was detailed to accompany the flagboat several miles downstream beginning a half hour later.[10] At 2:00 A.M. on December 3, with a severe storm threatening, the *Moose* and *Carondelet* tied up in the rain to the north bank below Hyde's Ferry and across from the picket line. This was a commanding position slightly to the right of the Army of Tennessee Detachment. When Fitch returned to Nashville, Capt. Miller had strict orders to assist Smith's troops in any way necessary.

The supply steamer *Magnet* came alongside the *Carondelet* and made fast just after 8:00 A.M. Two hours later, the *Moose*, beginning a series of patrols, rounded to abreast of the ironclad. The turtle's no. 2 gig hauled her captain out to the flagboat to report, allowing a reassured Fitch to steam on. A little while later, the *Carondelet* moved 500 yards upstream while the *Magnet* cast off and also went on up. The busy steamer *Magnet* again passed the stationary *Carondelet* in mid-afternoon, headed downriver. At 5:00 P.M., the patrolling *Moose* came upstream and landed briefly on the south side near the *Carondelet* before moving on up to Nashville. While the boats paddled back and forth on the river, Col. Kelley's battery, further down, made its inaugural attacks. Responding to warning shots from the bluffs above the Cumberland, the contract steamers *Prairie State* and *Prima Donna*, loaded with grain and cavalry animals, put into the bank, tied up and surrendered themselves into Confederate hands.

Gray-clad soldiers scrambled aboard their prizes; the 56 souls aboard the two vessels were made prisoner. Almost 200 horses and mules were led off while the Rebels pressed "into service the colored women onboard who were employed as cooks and chambermaids" and to help "liberate" items of value and to scatter and destroy the grain.

The naval supply steamer *Magnet* was fired into as she passed; she was hit upwards of 11 times and her wheel was shot away. A woman passenger was killed. The steamer's captain, a man named Harrol, continued beyond the first battery, but, finding another below, gave up. The *Magnet* ran into shore opposite the Southerners, tying up at a point about eight miles below Hyde's Ferry. There her crew ran into the woods to hide while help was sought. In the darkness of early evening, Capt. Harrol suddenly sought permission to board the *Carondelet.*

Obviously shaken, the steamboat captain told Acting Master Miller how his boat had been fired into and crippled near Bell's Mills. After the assault, the captain had traveled back to Hyde's Ferry, arriving where the ironclad was stationed about 7:30 P.M. Unable to move on his own without orders, Miller sent Acting Masters Mate L.W. Hastings with Harrol up to Nashville, where they could raise the alarm with Lt. Cmdr. Fitch.

The *Moose* had not been moored long at Nashville when, about 9:00 P.M., Hastings and Harrol came aboard. Harrol repeated his story. By the time of this interview, the strength of the audacious Confederates had grown in the telling from a few guns to elements of the enemy's entire left wing. The Rebels had, according to Harrol, struck the river and planted multiple batteries on its south side across from the Mills. Fitch, who had passed the location on many occasions over the past several years, was keenly aware of the location and knew it took far longer to reach by water than by land.

Even though it remained cloudy, threatening more rain, Fitch immediately determined to launch a night strike to wrest the two captured boats back from the enemy. He quickly stopped in to see Maj. Gen. Thomas and won his support to either recapture them or force their destruction — in either event taking the steamers away from the Southerners. A signal was made to the captains of the *Neosho*, *Brilliant*, *Fairplay*, *Reindeer*, and *Silver Lake* at 9:30 P.M. to get up steam and follow the *Moose* downriver at best speed.

Fitch's task group hove to near the *Carondelet* about 11:00 P.M. and the Pook turtle was

Captured prior to her conversion into a light draught gunboat, the *Fairplay* was photographed on the Cumberland River, ca. 1864, by Bell & Sheridan of Franklin Street, Clarksville, Tennessee. The earliest tinclad for which an image exists, the side wheeler joined the Mississippi Squadron in September 1862 as flagboat of the Mosquito Flotilla operated by Lt. Cmdr. Le Roy Fitch. She remained on the upper rivers through the war and in December 1864 joined the *Carondelet* in rescuing several steamers from the Confederates at Bell's Mills (Naval History and Heritage Command).

invited to join the parade. The *Neosho* took over the Hyde's Ferry station in support of the Army position, with the *Brilliant* detailed to operate with her (e.g., provide tow if necessary). Fifteen minutes later, Fitch steamed on with his boats arranged in this order: *Carondelet, Fairplay, Moose, Reindeer,* and *Silver Lake*. At 12:30 A.M., as the ironclad and four mosquito boats approached Bell's Mills, all hands aboard the warships were called to quarters. The boats moved down, as Fitch put it later, "perfectly quiet, with no lights visible."

The Indiana-born task group leader might be excused for that turn of phrase; steamboats were not quiet, but made puffing and chugging noises which were usually quite audible. There was no time to muffle the sounds, as Capt. Henry Walke did before taking the *Carondelet* past the Island No. 10 batteries in April 1862. What probably masked their approach was the myriad noises associated with a large city, sounds from the competing armies, general river traffic not yet completely stopped, and the crying of livestock.

Lugubriously coming down darkened (one can almost hear the music that played during the enemy battleship advance in John Wayne's World War II film *In Harm's Way*), the *Carondelet*, closely followed by the *Fairplay*, steamed towards Kelley's batteries. The night was cool, cloudy and devoid of natural light and hence the Confederates did not spot the Yankee craft, even though one was as big as a house.

About 12:45 A.M. December 4, the *Carondelet* opened with a hail of grape and canister as she passed the main Rebel camp in a hollow on the south side of the river opposite Bell's Mills. As her guns came to bear, a number of the men aboard could clearly see the *Prairie State* and *Prima Donna* tied up at the bank at Hillsboro Landing, two miles below. When the ironclad initiated the battle, the *Fairplay* was a little below the upper battery, with the *Moose* abreast of it, the *Reindeer* about 50 yards above, and the *Silver Lake* behind. As soon as the *Carondelet* started the fight, Kelley's men poured a "perfect shower of musketry" into all of the boats and began a responsive cannonade. The Pook turtle steamed slowly by the lower battery.

After passing, she rounded to and came up within about 300 yards of the Confederates, fired a few shots with her two 100-pdr. Parrotts and three big Dahlgrens, then passed up abreast before dropping back again. "The deafening roar of our 100 pounders," an officer aboard later recalled, "fairly made the ground tremble under them." The Confederates returned the ironclad's fire for about 20 minutes before falling back; *Carondelet* pumped occasional shells toward the last known Rebel locations until 2:30 A.M. When her gunners took stock of the magazine later in the morning, it was found that 26 rounds had been expended.

Undamaged, though hit three times, the *Carondelet* continued on. The Confederates continued to shoot at her, but, as earlier, most of their rounds passed over the ironclad. Her greatest damage was the loss of her flagstaff; although her National colors would be shown from a temporary spar, it would be three weeks before the boat's carpenters could erect a new one.

The thinly protected *Fairplay* could not possibly stand up to Kelley's rifled field guns and made no offensive effort to do so. Acting in concert with Miller's craft, her job was to get quickly past the Rebel gunners and to ensure the recapture of the transports at Hillsboro Landing. The side wheeler's gunners fired rapidly in passing. Hit twice, *Fairplay* turned the bend below, out of range.

The smoke from the guns and chimneys, combined with steam and the darkness of a starless night, quickly cut visibility for the other mosquito boats, which remained above. Fitch observed that, although the musketry along the bank and on the hillside was rather "annoying," the enemy artillery fire, though rapid, was not very telling because it was not well aimed. The task group commander later admitted it was a miracle "that amid so many shots and volleys of musketry, we should escape without the loss of a single man and no injury to the boats." By injury, the Fitch meant major damage. The lucky *Moose*, which also narrowly avoided a collision with the *Reindeer*, was, in fact, hit three times by shells, two of which could have sunk her.

The *Silver Lake* did not get close enough to actually engage the batteries. She did, according to Lt. Cmdr. Fitch, fire six rounds of canister and helped keep the musketry "silent along the bank above." Perhaps this explains how landsman Rowland S. True confused the actions of December 4 and 6 in his later account. Still, the Pennsylvanian witnessed what he later called "a grand display of fireworks." He would always remember the "thundering of the mighty guns, the shells screeching through the air back and forth, from one side to the other; sometimes bursting in the air, sometimes in the water throwing the water high in the air."

The first Bell's Mills engagement was not a great victory for either side. It is true that Fitch's task group was able to recapture the two steamers before they were destroyed. The navy man claimed his boats drove the Rebel guns back from the river and that it was his intervention which forced Kelley to destroy most of the prized grain before it could be transported and to free some of their crews. The Southerners claimed Kelley's caissons were out of ammunition. Although the fight was something of a tradeoff, in the end, the Rebels stayed away for less than a day and then, despite several more Fitch visits, closed the Cumberland tight for a week.

At 2:45 A.M. that Sunday, the *Carondelet* and *Fairplay* made fast to the *Prairie State* and

Prima Donna and towed them across the river. After they were made fast, the *Fairplay* came alongside them and the *Carondelet* dropped out into the river, offering defense in depth.

Navy sailors, led by Engineer Charles H. Caven, worked with the civilian crews of the two steamers to repair damages and put them in running order. The unmarried Caven, who was aboard the *Carondelet* for the entire war, here suffered a great financial reversal. Worried about his gunboat's chances, Caven, as he did before every battle, took all of his money (in this case $760) out of his locked trunk and put it in his pocket, thinking that if the *Carondelet* was sunk, he could get ashore and save his nest egg. In transferring aboard one of the recaptured steamers, the cash fell out of his pocket overboard.

The *Fairplay* got underway at 4:00 A.M. and proceeded four miles down the river to where the disabled *Magnet* was lying. Her damages were not as great as Captain Harrol had at first feared (and probably described). At 5:30 A.M., the two steamboats above were able to get up steam but did not depart. Instead, they waited for the *Carondelet*, which had also put down, to return towing the *Magnet*. At 6:00 A.M., the ironclad, trailed by the *Magnet*, and the *Fairplay*, convoying the *Prima Donna* and *Prairie State*, departed for up the river.

Three tinclads, meanwhile, arrived at Hyde's Ferry where the *Neosho* and *Brilliant* were tied up. Fitch informed the captains of the two guardians that the other units were trailing them from below and that they could depart upon their arrival. At 10:00 A.M., the *Carondelet*, *Fairplay*, and the civilian steamers departed with the *Neosho* and *Brilliant*. These vessels all arrived at Nashville at 4:45 P.M., about four hours behind the *Moose*. At Nashville, Fitch reported the engagement to Maj. Gen. Thomas and, by wire, to Acting Rear Adm. Lee. The enemy's establishment of heavy batteries at Bell's Mills was confirmed. It was now unsafe for transports to come up from Clarksville.

That evening, as hands were at supper, heavy cannonading was heard back of Nashville. About the same time, Lt. Cmdr. Fitch received a laudatory note from "Old Pap" Thomas, in which the theater commander confused Bell's Mills and Harpeth Shoals. The task group commander took the opportunity in reply to gently point out the difference. Harpeth Shoals was some 35 miles below Nashville, while Bell's Mills, he noted, was 12 to 18 river miles away (though just four by land) in the great bend of the Cumberland behind the city. Fitch had planned to start off for the former that evening, but when the bombardment back of the town was heard, he "thought perhaps there would be a general attack" and that his boats could assist on the right. "The heavy boats are so slow," he wrote, that if he had departed and Hood came on, "I would not have been able to reach here again until tomorrow afternoon."[11]

In a December 5 conference of gunboat captains aboard the *Moose*, Fitch outlined his plans to once again test the strength of the Rebel positions near Bell's Mills. With the Indiana-born sailor and his chief pilot, John Ferrell, embarked, the most powerful and best protected vessel available, the *Neosho*, would lead the assault, backed up by the Pook turtle. If their attack was successful, it would permit the tinclads to convoy a number of transports on toward Clarksville. While the monitor and the *Carondelet* were engaged, the steamer fleet would await the outcome some two to three miles above.

The major show got underway at 9:30 A.M. on a cold but clear December 6 when these boats moved out into the Cumberland and started downstream: the monitor *Neosho*; the stern-wheel transport *Metamora*; the tinclads *Moose* and *Reindeer*, lashed together; the stern wheelers *Prima Donna* and *Arizona*; the side wheelers *J. F. McComb* and *Mercury*; the tinclad *Fairplay*; the stern wheelers *Financier* and *Lilly*; the side wheelers *New York* and *Lady Franklin*; the tinclad *Silver Lake*; the side wheelers *Pioneer* and *Magnet*; and the ironclad *Carondelet*.

The parade moved peacefully on down past Hyde's Ferry and by Robertson's Island (Fitch, in his correspondence, mistakenly labeled the atoll Robinson's Island) until 11:15 A.M., when the *Neosho*'s lookouts spied a large Confederate force nearly opposite Bell's Mills apparently waiting for them. Col. Kelley's gunners and riflemen, replenished and ready for a fight, wasted no time in opening on the monitor from their protected emplacements behind the spurs of hills.

The *Neosho*, with Lt. Cmdr. Fitch embarked, went on down abreast of the lower battery, stopped, rounded to, and steamed back until abreast of the middle battery, which was nearly midway between the upper and lower emplacements. At that point, the monitor came to (about 20 to 30 yards off shore) and her 11-inch cannon spat grape and canister at Kelley's gunners, who were now all attempting to sink her. The dual between water and land continued for the next two and a half hours. During this time, the *Carondelet*, tinclads, and transports remained at the bank near Robertson's Island, with the men aboard the warships beat to quarters.

Believing that the *Neosho* could handle Kelley, approval was given for a St. Louis bound family (parents and two young ladies) aboard one of the civilian steamers to seek refuge aboard the *Carondelet*, the best-protected of the tied up vessels. When the shooting started, Acting Assistant Paymaster G.W. Robertson, who was not needed in any fight, encouraged them to join him in the relative safety of the coal bunker. Later, when it was obvious that there was no real danger, the family was invited to the wardroom for lunch with Capt. Miller and his officers.

From August 1862 to May 1865, Lt. Cmdr. Le Roy Fitch (1835–1875) served under Rear Adms. Davis, Porter, and Lee as operations officer for the Mosquito Flotilla, initially formed to pacify the upper tributaries of the Mississippi River, that eventually became the Tenth District of the Mississippi Squadron. Famous for his pursuit of the Rebel Morgan on the Ohio River in 1863, Fitch found himself in command of the naval defense of Nashville in December 1864. During this time, he employed the *Carondelet* on several occasions to fight masked Confederate batteries at Bell's Mills on the Cumberland River below the city (Naval Historical Center).

Unable to see much, Fitch eventually ordered the *Neosho* to disengage and steam back up the river. As Stanley Horn put it 90 years later, Kelley was "doing good work and thoroughly enjoying himself with his guns on the river bank." Moving out of range in the bend, the *Neosho* came up with the remainder of her task group, near Robertson's Island, still in the original order of sailing. Fitch, Miller, and Glassford reviewed the action. The task group commander wanted another daylight crack at Kelley and hoped that assistance from Miller's *Carondelet* might help him prevail. On the other hand, it was realized that sufficient Confederate cannon would probably survive the renewed battle to sink one or more of the light draughts or transports if they tried to make it past. As a result, Glassford was ordered to return with the mosquito boats and the steamers to Nashville. At this point, the *Carondelet*'s guests departed, "all in very good humor."

Fleet captain of the Western Flotilla and Mississippi Squadron, Alexander Pennock (1814–1876) handled the logistical and repair operations of those units, and stood in for the fleet commanders during their absence. While in temporary command of the Mississippi Squadron in mid–October 1864, he travelled to Memphis to oversee its defense against an expected attack by Maj. Gen. Nathan Bedford Forrest. Much of his stay was spent aboard the *Carondelet* (Library of Congress).

At 3:10 P.M., the transport convoy returned upriver. There is some irony in all of this. The water in the Cumberland near and over Harpeth Shoals was dropping rapidly. Even had the steamers gotten through — or Kelley had not been there — it is probable that they might have been forced back before reaching Clarksville.

As the light draughts and their charges disappeared toward Nashville, the *Carondelet* was ordered to drop down and tie up astern of the *Neosho*. There Fitch and Miller put the finishing touches on their attack plan. The *Carondelet* would follow down and make fast to the bank above the batteries while the *Neosho* went below, drawing the enemy's fire and showing their location to Miller's gunners. At 4:20 P.M., the two ironclads got underway.

The third round of Fitch's match versus Kelley opened at 4:30 P.M. when the *Neosho* steamed below the Confederate emplacements, rounded to, came back, and stopped in midstream as before, about 30 yards off the beach. Having drawn Rebel fire on her way down, the monitor easily succeeded in getting Kelley's men to show their locations to the *Carondelet*, which now joined Fitch in a spirited shelling. Unfortunately for them, the Union warships together had no great advantage, as the high enemy position allowed only one boat to engage the batteries at a time with any effect. That effect was minimal as the ironclads were forced to elevate their guns over the banks to clear them, thus missing the gray-clads.

Acting Ensign Donaldson, writing in the *Carondelet*'s logbook, called the Confederate response "feeble." Fitch himself did not find the contest quite as spirited as the earlier fight and thought his boats disabled two of Kelley's guns, believed to be 20-pdr. Parrott rifles.

About 5:30 P.M. as dusk launched another cold and, this time, cloudy night, the *Neosho* steamed up again, but was saluted by two only Confederate cannon as she passed and none as she continued, giving orders for the *Carondelet* to follow her upriver. Miller rounded to and joined his commander; at 10:00 P.M., the two ironclads made fast to the end of the line, astern of the *Reindeer* and *Moose*. In the most intense big gun duel of the Nashville campaign, Union navy casualties were "too trivial to mention."

After three engagements with Kelley, Fitch had to concede that his opponent still controlled the Cumberland. As Walter Durham put it, "the halt to navigation added to the siege mentality that recurrently threatened soldiers and civilians alike in Nashville."[12]

The in-port Nashville naval flotilla spent December 7 coaling and mending. Workers patched up the *Neosho*. A boiler leak aboard the *Carondelet* was slated for early repair. The wind was slight from the southwest and the day was cloudy, but warm.

In accordance with a plan for a two-pronged attack envisioned by Fitch, Lee and Thomas against Kelley's Bell's Mills batteries, the *Neosho*, *Carondelet*, and the still-lashed together *Moose* and *Reindeer* cast off and steamed downriver at 9:30 A.M. on December 8. It was hoped that the Pook turtle *Cincinnati*, with Acting Rear Adm. Lee embarked, would be able to steam up from Clarksville and join them.

As the result of an early morning visit with the Clarksville harbor master, Lee learned that the draft of the *Cincinnati* was too great to permit her to get across Davis' Ripple. Furthermore, and his own pilot confirmed it, unless the Pook turtle was taken back downriver to Smithland soon, the squadron leader risked her being stranded for the remainder of the winter. Lee definitely would not be joining Fitch in a cooperative attack against Kelley's batteries.

Downriver, the four warships from Nashville reached Robertson's Island and tied up to its bank in order of steaming. Fitch was rowed in the *Neosho*'s gig to the three other ships, going aboard each to confer with their captains. The two ironclads cast off at 11:30 A.M. and, as they continued down stream with the monitor in the lead, their crews were beat to quarters. The tinclads followed much further back. About an hour after starting down, the *Neosho* rounded to and turned back up, making a signal that the enemy was across the river. The *Carondelet* went back to warn the trailing light draughts and to remain with them until after lunch.

At 1:30 P.M., the *Moose* and *Reindeer* returned upriver and the *Neosho* and *Carondelet* went back down, the two ironclads steaming on until a brick house, seen earlier opposite Bell's Landing and perceived to be occupied by Confederate troops, came into view. The monitor and the turtle spent the next hour and a half alternatively shelling the place both "vigorously" and leisurely. After their shoot, Fitch's two iron monsters proceeded back up the Cumberland to Hyde's Ferry, where they arrived about 7:00 P.M. That evening, the task group commander informed his superiors that he would make another reconnaissance upriver the following morning.

Outside, the mercury was falling—fast. The north wind howled and the ground began to freeze. By morning, it was quite cold and stormy, with rain and snow. The executive officer was not concerned. "We have plenty of coal onboard and a plenty of stoves to burn it"—and, he continued, "a plenty of negroes to tend them." What was even better, Jordan revealed, was that "we have a plenty of time to sit by them and enjoy all the comforts there is to be derived from them."

Soldiers near Nashville continued to waltz towards combat for a fortnight. "Commodore Fitch," as Benjamin Truman told readers of the *New York Times*, "commands upon the Cumberland and assists in protecting our banks to a considerable extent." Noting the presence of two ironclads, the journalist also reported there were "also several other gunboats, of various shapes and sizes, patrolling the river." Another writer also praised the gunboats, asserting that "those who man them are celebrated in this section for their skill, bravery, and promptness in executing the part assigned them."

The opening of what all suspected to be the climactic ball was postponed for the better part of a week by the continuing severity of one of the worst winters in memory. The suffering from the cold, snow, and rain was intense among troops from both sides and civilians alike; for the next five days, the thermometer would not rise above 13 degrees Fahrenheit Nashville campaign literature is replete with stories of the woe and misery. Still, as Jordan noted, if any group within the city or without — besides a few privileged souls — did not endure major hardship from the weather in that period, it was the gunboatmen. Steam was, as always, kept up on the majority of the craft and those tars not on deck coaling or exposed for other duties were generally relatively warm.

During this idle time, the engineers aboard the *Carondelet* blew off steam in order to make the needed boiler repairs. Carpenters, despite the sleet and snow, were put to work rigging torpedo catchers, also known as torpedo rakes or "devils," even though there was no particular reason to believe Kelley or others had placed "torpedoes" in the river. Still, as the result of previous USN experience with these underwater mines and in preparation for a return downriver, both the *Neosho* and *Carondelet* were outfitted with the wrought-iron hooks and logs comprising the available countermeasure system.[13]

Often wearing icicles, the light craft of Fitch's Nashville flotilla remained active in the cold. The mighty *Neosho* and *Carondelet*, undoubtedly covered in some places topside with frozen snow, remained tied to the bank largely unable to move due to the low river stage. Each night, logbook entries reported "considerable picket firing around the line."

Aboard the *Carondelet*, "sitting 5 miles from Nashville at a fort with several other gunboats," John Hagerty wrote home from the engine room on December 13. "We had a fight with the Rebels on the 5th.... [S]ince then the monitor *Neosho* and us attacked the Rebel batteries and drove them back." "The monitor and us then went up to Nashville," he revealed, "and then returned on the 6th and they fired on us again ... [and] a shell from the monitor set a house on fire."

The Confederates had blockaded the river, Hagerty informed his wife, "and no mail can come from Cairo." Although there were gunboats at Clarksville "to help us," they couldn't come up because of the river stage. Like everyone else, the sailor was confident that "our land forces will drive them away.... [C]an hear the pickets firing from both sides.... [W]e are in front of 60,000–70,000 Rebels."

The river had fallen to a point where the *Carondelet*'s pilots did not believe it safe to try crossing the bars below. As the bottom was rocky, steam power alone, as seen on the Red River earlier in the year, could not get them through undamaged. Lt. Cmdr. Fitch, after hearing from Acting Master Miller and his pilots, agreed that only the light draught *Neosho* could be moved. To do that, he would have to drop her down below Robertson's Island with lines — slow, labor-intensive hand work as steam could not be trusted to take her through. If the weather changed even slightly, Fitch would get men aboard her to begin the task. Fortunately, the river stage began to ascend and that job was avoided.

A hoped for meteorological change began after midnight on December 14 when the winds warmed. At sunup, a slight rain fell and the entire city was covered until 11:00 a. m. by a thick blanket of fog. At midday, Maj. Gen. Thomas warned his corps commanders to prepare for an offensive according to the plan the high command had discussed throughout the cold snap. That afternoon, Thomas hosted a final conference at the St. Cloud Hotel to go over last minute details. Three hours later, Special Field Orders No. 342 were drawn up and dispatched for an all-out advance beginning the next morning as close to 6:00 A.M. as possible. Among the initial objectives for the offensive was the removal of the Confederate battery at Bell's Mills.

The major general commanding had a few last details to manage after dinner. At 8:00 P.M., he wired Maj. Gen. Halleck: "The ice having melted away today, the enemy will be attacked tomorrow morning." A large number of orders were now cut. About 8:00 P.M., a lengthy note was sent to Lt. Cmdr. Fitch (received two hours later) advising him that the enemy would be attacked at an early hour on Thursday morning. If it were possible for the Indiana-born sailor to "drop down the river and engage their batteries on the river bank," it would be "excellent cooperation."

By 11:00 P.M., Acting Master Miller and Fitch's other captains were aboard the flagboat *Moose*, actively reviewing Thomas' communication and making their plans for the morrow. The conference broke up after midnight and the gunboat skippers returned to their boats through banks of river mist thickened by campfire smoke. Heavy picket firing was heard from the river in the first hours after midnight.[14]

December 15 began cloudy, warm, and extremely foggy. This was a pea-soup fog familiar to residents of the eastern seacoast or London — or the hills of Tennessee in winter. The fog forced Maj. Gen. Thomas to wait out the perceptibility problem and led to some confusion in his ranks, including those bluecoats slated to cooperate with the navy.

From 6:00 A.M., the men aboard the navy vessels were able to hear, though not see, the apparent movement of the U.S. Army. At 7:20, the task group got underway in a moderate southern breeze and headed down the river with the *Neosho* in the lead. She was followed by the *Carondelet*, *Moose*, *Reindeer*, *Fairplay*, *Brilliant* and *Silver Lake*. Lt. Cmdr. Fitch remained aboard the flagboat, which was, together with the others, beat to quarters about an hour later.

Due to the delays and bafflement caused by the fog ashore, the honor of firing the first shots in the actual Battle of Nashville went to the U.S. Navy. This giant engagement was not only the last big clash of arms in the Civil War western theater, but also the climactic large-scale action for the Mississippi Squadron.

Fitch did not know for certain the location of Union cavalrymen from the 6th Division, whom he anticipated moving in behind the Confederate cannon opposite Bell's Mills. Expecting that they would soon be along, he determined to gain the attention of Col. Kelley's gunners until they rode up.

According to the plan worked out on the *Moose* around midnight, the *Neosho* was sent down below the batteries about 9:30 A.M. The monitor was not to knock out the guns but only feel their strength before returning above to report back to Fitch. The light draughts remained well out of range while the *Carondelet* followed the *Neosho* down and tied up to the bank within eyesight and extreme gun range.

The monitor easily attracted Rebel attention, carefully and deliberately engaging them for approximately 50 minutes. During this time, the Pook turtle above also sent four shells at Kelley's works. By 11:00 A.M., the two Yankee monsters had steamed back upstream and were anchored with the tinclads. The skippers reported to Fitch that Kelley had replied with only two guns of four spied and that no Federal cavalry was seen.

The gunboatmen were now convinced that this time they could easily silence Kelley's cannon and drive them away. Capture, however, and not dispersal, was the plan agreed to with Thomas. Because the Yankee horse soldiers had not arrived by noon, all hands were piped to lunch. All afternoon, the naval task group "maneuvered around above them" waiting for the bluecoated troopers to arrive behind the artillery.

For several reasons, the 6th Division horsemen, even though they had been waiting since 6:00 A.M., did not get started by the time the *Neosho* and *Carondelet* finished their shoot. On the Cumberland River flank before them a single Confederate brigade, with Brig. Gen. James R. Chalmers present, stood guard along the Charlotte Pike near Richland Creek. When Chalmers was seen across Richland Creek about noon, Union soldiers attempted to capture his barricades atop a ridge behind it. The riders stormed up the slope on the right flank. They were intent upon catching a portion of Kelley's artillery expected to be found at the summit — the same guns and same dismounted men thought to have been attacked by the *Neosho* and *Carondelet* earlier.

By the time the Northerners got through, the Rebel troopers behind the wall had moved off. The retreat was seen, at least partially, from the Cumberland. Acting Ensign Thomas A. Quinn, OOD aboard the *Carondelet*, wrote in the ship's deck log that "our cavalry charged over the hill and drove the enemy out of his works."

The 6th Division set off west along the Charlotte Pike after Chalmers. The pursuit went about four miles before the Federal cavalrymen once more ran into his Rebel brigade, posted in a strong position of long rail barricades located along a ridge beyond a small creek near Davidson's house overlooking Bell's Landing. This was, in fact, the true location of Kelley's artillery, which could now sweep the pike and the creek bridge.

An energetic attack on the Southern rear "directly into his works" about 3:00 P.M. was soon thereafter repulsed with heavy losses. "The rebs have chosen a good position," the division commander messaged headquarters. Thinking himself close enough to the Cumberland for the gunboats to make a difference, the cavalry advance was stopped and a messenger was dispatched to find Fitch and obtain his help.

About 3:40 P.M. the *Neosho* and *Carondelet* steamed down the river, rounded to, and began shelling what they perceived to be the Confederate positions. This attempt to enfilade the Confederate line was more noisy than effective. Many aboard the ironclads and among Johnson's troopers were convinced that the Rebels must be suffering great harm from the huge explosions.

According to contemporary and later reviews by Chalmers, Horn, and McDonough, the giant shells caused no damage to the butternut horsemen, but it did cut up a lot of nearby private property. The naval bombardment continued for 20 minutes, after which the *Carondelet* led the monitor back upstream. As the darkness of a winter evening approached, reaction to this cannonade was different from the perspectives of the three principles involved: Johnson, Chalmers, and Fitch.

As it would soon be dark, 6th Division commander Brig. Gen. Richard W. Johnson stayed put waiting for reinforcements. Of Fitch's shoot, the horseman believed "the tremendous discharges of his heavy guns contributed largely, I doubt not, to the already serious demoralization of the enemy." For his part, Brig. Gen. Chalmers was apprised that the Yankees were moving on his rear. To avoid being cut off, he ordered his men to abandon their present locations and hurry back toward the main Confederate army. At this point, Col. Kelley limbered up his guns and retired away from the Cumberland, finally shutting down his blockade.

Out on the water, the bluecoats believed that Kelley had found himself in a bad position and was attempting to remove his guns. He was "too late," they surmised, as "our cavalry closed in and took them with but little resistance." Satisfied that the combined arms objective had thus far "been successfully carried out," the USN task group moved down opposite Bell's Mills.

Replanting his cannon about a half mile back from the river near Davidson's landing, Kelley lobbed a few shells toward the cavalrymen and towards the *Carondelet* before continuing his exodus. This behavior was taken as an affront not only by the Federal riders, but by the Northern tars. "A few rounds of shell and shrapnel from our heavy guns," Lt. Cmdr. Fitch later wrote, "soon silenced the Rebels."

The rapid arrival of darkness brought an end to naval maneuvering in the Cumberland off Bell's Mills. "Not knowing the exact position our forces had taken, the firing on our part ceased and the boats were withdrawn a short distance above" the suspected Confederate gun emplacement. At 5:00 P.M., the gunboats landed at the bank, headed downstream.[15]

13

War's End

Under cover of heavy mist and poor visibility, the Federal army of Maj. Gen. George Thomas launched a counterattack out of Nashville on December 15 against the lines of Confederate Gen. John Bell Hood. The bluecoats were supported on the Cumberland at Bell's Mills by the *Carondelet* and *Neosho*, whose heavy shell firing actually opened the contest. Within a day, the Rebels were in full flight south.

The situation with Gen. Hood's main army deteriorated throughout the 16th to a point where the shattered graycoats rushed pell-mell in sleet and rain, not stopping until they were south of Brentwood after dark. Only then, in terrible weather that spared them instant Union pursuit, were scattered units able to commence their regrouping process. "The night that followed was strangely silent," wrote Walter Durham in 1987, "the last cannonading having stopped at dark with the flight of the rebels." As occasional lightning flashes rent the darkness, stragglers could be seen exiting the battlefield, either south or toward Nashville.[1]

On the evening of December 17, with Gen. Hood in full retreat and bluecoats in pursuit from several points, Maj. Gen. Thomas from the field, near Franklin, wrote to Mississippi Squadron commander Acting Rear Adm. Samuel Phillips Lee asking for help in another direction. If feasible, could the navy send one or two ironclads and several gunboats up the Tennessee to destroy the pre-positioned Confederate pontoon bridge believed functional at Florence? If the Federal gunboats could make it by Christmas Eve, Thomas reasoned, they had a good chance of intercepting the arriving Confederates and preventing their escape over the Tennessee.

Upon receipt of the message next morning, Lee, who had been detained by low water at Clarksville for almost two weeks, quickly consulted a chart. Geography dictated that he would be in a better position to oversee such an advance from Paducah, so he made a fast passage downriver. Fortunately, the rivers were beginning to rise and the weather, though rainy, was pleasant. One gunboat officer from Maine pointed out in a letter home that it "has been as warm as it is in June at home."

Observed by a good crowd of dockworkers and others watching from the bank, the first post-battle return convoy from Nashville to Smithland departed in two waves beginning at 11:30 A.M. The parade was led by the *Neosho*, under tow of the supply boat *Magnet.* The monitor was followed ten minutes later by the *Moose and Reindeer*, which led 11 transports and a hospital boat. The tinclad *Fairplay* brought up the rear. "We open the Cumberland today," Nashville quartermaster Col. James L. Donaldson cheerfully wrote to Quartermaster General Montgomery C. Meigs after witnessing the departure. "Transports here have left under convoy of the gunboats." The weather was cloudy, threatening rain. As the river continued to rise, the *Carondelet* was the only USN warship still anchored off the Tennessee capital.

While this return convoy exited out of the immediate war zone, Acting Rear Adm. Lee wired Maj. Gen. Thomas, agreeing to push a suitable naval force up the Tennessee River

The naval station at Mound City was the location where the *Carondelet* was decommissioned, dismantled and sold in the period between May and September 1865 (U.S. Army Military History Institute).

as soon as the boats arrived and the thick fog dissipated. If there was water enough in the river, it was anticipated that the gunboats could help cut off Hood's retreat. After battling rain, wind, and the shifting currents of the Cumberland for 18 hours, the Smithland-bound convoy reached Clarksville at dark on December 19. Appreciating the continuing necessity for well-organized and conducted upper river convoys, Fitch asked his superior to take over the gunboat advance while he remained on the Nashville–Smithland run. Agreeing, Acting Rear Adm Lee jumped at the chance to participate, operationally, in the final pursuit of Gen. Hood. For his part, Fitch, from his knowledge of the rivers gained in two years of war, may also have suspected that, based on intelligence reports, the Confederates were headed for Alabama via Great Muscle Shoals. Water levels over the obstruction would probably prevent any naval pursuit into the upper Tennessee.[2]

Thomas and Lee, urged on by Washington, D.C., generals and other leaders, pursued the retreating Confederates as they sped back to Alabama. Two days into Hood's retreat, Maj. Gen. Nathan Bedford Forrest took over as Confederate rear guard and provided spirited cover as the Rebels moved toward the bridge across the Tennessee at Florence, the head of steamboat navigation at that time. According to Stanley Horn, the butternut soldiers sang a parody of "The Yellow Rose of Texas":

> But now I'm going to leave you;
> My heart is full of woe.
> I'm going back to Georgia to see my Uncle Joe.
> You may talk about your Beauregards and sing of General Lee
> But the gallant Hood of Texas played hell in Tennessee.

Acting Rear Adm. Lee's expedition departed from Paducah up the Tennessee on December 20. Over the next week, the lead five gunboats would proceed with speed, destroying flatboats and ferrys en route. Simultaneously, the *Carondelet* departed Nashville for Fort Donelson, 45 miles downriver. While en route, she was also to prevent unauthorized river crossings, should she happen upon any. In particular, her crew were to watch for a Confederate force under Brig. Gen. Hylan B. Lyon that had been raiding in the Cumberland River region during the Nashville campaign. In late afternoon, she rounded to and anchored off Bowling Green, where two steamers awaited convoy. From her decks, the men could see six houses (only one of substance), large numbers of hogs, and four ladies waving white handkerchiefs.

It was anchors aweigh for the trio at daylight on December 22. About 9:00 A.M., the ironclad encountered the tinclad *Fairplay*, bound for Nashville with a convoy. The side wheeler also carried a new captain for the *Carondelet*, Acting Volunteer Lt. Charles P. Clark. The Portland, Maine, native was immediately rowed over, climbed aboard via the fantail, and read himself into command. Acting Master Miller willingly returned to his previous post of executive officer. The two gunboats next traded duties and the *Carondelet* took over the *Fairplay*'s charges, leading them back toward Clarksville.

As Lee's craft dropped anchor off Chickasaw, above Eastport but below Florence, on Christmas Eve, a message was dispatched from Maj. Gen. Thomas recommending that the follow-on boats, which he expected to convoy troop transports to Eastport, remain at that point until Hood's intentions were clearly known.

The *Carondelet* was not among these late arrivals, as she was kept in the Cumberland as heavy cover for the convoys on that river. During this mission, the ironclad fired her guns for the last two times while under steam. On both occasions, these were warning shots fired across the bows of Union transports disobeying the rules of convoy. Most of her time was spent anchored off Clarksville, where the new captain, Clark, drilled his men and exercised vigilance.

Between December 25 and 30, the wet weather turned cold. The remnants of the Confederate Army of Tennessee managed to cross over the Tennessee at Bainbridge and make for its final rendezvous at Tupelo, Mississippi. The Federal army, in warm if not hot pursuit, could not catch up, though it did manage to pick up many prisoners and much Confederate supply.

The frustrated Union generals were, with the exception of Thomas, not particularly happy with the role played by the Mississippi Squadron in this campaign. Cavalry chief Maj. Gen. James Wilson, who led the charge, was blunt in his contribution to the *Battles and Leaders* series. "The failure of the light draught gunboats on the Tennessee River to reach and destroy the pontoon bridge which Hood had kept in position," he wrote, "insured his safe retreat."[3]

The *Carondelet* moved to Smithland on January 4, 1865, and thence immediately thereafter to Johnsonville, on the Tennessee River. Once a thriving Union army depot operated by both military and civilian workers, the storage facility was largely destroyed in the wake of an attack by Forrest in November. Scott Jordan, now the ironclad's second lieutenant, reported that there were presently no civilian inhabitants, "except for three young ladies who occupy a house about 200 yards from our anchorage."

On January 14, in company with four tinclads, the *Carondelet* weighed for Eastport, 156 miles above. As convoy flagboat, she led four tinclads and 20 USQMD troop transports, aboard one of which was Maj. Gen. Thomas and his staff. The group arrived at its destination early next morning, finding the admiral and his gunboats, about 50 other steamers, and "the hills in the vicinity white with camp tents."

Lee remained on the Tennessee in support of Thomas through mid–January 1865. With the close of the Nashville campaign, he reported to navy secretary Gideon Welles that army-navy cooperation in the recent operation had "been of a most pleasing and cordial character."

By the end of January, Gen. Hood's Army of Tennessee had completed its retreat back into Mississippi. Pursuing Union forces, knowing that it was spent, allowed it to melt away, content in the knowledge that their actions since mid–December had all but finished the campaign in the west. Indeed, as historian Richard Gildrie has put it, the massive Union victory "effectively ended the war between the Mississippi River and the Appalachian Mountains."

Saluting the admiral with kind remarks, Lee's recent biographers concluded that "It is difficult to find anywhere in the history of the American Civil War a better demonstration of combined operations in which the army and the navy worked together with fewer problems and more impressive results." On the other hand, Craig Symonds reminds us that Lee "never won his great victory or obtained the formal thanks of Congress, and remained an acting rear-admiral until the end of the war."

Nathan Bedford Forrest (1821–1877) was one of a handful of western cavalry leaders who understood the importance of interdicting Federal waterborne commerce. In February 1862, he witnessed the failure of the *Carondelet* and her sisters at Fort Donelson and spent the war perfecting methods to bedevil the inland Union navy. Although he never directly took on any of the Pook turtles, one of his feints toward Memphis in October caused the *Carondelet* to be readied for the town's defense. Forrest later assisted Gen. John Bell Hood in his Nashville offensive in December 1864 and January 1865, providing gunners to fight her on the Cumberland and then covering the retreat of the shattered Confederate army (Library of Congress).

Military action along the western waters subsided almost daily from this time on through the conclusion of the war in April. Just as it was reported that Confederate soldiers were deserting from the lines in the east, so too did many disappear from duty in the Tennessee Valley — but not all. "The guerrilla war continued," observed Gildrie, "having a logic of its own, even though the military purposes were negligible." Though not as ferocious as in previous years, partisan and guerrilla activities remained a major concern for the Federal gunboatmen, as did the need to interrupt or counter them. Rebel hit and run attacks continued to be made. Many of the raids originated out of western Kentucky and were aimed at rail connections.

While maintaining often minimal patrols, the Mississippi Squadron was gradually altered from a war-fighting command to a coast guard force, which handled various police duties, some counterinsurgency activities, and customs inspections. When 1865 began, the U.S. Navy Department, believing that the rebellion would soon be over, sought significant economy in its operations.[4]

While Hood was in Tennessee, Maj. Gen. William T. Sherman's march to the sea virtually destroyed Rebel ability to send food and fuel to Virginia from the lower South via Georgia. The focus for Civil War military action now turned east, where Lt. Gen. Ulysses S. Grant had besieged the Army of Northern Virginia at Petersburg while Sherman and Rear Adm. David Dixon Porter set about shutting down Confederate succor from the sea by capturing Fort Fisher and Wilmington.

The *Carondelet* remained tied to the bank at Eastport, where her captains were also port commandants, technically part of the Ninth District under Lt. Commander Robert Boyd. In charge of the *Carondelet* only briefly, Capt. Clark was transferred to command of the *Benton* on February 1. The following morning, Acting Volunteer Lt. John Rogers came aboard and assumed command. He was not unfamiliar to Acting Master Miller and Acting Ensign Jordan, both of whom had met him when he commanded the *Naumkeag* at Clarendon the previous summer.

The ironclad's engines, never noted for their efficiency or endurance, were in very bad condition. Their last overhaul had been hasty and provided just sufficient power to get her through the Nashville campaign. In February, the *Carondelet*'s power plant was condemned by survey, necessitating extensive repairs. Unable to utilize his vessel, Rogers found it necessary to conduct his business aboard his old tinclad, the *Naumkeag*. The fighting days of the old lady were over. While repairs to her engines went slowly forward, she was little more than a floating battery.

Very little of interest occurred aboard the immobile gunboat as her sailors watched spring arrive and the foliage blossom. In addition to the daily shipboard routine of drill and hull and deck maintenance, there was ample opportunity for play, reading, or checkers. The junior officers regularly went ashore to hunt squirrel and pigeons (in one February week, over 40 squirrel were shot for the cook's pot) and fishing was great sport.

On April 7, Capt. Rogers had the entire crew mustered on the spar deck and read them the news that Richmond and Petersburg had fallen, the former three days earlier. The announcement was followed by huzzahs from every jack aboard. The boat's skipper now went ashore, but not before leaving orders for Ensign Jordan to expend a half dozen rounds of 100-pdr. shrapnel "as far back into the country" as possible, supposedly to get the attention of a band of "guerrillas" believed camped about four miles inland. Nearby Federal troops, supposing that a salute was being fired, cheered as each cannon roared a projectile overhead. They also cheered when they hit in some unknown spot and exploded with a distant noise that shook the ground.

On April 9, Gen. Lee surrendered to Lt. Gen. Grant at Appomattox Court House, Virginia, a fact soon communicated to friend and foe alike. As might be imagined, more naval gunfire sounded.

It was only a matter of time before the fruits of Northern victory spread across the land. In these heady early days of Union joy, unregulated navigation on the western rivers was fully reopened and military responsibility to police them was significantly reduced. Resources devoted to war were now reduced by the Federals accordingly. On Good Friday, April 14, General Order 60 was received by district commanders of the Mississippi Squadron. Henceforth, the remaining gunboats were not required to cover the landings by steamboats engaged in lawful trade unless desired by military authorities or the parties making the landings. In short, convoy escort was ended and any conflicting squadron orders on this point were revoked.

President Lincoln was shot shortly after 10:00 P.M. that day while watching *Our Amer-*

ican Cousin at Ford's Theatre. He died at 7:22 A.M. the next morning. While the nation came to grips with the enormity of the assassination and Vice President Andrew Johnson became president, plans were put in place to honor the late chief executive. On Sunday, navy secretary Welles wired all of his squadron commanders requiring them to observe the funeral with appropriate respect. More complete special orders were sent by mail. Commanders of the various squadrons passed word of Lincoln's death to all of their commanders. On most ships and boats, including the *Carondelet*, crews were assembled and the official announcement was read, along with the order for mourning. All officers began to wear crape, something which would adorn their uniforms for the next six months.

Toward the end of April, the engineers completed their overhaul of the *Carondelet*. On April 30, Capt. Rogers passed the order to raise steam. After rounding to, the *Carondelet* churned slowly downstream toward Paducah, arriving off that Kentucky town two days later. There the crew received its final liberty of the war.[5]

As after every war through the Vietnam conflict, the U.S. began to rapidly downsize its large military establishment. As the civilian leader of the naval establishment, Secretary Gideon Welles, a fiscal conservative, "determined to dismantle the Navy as efficiently as it had been built up." This would, however, be no haphazard enterprise. Care had to be taken to scale back in such a fashion as to not harm material and human requirements

Implementation of plans to reduce the overall size of the U.S. Navy were in full swing by the start of May. On the third day of the month, Secretary Welles ordered Acting Rear Adm. Lee to cut the expenses of the Mississippi Squadron as far as possible. To start with, only 25 vessels of all types were to be kept in commission. The resignations of any officers who wished to leave the service were to be approved. Requests for leave or transfer would also be considered, as long as a sufficient number of officers were retained to man the dwindling number of boats.

Lee took the opportunity on May 19 to pen a long report that provided his scenario "regarding the reduction of the squadron." It began with the suggestion that most of the ironclads be laid up in ordinary and all withdrawn once the last Confederate Trans-Mississippi area forces surrendered, probably within the month. It was also pointed out that only a handful of craft needed to be retained for service work and that all of the others could be brought to a central location. Mound City was desired, not only because it had workmen and facilities, but also because it would be convenient for later civilian surplus purchasers.

Casemate armor could be quickly and easily removed by the boats' crews for separate sale or storage. The guns could similarly be withdrawn — along with the heavy anchors, cables, and other items not required for commercial purposes— and shipped to New York for storage or use by other squadrons. Small arms and powder could be dispatched to magazines and basic engine repairs completed.

As withdrawn ironclads reported to Mound City, they would be taken in hand by laborers contracted for by Com. John W. Livingston, acting under order of the Bureau of Construction. In an orderly manner, the vessels would be decommissioned and demobilized. Several, like the *Cincinnati*, were earlier transferred to the West Gulf Coast Blockading Squadron and would go out of service at New Orleans.

After the vessels were stripped, a grand public sale (terms cash) should be held to gain as much return as possible on their original purchase prices. It was further recommended that, for 15 days in advance of whatever auction date was chosen, newspaper advertisements be placed in the daily newspapers of the principal river cities, including Pittsburgh, Cincinnati, Louisville, Cairo, St. Louis, Memphis, and New Orleans. For a week or so prior to the sale, prospective buyers would be allowed to inspect the boats.

Welles, in general, agreed with Lee's proposals for squadron downsizing. In responding on May 22, he noted that the surplus vessels would be sold under the direction of the Department's Bureau of Construction. He also named three vessels he thought should definitely be laid up early. Heading the list was the *Carondelet.* A week later, from Mound City, the flotilla commander replied in agreement and then wired Capt. Rogers: "Report here with the *Carondelet* tomorrow, 31st instant."[6]

The process by which Mississippi Squadron ironclads were recalled, dismantled, laid in ordinary, and eventually sold can be illustrated by tracing the end of the career of the *Carondelet.* Her fate and the manner of its occurrence represents, in the main, that which befell her sisters and, indeed, the entire inland fleet. Shortly after dawn on the last morning of May, less than a week after the surrender of Gen. E. Kirby Smith's Confederate Trans-Mississippi command, Acting Volunteer Lt. Rogers ordered his men to cast off for their final voyage. An hour after noon, the *Carondelet* arrived at Mound City. Aided by a pair of steam tugs, the ironclad came to anchor astern of the tinclad *St. Clair,* while the squadron flagboat — another light draught — the *Tempest,* fired a nine-gun salute.

Acting Rear Adm. Samuel Phillips Lee (1812–1897) succeeded Rear Adm. David D. Porter in command of the Mississippi Squadron during October 1864. Lee was prevented by low water from direct participation in the Battle of Nashville prior to the Confederate withdrawal. He pushed up the Tennessee River after the retreating Rebels in January 1865 but was unable to come to grips with the Southerners, many of whom escaped via the shoals. He was subsequently blamed in certain Union army circles for letting Gen. John Bell Hood escape. It fell to Lee to disband the squadron from April to August 1865, an unhappy task he performed with great efficiency (Naval History and Heritage Command).

The *Carondelet*'s commission now had less than three weeks to run. On Friday, June 2, after receiving his instructions, her captain ordered part of the crew to begin removing the huge cannon onto a barge moored alongside. Late in the afternoon, Acting Rear Adm. Lee came aboard to see how the work was progressing. After a brief inspection, he returned onboard the *Tempest,* convinced that the "cost" of this particular ironclad would be reduced in short order.

Within the next few days, all of the *Carondelet*'s great guns and small arms were turned over to the fleet's ordnance department. As there was no suitable place on the base for long-term storage of the large quantity of cannon, small arms, and pow-

During the Union Army pursuit of Confederate forces retreating from Nashville in January 1865, elements of the Mississippi Squadron under Acting Rear Adm. Samuel Phillips Lee provided active assistance, much of it centered on the Tennessee River town of Eastport, Mississippi. The *Carondelet* was posted at the town as station vessel from January 15 to April 30, 1865 (*Harper's Weekly*, February 28, 1865).

der being removed from withdrawn vessels, Rogers learned that those from his craft would be transported to the Union army barracks at Jefferson City, Missouri. At the same time, the gunboat's stores were broken out and, following what was becoming squadron-wide practice, invoiced and sent ashore. When the guns and provisions were nearly all offloaded, large numbers of enlisted sailors were sent to receiving ships and paid off. Many of the officers were given berths on other vessels or sent home to await discharge.

During the afternoon of June 16, a work party reported aboard the *Carondelet* from the naval facility. These men had orders to effect the few changes necessary to convert her into an "ordnance boat," or floating ammunition dump. The following day, with carpenters pounding around him, Capt. Rogers saluted the flag and went ashore. There he would wait the termination of his appointment. The whipping boy of several captains, Acting Ensign and Executive Officer Oliver Donaldson, who had come aboard with Capt. Walke from the *Tyler* in 1861 and for some time had been the senior officer aboard in time of service, was left in charge. He was the *Carondelet*'s last captain—for four days.

Sometime in the evening of June 20, Acting Rear Adm. Lee received a large package and letter from Capt. Rogers. Opening the communication, he read: "This vessel [*Carondelet*] is being fitted for an ordnance store ship by authority of Commodore Livingston. I therefore consider her cruise as a gunboat at an end and respectfully forward through you the logbook of this ship to the [Navy] Department. Allow me, sir, to tender my congratulations to you and the Department on the successful termination of the war, and the many hazardous enterprises this ship has passed through."

From the time Lee received her logbook, the *Carondelet* was decommissioned and her naval career was finished. Much of the century-long mystery that surrounded her eventual fate began at this point. Many of the government's documents, some of which were later printed in the Navy's *Official Records*, shed very little light on the boat—except for her sale—after the first day of summer 1865. No other mention is made regarding the vessel's duty as an ordnance store ship. This was probably only a temporary expedient while the guns of the boats coming into Mound City were held prior to their transfer to the Jefferson City barracks facility.

By August 2, we know that nine decommissioned ironclads, including the *Carondelet*, were inspected and moored in the towhead chutes above the naval station. All were "laid up in ordinary," the ancient term for an out-of-commission naval vessel being held in reserve for some future purpose. It was a state requiring only minimum maintenance and not dissimilar from the modern concept of "mothballing." Acting Volunteer Lt. George P. Lord, late skipper of the *Chillicothe*, a few other officers, and a handful of ratings were assigned to the skeleton upkeep crews.[7]

During the second week of August, Acting Rear Adm. Lee reported to Washington that all of the vessels which were to be liquidated were now in the hands of Com. Livingston. The Mississippi Squadron ceased to exist on August 14 when its commander hauled down his flag and returned east. Three days later, many of the tinclads, supply, and auxiliary craft were sold at a great auction attended by citizens from throughout the Mississippi Valley.[8]

In the months after Lee quit the west, Com. Livingston continued to sell off the equipment, stores, and vessels of the ex-squadron. The naval base at Memphis was also quietly closed out; that at Cairo followed. During this period, local contract Illinois workmen finished stripping the ironclads in ordinary. Armor plate and any items not required elsewhere and which might show a profit if sold separately were removed. By the middle of November, the City Series gunboats, as well as the other ironclad units, were little more than hulks.

The year would be truly profitable for one Daniel Jacobs of St. Louis, a buyer and seller of steamboats and their equipment. A competent man by all accounts, he participated in the August gunboat sales and knew that Livingston planned to sell the former ironclads. By November 21, he knew for sure, as the commodore advertised their auction in most of the river papers. That morning, the *St. Louis Daily Missouri Democrat* and the *St. Louis Daily Missouri Republican* both advised the public that some of the remaining vessels of the late fleet were going under the gavel. The selling would begin promptly at noon on Wednesday, November 29. All would be sold to the highest bidder, "together with their engines, tackle, and furniture."[9]

We do not know for certain exactly how this particular ship sale progressed. It was one of many surplus auctions held around the country from 1865 to 1867 by the Navy and the Army Quartermaster Department. Although there are no accounts of it in known diaries or correspondence and it was not widely covered by the public press, it undoubtedly unfolded much like the August sale, which was fully reported by several newspapers.

Possible future uses for the *Carondelet* and her sisters may have been surmised by many of their prospective buyers, who saw them either during the war or at the time of the great August auction. Also, since the government was taking rather large losses to be rid of this surplus, the purchasers probably did not anticipate making large bids. One thing is certain, Daniel Jacobs and his competitors had their financial arrangements completed. The advertisements specifically required that each bidder be able to place a 5 percent down payment on each vessel successfully won, the balance to be paid within a few months.

The morning of the appointed day dawned cold in Mound City; it was now less than a month until Christmas. Upriver at Cincinnati, ice was reported in the Ohio River as well as other tributaries. Although they may have had the opportunity over the past week to inspect the boats and other surplus items, Jacobs and the other buyers undoubtedly arrived at the naval station fairly early and may even have attended the coal barge sale the day before. Some would stay for the armor sale next day.[10]

The chief auctioneer, Solomon A. Silver, had presided over the August gunboat sale. The no-nonsense salesman, surrounded by naval station staff, gaveled the sale into session at noon. With 21 vessels and tons of equipment to be sold, a long afternoon was ahead.

It is quite probable that, as at the August sale, the one-time ironclads were unloaded alphabetically. With the *Baron de Kalb* and *Cairo* sunk, only the *Benton* kept the *Carondelet* from being the first vessel sold. When the name of the veteran, still distinguished by her chimneys with their distinctive but faded red identification bands, was placed before the buyers, all assembled knew her story well, including the troubles engineer James B. Eads had encountered finishing her and collecting government payment. After a short period of back-and-forth, Jacobs pledged $3,600 and emerged the high bidder. Moving to the closing table, he paid cash and was awarded a bill of sale. Triumphant, he went on to purchase three other craft before the proceedings closed.[11]

For years after the sale, few people knew or cared what fate now befell the once proud gunboat. In time, knowledge of her postwar history faded into obscurity. About half a century ago, Mr. William Tippitt, of Hernando, MS, while compiling data for a history of western steamboating, happened to solve part of the mystery. When placed in contact with the Southerner by Edwin C. Bearss, this writer was gratified by the information so kindly given. A check of other records and editions soon revealed sufficient material to advance the account of her destiny.[12]

Although Jacobs took possession of the *Carondelet* in early December 1865, because of the winter weather nothing was done with her until the following spring. As she still contained valuable parts, mainly the iron in her hull and the old engines, she was towed up the Ohio River to a Cincinnati wrecking yard in late May. Presumably, she was sold again as, upon reaching the Queen City, she was not demolished. However, in 1867, her engines were taken out and placed in the 50-ton towboat *Quaker*, a stern wheeler originally built

Mound City and Cairo, Illinois, were the operational and support centers of the Mississippi Squadron, with the former station center for the dissolution of the command in July and August 1865. The identity of the vessel pictured in the foreground is unknown (Miller's *Photographic History of the Civil War*).

A well-known photo showing two of the Pook turtles anchored in the Ohio River off Cairo in 1863. We enter it here for the depiction of the wharf boat in the foreground. This is the sort of vessel into which the hull of the *Carondelet* was converted following her sale in September 1865 (Naval History and Heritage Command).

at Antwerp, Ohio, in 1863 as the *John Perden* and renamed on January 1, 1865. She would be lost in 1877.

In the period after 1867, the former gunboat was outfitted as a wharfboat and probably remained at Cincinnati for the next three years. In 1870, however, the craft showed up roughly 150 miles further up the Ohio at Gallipolis, Ohio, under the ownership of Capt. John Hamilton of that city, owner of several floating storehouses tightly moored to the riverbank. There is no way to know whether he knew her Civil War identity.[13] In the years following, the unnamed warehouse deteriorated until she could be of no further commercial use. Eventually, she lay in a "sunken condition." By the spring of 1873, Hamilton had decided to scrap her for her remaining iron, "worth several thousand dollars." Before he could execute his plan, nature stepped in and the spring floods of that year washed her away downstream. The rising waters carried the hulk about 130 miles to a point near Manchester, in Adams County, Ohio. There she grounded at the head of Manchester Island, bows upstream, deck out of water, and lay "straight up and down the river."

During the last week of April, Capt. Hamilton arrived at Manchester, "a thriving village" of about 600 souls, to claim his wreck. Going over to the island, he found her "covered with pirates intent on tearing her to pieces for the old iron." After chasing these away, he procured the services of a watchman and sent him aboard as guard until the river fell, a service reminiscent of the time, after the fall of Vicksburg, when the *Carondelet* guarded the wreck of the sunken *Indianola*. Hamilton would, he promised, return later to burn her for the ore and what little profit remained in her bones.[14]

After 12 years of hard treatment and unflinching service, the *Carondelet* was no more. There is, however, one more postscript to her story, one which details her physical end.

The noted novelist and underwater explorer Clive Cussler contacted this author in May 1981 to suggest that the *Carondelet*'s hulk might not have been burnt and that he suspected that pieces of the boat might still exist, buried in the sands off Manchester Island. He intended to take a look and wondered if I had learned anything more. Unfortunately, I could not help, beyond offering assurance that such an expedition would be a worthy project.[15]

In the course of his research of old and new Ohio River charts, Cussler determined that over the last century and a quarter Manchester Island had receded approximately 200 yards west. Using a set of overlays, the physical search began about a year after our conversation. The novelist wreck hunter and a friend, employing a 22-foot boat loaned by the Manchester fire chief, dragged a Schonstedt gradiometer up and down the channel off Manchester Island, as well as its shoreline.

After half a day of trolling, projections indicated that the hulk of the *Carondelet* was found. The location was about 120 yards off the state of Ohio and 250 yards "east and slightly north" off the eastern tip of Manchester Island. To cover the use of the boat, the two adventurers agreed to take time out to search, on behalf of the sheriff, for a car reported missing in the river nearby. After doing so, Cussler and his colleague resumed their mission fully expecting to find some kind of largely intact sunken vessel. Unhappily, as they came to the eastern tip of Manchester Island they observed a large dredge boat. It had just passed over the wharf-boat's grave.

Running up to and going aboard the vessel, Cussler talked with her captain, who thought he had merely mashed an old barge. Rusty iron hardware and pieces of wood retrieved and saved by dredge crewmen was produced. After pointing out the location of the wreck he had dug through, the captain was crushed when the writer confirmed that it was the same spot where he believed the *Carondelet* lay.

Returning to their fire boat, the two explorers steered over to the wreck site and once more dragged their sensor over the riverbed. The gradiometer readings revealed hundreds of small objects scattered over the bottom. Still, there was something left. Fairly large but shattered fragments of the lower part of the *Carondelet*'s hull and keels remained intact two feet below the riverbed level at which the dredge was digging (18 feet below the surface). Successful in many other searches, the explorer was severely disappointed, as was this writer when he heard the news. "God, can you imagine?" Cussler later wrote. "After the *Carondelet* had rested undisturbed in the mud for a hundred and nine years, Cussler had to show up two days too late to save her."[16]

Chapter Notes

Introduction

1. Myron J. Smith, Jr., "A Construction and Recruiting History of the U.S. Steam Gunboat *Carondelet*, 1861–1861," (master's thesis, Shippensburg State University, 1969). My concern regarding the shortage of published nautical studies was intensified during work to compile the first published bibliography on the topic, *American Civil War Navies: A Bibliography* (Metuchen, NJ: Scarecrow, 1972).

2. Henry Walke, *Naval Scenes and Reminiscences of the Civil War in the United States on the Southern and Western Waters during the Years 1861, 1862 and 1863, with the History of That Period Compared and Corrected from Authentic Sources* (New York: F.R. Reed, 1877), 53; H. Allen Gosnell, *Guns on the Western Rivers* (Baton Rouge: Louisiana State University Press, 1949), ii; Pratt to writer, August 21, 1969; Catton to writer, November 5, 1969; Donald to writer, June 2, 1970.

3. Edwin C. Bearss, National Park Service, interview with writer, May 29, 1969. Then working out of the Office of Archeology and Historical Preservation at the National Park Service headquarters in the Department of the Interior, Mr. Bearss accompanied this writer on a D.C. city bus to visit the Smithsonian Institution where Mr. William E. Geoghegan had constructed a model of the *Carondelet*. Having recently salvaged the hulk of the *Carondelet*'s sister, the *Cairo*, from the Yazoo River, Bearss was—and remains—one of the country's foremost experts on the vessel type. He pointed out, during our ride, that despite subsequent difficulties in identification, whatever could be said about one of these craft during their construction period could be said of all—as they were almost, if not quite, carbon copies of one another. Thus, for example, if one gunboat had two rudders, they all did.

4. Myron J. Smith, Jr., *U.S.S. "Carondelet," 1861–1865* (Manhattan, KA: MA/AH Publishing for the USAF Historical Foundation, 1982).

5. Virgil Carrington Jones, "The Navy War: Introduction," *Civil War History* 9 (June 1963), 117.

Chapter 1

1. Louis S. Gerteis, *Civil War St. Louis* (Lawrence: University Press of Kansas, 2001), 78–79, 91–92; "James Buchanan Eads," in *Appleton's Cyclopedia of American Biography*, ed. James Grant Wilson and John Fisk (5 vols.; New York: D. Appleton, 1888) (vol. 2), 287; "James Buchanan Eads," University of Illinois at Urbana–Champagne Riverweb Site, http://www.riverweb.uiuc.edu/TECH/TECH20.htm (accessed September 18, 2006); John D. Milligan, *Gunboats Down the Mississippi* (Annapolis, MD: Naval Institute Press, 1965), 3; Richard Webber and John C. Roberts, "James B. Eads: Master Builder," *The Navy* 8 (March 1965), 23–25; Elmer L. Gaden, "Eads and the Navy of the Mississippi," *American Heritage of Invention & Technology* 9 (Spring 1994), 26–27. By 1860, Lawrenceburg, IN, native Eads (1820–1887), whose mother was a cousin of former president James Buchanan, was a highly regarded Missouri entrepreneur, a "rags-to-riches" businessman who got his financial start by selling apples on river packets. There being many wrecks along the river during those early steamboating days, Eads saw a chance to make money by salvaging some of them. Becoming knowledgeable about the shipping business while employed as a steamboat purser, he demonstrated an early mechanical aptitude when, in 1842, he devised a successful diving bell which could be operated from a special "snag-boat" that he called a "submarine." After entering into a partnership with Case & Nelson of St. Louis, the men became rich cleaning out river bottom wrecks. To satisfy his new bride and to alleviate health problems doubtless caused by his pioneering underwater salvage work, Eads quit the Mississippi. New energy and his fortune were poured into the establishment, at St. Louis, of the first glassworks west of the Ohio River; but the business failed and he was financially ruined, at age 37, by the Mexican War. Required by fate to replenish his empty bank accounts, Eads returned to the salvage business, improved his earlier innovations, and earned a second fortune. In 1855, poor health forced him to retire from active business at the age of 55. Later (1867–1874), he would construct the still-employed steel Mississippi River arch bridge at St. Louis and oversee river jetty improvement projects at New Orleans. At the time of his death, he was planning a ship-railway across Mexico's isthmus of Tehuantepec. Lincoln's navy secretary, Gideon Welles, and Eads struck up a friendship which continued over the years. When the Connecticut native left office in 1869, he contacted the engineer, then constructing his famous bridge, for advice on western railroad investments; John Niven, *Gideon Welles: Lincoln's Secretary of the Navy* (New York: Oxford University Press, 1973), 569; Robert J. Rombauer, *The Union Cause in St. Louis in 1862* (St. Louis, MO: Press of Nixon-Jones, 1909), 222. Edward Bates (1793–1869), prominent Missouri politician and former U.S. congressman, served as attorney general from 1861 to 1864; member of a noted Missouri family and Dred Scott's attorney during the famous Supreme Court case, Montgomery Blair (1813–1883), like Bates, served in Lincoln's cabinet from 1861 to1864. Mark M. Boatner III, *The Civil War Dictionary* (New York: David McKay, 1959), 50, 67; "Edward Bates, 1793–1869," in *Biographical Directory of the United States Congress, 1774–Present*, http://bioguide.congress.gov/scripts/biodisplay.pl?index=B000231 (accessed October 1, 2006).

2. Bates to Eads, April 16, 1861; James B. Eads Papers, Missouri Historical Society, St. Louis, cited hereafter as Eads Papers, with date; Charles Dana Gibson, with E. Kay Gibson, *Assault and Logistics*, vol. 2, *Union Army Coastal and River Operations, 1861–1866* (Camden, ME: Ensign Press, 1995), 54; Fletcher Pratt, *The Navy—a History: The Story of a Service in Action* (Garden City, NY: Garden City, 1941), 282; Webber and Roberts, "Master Builder"; Charles B. Boynton, *History of the Navy During the Rebellion*, 2 vols. (New York: D. Appleton, 1867), vol. 1, 498; James B. Eads, "Recollections of Foote and the Gunboats," in *Battles and Leaders of the Civil War*, ed. Robert V. Johnson and Clarence C. Buel, 4 vols. (New York: Century, 1884–1887, reprt. Thomas Yoseloff, 1956), vol. 1, 338–339, cited hereafter as *B&L*, followed by a comma, the volume number, a comma, and the page numbers; U.S. Navy Department, Naval History Division, *Riverine Warfare* (Washington, DC: GPO, 1968), 21; U.S. Navy Department, *Official Records of the*

Union and Confederate Navies in the War of the Rebellion, 31 vols. (Washington, DC: GPO, 1894–1922), Series I, Vol. 22, 278, 280, cited hereafter as ORN, followed by a comma, the series number in Roman numerals, a comma, the volume number in Arabic, a colon, and the page in Arabic; Louis How, *James B. Eads* (Boston: Houghton, Mifflin, 1900), 23–27; Phyllis F. Dorsett, "James B. Eads: Navy Shipbuilder, 1861," *U.S. Naval Institute Proceedings* 101 (August 1975), 76; Edwin C. Bearss, *Hardluck Ironclad: The Sinking and Salvage of the Cairo* (Baton Rouge: Louisiana State University Press, 1966), 10–12; Gaden, "Navy of the Mississippi," 28; William E. Geoghegan, "Study for a Scale Model of the U.S.S. *Carondelet*," *Nautical Research Journal* 17 (Summer 1970), 147–148; The West in Civil War literature refers generally to the western theater of operations beyond the Allegheny Mountains. See Bruce Catton, "Glory Road Began in the West," *Civil War History* 6 (June 1960), 229–237. Cairo, which would, indeed, become the key point on the Mississippi, was not a particularly likeable town. Seized on April 23, 1861, by Chicago troops, it was home to mosquitoes, malaria, rats, and mud. Despite its legendary shortcomings, the little hamlet would become the arsenal and depot of the western navy. William A. Pitkin, "When Cairo was Saved for the Union," *Illinois State Historical Society Journal* 51 (Autumn 1958), 384–305. Powerful Pennsylvania senator Simon Cameron (1779–1889) received his cabinet position as a payoff for his support in Lincoln's 1860 campaign. Ineffective and embarrassing, he was packed off as soon as possible (to Russia as ambassador, 1862–1866); reelected to the Senate in 1867, he remained in that body through Reconstruction. Boatner, *Dictionary*, 115. Eads' address was given in an ad for ships' carpenters placed in the *St. Louis Daily Missouri Democrat* on August 22, 1861.

3. Eads Papers, 339; ORN, I, 22: 278; Boynton, *History of the Navy;* Gaden, "Navy of the Mississippi"; Bearss, *Hardluck*; Geoghegan, "Study for a Scale Model"; How, *Eads.*

4. George B. McClellan, *The Civil War Papers of George B. McClellan: Selected Correspondence, 1860–1865*, ed. Stephen W. Sears (New York: Ticknor and Fields, 1989), 6–7; Ethan S. Rafuse, *McClellan's War: The Failure of Moderation in the Struggle for the Union* (Bloomington: Indiana University Press, 2005), 93; Bearss, *Hardluck*. George Brinton McClellan (1826–1885) became a central military figure of the Civil War. Better known as an organizer than as a field commander, his 1862 Peninsula campaign was a failure and he was relieved after failing to follow up after the Battle of Antietam. He was the Democratic presidential candidate in 1864. Boatner, *Dictionary*, 524.

5. Rafuse, *McClellan's War*, 94–99; Rafuse, "Impractical? Unforgivable?: Another Look at George B. McClellan's First Strategic Plan," *Ohio History* 110 (Summer–Autumn 2001), 153–164; Stephen W. Sears, *George B. McClellan: The Young Napoleon* (New York: Ticknor and Fields, 1988), 73–77.

6. Edward Townsend, *Anecdotes of the Civil War in the United States* (New York: D. Appleton, 1884), 56; U.S. War Department, *The War of the Rebellion: A Compilation of the Official Records of the Union and Confederate Armies*, 128 vols. (Washington, DC: GPO, 1880–1901), Series I, Vol. 51, 369–370, cited hereafter as OR, followed by a comma, the series number in Roman numerals, a comma, the volume number in Arabic, a colon, and the page in Arabic; Scott to McClellan, May 3, 1861, George B. McClellan Papers, Library of Congress; Timothy D. Johnson, *Winfield Scott: The Quest for Military Glory* (Lawrence: University Press of Kansas, 1998), 226–228; T. Harry Williams, *Lincoln and His Generals* (New York: Alfred A. Knopf, 1952; reprnt. Vintage Books, 1962), 16; Bern Anderson, "The Naval Strategy of the Civil War," *Military Affairs* 26 (Spring 1962), 15; Anderson, *By Sea and By River*, 33–34; Bearss, *Hardluck*, 13–14; Geoghegan, "Study for a Scale Model"; Milligan, *Gunboats*, 3–4; Gideon Welles, *The Diary of Gideon Welles, Secretary of the Navy Under Lincoln and Johnson*, ed. John T. Morse, Jr., 3 vols. (Boston: Houghton Mifflin, 1911), vol. 1., 242; *St. Louis Daily Missouri Democrat*, May 10, 1861. For a modern review of the Anaconda and later Union plans, see Brian Holden Reid, "Rationality and Irrationality in Union Strategy, April 1861–March 1862," *War in History* 1 (March 1994), 25–29.

7. Pratt, *The Navy*, 282; Charles Henry Ambler, *A History of Transportation in the Ohio Valley* (Glendale, CA: Arthur H. Clark, 1932), 248; James Monaghan, *Civil War on the Western Border, 1854–1865* (Boston: Little, Brown, 1955), 130–132; Bearss, *Hardluck*, 12; John W. Allen, *Legends and Lore of Southern Illinois* (Carbondale, IL: University Graphics, 1978), 288–289; T.K. Kionka, *Key Command: Ulysses S. Grant's District of Cairo* (Shades of Blue and Gray Series; Columbia: University of Missouri Press, 2006), 49; *Chicago Daily Tribune*, May 21, 1861; U.S. Navy Department, Naval History Division, *Civil War Naval Chronology, 1861–1865* (Washington, DC: GPO, 1966), 12–13; S. Chamberlain, "Opening of the Upper Mississippi and the Siege of Vicksburg," *Magazine of Western History* 5 (March 1887), 611–613; Milford M. Miller, "Evansville Steamboats During the Civil War," *Indiana Magazine of History* 37 (December 1941), 363; *Cincinnati Daily Commercial*, May 8, 1861; *New York Evening Post*, May 11, 1861; Evansville *Daily Journal*, May 14, 1861; How, *Eads*, 27; Niven, *Gideon Welles*, 378. According to the Valley of the Shadows Resource Center's 1861 timeline, the river blockade was officially launched on May 13, almost a month after President Lincoln had ordered establishment of a coastal blockade (Valley of the Shadow home page, http://valley.vcdh.virginia.edu/reference/timelines/timeline1861.html (accessed September 1, 2006)).

8. OR, I, 53: 490–491; ORN, I, 22, 277–280; Gibson, *Coastal and River Operations*, 160; Bearss, *Hardluck*, 12; Milligan, *Gunboats*, 5; Paul W. Gates, *The Illinois Central Railroad and Its Colonization Work* (Cambridge, MA: Harvard University Press, 1934), 275; Rafuse, *McClellan's War*, 100; McClellan, *The Civil War Papers of George B. McClellan*, 37; Dave Dawley, "William J. Kountz," Steamboat home page, http://members.tripod.com/~Write4801/captains/k.html (accessed September 15, 2006). A veteran of the War of 1812 and Scott's chief engineer during the Mexican War, Totten (1788–1864) had commanded the Corps of Engineers for years and would die on active duty (Boatner, *Dictionary*, 843–844).

9. Boynton, *History of the Navy;* ORN, I, 22: 280; Geoghegan, "Study for a Model,"; Milligan, *Gunboats;* Robert E. Johnson, *Rear Admiral John Rodgers, 1812–1882* (Annapolis, MD: Naval Institute Press, 1967), 156–157; Donald L. Canney, *The Old Steam Navy*, vol. 2: *The Ironclads, 1842–1885* (Annapolis, MD: Naval Institute Press, 1993), 47; Gaden, "Navy of the Mississippi," 29; Bearss, *Hardluck*, 13. The son of Com John Rodgers (1772–1838) of War of 1812 fame and brother-in-law of the army's brand new quartermaster general, Montgomery C. Meigs, the clean-shaven and balding 49-year-old Maryland-born Rodgers was a large man "who considered himself fit when his weight was below 200 pounds." A dedicated professional with a reputation for generosity toward his subordinates, Rodgers had been originally appointed as a midshipman 33 years earlier. An accomplished and dutiful seaman, known as "the scientific sailor," Rodgers (1812–1882) had won fame as second commander of the North Pacific Exploring Expedition (1854–1856) and was familiar with ocean steam navigation. While availability, nautical knowledge, family connections, and command experience were all decided pluses in his new appointment, a major negative was one the straight-shooting sailor shared with almost every other Federal naval officer: he "knew virtually nothing of riverine warfare." One might add that he was also very independent and politically inexperienced; and he steamed full-speed ahead into uncharted human shoals that, in less than a calendar quarter, forced Welles to make a leadership change. Following his Midwestern posting, Rodgers served on the Atlantic

coast, beginning in the experimental ironclad gunboat *Galena*. He was promoted to the rank of captain in June 1862. Twelve months later, while in command of the monitor *Weehawken*, he defeated and captured the Confederate armorclad *Atlanta*, for which he received the thanks of Congress and a promotion to commodore. Following his 1869 promotion to the rank of rear admiral, he commanded the Asiatic Squadron, served as president of the U.S . Naval Institute, from 1879 until his death, and was first president of the Naval Advisory Board, 1881. Rodgers was the subject of a flattering profile in *Harper's Weekly*, August 15, 1863. William B. Cogar, *Dictionary of Admirals of the U.S. Navy*, 2 vols. (Annapolis, MD: Naval Institute Press, 1989), vol. 1, 150–152; Edward W. Callahan, *List of Officers of the Navy of the United States and of the Marine Corps, from 1775 to 1900, Comprising a Complete Register of All Present and Former Commissioned, Warranted, and Appointed Officers of the United States Navy, and of the Marine Corps, Regular and Volunteer, Compiled from the Official Records of the Navy Department* (New York: L.R. Hamersly, 1901; Reprt., New York: Haskell House, 1969), 469; Lewis R. Hamersly, *The Records of Living Officers of the U.S. Navy and Marine Corps, Compiled from Official Sources* (Rev. ed., Philadelphia: J.B. Lippincott, 1870), 21–22; Milligan, *Gunboats*, 5; Spencer C. Tucker, *Blue & Gray Navies: The Civil War Afloat* (Annapolis, MD: U.S. Naval Institute, 2006), 114; Pratt, *The Navy;* Cogar, *Dictionary of Admirals*, 150–152; James R. Soley, "Rear Admiral John Rodgers, president of the Naval Institute, 1870–1882," *U.S. Naval Institute Proceedings* 20 (1882), 251–265. The efficient and politically adroit Meigs (1816–1892) was named quartermaster general on May 15, 1861, and held that post through the war, winning appointment as a brevet major general in July 1864. His name would appear often in support of the western river war. He was also brother-in-law to Postmaster General Blair. Boatner, *Dictionary*, 542; David W. Miller, *Second Only to Grant: Quartermaster General Montgomery C. Meigs* (Shippensburg, PA: White Mane Books, 2000).

10. ORN, I, 22: 284–286; Johnson, *Rear Admiral John Rodgers, 1812–1882*, 157; *Chicago Daily Tribune*, May 21, 1861; Milligan, *Gunboats*, 5–6; McClellan, *The Civil War Papers of George B. McClellan*, 22; ORN, I, 22:281; Gaden, "Navy of the Mississippi," 28; Louis C. Hunter, *Steamboats on the Western Rivers: An Economic and Technological History* (Cambridge, MA: Harvard University Press, 1949), 485; Miller, *Second Only to Grant*, 124; Robert C. Suhr, "Converted River Steamers Dubbed 'Timberclads' Gave the Union Navy an Important Presence on Southern Waters," *America's Civil War* 11 (July 1998), 20. I tell the full story of Rodgers' wooden gunboats in *The Timberclads in the Civil War: The "Lexington," "Conestoga," and "Tyler" on the Western Waters* (Jefferson, NC: McFarland, 2008); Geoghegan, "Study for a Scale Model." Bostonian Samuel Moore Pook (1804–1878) started working at the Brooklyn Navy Yard in 1825 as a shipwright's apprentice. Named a naval constructor (the last of the great designers of U.S. wooden sailing warships given that title) in 1841, he built, among others, the sloops-of-war *Preble* and *Saratoga*, the frigates *Congress* and *Franklin*, and the steamers *Merrimack* and *Princeton*. In 1852, he rebuilt "Old Ironsides," the U.S. frigate *Constitution*. Interestingly, the obituary in the *Times* does not mention Pook's western service. His son, Samuel H. Pook, designer of such noted clipper ships as the *Red Jacket*, also labored at the Brooklyn yard ("Samuel Moore Pook," in Wilson and Fisk, *Appleton's Cyclopedia of American Biography* 64; *New York Times*, December 4, 1878; Howard I. Chapelle, *The History of American Sailing Ships* (New York: W.W. Norton, 1935), 129; Chapelle, *The Search for Speed Under Sail* (New York: W.W. Norton, 1967), 362–363).

11. OR, I, 3, 1: 164–165; OR, I, 3, 2: 814–815; Lenthall to Totten, June 1, 1861, Records of the Office of the Quartermaster General (U.S. National Archives and Records Service, Record Group 92), cited hereafter as QMG Records; Totten to Scott, June 3, 1861, QMG Records; OR, I, 51, 1:157–160, 164–168; OR, I, 52, 1: 164–167; David D. Porter, *Naval History of the Civil War* (New York: Sherman, 1886; reprt., Secaucus, N.J.: Castle, 1984) 268; Hunter, *Steamboats*, 548; John D. Milligan, "The First American Ironclads: The Evolution of a Design," *Missouri Historical Society Bulletin* 22 (October 1965), 3–13; Milligan, "From Theory to Application: The Emergence of the American Ironclad War Vessel," *Military Affairs* 48 (July 1984), 126; Geoghegan, "Study for a Scale Model," 150–151; Ambler, *History of Transportation*, 245–246; Canney, *The Ironclads*; *St. Louis Daily Democrat*, June 5, 1861. Well-known naval architect John Lenthall (1807–1882) was chief of his bureau from 1853 to 1871. During this time, he compiled a large collection of ship plans, all but Totten's for blue water vessels. In 1991, the Library of the Philadelphia Maritime Museum released the 52-page booklet *John Lenthall, Naval Architect: A Guide to Plans and Drawings of American Naval and Merchant Vessels, 1790–1874, With a Bibliography of Works on Shipbuilding ... Collected by John Lenthall (b. 1807–d.1882).*

12. OR, I, 52, 165, 167–168; ORN, I, 22: 284; Geoghegan, "Study for a Scale Model." At the time Cameron made his offer, the Army Ordnance Department was having the smoothbore 42-pounders on hand rifled according to the ideas of Gen. Charles T. James. Converted possibly by Ames at Chicopee, MA, they could fire 81-pound solid shot or 64-pound shells. The James rifles later making their way aboard the Eads ironclads were often called 64-pounders (Eugene Canfield, *Civil War Naval Ordnance* (Washington, DC: Naval History Division, U.S. Navy Department, 1969), 6).

13. ORN, I, 22: 285–287; Bearss, *Hardluck*, 15–16; Meigs to McClellan, June 13, 1861, QMG Records; Meigs to McClellan, June 17, 1861, Montgomery C. Meigs Papers, Library of Congress, cited hereafter as Meigs Papers; Canney, *Ironclads*, 48; Geoghegan, "Study for a Scale Model"; Gaden, "Navy of the Mississippi," 28.

14. OR, III, 2: 816–819; *New York Times*, December 31, 1861; Milligan, *Gunboats*, 13; Milligan, "From Theory to Application," 126–127; Geoghegan, "Study for a Scale Model," 155–161; Caney, *Ironclads*. Readers should be warned that this interchangeable use of the word "wheelhouse" for pilothouse can cause difficulty when reading accounts of the ironclads' exploits. Technically, the "wheelhouse" enclosed the vessel's paddle wheel, while the "pilothouse" covered and protected her steering wheel. H. Allen Gosnell, *Guns on the Western Waters* (Baton Rouge: Louisiana State University Press, 1959), 74.

15. OR, III, 2: 819–820; Rombauer, *The Union Cause*; Geoghegan, "Study for a Scale Model"; *New York Times*, December 31, 1861; Canney, *Ironclads*. The armor, when finally placed aboard the *Carondelet* and her sisters, would prove far from sufficient: "on the upper deck, there was no armor at all; only water-level combat was envisaged" (Pratt, *The Civil War on Western Waters* (New York: Holt, 1956), 20–21).

16. These ports were made too large in every direction except upwards. Pook's original call for 20 gun ports was later reduced to 13. Although much of the interior lighting came from these ports, they were often kept closed in combat for fear of sniping, or because of cold weather. On those occasions, light came from oil or kerosene lanterns (Pratt, *Civil War on Western Waters*; OR, III, 2: 280; Geoghegan, "Study for a Scale Model").

17. Miligan, *Gunboats Down the Mississippi*, 14; Geoghegan, "Study for a Scale Model," 155; Pook to McClellan, July 2, 1861, QMG Records; Rodgers to Meigs, July 6, 1861, QMG Records; Canney, *Ironclads*, 52; Johnson, *Rear Admiral John Rodgers, 1812–1882*, 160–161; Parker to writer, March 13, 1969; William M. Fowler, Jr., *Under Two Flags: The American Navy in the Civil War* (Annapolis, MD: Naval Institute Press, 2001), 134–135; Gary D. Joiner, *Mr. Lincoln's Brown Water Navy: The Mississippi Squadron* (Lanham, MD: Row-

man & Littlefield, 2007), 25. Pratt, *Civil War on Western Waters*, was exceedingly complimentary of the middle-aged naval constructor's work: "at the time, with the materials and knowledge available, and under the burning urgency of war, it was not a far-from-discretable performance on the part of old Sam Pook." Geoghegan tells us that the Lenthall plans and two tracings of Pook's ideas submitted to Rodgers on July 2, 1861, are found in the QMG Records. The seven City Series plans, nos. 28-6-1B, 28-6-4D, 28-6-4F, 28-6-4M, 80-1-12, 80-1-14, and 80-1-16, are located in the records of the Bureau of Steam Navigation, Record Group 19, National Archives and Records Service. Pook's own "Specifications for Building a Gun Boat" are in Box 39 of the QMG Papers. Whitmore's drawings and "Description of Drawings for Engines," and Merritt's drawings and a description of them are in the QMG Records.

18. Meigs to Gideon Welles, July 19, 1861, QMG Records; Isherwood to Gideon Welles, July 20, 1861, QMG Records; Welles to Meigs, July 21, 1861, QMG Records; *New York Times*, December 31, 1861; Miller, *Second Only to Grant* 124–125; Milligan, *Gunboats*, 21; Milligan, "From Theory to Application"; *U.S. Statutes at Large* 12 (July 17, 1861), 261–263: Bearss, *Hardluck*, 16, 18–19. The vessels, according to Merritt's plans and explanation, would each have five boilers, 36 inches in diameter and 24 feet long. Atop the boilers would be a steam drum, employed to collect vapor-laden water and keep it out of the engine cylinders. Beneath the boilers would be the firebox and in front of them would be two "chimneys" (smokestacks), designed to be 44 inches in diameter and 28 feet high (for some unknown reason, the chimneys of the *Pittsburg*, *Mound City*, and *Louisville* rose to 33 feet). The exhaust from the reciprocating engines fed into the chimneys and in motion "a noisy locomotive-like puff-puff" sound much like that made by civilian riverboats would result. The noise could be heard for miles. Each gunboat would have two Merritt engines with cast-iron cylinders having bores of 22 inches. Each cylinder was to be "of suitable length for a stroke of piston of six feet" and then mounted at a 15 degree angle. The necessary piston, also of cast-iron, was to be attached to a rod 4 inches in diameter and 110 inches long. These proposals were accepted by the government and became the official blueprints for the power plants of Eads' gunboats. Unfortunately, when mounted in the boats' holds, these engines were installed too close to the decks above and, as a result of this installation fault, it was necessary to sand and wet the decks to keep them from taking fire when full speed was rung. Four of Merritt's plans are in the QMG Records (OR, III, 2: 820–832; William H. King, *Lessons and Practical Notes on Steam*, revised by James W. King (New York: D. Van Nostrand, 1864), 158–160; Canney, *Ironclads*; Bruce Catton, *The Terrible Swift Sword* (Garden City, NY: Doubleday, 1963), 242; and Henry Walke, *Naval Scenes and Reminiscences of the Civil War in the United States on the Southern and Western Waters during the Years 1861, 1862 and 1863 with the History of That Period Compared and Corrected from Authentic Sources* (New York: F.R. Reed, 1877), 95).

19. ORN, I, 22: 295; Allen Nevins, *Fremont: Pathmarker of the West* (New York: D. Appleton-Century, 1939), 492; Miller, *Second Only to Grant*; Boynton, *History of the Navy*, vol. 1, 503; *St. Louis Daily Missouri Democrat*, July 29, August 1, 1861; Francis Blair, Jr., James S. Rollins, and John W. Noell to Meigs, July 15, 1861, QMG Records; Montgomery Blair to Meigs, July 31, 1861, QMG Records; Johnson, *Rear Admiral John Rodgers, 1812–1882*, 165; William E. Smith, *The Francis Preston Blair Family in Politics* (2 vols.; New York: Macmillan, 1933), II, 52.

20. Eliot Callender, "What a Boy Saw on the Mississippi River," in Vol. I of *Military Essays and Recollections: Papers Read before the Illinois Commandery, Military Order of the Loyal Legion of the United States* (Chicago: A.C. McClurg, 1891), 51; Milligan, *Gunboats*, 11–13; Eads to Meigs, August 1, 1861, QMG Records; Gaden, "Navy of the Mississippi, 29; Canney, *Ironclads*; Miller, *Second Only to Grant*. Other bidders included Hambleton, Collier, and Company of Mound City, IL (where some of the hull work would eventually be sublet); Hartupee and Company of Pittsburgh, PA (where some of the Merritt engines would be built); and seven builders from New Albany, IN (Webber and Roberts, "Master Builder," 24).

21. The Treasury would meet the Missourian's asking price, but just to insure timely completion, a stipulation was inserted into the contract requiring that the builder forfeit $250 per day for each boat that was delayed beyond that time. The money due Eads would be paid in stipulated installments for each boat. To guard against fraud, every 20 days the government (in the person of specified superintendents) would "estimate," or check, the work and if it was satisfactory, 75 percent of the estimate would be paid. If the government determined that the builder was irregular or negligent, it reserved the right to cancel the contract and be "exonerated from every obligation thence arising, and the reserved percentage on the contract price, as well as all the material furnished, upon which no estimate or payment may have been made, shall be forfeited to and become the right and property of the United States." If it did cancel his contract, the government could then hire another builder to finish the project and Eads would have no right to question the determination "in any place or under any circumstance, whatsoever." He could even be sued, according to these terms, for the damages caused by his failure to complete his end of the deal. Even though the Treasury could retain 25 percent of the money at any time due him, Eads could, however, expect to be paid in full when the contract was fulfilled — if it was completed on time. The government lastly stated in the contract that it would appoint a project superintendent whose duties would be to inspect the material used in constructing the boats as the work progressed and to reject all the elements he deemed defective. If the ironclads were built in different yards, an assistant superintendent would be named to each of the extra facilities. All additional work was to be estimated by these superintendents and paid by the U.S. Treasury. Eads was happy to have a codicil added to the contract which provided that no deviation from the specifications would be required by the superintendents which might delay the Missourian from completing his contract on time (OR, III, 2: 816–817; *New York Times*, December 31, 1861; Bearss, *Hardluck*, 18).

22. "Abstract of Bids, August 6, 1861," QMG Records; Temple to Lane, August 14, 1861, QMG Records; Bearss, *Hardluck*, 19–20; Phyllis F. Dorset, "James B. Eads, Navy Shipbuilder, 1861," *U.S. Naval Institute Proceedings* 101 (August 1975), 77.

Chapter 2

1. U.S. War Department, *The War of the Rebellion: A Compilation of the Official Records of the Union and Confederate Armies*, 128 vols. (Washington, DC: GPO, 1880–1901), Series III, Vol. 2, 816, cited hereafter as OR, followed by a comma, the series number in Roman numerals, a comma, the volume number in Arabic, a colon, and the page in Arabic; Eads to Meigs, August 30, 1861, Records of the Office of the Quartermaster General (U.S. National Archives and Records Service, Record Group 92; cited hereafter as QMG Records).

2. Dorset, "Navy Shipbuilder," 77; Mary Emerson Branch, "A Story Behind the Story of the *Arkansas* and the *Carondelet*," *Missouri Historical Review* 79 (April 1985), 314. In the accounts of the building of the Eads gunboats found in the Official Records and elsewhere, the geographical names of St. Louis and Carondelet are used interchangeably. Carondelet residents have always pronounced the lyrical community name with "the 'a' nearly swallowed and a hard

't'" (Robert D. Huffstot, "The *Carondelet,*" *Civil War Times Illustrated* 6 (August 1967), 7). This booming little river town of the 1850s and 1860s, took its name from Francisco Luis Hector, Baron de Carondelet (c. 1748–1807), the last pre–American governor of Louisiana ("Carondelet," *Dictionary of American Naval Fighting Ships*, http://www.history.navy.mil/danfs/c4/carondelet-i.htm (accessed January 31, 2009)). It is interesting to note that Baron de Carondelet built several gunboats for the suppression of "savages" and squatters over a half a century before Eads began his project. For an interesting account of this early flotilla, see Abraham Nasatir, *Spanish War Vessels on the Mississippi, 1792–1796* (New Haven, CT: Yale University Press, 1968).

3. Branch, "Story," 314–318; *St. Louis Daily Missouri Democrat*, August 14, 1861; Jack D. Coombe, *Thunder Along the Mississippi: The River Battles That Split the Confederacy* (New York: Bantam, 1996), 18–19; Roland L. Meyer, Jr., "Inland Shipyard Saga," *Marine Engineering and Shipping Review* 51 (February 1946), 127–129; James M. Merrill, "Union Shipbuilding on Western Waters During the Civil War," *Smithsonian Journal of History* 3 (Winter 1968–1969), 17–44; Edwin C. Bearss, *Hardluck Ironclad: The Sinking and Salvage of the Cairo (*Baton Rouge: Louisiana State University Press, 1968), 19–20; Kendall D. Gott, *Where the South Lost the War: An Analysis of the Fort Henry–Fort Donelson Campaign, February 1862* (Mechanicsburg, PA: Stackpole, 2003), 27. A native of Maine who served his apprenticeship at Cincinnati and then relocated to Indiana, Primus Emerson (1815–1877) became one of the West's most famous steamboat builders. From 1836 to1841, when he moved to St. Louis, Emerson operated what became the important Madison, Indiana, boatyard in partnership with James Howard, who took its name upon his partner's departure. Over the next decade and a half, Emerson constructed and repaired boats at several cities. With several partners, the constructor purchased Carondelet riverfront property and incorporated his yard in 1855, growing it over the next four years into a $150,000 per year operation. When the yard was completed in 1859, it featured Emerson's patented marine railway. Centered on a 50 horsepower steam engine, the railway could pull the largest craft out of the water and had a simultaneous capacity of three big or six small boats. When war came and the steamboat business initially dried up, Emerson, with Southern political leanings, accepted a steamboat repair contract at Memphis. Ironically, through his association with John T. Shirley of that city, he became the prime builder of the Confederate armorclad *Arkansas*, which would later deal harshly with Eads' boat, the *Carondelet* (Branch, "Story"; *St. Louis Daily Missouri Republican*, January 12, 1877; *Memphis Daily Avalanche*, September 10, 1873.

4. Merritt to Meigs, July 22, 1861, QMG Records; OR, III, 2: 816; Rodgers to Litherbury, August 8, 1861, QMG Records; John D. Milligan, "From Theory to Application: The Emergence of the American Ironclad War Vessel," *Military Affairs* 48 (July 1984), 127; Bearss, *Hardluck*. According to his arrangement with Rodgers, Litherbury was to report to Eads and "inspect the materials used in construction" of the ironclads and to "reject all that he may deem defective." He was also to be sure all work was faithfully completed. For each boat, Litherbury was told to name a subcontractor at a salary of $3 per day.

5. U.S. Navy Department, *Official Records of the Union and Confederate Navies in the War of the Rebellion*, 31 vols. (Washington, DC: GPO, 1894–1922), Series I, Vol. 22, 284, 298, 308, cited hereafter as ORN, followed by a comma, the series number in Roman numerals, a comma, the volume number in Arabic, a colon, and the page in Arabic; Rodgers to Meigs, August 29, 1861, QMG Records; Bearss, *Hardluck*, 20–21.

6. ORN, I, 22: 306, 308; Donald L. Canney, *The Old Steam Navy*, vol. 2, *The Ironclads, 1842–1885* (Annapolis, MD: Naval Institute Press, 1993), 49–51; William E. Geoghegan, "Study for a Scale Model of the U.S.S. *Carondelet,*" *Nautical Research Journal* 17, no. 4 (1970): 234; Tom McGrath and Doug Ashley, *Historic Structure Report: U.S.S. "Cairo"* (Denver, CO.: National Park Service, U.S. Department of the Interior, 1981), 73–74; Gary D. Joiner, *Mr. Lincoln's Brown Water Navy: The Mississippi Squadron* (Lanham, MD: Rowman & Littlefield, 2007), 27–28; NiNi Harris, *History of Carondelet* (St. Louis, MO: Southern Commercial Bank, 1991), 25–26; Huffstot, "*Carondelet*"; Bearss, *Hardluck*. Rodgers' gun carriages (or trucks) were to accommodate 9-inch guns and 42-pounders and be made from high quality seasoned oak. Actual construction was to be made of two thicknesses riveted together. As the thickness of oak board to be riveted together into the carriages was not specified in the contract Rodgers advertised, one might assume that it was the same thickness as that used for all 9-inch naval guns of the period. The side pieces, known as "cheeks," were a caliber in thickness, so the larger the gun the larger the total carriage. American and British construction manuals called for a built-up cheek of two or more planks, which were cleverly "jogged or mortised together to prevent starting under the strain of firing." For a good discussion of gun carriages and implements, see Albert Manucy, *Artillery through the Ages* (National Park Service Interpretive Series, no. 3; Washington, DC: GPO, 1956), 46–52, 73–78. Interestingly, there were apparently no publications available at Cincinnati that summer explaining the fine points of gun carriage construction. Completion was delayed when Mr. Thom, in inquiring of the Navy Department for a *Naval Ordnance Manual*, was advised that no such publication as he described existed and he would have to ask Cmdr. Rodgers for plans (ORN, I, 22: 336, 344; Bearss, *Hardluck*, 21).

7. *St. Louis Daily Missouri Democrat*, August 20, 22, 1861; Rodgers to Frémont, August 28, 1861, QMG Records; Eads to Meigs, August 27, 1861, QMG Records. On October 29, Eads would be told that the vessels would be named after various western cities and towns and, on this basis, the seven gunboats are collectively known as the City Series (ORN, I, 22: 387).

8. ORN, I, 22: 297–298, 307, 320; Rodgers to Litherbury, August 30, 1861, Rodgers Family Papers, Naval Historical Foundation Collection, Library of Congress, cited hereafter as Rodgers Family Papers; Bearss, *Hardluck*, 27; Milligan, "From Theory to Application"; Canney, *Ironclads*, 51; Jay Slagle, *Ironclad Captain: Seth Ledyard Phelps and the U.S. Navy* (Kent, OH: Kent State University Press, 1996), 122; Charles B. Boynton, *History of the Navy during the Rebellion*, 2 vols. (New York: D. Appleton, 1867–1868), vol. 1, 501–503; Robert E. Johnson, *Rear Admiral John Rodgers, 1812–1882* (Annapolis, MD: Naval Institute Press, 1967), 161–163; *St. Louis Daily Missouri Democrat*, September 7, 1861; *Louisville Daily Journal*, August 8, 1861; *Evansville Daily Journal*, August 9, 1861; John F. Dillon, "The Role of Riverine Warfare in the Civil War," *Naval War College Review* 25 (March-April 1973): 62–63. Interestingly, the Blairs and Meigs would become major opponents of Maj. Gen. Frémont, though for reasons having nothing to do with the navy man, shortly after the Rodgers recall request was sent (Johnson, *Rear Admiral John Rodgers, 1812–1882*, 165–166; Nevins, *Fremont*, 512–514). Robert Johnson also quotes an undated note from Frémont to Blair that is far less diplomatic. "I don't like Commander Rodgers who is in charge of the Gun boat operations," he complained, "will you ask to have him removed and some younger officer put in his place" (Johnson, *Rear Admiral John Rodgers, 1812–1882*, 391). Welles' choice to succeed Cmdr. Rodgers was a "quiet, grey-haired veteran" with an enviable reputation even before this selection. Born in New Haven, Connecticut, the son of a governor and U.S. senator, Foote (1806–1863), promoted to captain only in June 1861, became a USN midshipman in 1822 and a commander in 1852. Known for his Christian bearing and dedication to the temperance move-

ment, he worked to abolish flogging during the 1840s, was one of the few members of the infamous 1850s retiring board to avoid major condemnation by his colleagues, and personally led an assault force against the barrier forts at Canton, China, in 1856. Later wounded in action at Fort Donelson, he was promoted to the rank of rear admiral, served as chief of the Bureau of Equipment and Recruiting, and was en route to take command of the South Atlantic Blockading Squadron at the time of his death (Spencer C. Tucker, *Andrew Foote: Civil War Admiral on Western Waters* (Annapolis, MD: Naval Institute Press, 2000), 114; "Sketches of the Officers of the Fort Donelson Fleet," *Philadelphia Inquirer*, February 18, 1862; William B. Cogar, *Dictionary of Admirals of the U.S. Navy*, 2 vols. (Annapolis, MD: Naval Institute Press, 1989), vol. 1, 63–65; and James Mason Hoppin, *Life of Andrew Hull Foote, Rear Admiral United States Navy* (New York: Harper & Brothers, 1874).

9. ORN, I, 22: 322; Fletcher Pratt, *The Navy: A History* (New York: Garden City Publishing, 1941), 286; Huffstot, "*Carondelet*," 8; *Chicago Daily Tribune*, September 11, 1861;Coombe, *Thunder*, 60; *New York Times*, April 10, 1862, and March 9, 1896; *New York Tribune*, July 6, 1896. Known as something of a maverick and a great artist, the taciturn Virginian Henry Walke (1808–1896), arguments to the contrary accepted, became one of the most successful and under-celebrated of all Civil War naval officers. A midshipman with Capt. Foote on the *Natchez* in 1827, Walke served in numerous ships and squadrons and was promoted to the rank of commander in 1855. One of many officers involuntarily retired by the infamous Naval Retiring Board set up under congressional legislation of that year, he was eventually returned to duty. Like all "restored officers," he was placed on half pay and throughout the Civil War received only 50 percent of the income his rank would ordinarily provide. In early 1861, while commanding the store ship *Supply* off Pensacola, he elected to remove personnel from the guardian forts and the navy yard rather than allow them to become POWs. His actions, technically violating previous orders, resulted in his court-martial, a "complimentary reprimand," and temporary banishment to the post of lighthouse inspector at Williamsport, New York. Later, in command of the famous Pook turtle *Carondelet*, he fought at Forts Henry and Donelson and ran the batteries at Island No. 10. Walke skippered several other vessels during the war, was promoted to captain in 1862 and commodore in 1866. He commanded the Mound City naval station from 1868 to 1870. After becoming a rear admiral in 1870, he retired in 1871, contributing his drawings and memories to books and articles on the conflict. His memoirs were perhaps the most acerbic of any penned by veteran officers of the Civil War Union navy, but they remain among the most useful. Walke died in New York in early 1896 (Alan Westcott, "Henry Walke," in *The Dictionary of American Biography* (New York: Scribner's, 1930), vol. 19, 336–337; "The Walke Family of Lower Norfolk County, Virginia," *The Virginia Magazine of History and Biography* 5 (October 1897), 149–150; "Sketches of the Officers of the Fort Donelson Fleet," *Philadelphia Inquirer*, February 18, 1862; Callahan, *List of Officers*, 564; Lewis R. Hamersly, *The Records of Living Officers of the U.S. Navy and Marine Corps, Compiled from Official Sources*, rev. ed. (Philadelphia: J. B. Lippincott, 1870), 178–179; Cogar, *Dictionary of Admirals*, vol. 1, 200–201). Walke's development as an artist is stressed by Audrey Gardner in her "Henry Walke, 1809–1896, Romantic Painter and Naval Hero" (master's thesis, George Washington University, 1971). His tremendous drive aboard his river commands, the *Carondelet* and *Lafayette*, was occasionally taken out in the form of tempers as recorded by his clerk, Thomas Lyons, in his *Anonymous Journal Kept on Board of the U.S. Steam Gunboat Carondelet, 1862–1863, Capt. Henry Walke Commanding* (Manuscript Division, Library of Congress, n.d.).

10. Eads to Meigs, August 30, 1861, QMG Records; Eads to Meigs, September 14 and 18, 1861, and January 27, 1862, QMG Records; Hartupee and Company to Meigs, September 18, 1861, QMG Records; *St. Louis Daily Missouri Democrat*, September 18, 1861; *St. Louis Daily Missouri Republican*, September 21, 1861; Bearss, *Hardluck*, 23–24; David W. Miller, *Second Only to Grant: Quartermaster General Montgomery C. Meigs* (Shippensburg, PA: White Mane Books, 2000), 125. In addition to Hartupee and Company, engines were also built by the Eagle Foundry and the Fulton Foundry, both of St. Louis. Because Meigs also had to pay for the *Benton*, *Essex*, and mortar boats out of the original appropriation, his invoice ledger was much larger than anticipated. In December, he explained this matter to the U.S. Congress, which obligingly provided another $1 million on Christmas Eve for "gunboats on the Western Rivers" (OR, I, 52, 1: 199; Miller, *Second Only to Grant*; *U.S. Statutes at Large* 12 (December 24, 1861), 331. New Yorker Wise (?–1881), was promoted to the rank of colonel in 1864 and named a brevet brigadier general of volunteers for war service in 1867 (Mark M. Boatner III, *The Civil War Dictionary* (New York: David McKay, 1959), 943).

11. Rodgers to Eads, August 10, 1861, Rodgers Family Papers (and also in James B. Eads Papers, Missouri Historical Society, St. Louis, cited hereafter as Eads Papers); Rodgers to Litherbury, August 30, 1861, Rodgers Family Papers; Rodgers to Meigs, August 10, 1861, QMG Records; Eads to Meigs, October 2, 1861, QMG Records; Merritt to Meigs, October 6 and 8, 1861, QMG Records; ORN, I, 22: 359–360; ORN, I, 23: 543; Louis S. Gerteis, "Wartime Production and Labor Unrest in Civil War St. Louis," *Gateway Heritage* 22, no. 3 (2001–2002): 9 (6–13); *St. Louis Daily Missouri Democrat*, September 21 and October 14, 1861; *St. Louis Daily Missouri Republican*, October 13, 1861; *New York Times*, February 8, 1862; Geoghegan, "Study," 234; McGrath and Ashley, *Structure Report*, 33, 39; Gott, *Lost the War*, 28–31; Angus Konstam and Tony Bryan, *Union River Ironclad, 1861–65* (New Vanguard Series, no. 56; London, Eng.: Osprey, 2002), 8; The American Society of Mechanical Engineers, *U.S.S. "Cairo" Engine and Boilers, 1862, The U.S.S. "Cairo" and Museum, Vicksburg National Military Park, A National Historical Mechanical Engineering Landmark, Vicksburg, MS, June 15, 1990*, http://scholar.google.com/scholar?hl=en&lr=&ie=UTF-8&q=cache:WLW3MwJtYK0J:mfnl.x.../h143.pdf+gunboat (accessed April 6, 2005); Robert E. Johnson, *Rear Admiral*, 126–127, 162; Canney, *Ironclads*, 51–54; Huffstot, "*Carondelet*," 6–7; Bearss, *Hardluck*. Years ago when first reviewing the *Carondelet* story, this writer corresponded with Mr. Geoghegan, a recognized expert on Civil War river ironclads then with the Division of Transportation of the Smithsonian Institution. In a 1969 letter, he noted that "wharf boats were in (and are in) general use along the Western rivers due to the great variation between high and low water." The craft "was just a hull (sometimes a worn-out steamer with her upper decks removed) with a warehouse built on the deck." He also went on to remind a then-young correspondent that all of the Eads gunboats, like many commercial steamers, were launched sideways via the marine railway (Geoghegan to writer, July 3, 1969). Perry (?–1880) was yet another "restored" officer. Having joined the USN from Maryland in 1828 and after years of sea service, he held shore billets during the Civil War, retired in 1865, was promoted to captain in 1867, and died in November 1880 (Callahan, *List of Officers*, 432). Incidentally, George R. Stewart tells us the reason why the name of the gunboat *Pittsburg* did not end with an "h." During the Civil War, the name of the town was usually spelled without an "h" and the "h" was not officially added until 1911 (for the benefit of the modern reader, we will use the "h" when speaking of the city) (Stewart, *Names on the Land: A Historical Account of Placenaming in the United States* [New York: Random House, 1945], 344).

12. While it is generally believed that the *St. Louis* (later *Baron de Kalb*) was the first ironclad launched, she was,

rather, the first to finish fitting out. Capt. Foote, in a letter from his St. Louis office to contractor Eads, had specifically ordered that "the following will be the names of the five gunboats building here as they are launched respectively: *Carondelet, St. Louis, Louisville, Pittsburg,* and *Benton.*" The Confederate armorclad *Virginia* (*Merrimack*) was the first American ship to be entirely protected; her 4-inch iron plating made her a completed rather than a partial ironclad like the *Carondelet* (ORN, I, 22: 387; Bearss, *Hardluck*, 26–27; Huffstot, "*Carondelet*"; Philip Melville, "*Carondelet* Runs the Gauntlet," *American Heritage* 10 (October 1959), 67).

13. Foote to Meigs, October 26, 1861, QMG Records; Eads to Meigs, January 27, 1862, QMG Records; ORN, I, 22: 395, 429, 446, 452; Bearss, *Hardluck*, 43; *Ashland (Ohio) Union*, December 4, 1861; *Cairo City Gazette*, December 12, 1861; *St. Louis Daily Missouri Democrat*, December 22, 1861; Gary D. Joiner, *Mr. Lincoln's*, 28; Dana M. Wegner, "Little Egypt's Naval Station," *U.S. Naval Institute Proceedings* 98 (March 1972), 74–76. The capstan, which hoisted the anchor, drew its power from an auxiliary, or "doctor," engine that worked from steam provided by the main boilers. Eads may have seen the value in such from his days in the salvage business when extra pulling strength was needed to bring up stumps or haul stricken vessels off sandbars or wrecks from channels (Canney, *Ironclads*, 53); The American Society of Mechanical Engineers, *U.S.S. "Cairo" Engine and Boilers, 1862, The U.S.S. "Cairo" and Museum, Vicksburg National Military Park, A National Historical Mechanical Engineering Landmark, Vicksburg, MS, June 15, 1990*, http://scholar.google.com/scholar?hl=en&lr=&ie=UTF-8&q=cache:WLW3MwJtYK0J:mfnl.x.../h143.pdf+gunboat (accessed April 6, 2005).

14. ORN, I, 22: 463, 485, 489, 493; Litherbury and Foote to Eads, December 21, 1861, QMG Records; Eads to Meigs, December 28, 1861; QMG Records; *St. Louis Daily Missouri Democrat*, June 26, 28, 1862; Florence Dorsey, *Road to the Sea: The Story of James B. Eads and the Mississippi River* (New York: Rinehart, 1947), 65; Eliot Callender, "What a Boy Saw on the Mississippi River," in (vol. 1) *Military Essays and Recollections: Papers Read before the Illinois Commandery, Military Order of the Loyal Legion of the United States* (Chicago: A.C. McClurg, 1891), 52; Charles Carleton Coffin, *Drumbeat of the Nation* (New York: Harper, 1886), 136. Light entered the casemates through the gun ports, and when they were closed for combat or to avoid snipers, the only illumination came from overhanging kerosene or oil lanterns. The gun ports also let in air during all weather and the casemates grew stifling when they were secured. When the *Carondelet*'s heavy cannon were mounted, the weight caused her knuckle to drop below the waterline. When she was completely finished, her gun ports rode just a foot above the waterline (Konstam and Bryan, *Union River*).

15. Henry Walke, *Naval Scenes and Reminiscences of the Civil War in the United States on the Southern and Western Waters during the Years 1861, 1862 and 1863, with the History of That Period Compared and Corrected from Authentic Sources* (New York: F.R. Reed, 1877), 54. On various occasions during the war, some of the 42-pounders burst. When the time came to replace them, "many were not turned into store, but thrown with a sigh of relief, into the waters of the Mississippi Alfred (T. Mahan, *The Gulf and Inland Waters* [New York: Scribner's, 1883], 14; ORN, I, 22: 777).

16. The *Carondelet* and her sisters also carried a 12-pounder Dahlgren boat howitzer for operations ashore. Huffstot, "*Carondelet.*" In its issue of February 22, 1862, *Harper's Weekly* includes an illustration of the gun deck of one of the turtles. The picture is quite accurate, "except for a few distortions" (Edwin C. Bearss to author, August 9, 1969). It appears brighter than when its entire length was lit only by kerosene lanterns. There is also insufficient depiction of the chests and side racks for such items as priming wires, fuse wrenches, gunlocks, shot tongs, cups, rammers, sponges, and shell bearers as well as the correct placement of coiled breeching and preventer gear, training tackles, and other hawsers.

17. Bearss, *Hardluck*, 105, 111; McGrath and Ashley, *Structure Report*, 33; Charles Carleton Coffin, *My Days and Nights on the Battlefield* (Boston: Estes and Lauriat, 1887), 75. The "peep-holes" were briefly alluded to by Albert D. Richardson on page 231 of his *Secret Service, the Field, the Dungeon, and the Escape* (Hartford, CT: American, 1866), but no details were provided. The *Carondelet* carried two logbooks during her period of commission. The deck log in the pilot house was conveniently placed, in an open position, so that the regularly scheduled officer of the deck could record his observations at the end of each watch. A survey of the existing copies of the deck log reveals a gold mine of information for scholars of the war on western waters. Periodically, the gunboat's skipper would read and approve (often with comments) the entries in the deck log. These entries were then recorded in a smooth log kept in the captain's cabin by the boat's clerk. At various times, both logs would be closed and forwarded to the secretary of the navy. At those times, new books would be opened and the record-keeping process renewed (deck logbooks of the U.S.S. *Carondelet*, May 1862–June 1865 (Records of the Bureau of Ships, Record Group 19, U.S. National Archives and Records Service), cited hereafter as *Carondelet* Logbook, with date). Prior to the establishment of the National Archives during the administration of President Franklin D. Roosevelt, logbooks of various vessels were deposited in the Navy Department's Bureau of Navigation. A problem for historians has developed, as parts of these logs were never turned over to the new agency or were lost. Accordingly, the front cover of the first of the existing *Carondelet* logbooks reveals that the Bureau of Navigation received all of that craft's deck logs—minus entries prior to May 28, 1862—on May 2, 1890. When the National Archives received these parts of the gunboat's record, along with other logbooks and associated records from the Navigation people, the pre–May 28, 1862, deck logs and all of the smooth logs were still missing. Forty years ago, when this writer first made inquiry concerning the missing parts, Elmer O. Parker of the Old Military Records Division of the National Archives confirmed their loss. We take heart, however. Had we chosen to tell the story of the Pook turtle *Cincinnati* from her logbooks, we would have found available only those from the November 1864–August 1865 period—all others missing (Kenneth W. Munden and Henry Putney Beard, *Guide to Federal Archives Relating to the Civil War* (Washington, DC: GPO, 1962), 461–463; Parker to writer, March 5, 1970).

18. ORN, I, 22: 504; *St. Louis Daily Missouri Democrat*, January 18, 24 and June 27, 1862; *Cincinnati Daily Gazette*, January 18, 1862; *Philadelphia Inquirer*, January 21, 1862; Bearss, *Hardluck*, 35–36; Milligan, "From Theory to Application," 127; Anthony Trollope, *North America* (New York: St. Martin's, 1986), 102; Bearss to writer, June 18, 1969; Geoghegan to writer, June 3, 1969. Roger N. Stembel (1810–1900) who, like Cmdr. Rodgers, was a Marylander, received his midshipman appointment (in 1832) from Ohio. Prior to the war, he, too, had seen his share of service on vessels in the Atlantic and prior to going West, had served at the Philadelphia naval asylum. He hoped for a blockade command, but, despite his forthcoming July promotion to the rank of commander, sea duty never came. Instead, he was given the timberclad *Lexington*, followed by the Pook turtle *Cincinnati.* He headed various shore activities from August 1862 through Appomattox. After the war, he did receive squadron commands prior to his 1872 retirement and promotion, two years later, to the rank of rear admiral. Cmdr. Pennock was, like Cmdr. Walke, a native of Virginia. Both men, like Tennessee's David Farragut, had remained loyal to the Union. After years at sea (1828–1859), Pennock

(1814–1876), like Walke, served as a lighthouse inspector in New York state. Pucked back into the mainstream by the Navy Department in September 1861, he was sent West with FO Foote to help oversee the construction of the Pook turtles and to handle flotilla equipment; he became fleet captain that October 20. In January 1862, he took over command of the Cairo naval station. Pennock would hold his post through 1864, gaining during his tenure "a reputation as one of the best wartime executives of the navy." While serving at Cairo, Pennock, who had brought out his wife to be with him, lived in quarters on the receiving ship, where he frequently enjoyed the company of junior officers and visitors at dinner. A postwar highlight for him was command of the European Squadron flagship *Franklin* (1867–1869) and commands of the Pacific and Asian stations (1872–1875), plus key shore installations at New York and Portsmouth, New Hampshire ("Sketches of the Officers of the Fort Donelson Fleet," *Philadelphia Inquirer*, February 18, 1862; Cogar, *Dictionary of Admirals*, vol. 1, 126–127, 179; Callahan, *List of Officers*, 519; Hamersly, *Living Officers*, 54, 90; Alan Westcott, "Alexander Mosely Pennock," in (vol. 14) *Dictionary of American Biography*, 10 vols. (New York: Scribner's, 1937), 444.

19. Bearss to writer, August 9, 1969; *Carondelet* Logbook, May 1862–June 1865, passim; Gott, *Lost the War*, 28; John D. Milligan, ed., *From the Fresh Water Navy, 1861–1864: The Letters of Acting Master's Mate Henry R. Browne and Acting Ensign Symmes E. Brown* (Naval Letters Series, volume 3; Annapolis, MD: Naval Institute Press, 1970), 111; Brig. Gen. Joseph G. Totten pointed out in his earlier memorandum to Lt. Gen. Winfield Scott that "Pittsburgh coal is the best. Pomeroy coal nearly if not quite as good (Pomeroy is half way between Pittsburgh and Cincinnati)." He also noted that there were about 200 coal barges available on the Ohio River, each able to carry an average load of 10,000 bushels. The naval base at Cairo did not have a significant coal depot and the "nearest considerable coal supply above Cairo," was at Caseyville, about 120 miles up the Ohio River (OR, I, 52, 1: 164). A view of the type of coal barges used and of the Essex coaling can be seen in John C. Roberts and Richard H. Webber, "Gunboats in the River War, 1861–1865," *U.S. Naval Institute Proceedings* 91 (March 1965), 98.

20. Bearss to writer, August 9, 1969; Gott, *Lost the War*, 30; Huffstot, "*Carondelet*," 48; Mahan, *Inland Waters*; Eliot Callender, "What a Boy Saw on the Mississippi," in *Military Essays and Recollections: Papers Read Before the Commandery of the State of Illinois, Military Order of the Loyal Legion of the United States* (Chicago: A.C. McClurg, 1891). "*Cairo* was known as the lightest and fastest of the Eads boats; *Carondelet* as the slowest," though historian Bearss saw little difference in their speeds. Seaman Callender reported that, moving upriver, the "racer [*Cairo*] in the fleet ... made two miles an hour upstream." This does not fit with the July 28, 1862, entry in the *Carondelet*'s deck log: "Steaming up the river, making about four miles an hour"—and this in poor condition as a result of the ironclad's run-in with the Confederate armorclad *Arkansas* (Callender; *Carondelet* Logbook, July 28, 1862).

21. Eads to Miegs, January 27, February 5, 1862, QMG Records (also in the Eads Papers); Dorman to Meigs, February 12, 1862, QMG Records; Meigs to Cutts, February 15, 1862, QMG Records; Cutts to Meigs, February 20, 1862, QMG Records. The gunboats, still technically Eads' property, were badly cut up at Fort Donelson on February 14. He undoubtedly wondered at the time if one of them had been sunk (as was very nearly the case) whether he would actually have been paid for it. In the end, the contractor was paid an average of $101,808 for each Pook turtle (U.S. National Park Service, Vicksburg National Military Park, *For Teachers: The USS "Cairo,"* http://www.nps.gov/vick/forteachers/upload/Cairo%20Pamphlet.pdf [accessed January 15, 2009]).

Chapter 3

1. U.S. Navy Department, *Official Records of the Union and Confederate Navies in the War of the Rebellion*, 31 vols. (Washington, DC: GPO, 1894–1922), Series I, Vol. 22, 374, 384, 390, 432–433, 436–437, 441–442, 435, 452, 464–465, 473–475, 478, 580, cited hereafter as ORN, followed by a comma, the series number in Roman numerals, a comma, the volume number in Arabic, a colon, and the page in Arabic; Phelps to Col. Cook, August 13, 1863, Seth Ledyard Phelps Papers, Missouri Historical Society, St. Louis, cited hereafter as Phelps Papers, with date; Henry Walke, *Naval Scenes and Reminiscences of the Civil War in the United States on the Southern and Western Waters during the Years 1861, 1862 and 1863 with the History of That Period Compared and Corrected from Authentic Sources* (New York: F.R. Reed, 1877), 30–31; John D. Milligan, *Gunboats Down the Mississippi* (Annapolis, MD: Naval Institute Press, 1965), 14–15; William N. Still, Jr., "The Common Sailor, Part I: Yankee Blue Jackets," *Civil War Times Illustrated* 23 (February 1985), 26. Under supervision, 600 sailors from New England and the Washington, D.C., area departed Washington for Cairo on November 17. Many were "good men, mostly fishermen," but many were "without drill." During the five-day train trip west, they had plenty of cooked provisions in the mess chests onboard, but, according to Cmdr. Walke, "they never tasted any warm liquid except at Seymour, Indiana, where the citizens generously gave them two barrels of hot coffee." The sailors duly arrived at the tip of Illinois on November 21, with 58 desertions en route.

2. ORN, I, 22: 493–494, 504, 516, 555, 579, 613, 642; Charles B. Boynton, *History of the Navy During the Rebellion*, 2 vols. (New York: D. Appleton, 1867), vol. 1, 525, 531; *St. Louis Daily Missouri Democrat*, January 24, 1862; Henry R. Browne and Symmes E. Browne, *From the Fresh Water Navy, 1861–1864: Letters of Acting Master's Mate Henry R. Browne and Acting Ensign Symmes E. Browne*, ed. John D. Milligan (Naval Letters Series, vol. 3, Annapolis, MD: Naval Institute Press, 1970), 23. At the end of 1861, Brig. Gen. Grant specifically ordered that men in the Cairo guardhouse be transferred "in view of the difficulty of getting men for the gunboat service" and that discipline cases up to and including desertion be handled the same way in the future. Many army transfers did not adjust to shipboard regiment, and Flag Officer Foote despaired of his initial draft, saying he'd rather "go into action half manned than to go with such men" (U.S. War Department, *The War of the Rebellion: A Compilation of the Official Records of the Union and Confederate Armies*, 128 vols. (Washington, DC: GPO, 1880–1901), Series I, Vol. 7, 534, cited hereafter as OR, followed by a comma, the series number in Roman numerals, a comma, the volume number in Arabic, a colon, and the page in Arabic; Charles B. Hirsch, "Gunboat Personnel on the Western Waters," *Mid-America* 34 (April 1952), 79–85; ORN, I, 22: 632).

3. Edwin C. Bearss, *Hardluck Ironclad: The Sinking and Salvage of the Cairo* (Baton Rouge: Louisiana State University Press, 1968), 176–177; Jack D. Coombe, *Thunder Along the Mississippi: The River Battles That Split the Confederacy* (New York: Sarpedon, 1996), 49; ORN, I, 22: 470, 501, 773; Walke, *Naval Scenes*, 424; James M. Merrill, "Cairo, Illinois: Strategic Civil War River Port," *Journal of Illinois History* 76 (Winter 1983), 252.

4. Richard West, "The Navy and the Press During the Civil War," *U.S. Naval Institute Proceedings* 63 (February 1937), 37–38; Albert D. Richardson, *The Secret Service, the Field, the Dungeon, and the Escape* (Hartford, CT: American, 1866), 220. The ironclad's initial group of volunteer officers through at least the Island No. 10 campaign, in order of rank aside from Walke, included the following: First Master Richard M. Wake; Second Master John Doherty; Third Master Charles C. Gray; Fourth Master Henry A. Walke (no relation to the skipper); Pilots William Hinton

and Daniel Weaver; Assistant Surgeon (the boat did not rate a full surgeon) James S. McNeeley; Assistant Paymaster (nor did it rate a full paymaster) George J. W. Nexsen; Chief Engineer William D. Faulkner; First Assistant Engineer Charles H. Caven; Second Assistant Engineer Samuel S. Brooks; Third Assistant Engineer Augustus G. Crowell; Masters Mates Theodore S. Gillmore and Edward E. Brennand; Gunner Richard Adams; Carpenter Oliver Donaldson; and Armorer N.H. Rhodes. Several would remain with the boat throughout her service (ORN, I, 22: 551; ORN, I, 24: 187; Deck Logbooks of the U.S.S. *Carondelet*, May 1862–June 1865 (Records of the Bureau of Ships, Record Group 19, U.S. National Archives and Records Service), cited hereafter as *Carondelet* Logbook, with date). According to the *Pittsburgh Evening Chronicle* of April 20, 1862, Brennand, Faulkner, Caven, Brooks, and Crowell were all from what would later be called the "Steel City."

5. Walke, *Naval Scenes*, 20–21.

6. Bearss, *Hardluck*, 122; Scott D. Jordan to wife, April 12, July 5, August 12, December 6, 1863, in *Civil War Letters of Scott D. Jordan, Produced for Eleanor Jordan West* (CD-ROM; Glendale, AZ: doug@bellnotes.com, 2007), cited hereafter as Jordan Letters, with date. When the *Carondelet*'s sister, the *Cairo*, was raised in 1865, many items of common usage were found and cataloged by the U.S. National Park Service. As provisions and implements for the City Series gunboats were ordered in bulk, it may be assumed that those types found on the salvaged boat were also aboard Capt. Walke's (Bearss, *Hardluck*, 156–157). Nearly 200 photos with descriptions of the arms, ordnance, medical equipment, uniform items, cooking gear, and personal effects salvaged from the *Cairo* are described in Elizabeth Hoxie Joyner's *The USS Cairo: History and Artifacts of a Civil War Gunboat* (Jefferson, NC: McFarland, 2006).

7. U.S. Naval Historical Center, *Civil War Naval Chronology*, 6 vols. (Washington, DC: GPO, 1966), vol. 6, 108–109; Allen Westcott, "Henry Walke," in *The Dictionary of American Biography*, 30 vols. (New York: Scribner's, 1930), vol. 19, 337.

8. Walke, *Naval Scenes*, 423–424; *Carondelet* Logbook, July 15, 1863; Herbert Aptheker, "The Negro in the Union Navy," *Journal of Negro History* 32 (April 1947), 169–200. For a list of crewmen and soldiers transferred to the *Carondelet* in early 1862, see ORN, I, 22: 736.

9. *Carondelet* Logbook, passim; Jordan Letters, May 28, 1863; Alfred T. Mahan, *The Gulf and Inland Waters* (New York: Scribner's, 1883), 18; Dennis J. Ringle, *Life in Mr. Lincoln's Navy* (Annapolis, MD: Naval Institute Press, 1998), 73–74; Bearss, *Hardluck*, 154; Richardson, *Secret Service*, 230; Jack Coggins, *Arms and Equipment of the Civil War* (Garden City, NY: Doubleday, 1962), 127; U. Levy, *Manual of Internal Rules and Regulations for Men-of-War* (New York: D. Van Nostrand, 1862), 9. Porter's General Order No. 4 of October 18, 1862, Porter read as follows: "(1) Every precaution must be taken against a surprise by the rebels; (2) The guns must always be kept loaded with grape or canister, and the small arms at hand, loaded and ready to repel boarders; (3) Boats are never to land at places were rebels are likely to cut off the men or fire on the boats without their being completely protected by the guns of the vessel; (4) Protected lookouts must be kept on the alert at all times; (5) Boats are not allowed to go on shore to get provisions, except at places occupied by United States troops; (6) No persons will be allowed to pillage under any circumstances, and all who do so are to be reported to me; (7) Vessels will show as few lights as possible in navigating the river at night, and not allow the men to congregate in conspicuous places in daytime, when in suspicious looking neighborhoods; (8) When any of our vessels are fired on, it will be the duty of the commander to fire back with spirit and to destroy everything in that neighborhood within reach of his guns. There is no impropriety in destroying houses supposed to be affording shelter to rebels, and it is the only way to stop guerrilla warfare. Should innocent persons suffer, it will be their own fault, and teach others that it will be to their advantage to inform the Government when guerrillas are about certain localities; (9) Every evening at sunset all vessels will go to quarters, with everything ready for action and guns pointed for the bank. At night the watch must always be on deck, and unless otherwise ordered, no vessel will lie without low steam; (10) This general order is to be passed over to any other commander who may be ordered to the vessel" (ORN, I, 23: 406).

10. Browne, *From the Fresh Water Navy*, 6–7; Jordan Letters, June 30, December 6, 1863; Bearss, *Hardluck*, 157–160; ORN, I, 22: 467; ORN, I, 23: 425. Crewmen were responsible for the repair of their own clothing. Most kept the items required for the task in a little sewing kit called a "housewife." Pine scraps were used to make primitive stencils to mark clothes as a protection from petty theft.

11. *Carondelet* Logbook, March 28, 1863; Thomas Lyons, *Anonymous Journal Kept on Board the U.S. Steam Gunboat Carondelet, Captain Henry Walke Commanding*, January 8–9, 1863 (Manuscript Division, Library of Congress, n.d.), cited hereafter as Anonymous Journal with the date; Bearss, *Hardluck*, 156; Charles Carleton Coffin, *My Days and Nights on the Battlefield* (Boston: Estes and Lauriat, 1887), 75; Coffin, *Drum-beat of the Nation* (New York: Harper, 1888), 229.

12. ORN, I, 22: 465–466, 467, 535; *Anonymous Journal*, January 11, 1863; *Carondelet* Logbook, June 10, September 17 and 27, and October 29, 1863; U.S. Navy Department, Mississippi Squadron, *Internal Rules and Regulations for Vessels of the Mississippi Fleet in the Mississippi River and Tributaries* (Cincinnati: Rickey and Carroll, 1862), 6; Milligan, *Gunboats Down the Mississippi*, 13, 171; Richardson, *Secret Service*, 231; Ringle, *Mr. Lincoln's Navy*, 58; Lester L. Swift, "Letters from a Sailor on a Tinclad," *Civil War History* 10 (March 1961), 51–52 948–62); James Edwin Campbell, "Recent Addresses of James Edwin Campbell: The Mississippi Squadron," *Ohio Archaeological and Historical Quarterly* 34 (January 1925), 60 (29–62); Coffin, *My Days*, 233. The watches were changed every night so that a man who had the first watch on Monday night would have the second watch on Tuesday night and so on throughout the week. Following his promotion to acting ensign on October 1, 1862, Donaldson remained with the *Carondelet* at that rank throughout her commission, often serving as executive officer or even acting commander. He was honorably discharged on January 1, 1866. Ammerman spent his short career entirely aboard the *Carondelet*, arriving as an acting ensign in January and receiving promotion at the end of July (Callahan, *List of Officers*, 24, 166).

13. ORN, I, 22: 466–467; *Civil War Naval Chronology* 6, 106–107; Bearss, *Hardluck*, 160–162; Junius Henri Browne, *Four Years in Secessia* (Hartford, CT: O.D. Case, 1865), 120–121; William H. Russell, *My Diary North and South* (New York: Felt, 1863), 516. Recent studies of gunboat life, in whole or in part, include the following: David F. Riggs, "Sailors of the U.S.S. *Cairo*: Anatomy of a Gunboat Crew," *Civil War History* 28 (September 1982), 266–273; William N. Still Jr.'s already cited "The Common Sailor, Part I: The Yankee Blue Jackets," *Civil War Times Illustrated* 23 (February 1985), 24–29, reprt. in William N. Still, Jr., John M. Taylor, and Norman C. Delaney, eds., *Raiders and Blockaders: The American Civil* War Afloat (Dulles, VA: Brassey's, 1998), 52–79; Ella Lonn, Foreigners in the Union Army and *Navy* (Baton Rouge: Louisiana State University Press, 1951); Herbert Aptheker, "The Negro in the Union Navy," *Journal of Negro History*, 32 (April 1947), 169–200; Charles C. Brewer, "African American Sailors and the Unvexing of the Mississippi River," *Prologue* 30 (Winter 1998), 279–286; W. Jeffrey Bolster, *Black Jacks: African American Seamen in the Age of Sail* (Cambridge, MA: Harvard University Press, 1997); and, perhaps the most helpful for this work, Michael J. Bennett, *Union Jacks: Yankee Sailors in the Civil War* (Chapel Hill: University of North Carolina Press, 2004).

Chapter 4

1. U.S. War Department, *The War of the Rebellion: A Compilation of the Official Records of the Union and Confederate Armies*, 128 vols. (Washington, DC: GPO, 1880–1901), Series I, Vol. 4: 362–363, 372–373, cited hereafter as OR, followed by a comma, the series number in Roman numerals, a comma, the volume number in Arabic, any part number in Arabic, a colon, and the page in Arabic; R.M. McMurry, *Two Great Rebel Armies* (Chapel Hill: University of North Carolina Press, 1989), 142; George Edgar Turner, *Victory Rode the Rails: The Strategic Place of Railroads in the Civil War* (Indianapolis: Bobbs-Merrill, 1953), 118; Anne J. Bailey, *The Chessboard of War: Sherman and Hood in the Autumn Campaigns of 1864* (Great Campaigns of the Civil War; Lincoln: University of Nebraska Press, 2000), 135; T.L. Connelly, *Civil War Tennessee* (Knoxville: University of Tennessee Press, 1979), 13–18; Byrd Douglas, *Steamboatin' on the Cumberland* (Nashville: Tennessee, 1961), 112; Benjamin F. Cooling, *Forts Henry and Donelson: The Key to the Confederate Heartland* (Knoxville: University of Tennessee Press, 1987), 13–14; *Harper's Weekly* 6 (March 15, 1862), 162.

2. Cooling, *Fort Donelson's Legacy*, 29, 42; Ulysses S. Grant, *Personal Memoirs of U.S. Grant: A Modern Abridgment* (New York: Premier, 1962), 80; Stanley F. Horn, comp., *Tennessee's War, 1861–1865: Described by Participants* (Nashville: Tennessee Civil War Centennial Commission, 1965), 29; Jack D. Coombe, *Thunder Along the Mississippi: The River Battles That Split the Confederacy* (New York: Bantam, 1996), 43–44; Peter Franklin Walker, "Command Failure: The Fall of Forts Henry and Donelson," *Tennessee Historical Quarterly* 16 (December 1957), 335–336; R.M. Kelly, "Holding Kentucky for the Union," in *Battles and Leaders of the Civil War*, ed. Robert V. Johnson and Clarence C. Buel, 4 vols. (New York: Century, 1884–1887, reprt. Thomas Yoseloff, 1956), vol. 1, 386–387; Charles Roland, *Albert Sidney Johnston: Soldier of the Republics* (Austin: University of Texas Press, 1964), 271.

3. Allan Nevins, *The War for the Union: War Becomes Revolution* (New York: Scribner's, 1960), 14–15; Stephen E. Ambrose, "The Union Command System and the Donelson Campaign," *Military Affairs* 24 (Summer 1960), 78–86; Cooling, *Fort Donelson's Legacy*, xiv. Rowena Reed also reviews Yankee strategy for Tennessee and the tangled relationships between Federal generals in her *Combined Operations in the Civil War* (Annapolis, MD: Naval Institute Press, 1978), 64–84.

4. OR, I, 3: 317–324; OR, I, 4:491–492, 504–505, 513; OR, I, 7: 144, 689, 711; Coombe, *Thunder Along the Mississippi*; Thomas Lawrence Connelly, *Army of the Heartland: The Army of Tennessee, 1861–1862* (Baton Rouge: Louisiana State University Press, 1967), 106. General Polk's wartime career is detailed in Joseph H. Parks, *General Leonidas Polk, C.S.A.: The Fighting Bishop* (Baton Rouge: Louisiana State University Press, 1962).

5. Fletcher Pratt, *The Civil War on Western Waters* (New York: Holt, 1956), 30; U.S. Navy Department, *Official Records of the Union and Confederate Navies in the War of the Rebellion*, 31 vols. (Washington, DC: GPO, 1894–1922), Series I, Vol. 22, 480–486, 503, 507, 773, 781, 813, cited hereafter as ORN, followed by a comma, the series number in Roman numerals, a comma, the volume number in Arabic, a colon, and the page in Arabic; OR, I, 7: 527–529, 532–534, 850–851; OR, I, 52, 2: 248, 252, 257–259; *New York Times*, January 6, 8, 12, 1862; *Memphis Daily Appeal*, January 9, 12, 1862; *Chicago Daily Tribune*, January 31, 1862; *Philadelphia Inquirer*, April 17, 1862; Bruce Catton, *Grant Moves South* (Boston: Little, Brown, 1960), 118–119; Walker, *Vicksburg*, 337; Ethan S. Rafuse, *McClellan's War: The Failure of Moderation in the Struggle for the Union* (Bloomington: Indiana University Press, 2005), 168–169; Ulysses S. Grant, *Personal Memoirs of U.S. Grant*, 2 vols. (New York: C. L. Webster, 1885–1886, reprt. [2 vols. in 1], New York: Penguin, 1999), vol. 1, 286–287; Ulysses S. Grant, *The Papers of Ulysses S. Grant*, vol. 3, *October 1, 1861–January 7, 1862*, ed. John Y. Simon, 24 vols. to date (Edwardsville: Southern Illinois University Press, 1970), 375–377; Jean Edward Smith, *Grant* (New York: Simon & Schuster, 2001), 137; Cooling, *Fort Donelson's Legacy*, 91; William B. Feis, *Grant's Secret Service: The Intelligence War from Belmont to Appomattox* (Lincoln: University of Nebraska Press, 2002), 60–61; Steven E. Woodworth, *Nothing But Victory: The Army of the Tennessee, 1861–1865* (New York: Alfred A. Knopf, 2005), 65–66; Milton F. Perry, *Infernal Machines: The Story of Confederate Submarine and Mine Warfare* (Baton Rouge: Louisiana State University Press, 1965), 10–11.

6. Feis, *Grant's Secret Service*, 62–66; ORN, I, 22: 512–513, 524–526; OR, I, 7: 120–122, 440, 561, 571; OR, I, 8: 509; *New York Times*, January 28, February 5, 1862; *Chicago Daily Tribune*, January 29, 1862; Cooling, *Fort Donelson's Legacy*, 44–46, 66; Grant, *The Papers of Ulysses S. Grant*, vol. 4, 90–91, 99, 103–104, 121–122; Grant, *Personal Memoirs of U.S. Grant*, 287–288; Gustavus Vasa Fox, *Confidential Correspondence of Gustavus Vasa Fox, Assistant Secretary of the Navy, 1861–1865*, ed. Robert Means Thompson and Richard Wainwright, 2 vols. (New York: De Vinne, 1918–1919), vol. 2, 32; Coombe, *Thunder Along the Mississippi*, 46; Herman Hattaway and Archer Jones, *How the North Won: A Military History of the Civil War* (Urbana: University of Illinois Press, 1983), 61–62; Woodworth, 68–69; Johnston, 420; Walker, *Vicksburg*, 335; Manning F. Force, *From Fort Henry to Corinth* (Campaigns of the Civil War, no. 2; New York: Scribner's, 1881; Rpr. New York: T.Y. Yoseloff, 1963), 25–28; William S. McFeely, *Grant: A Biography* (New York: W.W. Norton, 1981), 97; Edwin C. Bearss and Howard Nash, "Fort Henry," *Civil War Times Illustrated* 4 (November 1965), 11; Charles Carleton Coffin, *My Days and Nights on the Battlefield: A Book for Boys*, by "Carlton," pseud., 2nd ed. (Boston: Ticknor and Fields, 1864), 69; Jay Carlton Mullen, "The Turning of Columbus," *The Register of the Kentucky Historical Society* 64 (July 1966), 221–222. Gen. Beauregard did come west. He arrived at Bowling Green, Kentucky, on February 5 accompanied by two staff officers (Stanley F. Horn, *The Army of Tennessee* (Indianapolis: Bobbs-Merrill, 1941), 74; T. Harry Williams, *G. T. Beauregard: Napoleon in Gray* (Baton Rouge: Louisiana State University Press, 1955), 116).

7. ORN, I, 22: 528, 556; OR, I, 7: 120, 131–132, 140, 148–149, 843, 849, 855; Donald Davidson, *The Tennessee*, vol. 2, *New River, Civil War to TVA* (Rivers of America; New York: Rinehart, 1948), 16–19; James J. Hamilton, *The Battle of Fort Donelson* (New York: Thomas Yoseloff, 1968), 25; John S.C. Abbott, *The History of the Civil War in America*, 2 vols. (New York: H. Bill, 1863), vol. 1, 449; Cooling, *Fort Donelson's Legacy*, 88; Coombe, *Thunder Along the Mississippi*, 44; Henry Walke, "The Gunboats at Belmont and Fort Henry," *B&L*, vol. 1, 364; Taylor, "The Defense of Fort Henry," *B&L*, vol. 1, 369–370; John L. Holcombe and Walter J. Buttgenbachli, "Coast Defense in the Civil War: Fort Henry, Tennessee," *Journal of the United States Artillery* 39 (January 1913), 84–86, 89; Kenneth R. Johnson, "Confederate Defense and Union Gunboats on the Tennessee River," *The Alabama Historical Quarterly* 64 (Summer 1968), 41; Walker, *Vicksburg*, 338, 341; Alfred T. Mahan, *The Navy in the Civil War*, vol. 3, *The Gulf and Inland Waters* (New York: Scribner's, 1883), 22.

8. ORN, I, 22: 530, 534–537; *Cincinnati Daily Gazette*, February 3, 1862; Walke, "The Gunboats at Belmont and Fort Henry," *B&L*, vol. 1, 363; Allen Morgan Geer, *The Civil War Diary of Allen Morgan Geer, 20th Regiment, Illinois Volunteers*, ed. Mary Ann Anderson (Denver: Robert C. Appleman, 1977), 5, 15; Lew Wallace, *Smoke, Sound & Fury: The Civil War Memoirs of Major General Lew Wallace, U.S. Volunteers*, ed. Jim Leeke (Portland, OR: Strawberry Hill, 1998), 60; Coombe, *Thunder Along the Mississippi*, 46; John

D. Milligan, *Gunboats Down the Mississippi* (Annapolis, MD: Naval Institute Press, 1965), 38; Mahan, *Inland Waters*, 21; Douglas, *Steamboatin'*, 118–119. Although Foote wrote in SO-1 that his only major concern with his officers was that they might grow too enthusiastic in their attack and their firing become "too rapid for precision," he, in fact, laid out a host of other cautions, here enumerated: (1) Before going into action, the hoods covering the gratings of the hatches were to be removed to avoid concussion when the cannon were fired; (2) the anchors were to be unstocked to avoid interference with the range of the bow guns; (3) keying on the flagboat, the vessels were not to keep a strictly parallel line, but were to continuously move slightly ahead or astern, making it difficult for the Rebels to get an accurate range; (4) each boat was to observe an equal distance from the next; (5) the flagboat would open fire first; (6) boats were not to fire until correct sightings could be obtained "as this would not only be throwing away ammunition, but it would encourage the enemy to see us firing wildly and harmlessly at the fort"; (7) though a first shot might go wild, there was no excuse for a properly aimed second shot doing so; (8) when the flagboat ceased firing, the fort had surrendered or its surrender was imminent; all other gunboats were to cease firing; (9) as the boats would be close by one another, communications were to be verbal (no doubt through speaking trumpets) (ORN, I, 22: 535–536).

9. ORN, I, 22: 529, 531–537, 552–554, 565–567; OR, I, 7: 121–122, 136–140, 149, 151, 579, 581, 858; Steven E. Woodworth, *Nothing but Victory*, 71–74; *Clarksville Chronicle*, February 7, 1862; *New York Times*, February 8–9, 12, 1862; Coombe, *Thunder Along the Mississippi;* Grant, *The Papers of Ulysses S. Grant*, vol. 4, 141, 145–146, 148–149; Grant, *Personal Memoirs of U.S. Grant*, 290; Abbott, *Civil War*, vol. 1, 451; Edwin C. Bearss, "The Fall of Fort Henry," *West Tennessee Historical Society Publications* 17 (1963), 85–95; Daniel L. Ambrose, *History of the Seventh Regiment Illinois Volunteer Infantry* (Springfield: Illinois Journal, 1868), 25; Franc B. Wilkie, *Pen and Powder* (Boston: Ticknor, 1888), 99; Cooling, *Fort Donelson's Legacy*, 89, 92–93; Jay Slagle, *Ironclad Captain: Seth Ledyard Phelps and the U.S. Navy* (Kent, OH: Kent State University Press, 1996), 158; Henry Walke, "The Gunboats at Belmont and Fort Henry," *B&L*, vol. 1, 362; Spencer C. Tucker, "Timberclads Attack Up the Tennessee," *Naval History* 16 (February 2001), 27; Tucker, *Andrew Foote: Civil War Admiral on Western Waters* (Annapolis, MD: Naval Institute Press, 2000), 136–140; *Cincinnati Daily Gazette*, February 10, 1862. The *Gazette* story is reprt. in Frank Moore, ed., *The Rebellion Record: A Diary of American Events*, 12 vols. (New York: G. Putnam, 1861–1863; D. Van Nostrand, 1864–1868; Rpr. Arno, 1977), 4: 69–73.

10. ORN, I, 22: 534–536, 555–557, 567, 781–782; OR, I, 7: 580–587; *New York Times*, February 12, 1862; *Cincinnati Daily Gazette*, February 10, 1862; *Boston Morning Journal*, February 12, 1862; Donald Davidson, *The Tennessee*, 19; Steven E. Woodworth, *Nothing but Victory*, 74–76; Albert D. Richardson, *The Secret Service: The Field, the Dungeon and The Escape* (Hartford, CT: American, 1866), 214; Charles Carleton Coffin, *My Days and Nights*, 76–77; Mahan, *Inland Waters*, 22; Taylor, "The Defense of Fort Henry," *B&L*, vol. 1, 369; Coombe, *Thunder Along the Mississippi*, 47–48; Myron Smith, *The Timberclads*, 144–145; Slagle, *Ironclad Captain;* Walke, "The Gunboats at Belmont and Fort Henry," *B&L*, vol. 1, 362; Walke, *Naval Scenes*, 54–55, 60; The *Morning Journal* story is reprt. in Frank Moore, ed. *The Rebellion Record* 4: 69–73. Later, toward evening on February 5, the *Conestoga* came abreast of the flagboat *Cincinnati* to show one of the "infernal machines" to Flag Officer Foote, who was then in conference with visiting Brig. Gen. Grant. The submarine battery was manhandled over and onto the fantail of the ironclad. When Grant and his staff officers finished their meeting and were headed toward their yawl, they, together with Foote, spied the mine and expressed a desire to inspect it. This was the first of these "infernal machines" anyone in the U.S. Army high command had ever seen and Grant was particularly interested in its arming mechanism. The *Cincinnati's* armoror was summoned and proceeded to loosen the iron business end, along with a cap underneath. As he did so, it vented "a quantity of gas inside, probably generated from the wet powder, which rushed out with a loud sizzling noise." Everyone, including young witness Eliot Callender, naturally thought that the device was about to explode. The two army staffers hit the deck, while Foote began to rapidly climb the nearby ship's ladder, followed by Grant, who had never ascended a ship's ladder before and "was displaying more energy than grace." As they approached the top, the danger was past. Chuckling, Foote turned and asked, "General, why this haste?" Not missing a beat, the brigadier, already climbing back down, replied, "That the navy may not get ahead of us." The dissection was completed, the pieces carefully removed, and the visitors all departed. Eliot Callender, "What a Boy Saw on the Mississippi," in vol. 1 of *Military Essays and Recollections: Papers Read Before the Commandery of the State of Illinois, Military Order of the Loyal Legion of the United States* (Chicago: A.C. McClurg, 1891), 53–55. As the ironclad attack was finally launched, 12 more torpedoes were set out by Fort Henry's defenses, but, due to the current, they proved useless. For further information on these primitive underwater mines, see Edwin C. Bearss, *Hardluck Ironclad: The Sinking and Salvage of the Cairo* (Baton Rouge: Louisiana State University Press, 1966), 95–97, and Eugene Canfield, *Notes on Naval Ordnance of the American Civil War, 1861–1865* (Washington, DC: American Ordnance Association, 1960), 11–18.

11. OR, I, 7: 124, 138–153, 858, 861; ORN, I, 22: 133–146, 151, 538–539, 541–542, 545, 557–561, 567–569, 782; Smith, 144, 147; Richardson, 215–216; Steven E. Woodworth, *Nothing but Victory*, 75–78; Force, 30–31; Coombe, *Thunder Along the Mississippi*, 49–50; Cooling, *Steamboatin,'* 101–113; Walker, *Vicksburg*, 340–344; Johnston, *General Johnston*, 429–436; Coffin, *Drum-beat*, 77–87, 139–140; Bruce Catton, *Grant Moves South*, 145, 150; *Memphis Daily Appeal*, February 8, 1862; *Nashville Union and American*, February 8, 1862; *Chicago Daily Tribune*, February 8, 1862; *New York Herald*, February 14, 1862; *Philadelphia Enquirer*, February 11, 1862; *New York Times*, February 8, 12, 1862; *New York Tribune*, February 12, 1862; *Boston Morning Journal*, February 12, 1862; *Cincinnati Daily Gazette*, February 10, 1862; *St. Louis Daily Missouri Democrat*, February 9, 1862; Taylor, "The Defense of Fort Henry," *B&L*, vol. 1, 370–372, 380; Abbott, *Civil War*, vol. 1, 452–453; Force, *Fort Henry to Corinth*, 29–31; Wallace, *Smoke, Sound & Fury*, 62, 70; Slagle, *Ironclad Captain*, 160–162; Wilkie, *Pen and Powder*, 99–100; Walke, "The Gunboats at Belmont and Fort Henry," *B&L*, vol. 1, 363–367; Walke, *Naval Scenes*, 54–68; Spencer C. Tucker, *Unconditional Surrender: The Capture of Forts Henry and Donelson* (Abilene: McWhiney Foundation, 2001), 47–60; Tucker, *Andrew Foote*, 140–145; Bearss, "The Fall of Fort Henry," 96–107; Milligan, *Gunboats Down the Mississippi*, 37–42; Mahan, *Inland Waters*, 20–24; Mullen, "Pope's Campaign," 222; Kenneth R. Johnson, "Confederate Defenses and Union Gunboats on the Tennessee River," *The Alabama Historical Quarterly* 64 (Summer 1968), 49–50. The "G.W.B." *Democrat* story is reprt. in Frank Moore, ed., *The Rebellion Record* 4: 69–73, though Moore's printer mistakenly changed the final letter of the reporter's initials from "B" to "F." Concerning Fort Henry's evacuation, Gene Smith wrote the following: "Traditional Civil War historiography has accepted the revised Rebel version that Tilghman ordered the men to Fort Donelson before the Union attack began. In reality, the troops were in the trenches when Foote launched his barrage and panicked at the destructive force of the incoming artillery. Discipline collapsed, and the men deserted their posts, desperate to reach the safety of Fort Donelson. The South could scarcely admit that after 10 months of preparation its principal bastion on the Ten-

nessee surrendered after only one hour, or that the garrison ran away; thus the story was concocted that Tilghman ordered the withdrawal and simply maintained a covering fire from the fort to let the garrison escape. Grant was perfectly happy to accept the revised version.... [I]f the troops at Fort Henry had already departed, it freed him of blame for their escape." Smith's position is supported by any number of Northern newspaper correspondents, some of whom scrambled into the smoking ruins of Fort Henry even before many soldiers. Most remarks were similar to those in the *Philadelphia Enquirer* of February 11: "The infantry fled from their quarters, leaving bag and baggage." In his memoirs, Boston newsman Charles Carlton Coffin recorded that the Confederates were "terror-stricken." Both officers and men ran "to escape the fearful storm" and poured "out of the intrenchments into the road leading to Dover, a motley rabble." After the battle, *New York Tribune* journalist Richardson interviewed an elderly African American lady who "stood rubbing her hands with glee." Where were all the soldiers, he inquired, expecting to find many more POWs. "Lord A'mighty knows," she replied. "Dey jus' runned away like turkeys—nebber fired a gun!" The text of Arthur's CMOH citation, issued under G.O. 17, July 10, 1863, reads as follows: "Signal quartermaster onboard of the U.S.S. *Carondelet*, at the reduction of Forts Henry and Donelson, February 6 and 14, 1862, and other actions, most faithfully, effectively, and valiantly performed all the duties of signal quartermaster and captain of rifled bow gun, and was conspicuous for valor and devotion" (U.S. Navy Department, Bureau of Navigation, Record of Medals of Honor Issued to the Officers and Enlisted Men of the United States Navy, Marine Corps, and Coast Guard, 1862–1917 [Washington, DC: GPO, 1917], 9). Seaman Dorman's CMOH was awarded under G.O. 32, April 18, 1864 and, quoted from the same source as Arthur's award, reads: "Served onboard the U.S.S. *Carondelet* in various actions of that vessel. Carrying out his duties courageously throughout the actions of the *Carondelet*, Dorman, although wounded several times invariably returned to duty and constantly presented an example of devotion to the flag."

12. ORN, I, 22: 571–572, 574–575, 583; *Chicago Daily Tribune*, February 10, 1862; *Cincinnati Daily Gazette*, February 10, 1862; Grant, *The Papers of Ulysses S. Grant*, vol. 4, 172–173; Grant, *Personal Memoirs of U.S. Grant*, vol. 1, 293; Pratt, 57–58.

Chapter 5

1. *Atlanta Confederacy*, n.d., quoted in the *Macon Daily Telegraph*, February 10, 1862; Joseph H. Parks, *General Leonidas Polk, C.S.A.: The Fighting Bishop* (Baton Rouge: Louisiana State University Press, 1962), 209–210; William S. McFeely, *Grant: A Biography* (New York: W.W. Norton, 1981), 98–99; William Johnston, *The Life of Gen. Albert Sidney Johnston* (New York: D. Appleton, 1878), 435–439; Jean Edward Smith, *Grant* (New York: Simon & Schuster, 2001), 148–150; Benjamin F. Cooling, *Forts Henry and Donelson: The Key to the Confederate Heartland* (Knoxville: University of Tennessee Press, 1987), 123–125; T. Harry Williams, *G.T. Beauregard* (Baton Rouge: Louisiana State University Press, 1954), 151–154; Charles Roland, *Albert Sidney Johnston: Soldier of Three Republics* (Austin: University of Texas Press, 1964), 289–291; Jack D. Coombe, *Thunder Along the Mississippi: The River Battles That Split the Confederacy* (New York: Bantam, 1996), 52.

2. U.S. Navy Department, *Official Records of the Union and Confederate Navies in the War of the Rebellion*, 31 vols. (Washington, DC: GPO, 1894–1922), Series I, Vol. 22, 578, 583–585, 587, 592, 783, cited hereafter as ORN, followed by a comma, the series number in Roman numerals, a comma, the volume number in Arabic, a colon, and the page in Arabic; U.S. War Department, *The War of the Rebellion: A Compilation of the Official Records of the Union and Confederate Armies*, 128 vols. (Washington, DC: GPO, 1880–1901), Series I, Vol. 7: 156, 596–600; 894, cited hereafter as OR, followed by a comma, the series number in Roman numerals, a comma, the volume number in Arabic, any part number in Arabic, a colon, and the page in Arabic; OR, I, 2, 154–156; Coombe, *Thunder Along the Mississippi*, 59; Ulysses S. Grant, *The Papers of Ulysses S. Grant*, vol. 4, *January 8–March 31, 1862*, ed. John Y. Simon, 24 vols. to date (Edwardsville, IL: Southern Illinois University Press, 1972), 182–183; Grant, *Personal Memoirs of U.S. Grant*, 2 vols. (New York: C.L. Webster, 1885–1886, reprt. [2 vols. in 1], New York: Penguin, 1999), vol. 1, 291, 297–298, 307; James Marshall-Cornwall, *Grant as Military Commander* (New York: Van Nostrand-Reinhold, 1970), 56–57; Bruce Catton, *Grant Moves South* (Boston: Little, Brown, 1960), 148; *St. Louis Daily Missouri Democrat*, February 13, 1862; *Cincinnati Daily Gazette*, February 17, 1862; J. Haden Alldredge, et al., *A History of Navigation on the Tennessee River* (Washington, DC: GPO, 1937), 84–85; Jay Slagle, *Ironclad Captain: Seth Ledyard Phelps and the U.S. Navy* (Kent, OH: Kent State University Press, 1996), 170–176; Henry Walke, "The Western Flotilla at Fort Donelson, Island Number Ten, Fort Pillow and Memphis," in *Battles and Leaders of the Civil War*, ed. Robert V. Johnson and Clarence C. Buel, 4 vols. (New York: Century, 1884–1887, reprt. Thomas Yoseloff, 1956), vol. 1, 430; Walke, *Naval Scenes and Reminiscences of the Civil War in the United States on the Southern and Western Waters During the Years 1861, 1862 and 1863 with the History of That Period Compared and Corrected from Authentic Sources* (New York: F.R. Reed, 1877), 68, 82; Edwin C. Bearss, "The Ironclads at Fort Donelson," *The Register of the Kentucky Historical Society* 74 (January–July 1976), 1–3; Kenneth R. Johnson, "Confederate Defense and Union Gunboats on the Tennessee River." *The Alabama Historical Quarterly*, LXIV (Summer 1968), 57–60. Returning aboard the *Conestoga* after his February 10 visit with Grant, Phelps opened his mail, which included a message from Flag Officer Foote written the previous day. In it, the flotilla chief told his timberclad division leader that all available gunboats, meaning the lieutenant's, should cooperate with Grant in any Donelson assault. Once that was accomplished, they were then to move up the Cumberland to Clarksville in a raid reminiscent of the just-finished push. On the other hand, the letter Phelps received, which is reprt. in the *Navy Official Records* and was undoubtedly read by him after his interview with Grant, also states that the flag officer wanted to come to Cairo with the *Conestoga*. Phelps was to show the communication to Walke, and in his absence to Grant or his deputy. After hearing the details of Gwin's visit aboard the *Carondelet* and reporting ashore, Phelps decided, despite the lateness of the hour, to weigh for Cairo. When the timberclads failed to reach Paducah by twilight, Cmdr. Walke ordered a stout hawser passed from the *Carondelet* to the steamer *Alps*. She then towed the ironclad up and into the Cumberland alone. Walke, believing Phelps a Foote favorite who considered himself above the orders of a mere commander, was livid years later about what he considered to be a deliberate act of defiance on the lieutenant's part. In his memoirs he bluntly stated that "Professional men may understand this conduct on the part of naval officers to be an act of insubordination." Walke, a "restored officer" perhaps more conscious than most regarding his reputation, most likely made his observations based half on professional frustration and half on ignorance. A member of his own ship's company summed up the frustration felt aboard a number of the ironclads after the Fort Henry fight. "We are scarcely mentioned in the Fort Henry affair," he exclaimed, "while those western bandboxes, the *Conestoga*, *Lexington*, and *Tyler*, were puffed up by the papers when they were astern during the whole of the fight." And just days ago, hadn't the mighty ironclad steamed up to Danville and put right the

destruction of the railroad bridge that Lt. Phelps' old boat boys had muffed. Additionally, Cmdr. Walke probably never knew about the Foote letter to Phelps requiring that the *Conestoga* visit Cairo. He was likely unaware that the *Lexington* needed dockyard work and it is also highly probable that he received no word on these matters from the busy Grant or other soldiers, who, like Phelps, would also not have been able to reach him on the river.

3. Catton, 146, 150; ORN, I, 22: 391; OR, I, 7: 124, 165, 388–389, 397–398, 409–410, 832–833; *St. Louis Daily Missouri Democrat*, February 14, 1862; *Cincinnati Daily Times*, February 13, 1862; *Chicago Daily Tribune*, February 14, 19–20, 1862; Coombe, *Thunder Along the Mississippi*, 63–64; John S. C. Abbott, *The History of the Civil War in America*, 2 vols. (New York: H. Bill, 1863), vol. 1, 458; Spencer C. Tucker, *Andrew Foote: Civil War Admiral on Western Waters* (Annapolis, MD: Naval Institute Press, 2000), 146–150; Albert D. Richardson, *The Secret Service: The Field, the Dungeon and The Escape* (Hartford, CT: American, 1866), 213; Smith, 149–152; Jay Carlton Mullen, "The Turning of Columbus," *The Register of the Kentucky Historical Society* 64 (July 1966), 223; Slagle, *Ironclad Captain*, 176; Walter J. Buttgenbach, "Coast Defense in the Civil War: Fort Donelson," *Journal of the U.S. Artillery* 39 (March 1913), 211; Alfred T. Mahan, *Navy in the Civil War*, vol. 3, *The Gulf and Inland Waters* (New York: Scribner's, 1883), 26; William B. Feis, *Grant's Secret Service: The Intelligence War from Belmont to Appomattox* (Lincoln: University of Nebraska Press, 2002), 68–70; James J. Hamilton, *The Battle of Fort Donelson* (New York: Yoseloff, 1968), 50; Cooling, *Fort Donelson's Legacy*, 116,140; Hugh S. Bedford, "Fight Between the Batteries and Gunboats at Fort Donelson," *Southern Historical Society Papers* 13 (January–December 1885), 167 (165–173); Reuben R. Ross, "River Batteries at Fort Donelson," *Confederate Veteran* 4 (1896), 393 (393–398); Edwin C. Bearss, *Ironclads at Fort Donelson*, 73–78.

4. ORN, I, 22: 587–588, 592; OR, I, 7: 185, 389, 391, 393–394, 396, 398, 410–411, 594; Grant, *Personal Memoirs*, vol. 1, 302; Mahan, *The Gulf and Inland Waters*, 22; Abbott, *Civil War*, 462–463; Manning F. Force, *From Fort Henry to Corinth* (Campaigns of the Civil War, no. 2; New York: Scribner's, 1881; Rpr. New York: T.Y. Yoseloff, 1963), 43–44; Coombe, *Thunder Along the Mississippi*, 62–65; Kendall D. Gott, *Where the South Lost the War: An Analysis of the Fort Henry–Fort Donelson Campaign, February 1862* (Mechanicsburg, PA: Stackpole, 2003), 159–160; John D. Milligan, *Gunboats Down the Mississippi* (Annapolis, MD: Naval Institute Press, 1965), 45–46; Fletcher Pratt, *Short History of the Civil War* (New York: Pocket Books, 1952), 53; Catton, *Grant Moves South*, 153, 158; Walke, "The Western Flotilla," *B&L*, vol. 1, 431–433; Walke, *Naval Scenes*, 72–73, 75–76; *Cincinnati Daily Times*, February 13, 1862; *St. Louis Daily Missouri Democrat*, February 13, 18, 24, 1862; *Chicago Daily Tribune*, February 19, 1862; *New York Times*, February 22, 1862; Ross, "River Batteries"; Bedford, "Fight," 167, 170; Charles Carleton Coffin, *Drum-beat of the Nation* (New York: Harper, 1888), 144–146; Coffin, *My Days and Nights on the Battlefield: A Book for Boys*, by "Carlton," pseud. (Boston: Ticknor and Fields, 1864), 98; Bearss, *Ironclads at Fort Donelson*, 6–7, 79–84; Cooling, *Fort Donelson's Legacy*, 1432–143.

5. ORN, I, 22: 584–587, 591–593; 598, 622, 627–628; OR, I, 7: 163, 166 172–174, 236–240, 262–263, 265–266, 281–283, 316–329, 332–333, 365, 391–396, 399–401, 629, 940; Grant, *Personal Memoirs of U.S. Grant*, I, .242–248, 301–309; Grant, *The Papers of Ulysses S. Grant*, vol. 4, 230–231; *New York Herald*, February 17, 1862; *New York Times*, February 17, 22, 1862; *St. Louis Daily Missouri Democrat*, February 16–17, 1862; *Chicago Daily Tribune*, February 16–17, 19–20, 1862; *Philadelphia Inquirer*, February 17, March 3, 1862; *Charleston Mercury*, February 17, 1862; Walke, "The Western Flotilla at Fort Donelson, Island Number Ten, Fort Pillow and Memphis," *B&L.*, vol. 1, 433–437; Lew Wallace, "The Capture of Fort Donelson," *B&L*, vol. 1, 414, 420–423; Force, "Fort Henry to Corinth," 49–56, 60, 64; Walke, *Naval Scenes*, 77–79, 84–97; Bearss, *Ironclads at Fort Donelson*, 167–183; Lew Wallace, *Smoke, Sound & Fury, U.S. Volunteers*, Jim Leeke, ed. (Portland, OR: Strawberry Hill Press, 1998), p. 75; Johnston, *General Johnston*, 449–452; Woodworth, *Jefferson Davis*, 88–120; Abbott, *Civil War*, 465; Bedford, "Fight," 171–173; Charles C. Nott, *Sketches of the War: A Series of Letters to the North Moore Street School of New York*, cited in E. McCleod Johnson, *A History of Henry County, Tennessee* (Paris, TN: Priv. Print, 1958), 90; Catton, *Grant Moves South*, 153; Cooling, *Fort Donelson's Legacy*, 155–160; Coombe, *Thunder Along the Mississippi*, 65–73; Smith, *The Timberclads*, 153–155; Peter Franklin Walker, "Command Failure: The Fall of Forts Henry and Donelson," *Tennessee Historical Quarterly* 16 (December 1957), 348–349; Thomas Lawrence Connelly, *Army of the Heartland: The Army of Tennessee, 1861–1862* (Baton Rouge: Louisiana State University Press, 1967), 120; Jack H. Lepa, *The Civil War in Tennessee, 1862–1863* (Jefferson, NC: McFarland, 2007), 24–25; Scott W. Stucky, "Joint Operations in the Civil War," *Joint Forces Quarterly*, no. 6 (Autumn-Winter 1994–1995), 98; Gott, *Lost the War*, 167, 177–183; Jesse Bowman Young, "What a Boy Saw in the Army," quoted in Otto Eisenschiml and Ralph Newman, *The American Iliad: The Epic Story of the Civil War as Narrated by Eyewitnesses and Contemporaries*, rev. ed. (Indianapolis: Bobbs-Merrill, 1947), 156; Wesley Smith Dorris quoted in David C. Allen, *Winds of Change: Robertson County, Tennessee in the Civil War* (Nashville: Land Yacht Press, 2000), 25–26; Walter F. Meier, "A Confederate Private ['Spot' F. Terrell] at Fort Donelson, 1862," *American Historical Review* 31 (April 1926), 478 (477–484); Wilkie, *Pen and Powder*, 100–101, 104, 110–112; James M. Hoppin, *The Life of Andrew Hull Foote, Rear Admiral, United States Navy* (New York: Harper and Brothers, 1874), 223; Spencer C. Tucker, *Unconditional Surrender: The Capture of Forts Henry and Donelson* (Abilene: McWhiney Foundation, 2001), 61–104; Tucker, *Andrew Foote*, 154–158; Buttgenbach, "Coast Defense," 213. Sometime later when he heard of the defeat, Cmdr. John Rodgers II, replaced by Foote in command of the timberclad flotilla back in September, suggested his successor's tactics were faulty. Ironclads, he noted, were to fight wooden vessels and forts from a distance great enough to insure the ironclads remained unscathed. They were not to close and, as in the old school of sailing ships, exchange smashing broadsides. Robert E. Johnson, *Rear Admiral John Rodgers, 1812–1882* (Annapolis, MD: Naval Institute Press, 1967), 167–168.

Chapter 6

1. U.S. Navy Department, *Official Records of the Union and Confederate Navies in the War of the Rebellion*, 31 vols. (Washington, DC: GPO, 1894–1922), Series I, Vol. 22, 624–640, 654, 783, cited hereafter as ORN, followed by a comma, the series number in Roman numerals, a comma, the volume number in Arabic, a colon, and the page in Arabic; U.S. War Department, *The War of the Rebellion: A Compilation of the Official Records of the Union and Confederate Armies*, 128 vols. (Washington, DC: GPO, 1880–1901), Series I, Vol. 7: 153–156, 424, 436–438, 677, 683, 860–861, 890–892, 896–897, 944–945, cited hereafter as OR, followed by a comma, the series number in Roman numerals, a comma, the volume number in Arabic, any part number in Arabic, a colon, and the page in Arabic; *Memphis Avalanche*, February 26, 1862; *New York Times*, March 1, 5, 1862; *Chicago Daily Tribune*, February 25, 1862; *Cincinnati Daily Commercial*, March 1, 1862; Thomas Lawrence Connelly, *Army of the Heartland: The Army of Tennessee, 1861–1862* (Baton Rouge: Louisiana State University Press, 1967), 136–142;

Ulysses S. Grant, *Personal Memoirs of U.S. Grant*, 2 vols. (New York: C.L. Webster, 1885–1886, reprt. [2 vols. in 1], New York: Penguin, 1999), vol. 1, 215–217; Grant, *The Papers of Ulysses S. Grant*, vol. 4, *January 8–March 31, 1862*, ed. John Y. Simon, 24 vols. to date (Edwardsville: Southern Illinois University Press, 1972), 278–280, 282–283; Jean Edward Smith, *Grant* (New York: Simon & Schuster, 2001), 168–174; Henry Walke, *Naval Scenes and Reminiscences of the Civil War in the United States on the Southern and Western Waters during the Years 1861, 1862 and 1863 with the History of That Period Compared and Corrected from Authentic Sources* (New York: F.R. Reed, 1877), 94–95; Alfred T. Mahan, *Navy in the Civil War*, vol. 3, *The Gulf and Inland Waters* (New York: Scribner's, 1883), 29; Joseph H. Parks, *General Leonidas Polk, C.S.A.: The Fighting Bishop* (Baton Rouge: Louisiana State University Press, 1962), 208–219; Robert D. Whitsell, "Military and Naval Activities between Cairo and Columbus," *The Register of the Kentucky Historical Society* 61 (April 1963), 120–121; Spencer C. Tucker, *Andrew Foote: Civil War Admiral on Western Waters* (Annapolis, MD: Naval Institute Press, 2000), 165–167; Jay C. Mullen, "The Turning of Columbus." *Register of the Kentucky Historical Society* 64 (July 1966), 223–225; Daniel, *Cannoneers*, 67–71; Benjamin F. Cooling, *Forts Henry and Donelson: The Key to the Confederate Heartland* (Knoxville: University of Tennessee Press, 1987), 226–239; Henry R. Browne and Symmes E. Browne, *From the Fresh Water Navy, 1861–1864: Letters of Acting Master's Mate Henry R. Browne and Acting Ensign Symmes E. Browne*, ed. John D. Milligan, vol. 3 (Naval Letters Series; Annapolis, MD: Naval Institute Press, 1970), 31–32. On March 2, the last cavalrymen out set fire to all of the abandoned buildings. Just before departing, Maj. Gen. Polk wired Confederate War Secretary Judah Benjamin: "The work is done. Columbus gone."

2. ORN, I, 22: 643, 646, 649–666, 688, 693, 770; ORN, I, 23: 279; OR, I, 7: 437–438; OR, I, 8: 149–151, 179, 186, 726, 760, 762; *St. Louis Daily Missouri Democrat*, March 19, 1862; *St. Louis Daily Missouri Republican*, March 17, 1862; *Philadelphia Inquirer*, March 3, 20, 1862; *New York Times*, March 2, 10,17, 1862; *New York Tribune*, March 24, 1862; *New Orleans Daily Crescent*, March 26, 1862; *Chicago Daily Tribune*, March 4, 17, 19, 21, 24, 1862; Steven E. Woodworth, *Nothing but Victory: The Army of the Tennessee, 1861–1865* (New York: Alfred A. Knopf, 2005), 128; Grant, *The Papers of Ulysses S. Grant*, vol. 4, 310–312; Daniel and Bock, *Island No. 10*, 28–30, 34, 68–78, 153; Jack D. Coombe, *Thunder Along the Mississippi: The River Battles That Split the Confederacy* (New York: Bantam, 1996), 85–86; *Philadelphia Inquirer*, March 9, 1862; Parks, *Polk*, 214–215; William M. Polk, *Leonidas Polk, Bishop and General*, 2 vols. (New York: Longmans, Green, 1915), vol. 2, 75–81; Mahan, *Inland Waters*, 29–30; *Cincinnati Daily Gazette*, March 5, 8, 1862; *Cincinnati Daily Commercial*, March 18, 1862; *Wisconsin State Journal*, March 19, 1862; Franc B. Wilkie, *Pen and Powder* (Boston: Ticknor, 1888), 148–153; Henry Walke, "The Western Flotilla at Fort Donelson, Island Number Ten, Fort Pillow and Memphis," in *Battles and Leaders of the Civil War*, ed. Robert V. Johnson and Clarence C. Buel, 4 vols. (New York: Century, 1884–1887, reprt. Thomas Yoseloff, 1956), vol. 1, 437–439; Walke, *Naval Scenes*, 94–95, 98, 112; Gary D. Joiner, *Mr. Lincoln's Brown Water Navy: The Mississippi Squadron* (Lanham, MD: Rowman & Littlefield, 2007), 59; R. Thomas Campbell, *Confederate Naval Forces on Western Waters* (Jefferson, NC: McFarland, 2005), 41; James M. Hoppin, *The Life of Andrew Hull Foote, Rear Admiral, United States Navy* (New York: Harper and Brothers, 1874), 266; Spencer C. Tucker, *Andrew Foote: Civil War Admiral on Western Waters.* (Annapolis, MD: Naval Institute Press, 2000), 168–177; Allen C. Guelzo, *The Crisis of the American Republic: A History of the Civil War and Reconstruction* (New York: St. Martin's, 1995), 153–154; Jay Slagle, *Ironclad Captain: Seth Ledyard Phelps and the U.S. Navy* (Kent, OH: Kent State University Press, 1996), 194–195; Peter Cozzens, "Roadblock on the Mississippi," *Civil War Times Illustrated* 41 (March 2002), 42–43 (40–49); Junius Henri Browne, *Four Years in Secessia: Adventures Within and Without the Union Lines* (Hartford, CT: O.D. Case, 1865), 87–90, 117–118; William T. Sherman, *Sherman's Civil War: Selected Correspondence of William T. Sherman, 1860–1865*, ed. Brooks D. Simpson and Jean V. Berlin (Chapel Hill: University of North Carolina Press, 1999), 195; Tucker, 168. On March 11, by Presidential War Order No. 3, Maj. Gen. George B. McClellan was demoted from general in chief to head of the Army of the Potomac while the Department of the Ohio and the Department of the Missouri were combined into the Department of the Mississippi, under Maj. Gen. Henry W. Halleck (Curt Anders, *Henry Halleck's War: A Fresh Look at Lincoln's Controversial General-in-Chief* (Indianapolis: Guild Press of Indiana, 1999), 76–88; Stephen E. Ambrose, *Halleck: Lincoln's Chief of Staff* (Baton Rouge: Louisiana State University Press, 1962), 33). A number of well-remembered newsmen were embedded aboard the vessels of Foote's armada. Men like Junius Henri Browne of the *New York Tribune, Cincinnati Daily Times, Chicago Daily Tribune* reporter George ("G.P.U.") Upton, and Joseph ("Mack") McCallagh of the *Cincinnati Daily Gazette/Commercial* were aboard transports; Albert H. Bodman of the *Chicago Daily Tribune*, William E. Webb of the *St. Louis Daily Missouri Republican*, Franc B. ("Galway") Wilkie of the *New York Times* aboard the *Conestoga*; and Albert D. Richardson of the *New York Tribune* and Frank Chapman of the *New York Herald* aboard the *Benton.* Quite pleased with his Fort Donelson coverage within the pages of the *St. Louis Daily Missouri Democrat*, Capt. Walke entertained that paper's reporter William A. "F" Fayel. A native of Ostego County (NY) and former editor of the *Lockport (New York) Journal*, Fayel, a well-known Frémont supporter, transferred to St. Louis in July 1861 and took a job with the *Daily Missouri Democrat.* Following a stint as a front line war correspondent, he became the paper's city editor and then, in 1867, he moved over to the *St. Louis Daily Missouri Republican.* From November 1862 to 1872, he reported from the Missouri legislature, becoming "the best known of all the newspaper gentlemen at the capital." During the 1870s, he would serve as secretary to several U.S. commissions negotiating with the Plains Indians (J.T. Pratt, *Pen-Pictures of the Officers and Members of the House of Representatives, 26th General Assembly of Missouri* [Jefferson City, MO: Priv. print, 1872], 100–101).

3. ORN, I, 22: 685–689, 693–694; OR, I, 8: 125, 150, 154–156, 160–161, 174–175, 180–181,739; Daniel and Bock, *Island No. 10*, 98; *St. Louis Daily Missouri Democrat*, March 21, 1862; Coombe, *Thunder Along the Mississippi*, 86–87; Charles B. Boynton, *History of the Navy During the Rebellion*, 2 vols. (New York: D. Appleton, 1867), vol.1, 537; Walke, *Naval Scenes*, 100–102, 104–106; Tucker, *Foote*, 178–179, 182; *New York Tribune*, March 24, 1862; *New York Times*, March 19, 23, 29, 1862; *Philadelphia Inquirer*, March 24, 1862; *Cincinnati Daily Commercial*, March 21, April 19, 1862; *Memphis Daily Appeal*, March 20–21, 28, 1862; *New Orleans Daily Crescent*, March 16, 26, 1862; *New Orleans Delta*, March 25, 1862; Albert D. Richardson, *The Secret Service: The Field, the Dungeon and the Escape* (Hartford, CT: American, 1866), 226–228; Mahan, *Inland Waters*, 31; Charles Carleton Coffin, *The Boys of '61, or Four Years of Fighting* (Boston: Estes and Lauriat, 1885), 90; Browne, *From the Fresh Water Navy*, 43–44. Despite earlier hopes, the thousands of mortar bombs and gunboat shells being dropped in and around the river fortress were not having the intended effect. Indeed, one later analysis bluntly stated that the greatest failure from a Union perspective during the campaign was "the complete ineffectiveness of long-range shelling." The mortar shells forced the defenders to move their camps out of range and dig bombproof shelters for the batteries. Captured prisoners confessed that the fire-

works were a "great annoyance to the daily labors of the garrison," but otherwise caused little actual damage.

4. ORN, I, 22: 697, 703–705, 776, 822; OR, I, 8: 81–84, 156, 643–646, 660, 782; Daniel and Bock, *Island No. 10*, 90, 94–96, 119–120; Browne, *From the Fresh Water Navy*, 49; *St. Louis Daily Missouri Democrat*, March 18, 22, 1862; *St. Louis Daily Missouri Republican*, March 18, 22, April 3, 1862; *Chicago Daily Tribune*, March 19, 22, 1862; *New York Herald*, March 28, 1862; *New York Times*, March 22–23, 25–26, April 1, 10, 1862; *Philadelphia Inquirer*, March 22, 26, 1862; Walke, "The Western Flotilla," vol. 1, 441–442; Walke, *Naval Scenes*, 117–118; H. Allen Gosnell, *Guns on the Western Waters: The Story of the River Gunboats in the Civil War* (Baton Rouge: Louisiana State University Press, 1949), 73; Tucker, 184; Coombe, *Thunder Along the Mississippi*, 88–90; Edward W. Crippen, "Diary of Edward W. Crippen, Private, 27th Illinois Volunteers, War of the Rebellion, August 7, 1861–September 19, 1863," ed. Robert J. Kerner, in *Transactions of the Illinois State Historical Society for the Year 1910* (Springfield: Illinois Historical Society, 1910), 239; John D. Milligan, *Gunboats Down the Mississippi* (Annapolis, MD: Naval Institute Press, 1965), 56. Daniel and Bock (*Island No. 10*, 84–86) point out that there is considerable debate concerning Foote's March 20 opinion-gathering review session, who attended, and whether or not it may actually have occurred on March 18. The latter date is supported by several correspondents (*Chicago Daily Tribune*, March 22, 1862; *New York Tribune*, March 28, 1862) and on page 41 of historian W.A. Neal's *An Illustrated History of the Missouri Engineers and the 25th Infantry Regiment* (Chicago: Donohue and Henneperry, 1889). Several sources note that Lt. Cmdr. Phelps was quite eager to make the passage, but the flag officer refused to risk his most important gunboat (Slagle, *Ironclad Captain*, 202–205; Tucker, *Foote*, 181. On page 117 of his *Naval Scenes*, Walke indicates that neither he nor any of the *Carondelet*'s officers knew of a meeting, whether on the 18th or the 20th, though in his "Western Flotilla" piece for the Battles and Leaders series (vol. 1, 441) he confirms that Foote sent Capt. Stemble on the latter date to elicit comments. Tucker also states that "Foote met with his subordinate commanders" on the 20th. When Franc Wilkie told the island dash story in the April 10 issue of the *New York Times*, he frankly confessed that he did not know why Walke received the assignment. "Some boat had to go, and Captain Walke, being nearly the oldest officer in the fleet ... was dispatched." The choice was seen differently In the April 15 issue of the *New York Herald*. "I need not say to the friends and acquaintances of Captain Walke why he and his boat were selected for such hazardous work," commented reporter Frank Chapman. "The Commodore desired the experiment to be a success, and selected such a man and such a crew, and such a boat as should secure it."

5. ORN, I, 22: 706–708, 745–746; ORN, II, 1: 52; OR, I, 8: 653, 656, 659; *Cincinnati Daily Commercial*, April 5, 7, 10, 1862; *New York Herald*, April 15, 1862; *New York Times*, April 4–6, 10, 1862; *New York Tribune*, April 4, 9, 1862; *St. Louis Daily Missouri Democrat*, April 10, 1862; Walke, "The Western Flotilla," *B&L*, vol. 1, 442–444; Walke, *Naval Scenes*, 118, 124, 135; Charles Swigert, "Record of Charles Swigert, Late Private, Co. H., 42nd Ill. Infantry," Papers of George H. Thomas Post, Grand Army of the Republic, Department of Illinois, n.d., Chicago Historical Society Library, Chicago, cited hereafter as Swigert Record; Mahan, *Inland Waters*, 32; Tucker, *Foote*, 184–185; Daniel and Bock, *Island No. 10*, 92–93, 120–126; Gosnell, *Guns*, 74–75; Coombe, *Thunder Along the Mississippi* 90–91; Slagle, *Ironclad Captain*; Mike West, "Island No. 10 Hero [Col. George W. Roberts] Dies Valiant Death at Stones River," *Murfreesboro Post*, March 25, 2009. Buckeye steamboat pilot William R. Hoel (1825–1879) joined the Western Flotilla in October 1861, becoming pilot of the Pook turtle *Cincinnati*, aboard which he was wounded during the Battle of Fort Henry on February 6. Following the passage of the Island No. 10 batteries, Hoel was named an acting Volunteer lieutenant at the end of April and eventually rose to the prized rank of acting Volunteer lieutenant commander in 1864. Succeeding Cmdr. Stembel, he took over the *Cincinnati* in May and in October, the turtle *Pittsburg*. Hoel participated in the battles of Memphis, Vicksburg, and Grand Gulf. After commanding the ram *Vindicator*, he was honorably discharged on December 30, 1865. Regarded as a Civil War hero, he was also "widely known for his jealous temper and violent ways." Following the war, Hoel became a gentleman farmer north of Cincinnati and as the result of a romantic entanglement involving his wife and a local doctor, was shot dead in an altercation with the paramour (Karen Campbell, "Another Murder in Waynesville?: Capt. William Rion Hoel," Waynesville, Ohio: Connections with the Past, August 29, 2005, http://waynesgenhis.blogspot.com/2005/08/another-murder-in-waynesville-captain.html (accessed March 27, 2009). The left side of a vessel is now — and was then — known in the USN as the "port" side; however, on the western rivers and in some of the oceangoing merchant service, it was known as the "larboard" side. The logbook of the *New Orleans* was captured after the fall of Island No. 10 and extracts from it were published in the *Philadelphia Inquirer*, April 17, 1862.

6. ORN, I, 22: 709–713; OR, I, 8: 171–175; Swigert Record; *Chicago Daily Times*, April 6, 1862; *New York Times*, April 7, 1862; *St. Louis Daily Missouri Democrat*, April 10, 1862; *St. Louis Daily Missouri Republican*, March 23, April 10, 1862; *New York Herald*, April 15, 1862; *New York Tribune*, April 15, 1862; *Cincinnati Daily Commercial*, April 10, 1862; *New Orleans Delta*, April 9, 1862; Slagle, *Ironclad Captain*, 207–208; Mahan, *Inland Waters*, 32–33; Walke, "The Western Flotilla," *B&L*, vol. 1, 443–445; Walke, *Naval Scenes*, 124–125, 130–136; Browne, *Four Years in Secessia*, 124–129; Boynton, *History of the Navy*, vol. 1, 549–553; Daniel and Bock, *Island No. 10*, 123–126; Tucker, *Foote*, 185; Coombe, *Thunder Along the Mississippi*, 91–93; Gosnell, *Guns*, 75–78; John Fiske, *The Mississippi Valley in the Civil War* (New York: Houghton Mifflin, 1900), 104; Robert D. Huffstot, "The *Carondelet* and Other Pook Turtles," *Civil War Times Illustrated* 6 (August 1967), 10 (5–11). Although the St. Louis correspondent was the only one officially accredited to the *Carondelet*, another soul aboard kept a record of the passage and events of the next few days following. These were published in the *Pittsburgh Evening Chronicle* on April 20 and quoted in Walke's *Naval Scenes*, 176–177. It is possible that the writer was the newspaper's editor-correspondent Daniel O'Neill, but we do not know for certain that he was in the Western theater at this time, let alone aboard the gunboat.

7. OR, I, 8: 78–79; Fisk, *Geological Investigations*, 107; Coombe, *Thunder Along the Mississippi*; Mahan, *Inland Waters*, 33–35; William H. Fowler, *Under Two Flags: The American Navy in the Civil War* (New York: W.W. Norton, 1990), 151, 172–173; Daniel and Bock, *Island No. 10*, 148; Eliot Callender, "What a Boy Saw on the Mississippi River," in vol. 1 of *Military Essays and Recollections: Papers Read before the Illinois Commandery, Military Order of the Loyal Legion of the United States* (Chicago: A.C. McClurg, 1891), 58; Charles W. Read, "Reminiscences of the Confederate States Navy," *Southern Historical Society Papers* 1, no. 5 (1876), 338–339 (333–362); Campbell, "Recent Addresses," 47–49.

8. ORN, I, 22: 715–717, 719, 726–727, 777; OR, I, 8: 88, 666, 727, 887; Swigert Record; Walke, *Naval Scenes*, 144–145, 176–177; Walke, "The Western Flotilla," *B&L*, vol. 1, 445; *New York Times*, April 7, 1862; *St. Louis Daily Missouri Democrat*, April 8, 1862; *Memphis Daily Appeal*, April 9, 11–12, 1862; *Chicago Daily Tribune*, April 10, 1862; *Philadelphia Inquirer*, April 11, 1862; *New York Tribune*, April 14, 1862; Browne, *From the Fresh Water Navy*, 55; John M. Palmer, *Personal Recollections of General John M. Palmer: The Story of an Earnest Life* (Cincinnati: Robert Clarke, 1901), 99; Daniel and Bock, *Island No. 10*, 126–127. In writing his memoirs, Rear Adm. Walke had access to the deck logs of the *Carondelet* prior to late May 1862, the period after which

copies are held by the National Archives. Extracts from these early volumes are quoted in his memoirs, *Naval Scenes and Incidents*. Although Walke used these to bolster his reports, this writer accepts them as genuine.

9. ORN, I, 22: 718, 727; OR, I, 8: 78, 89, 98, 109, 670; Swigert Record; *St. Louis Daily Missouri Democrat*, April 8, 1862; *New York Times*, April 8, 1862; *Chicago Daily Tribune*, April 8, 12, 1862; *Richmond Press*, April 14, 1862; Walke, *Naval Scenes*, 148–151, 177; Walke, "The Western Flotilla," *B&L*, vol. 1, 445–446; Daniel and Bock, *Island No. 10*, 128, 130, 132; David S. Stanley, *Personal Recollections of Major General David S. Stanley* (Cambridge, MA: Harvard University Press, 1917), 90. When Lt. Thompson reported aboard the *Carondelet* after the batteries were captured, he reportedly told his superior that he had not followed Walke into the battle early on because "there was no fighting going on" (Walke, *Naval Scenes*, 151).

Chapter 7

1. U.S. Navy Department, *Official Records of the Union and Confederate Navies in the War of the Rebellion*, 31 vols. (Washington, DC: GPO, 1894–1922), Series I, Vol. 23, 3–4, 9–11, 667, 675, cited hereafter as ORN, followed by a comma, the series number in Roman numerals, a comma, the volume number in Arabic, a colon, and the page in Arabic; U.S. War Department, *The War of the Rebellion: A Compilation of the Official Records of the Union and Confederate Armies*, 128 vols. (Washington, DC: GPO, 1880–1901), Series I, Vol. 10, Pt. 2: 106–107, cited hereafter as OR, followed by a comma, the series number in Roman numerals, a comma, the volume number in Arabic, any part number in Arabic, a colon, and the page in Arabic; Henry Walke, *Naval Scenes and Reminiscences of the Civil War in the United States on the Southern and Western Waters During the Years 1861, 1862 and 1863 with the History of That Period Compared and Corrected from Authentic Sources* (New York: F.R. Reed, 1877), 245; *New York Herald*, April 26, 1862; Henry Walke, "The Western Flotilla at Fort Donelson, Island Number Ten, Fort Pillow and Memphis," in *Battles and Leaders of the Civil War*, ed. Robert V. Johnson and Clarence C. Buel, 4 vols. (New York: Century, 1884–1887, reprt. Thomas Yoseloff, 1956), vol. 1, 446–447; Ben LaBree, ed., *The Confederate Soldier in the Civil War, 1861–1865* (Louisville, KY: Courier-Journal Job Printing, 1895), 400–401; J. Thomas Scharf, *History of the Confederate States Navy* (New York: Rodgers and Sherwood, 1887; reprt., New York: Fairfax Press, 1977), 253; Henry R. Browne and Symmes E. Browne, *From the Fresh Water Navy, 1861–1864: Letters of Acting Master's Mate Henry R. Browne and Acting Ensign Symmes E. Browne*, ed. John D. Milligan, vol. 3 (Naval Letters Series; Annapolis, MD: Naval Institute Press, 1970), 61–62; Edwin C. Bearss, *Hardluck Ironclad: The Sinking and Salvage of the Cairo* (Baton Rouge: Louisiana State University Press, 1968), 50–51; John S. C. Abbott, *The History of the Civil War in America*, 2 vols. (New York: H. Bill, 1863), vol. 1, 270; Spencer C. Tucker, *Andrew Foote: Civil War Admiral on Western Waters* (Annapolis, MD: Naval Institute Press, 2000), 190–194; Jack D. Coombe, *Thunder Along the Mississippi: The River Battles That Split the Confederacy* (New York: Bantam, 1996), 120–121; E.B. Long, "Plum Point Bend: The Forgotten Battle," *Civil War Times Illustrated* 11 (June 1972), 7; R. Thomas Campbell, *Confederate Naval Forces on Western Waters* (Jefferson, NC: McFarland, 2005), 83–86. The brainchild of two former riverboat captains, J.H. Townsend and James E. Montgomery, the Confederate River Defense Fleet (CRDF) was created at New Orleans during the first quarter of 1862. Employing 14 seized merchant steamers, the new unit was not a part of the Confederate States Navy but a direct creation of the Confederate congress, which funded it to the tune of $1 million. Once in hand during March to early April, the vessels, of different sizes, were all modified along similar lines into rams, craft designed like the warships of ancient times to run into other boats. The engines and boilers were lowered as far as possible into the holds and protected by bulkheads, cotton bales were stuffed into every conceivable space for protection, and few cannon of different caliber were mounted, usually no more than four. Uniquely, the bows were strengthened with railroad iron. Two divisions were created, a northern group under Montgomery's control and a southern under Capt. John A. Stephenson, Townsend's successor. It is the former which interests us here; Stephenson's division was destroyed by Flag Officer David G. Farragut in the Battle of New Orleans at the end of April. In the days just after the fall of Island No. 10, Com. George Hollins, who had guided CSN fortunes on the upper rivers since the beginning of the year, was recalled to New Orleans. Many of the vessels he controlled were dispersed; and within a few days, his regular force was replaced by Montgomery's seven vessels from the northern division of the CRDF. The creation and deployment of this new naval organization was unknown to Flag Officer Foote, or his successor, Capt. Charles H. Davis. Still, refugees warned Foote to expect a naval attack and orders, not strictly followed, were issued, requiring the ironclads keep up steam and remain prepared for battle on a moment's notice (OR, I, 6: 860–861; Bearss, *Hardluck Ironclad*, 57; Robert Burpo, "Notes on the First Fleet Engagement in the Civil War," *American Neptune* 19 (October 1959), 267–268); Michael L. Gillespie, "The Novel Experiment: Cottonclads and Steamboats," *Civil War Times Illustrated* 22 (December 1983), 34–36; Coombe, *Thunder Along the Mississippi*, 122–123).

2. ORN, I, 23: 5–7, 10–11, 62–63, 69–70, 84, 667–668; OR, I, 6, 809–817, 853; OR, I, 10, 2: 107–108; *St. Louis Daily Missouri Democrat*, April 18, 1862; *New York Herald*, April 26, 1862; Walke, "The Western Flotilla," B& L, vol. 1, 446; Walke, *Naval Scenes*, 245–249; Abbott, *Civil War*, 271; Bearss, *Hardluck Ironclad*, 52–53, 58; Burpo, "Notes on First Fleet," 269–270 (265–273); Long, "Plum Point Bend," 8–9. In the two months following the Battle of Fort Donelson, the wounds received by Flag Officer Foote refused to properly heal. His health steadily declining, the ill squadron commander sought relief (Junius Henri Browne, *Four Years in Secessia* [Hartford, CT: O.D. Case, 1865], 164–165). Capt. Charles H. Davis (1807–1877) temporarily assumed squadron command on May 9 from the injured Foote. Foote's choice to act as his deputy and successor if need be, David was a year younger than his friend and, in the Antebellum period, developed an enviable reputation, like the first Western Flotilla leader, Cmdr. John Rodgers, as a scientific officer. Born in Boston, Davis earned a degree from Harvard University, becoming superintendent of the Nautical Almanac Office located there. With sea service during the expedition to capture filibusterer Walker in Nicaragua and with the South Atlantic Blockading Squadron, Davis would succeed Foote in June 1862, only to be succeeded himself in command of the Mississippi Squadron by David Dixon Porter in October (effective July). Constantly on duty ashore and afloat, he would die at his desk as superintendent of the Naval Observatory. Our profile of Rear Adm. Davis is taken from William B. Cogar, *Dictionary of Admirals of the U.S. Navy*, 2 vols. (Annapolis, MD: Naval Institute Press, 1989), vol. 1, 41–43, and Charles Henry Davis, *Life of Charles Henry Davis, Rear Admiral, 1807–1877* (Boston and New York: Houghton Mifflin, 1899).

3. ORN, I, 23: 669; Walke *Naval Scenes*, 247–250; John D. Milligan, *Gunboats Down the Mississippi* (Annapolis, MD: Naval Institute Press, 1965), 64–68; Bearss, *Hardluck Ironclad*, 56–57; Abbott, *Civil War*; Burpo, 271; Long, "Plum Point Bend," 10; Tucker, *Foote*, 194–195. At 4:00 P.M. in the afternoon of April 9, Flag Officer Foote departed the Western Flotilla for the North on sick leave, temporarily turning the unit over to Capt. Davis. Foote would never re-

turn (ORN, I, 23: 669; Tucker, *Foote*, 195–196). That night, Com. Montgomery presided over a CRDF council of war aboard the flagboat *Little Rebel*, attended by Missouri State Guard commander Brig. Gen. M. Jeff Thompson. It was at this confab that the Rebel captains decided to attack the Federal mortar boat and its ironclad guardian the next morning (Bearss, *Hardluck Ironclad*, 57; Gillespie, "Novel Experiment," 38; Campbell, "Recent Addresses," 87–88).

4. ORN, I, 23: 14–19, 54–57, 669, 677; OR, I, 10: 888–890; Deck Logbook of the U.S.S. *Carondelet*, May 10–June 5, 1862, Deck Logbooks of the U.S.S. *Carondelet*, May 1862–June 1865 (Records of the Bureau of Ships, Record Group 19, U.S. National Archives and Records Service), cited hereafter as *Carondelet* Logbook, with date; *Cincinnati Times*, May 16, 1862; *St. Louis Daily Missouri Democrat*, May 17, 1862; *Memphis Daily Appeal*, May 13, 1862; Eliot Callender, "What a Boy Saw on the Mississippi River," in vol. 1 of *Military Essays and Recollections: Papers Read before the Illinois Commandery, Military Order of the Loyal Legion of the United States* (Chicago: A.C. McClurg, 1891), 60–63; Walke, "The Western Flotilla," B& L, vol. 1, 447–449; Walke, *Naval Scenes*, 249–272; Abbott, *Civil War*, 272–273; Davis, Papers, 223–227; Burpo, "Notes of First Fleet," 271–273; Campbell, "Recent Addresses," 88–91; Bearss, *Hardluck Ironclad*, 57–63; H. Allen Gosnell, *Guns on the Western Waters: The Story of the River Gunboats in the Civil War* (Baton Rouge: Louisiana State University Press, 1949), 89–91; Long, "Plum Point Bend," 11–12; Gillespie, "Novel Experiment," 38–39; Alfred T. Mahan, *The Navy in the Civil War*, vol. 3, *The Gulf and Inland Waters* (New York: Scribner's, 1883), 45; Coombe, *Thunder Along the Mississippi*, 123–125; Jay Monaghan, *Swamp Fox of the Confederacy: The Life and Military Service of M. Jeff Thompson* (Tuscaloosa: University of Alabama Press, 1956), 52; Tucker, *Foote*, 196; Milligan, *Gunboats Down the Mississippi*, 64–67; Jay Slagle, *Ironclad Captain: Seth Ledyard Phelps and the U.S. Navy* (Kent, OH: Kent State University Press, 1996), 219–225; Browne, *From the Fresh Water Navy*, 74–77. Once again, in preparing his memoirs, Rear Adm. Walke was able to make use of the *Carondelet*'s decklogs for the period; these volumes are not currently held by the National Archives.

5. ORN, I, 23:114–141, 218, 671, 674, 679, 684; *Carondelet* Logbook, June 6, 1862; *Memphis Daily Argus*, June 6, 1862; *Chicago Daily Tribune*, June 10, 1862; *Cincinnati Daily Commercial*, June 11, 1862; *New York Tribune*, June 11, 1862; *St. Louis Daily Missouri Democrat*, June 10–11, 17–18, 1862; *Charleston Daily Courier*, June 17, 1862; Mahan, *Inland Waters*, 48–49; Milligan, *Gunboats Down the Mississippi* 73–77; Coombe, *Thunder Along the Mississippi*, 130–135; Charles B. Boynton, *History of the Navy During the Rebellion*, 2 vols. (New York: D. Appleton, 1867–1868), vol. 1, 573–574; Walke, "The Western Flotilla," B& L, vol. 1, 449–452; Walke, *Naval Scenes*, 277–297; Slagle, *Ironclad Captain*, 233–241; Warren D. Crandall and Isaac D. Newell, *History of the Ram Fleet and Mississippi Marine Brigade* (St. Louis, MO: Buschart Brothers, 1907), 60–80; Chester G. Hearn, *Ellet's Brigade: The Strangest Outfit of All* (Baton Rouge: Louisiana State University Press, 2000), 27–42; Alfred W. Ellet, "Ellet and His Steam Rams at Memphis," *B&L*, vol. 1, 456–459, cited hereafter as B&L, followed by a comma, the volume number in Roman numerals, a comma, and the page numbers; Charles C. Coffin, *My Days and Nights on the Battlefield: A Book for Boys* (Boston: Ticknor and Fields, 1864), 291–311; Browne, *Four Years in Secessia*, 187; Charles Dana Gibson, with E. Kay Gibson, *Assault and Logistics*, vol. 2, *Union Army Coastal and River Operations, 1861–1866* (Camden, ME: Ensign Press, 1995), 111–115; Campbell, "Recent Addresses," 91–98; Bearss, *Hardluck Ironclad*, 64–76. At about the same time Com. Montgomery was fashioning the CRDF, engineer Charles Ellet approached Federal secretary of war Edwin Stanton with his ideas for a highly maneuverable ram fleet. Alerted by intelligence to Confederate ram-building activities at New Orleans, Stanton commissioned Ellet and ordered him to find and convert river steamers to the purpose he proposed. Eight were duly ready and at Fort Pillow by May 25; Ellett was ready for action and had authority to operate his Mississippi Marine Brigade as an autonomous War Department command (ORN, I, 23: 29–36; Ellet, "Ellet and His Steam Rams," *B&L*, vol. 1, 453–456; Campbell, "Recent Addresses," 92; Bearss, *Hardluck Ironclad*, 66; Hearn, *Ellet's Brigade*, 11–26).

Chapter 8

1. U.S. Navy Department, *Official Records of the Union and Confederate Navies in the War of the Rebellion*, 31 vols. (Washington, DC: GPO, 1894–1922), Series I, Vol. 18, 647–652, 716, 729, cited hereafter as ORN, followed by a comma, the series number in Roman numerals, a comma, the volume number in Arabic, a colon, and the page in Arabic; ORN, I, 23: 210, 234, 243; ORN, II, 1: 782–783; U.S. War Department, *The War of the Rebellion: A Compilation of the Official Records of the Union and Confederate Armies*, 128 vols. (Washington, DC: GPO, 1880–1901), Series I, Vol. 19: 37, 41, cited hereafter as OR, followed by a comma, the series number in Roman numerals, a comma, the volume number in Arabic, any part number in Arabic, a colon, and the page in Arabic; Isaac Newton Brown, "The Confederate Gun-Boat *Arkansas*," in *Battles and Leaders of the Civil War*, ed. Robert V. Johnson and Clarence C. Buel, 4 vols. (New York: Century, 1884–1887, reprt. Thomas Yoseloff, 1956), vol. 3, 572; Cynthia E. Moseley, "The Naval Career of Henry Kennedy Stevens as Revealed in His Letters, 1839–1863," (master's thesis, University of North Carolina, 1951), 303–306; George W. Gift, "The Story of the *Arkansas*," *Southern Historical Society Papers* 8 (1884), 48–49; John D. Milligan, *Gunboats Down the Mississippi* (Annapolis, MD: Naval Institute Press, 1965), 82; Harriet Castlen, *Hope Bids Me Onward* (Savannah: Chatham, 1945), 63–64; Charles W. Read, "Reminiscences of the Confederate States Navy," *Southern Historical Society Papers* 1 (1876), 349–353; *Philadelphia Inquirer*, July 25, 1862; Kevin Carson, "21 Days to Glory: The Saga of the Confederate Ram *Arkansas*," *Sea Classics* 34 (July 2006), 38–40; Spencer C. Tucker, *Blue & Gray Navies: The Civil War Afloat* (Annapolis, MD: Naval Institute, 2006), 210; Ivan Musicant, *Divided Waters: The Naval History of the Civil War* (New York: HarperCollins, 1995), 248; William N. Still, *Iron Afloat: The Story of the Confederate Armorclads* (Nashville: Vanderbilt University Press, 1971; reprt., University of South Carolina Press, 1985), 62–66; John Johnson, "Story of the Confederate Armored Ram *Arkansas*," *Southern Historical Society Papers* 1 (1905), 1–4; Mary Emerson Branch, "The Story Behind the Story of the *Arkansas* and the *Carondelet*," *Missouri Historical Review* 79 (1985), 322; Daniel Barnhart, Jr., "Junkyard Ironclad," *Civil War Times Illustrated* 40 (May 2001), 30–35, 37; J. Thomas Scharf, *History of the Confederate Navy from Its Organization to the Surrender of Its Last Vessel* (New York: Rodgers and Sherwood, 1887; reprt., New York: Fairfax Press, 1977), 306–309; Henry Walke, *Naval Scenes and Reminiscences of the Civil War in the United States on the Southern and Western Waters during the Years 1861, 1862 and 1863 with the History of That Period Compared and Corrected from Authentic Sources* (New York: F.R. Reed, 1877), 302–304; R. Thomas Campbell, *Confederate Naval Forces on Western Waters* (Jefferson, NC: McFarland, 2005), 103–111; Jack D. Coombe, *Thunder Along the Mississippi: The River Battles That Split the Confederacy* (New York: Bantam, 1996), 151–154. Although our purpose here has not been to tell the valiant story of the *Arkansas*'s construction, which we leave to those cited in the footnotes, we do pay tribute to the men with little means who built the single most formidable Confederate warship to see service on the inland rivers. In justice, we provide minimal detail. Laid down with the aborted

Tennessee at Memphis by John T. Shirley in October 1861, the *Arkansas* was launched there on April 25, 1862. Just a day or so before the arrival of the Federal fleet at Memphis, she was taken, under order of Secretary Mallory, for completion first to Greenwood, MS, and then to Yazoo City, where she was commissioned on May 26. The Yazoo River was then home to upwards of 30 steamboats that escaped the doomed Tennessee city. A 1,200-ton casemate armorclad with a ram bow built on a flat hull, the warship was seen as a "seagoing steamer ... built upon the most approved model...." Henry Bentley, in a lengthy *Philadelphia Inquirer* article on July 25, told Northern readers that her design was "a combination of the flat-bottomed boats of the West and the keel-built steamers designed for navigation in the ocean or deep inland waters." She was propelled by two independently acting screws seven feet in diameter that were to maneuver the boat in the absence of a rudder. Each four-bladed propeller was, said Bentley, powered by a shaft from an inefficient low-pressure engine. The cylinders were 24 inches in diameter and of seven-foot stroke. Although the screws, protected by a "network of iron rods" from logs and other debris, allowed great maneuverability, the 99 hp engines themselves were unreliable. Salvaged as they were from the steamer *Natchez*, these would, in the end, prove the vessel's Achilles heel. Sufficiently overhauled, the power plants initially allowed the *Arkansas* to be rated at 8 knots (4 knots against the current). A large single chimney protruded from the hurricane deck behind her small raised pilothouse. Protected by 18-inch dovetailed T-railroad plating bolted atop thick wood bulwarks and compressed cotton and timber casemating, the *Arkansas* was 165 feet long, ten feet shorter than the *Carondelet*. She had a 35-foot beam and an 11.6-foot depth of hold. Bentley's report was off a bit, calling her 180x60. Unlike the sloping protection of most of the other Confederate armorclads, her casemate sides were not slanted but stood perpendicular to the water. Her fore and aft shields, were, however, slanted. Iron also covered the stern and hurricane deck. Her cast-iron bow was shaped, bolted, and riveted into a nine-ton running beak that projected underwater as a battering ram four feet forward of the hull. There has been some discussion over the years as to the paint scheme of the *Arkansas*. After all, the *Carondelet* was painted black, as were many other Union vessels. In fact, the *Arkansas* was, as Donald Barnhart, Jr., tells us, a "dull brown" hue. One crewman confirmed that it was sort of a camouflage, which "could not been seen at a distance." Flag Officer Farragut later called it "chocolate."

2. ORN, I, 18: 584–585, 650, 675; ORN, I, 19: 4; ORN, I, 23: 130–131, 233, 243; OR, I, 15: 515; Deck Logbook of the U.S.S. *Carondelet*, July 1–13, 1862, Deck Logbooks of the U.S.S. *Carondelet*, May 1862–June 1865, Records of the Bureau of Ships, Record Group 19, U.S. National Archives and Records Service, cited hereafter as *Carondelet* Logbook, with date; *Chicago Daily Tribune*, July 9, 1862; *New York Times*, July 13, 1862; *Granada Appeal*, July 16, 23, 1862; *Philadelphia Inquirer*, July 16, 1862; *New Orleans Daily Delta*, July 22, 1862; *Cincinnati Daily Commercial*, July 17, 1862; *Vicksburg Daily Citizen*, June 20, 1862; Barnhart, "Junkyard Ironclad," 35; Milligan, ed., *From the Fresh Water Navy, 1861–1864*, 110; Isaac Newton Brown, "The Confederate Gun-Boat *Arkansas*," 572–574; Gift, *Arkansas*, 51; Coombe, *Thunder Along the Mississippi*, 234; Milligan, *Gunboats Down the Mississippi*; Michael B. Ballard, *Vicksburg: The Campaign That Opened the Mississippi* (Chapel Hill: University of North Carolina Press, 2004), 57; Scharf, *Confederate Navy*, 310–311; Campbell, "Recent Addresses," 110–112, 114–115; Charles H. Davis, *Life of Charles H. Davis, Rear Admiral, U.S.N.* (Boston: Houghton Mifflin, 1899), 262–263, 267–70; Chester G. Hearn, *Ellet's Brigade*, 46–47.

3. ORN, I, 19: 4, 6, 37–39, 44, 56, 60, 705; ORN, I, 23: 131, 244, 258, 636, 671, 685; OR, I, 15: 32; *New Orleans Daily Delta*, July 22, 1862; *New York Herald*, July 25, 1862; Junius Henri Browne, *Four Years in Secessia: Adventures Within and Beyond the Union Lines* (Hartford, CT: O.D. Case, 1865), 214; Thomas Williams, "Letters of General Thomas Williams, 1862," *American Historical Review* 14 (January 1909), 322–323; *Carondelet* Logbook, July 14–15, 1862; James R. Soley, "Naval Operations in the Vicksburg Campaign," *B&L*, vol. 3, 555; Barnhart, "Junkyard Ironclad," 35–36; Milligan, *Gunboats Down the Mississippi*; Silas B. Coleman and Paul Stevens, "A July Morning with the Rebel Ram *Arkansas*," *U. S. Naval Institute Proceedings* 88 (July 1962), 86; Scharf, *Confederate Navy*, 309–310; Musicant, *Divided Waters*, 249; Chester G. Hearn, *Ellet's Brigade: The Strangest Outfit of All* (Baton Rouge: Louisiana State University Press, 2000), 49–50; Campbell, "Recent Addresses," 113; Walke, *Naval Scenes*, 303–305. Supplementing formal reports, an unusually high number of participants wrote or offered for transcription accounts of the Yazoo river encounter between the *Arkansas* and the three Union steamers. In addition to those already noted aboard the Rebel armorclad, we are fortunate that Cmdr. Walke left us his impressions. In addition, and more to our point, Paymaster Coleman, also known in the ORN as William, was an eyewitness aboard the *Tyler*. In 1890, the Michigander revealed his unique view of the only major engagement between a timberclad and a Confederate armorclad for the Detroit chapter of the Loyal Legion of the United States. We have noted that version in the bibliography and quote here from a reprint.

4. ORN, I, 19: 36–39, 41, 68, 132; ORN, I, 23: 685–686; *Granada Appeal*, July 16, 23, 1862; *Philadelphia Inquirer*, July 22, 1862; *Chicago Daily Tribune*, July 22–23, 1862; *New York Herald*, July 25, 1862; *Philadelphia Inquirer*, July 22, 1862; *New Orleans Daily Delta*, July 22, 1862; *Jackson Mississippian*, July 15, 1862, quoted in *Columbus (Georgia) Daily Enquirer*, July 23, 1862; *Carondelet* Logbook, July 15, 1862; Coleman and Stevens, "July Morning," 86, 88; Gift, *Arkansas*, 51–54; Isaac Newton Brown, "The Confederate Gun-Boat *Arkansas*," 574–575; Gift, *Arkansas*, 50–54; Walke, *Naval Scenes*, 307–324; Soley, "Naval Operations in the Vicksburg Campaign"; Mary Emerson Branch, "A Story Behind the Story of the *Arkansas* and the *Carondelet*," *Missouri Historical Review* 79 (April 1985), 324–325; Samuel Carter III, *The Final Fortress: The Campaign for Vicksburg, 1862–1863* (New York: St. Martin's Press, 1980); Carson, "21 Days," 40; Chester G. Hearn, *Ellet's Brigade*, 51; Campbell, "Recent Addresses," 114–119; Tucker, *Foote*, 211; Jim Miles, *A River Unvexed: A History and Tour Guide of the Campaign for the Mississippi River* (Nashville: Rutledge Hill Press, 1994), 217; Samuel Carter III, *The Final Fortress: The Campaign for Vicksburg 1862–1863* (New York: St. Martin's Press, 1980), 69–70; Barnhart, "Junkyard Ironclad," 36; Robert G. Hartje, *Van Dorn: The Life and Times of a Confederate General* (Nashville: Vanderbilt University Press, 1967), 201; Charles S. Foltz, ed., *Surgeon of the Seas: The Adventures of Jonathan M. Foltz* (Indianapolis: Bobbs-Merrill, 1931), 247–248; James Duffy, *Lincoln's Admiral: The Civil War Campaigns of David Farragut* (Edison, NJ: Castle Books, 2006), 143–144; Michael B. Ballard, *Vicksburg: The Campaign That Opened the Mississippi* (Chapel Hill: University of North Carolina Press, 2004), 56–57; Musicant, 249–250; Milligan, *Gunboats Down the Mississippi*, 83–84; Junius Henri Browne, *Four Years in Secessia*, 214–217; William N. Still, *Iron Afloat*, 68; Coombe, *Thunder Along the Mississippi*, 155–156. Even the acerbic Walke originally admitted that Lt. Gwin sustained him "through the fight in a very gallant and effective manner" (ORN, I, 19: 41). Having enlisted at Lansingburg, New York, on April 24, 1861, Morrison joined the crew of the *Carondelet* on February 15, 1862. Honorably discharged on March 31, 1863, he returned to Brooklyn, New York. His CMH was awarded under General Order 59, June 22, 1865 ("John G. Morrison, Civil War Medal of Honor Recipient," American Civil War Website, http://americancivilwar.com/medal_of_honor6.html (accessed April 9, 2008).

5. ORN, I, 19: 37–40, 44, 56, 69–71, 686, 705; Isaac Newton Brown, "The Confederate Gun-Boat *Arkansas*," 575–576; *Granada Appeal*, July 16, 23, 1862; *St. Louis Missouri Daily Democrat*, July 22, 1862; *Cincinnati Times*, July 22, 1862; *Philadelphia Inquirer*, July 22, 25, 1862; *New York Herald*, July 25, 1862; *New Orleans Daily Delta*, July 22, 1862; *Vicksburg Evening Post*, July 1, 1961; Gift, *Ibid.;* Browne, 217–219; Coleman and Stevens, 86–89; Coombe, *Thunder Along the Mississippi*; Carter, *Final Fortress*, 70–71; William N. Still, *Iron Afloat*, 69–71; Barnhart, "Junkyard Ironclad"; Carson, "21 Days"; Davis, Papers, 263; Milligan, *Gunboats Down the Mississippi*, 84–85; Charles B. Boynton, *History of the Navy During the Rebellion*, 2 vols. (New York: D. Appleton, 1867–1868), vol. 2, 246; Branch, "Story Behind the Story"; William N. Still, *Iron Afloat*, 68–69; Castlen, 145–148; Musicant, *Divided Waters*, 250–252; Scharf, *Confederate Navy*, 312–315; Campbell, "Recent Addresses," 120–135. Paymaster Coleman of the *Tyler*, along with many others in the years since, paid high tribute to the *Arkansas*, frankly stating that there was "no pluckier exploit in the war." In the process, she disabled the *Carondelet* and "badly injured and all but sunk *Tyler*" before passing through the fleet "without material injury." The armorclad was eventually lost during the August 1862 campaign for Baton Rouge. Her weak engines failed and rather than surrender, her crew blew her up (Coleman and Stevens, "July Morning," 88–89; William N. Still, *Iron Afloat*, 76–78). The *Arkansas*, from the combined Federal return fire, lost 10 dead and 15 wounded. Although there was no "Thanks of Congress" for the Federal officers involved in this particular episode, the highest legislative accolade available to naval men on both sides was awarded to Lt. Isaac Brown. A joint resolution of appreciation was sent to the daring commander by the Confederate congress on October 2. Brown had been earlier promoted to the rank of commander (ORN, I, 19: 36).

6. ORN, I, 19: 15; ORN, I, 23: 37–38, 41, 260–263, 268, 270–272; *Carondelet* Logbook, July 15–August 5, 1862; Scott D. Jordan to wife, April 12, 1863, in *Civil War Letters of Scott D. Jordan, Produced for Eleanor Jordan West* (CD-ROM; Tucson: doug@bellnotes.com, 2007), cited hereafter as Jordan Letters, with date; *St. Louis Missouri Daily Democrat*, July 22, 1862; *Cincinnati Times*, July 22, 1862; *Philadelphia Inquirer*, July 22, 25, 1862; *Chicago Daily Tribune*, July 22–23, 1862; *New York Herald*, July 25, 1862; *New Orleans Daily Delta*, July 22, 1862; Gift, *Arkansas*, 53; Foltz, ed., *Surgeon of the Seas*, 248; Jay Slagle, *Ironclad Captain: Seth Ledyard Phelps and the U.S. Navy* (Kent, OH: Kent State University Press, 1996), 305; Walke, *Naval Scenes*, 300–305; Davis, Papers, 267–270; A.B. Donaldson to secretary of the navy (Charles F. Adams), June 28, 1929 (Files of the U.S. Naval Academy Museum, Annapolis, MD); William D. Puleston, Mahan (New Haven, CT: Yale University Press, 1939), 64–65; Alfred T. Mahan, *The Gulf and Inland Waters*, vol. 3, *The Navy in the Civil War* (New York: Scribner's, 1883), 99–100; Mahan, *Admiral Farragut* (New York: D. Appleton, 1895), 191; Musicant, *Divided Waters*, 249; William L. Shea and Terrence J. Winschel, *Vicksburg Is the Key: The Struggle for the Mississippi Valley* (Great Campaigns of the Civil War Series; Lincoln: University of Nebraska Press, 2003), 24; George Wright. "USS *Carondelet* vs. CSS *Arkansas*," Civil War Navy Messageboard, http://history-sites.com/cgi-bin/bbs53x/cwnavy/webbbs_config.pl?read=1580 (accessed April 4, 2009).

7. ORN, I, 23: 330, 351, 388, 395; *Carondelet* Logbook, August 24, 1862; Walke, *Naval Scenes*, 445. When her repairs were completed, the ordnance of the *Carondelet* included six 32-pdr., 42 cwt smoothbores; one 42-pdr., 80 cwt army rifle; four 8-inch, 63 cwt smoothbores; one each 30-pdr. and 50 pdr. Dahlgren rifles; and one 12-pdr. Dahlgren boat howitzer (ORN, II, 1: 52).

8. ORN, I, 23: 377; 388, 392, 395, 433; *Carondelet* Logbook, October 9, 15, 1862; Walke, *Naval Scenes* 328, 333; Gustavus Vasa Fox, *Confidential Correspondence of Gustavas Vasa Fox, Assistant Secretary of the Navy, 1861–1865*, ed. Robert M. Thompson and Richard Wainwright, 2 vols. (New York: Naval History Society, 1919; reprt., Freeport, NY: Books for Libraries, 1972), vol. 2, 140; Chester G. Hearn, *Admiral David Dixon Porter: The Civil War Years* (Annapolis, MD: Naval Institute Press, 1996), 150–151.

9. ORN, I, 23: 439–440, 489–490, 495, 507, 521, 546, 588–590, 597, 656; OR, I, 17, 2: 500; *Carondelet* Logbook, October 23–December 31, 1862; *St. Louis Missouri Daily Democrat*, December 30–31, 1862; David Dixon Porter, *Incidents and Anecdotes of the Civil War* (New York: Sherman, 1886), 127; Bruce Catton, *Grant Moves South* (Boston: Little, Brown, 1960), 336–337, 340, 342.

Chapter 9

1. U.S. Navy Department, *Official Records of the Union and Confederate Navies in the War of the Rebellion*, 31 vols. (Washington, DC: GPO, 1894–1922), Series I, Vol. 23: 597, cited hereafter as ORN, followed by a comma, the series number in Roman numerals, a comma, the volume number in Arabic, a colon, and the page in Arabic; Deck Logbook of the U.S.S. *Carondelet*, January 1, 1863, Deck Logbooks of the U.S.S. *Carondelet*, May 1862–June 1865 (Records of the Bureau of Ships, Record Group 19, U.S. National Archives and Records Service), cited hereafter as *Carondelet* Logbook, with date; *St. Louis Missouri Daily Democrat*, December 31, 1862.

2. ORN, I, 23: 589; *Carondelet* Logbook, January 1, 1863. On March 17, 1863, Fentress was named commander of the tinclad *Rattler*, with Bath as his executive officer. The subsequent career of the new light draught captain was exceptionally checkered.

3. *Carondelet* Logbook, January 2–4, 1863; David Dixon Porter, *Incidents and Anecdotes of the Civil War* (New York: Sherman, 1886), 123; Bruce Catton, *Grant Moves South* (Boston: Little, Brown, 1960), 343. In General Order No. 29 issued just after Walke's departure upriver, Porter indicated that burning wood would be necessary for the ironclads at that moment. Additionally, the contract transports were to supply tows, thereby allowing the big gunboats to conserve coal. A red flag would indicate the need for a tow. Increasingly, the new tinclads would also be required to provide this service (ORN, I, 24: 98–99).

4. ORN, I, 24: 142, 144–145, 147–148, 202; *Carondelet* Logbook, January 5–8, 1863; Thomas Lyons, *Anonymous Journal Kept on Board the U.S. Steam Gunboat Carondelet, Captain Henry Walke Commanding*, January 8, 1863 (Manuscript Division, Library of Congress), cited hereafter as *Anonymous Journal*. At Helena, the gunboat's diarist and captain's clerk, Thomas Lyons, "saw Capt. Wade of the steam transport *Swallow*"— the same Richard M. Wade who was replaced as the ironclad's first master prior to her passage of the Island No. 10 batteries the previous April (*Anonymous Journal*, January 8, 1863).

5. ORN, I, 24: 162–163, 511; Thomas Lyons, *Anonymous Journal*, January 8–16, 1862; *Carondelet* Logbook, January 9–16, 1862; Henry Walke, *Naval Scenes and Reminiscences of the Civil War in the United States on the Southern and Western Waters during the Years 1861, 1862 and 1863 with the History of That Period Compared and Corrected from Authentic Sources* (New York: F.R. Reed, 1877), 341; Thomas O. Selfridge, Jr., *Memoirs of Thomas O. Selfridge, Jr., Rear Admiral, U.S. N.* (New York: G. Putnam, 1924), 76. Seventeen years earlier an observer named Thomas Bangs Thorpe described snags in an interesting travel volume. The writer related that some trees became attached to the bottom of the river. Because of their buoyancy and the strong river current, these would constantly surface and submerge, waving "upward and downward with the gracefulness of motion which would not disgrace a beau of the old school." Some

steamboats passed over these "sawyers," but many were not so lucky. It was recorded that once the snag hit an oncoming boat — usually with disastrous consequences— it would often rise above the wreck, "shake the dripping water from its forked limbs, and sink again, as if rejoicing in its strength." There was no way to guard against these "sawyers" since the timing of their appearance was totally unpredictable. (Thomas Bangs Thorpe, *The Mysteries of the Backwoods; or, Sketches of the Southeast, Including Character, Scenery, and Rural Sports* [Philadelphia, PA: Carey & Hart, 1846], 173–174).

6. ORN, I, 22: 551; ORN, I, 23: 117, 417, 424, 588; ORN, I, 24: 131, 137, 149, 193, 195–196, 467, 645–646, 649; *Carondelet* Logbook, January 17–25, 1863; Thomas Lyons, *Anonymous Journal*, January 17–18, 1863; *St. Louis Daily Missouri Democrat*, January 13–19, 1863; Walke, *Naval Scenes*, 379; Roy Basler, chief, Manuscript Division, Reference Department, Library of Congress, to writer, March 14, 1969. Shortly after his transfer to the *Lafayette*, Capt. Walke sent a "meritorious service list" to Acting Rear Adm. Porter. Despite his reputation for sometimes harsh treatment of his crew, Walke was always fairly lavish in his praise of those sailors he considered outstanding. It has been said that he was even more fair toward his men than the likes of Porter or Farragut. Eight petty officers and seaman, with Walke since the commissioning of the *Carondelet* over a year before, were pictured as having "faithfully, valiantly, and efficiently served their country" aboard the ironclad. Michael Reilly, James Whalen, Charles Wilson, George Midlam, John Ford, Thomas White, John G. Morrison, and Matthew Arthur (sometimes called Arnold) were singled out for notice by Congress under section seven of the July 1862 Navy Act, the section which began "To Further Promote the Efficiency of the Navy." Of the eight, the last two were awarded the Congressional Medal of Honor. In his memoirs, Walke wrongly blamed this small percentage on the negligence and bad judgment of his first full-time successor, a man with a hybrid navy-army past (ORN, I, 24: 193; Walke, *Naval Scenes*, 399–400; U.S. Congress, Senate, Committee on Veteran's Affairs, *Medal of Honor, 1863–1968: "In the Name of the Congress of the United States,"* 90th Cong., 2nd sess. (Washington, DC: GPO, 1968), 12–275; William E. Geoghegan, Museum Specialist, Division of Transportation, Smithsonian Institution, to writer, February 18, 1970.

7. ORN, I, 23: 645–646, 649; *St. Louis Missouri Daily Democrat*, December 9 and 27, 1862; *New York Herald*, December 19–20, 1862. In volumes dealing with the river war, in correspondence, and in the army and navy *Official Records*, Murphy is referred to as either J. McLeod Murphy or just McLeod Murphy. This writer, however, prefers to employ his entire name. Murphy was very proud of his men, men of the type badly needed in the Mississippi Squadron. To Porter, he extolled their virtues, pointing out that they could "patch a boiler, drive an engine, point a hawser, reeve a tackle, make a splice, fit a gun-breeching, pull an oar, feel a tree, dig a trench, shoe a horse, or do anything else that may be required." Additionally, "they have been baptized by the fire of 12 battles." Porter, who also did not know that Brennand was able to get the *Carondelet* away as quickly as he did, expected that the Pook turtle would be at Cairo, where Murphy could join her. Another month would pass, however, before Murphy could reach the ironclad (ORN, I, 23: 535, 645; ORN, I, 24: 131, 197, 324–325, 545).

8. ORN, I, 23: 645; ORN, I, 24: 207, 446–447. John McLeod Murphy was a man of many talents and author of a remarkable career. Born on Long Island in 1827, he entered the U.S. Naval Academy as a midshipman in early 1841. Eight years later, he and W N. Jeffers coauthored *Nautical Routine and Stowage, with Short Rules in Navigation* for the New York publisher N. Spear. After wide circulation in naval circles, it was reissued in 1861 by D. Van Nostrand and was passed out as an item of required reading by new naval officers, regular and volunteer alike. In 1851, the passed midshipman was detailed as hydrographic assistant on Maj. John G. Barnard's survey of the Isthmus of Tehuantepec. Murphy resigned from the sea service the following year to enter into a civilian career as a surveyor and engineer. Three years later, he was named surveyor of New York City. As his heart was still with ships and the sea, Murphy quit this position a year later to become the civilian constructing engineer at the Brooklyn Navy Yard. In 1860, friends persuaded him to try his luck in politics; and in the fall elections, he won a seat in the New York State senate. While performing his duties in Albany, he wrote (alone) *American Ships and Ship-building* for the New York publisher C.W. Baker. After Fort Sumter, he resigned his seat to serve as colonel of the 15th Regiment, New York Volunteer Engineers. With this rank and force, the former naval officer saw hard service with the Army of the Potomac, especially during the Peninsular Campaign. His December 1862 letter to Acting Rear Adm. Porter, supported by letters of reference from Capt. Henry A. Wise of the Navy's Ordnance Bureau, and Rear Adm. Andrew Hull Foote, former inland navy chief, resulted in his seconding to the *Carondelet*. Acting Volunteer Lt. Murphy relinquished command of the gunboat on 1 September and resigned his commission 30 July 1864. He returned to New York City, resumed his profession as a civil engineer, married, and had four children. Murphy was a frequent contributor to the newspaper and periodical press on subjects connected with his specialty. The apparent victim of a heart attack, Murphy died at his New York City home on June 2, 1871. In its obituary of him, the *New York Times* honored the 44-year old as "a brave, benevolent, and gifted man" ("John McCleod Murphy," in James Wilson and John Fiske, eds., *Appleton's Cyclopedia of American Biography*, 6 vols. (New York: D. Appleton, 1888), vol. 4, 466–467; *New York Times*, June 2, 1871). Henry Walke did not like Murphy, or any of the more ambitious volunteer officers for that matter. He styled Murphy as a man "of political fame." In his memoirs, the *Carondelet*'s first commander was particularly critical of his successor in relation to the Medal of Honor business cited in footnote 6 above (Walke, *Naval Scenes*, 348, 378, 399–400).

9. ORN, I, 24: 208, 211, 244, 321, 324–325, 351, 431; *Carondelet* Logbook, February 3, 5–6, 8, 1863; Thorpe, *Mysteries of the Backwoods*, 172; Alfred T. Mahan, *The Gulf and Inland Waters*, 141, 144–147; U.S. War Department, *The War of the Rebellion: A Compilation of the Official Records of the Union and Confederate Armies*, 128 vols. (Washington, DC: GPO, 1880–1901), Series I, Vol. 24, Pt. 1: 37, cited hereafter as OR, followed by a comma, the series number in Roman numerals, a comma, the volume number in Arabic, any part number in Arabic, a colon, and the page in Arabic; John D. Milligan, *Gunboats Down the Mississippi* (Annapolis, MD: Naval Institute Press, 1965), 132–135. About this time, Acting Rear Adm. Porter sent a report to Navy Secretary Gideon Welles praising the "old Pook turtles," including the *Carondelet*. Despite the fact that they were "fast wearing out," these City Series boats were more serviceable than the new ironclads *Indianola* and *Chillicothe*. Except for the obvious value of the 11-inch guns they mounted, many believed the newer craft would fail under fire. In both cases, history would prove their critics correct (ORN, I, 24: 322).

10. ORN, I, 24: 187, 207, 442–443, 452; *Carondelet* Logbook, February 18, 1863; Walke, *Naval Scenes*, 348.

11. ORN, I, 24: 453; *Carondelet* Logbook, March 4, 1863; Scott D. Jordan to wife, April 12, 1863, in *Civil War Letters of Scott D. Jordan, Produced for Eleanor Jordan West* (CD-ROM; Glendale, AZ: doug@bellnotes.com, 2007), cited hereafter as Jordan Letters, with date; Porter, Papers, 145. Gibson, Caven, Donaldson, Gunner Beauford, and Miller were all promoted by Capt. Walke on December 8, 1862. Miller would eventually replace Gibson as acting master; in fact, he would be in command of the ironclad during her last offensive action of the war, the fight with the Bell's Mills

batteries at Nashville in December 1864 (ORN, I, 26: 643–644). An Atlantic Ocean mariner from 1847 to 1852 and a farmer until Fort Sumter, Scott D. Jordan (1825–1899) of Cape Elizabeth, Maine, was appointed an acting ensign effective April 22, 1863. Like many Civil War gunboatmen, he would maintain an active correspondence with his family (primarily his wife, Judith) at home through his honorable discharge on November 22, 1865. After the Civil War he returned to farming and, in the 1870s, patented a pie rack that he sold around New England. His gunboat letters, written mostly aboard the *Carondelet*, were saved by the family and collected by his great-granddaughter, Eleanor Jordan West; they were transcribed and, with the help of Ensign Jordan's great great-grandson Douglas Bell, were printed and burned onto CD-ROMs to be passed to family members and other interested parties. Late in 2008, a copy made its way to this writer (Edward W. Callahan, *List of Officers of the Navy of the United States and of the Marine Corps, from 1775 to 1900, Comprising a Complete Register of All Present and Former Commissioned, Warranted, and Appointed Officers of the United States Navy, and of the Marine Corps, Regular and Volunteer, Compiled from the Official Records of the Navy Department* (New York: L.R. Hamersly, 1901; reprt., New York: Haskell House, 1969), 304.

Chapter 10

1. Richard S. West, Jr., "Gunboats in the Swamps: the Yazoo Pass Expedition," *Civil War History*, 9 (June 1963), 157–166; Francis V. Green, *The Mississippi*, vol. 8 of Campaigns of the Civil War (New York: Scribner's, 1883), 91–97; David Dixon Porter, *Incidents and Anecdotes of the Civil War* (New York: Sherman, 1885), 144–145; Ulysses G. Grant, *Personal Memoirs of U.S. Grant*, 2 vols. (New York: C.L. Webster, 1885–1886; reprt. [2 vols. in 1], New York: Penguin, 1999), vol. 1, 437–452; Samuel Carter III, *The Final Fortress: The Campaign for Vicksburg, 1862–1863* (New York: St. Martin's, 1980), 140; William L. Shea and Terrence J. Winschel, *Vicksburg Is the Key: The Struggle for the Mississippi Valley* (Great Campaigns of the Civil War Series; Lincoln: University of Nebraska Press, 2003), 72; Chester G. Hearn, *Admiral David Dixon Porter: The Civil War Years* (Annapolis, MD: Naval Institute Press, 1996),178–179; Michael B. Ballard, *Vicksburg: The Campaign That Opened the Mississippi* (Chapel Hill: University of North Carolina Press, 2004), 184.

2. U.S. Navy Department, *Official Records of the Union and Confederate Navies in the War of the Rebellion*, 31 vols. (Washington, DC: GPO, 1894–1922), Series I, Vol. 24: 474, cited hereafter as ORN, followed by a comma, the series number in Roman numerals, a comma, the volume number in Arabic, a colon, and the page in Arabic; Porter, Papers, 137; Carter, *Final Fortress*, 141; Shea and Winschel, *Vicksburg Is the Key*; *New York Times*, April 16, 1863. Franc B. Wilkie, who signed his accounts "Galway," wrote the clearest press reports of the naval aspects of the Steele's Bayou campaign. His dispatches and memoirs provide extensive information, e.g., see *Pen and Powder* (Boston: 1888), 306–310.

3. ORN, I, 20: 7; ORN, I, 24: 479; U.S. War Department, *The War of the Rebellion: A Compilation of the Official Records of the Union and Confederate Armies*, 128 vols. (Washington, DC: GPO, 1880–1901), Series I, Vol. 24, Pt. 1: 21, cited hereafter as OR, followed by a comma, the series number in Roman numerals, a comma, the volume number in Arabic, any part number in Arabic, a colon, and the page in Arabic; Alfred T. Mahan, *The Gulf and Inland Waters*, 147; Chester G. Hearn, *Admiral David Dixon Porter*, 183–184; Jack D. Coombe, *Thunder Along the Mississippi: The River Battles That Split the Confederacy* (New York: Bantam, 1996), 209; William L. Shea and Terrence J. Winschel, *Vicksburg Is the Key*; Ballard, *Vicksburg*.

4. ORN, I, 24: 681, 687; OR, I, 24, 3, 112, 123; Henry R. Browne and Symmes E. Browne, *From the Fresh Water Navy, 1861–1864: Letters of Acting Master's Mate Henry R. Browne and Acting Ensign Symmes E. Browne*, edited by John D. Milligan, vol. 3 (Naval Letters Series; Annapolis, MD: Naval Institute Press, 1970), 155; Chester G. Hearn, *Admiral David Dixon Porter*, 185–186; Ulysses G. Grant, *Personal Memoirs of U.S. Grant*, vol. 1, 453; Ballard, *Vicksburg*, 185; Shea and Winschel, *Vicksburg Is the Key*; Porter, Papers, 137; Deck Logbook of the U.S.S. *Carondelet*, March 13, 1863, Deck Logbooks of the U.S.S. *Carondelet*, May 1862–June 1865 (Records of the Bureau of Ships, Record Group 19, U.S. National Archives and Records Service), cited hereafter as *Carondelet* Logbook, with date.

5. ORN, I, 24: 474–475, 480–481, 493, 687; OR, I, 24, 3: 112; *Carondelet* Logbook, April 14–16, 1863; Mahan, *Inland Waters*, 148; William T. Sherman, *Memoirs of General W.T. Sherman, Written by Himself*, 2 vols. (New York: Appleton, 1875; reprt., Penguin Classics. New York: Penguin Books, 2000), vol. 1, 307; Carter, *Final Fortress*; Bruce Catton, *Grant Moves South* (Boston: Little, Brown, 1960), 385; *New York Times*, April 4, 16, 1863; Porter, Papers, 153–154; Ulysses G. Grant, *Personal Memoirs of U.S. Grant*; William H.C. Michael, "How the Mississippi Was Opened," *Civil War Sketches and Incidents; Papers Read before the Nebraska Commandery, Military Order of the Loyal Legion of the United States* (Omaha: The Commandery, 1902), 45; (34–58); Chester G. Hearn, *Admiral David Dixon Porter*, 187; Ballard, *Vicksburg*; Coombe, *Thunder Along the Mississippi*, 209–210; Shea and Winschel, *Vicksburg Is the Key*, 73; John D. Milligan, "Expedition into the Bayous," *Civil War Times Illustrated* 15 (January 1977), 16.

6. ORN, I, 24: 479, 493–494; OR, I, 24, 1: 432, 465–466; OR, I, 24, 3: 675–676; *Carondelet* Logbook, March 17–18, 1863; Ulysses G. Grant, *Personal Memoirs of U.S. Grant*, 154; Carter, *Final Fortress*, 142–145; Porter, Papers, 148; *New York Times*, April 16, 1863; Shea and Winschel, *Vicksburg Is the Key*; Michael, "How the Mississippi Was Opened," 46; Ballard, *Vicksburg*, 186; Chester G. Hearn, *Admiral David Dixon Porter*, 188; Coombe, *Thunder Along the Mississippi*; Mahan, *Inland Waters*, 149; Porter, Papers, 155–156; John D. Milligan, *Gunboats*, 16–17.

7. ORN, I, 24: 475–476, 688; OR, I, 24, 1: 465–466; *Carondelet* Logbook, March 19, 1863; *New York Times*, April 16, 1863; Chester G. Hearn, *Admiral David Dixon Porter*, 189. That night, Capt. Murphy returned to his ironclad, leaving the mound's defense to one of his ensigns. Upon his arrival, he found Porter sending off a message to Maj. Gen. Sherman asking the latter to "come to [my] rescue as quickly as possible." Its delivery was entrusted to the admiral's personal secretary, Charles Guild (Sherman, *Memoirs*, vol. 1, 308).

8. OR, I, 24, 1: 458, 466–467; ORN, I, 24: 459, 476, 494, 688; *New York Times*, April 16, 1863; *Carondelet* Logbook, March 20, 1863; Shea and Winschel, *Vicksburg Is the Key*, 74; Chester G. Hearn, *Admiral David Dixon Porter*; Carter, *Final Fortress*, 146–147; Ballard, *Vicksburg*; Coombe, *Thunder Along the Mississippi*; John D. Milligan, "Expedition into the Bayous," 17–18; Porter, Papers, 160–161. As the fleet withdrew, some of Featherston's artillery was mounted atop Murphy's mound. Downriver, Maj. Gen. Sherman, hearing the fire, thought the "booming more frequent than seemed consistent with mere guerrilla operations" (William T. Sherman, *Memoirs*).

9. OR, I, 24, 1: 250, 432–440, 459–460, 466–467; OR, I, 24, 3: 152, 701; ORN, I, 24: 477, 488–489, 495, 688; ORN, I, 25: 29; *Carondelet* Logbook, March 21–27, 1863; *New York Times*, April 4, 16, 1863; *Chicago Daily Tribune*, April 4,1863; Shea and Winschel, *Vicksburg Is the Key*, 74–75, 90–91; Ballard, *Vicksburg*, 186–187; Chester G. Hearn, *Admiral David Dixon Porter*, 190–192, 207–208; Carter, *Fuinal Fortress*, 147–149; Coombe, *Thunder Along the Mississippi*, 210–211; Porter, Papers, 163–165; William T. Sherman, *Memoirs*,

309–310; Michael, "How the Mississippi Was Opened," 48; John D. Milligan, "Expedition into the Bayous," 19–21; Green, *The Mississippi*, 178; James R. Soley, *Admiral Porter* (New York: D. Appleton, 1903), 311; Edwin C. Bearss and Warren E. Grabau, "How Porter's Flotilla Ran the Gauntlet Past Vicksburg," *Civil War Times Illustrated* 1 (December 1962), 38 (38–47); James R. Arnold, "Rough Work on the Mississippi," *Naval History* 13, no. 5 (1999), 38 (38–43). In his response to Grant, Porter pointed out that, once below, the heavy ironclads would not be able to return upstream against the current. Porter's other concerns regarding logistics and fleet composition were expressed in a letter to navy assistant secretary Gustavus Vasa Fox, but an added spur to action came directly from navy secretary Welles, who wrote quite bluntly: "The Department wishes you to occupy the river below Vicksburg..." (OR, I, 24: 1: 25; OR, I, 24, 3: 151–152; Gustavus Vasa Fox, *Confidential Correspondence of Gustavas Vasa Fox, Assistant Secretary of the Navy, 1861–1865*, ed. Robert M. Thompson and Richard Wainwright, 2 vols. [New York: Naval History Society, 1919; reprt., Freeport, NY: Books for Libraries, 1972], vol. 2, 172; ORN, I, 24: 520, 552).

10. ORN, I, 24: 521, 553–555, 690; OR, I, 24, 2: 336–337; OR, I, 24, 3: 688; *Carondelet* Logbook, April 10–15, 1863; Chester G. Hearn, *Admiral David Dixon Porter*, 208–209; Arnold, "Rough Work," 39–41; Edwin C. Bearss, *The Campaign for Vicksburg*, 3 vols. (Dayton: Morningside, 1986), vol. 2, 64; Ballard, *Vicksburg*, 197–198; Coombe, *Thunder Along the Mississippi*, 211–213; Bearss and Grabau, "Porter's Flotilla," 39–41.

11. ORN, I, 24: 521, 553–555, 561–567, 682, 690, 717; *Carondelet* Logbook, April 16–17, 1863; *New York Times*, April 23, 1863; *National Tribune*, January 20, 1887; Henry Walke, *Naval Scenes and Reminiscences of the Civil War in the United States on the Southern and Western Waters during the Years 1861, 1862 and 1863 with the History of That Period Compared and Corrected from Authentic Sources* (New York: F.R. Reed, 1877), 354–355, 363; James T. Hogane, "Reminiscences of the Siege of Vicksburg," *Southern Historical Society Papers* 11 (April-May 1883), 4854–4886; Chester G. Hearn, *Admiral David Dixon Porter*, 209–219; Charles Heckman "Heck" Gulick, "Letters from 'Heck,'" ed. Stan Hamper, *Civil War Times Illustrated* 21 (June 1982), 24–26 (24–31); Shea and Winschel, *Vicksburg Is the Key*, 98–100; Arnold, "Rough Work," 41–42; Bearss, *The Campaign for Vicksburg*, vol. 2, 64–74; Coombe, *Thunder Along the Mississippi*, 213–214; Bearss and Grabau, "Porter's Flotilla," 40–46; Ballard, *Vicksburg*, 199–202; Peter F. Walker, *Vicksburg: A People at War, 1860–1865* (Chapel Hill: University of North Carolina Press, 1960), 151–152; James R. Soley, "Naval Operations in the Vicksburg Campaign," in *Battles and Leaders of the Civil War*, ed. Robert V. Johnson and Clarence C. Buel, 4 vols. (New York: Century, 1884–1887, reprt. Thomas Yoseloff, 1956), vol. 3, 566 .

12. ORN, I, 24: 606–609, 612, 626–628, 682–683; OR, I, 24, 1: 27–28, 79–82, 142, 663–664; OR, I, 24, 3: 204–205, 211, 221, 225–226, 228, 231, 237–238; *Carondelet* Logbook, April 22–28, 1863; Walke, *Naval Scenes*, 366, 372–373; Shea and Winschel, *Vicksburg Is the Key*, 100–103; Charles A. Dana, *Recollections of the Civil War* (New York: D. Appleton, 1898), 41–42; Soley, "Navy in the Vicksburg Campaign," *B&L*, vol. 3, 567; Ulysses G. Grant, *Personal Memoirs of U.S. Grant*, vol. 1, 395; Mahan, *Inland Waters*, 158–159; Arnold, "Rough Work," 43; Ballard, *Vicksburg*, 214–217; Coombe, *Thunder Along the Mississippi*, 215; Chester G. Hearn, *Admiral David Dixon Porter*, 220–223; Bearss, *The Campaign for Vicksburg*, vol. 2, 271–274, 277; Bearss, "Grand Gulf's Role in the Civil War," *Civil War History* 5 (March 1959), 20–22 (5–29). To help prevent the reinforcement of Grand Gulf, Maj. Gen. Sherman, with support from the squadron's upper division, conducted a two-day feint up the Yazoo (Shea and Winschel, *Vicksburg Is the Key*, 102–103).

13. ORN, I, 24: 607–628, 684, 690, 699, 702; OR, I, 24, 1, 142, 574–576; OR, I, 24, 3: 792–793, 797, 800; *Carondelet* Logbook, April 29, 1863; Scott D. Jordan to wife, May 28, 1863, in *Civil War Letters of Scott D. Jordan, Produced for Eleanor Jordan West* (CD-ROM; Glendale, AZ: doug@bellnotes.com, 2007), cited hereafter as Jordan Letters, with date; Walke, 374–376; Coombe, *Thunder Along the Mississippi*, 215–216; Ballard, *Vicksburg*, 218–219; Shea and Winschel, *Vicksburg Is the Key*, 102–105; Mahan, *Inland Waters*, 160–162; Ulysses G. Grant, *Personal Memoirs of U.S. Grant*, vol. 1, 396–397; Dana, *Recollections*, 43; Arnold, "Rough Work,"; Chester G. Hearn, *Admiral David Dixon Porter*, 223–225; Bearss, *The Campaign for Vicksburg*, vol. 2, 285–289; Bearss, "Grant Gulf's Role," 23–27; *Pine Bluff (MS) Commercial*, December 17, 1904.

14. ORN, I, 24: 626–627; OR, I, 24, 1: 663–666; OR, I, 24, 3: 816; *Carondelet* Logbook, April 30–July 4, 1863; Walke, 374–378; Ulysses G. Grant, *Personal Memoirs of U.S. Grant*, vol. 1, 409–410; Shea and Winschel, *Vicksburg Is the Key*, 106–108; Ballard, *Vicksburg*; Bearss, *The Campaign for Vicksburg*, vol. 2, 311–314; Bearss, "Grant Gulf's Role," 27–28.

Chapter 11

1. U.S. Navy Department, *Official Records of the Union and Confederate Navies in the War of the Rebellion*, 31 vols. (Washington, DC: GPO, 1894–1922), Series I, Vol. 24: 672, cited hereafter as ORN, followed by a comma, the series number in Roman numerals, a comma, the volume number in Arabic, a colon, and the page in Arabic; ORN, I, 25: 124–125; Scott D. Jordan to wife, May 16, 1863, in *Civil War Letters of Scott D. Jordan, Produced for Eleanor Jordan West* (CD-ROM; Glendale, AZ: doug@bellnotes.com, 2007), cited hereafter as Jordan Letters, with date; Deck Logbook of the U.S.S. *Carondelet*, May 15, 1863, Deck Logbooks of the U.S.S. *Carondelet*, May 1862–June 1, 1865 (Records of the Bureau of Ships, Record Group 19, U.S. National Archives and Records Service), cited hereafter as *Carondelet* Logbook, with date; *Chicago Daily Tribune*, November 22, 1863; Richard E. Beringer, Herman Hattaway, Archer Jones, and William N. Still, Jr., *Why the South Lost the Civil War* (Athens: University of Georgia Press, 1986), 191–192; Gary D. Joiner, *Mr. Lincoln's Brown Water Navy: The Mississippi Squadron* (Lanham, MD: Rowman and Littlefield, 2007), 173; David Dixon Porter, *Naval History of the Civil War* (New York: Sherman, 1886; reprt., Secaucus, NJ: Castle, 1984), 339. The district scheme was first modified in mid–August, when a new disposition was announced: DISTRICT # LOCATION: (1) New Orleans to Donaldsonville, LA; (2) Donaldsonville to Red River; (3) Red River to Natchez, MS; (4) Natchez, MS, to Vicksburg, MS; (5) Vicksburg, MS, to White River; (6) White River to Cairo, IL; (7) Cairo, IL, to head of Tennessee River; (8) Cumberland River to its source + Upper Ohio River. Creation and administration of the district arrangement of the Mississippi Squadron is worthy of further study, perhaps a lengthy article or PhD dissertation.

2. ORN, I, 25: 28–29, 54–55, 59, 147–148; *Carondelet* Logbook, May 21–23, 30–June 1, 1863; Richard Taylor, *Destruction and Reconstruction: Personal Experiences of the Late War* (New York: D. Appleton, 1879), 137–139; Joseph Blessington, *The Campaigns of Walker's Texas Division* (Austin: Pemberton, 1968), 79–93; John D. Winters, *The Civil War in Louisiana* (Baton Rouge: Louisiana State University Press, 1963), 198–203; Joseph H. Parks, *General Edmund Kirby Smith, C.S.A.* (Baton Rouge: Louisiana State University Press, 1954), 277–278; Robert L. Kerby, *Kirby Smith's Confederacy: The Trans-Mississippi South, 1863–1865* (New York: Columbia University Press, 1972), 112–114.

3. ORN, I, 25: 182–183, 218; *Carondelet* Logbook, June

1–July 7, 1863; Jordan Letters, June 30, July 5, 1863. Nelson was correct; it would be well over a year before the *Indianola* was raised and she would not be repaired before the war was over.

4. ORN, I, 25: 301–302; *Carondelet* Logbook, July 14–15, August 1–7, 1863; Jordan Letters, August 8, 12, 1863.

5. *Carondelet* Logbook, October 15–28, 1863; Jordan Letters, October 24, 27, December 6, 1863, January 6, 1864.

6. ORN, I, 25: 378, 383, 401, 507, 583, 609, 624–625, 638, 678, 692, 726; *Carondelet* Logbook, August 25–September 8, 1863, December 11–31, 1864; January 1–6, 26–31, 1864; Jordan Letters, August 8, 1863, January 6, February 6, 1864; William H. Elder, "September 1, 1863," in his *Civil War Diary (1862–1863) of Bishop William Henry Elder, Bishop of Nashville* (Jackson, MS: R.O. Gerow Bishop of Natchez-Jackson, 1960), 125. Though hope for his return was retained by *Carondelet* crewmen, the popular Murphy was unable to return; indeed, he eventually resigned his commission on July 30, 1864. Having been appointed an acting ensign the previous October, James C. Gipson would be promoted to acting master on October 24. When Lt. Cmdr. Mitchell assumed command of the *Carondelet* in November, Gipson was given the new tinclad *Exchange*. Near Greenville, MS, on June 5, 1864, his light draught was attacked by Confederate masked batteries. She was heroically fought and took severe damage. For his gallantry, Gipson was appointed an acting Volunteer lt. on July 9. He would be honorably discharged on November 14, 1865 (Edward W. Callahan, *List of Officers of the Navy of the United States and of the Marine Corps, from 1775 to 1900, Comprising a Complete Register of All Present and Former Commissioned, Warranted, and Appointed Officers of the United States Navy, and of the Marine Corps, Regular and Volunteer, Compiled from the Official Records of the Navy Department* [New York: L.R. Hamersly, 1901; reprt., New York: Haskell House, 1969], 220; ORN, I, 26: 354–355, 385).

7. U.S. War Department, *The War of the Rebellion: A Compilation of the Official Records of the Union and Confederate Armies*, 128 vols. (Washington, DC: GPO, 1880–1901), Series I, Vol. 26, Part 1: 384, 559, 653, 673, cited hereafter as OR, followed by a comma, the series number in Roman numerals, a comma, the volume number in Arabic, any part number in Arabic, a colon, and the page in Arabic; ORN, I, 25: 734–736, 770–773; ORN, I, 26: 773; *Carondelet* Logbook, January 15–February 20, 1864; Jordan Letters, January 6, February 6, 14, 18, 1864; U.S. Congress, Joint Committee on the Conduct of the War, *Report: Red River* (38th Cong., 2nd sess.; Washington, D.C.: GPO, 1864; reprt., Greenwood Press, 1971), 5, cited hereafter as *Joint Committee*, with page number in Arabic; Gary D. Joiner, *Through the Howling Wilderness: The 1864 Red River Campaign and Union Failure in the West* (Knoxville: University of Tennessee Press, 2006), 52; Thomas O. Selfridge, *Memoirs of Thomas O. Selfridge, Jr., Rear Admiral, U.S.N.* (New York: Knickerbocker, 1924; reprt. Columbia, University of South Carolina Press, 1987), 87–88; William Riley Brooksher, *War Along the Bayous: The 1864 Red River Campaign in Louisiana* (Washington, DC: Brassey's, 1998), xi–xii, 1–24; Myron J. Smith, Jr., *The Timberclads in the Civil War: The "Lexington," "Conestoga" and "Tyler" on the Western Rivers* (Jefferson, NC: McFarland, 2008), 432. New to the squadron from the East, Lt. Cmdr. John G. Mitchell joined the USN as a midshipman in 1850. After his naval academy graduation in 1856, he was promoted through the ranks, becoming a lieutenant in 1858 and a lieutenant commander in July 1862. There is little additional information on Mitchell save that he was, according to Callahan, "killed, 22 October 1868" (Edward W. Callahan, *List of Officers of the Navy of the United States and of the Marine Corps, from 1775 to 1900, Comprising a Complete Register of All Present and Former Commissioned, Warranted, and Appointed Officers of the United States Navy, and of the Marine Corps, Regular and Volunteer, Compiled from the Official Records of the Navy Department* (New York: L.R. Hamersly, 1901; reprt., New York: Haskell House, 1969), 398. The woman suspect was sent down to Lt. Cmdr. Owen aboard the same boat that dropped off Mitchell. Her fate is unknown.

8. Joiner, *Through the Howling Wilderness*, 24–26, 52–53; ORN, I, 25: 787–788; ORN, I, 26: 747–748, 783, 788; OR, I, 34, 1: 155–160; *New York Times*, March 15, 17, 1864; *Philadelphia Inquirer*, March 15, 1864; *Chicago Daily Tribune*, March 15, 1864; Smith, *The Timberclads in the Civil War*, 433–440; "Surgeon Mixer's Account, March 2, 1864," in Frank Moore, ed., *The Rebellion Record: A Diary of American Events*, 12 vols. (New York: Putnam, 1861–1863; D. Van Nostrand, 1864–1868; reprt. Arno, 1977), vol. 8, 445–446; Hiram H. Martin, "Service Afield and Afloat: A Reminiscence of the Civil War," ed. Guy R. Everson, *Indiana Magazine of History* 89 (March 1993), 52–53; David Dixon Porter, *Naval History of the Civil War, 556*; Taylor, *Destruction and Reconstruction*, 153–154; Alwyn Barr, *Polignac's Texas Brigade*, 2nd. ed. (College Station: Texas A&M University Press, 1998), 1–30; Mark M. Boatner III, *The Civil War Dictionary* (New York: David McKay, 1959), 657.

9. OR, I, 34, 1: 168, 304, 476; OR, I, 34, 2: 448–449, 494–496, 554, 616; ORN, I, 26: 23–26, 789; *Carondelet* Logbook, March 5–12, 1864; Jordan Letters, February 29–March 7, 1864; *Dickinson Diary*, March 16–17, 1864; *Chicago Daily Tribune*, March 13, 19, 1864; *New York Tribune*, March 28, 1864; *St. Louis Daily Missouri Republican*, March 28, 1864; *Philadelphia Inquirer*, March 30, 1864; U. S. Congress, Joint Committee on the Conduct of the War, *Report: Red River* (38th Cong., 2nd sess.; Washington, DC: GPO, 1864; reprt., Greenwood Press, 1971), 21, cited hereafter as *Joint Committee*, with page number in Arabic; Mahan, *Inland Waters*, 189–190; Porter, *Naval History*, 494–496, 559–560; Porter, *Incidents and Anecdotes of the Civil War* (New York: D. Appleton, 1885; reprt., Harrisburg PA: Archive Society, 1997), 213; Taylor, *Destruction and Reconstruction* 180–181; Richard B. Irwin, "The Red River Campaign," in *Battles and Leaders of the Civil War*, ed. Robert V. Johnson and Clarence C. Buel, 4 vols. (New York: Century, 1884–1887, reprt. Thomas Yoseloff, 1956), vol. 4, 349–351; Thomas O. Selfridge, Jr., "The Navy in the Red River," *B&L*, vol. 4, 362; Smith, *The Timberclads in the Civil War*, 443–444; David Dixon Porter, "The Mississippi Flotilla in the Red River Expedition," *B&L*, vol. 4, 367; Walter G. Smith, ed., *Life and Letters of Thomas Kilby Smith* (New York: Putnam, 1898), 356; Joiner, *Through the Howling Wilderness*, 54–57; Joiner and Charles E. Vetter, "The Union Naval Expedition on the Red River, March 12–May 22, 1864," *Civil War Regiments: A Journal of the American Civil War* 4 (1994), 26–41; Curtis Milbourn and Gary D. Joiner, "The Battle of Blair's Landing," *North and South* 9 (February 2007), 12; Chester G. Hearn, *Admiral David Dixon Porter: The Civil War Years* (Annapolis, MD: Naval Institute Press, 1996), 245–246; Saunders, "Civil War Letters," 20–21; Morris, *Recollections of a Rebel Reefer*; Mahan, *Inland Waters*, 190–191.

10. OR, 34, 1: 305, 313, 338–339, 500, 506, 561; OR, I, 34, 2: 494, 610–611; ORN, I, 26: 29–31, 35, 41, 50, 773–774, 781, 784–785, 789, 792; *Carondelet* Logbook, March 14–20, 1864; Jordan Letters, March 12, 20, 1864; Mahan, *Inland Waters*, 190–191; Smith, *The Timberclads in the Civil War*, 444–445; *Chicago Daily Tribune*, March 29 and April 1, 1864; *New York Daily Tribune*, April 4, 1864; *St. Louis Daily Missouri Republican*, March 26, 1864; *Columbus (WI) Democrat*, May 29, 1895; Porter, *Naval History*, 499–500; Taylor, *Destruction and Reconstruction*, 156, 181–183; Joint Committee, 8–9, 18, 71, 74, 224–225; Joiner and Vetter, 41–49; Selfridge, "The Navy in the Red River," *B&L*, vol. 4; Selfridge, *Memoirs*, 96–98; Mahan, *Inland Waters*, 193–194; Harris H. Beecher, *Record of the 114th Regiment, New York State Volunteer Infantry* (Norwich, NY: J.F. Hubbard, Jr., 1866), 299–300; John D. Winters, *The Civil War in Louisiana* (Baton Rouge: Louisiana State University Press, 1963), 330–331; Ludwell H. Johnson, *Red River Campaign: Politics & Cotton in the Civil*

War. (Kent, OH: Kent State University Press, 1993), 99–105; Ivan Musicant, *Divided Waters: The Naval History of the Civil War* (New York: HarperCollins, 1995), 295–296; Irwin, "The Red River Campaign," *B&L*, vol. 4, 349–350; L. Kerby, *Smith's Confederacy*, 297; Hearn, *Admiral David Dixon Porter*, 246–248.

11. ORN, I, 26: 774–775, 792; OR, I, 34, 1: 179–180; 282, 308–309, 322, 324, 331, 341, 380–381, 384, 388–393, 407, 428, 445, 452, 468, 471–472, 633–634; OR, I, 34, 2: 610–611; OR, I, 34, 3: 98–99; *Carondelet* Logbook, March 28–April 8, 1864; Jordan Letters, March 30, April 7, 22 1864; *New York World*, April 16, 1864; *Columbus (WI) Democrat*, May 29, 1895; Joint Committee, 35, 210, 275–276, 282, 286–287, 323; ORN, I, 26: 38–39, 42–43, 46, 50–51, 54, 60–61, 777–778, 781, 785, 789; Musicant, *Divided Waters*, 296–297; Thomas O. Selfridge, Jr., "The Navy in the Red River," *B&L*, vol. 4, 363; Selfridge, *Memoirs*, 99–101; Mahan, *Inland Waters*, 195–196; Brooksher, *War Along the Bayous*, 69–78; Irwin, "The Red River Campaign," *B&L*, vol. 4, 351–356; Porter, *Naval History*, 502, 511–512; Joiner, *Through the Howling Wilderness*, 32, Joiner and Vetter, "Union Naval Expedition," 49–51; Mahan, *Inland Waters*, 193–196; Hearn, *Admiral David Dixon Porter*, 248–250; Steven D. Smith and George J. Castille III, "Bailey's Dam," Louisiana, Department of Culture, Recreation and Tourism Anthropological Study No. 8, March 1986, http://www.crt.state.la.us/archaeology/BAILEYS/baileys.htm (accessed August 7, 2006).

12. OR, I, 34, 1: 310, 382–383; ORN, I, 26: 66, 69, 72–78, 775, 790, 792; *Carondelet* Logbook, April 14–26, 1864; *Philadelphia Press*, April 29, 1864; *St. Louis Daily Missouri Democrat*, May 10, 1864; *Columbus (WI) Democrat*, May 29, 1895; Musicant, *Divided Waters*, 300–301; Mahan, *Inland Waters*, 198; Brooksher, *War Along the Bayous*, 158–159; Joiner and Vetter, "Union Naval Expedition," 58–59; Selfridge, Jr., "The Navy in the Red River," *B&L*, vol. 4, 364; Selfridge, *Memoirs*, 99–101; Jay Slagle, *Ironclad Captain: Seth Ledyard Phelps and the U.S. Navy* (Kent, OH: Kent State University Press, 1996), 365–367; Hearn, *Admiral David Dixon Porter*, 253–254; Porter, *Naval History*, 515–519; Porter, *Incidents and Anecdotes*, 235–239; Pellet, *114th Regiment*, 222; *Joint Committee*, 247–248.

13. ORN, I, 26: 92–95, 130–132, 137–138, 142–145, 775–776, 793; OR, I, 34, 1: 209, 310, 402–406, 491, 585–586; *Carondelet* Logbook, April 28–May 21, 1864; Jordan Letters, May 22, 1864; *New Orleans Era*, May 17, 1864; *New Orleans Times*, May 18, 1864; *Columbus (WI) Democrat*, May 29, 1895; Mahan, *Inland Waters*, 203–207; Steven D. Smith and George J. Castille III, "Bailey's Dam," Louisiana, Department of Culture, Recreation and Tourism Anthropological Study No. 8, March 1986, http://www.crt.state.la.us/archaeology/BAILEYS/baileys.htm (accessed August 7, 2006); Porter, *Incidents and Anecdotes*, 248–249; Porter, *Naval History*, 525–534; Johnson, *Red River Campaign*, 256–262; Musicant, *Divided Waters*, 303–304; Kerby, *Smith's Confederacy*, 318; Taylor, *Destruction and Reconstruction*, 186–189; Irwin, "The Red River Campaign," *B&L*, vol. 4, 358–362; Hearn, *Admiral David Dixon Porter*, 258–265; Slagle, *Ironclad Captain*, 378–381; Joiner and Vetter, "Union Naval Expedition," 64–67; Selfridge, Jr., "The Navy in the Red River," *B&L*, vol. 4, 365–366; Selfridge, *Memoirs*, 109–111; Brooksher, *War Along the Bayous*, 209–215. With her side armor removed, the speed of the *Carondelet* was increased by approximately two knots.

14. OR, I, 34, 1: 1044–1045, 1051–1052; ORN, I, 26: 330, 375, 402–403, 415–434, 447–448, 451–454, 453–454, 461, 464, 467, 469–470, 478, 480, 791; *Carondelet* Logbook, May 27, June 29–July 1–9, 1864; Jordan Letters, June 10, 25, 28, July 3–4, 1864; Slagle, *Ironclad Captain* 385; Smith, *The Timberclads*, 469–477; *New York Times*, June 29, 1864; *St. Louis Daily Missouri Democrat*, July 2, 1864; *Chicago Daily Tribune*, July 3–4, 1864; *Baltimore Sun*, July 4, 1864; *Cleveland Daily Herald*, July 5, 1864; *Chattanooga Daily Gazette*, July 12, 1864; *Memphis Argus*, July 12, 1864; "Where We've Been: U.S.S. *Queen City* Sinking," Clarendon, Arkansas, Homepage, http://www.clarendon-ar.com/been/uss_queen_city/index.html (accessed July 6, 2007); Mahan, *Inland Waters*, 212–213; John N. Edwards, *Shelby and His Men, or the War in the West* (Cincinnati: Miami, 1867, reprt., Waverly, MO: General J.O. Shelby Memorial, 1993), 321–326.

Chapter 12

1. William Tecumseh Sherman, *Memoirs* (New York: Penguin, 2000), 519; U.S. War Department, *The War of the Rebellion: A Compilation of the Official Records of the Union and Confederate Armies*, 128 vols. (Washington, DC: GPO, 1880–1901), Series I, Vol. 39, Pt. 3: 162, cited hereafter as OR, followed by a comma, the series number in Roman numerals, a comma, the volume number in Arabic, a colon, and the page in Arabic; Lloyd Lewis, *Sherman: Fighting Prophet* (New York: Harcourt, Brace and World, 1960), 430.

2. Deck Logbooks of the U.S.S. *Carondelet*, September 23–October 3, 1864, Deck Logbooks of the U.S.S. *Carondelet*, May 1862–June 1, 1865 (Records of the Bureau of Ships, Record Group 19, U.S. National Archives and Records Service), cited hereafter as *Carondelet* Logbook, with date; Scott D. Jordan to wife, September 23, October 5, 1864, in *Civil War Letters of Scott D. Jordan, Produced for Eleanor Jordan West* (CD-ROM; Glendale, AZ: doug@bellnotes.com, 2007), cited hereafter as Jordan Letters, with date; Bruce Catton, *Never Call Retreat* (New York: Pocket Books, 1973), 388; John Bell Hood, *Advance and Retreat: Personal Experiences in the United States and Confederate States Armies* (New Orleans, LA: Pub. for the Hood Orphan Memorial Fund, 1880), 263–269; Hood, "The Invasion of Tennessee," in *Battles and Leaders of the Civil War*, ed. Robert V. Johnson and Clarence C. Buel, 4 vols. (New York: Century, 1884–1887, reprt. Thomas Yoseloff, 1956), vol. 4, 425; OR, I, 39, 2: 121; Lonnie E. Maness, *An Untutored Genius: The Military Career of General Nathan Bedford Forrest* (Oxford, MS: Guild Bindery Press, 1990), 317–322; Benson J. Lossing, *Pictorial Field Book of the Civil War: Journeys through the Battlefields in the Wake of Conflict*, 3 vols. (Hartford, CT: T. Belknap, 1874, reprt. Johns Hopkins University Press, 1997), vol. 3, 398–399; Myron J. Smith, Jr., *Le Roy Fitch: The Civil War Career of a Union Gunboat Commander* (Jefferson, NC: McFarland, 2007), 267–268; Dudley Taylor Cornish and Virginia Jeans Laas, *Lincoln's Lee: The Life of Samuel Phillips Lee, United States Navy, 1812–1897* (Lawrence: University Press of Kansas, 1986), 140; Johnny H. Whisenant, "Samuel Phillips Lee, U.S.N.: Commander, Mississippi Squadron (October 19, 1864–August 14, 1865)," (master's thesis, Kansas State College of Pittsburg, 1968), 12–20; "Samuel Phillips Lee," in William B. Cogar, *Dictionary of Admirals of the U.S. Navy*, 2 vols. (Annapolis, Md.: Naval Institute Press, 1989), vol. 1, 96–97. During the transition between Porter and Lee, Capt. Alexander M. Pennock, the Cairo base commander, served as squadron commander pro tem.

3. U.S. Navy Department, *Official Records of the Union and Confederate Navies in the War of the Rebellion*, 31 vols. (Washington, DC: GPO, 1894–1922), Series I, Vol. 26, 632, 694, 721 732–733, cited hereafter as ORN, followed by a comma, the series number in Roman numerals, a comma, the volume number in Arabic, a colon, and the page in Arabic; *Carondelet* Logbook, October 16–18, November 11–15, 1864; Jordan Letters, October 17, November 12, 19, 1864.

4. *Carondelet* Logbook, November 13–19, 1864; Jordan Letters, November 19, 1864; John Hagerty to wife, September 16, November 15, 1864, in "Dear Maggie…: The Letters

of John Hagerty, 1st Class Fireman, U.S.S. *Carondelet*," Letters of John Hagerty, http://www.webnation.com/~spectrum/usn-cw/diaries/HagertyJohnHome.htm (April 3, 2000), cited hereafter as Hagerty Letters, with date. Hagerty (?–1918) was honorably discharged in August 1865 and lived thereafter in Dawson, PA, with his wife and 10 children.

5. The younger half brother of Col. Graham Newell Fitch of Logansport, IN, and an 1856 USNA graduate, Le Roy Fitch (1835–1875) spent most of the war in command of the tinclads operating on the Upper Rivers, particularly the Ohio and Cumberland. He is remembered for blocking Maj. Gen. John Hunt Morgan's return South from his great Indiana-Ohio Raid (1863), his aggressive duels with Maj. Gen. Nathan Bedford Forrest and his several combats with Rebel gunners during the Battle of Nashville (1864). Fitch died of a mysterious illness at home just before his 40th birthday. He is profiled in my *Le Roy Fitch: The Civil War Career of a Union Gunboat Commander* (Jefferson, NC: McFarland, 2007) and "Le Roy Fitch Meets the Devil's Parson: The Battle of Bell's Mills, December 4–6, 1864," *North & South* 10 (January 2008), 44.

6. Byrd Douglas, *Steamboatin' on the Cumberland* (Nashville: Tennessee Book, 1961), 162–163; *Chicago Daily Tribune*, November 24, 1864; Jordan Letters, November 23, 1864. Luckily for the Union, Gen. Hood elected to keep Forrest with him, allowing only a few mounted units to be split off and sent against logistical targets along the Cumberland. "No longer would this ingenious leader be left," wrote Douglas, "to harass Thomas." On the other hand, Maj. Gen. Thomas would continue to overestimate Forrest's strength and threat, with his concern for "the devil" a major reason Nashville was placed into a defensive position (Douglas, *Steamboatin,'* 164; Wiley Sword, *Embrace an Angry Wind: The Confederacy's Last Hurrah — Spring Hill, Franklin & Nashville* (New York: HarperCollins, 1992), 278. The *Neosho* was the other ironclad involved in the defense of Nashville. Designed by James B. Eads, she and her sister *Osage* were the only stern-wheel monitors. Both were laid down at Carondelet, MO, in 1862; the former cost $194,757.67 and was commissioned in May 1863. With a "turtleback" design on wooden hulls, both came in at 523 tons. The pair, both of which participated in the Red River Expedition, measured 180 feet, with beams of 45 feet and depths of hold of 4.6 feet; each had a single forward-mounted revolving turret and one tall chimney amidships. The two were each powered with a pair of horizontal high-pressure engines and four boilers and were designed to steam at a top speed of 12 mph. Armament comprised two 11-inch Dahlgren smoothbores in the turrets, which were shielded by six inches of armor. Armor protection on the sides was 2.5 inches thick, with 1.25 inches on the deck (ORN, II, 1: 157; Paul H. Silverstone, *Warships of the Civil War Navies* (Annapolis, MD: Naval Institute Press, 1989), 149; Donald L. Canney, *The Old Steam Navy*, vol. 2, *The Ironclads, 1842–1885* (Annapolis, MD: Naval Institute Press, 1993), 107–110). Acting Volunteer Lt. Samuel Howard, *Neosho*'s captain, remained with the USN until honorably discharged on November 4, 1868 (Edward W. Callahan, *List of Officers of the Navy of the United States and of the Marine Corps, from 1775 to 1900, Comprising a Complete Register of All Present and Former Commissioned, Warranted, and Appointed Officers of the United States Navy, and of the Marine Corps, Regular and Volunteer, Compiled from the Official Records of the Navy Department* (New York: L.R. Hamersly, 1901; reprt., New York: Haskell House, 1969), 278).

7. The Rev. Dr. David Campbell Kelley of the 26th Tennessee was born at Leeville, TN, on Christmas Day, 1833. An 1851 graduate of Cumberland University, in 1853, he became a medical doctor, graduating from the University of Nashville. That same year he traveled to China as a Methodist medical minister. Nicknamed "the Parson," Kelley began his war service at Huntsville, AL, as captain of "The Kelly Rangers/Kelly Troopers," Company F, Forrest's Battalion (3d Tennessee Cavalry). It was Kelley whom Forrest asked to pray for the troops at Fort Donelson in February 1862, becoming thereafter, according to Dr. Wyeth, one of the cavalry leader's intimate associates. One Ohio reporter characterized Kelley as "a bold, desperate, and notorious partisan." He was a man who "threatened to blow every gunboat out of the river, whenever the opportunity presented itself." After the Civil War, the colonel took a D.D. degree from Cumberland University in 1868 and served the Methodist Episcopal church at Gallatin, TN, and at other towns thereafter in the Nashville area. Kelley was one of the founders of Vanderbilt University (1873) and served on its board of trustees from 1875 to 1891. Fitch's wartime opponent held numerous posts within his church hierarchy and ran (unsuccessfully) as Prohibition Party candidate for governor of Tennessee in 1890. Kelley, who died at Nashville on May 14, 1909, "was a vocal force," according to John E. Fisher, "in urging upon whites reasoned and informed views of blacks and relations between the races" (W. Calvin Dickinson, "Temperance," in *The Tennessee Encyclopedia of History and Culture*, edited by Carroll Van West [Nashville: Rutledge Hill Press for the Tennessee Historical Society, 1998]), 913; "'The Kelly Rangers/Kelly Troopers," Company F, Forrest's Battalion (3d Tennessee Cavalry) and Company K, 4th Alabama Cavalry Regiment," Confederate Units of Madison County homepage, http://www.rootsweb.com/~almadiso/confunit.htm (accessed March 4, 2006); John E. Fisher, *They Rode with Forrest and Wheeler: A Chronicle of Five Tennessee Brothers' Service in the Confederate Western Cav*alry (Jefferson, NC: McFarland, 1995), 244–245, 250; the "Reverend Dr. D.C. Kelley," *The Vanderbilt University Quarterly* 9 (October 1909), 236; Teresa Gray, public services archivist, Special Collections and University Archives, Jean and Alexander Heard Library, Vanderbilt University, "Re: David Campbell Kelley," March 13, 2006, personal e-mail to author, March 13, 2006; Smith, "Le Roy Fitch Meets the Devil's Parson," 43; *Cincinnati Daily Gazette*, December 8, 1864.

8. ORN, I, 26: 632–635, 647, 746; OR, I, 45, 1, 1032–1033, 1056–1057, 1075, 1104, 1131–1132, 1135; *Carondelet* Logbook, November 27–29, 1864; Deck Logbook of the U.S.S. *Moose*, November 27, 29, 1864, Deck Logbook of the U.S.S. *Moose*, June 15, 1863–August 10, 1865 (Records of the Bureau of Navigation, Record Group 19, U.S. National Archives), cited hereafter as *Moose* Logbook, with date; Jordan Letters, November 23, 28, 30, 1864; *Nashville Daily Union*, November 25, 1864; Walter T. Durham, *Reluctant Partners: Nashville and the Union — July 1, 1863, to June 30, 1865* (Nashville: Tennessee Historical Society, 1987), 206; Douglas, *Steamboatin'*; Henry Stone, "Repelling Hood's Invasion of Tennessee." in *Battles and Leaders of the Civil War*, ed. Robert V. Johnson and Clarence C. Buel, 4 vols. (New York: Century, 1884–1887, reprt., New York: Thomas Yoseloff, 1956), 443; Minnesota, Board of Commissioners on Publication of History of Minnesota in the Civil and Indian Wars, *Minnesota in the Civil and Indian Wars, 1861–1865*, 2 vols. (St. Paul, MN: Pioneer, 1889), vol. 1, 274; Smith, *Le Roy Fitch*, 297–300.

9. ORN, I, 26: 636–637, 647–648; OR, I, 45, 1: 34; OR, I, 45, 2: 3, 17; Minnesota, *Minnesota*, vol. 1, 274; Edwin G. Huddleston, *The Civil War in Middle Tennessee* (Nashville: Nashville Banner, 1965), 118–119; *Moose* Logbook, November 30–December 1, 1864; *Carondelet* Logbook, November 30–December 1, 1864; Jordan Letters, November 30, December 1, 1864; *Nashville Daily Press*, November 30–December 2, 1864; Fisher, *They Rode with Forrest*, 161; Smith, *Le Roy Fitch*, 300–303; Stanley F. Horn, *The Army of Tennessee: A Military History* (Indianapolis: Bobbs-Merrill, 1941, reprt., Norman: University of Oklahoma Press, 1968), 404; Horn, *The Decisive Battle of Nashville* (Baton Rouge: Louisiana State University Press, 1956), 30–31; James F. Rusling, *Men and Things I Saw in Civil War Days*, new ed.

(New York: Methodist Book Concern, 1914), 87–88; Stanley F. Horn, comp., *Tennessee's War, 1861–1865: Described by Participants* (Nashville: Tennessee Civil War Centennial Commission, 1965), 321–322; Sword, *Embrace an Angry Wind*, 272–274; Durham, *Reluctant Partners*, 211–214. Smith's units, now collectively named with several other provisional groups as the Army of the Tennessee Detachment, were debarked from their boats on December 1–2 and were moved into line of battle on a range of hills two miles southwest of town. There they threw up earthworks and settled down to wait, guarding the right of the Union defense. The center was held by the IV Corps while the XXIII Corps was on the left.

10. OR, I, 45, 1: 79–83, 764; OR, I, 45, 2: 18, 27, 191; ORN, I, 26: 636–639, 646; Sword, *Embrace an Angry Wind*, 281; *Moose* Logbook, December 2, 1864; *Carondelet* Logbook, December 2, 1864; Mark Zimmerman, *Battle of Nashville Preservation Society Guide to Civil War Nashville* (Nashville: Lithographics, 2004), 49; Stanley F. Horn, "Nashville during the Civil War," *Tennessee Historical Quarterly* 4 (March 1945), 19; Thomas L. Connelly, *Autumn of Glory: The Army of Tennessee, 1862–1865* (Baton Rouge: Louisiana State University Press, 1971), 508; James Lee McDonough, *Nashville: The Western Confederacy's Final Gamble* (Knoxville: University of Tennessee Press, 2004), 141–142; Steven E Woodward, *Jefferson Davis and His Generals: The Failure of Confederate Command in the West* (Lawrence: University Press of Kansas, 1990), 301; Douglas, *Steamboatin,'* 165; Smith, *Le Roy Fitch*, 303–305; Durham, *Reluctant Partners*, 214–215; John E. Fisher, *They Rode with Forrest and Wheeler: A Chronicle of Five Tennessee Brothers' Service in the Confederate Western Cavalry* (Jefferson, NC: McFarland, 1995), 162; John Allan Wyeth, *Life of General Nathan Bedford Forrest* (New York: Harper & Bros., 1904), 547; Thomas Jordan and J. Pryor, *The Campaigns of Lieut. Gen. N.B. Forrest and of Forrest's Cavalry* (New Orleans and New York: Blelock, 1868, reprt., New York: Da Capo, 1996), 636; Smith, "Le Roy Fitch Meets the Devil's Parson," 44.

11. ORN, I, 26: 641–647; OR, I, 45, 2: 37, 43, 48–49, 51–52, 54; *Carondelet*, Logbook December 3–4, 1864; *Moose* Logbook, December 3–4, 1864; Jordan Letters, December 3, 21, 1864; David Dixon Porter, *Naval History of the Civil War* (New York: Sherman, 1886; reprt., Mineola, NY: Dover, 1998), 803–804; Alfred T. Mahan, *Navy in the Civil War*, vol. 3, *The Gulf and Inland Waters* (New York: Scribner's, 1883), 215–216; Rowland Stafford True, "Life Aboard a Gunboat," *Civil War Times Illustrated* 9 (February 1971), 39–40; Jordan and Pryor, *Campaigns*, 636; Wyeth, *General Forrest*, 547–548; Henry Walke, *Naval Scenes and Reminiscences of the Civil War in the United States on the Southern and Western Waters during the Years 1861, 1862 and 1863 with the History of That Period Compared and Corrected from Authentic Sources* (New York: F.R. Reed, 1877), 124. The firing heard by the gunboatmen, and for that matter nearly everyone else in the area, was from the attack made by Morton's artillery and BG Tyree Bell's brigade on Blockhouse No. 3 south of Nashville. The cannonade heralded the fall of one more of the seven small fortifications established to guard bridges along the Nashville & Chattanooga Railroad route to Murfreesboro. Most of these had been ordered evacuated, but, with Rebel cavalry about and the telegraph down, the word did not get to the defenders of several outposts. Nos. 1–2 had been taken since Friday. Between 2:30 A.M. and 3:15 A.M. on December 5, men aboard the Nashville gunboats again heard "heavy firing on the left of the line," a cannonade which resumed at 8:45 P.M., with the sound of drums and bugles coming from the direction of the Tennessee state house. During the day, Federal artillery blasted the high ground and hills in front of their defense line to remove cover that attacking Confederates might employ. Walter Durham tells us that "the rumble of cannons was heard in Nashville all day long" and that many houses were destroyed (*Carondelet* Logbook, December 4–5, 1864; Durham, *Reluctant Partners*, 226).

12. OR, I, 45, 1: 631–632, 650–652, 654, 658, 660, 744, 754–755; OR, I, 45, 2: 651, 657, 758; ORN, I, 26: 648, 758; *Carondelet* Logbook, December 5–6, 1864; Jordan Letters, December 6, 1864; *Moose* Logbook, December 5–6, 1864; *Nashville Dispatch*, December 6, 1864; *Nashville Daily Times and True Union*, December 8, 1864; McDonough, *Nashville*, 144; Jordan and Pryor, *Campaigns*, 630–631; Mike Fitzpatrick, "Miasma Fogs and River Mists," *Military Images* 25 (January-February 2004), 29; Wyeth, *General Forrest*, 548; Bern Anderson, *By Sea and By River: The Naval History of the Civil War* (New York: Knopf, 1962), 266; Durham, *Reluctant Partners*, 218; True, "Life Aboard," 40; James McCague, *The Cumberland* (Rivers of America; New York: Holt, Rinehart and Winston, 1973), 180; Horn, *The Decisive Battle of Nashville*, 80; Zimmerman, *Civil War Nashville*, 9; Smith, *Le Roy Fitch*, 305–310; Smith, "Le Roy Fitch Meets the Devil's Parson," 45–48.

13. OR, I, 45, 2: 97–101, 105–106, 117; ORN, I, 26: 184, 654–659, 662; *Carondelet* Logbook, December 7–14, 1864; *Moose* Logbook, December 7–14, 1864; Jordan Letters, December 9, 1864; *Nashville Daily Press*, December 8, 1864; *New York Times*, December 12, 18–19, 24–25, 1864; Smith, *Le Roy Fitch*, 311–319; McDonough, *Nashville*, 149–151; Tamara Moser Melia, *"Damn the Torpedoes": A Short History of U.S. Naval Mine Countermeasures, 1777–1991* (Contributions in Naval History, no. 4; Washington, DC: Naval Historical Center, Department of the Navy, 1991), 12. As part of a continuing series on the Nashville siege, an eastern newspaper reported that the Confederates had "established a battery on a bluff 14 miles down the river." It continued: "Seven gunboats went down and engaged this battery without dislodging the rebels from their position. The gunboats returned ... one of them considerably damaged." The gunboat supposedly damaged was the *Carondelet*. When he saw the story, Acting Ensign Jordan hastened a letter north over the L&N Railroad to assure his Maine family that it was false (*New York Times*, December 9, 1864; Jordan Letters, December 9, 1864).

14. ORN, I, 26: 652–653, 662–664, 688, 803–806; OR, I, 45, 2: 160, 168–171, 180–184, 191–192; OR, I, 45, 2: 168–171; Smith, *Le Roy Fitch*, 319–325; Rusling, *Men and Things*, 340; *Carondelet* Logbook, December 12–15, 1864; *Moose* Logbook, December 12–15, 1864; Hagerty Letters, December 13, 1864; Douglas, *Steamboatin,'* 164–165.

15. OR, I, 45, 1, 37–38, 128, 599–600, 606, 765; OR, I, 45, 2: 185,197, 205–206; ORN, I, 26: 650–651; ; *Moose* Logbook, December 15, 1864; *Carondelet* Logbook, December 15, 1864; Jordan Letters, December 15, 1864; Sword, *Embrace an Angry Wind*, 319–322, 326–328; Horn, *The Decisive Battle of Nashville*, 39, 84; McDonough, *Nashville*, 157, 175–176; Smith, *Le Roy Fitch*, 325–328; McCague, *The Cumberland*; Zimmerman, *Civil War Nashville*, 69; Durham, *Reluctant Partners*, 245.

Chapter 13

1. U.S. Navy Department, *Official Records of the Union and Confederate Navies in the War of the Rebellion*, 31 vols. (Washington, DC: GPO, 1894–1922), Series I, Vol. 26, 184, 650–651, 653, 661–662, 668, cited hereafter as ORN, followed by a comma, the series number in Roman numerals, a comma, the volume number in Arabic, a colon, and the page in Arabic; ORN, I, 27: 153; U.S. War Department, *The War of the Rebellion: A Compilation of the Official Records of the Union and Confederate Armies*, 128 vols. (Washington, DC: GPO, 1880–1901), Series I, Vol. 45, Pt. 1: 37–39, 45, 128, 599–601, 606,765, cited hereafter as OR, followed by a comma, the series number in Roman numerals, a comma, the volume number in Arabic, a colon, and the page in Ara-

bic; OR, I, 45, 2: 117, 154, 160, 180–185, 191–192, 194, 196–197, 205–206, 210, 213, 231, 245, Deck Logbook of the U.S.S. *Carondelet*, December 15–17, 1864; Deck Logbooks of the U.S.S. *Carondelet*, May 1862–June 1, 1865 (Records of the Bureau of Ships, Record Group 19, U.S. National Archives and Records Service), cited hereafter as *Carondelet* Logbook, with date; Deck Logbook of the U.S.S. *Moose*, December 15–17, 1864, Deck Logbook of the U.S.S. *Moose*, June 15, 1863–August 10, 1865 (Records of the Bureau of Navigation, Record Group 19, U.S. National Archives), cited hereafter as *Moose* Logbook, with date; *Nashville Daily Union*, December 20, 22, 1864; *Cincinnati Daily Gazette*, December 8, 1864; *Milwaukee Daily Sentinel*, December 14, 24, 1864; *Nashville Daily Press*, December 12, 14, 1864; *New York Times*, December 12, 18–19, 24–25, 1864; *Chicago Daily Tribune*, December 16, 19, 1864; James H. Wilson, *Under the Old Flag*, 2 vols. (New York: D. Appleton, 1912), vol. 2, 109–112; Wyeth, *General Forrest*, 555–559; Isaac R. Sherwood, *Memories of the War* (Toledo: H.J. Crittenden, 1923), 149; Walter T. Durham, *Reluctant Partners: Nashville and the Union — July 1, 1863, to June 30, 1865* (Nashville: Tennessee Historical Society, 1987), 237, 245, 261, 266, 268; James Lee McDonough, *Nashville: The Western Confederacy's Final Gamble* (Knoxville: University of Tennessee Press, 2004), 149–151, 157,176–177; Stanley Horn, *The Decisive Battle of Nashville* (Baton Rouge: Louisiana State University Press, 1956), 39, 84, 150–152; Wiley Sword, *Embrace an Angry Wind: The Confederacy's Last Hurrah — Spring Hill, Franklin & Nashville* (New York: HarperCollins, 1992), 319–350; Mark Zimmerman, *Battle of Nashville Preservation Society Guide to Civil War Nashville* (Nashville: Lithographics, 2004), 69; Myron J. Smith, Jr., *Le Roy Fitch: The Civil War Career of a Union Gunboat Commander* (Jefferson, NC: McFarland, 2007), 310–331.

2. OR, I, 45, 1: 618–619, 632, 755; OR, I, 45, 2: 231, 251; ORN, I, 26: 670–673; Nashville *Daily Union*, December 17, 1864; *Moose* Logbook, December 18–19, 1864; *Carondelet* Logbook, December 18–19, 1864; Scott D. Jordan to wife, December 18, 1864, in *Civil War Letters of Scott D. Jordan, Produced for Eleanor Jordan West* (CD-ROM; Glendale, AZ: doug@bellnotes.com, 2007), cited hereafter as Jordan Letters, with date; Sword, *Embrace an Angry Wind*, 401, 416; Smith, *Le Roy Fitch*, 331–333; Dudley Taylor Cornish and Virginia Jeans Laas, *Lincoln's Lee: The Life of Samuel Phillips Lee, United States Navy, 1812–1897* (Lawrence: University Press of Kansas, 1986), 148.

3. OR, I, 45, 1: 674, 732; OR, I, 45, 2: 357,371, 507, 731; ORN, I, 26: 672–679. 690; ORN, I, 27: 9–28; *Carondelet* Logbook, December 18–30, 1864; Jordan Letters, December 21, 29, 1864; *Chicago Daily Tribune*, January 10, 1865; McDonough, *Nashville*, 273–274; Sword, *Embrace an Angry Wind*, 401, 421, 423; Smith, *Le Roy Fitch*, 333–334; Robert Selph Henry, *"First with the Most" Forrest* (Indianapolis: Bobbs-Merrill, 1944), 416; Stanley F. Horn, *The Army of Tennessee* (Indianapolis: Bobbs-Merrill, 1941), 420–421; Wilson, *Under the Old Flag*, vol. 2, 142; Wilson, "The Union Cavalry in the Hood Campaign," in *Battles and Leaders of the Civil War*, ed. Robert V. Johnson and Clarence C. Buel, 4 vols. (New York: Century, 1884–1887); reprt. Thomas Yoseloff, 1956), vol. 4, 471; Donald Davidson, *The Tennessee*, vol. 2, *New River, Civil War to TVA* (Rivers of America; New York: Rinehart, 1948), 106. A New Hampshire native, Clark (1836–1901) spent several years in the commercial maritime industry during the 1850s. Appointed an acting ensign in October 1862, Clark became an acting master the following July and commander of the sloop *Rosalie* of the West Gulf Coast Blockading Squadron. Promoted to his last rank on August 9, 1864, he would be honorably discharged in November 1865. After several years as a St. Louis merchant, he entered the railroad business as a clerk in 1870, rising to become president of the New York, New Haven, and Hartford Railroad in 1887. The executive died of a heart attack while touring southern France. Married, he had one son, who followed him into the transportation arena with the same railroad (Edward W. Callahan, *List of Officers of the Navy of the United States and of the Marine Corps, from 1775 to 1900, Comprising a Complete Register of All Present and Former Commissioned, Warranted, and Appointed Officers of the United States Navy, and of the Marine Corps, Regular and Volunteer, Compiled from the Official Records of the Navy Department* (New York: L.R. Hamersly, 1901; reprt., New York: Haskell House, 1969), 115; *New York Times*, March 22, 1901.

4. ORN, I, 27: 15–16, 36, 41, 47–53, 85; *Carondelet* Logbook, January 3–30, 1865; Jordan Letters, January 7, 12, 1865; Lewis B. Parsons, *Reports to the War Department* (St. Louis, MO: George Knapp, 1867), 38; Cornish and Laas, *Lincoln's Lee*, 149–150; Craig L. Symonds, *Lincoln and His Admirals: Abraham Lincoln, the U.S. Navy, and the Civil War* (New York: Oxford University Press, 2008), 331; Richard Gildrie, "Guerrilla Warfare in the Lower Cumberland River Valley, 1862–1865," *Tennessee Historical Quarterly* 49 (Fall 1990), 173; Thomas Connelly, *Autumn of Glory: The Army of Tennessee, 1862–1865* (Baton Rouge: Louisiana State University Press, 1971), 513; Allen C. Guelzo, *The Crisis of the American Republic: A History of the Civil War and Reconstruction* (New York: St. Martin's, 1995), 368–369.

5. ORN, I, 27: 141, 148–149, 711; *Carondelet* Logbook, January 31, February 1–19, April 7–19 1865; Jordan Letters, January 30, February 11, 17, March 9, April 8, 1865; *Milwaukee Daily Sentinel*, April 14, 1865; Guelzo, *Crisis*, 377–379. Acting Volunteer Lt. John Rogers, like Clark, was initially appointed an acting ensign in October 1862. He became an acting master in August 1863 and skippered the tinclad *Queen City*. Rogers was promoted to his last rank in July 1864. He would be honorably discharged on December 4, 1865. One of his subordinates praised the 238-lb. skipper for his kindnesses to the local populace, though mentioning that he was a bit rough in his conversation (Callahan, *List of Officers*, 471; Jordan Letters, April 8, 1865).

6. ORN, I, 27: 172–175, 185, 210–213, 217, 252–255; John Niven, *Gideon Welles: Lincoln's Secretary of the Navy* (New York: Oxford University Press, 1973), 506–507; Charles Oscar Paullin, *Paullin's History of Naval Administration, 1775–1911* (Annapolis, MD: U.S. Naval Institute, 1968), 312.

7. ORN, I, 27: 278–279; *Carondelet* Logbook, May 31–June 1, June 9–20, 1865; David Stephen Heidler, *Encyclopedia of the War of 1812* (Annapolis, MD: Naval Institute Press, 2004), 591. The Rogers letter to Lee reprinted here is the final entry in the *Carondelet*'s last deck log. This volume, together with several others, now rests in the National Archives.

8. ORN, I, 27: 344; *St. Louis Daily Missouri Democrat*, August 9–20, 1865; *Chicago Daily Tribune*, August 18, 21, 1865; Myron J. Smith, Jr., *The Timberclads in the Civil War: "Lexington," "Conestoga" and "Tyler" on the Western Waters* (Jefferson, NC: McFarland, 2008), 480. While the fleet that began as the Western Flotilla was no more, the naval station at Mound City continued to function into the 1870s. The *Carondelet*'s first captain, Henry Walke, served as base CO during 1868 and 1869, his last active billet before retiring ("Rear Admiral Henry Walke, U.S.N.," *United Service* 7 (March 1892), 320).

9. The newspapers also advertised the auction of 5,000 tons of the ex-fleet's coal and a number of coal barges for November 28 and the sale of 250–300 tons of "T" railroad iron — this being the armor of the dismantled ironclads— on November 30.

10. *St. Louis Daily Missouri Democrat*, November 21, 30, 1865; *Cincinnati Daily Commercial*, December 19, 1865.

11. ORN, II, 1: 52.

12. Tippett to writer, June 8, 1970.

13. *Cincinnati Daily Commercial*, May 25, 1873; *Memphis Public Ledger*, April 23, 1873; Paul H. Silverstone, *Civil War*

Navies, 1855–1883 (U.S. Navy Warship Series; New York: Routledge, 2006), 113; William C. Lytle, *Merchant Steam Vessels of the United States, 1807–1868, "The Lytle List."* (Publication No. 6; Mystic, CT: Steamship Historical Society of America, 1952), 101; Frederick Way, Jr., *Way's Packet Directory, 1848–1994: Passenger Steamboats of the Mississippi River System since the Advent of Photography in Mid-Continent America* (Athens: Ohio University Press, 1983; rev. ed., Athens: Ohio University Press, 1994), 72.

14. *Cincinnati Daily Commercial*, April 18, 22, 1873; Myron J. Smith, Jr., "The Final Fate of the U.S.S. *Carondelet*," *Nautical Research Journal* 20 (January 1974), 50–58.

15. Clive Cussler, telephone interview with the author, May 6, 1981.

16. Clive Cussler, "U.S.S. *Carondelet*: The Hunt for the Famous Union Ironclad River Gunboat *Carondelet* in the Ohio River, May 1982," NUMA: National Underwater and Marine Agency home page, http://www.numa.net/expeditions/carondelet.html (accessed May 2009); Cussler and Craig Dirgo, *The Sea Hunters* (New York: Simon & Schuster, 1996), 168–177.

Bibliography

Primary Sources

Bache, George M. Collection. Navy Department Library, Naval Historical Center, Washington, DC.

Bock, William N. Papers. Illinois State Historical Society, Springfield.

Browne, Symmes. Papers. Ohio Historical Society, Columbus.

Callender, Eliot. "What a Boy Saw on the Mississippi." In *Military Essays and Recollections: Papers Read before the Commandery of the State of Illinois, Military Order of the Loyal Legion of the United States* (Chicago: A.C. McClurg, 1891).

U.S.S. *Carondelet*, Deck Logbook: May 1862–June 1865. Record Group 24: U.S. Navy Department, Records of the Bureau of Naval Personnel. National Archives, Washington, DC.

Civil War, Confederate and Federal. Collection. Tennessee State Library and Archives, Nashville.

Civil War Times Illustrated. Collection. U.S. Army Military History Institute, Carlisle Barracks, PA.

Clark, Charles Peter. Papers. Coll. 135, Manuscripts Collection, G.W. Blunt White Library, Mystic Seaport Museum, Inc., CT.

Confederate States of America Congress. House of Representatives. Special Committee on the Recent Military Disasters. *Report of the Special Committee on the Recent Military Disasters at Forts Henry & Donelson & the Evacuation of Nashville.* Richmond, VA: Enquirer, 1862.

Confederate States of America War Department. *Official Reports of Battles.* Richmond, VA: Enquirer, 1862.

Davis, Frederic E. Papers. Emory University. Atlanta.

Eads, James B. Papers. Missouri Historical Society, St. Louis.

Johnson, Robert V., and Clarence C. Buell, eds. *Battles and Leaders of the Civil War.* 4 vols. New York: Century, 1884–1887. Reprint Thomas Yoseloff, 1956.

Jordan, Scott D. *Civil War Letters of Scott D. Jordan, Produced for Eleanor Jordan West.* CD-ROM. Glendale, AZ: doug@bellnotes.com, 2007.

Lyons, Thomas. *Anonymous Journal Kept on Board of the U.S. Steam Gunboat "Carondelet," Captain Henry Walke Commanding, 1862–1863.* Manuscript Division, Library of Congress, n.d.

Meigs, Montgomery C. Papers. Manuscript Division, Library of Congress, Washington, DC.

U.S.S. *Moose*, Deck Logbook. June 15, 1863–August 10, 1865. Records of the Bureau of Navigation, Record Group 19, U.S. National Archives, Washington, DC.

Pennock, Alexander Mosley. Papers. Illinois State Historical Society, Springfield.

Phelps, Seth Ledyard. Papers. Missouri Historical Society, St. Louis (SLPC).

Porter, David Dixon. Papers. Manuscript Division, Library of Congress, Washington, DC.

_____. Papers. Missouri Historical Society, St. Louis.

Records of the Office of the Quartermaster General. Record Group 92. National Archives, Washington DC.

Rodgers Family. Papers, Library of Congress.

Rodgers, John. Collection. Library of Congress (JRC).

Swigert, Charles P. "Record of Charles P. Swigert, Late Private, Co. H., 42nd Ill. Infantry." Papers of George H. Thomas Post, Grand Army of the Republic, Department of Illinois, n.d, Chicago Historical Society Library, Chicago.

United States Congress. Joint Committee on the Conduct of the War. *Report: Red River.* 38th Cong., 2nd sess. Washington, DC: GPO, 1864. Reprint, Greenwood, 1971.

United States Navy Department. *Official Records of the Union and Confederate Navies in the War of the Rebellion (ORN).* 31 vols. Washington, DC: GPO, 1894–1922.

United States Records of the Bureau of Naval Personnel: Record Group 24. National Archives, Washington, DC.

United States Records of the Office of Naval Records and Library, Naval Records Collection: Record Group 45. National Archives, Washington, DC.

United States War Department. *Atlas to Accompany the Official Records of the War of the Rebellion.* Compiled by Calvin D. Cowles. 3 vols. Washington, DC: GPO, 1891–1895.

United States. *The War of the Rebellion: A Compilation of the Official Records of the Union and Confederate Armies (OR).* 128 vols. Washington, DC: GPO, 1880–1901.

Watson, Theodore. Letters. Newberry Library (Chicago).

Welles, Gideon. Papers. Manuscript Division, Library of Congress, Washington, DC.

Newspapers

Atlantic (NJ) *Democrat*
Boston Morning Journal
Cairo City (IL) *Weekly Gazette*
Charleston (SC) *Daily Courier*
Charleston (SC) *Mercury*

Chicago Daily Post
Chicago Daily Times
Chicago Daily Tribune
Chicago Evening Journal
Cincinnati Daily Commercial
Cincinnati Daily Enquirer
Cincinnati Daily Gazette
Cincinnati Times
Clarksville (TN) *Chronicle*
Cleveland (OH) *Daily Plain Dealer*
Columbus (OH) *Crisis*
Columbus (GA) *Daily Enquirer*
Evansville Daily Journal
Florence (AL) *Gazette*
Frank Leslie's Illustrated Newspaper
Granada (MS) *Appeal*
Harper's Weekly
Houston Daily Telegraph
Houston Tri-Weekly Telegraph
Illinois Weekly State Journal
Indiana Herald
Indianapolis Daily Journal
Indianapolis News
Jackson Mississippian
Little Rock True Democrat
Louisville (KY) *Courier*
Louisville (KY) *Daily Journal*
Macon (GA) *Daily Telegraph*
Macon (GA) *Weekly Telegraph*
Memphis Argus
Memphis Daily Appeal
Memphis Daily Avalanche
Memphis Bulletin
Mobile Daily Advertiser & Register
Mobile Daily Tribune
Mobile Evening News
Nashville Banner
Nashville Daily Patriot
Nashville Daily Union
Nashville Dispatch
Nashville Times
Nashville Union and American
National Intelligencer
Natchitoches (LA) *Union*
New Albany (IN) *Ledger*
New Orleans Daily Crescent
New Orleans Daily Delta
New Orleans Daily Picayune
New Orleans Era
New Orleans Times
New York Herald
New York Times
New York Tribune
New York World
Pine Bluff (MS) *Commercial*
Richmond Dispatch
St. Louis Daily Missouri Democrat
St. Louis Daily Missouri Republican
Savannah Republican
Vicksburg Evening Post
Vicksburg Sunday Post
Wisconsin State Journal

Internet Sources

American Society of Mechanical Engineers. *U.S.S. "Cairo" Engine and Boilers, 1862, the U.S.S. "Cairo" and Museum, Vicksburg National Military Park, A National Historical Mechanical Engineering Landmark, Vicksburg, MS, June 15, 1990.* http://scholar.google.com/scholar?hl=en&lr=&ie=UTF-8&q=cache:WLW3MwJtYK0J:mfnl.x.../h143.pdf+gunboat (accessed April 6, 2005).

Aronson, Alan. "Strategic Supply of Civil War Armies." *General Histories of the American Civil War.* http://members.cox.net/rb2307/content/STRATEGIC_SUPPLY_OF_CIVIL_WAR_ARMIES.htm (accessed March 30, 2000).

Bailey, Anne J. "Parson's Texas Cavalry." *Handbook of Texas Online.* http://www.tsha.utexas.edu/handbook/online/articles/PP/qkp1.html (accessed July 22, 2007).

Bering, John A., and Thomas Montgomery. *History of the Forty-Eighth Ohio Vet. Vol. Inf.* On 48th OVVI home page (Don Worth). http://www.riovvi.org/oh48hist.html (accessed January 25, 2007).

Biographical Directory of the United States Congress, 1774–Present. http://bioguide.congress.gov/scripts/biodisplay.pl?index=B000231 (accessed October 1, 2006).

Campbell, Karen. "Another Murder in Waynesville?: Capt. William Rion Hoel." *Waynesville, Ohio: Connections with the Past,* August 29, 2005. http://waynesgenhis.blogspot.com/2005/08/another-murder-in-waynesville-captain.html (accessed March 27, 2009).

"The Civil War Diary of Michael Sweetman, Co. K 114th O.V.I." Edited by Johnda T. Davis. *Fortunecity.* http://www.fortunecity.com/westwood/makeover/347/id229.htm (accessed May 5, 2007).

Cussler, Clive. "U.S.S. *Carondelet*: The Hunt for the Famous Union Ironclad River Gunboat *Carondelet* in the Ohio River, May 1982." *NUMA: National Underwater and Marine Agency* home page. http://www.numa.net/expeditions/carondelet.html (accessed May 2009).

Dawley, Dave. "William J. Kountz," Steamboat home page. http://members.tripoDCom/~Write4801/captains/k.html (accessed September 15, 2006).

Hagerty, John. "Dear Maggie...": The Letters of John Hagerty, 1st Class Fireman, U.S.S. *Carondelet.*" Letters of John Hagerty http://www.webnation.com/~spectrum/usn-cw/diaries/HagertyJohnHome.htm (accessed April 3, 2000).

Hogan, Brian, Conrad Bush, and Mike Brown. "The 76th New York and the Navy." 76th New York Infantry Regiment home page. http://www.bpmlegal.com/76NY/76navy.html accessed (July 12, 2005).

"James Buchanan Eads." University of Illinois at Urbana-Champagne Riverweb site. http://www.riverweb.uiuc.edu/TECH/TECH20.htm (accessed September 18, 2006).

"John G. Morrison, Civil War Medal of Honor Recipient." American Civil War Website. http://americancivilwar.com/medal_of_honor6.html (accessed April 9, 2008).

"The 'Kelly Rangers/Kelly Troopers,' Company F, Forrest's Battalion (3d Tennessee Cavalry) and Company K, 4th Alabama Cavalry Regiment." Confederate Units of Madison County home page. http://www.rootsweb.com/~almadiso/confunit.htm (accessed March 4, 2006).

"The Origin of the Ranks and Rank Insignia Now Used by the United States Armed Forces, Officers: Lieutenants." *Traditions of the Naval Service*. http://www.history.navy.mil/trivia/triv4-5d.htm (accessed July 7, 2005).

"Red River." *LoveToKnow 1911*. http://www.1911encyclopedia.org/Red_River (accessed September 3, 2006).

Smith, Steven D., and George J. Castille III. "Bailey's Dam." Louisiana Department of Culture, Recreation and Tourism Anthropological Study No. 8, March 1986. http://www.crt.state.la.us/archaeology/BAILEYS/baileys.htm (accessed August 7, 2006).

United States National Park Service. Vicksburg National Military Park. *For Teachers: The USS "Cairo."* http: www.nps.gov/vick/forteachers/upload/Cairo%20Pamphlet.pdf (accessed December 21, 2008).

United States Navy Department. Mississippi Squadron. *Internal Rules and Regulations for Vessels of the Mississippi Fleet in the Mississippi River and Tributaries*. Cincinnati: Rickey and Carroll, 1862.

_____. Naval Historical Center. "Commander Isaac Newton Brown, CSN (1817–1889)," *OnLine Library of Selected Images— People— United States*. http://www.history.navy.mil/photos/pers-us/uspers-b/in-brwn.htm (accessed March 30, 2007).

_____. *Frequently Asked Questions, No. 63: Ship Naming in the United States Navy, a Note on Navy Ship Name Prefixes*. http://www.history.navy.mil/faqs/faq63-1.htm (accessed April 16, 2007).

"Where We've Been: U.S.S. *Queen City* Sinking." Clarendon Arkansas home page. http://www.clarendon-ar.com/been/uss_queen_city/index.html (accessed July 6, 2007).

Wiener, James G., et al. "Mississippi River." U.S. Geological Survey, Biological Resources Division home page. http://biology.usgs.gov/s+t/SNT/noframe/ms137.htm (accessed August 26, 2006).

Williams, Scott K. "St. Louis' Ships of Iron: The Ironclads and Monitors of Carondelet (St. Louis), Missouri." Missouri Civil War Museum home page. http://www.moissouricivilwarmuseum.org/1ironclads.htm (accessed July 12, 2005).

Wright, George. "Re: Confederate River Gunboats." Civil War Navies Messageboard. http://history-sites.com/mb/cw/cwnavy/index.cgi?read=1948 (accessed November 10, 2006).

_____. "USS *Carondelet* vs. CSS *Arkansas*." Civil War Navies Messageboard. http://history-sites.com/cgi-bin/bbs53x/cwnavy/webbbs_config.pl?read=1580 (accessed April 4, 2009).

Books

Abbott, John S.C. *The History of the Civil War in America*. 2 vols. New York: H. Bill, 1863.

Alden, Carroll Storrs, and Ralph Earle. *Makers of Naval Tradition*. Boston: Ginn, 1925.

Allardice, Bruce S. *More Generals in Gray*. Baton Route: Louisiana State University Press, 1995.

Allen, John W. *Legends and Lore of Southern Illinois*. Carbondale, IL: University Graphics, 1978.

Ambler, Charles Henry. *A History of Transportation in the Ohio Valley*. Glendale, CA: Arthur H. Clark, 1932.

Ambrose, Daniel L. *History of the Seventh Regiment Illinois Volunteer Infantry*. Springfield: Illinois Journal, 1868.

Ambrose, Stephen E. *Halleck: Lincoln's Chief of Staff*. Baton Rouge: Louisiana State University Press, 1962.

Anders, Curt. *Disaster in Damp Sand: The Red River Expedition*. Carmel: Guild Press of Indiana, 1997.

_____. *Henry Halleck's War: A Fresh Look at Lincoln's Controversial General-in-Chief*. Indianapolis: Guild, 1999.

Anderson, Bern. *By Sea and By River: The Naval History of the Civil War*. New York: Knopf, 1962.

Andrews, J. Cutler. *The North Reports the Civil War*. Pittsburgh: University of Pittsburgh Press, 1985.

_____. *The South Reports the Civil War*. Pittsburgh: University of Pittsburgh Press, 1985.

Angle, Paul M., ed. *Illinois Guide and Gazetter: Prepared Under the Supervision of the Illinois Sesquicentennial Commission*. Chicago: Rand McNally, 1969.

Austin, J.P. *The Blue and the Gray: Sketches of a Portion of the Unwritten History of the Great American Civil War*. Atlanta: Franklin, 1899.

Bacon, Benjamin W. *Sinews of War: How Technology, Industry and Transportation Won the Civil War*. Novato, CA: Presidio, 1997.

Badeau, Adam. *Military History of Ulysses S. Grant*. 3 vols. New York: D. Appleton, 1868–1881.

Bailey, Anne J. *Between the Enemy and Texas: Parsons's Texas Cavalry in the Civil War*. Fort Worth: Texas Christian University Press, 1989.

_____. *The Chessboard of War: Sherman and Hood in the Autumn Campaigns of 1864*. Great Campaigns of the Civil War. Lincoln: University of Nebraska Press, 2000.

Ballard, Michael B. *Vicksburg: The Campaign that Opened the Mississippi*. Chapel Hill: University of North Carolina Press, 2004.

Banta, Richard E. *The Ohio*. Rivers of America. New York: Rinehart, 1949.

Barrett, Edward. *Gunnery Instruction Simplified for the Volunteer Officers of the U.S. Navy, with Hints for Executive and Other Officers*. New York: D. Van Nostrand, 1863.

Barron, Samuel B. *The Lone Star Defenders: A Chronicle of the Third Texas Cavalry, Ross' Brigade*. New York and Washington, DC: Neale, 1908.

Bartols, Barnabas H. *A Treatise on the Marine Boilers of the United States*. Philadelphia: R.W. Barnard, 1851.

Bates, Edward. *The Diary of Edward Bates, 1859–1866*. Edited by Howard Kennedy Beale. Washington, DC: GPO, 1933. Reprint, Da Capo, 1971.

Beale, Howard K., ed. *Diary of Gideon Welles: Secretary of the Navy under Lincoln and Johnson*. 2 vols. New York: W.W. Norton, 1960.
Beard, William E. *The Battle of Nashville, Including an Outline of the Stirring Events Occurring in One of the Most Notable Movements of the Civil War — Hood's Invasion of Tennessee*. Nashville: Marshall & Bruce, 1913.
Bearss, Edwin C. *The Fall of Fort Henry*. Dover, TN: Eastern National Park and Monument Association, 1989.
_____. *Hardluck Ironclad: The Sinking and Salvage of the "Cairo."* Baton Rouge: Louisiana State University, 1966.
_____. *Unconditional Surrender: The Fall of Fort Donelson*. Dover, TN: Eastern National Park and Monument Association, 1991.
_____. *The Vicksburg Campaign*. 3 vols. Dayton: Morningside, 1985–1986.
Beecher, Harris H. *Record of the 114th Regiment, New York State Volunteer Infantry*. Norwich, NY: J.F. Hubbard, Jr., 1866.
Bennett, Frank M. *Steam Navy of the United States: A History of the Growth of the Steam Vessel of War in the U.S. Navy, and of the Naval Engineer Corps*. Pittsburgh, PA: Warren, 1896. Reprint, New York: Greenwood, 1970.
Bennett, Michael J. *Union Jacks: Yankee Sailors in the Civil War*. Chapel Hill: University of North Carolina Press, 2004.
Beringer, Richard E., Herman Hattaway, Archer Jones, and William N. Still, Jr. *Why the South Lost the Civil War*. Athens: University of Georgia Press, 1986.
Birtle, Andrew J. *U.S. Army Counterinsurgency and Contingency Operations Doctrine, 1860–1941*. Washington, DC: GPO, 1998.
Blessington, Joseph P. *The Campaigns of Walker's Texas Division*. Austin: Pemberton, 1968.
Boatner, Mark M., III. *The Civil War Dictionary*. New York: David McKay, 1959.
Bolster, W. Jeffrey. *Black Jacks: African American Seamen in the Age of Sail*. Cambridge, MA: Harvard University Press, 1997.
Boynton, Charles B. *History of the Navy during the Rebellion*. 2 vols. New York: D. Appleton, 1867–1868.
Bradford, Gershom. *The Mariner's Dictionary*. New York: Weathervane, 1970.
Bragg, Marion. *Historic Names and Places on the Lower Mississippi River*. Vicksburg: Mississippi River Commission, 1977.
Brandt, J.D. *Gunnery Catechism, as Applied to the Service of Naval Ordnance*, New York: D. Van Nostrand, 1864.
A Brief and Condensed History of Parsons' Texas Cavalry Brigade. Waxhachie, TX: J.M. Flemister, 1893.
Brock, Eric, and Gary D. Joiner. *Red River Steamboats*. Charleston, SC: Arcadia, 1999.
Brooksher, William Riley. *War Along the Bayous: The 1864 Red River Campaign in Louisiana*. Washington DC: Brassey's, 1998.
Browne, Henry R., and Symmes E. *From the Fresh Water Navy, 1861–1864: Letters of Acting Master's Mate Henry R. Browne and Acting Ensign Symmes E. Browne*. Edited by John D. Milligan. Naval Letters Series, volume 3. Annapolis, MD: Naval Institute, 1970.
Browne, Junius Henri. *Four Years in Secessia: Adventures Within and Without the Union Lines*. Hartford, CT: O.D. Case, 1865.
Brownlee, Richard S., III. *Gray Ghosts of the Confederacy: Guerrilla Warfare in the West, 1861–1865*. Baton Rouge: Louisiana State University Press, 1958.
Bucy, Carole. *A Path Divided: Tennessee's Civil War Years*. Nashville: Tennessee 200, 1996.
Callahan, Edward W. *List of Officers of the Navy of the United States and of the Marine Corps, from 1775 to 1900, Comprising a Complete Register of All Present and Former Commissioned, Warranted, and Appointed Officers of the United States Navy, and of the Marine Corps, Regular and Volunteer, Compiled from the Official Records of the Navy Department*. New York: L.R. Hamersly, 1901. Reprint, New York: Haskell House, 1969.
Calore, Paul. *Naval Campaigns of the Civil War*. Jefferson, NC: McFarland, 2002.
Campbell, R. Thomas. *Confederate Naval Forces on Western Waters: The Defense of the Mississippi River and Its Tributaries*. Jefferson, NC: McFarland, 2005.
_____. *Gray Thunder*. Exploits of the Confederate Navy. New Orleans: Burd Street, 1996.
_____. *Southern Thunder*. Exploits of the Confederate Navy. New Orleans: Burd Street, 1996.
Canfield, Eugene B. *Civil War Naval Ordnance*. Washington, DC: Naval History Division, U.S. Navy Department, 1969.
Canney, Donald L. *Lincoln's Navy: The Ships, Men and Organization, 1861–65*. London and New York: Conway Maritime, 1998.
_____. *The Old Steam Navy*. Vol. 2, *The Ironclads, 1842–1885*. Annapolis, MD: Naval Institute Press, 1993.
Capers, Gerald M. *The Biography of a River Town: Memphis — Its Heroic Age*. Chapel Hill: University of North Carolina Press, 1939. 292p.
Carter, Samuel, III. *The Final Fortress: The Campaign for Vicksburg 1862–1863*. New York: St. Martin's, 1980.
Castel, Albert. *General Sterling Price and the Civil War in the West*. Baton Rouge: Louisiana State University Press, 1968.
Castlen, Harriet (Gift). *Hope Bids Me Onward*. Savannah: Chatham, 1945.
Catton, Bruce. *The American Heritage Picture History of the Civil War*. New York: American Heritage, 1960.
_____. *The Centennial History of the Civil War*. 3 vols. Garden City, NY: Doubleday, 1961–1965.
_____. *Grant Moves South*. Boston: Little, Brown, 1960.
_____. *Never Call Retreat*. New York: Pocket Books, 1973.
_____. *This Hallowed Ground: The Story of the Union*

Side of the Civil War. Garden City, NY: Doubleday, 1956.

Chamberlain, William H., ed. *Sketches of War History, 1861–1865: Papers Prepared for the Ohio Commandery of the Military Order of the Loyal Legion of the United States*. 6 vols. Cincinnati: R Clarke, 1890–1908.

Chappelle, Howard I. *History of the American Sailing Navy*. New York: W.W. Norton, 1935.

_____. *The Search for Speed Under Sail*. New York: W.W. Norton, 1967.

Christ, Mark K., ed. *Rugged and Sublime: The Civil War in Arkansas*. Fayetteville: University of Arkansas Press, 1994.

Church, Frank L. *Civil War Marine: A Diary of the Red River Expedition, 1864*. Edited and annotated by James P. Jones and Edward F. Keuchel. Washington, DC: History and Museums Division, Headquarters, U.S. Marine Corps, 1975.

Clark, Orton. *The One Hundred and Sixteenth Regiment of New York Volunteers*. Buffalo: Matthews & Warren, 1868.

Cleaves, Freeman. *Rock of Chickamauga: The Life of General George H. Thomas*. Norman: University of Oklahoma Press, 1948.

Coffin, Charles C. *Drum-beat of the Nation*. New York: Harper, 1888.

_____. *My Days and Nights on the Battlefield: A Book for Boys*. By "Carlton," pseud. 2nd ed. Boston: Ticknor and Fields, 1864.

Cogar, William B. *Dictionary of Admirals of the U.S. Navy*. 2 vols. Annapolis, MD: Naval Institute Press, 1989.

Coggins, Jack. *Arms and Equipment of the Civil War*. Garden City, NY: Doubleday, 1962.

Coleman, Silas B. *A July Morning with the Rebel Ram "Arkansas."* War Papers Read before the Commandery of the State of Michigan, Military Order of the Loyal Legion of the United States, No. 1. Detroit: Winn & Hammond, 1890. Reprint, *Papers of the Military Order of the Loyal Legion of the United States*. Reprint ed., 56 vols. Wilmington, NC: Broadfoot, 1994.

Conger, Arthur L. *The Rise of U.S. Grant*. New York: Century, 1931.

Connelly, Thomas Lawrence. *Army of the Heartland: The Army of Tennessee, 1861–1862*. Baton Rouge: Louisiana State University Press, 1967.

_____. *Autumn of Glory: The Army of Tennessee, 1862–1865*. Baton Rouge: Louisiana State University Press, 1971.

_____. *Civil War Tennessee: Battles and Leaders*. Knoxville: University of Tennessee Press, 1979.

Connelly, Thomas W. *History of the 70th Ohio Regiment: From Its Organization to Its Mustering Out*. Cincinnati: Peak Bros., 1902.

Cooling, Benjamin F. *Fort Donelson's Legacy: War and Society in Kentucky and Tennessee, 1862–1863*. Knoxville: University of Tennessee Press, 1997.

_____. *Forts Henry and Donelson: The Key to the Confederate Heartland*. Knoxville: University of Tennessee Press, 1987.

Coombe, Jack D. *Thunder Along the Mississippi: The River Battles That Split the Confederacy*. New York: Sarpedon, 1996.

Cornish, Dudley Taylor, and Virginia Jeans Laas. *Lincoln's Lee: The Life of Samuel Phillips Lee, United States Navy, 1812–1897*. Lawrence: University Press of Kansas, 1986.

Coulter, E. Merton. *The Civil War and Readjustment in Kentucky*. Chapel Hill: University of North Carolina Press, 1926.

Cox, Douglas E. *Joint Operations during the Campaign of 1862 on the TN & Cumberland River*. Carlisle Barracks, PA: U.S. Army War College, 1989.

Cox, Jacob D. *March to the Sea: Franklin and Nashville*. Campaigns of the Civil War, no. 10. New York: Scribner's, 1882.

_____. *Military Reminiscences of the Civil War*. 2 vols. New York: Scribner's, 1900.

Crandall, Warren D., and Isaac D. Newell. *History of the Ram Fleet and Mississippi Marine Brigade*. St. Louis, MO: Buschart Brothers, 1907.

Currie, George E. *Warfare Along the Mississippi: The Letters of Lt. George E. Currie*. Edited by Norman E. Clark. Mount Pleasant: Central Michigan University, 1861.

Cussler, Clive, and Craig Dirgo. *The Sea Hunters*. New York: Simon & Schuster, 1996.

Dana, Charles A. *Recollections of the Civil War*. New York: D. Appleton, 1898.

Daniel, Larry J. *Cannoneers in Gray: The Field Artillery of the Army of Tennessee, 1861–1865*. Birmingham: University of Alabama Press, 1984.

_____ and Lynn N. Bock. *Island No. 10: Struggle in the Mississippi Valley*. Tuscaloosa: University of Alabama Press, 1996.

Davidson, Alexander, and Bernard Stuve. *A Complete History of Illinois from 1673 to 1873*. Springfield: Illinois Journal, 1874.

Davidson, Donald. *The Tennessee*. Vol. 2, *The New River, Civil War to TVA*. Rivers of America. New York: Rinehart, 1948.

Davis, Charles H. *Charles H. Davis: Life of Charles Henry Davis, Rear Admiral, 1807–1877*. Boston and New York: Houghton Mifflin, 1899.

Davis, Jefferson. *Rise and Fall of the Confederate Government*. 2 vols. New York: D. Appleton, 1881.

DeBlack, Thomas A. *With Fire and Sword: Arkansas, 1861–1874*. Fayetteville: University of Arkansas Press, 2003.

Dewey, George. *Autobiography of George Dewey: Admiral of the Navy*. New York: Scribner's, 1913.

Dickey, Thomas S., and Peter C. George. *Field Artillery Projectiles of the American Civil War, Revised and Supplemented 1993 Edition*(tm). Mechanicsville, VA: Arsenal II, 1993.

Dodson, W.C. *Campaigns of Wheeler and His Cavalry*. Atlanta: Hudgins, 1897.

Donald, David Herbert. *Lincoln*. New York: Simon & Schuster, 1995.

Dorsey, Florence. *Road to the Sea: The Story of James B. Eads and the Mississippi River*. New York: Rinehart, 1947.

Douglas, Byrd. *Steamboatin' on the Cumberland*. Nashville: Tennessee Book, 1961.

Driggs, George W. *Opening the Mississippi, or Two Years Campaigning in the Southwest.* Madison, WI: William J. Park, 1864.

Duaine, Carl L. *The Dead Men Wore Boots: An Account of the 32nd Texas Volunteer Cavalry, CSA, 1862–1865.* Austin: San Felipe, 1966.

Duffy, James P. *Lincoln's Admiral: The Civil War Campaigns of David Farragut.* Edison, NJ: Castle, 2006.

Dugan, James. *History of Hurlbut's Fighting Fourth Division.* Cincinnati: Morgan, 1863.

Dunnavent, R. Blake. *Brown Water Warfare: The U.S. Navy in Riverine Warfare and the Emergence of a Tactical Doctrine, 1775–1970.* New Perspectives on Maritime History and Nautical Archaeology. Gainesville: University of Florida Press, 2003.

Durham, Walter T. *Nashville: The Occupied City—the First Seventeen Months—February 16, 1862–June 30, 1863.* Nashville: Tennessee Historical Society, 1985.

_____. *Reluctant Partners: Nashville and the Union—July 1, 1863 to June 30, 1865.* Nashville: Tennessee Historical Society, 1987.

Dyer, Frederick H. *A Compendium of the War of the Rebellion.* 3 vols. Des Moines: Dyer, 1908. Reprint, New York: Thomas Yoseloff, 1959.

Eddy, T.M. *The Patriotism of Illinois: A Record of the Civil and Military History of the State in the War for the Union.* 2 vols. Chicago: Clarke, 1865.

Edwards, John N. *Shelby and His Men, or the War in the West.* Cincinnati: Miami, 1867. Reprint, Waverly, MO: General J.O. Shelby Memorial, 1993.

Ellicott, John M. *The Life of John Ancrum Winslow, Rear-Admiral, United States Navy, Who Commanded the U.S. Steamer "Kearsarge" in Her Action with the Confederate Cruiser "Alabama."* New York: Putnam's, 1905.

Engle, Stephen D. *Struggle for the Heartland: The Campaigns from Fort Henry to Corinth.* Lincoln: University of Nebraska Press, 2001.

Ericson, Peter. *Running the Batteries: The Union Gunboats on the Western Rivers.* Morrisville, NC: Lulu Enterprises, 2007.

Evans, Robley D. *A Sailor's Log: Recollections of a Naval Life.* New York: D. Appleton, 1901.

Faulk, Odie. *General Tom Green, Fightin' Texan.* Waco: Texian Press, 1963.

Faust, Patricia L. *Historical Times Illustrated Encyclopedia of the Civil War.* New York: HarperCollins, 1986.

Feis, William B. *Grant's Secret Service: The Intelligence War from Belmont to Appomattox.* Lincoln: University of Nebraska Press, 2002.

Ferguson, John L., ed. *Arkansas and the Civil War.* Little Rock: Arkansas Historical Commission, 1962.

Fisher, John E. *They Rode with Forrest and Wheeler: A Chronicle of Five Tennessee Brothers' Service in the Confederate Western Cavalry.* Jefferson, NC: McFarland, 1995.

Fisk, Harold. *Geological Investigations of the Alluvial Valley of the Lower Mississippi River.* Washington, DC: U.S. Army Corps of Engineers, 1944.

Fiske, John. *The Mississippi Valley in the Civil War.* New York: Houghton Mifflin, 1900.

Fitzhugh, Lester N. *Texas Batteries, Battalions, Regiments, Commanders and Field Officers, Confederate States Army, 1861–1865.* Midlothian, TX: Mirror, 1959.

Foltz, Charles S., ed. *Surgeon of the Seas: The Adventures of Jonathan M. Foltz.* Indianapolis: Bobbs-Merrill, 1931.

Foote, Shelby. *The Civil War: A Narrative.* 3 vols. New York: Random House, 1958–1974. Reprint, New York: Vintage Books, 1986.

Force, Manning F. *From Fort Henry to Corinth.* Campaigns of the Civil War, No. 2. New York: Scribner's, 1882. Reprint T.Y. Yoseloff, 1963.

Forsyth, Michael J. *The Red River Campaign of 1864 and the Loss by the Confederacy of the Civil War.* Jefferson, NC: McFarland, 2001.

Fort Henry & Fort Donelson Campaigns, February, 1862: Source Book. Fort Leavenworth: General Service Schools, 1923.

Fowler, William H. *Under Two Flags: The American Navy in the Civil War.* New York: W.W. Norton, 1990.

Fox, Gustavus Vasa. *Confidential Correspondence of Gustavus Vasa Fox, Assistant Secretary of the Navy, 1861–1865.* Edited by Robert Means Thompson and Richard Wainwright. 2 vols. New York: De Vinne, 1918–1919.

Frankignoul, Daniel. *Prince Camille de Polignac, Major General, C.S.A. "The Lafayette of the South."* Brussels: Confederate Historical Association of Belgium, 1999.

Franklin, Samuel R. *Memories of a Rear Admiral: Who Has Served for More Than Half a Century in the Navy of the United States.* New York: Harper and Brothers, 1898.

Freemon, Frank R. *Gangrene and Glory: Medical Care during the American Civil War.* Urbana: University of Illinois Press, 2001.

Gabel, Christopher R., and the Staff Ride Team. *Staff Ride Handbook for the Vicksburg Campaign, December 1862–July 1863.* Fort Leavenworth: Combat Studies Institute, U.S. Army Command and General Staff College, 2001.

Gallaway, H.P. *Ragged Rebel: A Common Soldier in W.H. Parsons' Texas Cavalry, 1861–1865.* Austin: University of Texas Press, 1988.

Gates, Paul W. *The Illinois Central Railroad and Its Colonization Work.* Cambridge, MA: Harvard University Press, 1934.

Geer, Allen Morgan. *The Civil War Diary of Allen Morgan Geer, 20th Regiment, Illinois Volunteers.* Edited by Mary Ann Anderson. Denver: Robert C. Appleman, 1977.

Gerteis, Louis S. *Civil War St. Louis.* Lawrence: University Press of Kansas, 2001.

Gibbons, Tony. *Warships and Naval Battles of the Civil War.* New York: Gallery, 1989.

Gibson, Charles Dana, with E. Kay Gibson. *Assault and Logistics.* Vol. 1, *Dictionary of Transports and Combat Vessels Steam and Sail Employed by the Union Army, 1861–1868.* Camden, ME: Ensign, 1995.

_____. *Assault and Logistics*. Vol. 2, *Union Army Coastal and River Operations, 1861–1866*. Camden, ME: Ensign, 1995.

Gildrie, Richard, Philip Kemmerly, and Thomas H. Winn. *Clarksville, Tennessee, in the Civil War: A Chronology*. Clarksville: Montgomery County Historical Society, 1984.

Glazier, Willard. *Battles for the Union*. Hartford, CT: Dustin, Gilman, 1875.

Goodspeed's General History of Tennessee. Chicago: Goodspeed, 1887. Reprint, Nashville, C. and R. Elder, 1973.

Gosnell, H. Allen. *Guns on the Western Waters: The Story of the River Gunboats in the Civil War*. Baton Rouge: Louisiana State University Press, 1949. Reprint, Louisiana State University Press, 1993.

Gott, Kendall D. *Where the South Lost the War: An Analysis of the Fort Henry-Fort Donelson Campaign, February 1862*. Mechanicsburg, PA: Stackpole, 2003.

Grant, Ulysses S. *The Papers of Ulysses S. Grant*. Edited by John Y. Simon. 24 vols. to date. Edwardsville: Southern Illinois University Press, 1967.

_____. *Personal Memoirs of U.S. Grant*. 2 vols. New York: C.L. Webster, 1885–1886. Reprint (2 vols. in 1), New York: Penguin, 1999.

_____. *Personal Memoirs of U.S. Grant: A Modern Abridgment*. New York: Premier, 1962.

Green, Francis Vinton. *The Mississippi*. Campaigns of the Civil War, vol. 8. New York: Scribner's, 1885. Reprint, The Blue & The Gray, n.d.

Griess, Thomas E., ed. *Atlas for the American Civil War*. West Point Military History Series. Wayne, NJ: Avery, 1986.

Grisamore, Silas T. *The Civil War Reminiscences of Major Silas T. Grisamore, C.S.A.* Edited by Arthur W. Bergeron, Jr. Baton Rouge: Louisiana State University Press, 1993.

Groom, Winston. *Shrouds of Glory: From Atlanta to Nashville— The Last Great Campaign of the Civil War*. New York: Atlantic Monthly Press, 1995.

Guelzo, Allen C. *The Crisis of the American Republic: A History of the Civil War and Reconstruction*. New York: St. Martin's, 1995.

Hackemer, Kurt. *The U.S. Navy and the Origins of the Military-Industrial Complex, 1847–1883*. Annapolis MD: Naval Institute Press, 2001.

Haites, Erik F., James Mak, and Gary M. Walton, *Western River Transportation: The Era of Early Internal Developments, 1810–1860*. Baltimore: Johns Hopkins University Press, 1975.

Hamersly, Lewis B. *The Records of Living Officers of the U.S. Navy and Marine Corps*. Philadelphia: J.B. Lippincott, 1870.

Hamilton, James J. *The Battle of Fort Donelson*. South Brunswick, NJ: Yoseloff, 1968.

Hancock, R.R. *Hancock's Diary, or A History of the Second Tennessee Cavalry, with Sketches of the First and Seventh Battalions*. Nashville: Brandon, 1887.

Harrington, Fred Harvey. *Fighting Politician: Major General N.P. Banks*. Westport, CT: Greenwood, 1948.

Harris, NiNi. *History of "Carondelet."* St. Louis, MO: Southern Commercial Bank, 1991.

Harrison, Lowell H. *The Civil War in Kentucky*. Lexington: University Press of Kentucky, 1975.

Hartjie, Robert C. *Van Dorn: Life and Times of a Confederate General*. Nashville: Vanderbilt University Press, 1967.

Hattaway, Herman, and Archer Jones. *How the North Won: A Military History of the Civil War*. Urbana: University of Illinois Press, 1983.

Hay, Thomas Robson. *Hood's Tennessee Campaign*. New York: Neale, 1929.

Hearn, Chester G. *Admiral David Glasgow Farragut: The Civil War Years*. Annapolis, MD: Naval Institute Press, 1998.

_____. *Admiral David Dixon Porter: The Civil War Years*. Annapolis, MD: Naval Institute Press, 1996.

_____. *The Capture of New Orleans, 1862*. Baton Rouge: Louisiana State University Press, 1995.

_____. *Ellet's Brigade: The Strangest Outfit of All*. Baton Rouge: Louisiana State University Press, 2000.

_____. *Rebels and Yankees: Naval Battles of the Civil War*. San Diego: Thunder Bay Press, 2000.

Hedley, F.Y. *Marching Through Georgia: Pen-Pictures of Every-Day Life in General Sherman's Army from the Beginning of the Atlanta Campaign Until the Closing of the War*. Chicago: Donohue, Henneberry, 1890.

Heidler, David Stephen. *Encyclopedia of the War of 1812*. Annapolis, MD: Naval Institute Press, 2004.

Henderson, Mary Bess McCain, Evelyn Janet McCain Young, and Anna Irene McCain Naheloffer. *"Dear Eliza": The Letters of Michel Andrew Thompson*. Ames, IA: Carter, 1976.

Henry, James P. *Resources of the State of Arkansas, with Description of Counties, Railroads, Mines, and the City of Little Rock*. Little Rock: Price & McClure, 1872.

Henry, Robert Selph. *"First with the Most" Forrest*. Indianapolis: Bobbs-Merrill, 1944.

Hicken, Victor. *Illinois in the Civil War*. Urbana: University of Illinois Press, 1991.

Hill, Jim Dan. *Sea Dogs of the Sixties*. Minneapolis: University of Minnesota, 1935. Reprint, New York: A.S. Barnes, 1961.

Hollandsworth, James G., Jr. *Pretense of Glory: The Life of General Nathaniel P. Banks*. Baton Rouge: Louisiana State University Press, 1998.

Hoobler, James A. *Cities Under the Gun: Images of Occupied Nashville and Chattanooga*. Nashville: Rutledge Hill Press, 1986.

Hood, John Bell. *Advance and Retreat: Personal Experiences in the United States and Confederate States Armies*. New Orleans: Published for the Hood Orphan Memorial Fund, 1880.

Hoppin, James M. *The Life of Andrew Hull Foote, Rear Admiral, United States Navy*. New York: Harper and Brothers, 1874.

Horn, Stanley F. *The Army of Tennessee: A Military History*. Indianapolis: Bobbs-Merrill, 1941.

_____. *The Decisive Battle of Nashville*. Baton Rouge: Louisiana State University Press, 1956.

Horn, Stanley F., comp. *Tennessee's War, 1861–1865: Described by Participants.* Nashville: Tennessee Civil War Centennial Commission, 1965.

Hosmer, James K. *A Short History of the Mississippi Valley.* New York: Houghton Mifflin, 1902.

How, Louis. *James B. Eads.* Boston: Houghton Mifflin, 1900.

Howard, Robert P. *Illinois: A History of the Prairie State.* Grand Rapids, MI: William B. Eerdmans, 1973.

Hubbell, John T., and James W. Geary, eds. *Biographical Dictionary of the Union: Northern Leaders of the Civil War.* Westport, CT: Greenwood, 1995.

Huddleston, Duane, Sammie Rose, and Pat Wood. *Steamboats and Ferries on White River: A Heritage Revisited.* Conway: University of Central Arkansas Press, 1995. Reprint, Fayetteville: University of Arkansas Press, 1998.

Huddleston, Edwin G. *The Civil War in Middle Tennessee.* Nashville: Nashville Banner, 1965.

Hughes, Nathaniel Cheairs, Jr., and Roy P. Stonesifer Jr. *The Life and Wars of Gideon J. Pillow.* Chapel Hill: University of North Carolina Press, 1993.

Huling, Edmund J. *Reminiscences of Gunboat Life in the Mississippi Squadron.* Saratoga Springs, NY: Sentinel Print, 1881.

Hunt, Roger D., and Jack R. Brown. *Brevet Brigadier Generals in Blue.* Gaithersburg, MD: Olde Soldier, 1997.

Hunter, Louis C. *Steamboats on the Western Waters: An Economic and Technological History.* Cambridge, MA: Harvard University Press, 1949. Reprint, New York: Dover, 1993.

Huston, James A. *The Sinews of War: Army Logistics, 1775–1953.* Army Historical Series. Washington, DC: Office of the Chief of Military History, United States Army, 1966.

James, Uriah Pierson. *James' River Guide.* Cincinnati: U.P. James, 1866.

Jessee, James W. *Civil War Diaries of James W. Jessee, 1861–1865, Company K, 8th Regiment of Illinois Volunteer Infantry.* Edited by William P. LaBounty. Normal, IL: McLean County Genealogical Society, 1997.

Johnson, Adam R. "Stovepipe." In *The Partisan Rangers of the Confederate Army,* edited by William J. Davis. Louisville, KY: George G. Fetter, 1904. Reprint, Austin: State House Press, 1995.

Johnson, Ludwell H. *Red River Campaign: Politics and Cotton in the Civil War.* Baltimore: Johns Hopkins University Press, 1958. Reprint, Kent, OH: Kent State University Press, 1993.

Johnson, Robert E. *Rear Admiral John Rodgers, 1812–1882.* Annapolis, MD: Naval Institute Press, 1967.

Johnson, Timothy D. *Winfield Scott: The Quest for Military Glory.* Lawrence: University Press of Kansas, 1998.

Johnston, William Preston. *The Life of Gen. Albert Sidney Johnston.* New York: D. Appleton, 1878.

Joiner, Gary, ed. *Little to Eat and Thin Mud to Drink: Letters, Diaries, and Memoirs from the Red River Campaigns, 1863–1864.* Knoxville: University of Tennessee Press, 2007.

Joiner, Gary. *Mr. Lincoln's Brown Water Navy: The Mississippi Squadron.* Lanham, MD: Rowman & Littlefield, 2007.

_____. *One Damn Blunder from Beginning to End: The Red River Campaign of 1864.* Lanham, MD: Rowman & Littlefield, 2003.

_____. *Through the Howling Wilderness: The 1864 Red River Campaign and Union Failure in the West.* Knoxville: University of Tennessee Press, 2006.

Jones, Archer. *Confederate Strategy: From Shiloh to Vicksburg.* Baton Rouge: Louisiana State University Press, 1961.

Jones, James P., and Edward F. Keuchel, eds. *Civil War Marine: A Diary of the Red River Expedition, 1864.* Washington, DC: Naval History Division, Navy Department, 1975.

Jones, Virgil C. *Gray Ghosts and Rebel Raiders.* New York: Holt, 1956.

Jordan, Thomas, and J.P. Pryor. *The Campaigns of Lieut. Gen. N.B. Forrest and of Forrest's Cavalry.* New Orleans and New York: Blelock, 1868. Reprint, New York: Da Capo, 1996.

Joyner, Elizabeth Hoxie. *The U.S.S. "Cairo": History and Artifacts of a Civil War Gunboat.* Jefferson, NC: McFarland, 2006.

Kane, Adam. *The Western River Steamboat.* College Station: Texas A&M University Press, 2004.

Kerby, Robert L. *Kirby Smith's Confederacy: The Trans-Mississippi South, 1863–1865.* Tuscaloosa: University of Alabama Press, 1972.

Killebrew, J.B. *Introduction to the Resources of Tennessee.* 2 vols. Nashville: Tavel, Eastman, and Howell, 1874.

King, William H. *Lessons and Practical Notes on Steam.* Revised by James W. King. New York: D. Van Nostrand, 1864.

Kionka, T.K. *Key Command: Ulysses S. Grant's District of Cairo.* Shades of Blue and Gray Series. Columbia: University of Missouri Press, 2006.

Kiper, Richard L. *Major General John Alexander McClernand: Politician in Uniform.* Kent, OH: Kent State University Press, 1999.

Kitchens, Ben Earl. *Gunboats and Cavalry: A History of Eastport, Mississippi, with Special Emphasis on Events of the War Between the States.* Florence, AL: Thornwood, 1985.

Klein, Benjamin F. *The Ohio River Atlas: A Collection of the Best Known Maps of the Ohio River, from 1713 to 1854.* Cincinnati: Picture Marine, 1954.

Knapp, David. *The Confederate Horsemen.* New York: Vantage, 1966.

Koerner, Gustave. *Memoirs of Gustave Koerner: Written at the Suggestion of His Children.* Edited by Thomas J. McCormick. 2 vols. Grand Rapids, IA: Torch, 1909.

Konstam, Angus, and Tony Bryan. *Confederate Ironclad, 1861–65.* New Vanguard Series 41. Oxford, UK: Osprey, 2001.

_____. *Mississippi River Gunboats of the American Civil War, 1861–1865.* New Vanguard Series 49. London, England: Osprey, 2002.

_____. *Union Monitor, 1861–1865.* New Vanguard Series. London, England: Osprey, 2002.

_____. *Union River Ironclad, 1861–1865*. New Vanguard Series 56. London, England: Osprey, 2002.
LaBree, Ben, ed. *The Confederate Soldier in the Civil War, 1861–1865*. Louisville, KY: Courier-Journal Job Printing, 1895.
Lane, Carl D, *American Paddle Steamboats*. New York: Coward-McCann, 1943.
Lansden, John M. *History of the City of Cairo, Illinois*. Chicago: R.R. Donnelley, 1910.
Lemcke, Julius A. *Reminiscences of an Indianian: From the Sassafras Log Behind the Barn in Posey County to Broader Fields*. Indianapolis: Hollenbeck, 1905.
Lepa, Jack H. *The Civil War in Tennessee, 1862–1863*. Jefferson, NC: McFarland, 2007.
Levy, U.P. *Manual of Internal Rules and Regulations for Men-of-War*. New York: D. Van Nostrand, 1862.
Lewis, Berkeley R. *Notes on Ammunition of the American Civil War, 1861–1865*. Washington, DC: American Ordnance Association, 1959.
Lewis, Charles Lee. *David Glasgow Farragut*. Annapolis, MD: Naval Institute Press, 1943.
Lewis, Lloyd. *Sherman: Fighting Prophet*. New York: Harcourt, Brace and World, 1960.
Logan, Mrs. John A. *Reminiscences of a Soldier's Wife*. New York: Scribner's, 1913.
Longacre, Edward G. *Mounted Raids of the Civil War*. New York: A.S. Barnes, 1975.
Lonn, Ella. *Foreigners in the Union Army and Navy*. Baton Rouge: Louisiana State University Press, 1951.
Lossing Benson J. *Pictorial Field Book of the Civil War: Journeys through the Battlefields in the Wake of Conflict*. 3 vols. Hartford, CT: T. Belknap, 1874. Reprint, Johns Hopkins University Press, 1997.
Lowe, Richard. *Walker's Texas Division, C.S.A.: Greyhounds of the Trans-Mississippi*. Baton Rouge: Louisiana State University Press, 2004.
Luraghi, Raimondo. *A History of the Confederate Navy*. Translated by Paolo E. Coletta. Annapolis MD: Naval Institute Press, 1996.
Lytle, William C., comp. *Merchant Steam Vessels of the United States, 1807–1868: "The Lytle List."* Publication no. 6. Mystic, CT: Steamship Historical Society of America, 1952.
Macartney, Clarence Edward. *Mr. Lincoln's Admirals*. New York: Funk and Wagnalls, 1956.
Mahan, Alfred T. *The Gulf and Inland Waters*. Vol. 3, *The Navy in the Civil War*. New York: Scribner's, 1883.
Maness, Lonnie E. *An Untutored Genius: The Military Career of General Nathan Bedford Forrest*. Oxford, MS: Guild Bindery, 1990.
Manucy, Albert. *Artillery through the Ages*. National Park Service Interpretive Series, no. 3. Washington, DC: GPO, 1956.
Marshall-Cornwall, James. *Grant as Military Commander*. New York: Van Nostrand Reinhold, 1970.
Marszalek, John F. *Commander of All Lincoln's Armies: A Life of General Henry W. Halleck*. Cambridge, MA: Belknap Press, 2004.
_____. *Sherman: A Soldier's Passion for Order*. New York: Free Press, 1993.
Marvel, William. *Burnside*. Chapel Hill: University of North Carolina Press, 1991.
Mayeux, Steven M. *Earthen Walls, Iron Men: Fort DeRussy, Louisiana, and the Defense of Red River*. Knoxville: University of Tennessee Press, 2006.
McCague, James. *The Cumberland*. Rivers of America. New York: Holt, Rinehart and Winston, 1973.
McCammack, Brian. "Competence, Power, and the Nostalgic Romance of Piloting in Mark Twain's *Life on the Mississippi*." *Southern Literary Journal* 39 (March 2006): 1–18.
McClellan, George B. *The Civil War Papers of George B. McClellan: Selected Correspondence, 1860–1865*. Edited by Stephen W. Sears. New York: Ticknor and Fields, 1989.
McCutchan, Kenneth P., ed. *"Dearest Lizzie": The Civil War as Seen Through the Eyes of Lieutenant Colonel James Maynard Shanklin, of Southwest Indiana's Own 42nd Regiment, Indiana Volunteer Infantry, and Recounted in Letters to His Wife*. Evansville, IN: Friends of Willard Library, 1988.
McDonough, James Lee. *Nashville: The Western Confederacy's Final Gamble*. Knoxville: University of Tennessee Press, 2004.
McDowell, Robert Emmett. *City of Conflict: Louisville in the Civil War, 1861–1865*. Louisville, KY: Civil War Roundtable, 1962.
McFeely, William S. *Grant: A Biography*. New York: W.W. Norton, 1981.
McGrath, Tom, and Doug Ashley, *Historic Structure Report: U.S.S. "Cairo."* Denver: National Park Service, U.S. Department of the Interior, 1981.
McMurry, Richard M. *John Bell Hood and the War for Southern Independence*. Lexington: University Press of Kentucky, 1982.
_____. *Two Great Rebel Armies*. Chapel Hill: University of North Carolina Press, 1989.
McPherson, James M. *Battle Cry of Freedom: The Civil War Era*. New York: Oxford University Press, 1988.
_____. *The Negro's Civil War*. New York: Ballantine, 1991.
Melia, Tamara Moser. *"Damn the Torpedoes": A Short History of U.S. Naval Mine Countermeasures, 1777–1991*. Contributions in Naval History, no. 4. Washington, DC: Naval Historical Center, Department of the Navy, 1991.
Melton, Maurice. *The Confederate Ironclads*. New York: Thomas Yoseloff, 1968.
Merrill, James M. *Battle Flags South: The Story of the Civil War Navies on Western Waters*. Rutherford, NJ: Fairleigh Dickinson University Press, 1970.
_____. *The Rebel Shore: The Story of Union Sea Power in the Civil War*. Boston: Little, Brown, 1957.
Miles, Jim. *A River Unvexed: A History and Tour Guide of the Campaign for the Mississippi River*. Nashville: Rutledge Hill, 1994.
Miller, David W. *Second Only to Grant: Quartermaster General Montgomery C. Meigs*. Shippensburg, PA: White Mane, 2000.
Miller, Francis Trevelyan, ed. *The Photographic History of the Civil War*. Vol. 6, *The Navies*. New York: Castle, 191. Reprint, New York: Thomas Yoseloff, 1957.

Milligan, John D. *Gunboats Down the Mississippi.* Annapolis, MD: Naval Institute Press, 1965.

Minnesota Board of Commissioners on Publication of History of Minnesota in the Civil and Indian Wars. *Minnesota in the Civil and Indian Wars, 1861–1865.* 2 vols. St. Paul: Pioneer, 1889.

Mitchell, Joseph B., ed. *The Badge of Gallantry: Recollections of Civil War Congressional Medal of Honor Winners.* New York: Macmillan, 1968.

Monaghan, James. *Civil War on the Western Border, 1854–1865.* Boston: Little, Brown, 1955.

Monaghan, Jay. *Swamp Fox of the Confederacy: The Life and Military Services of M. Jeff Thompson.* Tuscaloosa: Confederate Publishing, 1956.

Montgomery, Frank A. *Reminiscences of a Mississippian in Peace and War.* Cincinnati: Robert Clarke, 1901.

Moore, Frank, ed. *The Rebellion Record: A Diary of American Events.* 12 vols. New York: G.P. Putnam, 1861–1863; D. Van Nostrand, 1864–1868. Reprint, Arno, 1977.itchell,

Morgan, James Morris. *Recollections of a Rebel Reefer.* Boston: Houghton Mifflin, 1917.ome

Morton, John Watson. *The Artillery of Nathan Bedford Forrest's Cavalry.* Paris, TN: Guild Bindery, 1988.

Munden, Kenneth W., and Henry Putney Beard, *Guide to Federal Archives Relating to the Civil War.* Washington, DC: GPO, 1962.

Murphy, John McLeod. *American Ships and Shipbuilding.* New York: C.W. Baker, 1860.

_____ and W.N. Jeffers. *Nautical Routine and Stowage, with Short Rules in Navigation.* New York: D. Van Nostrand, 1861.

Musicant, Ivan. *Divided Waters: The Naval History of the Civil War.* New York: HarperCollins, 1995.

Musser, Charles O. *Soldier Boy: The Civil War Letters of Charles O. Musser, 29th Iowa.* Edited by Larry Popchock. Iowa City: Iowa State University Press, 1995.

Nasatir, Abraham P. *Spanish War Vessels on the Mississippi, 1792–1796.* New Haven, CT: Yale University Press, 1968.

The Navigator, Containing Directions for Navigating the Monongahela, Allegheny, Ohio and Mississippi Rivers. 8th ed. Pittsburgh, PA: Cramer, Speark and Eichbau, 1814; Reprint, University of Michigan Press, 1966.

Neuman, Frederick G. *The Story of Paducah, Kentucky.* Paducah: Young, 1927.

Nevins, Allan. *Fremont: The War for the Union: The Improvised War.* New York: Scribner's, 1959.

Nichols, James L. *Confederate Engineers.* Tuscaloosa: Confederate Publishing, 1957.

Niven, John. *Gideon Welles: Lincoln's Secretary of the Navy.* New York: Oxford University Press, 1973.

Oates, Stephen B. *Confederate Cavalry West of the River.* Austin: University of Texas Press, 1961.

O'Flaherty, Daniel. *General Jo Shelby: Undefeated Rebel.* Chapel Hill: University of North Carolina Press, 1954.

Olmstead, Edwin, Wayne E. Stark, and Spencer C. Tucker. *The Big Guns: Civil War Siege, Seacoast and Naval Cannon.* Bloomfield, Ontario: New York: Alexandria Bay: Museum Restoration Service, 1997.

Page, Dave. *Ships Versus Shore: Engagements Along Southern Shores and Rivers.* Nashville: Rutledge Hill, 1994.

Palmer, John M. *Personal Recollections of General John M. Palmer: The Story of an Earnest Life.* Cincinnati: Robert Clarke, 1901.

Palmer, Patricia J. *Frederick Steele: Forgotten General.* Stanford: Stanford University Press, 1971.

Parker, Foxhall A. *The Naval Howitzer Afloat.* New York: D. Van Nostrand, 1866.

_____. *The Naval Howitzer Ashore.* New York: D. Van Nostrand, 1865.

Parks, Joseph H. *General Edmund Kirby Smith, C.S.A.* Baton Rouge: Louisiana State University Press, 1954.

_____. *General Leonidas Polk, C.S.A.: The Fighting Bishop.* Baton Rouge: Louisiana State University Press, 1962.

Parrish, T. Michael. *Richard Taylor: Soldier Prince of Dixie.* Chapel Hill: University of North Carolina Press, 1992.

Parrish, Tom Z. *The Saga of the Confederate Ram "Arkansas": The Mississippi Valley Campaign, 1862.* Hillsboro, TX: Hill College Press, 1987.

Parsons, Lewis B. *Reports to the War Department.* St. Louis, MO: George Knapp, 1867.

Paullin, Charles Oscar. *Paullin's History of Naval Administration, 1775–1911.* Annapolis, MD: Naval Institute Press, 1968.

Pellet, Elias P. *History of the 114th Regiment, New York State Volunteers.* Norwich, NY: Telegraph & Chronicle Power, 1866.

Perry, James M. *A Bohemian Brigade: The Civil War Correspondents, Mostly Rough, Sometimes Ready.* New York: John Wiley, 2000.

Perry, Milton F. *Infernal Machines: The Story of Confederate Submarine and Mine Warfare.* Baton Rouge: Louisiana State University Press, 1965.

Peterson, Harold L. *Notes on Ordnance of the American Civil War, 1861–1865.* Washington, DC: American Ordnance Association, 1959.

Petrie, Donald A. *The Prize Game: Lawful Looting on the High Seas in the Days of Fighting Sail.* Annapolis, MD: Naval Institute Press, 1999.

Philadelphia Maritime Museum Library. *John Lenthall, Naval Architect: A Guide to Plans and Drawings of American Naval and Merchant Vessels, 1790–1874: With a Bibliography of Works on Shipbuilding ... Collected by John Lenthall (b. 1807–d.1882).* Philadelphia: Philadelphia Maritime Museum, 1991.

Plum, William R. *The Military Telegraph during the Civil War in the United States.* 2 vols. Chicago: Jansen, McClurg, 1882.

Polk, William M. *Leonidas Polk, Bishop and General.* 2 vols. New York: Longmans, Green, 1915.

Pollard, E.B. *The Lost Cause: A New Southern History of the War of the Confederates.* New York: E.B. Treat, 1867.

Ponder, Jerry. *Major General John S. Marmaduke, C.S.A.* Mason, TX: Ponder, 1999.

Porter, David D. *Incidents and Anecdotes of the Civil War*. New York: D. Appleton, 1885. Reprint, Harrisburg, PA: Archive Society, 1997.

_____. *Naval History of the Civil War*. New York: Sherman, 1886. Reprint, Secaucus, NJ: Castle, 1984.

Powers, Ron. *Mark Twain: A Life*. New York: Free Press, 2005.

Pratt, Fletcher. *The Civil War on Western Waters*. New York: Holt, 1958.

_____. *The Navy, a History: The Story of a Service in Action*. Garden City, NY: Garden City, 1941.

Pratt, J.T. *Pen-Pictures of the Officers and Members of the House of Representatives, 26th General Assembly of Missouri* . Jefferson City, MO: Private printing, 1872.

Prokopowicz, Gerald K. *All for the Regiment: The Army of the Ohio, 1861–1862*. Chapel Hill: University of North Carolina Press, 2001.

Prushankin, Jeffrey S. *A Crisis in Confederate Command: Edmund Kirby Smith, Richard Taylor, and the Army of the Trans-Mississippi*. Baton Rouge: Louisiana State University Press, 2005.

Puleston, William D. *Mahan*. New Haven, CT: Yale University Press, 1939.

Rae, Ralph R. *Sterling Price: The Lee of the West*. Little Rock: Pioneer, 1959.

Rafuse, Ethan S. *McClellan's War: The Failure of Moderation in the Struggle for the Union*. Bloomington: Indiana University Press, 2005.

Ramold, Steven J. *Slaves, Sailors, Citizens: African Americans in the Union Navy*. DeKalb: Northern Illinois University Press, 2002.

Reed, Rowena. *Combined Operations in the Civil War*. Annapolis, MD: Naval Institute Press, 1978.

Regimental Association. *History of the 46th Regiment, Indiana Volunteer Infantry, September 1861–September 1865*. Logansport, IN: Wilson, Humphries, 1888.

Reid, Whitelaw. *Ohio in the War: Her Statesmen, Her Generals, and Soldiers*. 2 vols. Cincinnati: Moore, Wilstach & Baldwin, 1868.

Rerick, John H. *The 44th Indiana Volunteer Infantry: History of Its Services in the War of the Rebellion*. Lagrange, IN: Private Printing, 1880.

Rice, Ralsa C. *Yankee Tigers: Through the Civil War with the One Hundred and Twenty-Fifth Ohio*. Edited by Richard A. Baumgartner and Larry M. Strayer. Huntington, WV: Blue Acorn, 1992.

Richardson, Albert D. *A Personal History of Ulysses S. Grant*. Hartford, CT: Winter and Hatch, 1885.

_____. *The Secret Service: The Field, the Dungeon and the Escape*. Hartford, CT: American, 1866.

Ringle, Dennis J. *Life in Mr. Lincoln's Navy*. Annapolis, MD: Naval Institute Press, 1998.

Roberts, William H. *Civil War Ironclads: The U.S. Navy and Industrial Mobilization*. Baltimore: Johns Hopkins University Press, 2002.

Roe, Francis Asbury. *Naval Duties and Discipline, with the Policy and Principles of Naval Organization*. New York: D. Van Nostrand, 1865.

Roland, Charles P. *Albert Sidney Johnston: Soldier of Three Republics*. Austin: University of Texas Press, 1964.

Roman, Alfred. *Military Operations of General Beauregard*. 2 vols. New York: Harper and Brothers, 1884.

Rombauer, Robert J. *The Union Cause in St. Louis in 1862*. St. Louis, MO: Nixon-Jones, 1909.

Rusling, James F. *Men and Things I Saw in Civil War Days*. New edition. New York: Methodist Book Concern, 1914.

Russell, William H. *My Diary North and South*. New York: Felt, 1863.

Safford, James M. *Geology of Tennessee*. Nashville: S.C. Mercer, 1869.

Schafer, Louis S. *Confederate Underwater Warfare: An Illustrated History*. Jefferson, NC: McFarland, 1996.

Scharf, J. Thomas. *History of the Confederate Navy from Its Organization to the Surrender of Its Last Vessel*. New York: Rodgers and Sherwood, 1887. Reprint, New York: Fairfax, 1977.

Schlay, Cora R. *Alexandria in the Civil War*. Four Louisiana Civil War Stories. Baton Rouge: Louisiana Civil War Centennial Commission, 1961.

Sears, Stephen W. *George B. McClellan: The Young Napoleon*. New York: Ticknor and Fields, 1988.

Selfridge, Thomas O., Jr. *Memoirs of Thomas O. Selfridge, Jr., Rear Admiral, U.S.N.* New York: Knickerbocker, 1924. Reprint, Columbia: University of South Carolina Press, 1987.

Shalhope, Robert E. *Sterling Price: Portrait of a Southerner*. Columbia: University of Missouri Press, 1971.

Shea, William L., and Terrence J. Winschel, *Vicksburg Is the Key: The Struggle for the Mississippi Valley*. Great Campaigns of the Civil War Series. Lincoln: University of Nebraska Press, 2003.

Sherman, William Tecumseh. *Memoirs*. 2 vols. New York: Appleton, 1875. Reprint, New York: Penguin, 2000.

_____. *Sherman's Civil War: Selected Correspondence of William T. Sherman, 1860–1865*. Edited by Brooks D. Simpson and Jean V. Berlin. Chapel Hill: University of North Carolina Press, 1999.

Sherwood, Isaac R. *Memories of the War*. Toledo: H.J. Crittenden, 1923.

Silverstone, Paul H. *Civil War Navies, 1855–1883*. U.S. Navy Warship Series. New York: Routledge, 2006.

_____. *The Sailing Navy, 1775–1854*. Annapolis, MD: Naval Institute Press, 2001.

_____. *Warships of the Civil War Navies*. Annapolis, MD: Naval Institute Press, 1989.

Simpson, Brooks D. *Ulysses S. Grant: Triumph Over Adversity, 1822–1885*. New York: Houghton Mifflin, 2000.

Simson, Jay W. *Naval Strategies of the Civil War: Confederate Innovations and Federal Opportunism*. Nashville: Cumberland House, 2001.

Slagle, Jay. *Ironclad Captain: Seth Ledyard Phelps and the U.S. Navy*. Kent, OH: Kent State University Press, 1996.

Smith, Jean Edward. *Grant*. New York: Simon & Schuster, 2001.

Smith, Myron J., Jr. *American Civil War Navies: A Bibliography*. Metuchen, NJ: Scarecrow, 1972.

_____. *Le Roy Fitch: The Civil War Career of a Union River Gunboat Commander.* Jefferson, NC: McFarland, 2007.

_____. *The Timberclads in the Civil War: The "Lexington," "Tyler" and "Conestoga" on the Western Waters, 1861–1865.* Jefferson, NC: McFarland, 2008.

_____. *U.S.S. "Carondelet," 1861–1865.* Manhattan, KA: MA/AH, 1982.

Smith, Walter G., ed. *Life and Letters of Thomas Kilby Smith, Brevet Major General United States Volunteers.* New York: Putnam, 1898.

Smith, William E. *The Francis Preston Blair Family in Politics.* 2 vols. New York: Macmillan, 1933.

Soley, James R, *Admiral Porter.* New York: D. Appleton, 1903.

Speer, Lonnie R. *Portals to Hell: Military Prisons of the Civil War.* Mechanicsburg, PA: Stackpole, 1997.

Stamp, Kenneth M. *And the War Came: The North and the Secession Crisis, 1860–1861.* Baton Rouge, Louisiana State University Press, 1970.

Stanley, David S. *Personal Recollections of Major General David S. Stanley.* Cambridge, MA: Harvard University Press, 1917.

Stanley, Henry M. *The Autobiography of Sir Henry Morton Stanley.* Edited by Dorothy Stanley. Boston: Houghton Mifflin, 1909.

_____. *Sir Henry Morton Stanley, Confederate.* Edited by Nathaniel C. Hughes, Jr. Baton Rouge: Louisiana State University Press, 2000.

Starr, Stephen. *The Union Cavalry in the Civil War.* Vol. 3, *The War in the West, 1861–1865.* Baton Rouge: Louisiana State University Press, 1985.

Stern, Philip Van Doren, ed. *Soldier Life in the Union and Confederate Armies.* New York: Premier, 1961.

Stewart, George R. *Names on the Land: A Historical Account of Placenaming in the United States.* New York: Random House, 1945.

Still, William N., Jr. *Confederate Shipbuilding.* Athens: University of Georgia Press, 1969. Reprint, Columbia: University of South Carolina Press, 1987.

_____. *Iron Afloat: The Story of Confederate Armorclads.* Nashville: Vanderbilt University Press, 1971. Reprint, Columbia: University of South Carolina Press, 1985.

_____, ed. *The Confederate Navy: The Ships, Men, and Organization, 1861–1865.* Annapolis, MD: Naval Institute Press, 1997.

Stotherd, R.H. *Notes on Torpedoes, Offensive and Defensive.* Washington, DC: Government Printing Office, 1872.

Surdam, David G. *Northern Naval Superiority and the Economics of the American Civil War.* Columbia: University of South Carolina, 2001.

Swedberg, Claire E., ed. *Three Years with the 92nd Illinois: The Civil War Diary of John M. King.* Mechanicsburg, PA: Stackpole, 1999.

Sword, Wiley. *The Confederacy's Last Hurrah: Spring Hill, Franklin and Nashville.* Lawrence: University Press of Kansas, 1993.

_____. *Embrace an Angry Wind: The Confederacy's Last Hurrah — Spring Hill, Franklin & Nashville.* New York: HarperCollins, 1992.

Symonds, Craig L. *Lincoln and His Admirals: Abraham Lincoln, the U.S. Navy, and the Civil War.* New York: Oxford University Press, 2008.

Taylor, Lenette S. *"The Supply for Tomorrow Must Not Fail": The Civil War of Captain Simon Perkins, Jr., a Union Quartermaster.* Kent, OH: Kent State University Press, 2004.

Taylor, Richard. *Destruction and Reconstruction: Personal Experiences of the Late War.* New York: D. Appleton, 1879.

Thomas, David Y. *Arkansas in War and Reconstruction, 1861–1874.* Little Rock: Central, 1926.

Thomas, Dean S. *Cannons: Introduction to Civil War Artillery.* Arendtsville, PA: Thomas, 1985.

Thompson, M. Jeff. *The Civil War Reminiscences of General M. Jeff Thompson.* Edited by Donal J. Stanton, Goodwin F. Berquist, and Paul C. Bowers. Dayton: Morningside Bookshop, 1988.

Thompson, M.S., ed. *General Orders and Circulars Issued by the Navy Department from 1863 to 1887.* Washington DC: Government Printing Office, 1887.

Thorpe, Thomas Bangs. *The Mysteries of the Backwoods, or Sketches of the Southeast, Including Character, Scenery, and Rural Sports.* Philadelphia: Carey & Hart, 1846.

Townsend, Edward. *Anecdotes of the Civil War in the United States.* New York: D. Appleton, 1884.

Trudeau, Noah Andre. *Like Men of War: Black Troops in the Civil War, 1862–1865.* Boston: Little, Brown, 1998.

Tucker, Louis L. *Cincinnati during the Civil War.* Publications of the Ohio Civil War Centennial Commission, no. 9. Columbus: Ohio State University Press, 1962.

Tucker, Spencer C. *Andrew Foote: Civil War Admiral on Western Waters.* Annapolis, MD: Naval Institute Press, 2000.

_____. *Arming the Fleet: U.S. Navy Ordnance in the Muzzle-Loading Era.* Annapolis, MD: Naval Institute Press, 1988

_____. *Blue & Gray Navies: The Civil War Afloat.* Annapolis, MD: U.S. Naval Institute, 2006.

_____. *Unconditional Surrender: The Capture of Forts Henry and Donelson.* Abilene: McWhiney Foundation, 2001.

Turner, George Edgar. *Victory Rode the Rails: The Strategic Place of Railroads in the Civil War.* Indianapolis: Bobbs-Merrill, 1953.

Twain, Mark. *Life on the Mississippi.* New York: Harper & Brothers, 1950.

United States. Congress. Senate Committee on Veteran's Affairs. *Medal of Honor, 1863–1968: "In the Name of the Congress of the United States."* 90th Cong., 2nd sess. Washington, DC: GPO, 1968.

_____. Navy Department. *Laws of the United States Relating to the Navy.* Washington, DC: GPO, 1866.

_____. _____. *Regulations for the Government of the United States Navy.* Washington, DC: GPO, 1865.

_____. _____. Bureau of Navigation. *Record of Medals of Honor Issued to the Officers and Enlisted*

Men of the United States Navy, Marine Corps, and Coast Guard, 1862–1917. Washington, DC: GPO, 1917.

_____. _____. Mississippi Squadron. *General Orders, Rear Adm. D. D. Porter, Commanding, From Oct. 16th 1862 to Oct. 26th 1864.* St. Louis, MO: R. P. Studley, 1864.

_____. _____. _____. *General Orders, Rear Adm. S. P. Lee Commanding, From Nov. 1st 1864 to April 24th, 1865.* St. Louis, MO: R. P. Studley, 1865.

_____. _____. Naval History Division. *Civil War Naval Chronology, 1861–1865.* 6 vols. in 1. Rev. ed. Washington, DC: GPO, 1966.

_____. _____. _____. *Dictionary of American Naval Fighting Ships.* 8 vols. Washington, DC: GPO, 1916–1981.

_____. _____. _____. *Riverine Warfare: The United States Navy's Operations on Inland Waters.* Rev. ed. Washington, DC: GPO, 1968.

_____. _____. Office of the Secretary of the Navy. *Report of the Secretary of the Navy.* 6 vols. Washington, DC: GPO, 1861–1866.

Van Doren Stern, Philip. *The Confederate Navy: A Pictorial History.* New York: Bonanza, 1961.

Villard, Henry. *Memoirs of Henry Villard, Journalist and Financier, 1835–1900.* 2 vols. Boston: Houghton Mifflin, 1904.

Walke, Henry. *Naval Scenes and Reminiscences of the Civil War in the United States on the Southern and Western Waters during the Years 1861, 1862 and 1863, with the History of That Period Compared and Corrected from Authentic Sources.* New York: F.R. Reed, 1877.

Walker, Peter F. *Vicksburg: A People at War, 1860–1865.* Chapel Hill: University of North Carolina Press, 1960.

Wallace, Lew. *An Autobiography.* 2 vols. New York: Harper & Brothers, 1906.

_____. *Smoke, Sound & Fury: The Civil War Memoirs of Major General Lew Wallace, U.S. Volunteers.* Edited by Jim Leeke. Portland, OR: Strawberry Hill, 1998.

Warner, Ezra. *Generals in Blue: Lives of Union Commanders.* Baton Rouge: Louisiana State University Press, 1964.

_____. *Generals in Gray. Lives of Confederate Commanders.* Baton Rouge: Louisiana State University Press, 1959.

Wash, W.A. *Camp, Field and Prison Life, Containing Sketches of Service in the South.* St. Louis, MO: Southwestern, 1870.

Waters, Charles M. *Historic Clarksville: The Bicentennial Story, 1784–1984.* Clarksville, TN: Historic Clarksville, 1983.

Way, Frederick, Jr. *Way's Packet Directory, 1848–1994: Passenger Steamboats of the Mississippi River System since the Advent of Photography in Mid-Continent America.* Athens: Ohio University Press, 1983. Revised edition, Athens: Ohio University Press, 1994.

Webster, William G. *The Army and Navy Pocket Dictionary.* Philadelphia: J.B. Lippincott, 1865.

Webster's Geographical Dictionary. Rev. ed. Springfield, MA: G.&C. Merriam, 1966.

Weigley, Russell F. *Quartermaster General of the Union Army: A Biography of M.C. Meigs.* New York: Columbia University Press, 1959.

Welcher, Frank J. *The Union Army, 1861–1865: Organization and Operations.* Vol. 3, *The Western Theater.* Bloomington: Indiana University Press, 1993.

Welles, Gideon. *The Diary of Gideon Welles, Secretary of the Navy under Lincoln and Johnson.* Edited by John T. Morse, Jr. 3 vols. Boston: Houghton Mifflin, 1911. Reprint, New York: W.W. Norton, 1960.

Wells, Tom H. *The Confederate Navy: A Study in Organization.* Tuscaloosa: University of Alabama Press, 1971.

West, Richard S. *Gideon Welles, Lincoln's Navy Department.* Indianapolis: Bobbs-Merrill, 1943.

_____. *Mr. Lincoln's Navy.* New York: Longman's, Green, 1957.

_____. *The Second Admiral: A Life of David Dixon Porter, 1813–1891.* New York: Coward-McCann, 1937.

Wideman, John C. *The Sinking of the U.S.S. "Cairo."* Jackson: University Press of Mississippi, 1993.

Wiley, Bell I. *The Life of Billy Yank, the Common Soldier of the Union.* New York: Bobbs-Merrill, 1952. Reprint, Baton Rouge: Louisiana State University Press, 1991.

_____. *The Life of Johnny Reb, the Common Soldier of the Confederacy.* New York: Bobbs-Merrill, 1943. Reprint. Baton Rouge: Louisiana State University Press, 1990.

Wiley, William. *The Civil War Diary of a Common Soldier.* Edited by Terrence J. Winschel. Baton Rouge: Louisiana State University Press, 2001.

Wilkie, Franc B. *Pen and Powder.* Boston: Ticknor, 1888.

Williams, T. Harry. *Lincoln and His Generals.* New York: Alfred Knopf, 1952. Reprint, New York: Vintage, 1962.

_____. *P.G.T. Beauregard.* Baton Rouge: Louisiana State University Press, 1954.

Wilson, James Grant, and John Fiske, eds. *Appleton's Cyclopaedia of American Biography.* 5 vols. New York: D. Appleton, 1888.

Wilson, James H. *The Life of John A. Rawlins.* New York: Neale, 1916.

_____. *Under the Old Flag.* 2 vols. New York: D. Appleton, 1912.

Winters, John D. *The Civil War in Louisiana.* Baton Rouge: Louisiana State University Press, 1963.

Winters, William. *The Musick of the Mocking Birds, the Roar of the Cannon: The Diary and Letters of William Winters.* Edited by Steven E. Woodworth. Lincoln, NE: University of Nebraska Press, 1998.

Woodworth, Steven E. *Jefferson Davis and His Generals: The Failure of Confederate Command in the West.* Lawrence: University Press of Kansas, 1990.

_____. *Nothing but Victory: The Army of the Tennessee, 1861–1865.* New York: Alfred A. Knopf, 2005.

_____, ed. *Grant's Lieutenants: From Cairo to Vicksburg.* Lawrence: University Press of Kansas, 2001.

Wyeth, John Allan. *Life of General Nathan Bedford Forrest*. New York: Harper & Bros., 1904 [c1899]. Reprint, New York: Harper, 1959.

Zimmerman, Mark. *Battle of Nashville Preservation Society Guide to Civil War Nashville*. Nashville: Lithographics, 2004.

Articles and Essays in Books or Journals

Ambrose, Stephen E. "The Union Command System and the Donelson Campaign." *Military Affairs* 24 (Summer 1960), 78–86.

Anderson, Bern. "The Naval Strategy of the Civil War." *Military Affairs* 26 (Spring 1962), 11–21.

Aptheker, Herbert. "The Negro in the Union Navy." *Journal of Negro History* 32 (April 1947), 169–200.

Arnold, James R. "Rough Work on the Mississippi." *Naval History* 13, no. 5 (1999), 38–43.

Bailey, Anne J. "Chasing Banks Out of Louisiana: Parson's Texas Cavalry in the Red River Campaign." *Civil War Regiments: A Journal of the American Civil War* 2 (1992), 212–233.

Barnhart, Donald, Jr. "Junkyard Ironclad." *Civil War Times Illustrated* 40 (May 2001), 31–37, 67–68.

Bastian, David F. "Opening of the Mississippi during the Civil War." In *New Aspects of Naval History: Selected Papers from the Fifth Naval History Symposium*. Edited by U.S. Navy Academy, Department of History. Baltimore: Nautical & Aviation, 1985.

Bearss, Edwin C. "The Construction of Forts Henry and Donelson." *West Tennessee Historical Society Publications*, 21 (1967), 24–47.

_____. "The Fall of Fort Henry, Tennessee." *West Tennessee Historical Society Publications* 17 (1963), 85–107.

_____. "Grand Gulf's Role in the Civil War." *Civil War History* 5 (March 1959), 5–29.

_____. "The Ironclads at Fort Donelson." *The Register of the Kentucky Historical Society* 74 (January, April, July 1976), 1–9, 73–84, 167–191.

_____. "The Trans-Mississippi Confederates Attempt to Relieve Vicksburg." *McNeese Review* 15 (1964), 46–70.

_____. "Unconditional Surrender: The Fall of Fort Donelson." *Tennessee Historical Quarterly* 21 (June 1962), 47–62.

Bearss, Edwin C., and Howard P. Nash. "Fort Henry." *Civil War Times Illustrated* 4 (November 1965), 9–15.

Bearss Edwin C., and Warren E. Grabau. "How Porter's Flotilla Ran the Gauntlet Past Vicksburg." *Civil War Times Illustrated* 1 (December 1962), 38–47.

Bedford, Hugh S. "Fight between the Batteries and Gunboats at Fort Donelson." *Southern Historical Society Papers* 13 (1885), 165–173.

Bergeron, Arthur W., Jr. "General Richard Taylor as a Military Commander." *Louisiana History* 23 (Winter 1982), 35–47.

Bigelow, Martha M. "The Significance of Milliken's Bend in the Civil War." *Journal of Negro History* 45 (Fall 1960), 156–163.

Billias, George A. "Maine Lumbermen Rescue the Red River Fleet." *New England Social Studies Bulletin*, no. 16 (January 1958), 5–8.

Blake, W.H. "Coal Barging in Wartime, 1861–1865." *Gulf States Historical Magazine* 1 (May 1903), 409–412.

Blume, Kenneth J. "'Concessions Where Concessions Could Be Made': The Naval Efficiency Boards of 1855–1857." In *New Interpretations in Naval History: Selected Papers from the 14th Naval History Symposium*. Edited by Randy Carol Balano and Craig L. Symonds. Annapolis, MD: Naval Institute Press, 2001.

Bogle, Robert V. "Defeat through Default: Confederate Naval Strategy for the Upper Tennessee and Its Tributaries, 1861–1862." *Tennessee Historical Quarterly* 18 (Spring 1968), 62–71.

Branch, Mary Emerson. "The Story Behind the Story of the *Arkansas* and the *Carondelet*." *Missouri Historical Review* 79 (1985), 313–331.

Brewer, Charles C. "African-American Sailors and the Unvexing of the Mississippi River." *Prologue* 30 (Winter 1996), 279–286.

Brown, H.D. "The First Successful Torpedo and What It Did." *Confederate Veteran* 18 (1910), 169.

Brown, Henry. "The Dark and the Light Side of the River War." Edited by John D. Milligan. *Civil War Times Illustrated* 9 (December 1970), 12–18.

Burpo, Robert. "Notes on the First Fleet Engagement in the Civil War." *American Neptune* 19 (October 1959), 265–273.

Buttgenbach, Walter J. "Coast Defense in the Civil War: Fort Donelson," *Journal of the U.S. Artillery* 39 (March 1913), 210–216.

Callender, Eliot. "What a Boy Saw on the Mississippi River." In *Military Essays and Recollections: Papers Read Before the Illinois Commandery, Military Order of the Loyal Legion of the United States*. 4 vols. Chicago: A.C. McClurg, 1891. Vol. 1, 51–68.

Campbell, James Edwin. "Recent Addresses of James Edwin Campbell: The Mississippi Squadron." *Ohio Archaeological and Historical Quarterly* 34 (January 1925), 29–64.

Carson, Kevin. "21 Days to Glory: The Saga of the Confederate Ram *Arkansas*." *Sea Classics* 39 (July 2006), 38–41, 58–59.

Catton, Bruce. "Glory Road Began in the West." *Civil War History* 6 (June 1960), 229–237.

Chamberlain, S. "Opening of the Upper Mississippi and the Siege of Vicksburg." *Magazine of Western History* 5 (March 1887), 609–624.

Chandler, Walter. "The Memphis Navy Yard." *West Tennessee Historical Papers* 1 (1947), 68–72.

Coggins, Jack. "Civil War Naval Ordnance: Weapons and Equipment." *Civil War Times Illustrated* 4 (November 1964), 16–20.

Coleman, Silas B., and Paul Stevens. "A July Morning with the Rebel Ram Arkansas." *U.S. Naval Institute Proceedings* 88 (July 1962), 84–97.

Conger, A.L. "Fort Donelson." *The Military Historical and Economis* 1 (January 1916), 33–62.

Cozzens, Peter. "Roadblock on the Mississippi." *Civil War Times Illustrated* 41 (March 2002), 40–49.

Davis, Steven R. "Workhorse of the Western Waters: The Timberclad *Tyler*." *Civil War Times Illustrated* 44 (February 2005), 34–40, 80.

DeBlack, Thomas A. "'We Must Stand or Fall Alone.'" In *Rugged and Sublime: The Civil War in Arkansas*. Edited by Mark K. Christ. Fayetteville: University of Arkansas Press (1994).

Dillon, John F. "The Role of Riverine Warfare in the Civil War." *Naval War College Review* 25 (March–April 1973), 62–63+.

Dorsett, Phyllis F. "James B. Eads: Navy Shipbuilder, 1861," *U.S. Naval Institute Proceedings* 101 (August 1975), 76–79.

East, Sherrod E. "Montgomery C. Meigs and the Quartermaster Department." *Military Affairs* 25 (Winter 1961–1962), 183–196.

Eisterhold, John A. "Fort Heiman: Forgotten Fortress." *West Tennessee Historical Society Papers* 28 (1974), 43–54.

Fitzhugh, Lester N. "Texas Forces in the Red River Campaign." *Texas Military History* 3 (Spring 1963), 15–22.

Fitzpatrick, Mike. "Miasma Fogs and River Mists." *Military Images* 25 (January-February 2004), 25–29.

Foreman, Grant. "River Navigation in the Early Southwest," *The Mississippi Valley Historical Review* 15 (June 1928), 34–55.

Gaden, Elmer L., Jr. "Eads and the Navy of the Mississippi." *American Heritage of Invention & Technology* 9 (Spring 1994), 24–31.

Geoghegan, William E. "Study for a Scale Model of the U.S.S. *Carondelet*." *Nautical Research Journal* 17 (Fall and Winter 1970), 147–163, 231–236.

Gerteis, Louis S. "Wartime Production and Labor Unrest in Civil War St. Louis." *Gateway Heritage* 22, no. 3 (2001–2002), 6–13.

Gift, George W. "The Story of the *Arkansas*." *Southern Historical Society Papers* 8 (1884), 48–54.

Gillespie, Michael L. "The Novel Experiment: Cottonclads and Steamboats." *Civil War Times Illustrated* 22 (December 1983), 34–36.

Goodwin, Martha. "The Ram *Arkansas*." *Confederate Veteran* 28 (January–December 1920), 263–264.

Gulick, Charles Heckman ("Heck"). "Letters from 'Heck.'" Edited by Stan Hamper. *Civil War Times Illustrated* 21 (June 1982), 24–31.

Hagerman, Edward. "Field Transportation and Strategic Mobility in the Union Armies." *Civil War History* 34 (June 1988), 143–171.

Hirsch, Charles B. "Gunboat Personnel on the Western Waters." *Mid-America* 34 (April 1952), 73–86.

Hogan, George M. "Parson's Brigade of Texas Cavalry." *Confederate Veteran* 33 (January 1925), 17–19.

Hogane, James T. "Reminiscences of the Siege of Vicksburg." *Southern Historical Society Papers* 11 (April–May 1883), 4854–4886.

Holcombe, John L., and Walter J. Buttgenbachli. "Coast Defense in the Civil War: Fort Henry, Tennessee." *Journal of the United States Artillery* 39 (January 1913), 83–90.

Horn, Stanley F. "Nashville during the Civil War." *Tennessee Historical Quarterly* 4 (March 1945), 3–22.

_____. "Nashville: The Most Decisive Battle of the War." *Civil War Times Illustrated* 3 (December 1964), 4–11, 31–36.

Huffstot, Robert S. "The *Carondelet* and Other 'Pook' Turtles." *Civil War Times Illustrated* 6 (August 1967), 4–11.

_____. "The Story of the C.S.S. *Arkansas*." *Civil War Times Illustrated* 7 (July 1968), 20–27.

Huston, James A. "Logistical Support of Federal Armies in the Field." *Civil War History* 7 (March 1961), 36–47.

Johnson, John. "Story of the Confederate Armored Ram *Arkansas*." *Southern Historical Society Papers* 33 (1905), 1–15.

Johnson, Kenneth R. "Confederate Defense and Union Gunboats on the Tennessee River." *The Alabama Historical Quarterly* 64 (Summer 1968), 39–60.

Joiner, Gary D. "The Congressional Investigation Following the Red River Campaign." *North Louisiana History* 35 (Fall 2004), 147–167.

_____. "The Red River Campaign." *Louisiana Cultural Vistas* (Fall 2006), 58–69.

_____. "Up the Red River and Down to Defeat." *America's Civil War* (March 2004), 22–29.

_____ and Charles E. Vetter. "The Union Naval Expedition on the Red River, March 12–May 22, 1864." *Civil War Regiments: A Journal of the American Civil War* 4, no. 2 (1994), 26–67.

Jones, Archer. "Tennessee and Mississippi: Joe Johnston's Strategic Problem." *Tennessee Historical Quarterly* 18 (June 1959), 134–147.

Jones, Virgil Carrington. "The Naval War: Introduction." *Civil War History* 9 (June 1963), 117–120.

Landers, H.L. "Wet Sand and Cotton: Banks' Red River Campaign." *Louisiana Historical Quarterly* 19 (January 1936), 150–195.

Long, E.B. "Plum Point Bend: The Forgotten Battle." *Civil War Times Illustrated* 11 (June 1972), 4–11.

Maness, Lonnie E. "Fort Pillow Under Confederate and Union Control." *West Tennessee Historical Society Papers* 38 (1984), 84–98.

Mangum, Ronald S. "The Vicksburg Campaign: A Study in Joint Operations." *Parameters* 21 (Autumn 1991), 74–86.

Martin, David. "The Red River Campaign." *Strategy and Tactics*, no. 106 (1986), 11–20.

Martin, Hiram H. "Service Afield and Afloat: A Reminiscence of the Civil War, Edited by Guy R. Everson." *Indiana Magazine of History* 89 (March 1993), 35–56.

Maury, D.H. "Sketch of General Richard Taylor." *Southern Historical Society Papers* 7 (1879), 343–345.

McClinton, Oliver W. "The Career of the Confederate States Ram *Arkansas*." *Arkansas Historical Quarterly* 7 (Winter 1948), 329–333.

McCreary, James Bennett. "Journal of My Soldier Life." *Register of the Kentucky State Historical Society* 33 (April–July 1935), 97–117, 191–211.

Meier, Walter F. "A Confederate Private ['Spot' F. Terrell] at Fort Donelson, 1862." *American Historical Review* 31 (April 1926), 477–484.

Melville, Philip. "*Carondelet* Runs the Gauntlet." *American Heritage* 10 (October 1959), 65–77.

Merrill, James M. "Cairo, Illinois: Strategic Civil War River Port." *Journal of the Illinois State Historical Society* 76 (Winter 1983), 242–257.

_____. "Capt. Andrew Hull Foote and the Civil War on Tennessee Waters." *Tennessee Historical Quarterly* 30 (1971), 83–93.

_____. "Union Shipbuilding on Western Waters during the Civil War." *Smithsonian Journal of History* 3 (Winter 1968–1969), 17–44.

Meyer, Roland L., Jr., "Inland Shipyard Saga." *Marine Engineering and Shipping Review* 51 (February 1946), 127–129.

Michael, William H.C. "How the Mississippi Was Opened." *Civil War Sketches and Incidents: Papers Read before the Nebraska Commandery, Military Order of the Loyal Legion of the United States* (Omaha: The Commandery, 1902).

_____. "The Mississippi Squadron in the Civil War." In *Civil War Sketches and Incidents: Papers Read by Companions of the Commandery of the State of Nebraska, Military Order of the Loyal Legion of the United States.* Omaha: The Commandery, 1902.

Miller, Milford M. "Evansville Steamboats during the Civil War." *Indiana Magazine of History* 37 (December 1941), 359–381.

Milligan, John D. "Expedition into the Bayous." *Civil War Times Illustrated* 15 (January 1977), 12–21.

_____. "From Theory to Application: The Emergence of the American Ironclad War Vessel." *Military Affairs* 48 (July 1984), 126–132.

_____. "Navy Life on the Mississippi River." *Civil War Times Illustrated* 33 (May–June 1994), 16, 66–73.

_____, ed. "The Dark and the Light Side of the River War." *Civil War Times Illustrated* 9 (December 1970), 12–19.

Mullen, Jay C. "Pope's New Madrid and Island No. 10 Campaign." *Missouri Historical Review* 49 (April 1965), 325–343.

_____. "The Turning of Columbus." *Register of the Kentucky Historical Society* 64 (July 1966), 209–225.

Nash, Howard P. "Island No. 10." *Civil War Times Illustrated* 5 (December 1966), 42–50.

Newcomer, Lee N. "The Battle of Memphis, 1862." *West Tennessee Historical Society Papers* 12 (1958), 41–57.

Nichols, George Ward. "Down the Mississippi." *Harper's New Monthly Magazine* 41 (November 1870), 836–845.

Paschall, Rod. "Tactical Exercises— Mission: Protection," *MHQ: The Quarterly Journal of Military History* 4 (Spring 1992), 56–58.

Patrick, Jeffrey L., ed. "A Fighting Sailor on the Western Waters: The Civil War Letters of [De Witt C. Morse] 'Gunboat.'" *Journal of Mississippi History* 58 (September 1996), 255–283.

Perret, Geoffrey. "Anaconda: The Plan That Never Was." *North and South* 6 (May 2003), 36–43.

Pitkin, William A. "When Cairo Was Saved for the Union." *Illinois State Historical Society Journal* 51 (Autumn 1958), 284–305.

Rafuse, Ethan S. "Impractical? Unforgivable?: Another Look at George B. McClellan's First Strategic Plan." *Ohio History* 110 (Summer-Autumn 2001), 153–164.

_____. "McClellan and Halleck at War: The Struggle for Control of the Union War Effort in the West, November 1861–March 1862." *Civil War History* 49 (January 2003), 32–51.

Read, Charles W. "Reminiscences of the Confederate States Navy." *Southern Historical Society Papers* 1 (1876), 333–362.

Reid, Brian Holden. "Rationality and Irrationality in Union Strategy, April 1861–March 1862," *War in History* 1 (March 1994), 25–29.

"Reverend Dr. D.C. Kelley." *Vanderbilt University Quarterly* 9 (October 1909), 236.

Riggs, David F. "Sailors of the U.S.S. *Cairo*: Anatomy of a Gunboat Crew." *Civil War History* 28 (September 1982), 266–273.

Ripley, C. Peter. "Prelude to Donelson: Grant's January 1862 March into Kentucky." *Register of the Kentucky Historical Society* 68 (October 1970), 311–318.

Roberts, John C., and Richard H. Webber. "Gunboats in the River War, 1861–1865." *U.S. Naval Institute Proceedings* 91 (March 1965), 83–100.

Rose, F.P. "The Confederate Ram *Arkansas.*" *Arkansas Historical Quarterly* 12 (Winter 1953), 333–339.

Ross, Reuben R. "River Batteries at Fort Donelson." *Confederate Veteran* 4 (1896), 393–398.

Roth, David E. "The Civil War at the Confluence: Where the Ohio Meets the Mississippi." *Blue & Gray Magazine* 2 (July 1985), 6–20.

Sanger, D.B. "Red River: A Mercantile Expedition." *Tyler's Quarterly Historical and Genealogical Magazine* 17 (October 1935), 70–81.

Saunders, Herbert. "The Civil War Letters of Herbert Saunders." Edited by Ronald K. Hutch. *Register of the Kentucky Historical Society* 69 (March 1971), 17–29.

Sawyer, William D. "The Western River Engine." *Steamboat Bill* 35 (1978), 71–80.

Smith, Myron J., Jr. "The Final Fate of the U.S.S. *Carondelet.*" *Nautical Research Journal* 20 (January 1974), 50–58.

_____. "Le Roy Fitch Meets the Devil's Parson: The Battle of Bell's Mills, December 4–6, 1864." *North & South* 10 (January 2008), 42–53.

Still, William N., Jr. "The Common Sailor — The Civil War's Uncommon Man: Part I, Yankee Blue Jackets." *Civil War Times Illustrated* 23 (February 1985), 25–39.

Stucky. Scott W. "Joint Operations in the Civil War." *Joint Forces Quarterly,* no. 6 (Autumn-Winter 1994–1995), 92–105.

Suhr, Robert C. "Personality: Charles Henry Davis'

Brilliant U.S. Navy Career Was Interrupted, Not Enhanced, by the Civil War." *Military History* 21 (January–February 2005), 74–75.

Swift, John. "Letters from a Sailor on a Tinclad." Edited by Lester L. Swift. *Civil War History* 10 (March 1961), 48–62.

Toplovich, Ann. "Cumberland River." In *The Tennessee Encyclopedia of History and Culture*. Edited by Carroll Van West. Nashville: Rutledge Hill for Tennessee Historical Society, 1998.

_____. "Tennessee River System." In *The Tennessee Encyclopedia of History and Culture*. Edited by Carroll Van West. Nashville: Rutledge Hill for Tennessee Historical Society, 1998.

True, Rowland Stafford. "Life Aboard a Gunboat [U.S.S. *Silver Lake*, No. 23]: A First-Person Account." *Civil War Times Illustrated* 9 (February 1971), 36–43.

Tucker, Spencer C. "Capturing the Confederacy's Western Waters." *Naval History* 20 (June 2006), 16–23.

_____. "Timberclads Attack Up the Tennessee." *Naval History* 16 (February 2001), 27–29.

United States Naval Historical Foundation. "River Navies in the Civil War." *Military Affairs* 18 (Spring 1954), 29–32.

Vitz, Carl. "Cincinnati: Civil War Port." *Museum Echoes* 34 (July 1961), 51–54.

"The Walke Family of Lower Norfolk County, Virginia." *The Virginia Magazine of History and Biography* 5 (October 1897), 149–150.

Walker, Peter F. "Building a Tennessee Army: Autumn, 1861." *Tennessee Historical Quarterly* 16 (June 1957), 99–116.

_____. "Command Failure: The Fall of Forts Henry and Donelson." *Tennessee Historical Quarterly* 16 (December 1957), 335–360.

_____. "Holding the Tennessee Line: Winter 1861–1862." *Tennessee Historical Quarterly* 16 (September 1957), 228–249.

Webber, Richard, and John C. Roberts, "James B. Eads: Master Builder," *The Navy* 8 (March 1965), 23–25.

Wegner, Dana S. "Little Egypt's Naval Station." *U.S. Naval Institute Proceedings* 98 (March 1972), 74–76.

_____. "S.X.: The Federal Gunboat *Essex*." *Nautical Research Journal* 19 (Spring 1972), 49–51.

Weigley, Russel F. "Montgomery C. Meigs: A Personality Profile." *Civil War Times Illustrated* 3 (November 1964), 42–48.

West, Richard, Jr. "Gunboats in the Swamps: the Yazoo Pass Expedition." *Civil War History* 9 (June 1963), 157–166.

_____. "Lincoln's Hand in Naval Matters," *Civil War History* 4 (June 1958), 175–181.

White, Lonnie J. "Federal Operations at New Madrid and Island No. 10." *West Tennessee Historical Society Papers* 17 (1963), 47–67.

Whitesell, Robert D. "Military and Naval Activity between Cairo and Columbus." *Register of the Kentucky Historical Society* 61 (April 1963), 107–121.

Williams, Thomas. "Letters of General Thomas Williams, 1862." *American Historical Review* 14 (January 1909), 309–328.

Winschel, Terrence J. "To Rescue Gibraltar: John G. Walker's Texas Division and the Relief of Fortress Vicksburg." *Civil War Regiments* 3, no. 3 (1993), 33–58.

Unpublished Sources

Barr, Alwyn. "Confederate Artillery in the Trans-Mississippi." Master's thesis, University of Texas, 1961.

Bogle, Victor M. "A 19th Century River Town: A Social-Economic Study of New Albany, Indiana." Ph.D. diss., Boston University, 1951.

Chapman, Jesse L. "The Ellet Family and Riverine Warfare in the West, 1861–1865." Master's thesis, Old Dominion University, 1985.

Getchll, Charles M., Jr. "Defender of Inland Waters: The Military Career of Isaac Newton Brown, Commander, Confederate States Navy, 1861–1865." Master's thesis, University of Mississippi, 1978.

Goodman, Michael Harris. "The Black Tar: Negro Seamen in the Union Navy." Ph.D. diss., University of Nottingham, 1975.

King, George L. "Campaign of Fort Henry & Fort Donelson, 1862." Fort Benning, GA, Infantry School, Fourth Section, Committee "H," 1989. 43 pp. from Google and TN State library page.

Moseley, Cynthia E. "The Naval Career of Henry Kennedy Stevens as Revealed in His Letters, 1839–1863." Master's thesis, University of North Carolina, 1951.

Parker, Theodore R. "The Federal Gunboat Flotilla on the Western Waters during Its Administration by the War Department to October 1, 1862." Ph.D. diss., University of Pittsburgh, 1939.

Polser, Aubrey Henry. "The Administration of the United States Navy, 1861–1865." Ph.D. diss., University of Nebraska, 1975.

Sharpe, Hal F. "A Door Left Open: The Failure of the Confederate Government to Adequately Defend the Inland Rivers of Tennessee." Master's thesis, Austin Peay State University, 1981.

Smith, Myron J., Jr. "A Construction and Recruiting History of the U.S. Steam Gunboat *Carondelet*, 1861–1862." Master's thesis, Shippensburg State University, 1969.

Stonesifer, Roy P., Jr. "The Forts Henry-Heiman & Fort Donelson Campaigns: A Study of Confederate Command." PhD diss., Pennsylvania State University, 1965.

Whisenant, Johnny H. "Samuel Phillips Lee, U.S.N.: Commander, Mississippi Squadron (October 19, 1864–August 14, 1865." Master's thesis, Kansas State College of Pittsburg, 1968.

Wright, Aubrey Gardner. "Henry Walke, 1809–1896: Romantic Painter and Naval Hero." Master's thesis, George Washington University, 1971.

Correspondence and Interviews

Bearss, Edwin C. (National Park Service). Interview with author, May 29, 1969.

_____. Letters to author. June 18, 1969; August 9, 1969.

Catton, Bruce. Letter to author, November 5, 1969.

Cussler, Clive. Telephone interview with author, May 6, 1981.

Donald, David. Letter to author, June 2, 1970.

Geoghegan, William E. (Smithsonian Institution). Letters to author. June 3, 1969; July 3, 1969.

Gray, Teresa (Public services archivist, Special Collections and University Archives, Jean and Alexander Heard Library, Vanderbilt University). "Re: David Campbell Kelley," March 13, 2006. Personal e-mail. March 13, 2006.

Parker, Elmer O. (National Archives). Letters to author. March 13, 1969; March 5, 1970.

Pratt, E.J. (National Park Service). Letter to author, August 21, 1969.

Tippett, William. Letter to author, June 8, 1970.

Index

Numbers in ***bold italics*** indicate pages with illustrations.

African-American crewmen *see* *Carondelet* (U.S. ironclad) officers and men
Alabama, CS regiments: Infantry: 40th 162
Alexandria, LA, falls and rapids of 184, 186, 189–192; *see also* Bailey, U.S. Lt. Col. Joseph; Red River Campaign (1864)
Alps (steamer) 73, 77, 94; *see also* Fort Donelson, TN, Battle of (1862); Island No. 10, Battle of (1862)
Ammerman, U.S. Acting Master Charles H. 46, 149, 168; *see also* *Carondelet* (U.S. ironclad)
"Anaconda Plan" (1861) 7–***8***, 9, 17, 50; *see also* Scott, U.S. Lt. Gen. Winfield
Arizona (steamer) 206; *see also* Nashville, TN, Battle of (1864)
Arkansas (C.S. ironclad) 30, 122–127, ***128***, 129–131, ***132***, 133–137, ***138***, 139–143, 145; *see also* Brown, C.S. Lt. Isaac Newton
Arkansas, CS regiments: Infantry: 12th 103; *see also* Island No. 10, Battle of (1862)
Arthur, U.S. Signal Quartermaster Matthew 66; *see also* *Carondelet* (U.S. ironclad); Fort Henry, TN, Battle of (1862)
Athinson, U.S. Acting First Assistant Engineer George N. 149; *see also* *Carondelet* (U.S. ironclad)

Bache, U.S. Lt. George M. 149, 157, 186, 193; *see also* *Cincinnati* (U.S. ironclad); *Lexington* (U.S. timberclad); *Tyler* (U.S. timberclad)
Bailey, U.S. Lt. Col. Joseph 190–192; *see also* Alexandria, LA, falls and rapids of; Red River Campaign (1864)
Bailey's Dam *see* Alexandria, LA, falls and rapids of; Bailey, U.S. Lt. Col. Joseph; Red River Campaign (1864)
Banks, U.S. Maj. Gen. Nathaniel 177, 181, 184–188, 190–191; *see also* Red River Campaign (1864)
Bannon, U.S. Acting Assistant Surgeon Douglas R. 149; *see also* *Carondelet* (U.S. ironclad)
Baron de Kalb (U.S. ironclad) 147–148, 223; *see also* *St. Louis* (U.S. ironclad)
Bates, Barton (bondsman) 20; *see also* City Series gunboats
Bates, U.S. Attorney Gen. Edward 5–6, 9
Bath, U.S. Acting Master's Mate John 144; *see also* *Carondelet* (U.S. ironclad)
Beauregard, C.S. Gen. P.G.T. 54, 70, 88, 94; *see also* Fort Donelson, TN, Battle of (1862); Island No. 10, Battle of (1862)
Bedford, C.S. Lt. Hugh S. 73–74, 80–81, 83; *see also* Fort Donelson, TN, Battle of (1862)
Bells Mills, TN, Battle of (1864) 202–209, 211–213; *see also* Fitch, U.S. Lt. Cmdr. Le Roy; Kelley, C.S. Col. David C. ("Parson"); Nashville, TN, Battle of (1864); *Neosho* (U.S. monitor)
Belmont, Battle of (1862) 40, 112; *see also* Walke, U.S. Capt. Henry
Benton (U.S. ironclad) 26, 89, 95, 97, 102, 111, 115–119, 125, 134, 153, 165, 170–171, 175, 218, 223; *see also* Clark, U.S. Acting Volunteer Lt. Charles P.; Grand Gulf, MS, Battle of (1863); Greer, U.S. Lt. Cmdr. James A.; Memphis, TN, Battle of (1862); Passage of Vicksburg batteries (1863); Plum Point Bend, Battle of (1862)
Benton, U.S. Senator Thomas Hart 17
Black Hawk (U.S. flagboat) 142, 144, 146, 163, 165, 178–179, 199–200; *see also* Lee, U.S. Acting RAdm. Samuel Phillips; Porter, U.S. RAdm. David Dixon
"Black List" *see* Discipline aboard ship
Blair, Francis P. 17
Blair, U.S. Col. Frank (bond guarantor) 20
Blair, U.S. Postmaster Gen. Montgomery 5, 19, 24
Bowen, C.S. Col. John S. 169; *see also* Grand Gulf, MS, Battle of (1863)
Brennand, U.S. Acting Volunteer Lt. Edward E. 146–147; *see also* *Carondelet* (U.S. ironclad); *Prairie Bird* (U.S. tinclad No. 10)
Briggs, C.S. Lt. H.H. 202; *see also* Bell's Mills, TN, Battle of (1864); Nashville, TN, Battle of (1864)
Brilliant (U.S. tinclad No. 18) 46, 199, 203, 206, 211; *see also* Bell's Mills, TN, Battle of (1864); Nashville, TN, Battle of (1864)
Brown, C.S. Lt. Isaac Newton 122, ***124***, 129, 131–135, 137; *see also* *Arkansas* (C.S. ironclad)
Brown, U.S. Acting Ensign Symmes 153; *see also* *Tyler* (U.S. timberclad)
Bruinsburg, MS Federal cross-river landing (1863) 172–174; *see also* Grand Gulf, MS, Battle of (1863); Vicksburg, MS, 3rd siege (winter-summer 1863)
Buell, U.S. Maj. Gen. Don Carlos 51, 53–54; *see also* Fort Donelson, TN, Battle of (1862)
Buffington, U.S. Lt. Albert 27
Buford, U.S. Col. Napoleon B. 98, 101; *see also* Island No. 10, Battle of (1862)

Cairo (U.S. ironclad) 35, 40, ***48***, 112, 118, 142, 223; *see also* City Series gunboats; Memphis, TN, Battle of (1862); Torpedoes
Callender, U.S. Seaman Eliot 34, 104; *see also* *Cincinnati* (U.S. ironclad)
Cameron, U.S. War Secretary Simon ***6***, 8–10, 13, 22
Campti, LA, Battle of (1864) 187–188; *see also* Red River Campaign (1864)
Carondelet (U.S. ironclad): acceptance inspection (January 1862) 35; Armament (April 1862) 99; Armament (December 1862) 180; Armament (January 1862) 35; arrives at Cairo, IL 32; at Battle of Memphis (1862) 118–121; Bell's Mills, TN, Battle of (1864) 202–209, 211–213; Bruinsburg, MS Federal cross-river landing (1863) 172–174; Clive Cussler hulk search expedition (1982) 225; coaling practice 37; commissioned 34; at Fort Donelson (1862) 70–87; at Fort Henry (1862) 50–69; at Fort Pillow (1862) 111–117; Grand Gulf, MS, Battle of

(1863) 169–174; *Indianola* (U.S. ironclad) salvage (1863) 174–175, 178, 180; at Island No. 10 (1862) 88–110; launched 31; life aboard 41–42, ***43***, 44–49, 175, 179–180, 194; Nashville, TN, Battle of (1864) 195–197, ***198***, 199–216; officers and men 40–42, 196; passage of Vicksburg batteries (1863) 165–166, ***167–168***, 169; Perkin's Landing, MS, Battle of (1863) 176–178; postwar fate 223–224; Red River Campaign (1864) 181, ***182***, 183–186, ***187***, 188–189, ***190***, 191–192; speed 37; stack band color: red 35; Steele's Bayou Expedition (1863) 151–155, 157–163; vs C.S. ram *Arkansas* (1862) 122–143; White River, AR, antishipping war (summer 1864) 192–194; withdrawal from service/sale 219–223; *see also* Ammerman, Acting Master Charles H.; Arthur, Signal Quartermaster Matthew; Athinson, Acting First Assistant Engineer George N.; Bannon, Acting Assistant Surgeon Douglas R.; Bath, Acting Master's Mate John; Brennand, Acting Volunteer Lt. Edward E.; Caven, Acting Ensign Charles H.; City Series gunboats; Clark, Acting Volunteer Lt. Charles P.; DeGroot, Acting Master's Mate William H.H.; Deming, Pilot John; Donaldson, Acting Ensign Oliver; Dorman, Seaman John Henry; Faulkner, Chief Engineer William D.; Fentress, Acting Ensign Walter E.H.; Gibson, Acting Ensign James C.; Gilmore, Master's Mate Theodore S.; Greer, Lt. Cmdr. James A.; Hagerty, Fireman John; Hall, Acting Gunner John; Hastings, Acting Master's Mate Lauren W.; Jordan, Acting Ensign Scott D.; Kantz, Pilot William; Keller, 2nd Lt. Lewis; Lyons, Captain's Clerk Thomas; McWilliams, Acting Third Assistant Engineer John; Miller, Acting Master's Mate Charles W.; Mitchell, Lt. Cmdr. John G.; Morrison, Coxswain John G.; Murphy, Acting Volunteer Lt. John McLeod; Murray, Pilot John; Nexsen, Paymaster George J.W.; Norton, Acting Second Assistant Engineer Michael; Quinn, Acting Ensign Thomas A.; Robertson, Acting Assistant Paymaster G.W.; Rogers, Acting Volunteer Lt. John; Russel, Seaman Saul; Wade, First Master Richard; Walke, Capt. Henry; Weaver, Pilot Daniel; Wilson, Boatswain's Mate Charles; Wilson, Acting Assistant Paymaster/Purser George; Worden, Acting Assistant Paymaster/Purser L.C.

Carondelet Marine Railway and Drydock Company 20–21, 24; *see also* Eads, James B.; Emerson, Primus

Caven, U.S. Acting Ensign Charles H. 68, 206; *see also Carondelet* (U.S. ironclad); Fort Henry, TN, Battle of (1862)

Chalmers, C.S. Brig. Gen. James 202, 212; *see also* Kelley, C.S. Col. David C. ("Parson"); Nashville, TN, Battle of (1864)

Chickasaw Bayou, Battle of (1862) 142–143, 147; *see also* Sherman, U.S. Maj. Gen. William T.; Vicksburg, MS, 2nd siege (fall–winter 1862)

Chillicothe (U.S. ironclad) 147–148

Choctaw (U.S. ironclad) 165

Cincinnati (U.S. ironclad) 34, 40, 56–58, 60, 64–65, 67–68, 71, 97, 111, 113, 116–117, 129, 147, 153–154, 157, 209, 219; *see also* Bache, U.S. Lt. George M.; *City Series* gunboats; Fort Henry, TN, Battle of (1862); Island No. 10, Battle of (1862); Nashville, TN, Battle of (1864); Plum Point Bend, Battle of (1862); Steele's Bayou Expedition (1863)

City Series gunboats: advertising/contracting 16–19; construction 20–***21***, 22–31, ***32–33***, 34–38; design 12–16; recruiting 39–40

Clarendon, AR, CS attack upon (summer 1864) 193–194; *see also Queen City* (U.S. tinclad No. 26); Shelby, C.S. Brig. Gen. Joseph O. ("Jo"); White River, AR, antishipping war (summer 1864)

Clark, U.S. Acting Volunteer Lt. Charles P. 216, 218; *see also Benton* (U.S. ironclad); *Carondelet* (U.S. ironclad)

Coleman, U.S. Paymaster Silas B. 126, 134; *see also Arkansas* (C.S. ironclad); *Tyler* (U.S. timberclad)

Conestoga (U.S. timberclad) 51, 53, 57, 62, 68, 71, 80, 85–86, 147; *see also* Fort Henry, TN, Battle of (1862); Phelps, U.S. Lt. Cmdr. S. Ledyard

Confederate River Defense Fleet 113–117; *see also General Beauregard*; *General Bragg*; *General Earl Van Dorn*; *General Jeff Thompson; General Lovell; Little Rebel*; Memphis, Battle of (1862); Plum Point Bend, Battle of (1862)

Cook, C.S. Lt. Col. W.D.S. 103; *see also* Island No. 10, Battle of (1862)

Corinth, MS, U.S. capture of (1862) 118; *see also* Halleck, U.S. Maj. Gen. Henry

Cricket (U.S. tinclad No. 6) 190; *see also* Red River Campaign (1864)

Cullum, U.S. Brig. Gen. George W. 71; *see also* Halleck, Maj. Gen. Henry

Cussler, Clive (novelist/explorer) 225; *see also Carondelet* (U.S. ironclad) Clive Cussler hulk search expedition (1982)

Cutts, U.S. comptroller J. Madison 38

Daily routine aboard ship 45–47

Dana, U.S. war department envoy Charles A. 176

Danville, TN, railroad bridge destruction (1862) 69

Davidson's Landing, TN *see* Bell's Mills, TN, Battle of (1864); Nashville, TN, Battle of (1864)

Davis, U.S. RAdm. Charles H. 112–113, 115–116, ***118***, 123, 125–126, 135, 140–141; *see also Arkansas* (C.S. ironclad); Fort Pillow, Battle of (1862); Memphis, TN, Battle of (1862); Plum Point Bend, Battle of (1862); Vicksburg, MS, 1st siege (spring–summer 1862)

Davis, C.S. Pres. Jefferson 53, 176; *see also* Vicksburg, MS, 3rd siege (winter-summer 1863)

Deer Creek Expedition (1863) *see* Steele's Bayou Expedition (1863); Vicksburg, MS, 3rd siege (winter-summer 1863)

DeGroot, U.S. Acting Master's Mate William H.H. 149; *see also Carondelet* (U.S. ironclad)

Deming, U.S. Pilot John 100, 108, 128, 146; *see also Carondelet* (U.S. ironclad); *Lafayette* (U.S. ironclad)

Dennis, U.S. Acting Master John S. 192, 194; *see also Huntress* (U.S. tinclad No. 58)

Dennison, Ohio Gov. William 6–7, 10

Diet aboard ship 44–45, 175, 179–180, 194; *see also Carondelet* (U.S. ironclad) life aboard

Discipline aboard ship 46–47; *see also Carondelet* (U.S. ironclad) life aboard

Divine Services 47

Dixon, C.S. Lt. Joseph 73, 76; *see also* Fort Donelson, TN, Battle of (1862)

Donaldson, U.S. Col. James L. 214; *see also* Nashville, TN, Battle of (1864)
Donaldson, U.S. Acting Ensign Oliver 46, 140, 145, 149, 174, 178, 196, 208, 221; *see also* *Carondelet* (U.S. ironclad)
Donelson, TN CS Attorney Gen. Daniel S. 51; *see also* Fort Donelson, TN, Battle of (1862)
Dorman, U.S. Seaman John Henry 66; *see also* *Carondelet* (U.S. ironclad); Fort Henry, TN, Battle of (1862)
Dorman, O.M. (accountant) 38
Dorris, CS Pvt. Wesley Smith 79, 86; *see also* Fort Donelson, TN, Battle of (1862)
Drunkenness *see* Discipline aboard ship

Eads, James B. (contractor) 5–11, ***14***, 17, 19–21, 23–24, 26–29, 31–34, 36–38, 50, 141, 145, 223; *see also* City Series gunboats; Missouri Wrecking Company
Eagle Iron Works 23; *see also* Thom, N.G. (engineer)
Eastport (C.S./U.S. ironclad) 122, 186–190; *see also* Red River Campaign (1864)
Elder, Bishop William Henry 179; *see also* Murphy, U.S. Acting Volunteer Lt. John McLeod
Ellet, U.S. Lt. Col. Alfred 125–127, 135; *see also* *Arkansas* (C.S. ironclad); Mississippi Marine Brigade, U.S.
Ellet, U.S. Col. Charles, Jr. 118–121, 127 *see also* Memphis, TN, Battle of (1862); Mississippi Marine Brigade, U.S.
Emerson, Primus 20; *see also* Carondelet Marine Railway and Drydock Company
Emerson's Ways *see* Carondelet Marine Railway and Drydock Company
Essex (U.S. ironclad) 26, 53, 56–58, 60, 66–68, 71, 125 *see also* *Arkansas* (C.S. ironclad); Fort Henry, TN, Battle of (1862)

Fairplay (U.S. tinclad No.17) 199, 203–***204***, 205–206, 211, 214, 216; *see also* Bell's Mills, TN, Battle of (1864); Fitch, U.S. Lt. Cmdr. Le Roy; Nashville, TN, Battle of (1864)
Farragut, U.S. RAdm. David G. 122–123, 125–126, 135, 140–141; *see also* *Arkansas* (C.S. ironclad); Vicksburg, MS, 1st siege (spring–summer 1862)
Faulkner, U.S. Chief Engineer William D. 74, 99, 101–102; *see also* *Carondelet* (U.S. ironclad)
Fawn (U.S. tinclad No. 30) 192–193; *see also* White River, AR, antishipping war (summer 1864)
Featherston, C.S. Brig. Gen. Winfield S. 159–162; *see also* Steele's Bayou Expedition (1863)
Fentress, U.S. Acting Ensign Walter E.H. 144–145; *see also* *Carondelet* (U.S. ironclad)
Ferguson, C.S. Col. Samuel W. 157–161; *see also* Steele's Bayou Expedition (1863)
Fern (U.S. tugboat) 155; *see also* Steele's Bayou Expedition (1863)
Ferrell, U.S. Pilot John 206; *see also* Bell's Mills, Battle of (1864); *Neosho* (U.S. monitor)
Filtry, Oliver B. (bondsman) 20, 27; *see also* City Series gunboats
Financier (steamer) 206; *see also* Nashville, TN, Battle of (1864)
Fitch, U.S. Lt. Cmdr. Le Roy 197, 199–206, ***207***, 208–213, 215; *see also* *Carondelet* (U.S. ironclad); Kelley, C.S. Col. David C. ("Parson"); Lee, U.S. Acting RAdm. Samuel Phillips; *Moose* (U.S. tinclad No. 34); *Neosho* (U.S. monitor); Thomas, U.S. Maj. Gen. George H. ("Old Pap")
Floyd, C.S. Brig. Gen. John B. 73, 79; *see also* Fort Donelson, TN, Battle of (1862)
Foote, U.S. RAdm Andrew Hull 24–***25***, 27–28, 31–32, 34–37, 39–40, 51, 53, 56–57, 59–60, 63, 65, 67–71, 79–81, 85, 87, 89, 92, 94–98, 104, 111–112; *see also* City Series gunboats; Fort Donelson, TN, Battle of (1862); Fort Henry, TN, Battle of (1862); Fort Pillow, TN, Battle of (1862); Island No. 10, Battle of (1862)
Forest Rose (U.S. tinclad No. 9) 179
Forrest, C.S. Maj. Gen. Nathan B. 144, 195–196, 202, 215–216, ***217***; *see also* Nashville, TN, Battle of (1864)
Forrest Queen (steamer); *see also* Perkin's Landing, MS, Battle of (1863)
Fort Cobun, MS *see* Grand Gulf, MS, Battle of (1863)
Fort Defiance, IL 56
Fort De Russy, LA 184–185; *see also* Red River Campaign (1864)
Fort Donelson, TN, Battle of (1862) 51, 70–73, ***74–76***, 77, ***78***, 79–80, ***81–82***, 83, ***84***, 85, ***86***, 87
Fort Henry, TN, Battle of (1862) 50–51, ***52***, 53–54, ***55***, 56–60, ***61–63***, 64–69
Fort Pillow, TN, Battle of (1862) 111–112, ***113–115***, 116–117; *see also* Plum Point Bend, Battle of (1862)
Fort Sumter, SC, Battle of (1861) 5, 43; *see also* Beauregard, C.S. Lt. Gen. P.G.T.
Fort Wade, MS *see* Grand Gulf, MS, Battle of (1863)
Fort Wright *see* Fort Pillow, TN
Fox, U.S. Assistant Navy Secretary Gustavus V. 6, 24, 35, 142
Franklin, TN, Battle of (1864) 200–201; *see also* Nashville, TN, Battle of (1864)
Free time aboard ship 47–48; *see also* Skylarking
Fremont, U.S. Maj. Gen. John C. 17, 19, 24–25
Frequa, C.S. Pvt. John G. 83; *see also* Fort Donelson, TN, Battle of (1862)
Fulkerson, C.S. Capt. Isaac D. 116; *see also* Confederate River Defense Fleet; *General Earl Van Dorn* (C.S. gunboat); Plum Point Bend, Battle of (1862)

Gaylord, Son & Company 23, 27
General Beauregard (C.S. gunboat) 117–119; *see also* Confederate River Defense Fleet; Plum Point Bend, Battle of (1862)
General Bragg (C.S./U.S. gunboat) 112–113, 116, 118, 136; *see also* Confederate River Defense Fleet; Plum Point Bend, Battle of (1862)
General Earl Van Dorn (C.S. gunboat) 112, 116–118; *see also* Confederate River Defense Fleet; Plum Point Bend, Battle of (1862)
General Jeff Thompson 117–118; *see also* Confederate River Defense Fleet; Plum Point Bend, Battle of (1862)
General Lovell 117–119; *see also* Confederate River Defense Fleet; Plum Point Bend, Battle of (1862)
General Sterling Price (C.S. /U.S. gunboat) 111, 116, 118–119, 153–154, 169; *see also* Confederate River Defense Fleet; Grand Gulf, MS, Battle of (1863); Passage of Vicksburg batteries (1863); Plum Point Bend, Battle of (1862); Steele's Bayou Expedition (1863)
General Sumter (C.S. gunboat) 112, 116, 118; *see also* Confederate River Defense Fleet; Plum Point Bend, Battle of (1862)
Geoghegan, U.S. Smithsonian Institution transportation specialist William E. 16
Getty, U.S. Acting Master Robert

144; *see also Marmora* (U.S. tinclad No. 2)
Gibbons, C.S. Pvt. Israel 91; *see also* Island No. 10, Battle of (1862)
Gibson, U.S. Acting Ensign James C. 149, 180–181; *see also Carondelet* (U.S. ironclad)
Gift, C.S. Lt. George W. 122, 125, 129–132, 134–135, 140, 142; *see also Arkansas* (C.S. ironclad)
Gilmer, C.S. Maj. Jeremy F. 60; *see also* Fort Henry, TN, Battle of (1862)
Gilmore, U.S. Master's Mate Theodore S. 102; *see also Carondelet* (U.S. ironclad); Island No. 10, Battle of (1862)
Glassford, U.S. Acting Volunteer Lt. Henry A. 207–208; *see also Reindeer* (U.S. tinclad No. 35)
Grace, C.S. Pvt. J.M. 101; *see also* Island No. 10, Battle of (1862)
Graham (wharfboat) 28
Grand Gulf, MS, Battle of (1863) 169–174; *see also* Vicksburg, MS, 3rd siege (winter-summer 1863)
Granger, U.S. Brig Gen. Gordon 105; *see also* Island No. 10, Battle of (1862)
Grant, U.S. Lt. Gen. 48, 51, 53, 55, 57–58, 60, 63–65, 68–69, 70–74, ***78***, 79–80, 147–148, 150–151, 153–155, 163, 166, 169–172, 174–175, 178, 181, 185, 218; *see also* Fort Donelson, TN, Battle of (1862); Fort Henry, TN, Battle of (1862); Grand Gulf, MS, Battle of (1863); Vicksburg, MS, 3rd siege (winter-summer 1863)
Greene, C.S. Col. Colton 192; *see also* White River, AR, antishipping war (summer 1864)
Greer, U.S. Pvt. Allen 56; *see also* Fort Henry, TN, Battle of (1862)
Greer, U.S. Lt. Cmdr. James A. 147–149, 175, 177; *see also Benton* (U.S. ironclad); *Carondelet* (U.S. ironclad)
Grimball, C.S. Lt. John 122, 131–132; *see also Arkansas* (C.S. ironclad)
Gulick, U.S. Acting Master's Mate Charles Heckman ("Heck") 166, 168; *see also Ivy* (U.S. tugboat); Passage of Vicksburg batteries (1863)
Gunnery drill ***28***, ***42***, 45, ***47***, 57, 149, 199; *see also Carondelet* (U.S. ironclad) life aboard
Gwin, U.S. Lt. William 40, 71, 125–131, 134–136, 140; *see also Arkansas* (C.S. ironclad); *Tyler* (U.S. timberclad)
Hagerty, U.S. Fireman John 196, 210; *see also Carondelet* (U.S. ironclad)
Hall, U.S. Acting Gunner John 85; *see also Carondelet* (U.S. ironclad)
Halleck, U.S. Maj. Gen. Henry 40, 51, 53, 55, 58, 69–71, 89, 94–95, 97, ***108***, 112, 118, 201–202, 211; *see also* Corinth, MS, U.S. capture of (1862); Fort Donelson, TN, Battle of (1862); Fort Henry, TN, Battle of (1862); Fort Pillow, Battle of (1862); Island No. 10, Battle of (1862); Nashville, TN, Battle of (1864)
Hamilton, Capt. John (postwar owner/wharf boat proprietor) 224; *see also Carondelet* (U.S. ironclad) postwar fate
Hardee, C.S. Maj. Gen. William J. 70
Harris, C.S. Tenn. Gov Isham G. 50–51
Harrol, Capt. 203, 206; *see also* Bell's Mills, TN, Battle of (1864); *Magnet* (steamer)
Hartford (U.S. sloop-of-war) 127, 135; *see also Arkansas* (C.S. ironclad); Farragut, U.S. RAdm. David G.
Hartupee and Company 26, 28; *see also* City Series gunboats
Harwood, U.S. Capt. Andrew A. 22
Hastings, U.S. Acting Master's Mate Lauren W. 149, 203; *see also Carondelet* (U.S. ironclad)
Haynes, C.S. Col. Milton A. 72, 76–77; *see also* Fort Donelson, TN, Battle of (1862)
Heiman, C.S. Col. Adolphus 64; *see also* Fort Henry, TN, Battle of (1862)
Henry, TN C.S. Senator Gustavus A. 51; *see also* Fort Henry, Battle of (1862)
Henry Clay (steamer) 169; *see also* Passage of Vicksburg batteries (1863)
Higgins, C.S. Col. Edward 166; *see also* Passage of Vicksburg batteries (1863)
Hodges, C.S. Pilot John G. 131; *see also Arkansas* (C.S. ironclad)
Hoel, U.S. Acting Volunteer Lt. William R. 100–103, 170; *see also Cincinnati* (U.S. ironclad); Grand Gulf, MS, Battle of (1863); Island No. 10, Battle of (1862); Pittsburg (U.S. ironclad)
Hogane, C.S. Maj. James T. 166; *see also* Passage of Vicksburg batteries (1863)
Hollins, C.S. Com. George N. 105; *see also* Island No. 10, Battle of (1862)
Hood, C.S. Gen. John Bell 195–197, 200–202, 214–217; *see also* Nashville, TN, Battle of (1864)
Hottenstein, U.S. Capt. John A. 98, 101, 107; *see also* Illinois, US regiments: Infantry: 42nd; Island No. 10, Battle of (1862)
Hovey, U.S. Brig. Gen. Alvin P. 142
Hull, U.S. Com. James B. 175, 178; *see also Indianola* (U.S. ironclad)
Hunter, U.S. Lt. James M. 126–127, 130, 134; *see also Arkansas* (C.S. ironclad); *Queen of the West* (U.S. ram)
Huntress (U.S. tinclad No. 58) 192; *see also* White River, AR, antishipping war (summer 1864)

Illinois (steamer) 69
Illinois, U.S. regiments: Infantry: 20th 56; 27th 98; 32nd 69; 42nd 98; 63rd 126
In Harm's Way (movie) 204
Indianola (U.S. ironclad) salvage (1863) 174–175, 178, 180
Iowa, U.S. regiments: Cavalry: 5th 78–79
Island No. 10, Battle of (1862) 50, 88–89, ***90***, 91–92, ***93–96***, 97–98, ***99–100***, 101–105, ***106–108***, 109–110
Ivy (U.S. tugboat) 166; *see also* Passage of Vicksburg batteries (1863)

J.F. McComb (steamer) 206; *see also* Nashville, TN, Battle of (1864)
Jacobs, Daniel (steamboat buyer) 222; *see also Carondelet* (U.S. ironclad) withdrawal from service/sale
John Warner (steamer) 188; *see also* Red River Campaign (1864)
Johnson, U.S. Vice President/President Andrew 219
Johnson, U.S. Brig. Gen. Richard W. 212; *see also* Nashville, TN, Battle of (1864)
Johnston, C.S. Lt. Gen. Albert Sidney 50, 51, 54, 70–71; *see also* Fort Donelson, TN, Battle of (1862)
Jones, U.S. Port of St. Louis Collector Asa (bond guarantor) 20
Jones, William (constructor) 19
Jordan, U.S. Acting Ensign Scott D. 41–42, ***148***–149, 171, 175, 178–180, 186, 191, 193–194, 196–197, 199, 216, 218; *see also Carondelet* (U.S. ironclad)
Juliet (U.S. tinclad No. 4) 144

Kantz, U.S. Pilot William 149, 168; *see also Carondelet* (U.S. ironclad)

Keller, U.S. 2nd Lt. Lewis 149; *see also Carondelet* (U.S. ironclad); Ohio, U.S. regiments: Infantry: 58th
Kelley, C.S. Col. David C. ("Parson") ***199***, 202–205, 207–213; *see also* Bell's Mills, TN, Battle of (1864); Fitch, U.S. Lt. Cmdr. Le Roy; Nashville, TN, Battle of (1864)
Kilty, U.S. Cmdr. Augustus 115, 117; *see also Mound City* (U.S. ironclad); Plum Point Bend, Battle of (1862)
Kirby Smith, C.S. Gen. E. 220
Kirby Smith, U.S. Col. J.L. 105, 176; *see also* Island No. 10, Battle of (1862); Perkin's Landing, MS, Battle of (1863)

Lady Franklin (steamer) 206; *see also* Nashville, TN, Battle of (1864)
Lafayette (U.S. ironclad) 145–147, 149, 165–166, 169–174; *see also* Grand Gulf, MS, Battle of (1863); Passage of Vicksburg batteries (1863); Walke, Capt. Henry
Lancaster (U.S. ram) 125, 127; *see also Arkansas* (C.S. ironclad)
Laurel (U.S. tugboat) 144
Lee, C.S. Lt. Gen. Robert E. 50, 218
Lee, U.S. Acting RAdm. Samuel Philips 195, 197, 199–200, 206, 209, 214–217, 219–***220***; *see also Black Hawk* (U.S. flagboat); Nashville, TN, Battle of (1864); Thomas, U.S. Maj. Gen. George H. ("Old Pap")
Lenthall, U.S. Naval Constructor John ***12***, 13–14, 30; *see also* City Series gunboats
Leonard, C.S. Capt. N.H.H. 116; *see also General Bragg* (C.S. gunboat); Memphis, TN, Battle of (1862); Plum Point Bend, Battle of (1862)
Lexington (U.S. timberclad) 32, 53, 57, 65, 71, 147, 186, 189, 191; *see also* Alexandria, LA, falls and rapids of; Red River Campaign (1864); Bache, U.S. Lt. George M.; Fort Henry, TN, Battle of (1862)
Lilly (steamer) 206; *see also* Nashville, TN, Battle of (1864)
Lincoln, U.S. President Abraham 5–7, 9, 218–219
Litherbury, John (construction superintendent) 22, 24, 34; *see also* City Series gunboats
Little Rebel (C.S. gunboat) 116, 118; *see also* Confederate River Defense Fleet; Plum Point Bend, Battle of (1862)
Livingston, U.S. Com. John W. 219; *see also Carondelet* (U.S. ironclad) withdrawal from service/sale
Louisiana, CS regiments: Infantry: 5th 91
Louisville (U.S. ironclad) 32, 71, 80, 84–85, 118, 147, 153–155, 160–162, 165, 171, 180, 187; *see also* City Series gunboats; Fort Donelson, TN, Battle of (1862); Grand Gulf, MS, Battle of (1863); Memphis, TN, Battle of (1862); Owen, U.S. Lt. Cmdr. Robert K.; Passage of Vicksburg batteries (1863); Steele's Bayou Expedition (1863)
Lynch, C.S. Flag Officer William F. 122, 134; *see also Arkansas* (C.S. ironclad)
Lyon, C.S. Brig. Gen. Hylan B. 216; *see also* Nashville, TN, Battle of (1864),
Lyons, U.S. Captain's Clerk Thomas 145–146; *see also Carondelet* (U.S. ironclad); *Lafayette* (U.S. ironclad); Walke, U.S. Capt. Henry

Mackall, C.S. Brig. Gen. William W. 89, 105; *see also* Island No. 10, Battle of (1862)
Magnet (steamer) 203, 206, 214; *see also* Bell's Mills, TN, Battle of (1864)
Mansfield, LA, Battle of (1864) 187; *see also* Red River Campaign (1864)
Marmaduke, C.S. Brig. Gen. John S. 192; *see also* White River, AR, antishipping war (summer 1864)
Marmora (U.S. tinclad No. 2) 144; *see also* Getty, U.S. Acting Master Robert
Massachusetts, U.S. regiments: Infantry: 13th 126
Maurepas (C.S. gunboat) 111
Maury Artillery *see* Tennessee, CS regiments: Artillery, 1st Heavy
McClellan, U.S. Maj. Gen. George B. 7, 9–11, 15–17, 24, 53–54
McCowan, C.S. Brig. Gen. John P. 89; *see also* Island No. 10, Battle of (1862)
McCulloch, C.S. Brig. Gen. Henry E. 177–178; *see also* Perkin's Landing, MS, Battle of (1863)
McGee, U.S. master carpenter James R. 35
McGill (steamer) 78
McGinnis, U.S. Brig. Gen. George F. 172; *see also* Vicksburg, MS, 3rd siege (winter-summer 1863)
McPherson, U.S. Col. James B. 69
McWilliams, U.S. Acting Third Assistant Engineer John 149; *see also Carondelet* (U.S. ironclad)
Meigs, U.S. Quartermaster General/Brig. Gen. Montgomery C. 13–17, 19–23, 26–28, ***29***, 32, 34, 38, 214; *see also* City Series gunboats
Memphis, TN, Battle of (1862) 118–121, 127; *see also* Confederate River Defense Fleet; Ellet, U.S. Col. Charles, Jr.; Mississippi Marine Brigade, U.S.; Montgomery, C.S. Com. J.E.
Mercury (steamer) 206; *see also* Nashville, TN, Battle of (1864)
Merritt, A. Thomas (engine contractor/construction superintendent) 16, 19, 21, 27–28, 34–35; *see also* City Series gunboats
Metamora (steamer) 206; *see also* Nashville, TN, Battle of (1864)
Miller, U.S. Acting Master's Mate Charles W. 149, 193, 196, 199, 202–205, 207, 209–211, 216, 218; *see also Carondelet* (U.S. ironclad)
Mines *see* Torpedoes
Mississippi, CS regiments: Infantry: 22nd 160; 23rd 160
Mississippi Marine Brigade, U.S. 118; *see also* Ellet, Lt. Col. Alfred; Ellet, Col. Charles, Jr.; Memphis, TN, Battle of (1862)
Missouri, US regiments: Infantry: 6th 171; 8th 155, 161–162; 10th 172; 30th 144
Missouri Wrecking Company 6, 10; *see also* Eads, James B. (contractor)
Mitchell, U.S. Lt. Cmdr. John G. 181, 184–185, 187–189, 191–194; *see also Carondelet* (U.S. ironclad)
Monarch (U.S. ram) 118–119; *see also* Memphis, TN, Battle of (1862); Mississippi Marine Brigade, U.S.
Montgomery, C.S. Com. J.E. 112, 117, 119, 121; *see also* Confederate River Defense Fleet; Memphis, TN, Battle of (1862); Plum Point Bend, Battle of (1862)
Moose (U.S. tinclad No. 34) 199–206, 209, 211, 214; *see also* Bell's Mills, TN, Battle of (1864); Fitch, U.S. Lt. Cmdr. Le Roy; Nashville, TN, Battle of (1864)
Morrison, U.S. Coxswain John G. 132–133; *see also Arkansas* (C.S. ironclad); *Cardondelet* (U.S. ironclad)
Mound City (U.S. ironclad) 30, 40, 92–93, 111, 115–117, 129, 153–154, 165, 171, 185; *see also* City Series gunboats; Grand Gulf, MS, Battle of (1863); Kilty, U.S. Cmdr. Augustus; Passage of Vicksburg batteries (1863);

Plum Point Bend, Battle of (1862); Red River Campaign (1864); Steele's Bayou Expedition (1863)
Murphy, U.S. Acting Volunteer Lt. John McLeod 146, ***148***, 149, 153, 157–161, 163, 168–169, 172–179; *see also Carondelet* (U.S. ironclad)
Murray, U.S. Pilot John 149, 168; *see also Carondelet* (U.S. ironclad)

Nashville, TN, Battle of (1864) 195–197, ***198***, 199–216; *see also* Fitch, U.S. Lt. Cmdr. Le Roy; Forrest, C.S. Maj. Gen. Nathan Bedford; Hood, C.S. Gen. John Bell; Kelley, C.S. Col. David C. ("Parson"); Lee, U.S. Acting RAdm. Samuel Phillips; Thomas, U.S. Maj. Gen. George H. ("Old Pap")
Naumkeag (U.S. tinclad No. 37) 192–194, 218; *see also* Rogers, U.S. Acting Volunteer Lt. John; White River, AR, antishipping war (summer 1864)
Nelson, William S. (bondsman) 20; *see also* City Series gunboats
Neosho (U.S. monitor) 199–202, 204, 206, 207–212; *see also* Bell's Mills, TN, Battle of (1864); Fitch, U.S. Lt. Cmdr. Le Roy; Nashville, TN, Battle of (1864)
New Era (U.S. tinclad No.7) 145–146, 192
New Falls City (steamer) 188; *see also* Red River Campaign (1864)
New Orleans (C.S. floating battery) 97–98, 103; *see also* Island No. 10, Battle of (1862)
New York (steamer) 206; *see also* Nashville, TN, Battle of (1864)
Newsboy (U.S. Army gunboat) 200–201; *see also* Nashville, TN, Battle of (1864)
Nexsen, U.S. Paymaster George J.W. 68; *see also Carondelet* (U.S. ironclad); Fort Henry, TN, Battle of (1862)
Norton, U.S. Acting Second Assistant Engineer Michael 149; *see also Carondelet* (U.S. ironclad)
Nott, U.S. Capt. Charles 78–79; *see also* Fort Donelson, TN, Battle of; Iowa, U.S. regiments: Cavalry: 5th

Oglesby, U.S. Col. Richard 77; *see also* Fort Donelson, TN, Battle of (1862)
Ohio, U.S. regiments: Infantry: 58th 149; 80th 172
O'Leary, U.S. Seaman James 183; *see also* Red River Campaign (1864)
*Osage (*U.S. monitor) 192
Owen, U.S. Col. Richard 177–178; *see also* Perkin's Landing, MS, Battle of (1863)
Owen, U.S. Lt. Cmdr. Robert K. 180; *see also Louisville* (U.S. ironclad)
Ozark (U.S. ironclad) 185; *see also* Red River Campaign (1864)

Paducah, KY, U.S. capture (1861) 51; *see also* Grant, U.S. Maj. Gen. Ulysses S.
Palmer, U.S. Brig. Gen. John M. 105, 109; *see also* Island No. 10, Battle of (1862)
Parker, U.S. National Archives historian Elmer O. 16
Passage of Vicksburg batteries (1863) 165–166, ***167–168***, 169; *see also* Porter, U.S. RAdm. David Dixon;
Paulding, U.S. Com. Hiram 6
Paw Paw (U.S. tinclad No. 31) 200; *see also* Nashville, TN, Battle of (1864)
Pearce, Albert (bondsman) 20; *see also* City Series gunboats
Pelican (floating battery) see *New Orleans* (C.S. floating battery)
Pemberton, C.S. Maj. Gen. John C. 158, 174–175; *see also* Steele's Bayou Expedition (1863); Vicksburg, MS, 3rd siege (winter-summer 1863)
Pennock, U.S. Cmdr. and Fleet Captain Alexander M. 35, 141–142, 145–146, 149, 196, ***208***
Peosta (U.S. tinclad No. 36) 199–200; *see also* Nashville, TN, Battle of (1864)
Perkin's Landing, MS, Battle of (1863) 176–178; *see also* McCulloch, C.S. Brig. Gen. Henry E.
Perry, U.S. Cmdr. Roger 28; *see also* City Series gunboats
Peters, U.S. Gunner Herman 128, 131; *see also Arkansas* (C.S. ironclad); *Tyler* (U.S. timberclad)
Phelps, U.S. Lt. Cmdr. S. Ledyard 39, 51, 53, 57, 68, 71, 95, 126–127, 136, 188–189, 192–194; *see also Benton* (U.S. ironclad); *Conestoga* (U.S. timberclad); *Eastport* (C.S./U.S. ironclad)
Pillow, C.S. Maj. Gen. Gideon 50; *see also* Fort Henry, TN, Battle of (1862)
Pilots 41
Pioneer (steamer) 206; *see also* Nashville, TN, Battle of (1864)
Pittsburg (U.S. ironclad) 32, 71, 78, 80, 84–85, 97, 102, 105, 107–109, 112, 117, 153–154, 165, 168, 170–171, ***183***, 185; *see also* City Series gunboats; Fort Donelson, TN, Battle of (1862); Grand Gulf, MS, Battle of (1863); Hoel, U.S. Acting Volunteer Lt. William R.; Island No. 10, Battle of (1862); Passage of Vicksburg batteries (1863); Plum Point Bend, Battle of (1862); Steele's Bayou Expedition (1863); Thompson, U.S. Lt. Egbert
Plum Point Bend, Battle of (1862) ***113–115***, 116–117, 129; *see also* Confederate River Defense Fleet; Fort Pillow, TN, Battle of (1862)
Polk, C.S. Maj. Gen. Leonidas 50–51, 60, 70
Pook, U.S. Naval Constructor Samuel M. 13–17, 19, 21, 23, 33, 36; *see also* City Series gunboats
Pope, U.S. Maj. Gen. John 89, 94–95, 99, ***103***, 104–105, 107, 109, 110, 112, 118; *see also* Island No. 10, Battle of (1862)
Porter, U.S. RAdm. David Dixon 46, 141–146, 148, 150, 153–155, 157–165, 169–***170***, 171–176, 178, 180–181, 183–186, 188–190, 193–195, 218; *see also Black Hawk* (U.S. flagboat); Grand Gulf, MS, Battle of (1863); Red River Campaign (1864); Steele's Bayou Expedition (1863); Vicksburg, MS, 3rd siege (winter-summer 1863)
Porter, U.S. Cmdr. William D. ("Dirty Bill") 56, 125, 145; *see also Arkansas* (C.S. ironclad); *Essex* (U.S. ironclad)
Prairie Bird (U.S. tinclad No. 10) 146; *see also* Brennand, U.S. Acting Volunteer Lt. Edward E.
Prairie State (steamer) 203–206; *see also* Bell's Mills, TN, Battle of (1864); Nashville, TN, Battle of (1864)
Prima Donna (steamer) 203–204, 206; *see also* Bell's Mills, TN, Battle of (1864); Nashville, TN, Battle of (1864)
Provisions *see* Diet aboard ship

Queen City (U.S. tinclad No. 26) 192–193; *see also* Shelby, C.S. Brig. Gen. Joseph O. ("Jo"); White River, AR, antishipping war (summer 1864)
Queen of the West (U.S. ram) 118–119, 126–127, 129–130, 134, 136–137; *see also Arkansas* (C.S. ironclad); Hunter, U.S. Lt. James M.; Memphis, TN, Battle of (1862); Mississippi Marine Brigade, U.S.
Quinn, U.S. Acting Ensign Thomas A. 149, 212; *see also Carondelet* (U.S. ironclad)

Rawlins, U.S. Capt. John A. 69
Read, C.S. Lt. Charles W. 105, 122; *see also* Island No. 10, Battle of (1862)
Recruiting *see* City Series gunboats
Red River Campaign (1864) 181, ***182***, 183–186, ***187***, 188–189, ***190***, 191–192; *see also* Porter, U.S. RAdm. David Dixon
Red Rover (U.S. hospital boat) 136, 141
Reindeer (U.S. tinclad No. 35) 199, 203–207, 209, 211, 214; *see also* Bell's Mills, TN, Battle of (1864); Glassford, U.S. Acting Volunteer Lt. Henry A.; Nashville, TN, Battle of (1864)
Rice, C.S. Capt. T.W. 202; *see also* Bell's Mills, TN, Battle of (1864); Nashville, TN, Battle of (1864)
Roaches 179; *see also Carondelet* (U.S. ironclad) life aboard
Rob Roy (steamer) 186; *see also* Red River Campaign (1864)
Robb, C.S. Lt. Col. Alfred 87; *see also* Fort Donelson, TN, Battle of (1862)
Roberts, U.S. Col. George W. 97, 101; *see also* Island No. 10, Battle of (1862)
Robertson, U.S. Acting Assistant Paymaster G.W. 207; *see also Carondelet* (U.S. ironclad)
Rodgers, U.S. Cmdr. John, II 10–11, 13–14, ***15***, 16, 19, 21–25, 27–28, 30, 36, 39; *see also* City Series gunboats
Rogers, U.S. Acting Volunteer Lt. John 194, 218, 220–221; *see also Carondelet* (U.S. ironclad); *Naumkeag* (U.S. tinclad No. 37)
Ross, C.S. Capt. Robert R. 73, 77; *see also* Fort Donelson, TN, Battle of (1862)
Rucker, C.S. Col. Edmund W. 202; *see also* Bell's Mills, TN, Battle of (1864); Nashville, TN, Battle of (1864)
Rusling, U.S. Col. James F. 201; *see also* Nashville, TN, Battle of (1864)
Russel, U.S. Seaman Saul 46–47; *see also Carondelet* (U.S. ironclad)

Sabine Crossroads, LA, Battle of (1864) 188; *see also* Red River Campaign (1864)
St. Clair (U.S. tinclad No. 19) 220
St. Louis (U.S. ironclad) 32, 34, 53, 56–58, 64, 67–68, 80, 84–85, 112, 118; *see also* City Series gunboats; Fort Donelson, TN, Battle of (1862); Fort Henry, TN, Battle of (1862); Memphis, TN, Battle of (1862)
St. Louis & Iron Mountain Railroad 20
Sallie Wood (steamer) 141
Samuel Orr (steamer) 55
Scott, U.S. assistant war secretary Thomas 104; *see also* Island No. 10, Battle of (1862)
Scott, U.S. Lt. Gen. Winfield 7–9, 11, 17, 50; *see also* "Anaconda Plan" (1861)
Selfridge, U.S. Lt. Cmdr. Thomas O. 184, 192; *see also* Red River Campaign (1864)
Shelby, C.S. Brig. Gen. Joseph O. ("Jo") 192–***193***, 194; *see also Queen City* (U.S. tinclad No. 26); White River, AR, antishipping war (summer 1864)
Sherman, U.S. Maj. Gen. William T. 142–143, 147, 155, ***160***, 161–163, 181, 184, 188, 195, 197, 218; *see also* Chickasaw Bayou, Battle of (1862); Red River Campaign (1864); Steele's Bayou Expedition (1863)
Silver, Solomon A. (auctioneer) 222–223; *see also Carondelet* (U.S. ironclad) withdrawal from service/sale
Silver Cloud (U.S. tinclad No. 28) 194; *see also* White River, AR, antishipping war (summer 1864)
Silver Lake (U.S. tinclad No. 23) 199, 203–206, 211; *see also* Bell's Mills, TN, Battle of (1864); Nashville, TN, Battle of (1864); True, U.S. Landsman Rowland S.
Silver Lake No. 2 (U.S. Army gunboat) 200; *see also* Nashville, TN, Battle of (1864)
"Skylarking," 46; *see also* Free time aboard ship
Smith, U.S. Maj. Gen. A.J. ("Whiskey") 184–188, 195, 197, 199–201; *see also* Nashville, TN, Battle of (1864); Red River Campaign (1864)
Smith, U.S. Col. Giles A. 155, 161–162; *see also* Steele's Bayou Expedition (1863)
Smith, U.S. Brig. Gen. T. Kilby 186–189; *see also* Red River Campaign (1864)
Smith, U.S. Lt. Cmdr. Watson 148–151; *see also* Yazoo Pass Expedition (1863)
Smithland, KY, US capture (1861) 51
Sparkman, C.S. Lt. J.M. 83; *see also* Fort Donelson, TN, Battle of (1862)
Spitfire (U.S. tugboat) 58
Springfield (U.S. tinclad No. 22) 199; *see also* Nashville, TN, Battle of (1864)
Stanley, U.S. Brig. Gen. David S. 109; *see also* Island No. 10, Battle of (1862)
Steele, U.S. Maj. Gen. Frederick 184, 194; *see also* Red River Campaign (1864); White River, AR, antishipping war (summer 1864)
Steele's Bayou Expedition (1863) 151–155, 157–163; *see also* Porter, U.S. RAdm. David Dixon; Vicksburg, MS, 3rd siege (winter-summer 1863)
Stembel, U.S. Cmdr. Roger N. 35, 95, 100, 113; *see also Cincinnati* (U.S. ironclad)
Stevens, C.S. Lt. Henry Kennedy 122, 125; *see also Arkansas* (C.S. ironclad)
Stevenson, C.S. Maj. Gen. Carter L. 158, 165; *see also* Steele's Bayou Expedition (1863); Vicksburg, MS, 3rd siege (winter–summer 1863)
Swigert, U.S. Pvt. Charles P. 98–99, 103; *see also* Illinois, US regiments: Infantry: 42nd; Island No. 10, Battle of (1862)

Taylor see *Tyler* (U.S. timberclad)
Taylor, C.S. Capt. Jesse 60, 65–68; *see also* Fort Henry, TN, Battle of (1862)
Taylor, C.S. Maj. Gen. Richard ("Dick") 175, ***177***, 184–185; *see also* Perkin's Landing, MS, Battle of (1863); Red River Campaign (1864)
Tempest (U.S. tinclad No. 1) 220; *see also* Lee, U.S. Acting RAdm. Samuel Phillips
Temple, A.F. (constructor) 19
Tennessee, CS regiments: Artillery: 1st Heavy 65, 73, 101; Cavalry 26, 199; Infantry: 10th 55, 60; 49th 87
Terrell, C.S. Pvt. "Spot" F. 84; *see also* Fort Donelson, TN, Battle of (1862)
Thistle (U.S. tugboat) 154–155, 157; *see also* Steele's Bayou Expedition (1863)
Thom, N.G. (engineer) 23; *see also* Eagle Iron Works
Thomas, U.S. Maj. Gen. George H. ("Old Pap") 195, 197, 199–203, 206, 209–211, 214–217; *see also* Lee, U.S. Acting RAdm. Samuel Phillips; Nashville, TN, Battle of (1864)
Thompson, U.S. Lt. Egbert 78, 105, 108–110, 117; *see also* Fort Donelson, TN, Battle of (1862); *Pittsburg* (U.S. ironclad)
Thompson, C.S. Brig. Gen. M. Jeff 121; *see also* Memphis, TN, Battle of (1862)
Tilghman, C.S. Brig. Gen. Lloyd

51, 53–54, 59, 65–68; *see also* Fort Henry, TN, Battle of (1862)
Torpedoes 55, 62, 142, 186–187, 189, 210; *see also Cairo* (U.S. ironclad); *Eastport* (C.S./U.S. ironclad); Fort Henry, TN, Battle of (1862); Nashville, TN, Battle of (1864); Red River Campaign (1864)
Totten, U.S. Brig. Gen. Joseph G. 9, 11, 13–14
Townsend, U.S. Cmdr. Robert 196; *see also* Forrest, C.S. Maj. Gen. Nathan B.
Treat, Judge Samuel (bond guarantor) 20
Trollope, Anthony (writer) 36
True, U.S. Landsman Rowland S. 205; *see also Silver Lake* (U.S. tinclad No. 23)
Tuscumbia (U.S. ironclad) 170–171; *see also* Grand Gulf, MS, Battle of (1863)
Tyler (U.S. timberclad) 25, 40, 53, 56–57, 62, 71, 80, 85–86, 125–132, 134–137, 153, 192–193; *see also Arkansas* (C.S. ironclad); Bache, U.S. Lt. George M.; Coleman, U.S. Paymaster Silas B.; Fort Henry, TN, Battle of (1862); Gwin, U.S. Lt. William; Peters, U.S. Gunner Herman; Walke, U.S. Capt. Henry; White River, AR, antishipping war (summer 1864)

Uniforms 44

V.F. Wilson (steamer) 144, 146
Van Dorn, C.S. Maj. Gen. Earl 124, 134; *see also Arkansas* (C.S. ironclad); Vicksburg, MS, 1st siege (spring-summer 1862)
Vicksburg, MS, 1st siege (spring-summer 1862) 123–143; *see also Arkansas* (C.S. ironclad); Van Dorn, C.S. Maj. Gen. Earl
Vicksburg, MS, 2nd siege (fall-winter 1862) 142; *see also Cairo* (U.S. ironclad); Chickasaw Bayou, Battle of (1862); Sherman, U.S. Maj. Gen. William T.
Vicksburg, MS, 3rd siege (winter-summer 1863) 147, 151, ***152***, 153–155, ***156***, 157–158, ***159***, 160–163, ***164***, 165–166, ***167–168***, 169–172, ***173***, 174–178; *see also* Grant, U.S. Maj. Gen. Ulysses S.; Passage of Vicksburg batteries (1863); Porter, U.S. RAdm. David Dixon
Victory (U.S. tinclad No. 33) 199; *see also* Nashville, TN, Battle of (1864)
Virginia (C.S. ironclad) 16

W.H. Brown (steamer) 58, 69
Wade, U.S. First Master Richard 84, 100; *see also Carondelet* (U.S. ironclad)
Wade, C.S. Col. William B. 170; *see also* Grand Gulf, MS, Battle of (1863)
Walke, U.S. Capt. Henry 25, ***36***, 40, 56, 60–69, 71, 73–74, 76–77, 81, 83–86, 88–89, 91–97, 100–105, 107, 112–113, 115–118, 122, 125–145, 149, 165, 170, 173, 200; *see also Arkansas* (C.S. ironclad); *Carondelet* (U.S. ironclad); *Lafayette* (U.S. ironclad)
Walker, C.S. Maj. Gen. John George 175; *see also* Perkin's Landing, MS, Battle of (1863)
Wallace, U.S. Brig. Gen. Lew 56, 67, 83; *see also* Fort Donelson, TN, Battle of (1862); Fort Henry, TN, Battle of (1862)
Watches aboard ship 42, 44
Weaver, U.S. Pilot Daniel 84, 100; *see also Carondelet* (U.S. ironclad)
Webster, U.S. Col. Joseph D. 69, 72; *see also* Fort Donelson, TN, Battle of (1862)
Welles, U.S. Navy Secretary Gideon 6, 8–11, ***12***, 13–14, 22, 24–25, 39–40, 57, 123, 136, 140, 151, 172, 186, 195, 219; *see also* City Series gunboats; Davis, U.S. RAdm. Charles H.; Foote, U.S. RAdm. Andrew Hull; Porter, U.S. RAdm. David Dixon
West Gulf Coast Blockading Squadron, U.S. *see Arkansas* (C.S. ironclad); Farragut, U.S. RAdm. David G.
White River, AR, antishipping war (summer 1864) 192–194
Whitmore, S.H. (paddlewheel contractor) 16; *see also* City Series gunboats
Williams, U.S. Brig. Gen. Thomas 125; *see also Arkansas* (C.S. ironclad); Vicksburg, MS, 1st siege (spring-summer 1862)
Wilson, U.S. Lt. Byron 149; *see also Mound City* (U.S. ironclad)
Wilson, U.S. Boatswain's Mate Charles 102–103; *see also Carondelet* (U.S. ironclad); Island No. 10, Battle of (1862)
Wilson, U.S. Acting Assistant Paymaster/Purser George 104; *see also Carondelet* (U.S. ironclad); Island No. 10, Battle of (1862)
Wilson, U.S. Maj. Gen. James 201, 216; *see also* Nashville, TN, Battle of (1864)
Wilson, C.S. Acting Master's Mate John A. 140; *see also Arkansas* (C.S. ironclad)
Wisconsin, US regiments: Infantry: 4th 131
Wise, U.S. Capt. George D. 26, 34
Wood, C.S. Lt. R.L. 159; *see also* Steele's Bayou Expedition (1863)
Woodford (U.S. hospital boat) 186; *see also* Red River Campaign (1864),
Worden, U.S. Acting Assistant Paymaster/Purser L.C. 149; *see also Carondelet* (U.S. ironclad)

Yazoo Pass Expedition (1863) 148–151; *see also* Smith, U.S. Lt. Cmdr. Watson; Vicksburg, MS, 3rd siege (winter-summer 1863)